Veterinary Notes
for Horse Owners

M. Horace Hayes, FRCVS

Revised by
P. D. Rossdale, MA, PhD, FACVSc, DESM, FRCVS

Illustrations by Fiona Silver

Stanley Paul
London Sydney Auckland Johannesburg

Stanley Paul & Co Ltd

An imprint of Century Hutchinson Ltd
62–65 Chandos Place, London WC2N 4NW

Century Hutchinson Australia (Pty) Ltd
89–91 Albion Street, Surry Hills, NSW 2010

Century Hutchinson New Zealand Limited
PO Box 40–086, Glenfield, Auckland 10

Century Hutchinson South Africa (Pty) Ltd
PO Box 337, Bergvlei 2012, South Africa

First edition 1877
Second edition 1880
Third edition 1884
Fourth edition 1889
Fifth edition 1897
Sixth edition 1903
Seventh edition 1906
Eighth edition 1915
Ninth edition 1921
Tenth edition 1924
Eleventh edition 1929
Twelfth edition 1934
Thirteenth edition 1938
Fourteenth enlarged edition 1950
Reprinted 1952, 1954, 1956, 1959, 1960
Fifteenth edition 1964
Reprinted 1965
Sixteenth edition 1968
Reprinted 1970, 1971, 1972, 1973, 1974,
1976, 1978, 1981, 1983, 1985, 1986
Seventeenth edition 1987
Reprinted 1988, 1989

© 1968 Revised edition Stanley Paul Ltd
© 1987 Revised edition P. D. Rossdale
Illustration © Fiona Silver

Designed by Roger Walker

Set in Linotron Sabon by Deltatype Ltd, Ellesmere Port, Cheshire

Printed and bound in Great Britain by
Butler & Tanner Ltd, Frome and London

British Library Cataloguing in Publication Data
Hayes, M horace
    Veterinary notes for horse owners. ——
    17th ed.
    1. Horses —— Diseases
    I. Title   II. Rossdale, Peter
    636.1'0896   SF951

ISBN 0 09 173701 X (cased)
    0 09 171511 3 (paper)

CONTENTS

Introduction   1
P. D. Rossdale, MA, PhD, FACVSc, DESM, FRCVS

The Organ Systems

1   The Digestive System   5
T. R. C. Greet, BVMS, MVM, FRCVS, and P. D. Rossdale

2   The Respiratory (Breathing) System   25
T. R. C. Greet and Jill Thomson, BVSc, PhD, MRCVS

3   The Heart and Circulation   53
P. D. Rossdale

3   The Lymphatic System   66
P. D. Rossdale

5   The Blood   70
P. D. Rossdale

6   The Urinary System   78
G. A. Munroe, BVSc, CertEO, CertESM, MRCVS

7   The Skin and Its Diseases   90
K. P. Baker, MA, MSc, PhD, FRCVS

8   Systems of Communication: The Central and Peripheral
Nervous Systems; The Autonomic Nervous System;
The Endocrine System; The Neuroendocrine System   106
P. D. Rossdale

9   The Optic System   125
John Parker, MA, VETMB, MRCVS

10 The Ear   135
T. R. C. Greet

The Musculoskeletal System

11 Lameness: An Introduction   141
    Sue J. Dyson, MA, VetMB, CertEO, FRCVS
12 Conditions of Bone   153
    Sue J. Dyson
13 The Joints   172
    Sue J. Dyson
14 Bursae, Tendons and Ligaments   206
    Sue J. Dyson
15 Muscle Problems   225
    Sue J. Dyson
16 The Feet   232
    Sue J. Dyson
17 Miscellaneous Conditions of Lameness   258
    Sue J. Dyson
18 The Neck, Back and Pelvis; Incoordination   264
    Sue J. Dyson
19 Flexural and Angular Limb Deformities in Foals   278
    Sue J. Dyson and A. S. Turner, DPhil
20 Shoeing   298
    C. M. Colles, BVetMed, PhD, MRCVS

The Reproductive System

21 The Male Genital Organs and Their Endocrine Glands   307
    J. E. Cox, BVetMed, BSc, PhD, MRCVS
22 The Female Genital Organs and Their Endocrine Glands   318
    P. D. Rossdale
23 The Oestrous Cycle   324
    P. D. Rossdale
24 Pregnancy   331
    D. H. Steven, MA, VetMB, FRCVS, and P. D. Rossdale
25 Parturition   344
    P. D. Rossdale
26 The Newborn Foal in Health   366
    P. D. Rossdale
27 Conditions of the Newborn Foal   378
    P. D. Rossdale

Infectious Diseases

28 The Causes of Infectious Diseases   397
    Mary E. Mackintosh, BSc, MSc, PhD

29 Diseases Caused by Bacteria   410
    Malcolm C. Roberts, BVSc, PhD, FRCVS, FASCVSc

30 Diseases Caused by Viruses   422
    Jenny A. Mumford, BSc, PhD

31 Diseases Caused by Protozoa   433
    Sheelagh Lloyd, PhD, MVB, MRCVS

32 Parasitic Conditions   438
    Sheelagh Lloyd

Medical and Surgical Matters

33 Routes of Administration of Medicines   477
    Deidre M. Carson, BVSc, MRCVS

34 Veterinary Medicines   483
    Deidre M. Carson

35 Methods of Restraint and Handling   494
    Deidre M. Carson

36 Inflammation   501
    W. N. Steven, BVMS, MRCVS

37 Poisoning in Horses   507
    D. L. Frape, PhD, DipAgric, CBiol, FIBiol

38 Preventive Medicine   522
    N. J. Wingfield Digby, BVSc, MRCVS

39 Surgery   530
    W. N. Steven and J. E. Cox

40 Wounds; The First-Aid Kit   547
    Deidre M. Carson and Jennifer M. Dykes, VN

41 Growths and Cysts   560
    P. D. Rossdale

Management and Husbandry

42 Behavioural Problems   569
    Sue J. Dyson
43 The Nutrition and Feeding of Horses   580
    H. F. Hintz, BS, DPhil
44 The Relationship between Soundness and Conformation   602
    H. W. Dawes, CBE, FRCVS
45 Genetics of the Horse   618
    Susan E. Long, BVMS, PhD, MRCVS
46 The Importance of Selective Breeding   630
    Hilary Legard
47 The Hunter   635
    W. Morgan

Miscellaneous

48 Exercise Physiology   655
    D. H. Snow, BVSc, BSc, PhD, MRCVS
49 The Purchase of Horses and Veterinary Certification   662
    N. J. Wingfield Digby
50 The Legal Implications of the Purchase of a Horse   672
    S. R. Hopes LL.B
51 The Role of the State Veterinary Service   678
    I. B. Dick, MRCVS
52 Veterinary Nurses in Practice   683
    Jennifer M. Dykes
53 The Examination of the Horse's Mouth for Age   686
    J. F. D. Tutt, FRCVS
54 Colours and Markings of British Horses for Identification
    Purposes   699
    Janet M. Anderson

Appendix 1: Proprietary Medicines   705
Appendix 2: FEI Prohibited Substances   708
Appendix 3: Notifiable Diseases   709
Glossary   710
Index   712

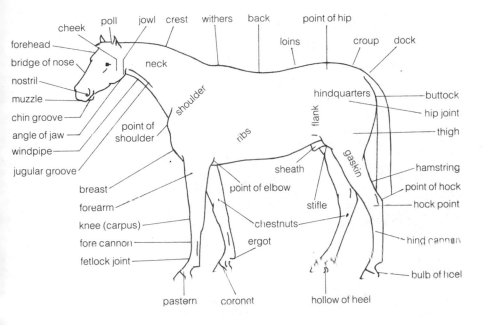

Figure 1 The points of a horse

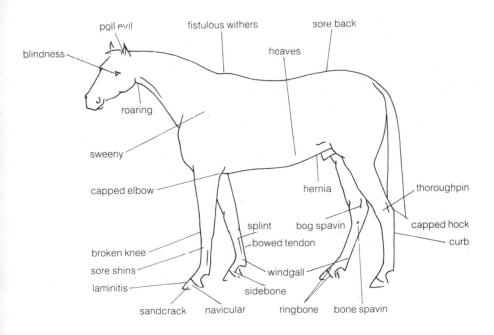

Figure 2 Location of unsoundness and blemishes

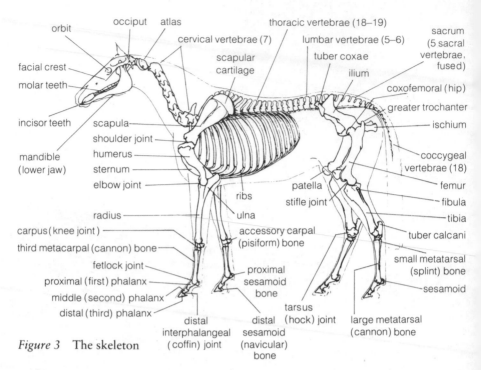

orbit
occiput   atlas
cervical vertebrae (7)
thoracic vertebrae (18–19)
lumbar vertebrae (5–6)
sacrum
(5 sacral
vertebrae,
fused)
facial crest
scapular
cartilage
tuber coxae
molar teeth
ilium
incisor teeth
scapula
shoulder joint
humerus
sternum
elbow joint
ribs
mandible
(lower jaw)
radius
ulna
coxofemoral (hip)
greater trochanter
ischium
coccygeal
vertebrae (18)
patella
stifle joint
femur
fibula
tibia
carpus (knee joint)
third metacarpal (cannon) bone
fetlock joint
proximal (first) phalanx
middle (second) phalanx
distal (third) phalanx
accessory carpal
(pisiform) bone
proximal
sesamoid
bone
tuber calcani
small metatarsal
(splint) bone
sesamoid
tarsus
(hock) joint
large metatarsal
(cannon) bone
distal
interphalangeal
(coffin) joint
distal
sesamoid
(navicular)
bone

Figure 3   **The skeleton**

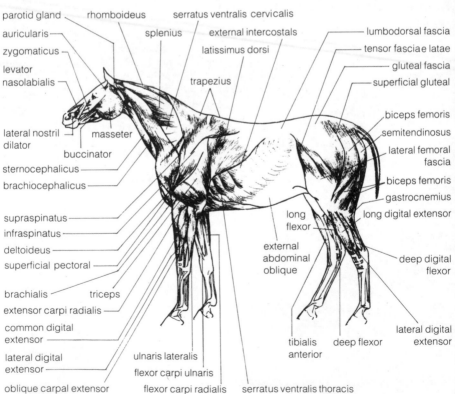

parotid gland
rhomboideus
serratus ventralis cervicalis
auricularis
splenius
external intercostals
lumbodorsal fascia
zygomaticus
latissimus dorsi
tensor fasciae latae
levator
nasolabialis
trapezius
gluteal fascia
superficial gluteal
lateral nostril
dilator
masseter
buccinator
biceps femoris
semitendinosus
lateral femoral
fascia
sternocephalicus
brachiocephalicus
biceps femoris
gastrocnemius
supraspinatus
infraspinatus
deltoideus
superficial pectoral
long
flexor
long digital extensor
external
abdominal
oblique
deep digital
flexor
brachialis
triceps
extensor carpi radialis
common digital
extensor
lateral digital
extensor
oblique carpal extensor
ulnaris lateralis
flexor carpi ulnaris
flexor carpi radialis
serratus ventralis thoracis
tibialis
anterior
deep flexor
lateral digital
extensor

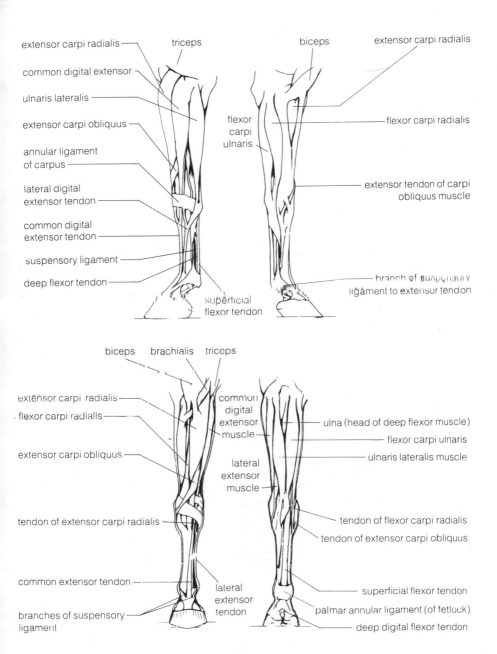

extensor carpi radialis — triceps — biceps — extensor carpi radialis

common digital extensor —

ulnaris lateralis —

extensor carpi obliquus — flexor carpi ulnaris — flexor carpi radialis

annular ligament of carpus —

lateral digital extensor tendon — extensor tendon of carpi obliquus muscle

common digital extensor tendon —

suspensory ligament —

deep flexor tendon — branch of suspensory ligament to extensor tendon

superficial flexor tendon

biceps   brachialis   triceps

extensor carpi radialis — common digital extensor muscle

flexor carpi radialis — ulna (head of deep flexor muscle)

flexor carpi ulnaris

extensor carpi obliquus — lateral extensor muscle — ulnaris lateralis muscle

tendon of extensor carpi radialis — tendon of flexor carpi radialis

tendon of extensor carpi obliquus

common extensor tendon — lateral extensor tendon — superficial flexor tendon

branches of suspensory ligament — palmar annular ligament (of fetlock)

deep digital flexor tendon

Figures 5 and 6   The muscles, tendons and ligaments of the forelimb

Figure 4   The muscle system

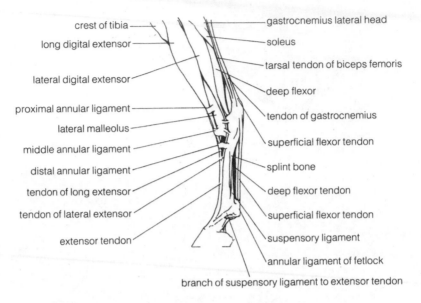

Figure 7 The muscles, tendons and ligaments of the hind limb

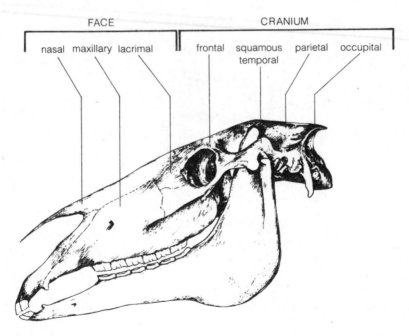

Figure 8 The skull

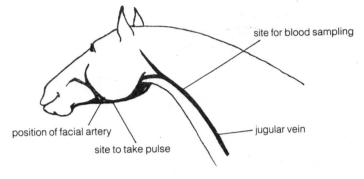

site for blood sampling

position of facial artery

site to take pulse

jugular vein

Figure 9 Jugular and site of pulse

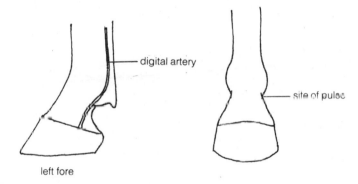

digital artery

site of pulse

left fore

Figure 10 Digital artery and site of pulse

INTRODUCTION

Veterinary Notes for Horse Owners by Horace Hayes first appeared in 1877. Since that time it has gone through sixteen editions, including two major revisions, in 1950 and 1968, by J. F. Donald Tutt. For this new edition, the seventeenth, the text has been completely revised once more, retaining only two chapters from the previous edition.

For more than a century, therefore, the book has been a source of reference for those concerned with the care and management of horses. The fact that it is still in demand today is evidence of the unrivalled value of a work to which its original author – Captain M. Horace Hayes, FRCVS – dedicated so much thought and time. An artillery officer and later in the Buffs, Hayes qualified as a veterinary surgeon in 1883. He wrote many books, including *Riding and Hunting, Stable Management and Exercise* and *Points of the Horse* – standard works which are still read today. *Veterinary Notes for Horse Owners* is perhaps his most useful work.

Hayes's successor, J. F. Donald Tutt, FRCVS, qualified as a veterinarian in 1914. He served with the Royal Army Veterinary Corps during the First World War and subsequently joined the family veterinary practice. A prolific writer, he had great experience of horses, including Thoroughbred studs and training stables. For his second revision of *Veterinary Notes for Horse Owners* he persuaded many eminent veterinarians of the time to contribute chapters on their special fields, a practice followed in this current edition.

When *Veterinary Notes for Horse Owners* first appeared, veterinary science was a pale shadow of its present self. Then the health of horses relied more on the art than on the science of management and veterinary skills. Experience was more important than knowledge because knowledge itself was constrained by the limited techniques available at the time. In the last twenty years these constraints have been lifted in all fields of medical science, and veterinary science has undergone a corresponding expansion, bringing with it a sophistication of knowledge and its application.

The metamorphosis of veterinary practice has been matched by changes in lay attitudes, understanding and knowledge. Horse owners are not only increasingly capable of comprehending the complicated background of biological science and veterinary practice but demonstrate an admirable ability to come to terms with the jargon of biological technology. Both vets and owners have, so to speak, come of scientific age.

Today's text has attempted to take account of these changes. The aim of the present edition is similar to that of the previous ones, namely to provide an informative account of veterinary facts relating to the horse. The emphasis, however, is on explanation rather than on do-it-yourself advice.

In revising the content for the present edition I have been fortunate to enlist the enthusiastic collaboration of a number of colleagues in the United Kingdom, Ireland and the United States of America. From the Animal Health Trust in Newmarket come Sue Dyson, Chris Colles, Mary Mackintosh, Jenny Mumford and David Snow. Tim Greet, Nicholas Wingfield Digby, Deidre Carson, Neil Steven, Graham Munroe and John Parker all work in equine general practice. Dr Sheelagh Lloyd is at the Department of Clinical Veterinary Medicine, University of Cambridge, Donald Steven works at the Subdepartment of Veterinary Anatomy, University of Cambridge, Dr John Cox is a member of the Department of Veterinary Clinical Science, University of Liverpool, Dr Jill Thomson works at the Veterinary Investigation Centre, Edinburgh, and Dr Sue Long is in the Department of Animal Husbandry, University of Bristol. Kenneth Baker is Associate Professor of Clinical Veterinary Medicine at University College, Dublin, Malcolm Roberts is Professor of Equine Medicine at North Carolina State University, Simon Turner is Professor of Surgery in the Department of Clinical Sciences, Colorado State University, and Harold Hintz Associate Professor of Nutrition at New York State College of Veterinary Medicine, Cornell University. David Frape is a consultant nutrition physiologist working for the CANTAB group and based at Hinchingbrooke Hospital, Huntingdon, Ian Dick is Ministry of Agriculture, Fisheries and Food Divisional Veterinary Officer for Suffolk, William Morgan is manager of the Limestone Stud, Lincolnshire, and Simon Hopes works in the International Department of Willis Faber & Dumas. Hilary Legard is a freelance journalist, Jenny Dykes is in charge of veterinary nursing at Beaufort Cottage Stables, Newmarket, and Janet Anderson is secretary to the trainer Michael Stoute. This broad representation of professional authorities enables the reader to draw from a wide variety of expert opinion.

Finally, I should particularly like to thank Janet Anderson and Jan Wade for all the hard work they have put into the compilation of this new edition. Their assistance has been invaluable. Thanks, too, must go to Fiona Silver for her excellent illustrations and to Rob Pilsworth, Sue Hogg and Dominique Shead for their work on the manuscript and proofs.

The publishers would also like to thank the *Equine Veterinary Journal* for permission to quote passages in chapter 50, and the Royal College of Veterinary Surgeons' library for supplying information on J. F. Donald Tutt.

Peter D. Rossdale
Newmarket, 1987

The Organ Systems

The life of any individual, man or animal, depends upon the functions of the organs of the body. You, the reader, are using the eyes to read this text; when you eat you employ the organs of the digestive system. In this section, therefore, the organ systems are described in terms of their functions. First, the digestive system, which consists of a tube running from the mouth to the anus along which food is propelled. This system is described by Tim Greet, and I have assisted him in this task by describing the glands, such as the liver, pancreas and salivary glands, which are involved in the digestive process either by secreting substances that break down food into more simple compounds for use by the body or which, as in the liver, receive the products of digestion and deal with them so as to make the constituents of the food useful to the body in terms of energy for body-building processes.

The respiratory system has, for the sake of description, been divided into the upper and lower parts, i.e. the airways of the head and neck and those of the lungs. Tim Greet describes the upper and Jill Thomson the lower parts of the respiratory system.

The heart and blood circulation, the blood and the lymphatic system form part of the means of transporting substances and gases around the body. I have described these separately, but they are, of course, interrelated systems, although, apart from the heart, they may not fit exactly the description of an organ.

The urinary system is described by Graham Munroe. This system is responsible for filtering the blood to divest it of noxious substances which would otherwise accumulate in the body. The kidneys are the organs which help to maintain a proper fluid and electrolyte balance in the body.

The skin is not generally regarded as an organ but it is none the less a collection of cells with a specialized function, namely to protect the body against outside influences such as injury, friction and the entry of microbes, while at the same time helping to maintain the integrity of the internal medium on which life depends. Skin represents the frontier between life outside and inside the body. Skin and its diseases are described by Kenneth Baker.

If the heart and blood circulation are the means of transport, so are hormones, and the glands that produce them together with the nervous system and neuroendocrine system enable one part of the body to control another, as for example, the pituitary controlling the oestrous cycle of the mare (see chapter 23). The nervous system contains not only the means of communicating action – for example, the forces required to deliver a kick by the hind leg – but also the sensory pathways – for example, sensation of the prick of a needle which causes the horse to deliver the kick. The eye, described by John Parker, and the ear, described by Tim Greet, are special organs of sense that communicate much of the sensory input by which an individual is made aware of its surroundings in terms of sight and hearing.

1
THE DIGESTIVE SYSTEM

The horse has a completely herbivorous (vegetable) diet and its digestive system has evolved to deal with this type of food material. For example, the large intestine contains a population of microbes which break down the vegetable cellulose. This chapter presents a brief outline of the functional anatomy of the digestive system and describes some of the more common problems affecting it.

Functional anatomy

Mouth   The mouth is specialized to enable a horse to grasp grasses and other vegetation and to grind them into a digestible pulp. The adult horse has forty or forty-two teeth (see Figure 11) (compared with twenty-four temporary teeth in the foal). These are classified into incisors (twelve), which grasp and shear the grass just above its roots, and premolars and molars (twenty-four), which are the specialized grinding teeth. The canine (tushes) and wolf (first premolar) teeth appear to have no function in the modern horse and are vestiges of a more primitive ancestor.

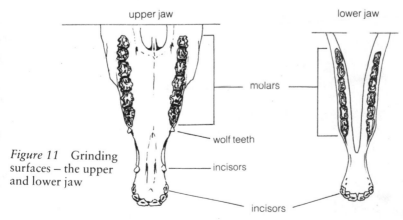

upper jaw   lower jaw

molars

wolf teeth

Figure 11   Grinding
surfaces – the upper
and lower jaw

incisors

incisors

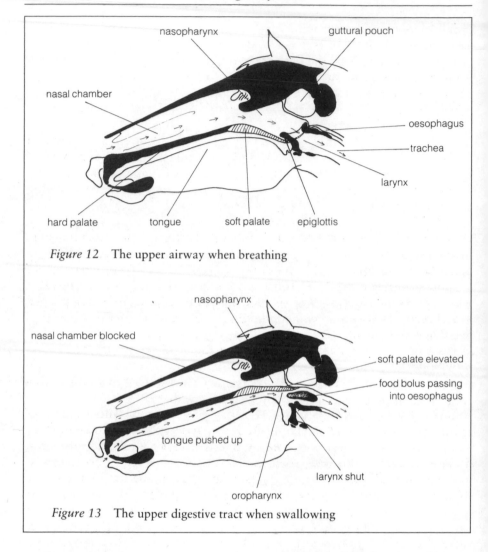

Figure 12 The upper airway when breathing

Figure 13 The upper digestive tract when swallowing

The muscular tongue acts with the hard and soft palates to propel food material from the incisor teeth to the grinding teeth and then to the back of the mouth (oropharynx), where food material accumulates prior to swallowing. The salivary glands discharge from tiny openings into the mouth and provide fluid containing special enzymes which aid in the degradation of food material.

Oropharynx (back of the mouth) The oropharynx is a muscular compartment which is continuous with the back of the mouth, and it is here that food material is stored prior to swallowing. The roof of the oropharynx is formed by the soft palate, a horizontal muscular sheet, which separates the oropharynx from the nasopharynx, which is only involved with breathing (see Figures 12 and 13). When a bolus of food material is swallowed, it is propelled backwards by the base of the tongue and the pharyngeal muscles from the oropharynx into the oesophagus (gullet). At this moment the soft palate is elevated to block off the back of the nose (Figure 13), and the larynx moves forward and closes so that food material cannot leak into the upper or lower respiratory tracts.

Swallowing is a highly coordinated activity in which the individual components or movements last only for a fraction of a second. The pharynx can be considered as the crossroads between food material and air. Any disturbance in its function can produce serious difficulties in swallowing and/or breathing.

Oesophagus (gullet) and stomach The muscular tube of the gullet transfers food material by means of wavelike movements which squeeze food in the direction of the stomach

Food material enters the stomach through a one-way muscular valve which prevents regurgitation of food material back up the oesophagus except under the most extreme conditions (for example, when the stomach is massively distended). Consequently a horse cannot vomit. The stomach lining is partly glandular and partly non-glandular. The glandular portion provides enzymes and acids which help to digest the food material. From the stomach ingesta pass through a valve into the small intestine (Figure 14).

Small intestine The small intestine is a long muscular tube with a glandular lining. In the upper part enzymatic fluids secreted by the liver and pancreas, along with the enzymes produced by the intestinal glands, help to break down the ingesta into their basic constituents. These constituents – fats, proteins and carbohydrates – are absorbed and transported by the blood stream to be utilized by the body to produce energy and materials for growth. The small intestine lies in coils in the left side of the abdomen and is connected to the large intestine (caecum and colon) by another muscular valve (ileocaecal). Food material is transported by muscular wave movement.

Caecum and large colon (large intestine) Ingesta are passed through the ileocaecal valve into the caecum and large colon, where the resident microbial population breaks down cellulose into its basic constituents. The muscular contractions of the caecum and large colon are rather complex, but these structures, the largest in the equine abdomen, are responsible for the absorption of a considerable amount of water from the ingesta.

The muscular coat of the caecum and large colon is complicated, having bands and sacculations, but ingesta are still moved by waves as in the simpler oesophagus and small intestine. The large colon is folded on itself and narrows at one of the bends (the pelvic flexure), predisposing this site to

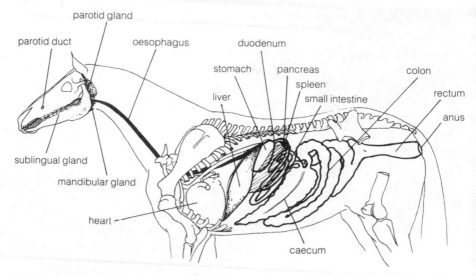

Figure 14   The digestive system and its accessory glands

blockage. The large colon is continuous with the transverse colon and the small colon.

Small colon, rectum and anus   The small colon continues the process of electrolyte and water absorption, its muscular structure having bands and sacculations similar to the large colon and caecum. It transfers the ingesta to the rectum, a simple muscular tube through which faecal material (dung) passes to the external environment. The anus is a muscular valve which regulates defaecation.

Conditions of the Digestive System

THE TEETH (see also chapter 53)

Overshot jaws (**parrot mouth**) are relatively common, whereas undershot jaws (**sow mouth**) are extremely rare. Horses affected with both types of incisor malocclusion cope well with grazing and mastication and rarely lose condition.

There is a variety of other congenital abnormalities of the mouth which involve **malocclusion** of the teeth. One of the more commonly encountered of these is absence of cheek teeth. This appears most frequently in ponies and usually involves the absence of one or two cheek teeth on each side of the lower jaw. This results in relative overgrowth of the teeth in the upper jaw, which develop very sharp points, which can cause oral discomfort and quidding of food.

Figure 15   A parrot mouth

Figure 16   Part of the skull, showing the sharp hooks of the first upper molar and last lower molar

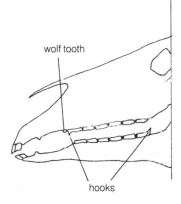

In the normal horse the upper cheek teeth are located more widely apart than the lower cheek teeth, and this results in the development of sharp points on the outside of the upper teeth and on the inside of the lower teeth. These can be smoothed by regular rasping. Dental irregularities also develop because of the manner in which the horse masticates. Thus a sharp point or hook forms on the first upper cheek tooth and the last lower cheek tooth on each side. Although regular rasping of the teeth will remove these, the sixth tooth on the lower jaw is more difficult to rasp. Eventually, in older horses, a sharp point develops which may cause discomfort during eating.

Figures 17 and 18   Teeth edges before and after rasping

The temporary or milk teeth (both incisors and cheek teeth) are usually shed without difficulty. However, occasionally a temporary cheek tooth may become wedged between the adjoining teeth, and this can result in difficulty with chewing, often producing a foul smell to the breath because of trapped food. Any horse which appears to salivate and drop food should be examined by a veterinarian who will remove the wedged tooth with a pair of forceps.

Dental disease in the horse is relatively uncommon and it is surprising how, when a genuine dental problem occurs, many horses appear to carry on eating without difficulty. The sign which usually attracts the owner's attention is either a swelling or a discharging wound on the lower jaw or a swelling on the side of the face. Sometimes there may be a foul-smelling discharge from one nostril, as described in sinusitis (see p. 29). If any of these signs develop, a vet should be called and it may be necessary to carry out a radiographic or endoscopic examination to identify the problem.

Removing permanent cheek teeth of a horse is a difficult job, requiring considerable force, and must be carried out under general anaesthesia. The one exception to this is the removal of wolf teeth, which may be indicated if there is a problem with mouthing the bit. These vestigial teeth are small, with short roots, and usually can be removed relatively easily without a general anaesthetic.

Rarely other congenital abnormalities of teeth may be noticed. The commonest of these is the so-called **dentigenous cyst**. Affected horses usually have a discharging sinus at the base of the ear which produces a honey-like or waxy substance. Sometimes this discharge may be associated with a tooth developing on the side of the skull at this point. This tooth cannot be seen by the naked eye but is visible on a radiograph. Removal of the tooth and the cystic lining can be carried out, usually under general anaesthesia, by a vet.

THE MOUTH

Other conditions which affect the mouth include **paralysis of the face**, which is usually the result of an injury to the side of the face in which the nerve supply to the facial muscles is damaged. Affected horses have a droopy lower lip on the affected side and the muzzle and nostrils are twisted to the other side. In most cases the problem gradually resolves without treatment over a period of six months to a year. During that time the affected horse can have some difficulty in masticating food.

Paralysis of the tongue is rare but has been seen in some cases of botulism (see p. 415) or following nerve damage after fungal infection of the guttural pouch (see p. 33).

THE PHARYNX

Pharyngeal diseases are relatively uncommon in horses but almost always produce some difficulty in swallowing. The usual signs of this are coughing during swallowing and a nasal discharge containing food material. In severe cases aspiration of food material can produce a gangrenous pneumonia with foul-smelling breath and usually considerable loss of bodyweight.

The commonest cause of pharyngeal disease is **paralysis of the pharyngeal muscles** after fungal infection of the guttural pouch (see p. 33). **Pharyngeal abscesses** may form in the wall in strangles infection (see p. 411). Foreign bodies may also lodge in the pharynx, typically if a horse swallows a hawthorn twig in hay. In such cases there is usually severe coughing.

Foals with a **cleft palate** usually discharge milk down their nostrils while suckling (see p. 31). Swallowing can be impaired in diseases which produce distension of the guttural pouch (i.e. infections producing accumulations of pus in the guttural pouch or, in foals, distension of the guttural pouch by air – see p. 31).

If a horse has difficulty in swallowing it is important to alert your vet immediately because this may be the first indication of a serious problem, such as fungal infection of the guttural pouch. In such cases early recognition is important if loss of life is to be prevented. It is quite common for vets to carry out an endoscopic or radiographic examination to try to identify the cause of pharyngeal disease; in particular the flexible fibre-optic endoscope has proved to be an invaluable tool for identifying the cause of pharyngeal obstruction.

OESOPHAGUS (GULLET)

The commonest condition affecting the oesophagus is **obstruction by impacted food material (choke)**, the most usual being dried sugar-beet pulp. An affected horse usually stands with its head and neck extended in a rather uncomfortable position and food material and saliva pour from both nostrils. **Recurrent oesophagal obstruction** may result in chronic dilatation of the oesophagus, which predisposes the horse to further bouts of blockage. In cases of oesophagal obstruction a vet must be called. He/she may choose to treat the horse conservatively with relaxant or sedative drugs, allowing the obstruction to clear itself; alternatively, he/she may free the obstruction by passing a stomach tube. Rarely foreign bodies may become lodged in the oesophagus and require surgical removal under general anaesthetic.

Rupture of the oesophagus occurs rarely, sometimes following a kick in the neck. Usually there is a wound which discharges food and saliva. Veterinary attention should be sought immediately in such a case, as a delay in treatment may have serious consequences.

Both fibre-optic endoscopy and radiography can be of immense help in examining the oesophagus.

COLIC

Colic is the general term given to abdominal pain which may be caused by a variety of different conditions affecting different organs in the abdominal cavity. This section refers only to those causes of colic resulting from diseases of the digestive system. Abdominal pain may occur in a variety of different degrees, but in all cases it should be recognized by the owner as a cause for concern and veterinary advice sought immediately.

The most frequent cause of abdominal pain is spasm of the muscular wall of the intestine; hence the name **spasmodic colic**. There are many causes for this: for example, damage to the intestinal wall by migrating parasitic larvae or feeding too soon after fast exercise. There are other less well-recognized causes and often the cause cannot be determined. Affected horses are usually moderately distressed, show signs of sweating and constantly lie down and get up; they may look frequently at their flanks, kick at their abdomen and roll; they may even become cast in the box. They usually pass few droppings, but the condition may come and go quite rapidly. In some cases there may be sounds of intestinal movement; in other cases these sounds may not be heard. Treatment with a relaxant (spasmolytic) drug usually alleviates the problem rapidly.

The next most common type of colic, **impactive colic**, is caused by impaction of food material in the large intestine. Most frequently this occurs in the large colon at the pelvic flexure, which is a relatively narrow point in the intestinal system. It occurs for a variety of reasons, often when a horse has eaten a large quantity of straw bedding. Affected horses are usually in less pain than those with spasmodic colic and tend to lie down or look off colour without signs of violent abdominal pain. They may get up and down in rather an uncomfortable manner, roll or look at their flanks. A vet will usually be able to identify the site of impaction by manual examination via the rectum (i.e. by feeling inside the horse's abdomen). Administration of large volumes of liquid paraffin, salt water and some agent to stimulate gut movement through a stomach tube is the usual method of treatment. It is also frequently necessary for painkilling drugs to be given to keep the horse out of discomfort while the impaction is being cleared.

A more unusual form of colic results from **gaseous distension (tympany) of the intestines**. There are several causes of this type of colic, which is usually particularly painful. Affected horses may show signs of severe abdominal pain, with sweating and violent rolling. Areas of gaseous distension may occur in front of an impaction, but there are other reasons for the development of gas in the intestine. The most common of these is a major obstruction to the flow of the material caused by the intestines becoming twisted (see below). Gaseous distension of the stomach and intestines also occurs if food material ferments within the intestines: this occurs, for example, when brewer's grain has been used as a feed. In such cases veterinary attention must be sought immediately. The pain associated with the condition can usually be relieved only when a tube is inserted into the stomach to allow gaseous release. In some cases it may be necessary to carry out general anaesthesia and laparotomy (opening the abdomen) to relieve gas-filled intestines.

The final major category of colic, and usually the most dramatic in presentation, is that of **intestinal catastrophy** (or what is popularly known as **twisted gut**). This includes twisting (volvulus) of the intestines, intussusception (one piece of intestine becomes telescoped into the following piece) or rotation of the intestine about its mesentary, which produces obstruction of the blood supply. In most of these cases the clinical signs are very dramatic and affected horses usually show severe pain or agony and sweating; they are often uncontrollably violent in their behaviour. Collapse, shock and death are the usual result if the condition is allowed to progress. As with other types of colic, immediate veterinary attention should be requested. In many cases a diagnosis can be made fairly rapidly because of the severity of clinical signs. Sometimes it is not possible to carry out any form of treatment and humane destruction should be performed as quickly as possible. However, in recent years considerable advances have been made in abdominal surgery in the horse and it is now possible for some cases to be saved if they can be referred quickly to a centre with the appropriate expertise. Despite improved techniques, a considerable number of cases still die or are destroyed humanely because of problems associated with surgical treatment.

ENTERITIS

This means literally 'inflammation of the intestines' and the usual presenting sign is that of **diarrhoea**. This can occur in any age or type of horse and there are many possible causes. The most frequent causes of diarrhoea are those produced by nutrition, such as overfeeding with highly proteinaceous food materials. Other causes include parasitic infestations (for example, *Strongyloides* species) in foals (see p. 450) and intestinal infections with bacteria and viruses (see chapters 29 and 30).

Recognition of the nutritional causes of diarrhoea and their correction usually result in a resolution of the problem. Probably the simplest method of treatment is to feed affected horses with hay and water only for a few days. However, if the diarrhoea is profuse or if it continues for more than twenty-four hours, it is essential to call a vet so that further investigation can be carried out. This usually involves collecting samples of dung for parasitic analysis or identification of pathogenic bacteria which may have caused the problem.

Appropriate treatment with anthelmintics can usually eliminate parasitic causes of diarrhoea but bacterial causes can be more difficult to treat. In particular the diarrhoea produced by *Salmonella* bacteria (see p. 417) has potentially serious public health risks, but a vet will be able to advise on the isolation of affected horses and the appropriate treatment in such cases.

In severe cases of enteritis it may be necessary for the horse to receive fluid intravenously and other forms of supportive therapy as recommended by the vet. Antibiotics may or may not be effective in treating bacterial causes of diarrhoea. A number of cases of diarrhoea appear to have no specific cause; some of these can be treated quite effectively with drugs. However, despite some advances in methods of treatment, enteritis remains one of the most difficult problems to manage in veterinary practice.

WEIGHT LOSS

There are many causes of weight loss, some of which involve diseases of the digestive system. Obviously any horse which is unable to eat or swallow will lose weight. Similarly horses with persistent diarrhoea will eventually lose bodily condition. Some horses are unable to absorb the nutrients from their feed although they may show no signs other than weight loss. Such horses may suffer from cancerous thickening and destruction of the intestinal lining or merely chronic inflammation of the intestines; occasionally no cause can be found for the problem. Undoubtedly the commonest cause of unthrift-iness or weight loss is severe intestinal parasitism or its after-effects. Subacute or chronic grass sickness (see below) may also produce dramatic loss of bodily condition.

GRASS SICKNESS

Grass sickness is a relatively common disease which affects horses and ponies at grass. The cause of the disease is unknown and symptoms are variable. However, the most usual presenting feature, and the one which draws the attention of the owner, is colic. Affected horses have constipation, usually associated with impaction of the colon. They may also show other signs, such as patchy sweating or trembling of the muscles of the shoulder, quarters or neck. Some horses may die rapidly (acute type), often after rupture of the stomach; in fact, some horses are found dead (peracute type). It is more usual for signs of colic and distress to be seen, followed by rapid loss of condition (subacute type). There is also a more chronic form of the disease in which the horse wastes away without showing signs of colic or the other typical features.

Although most horses which contract the disease die or are humanely destroyed, it appears that a few animals may show clinical signs and recover. It is important that a vet be contacted early. Treatment will usually be aimed at alleviating the impaction of the colon and relieving gastric distension by passing a stomach tube.

MISCELLANEOUS ABDOMINAL CONDITIONS

There are a number of relatively uncommon conditions which can affect the abdomen of the horse and produce signs of digestive disturbance or abdominal pain.

Peritonitis (inflammation of the lining of the abdominal cavity) is fortunately very rare in horses but can occur as a sequel to colic, parasitic larval migration, enteritis or surgical treatment for any abdominal condition. Affected horses usually show moderate abdominal pain not typical of colic; they stand depressed, are reluctant to move, and are very tender to being touched around the flanks. They usually turn rather stiffly, preferring to stand dejectedly in one position. A vet can usually confirm the presence of peritonitis by collecting a sample of peritoneal fluid (the fluid which lubricates the interior of the abdominal cavity) for laboratory analysis. Treatment is prolonged at best (antibiotics and anti-inflammatory or painkilling drugs) and many cases do not recover.

In young animals **lymphosarcoma** (see p. 565) of the intestines (usually occurring as a tumour of the bowel wall) can occur and affected horses may show diarrhoea or loss of condition. Occasionally **malignant tumours** of the stomach may cause signs of peritonitis and weight loss; usually these are associated with abdominal discomfort. In older horses **lipomas** (tumours of fat) occasionally twist round the intestine, producing the clinical signs of twisted gut. Such cases can be diagnosed by exploratory surgery and, in some animals, resection of the affected piece of intestine can result in complete recovery.

Abdominal abscesses which may or may not be associated with the intestines can produce clinical signs of colic. They are most usually seen in young foals but can occur in horses of any age. Diagnosis can be very difficult but a vet can attempt to ascertain the cause of the problem by collecting peritoneal fluid and a blood sample. Foals with abdominal abscesses usually do not thrive very well and have increased body temperature which may fluctuate. Treatment is by a prolonged course of antibiotics and this may resolve the milder cases, but a number of horses succumb to the problem.

Rupture of the stomach occurs occasionally in horses, usually as the end result of intestinal blockage. It most commonly occurs in association with intestinal twists or following grass sickness. Horses which have shown signs of violent abdominal pain and suddenly become quiet usually have just suffered rupture of the stomach. Signs of shock precede death, which is usually fairly rapid.

Rupture of the diaphragm is very uncommon in horses but may occur in brood mares following foaling or in horses after major accidents. It is a very difficult condition to diagnose, but affected horses may present with abdominal pain. Usually an exploratory operation is required for a diagnosis to be made, but the prognosis is usually poor.

A **hernia** is the passage of a loop of intestine or even of the fat associated with the abdomen through a natural or acquired hole in the body wall. The two most common sites are at the navel or through the inguinal ring into the groin. Any horse or foal found with a swelling in these regions should be examined by a vet as soon as possible in case a piece of intestine becomes entrapped through the hernia. This cuts off the blood supply to that piece of intestine, producing severe colic, and requires an emergency operation (see chapter 39).

Small pieces of intestine can also herniate through other sites within the abdomen, but these can only be diagnosed by a vet by an internal examination or an exploratory operation.

Prolapse of the rectum occurs rarely in horses and its cause is uncertain. The prolapse protrudes through the anal sphincter and immediate veterinary attention must be sought before serious damage is done to the wall of the intestine, as this can result in the death of the horse.

ACCESSORY GLANDS OF THE DIGESTIVE SYSTEM

The accessory glands of the digestive system comprise the liver, the pancreas and the salivary glands.

THE LIVER

The liver is a large organ, red-brown in colour and, in an adult horse, weighs about 10 lb (5 kg). It is found in the abdominal cavity sandwiched between the diaphragm, the stomach and the intestines. It has right, middle and left lobes and is attached by ligaments to the diaphragm and the abdominal wall. It is covered by a capsule and represents the largest gland in the body.

The liver is supplied by arteries, veins, nerves and lymph channels. In addition it possesses a duct which carries bile into the duodenum. Unlike other mammals, the horse has no gall bladder, a fact which has proved a trap to many a veterinary student during professional examinations.

About 75 per cent of the blood passing through the liver enters from the portal vein, which contains blood coming from the intestines. The liver thus receives the products of digested food which have been absorbed through the wall of the gut. The other 25 per cent of blood is carried into the liver by the hepatic artery and nourishes the liver cells.

After passing through the liver, blood flows out into the large veins leading to the heart. The organ is therefore strategically placed to act as a filter for the digestive processes that start in the gut.

The liver of the newborn foal is relatively large, weighing about 3 lb and the ratio of liver to bodyweight is about 1 to 5; in the adult the ratio is 1 to 100.

In foetal life the foal's liver receives blood from the umbilical vein, which carries blood from the placenta. All the blood from the placenta has to pass through the liver. This is in contrast to other species, in which a duct (the ductus venosus) allows a substantial proportion of the blood flow to bypass the liver. There is no ductus venosus in the horse.

Following foaling and severance of the umbilical cord the vein has no further function and it shrivels, leaving a cord known by anatomists as the round ligament of the liver.

The liver cleanses the blood of noxious substances, such as drugs and poisons, and forms part of the defence mechanism against microbes. It is capable of over a hundred different functions. These may be classed as (a) excretory to the exterior, as in the excretion of bile into the intestines; (b) excretory into the blood; (c) metabolic processes such as those concerned with the storage of sugar and the regulation of blood levels of carbohydrates, protein and fat.

The minute structure of the liver is composed of cells arranged in sheets between which blood circulates freely. Between adjacent sheets of liver cells there are tiny canals into which bile is secreted. The canals join together and eventually deliver bile into the common bile duct. Each liver cell has, therefore, a passage containing blood on one side, into which secretory products of the cells can pann, and a system of bile canals on the other side.

Under the microscope a section of liver reveals cells arranged in lobules which form columns radiating from a central vein. The vein thus receives blood that has passed between the sheets of liver cells. The central veins collect together and carry blood to the great veins passing to the heart. On the periphery of the lobule strands of fibrous tissue act as scaffolding. These contain the portal vein and bile canals.

A fine network of special cells is present in liver. These cells are responsible for taking up bacteria and other unwanted particles. This system is similar to that in other parts of the body and is known as the reticulo-endothelial (RE) system.

Some functions of the liver

Storage   Liver cells take up sugar and convert it into glycogen. In this form it is suitable for storage and can be converted to sugar when required for metabolism. The liver converts amino acids into protein, which can be stored or utilized in various parts of the body for growth or converted into sugar for energy. The liver also stores fat and vitamins.

Regulating blood content   The liver helps to regulate the concentration of fat, sugar and amino acids in the bloodstream. According to the amount present in the blood received by the liver, the cells take up these substances or deliver them back into the bloodstream as required.

Converting substances and metabolism   The liver can transform various substances into simple compounds or convert them into more complex ones. Thus they can protect the body against poisons by changing them into harmless substances. For example, the liver prevents the accumulation of ammonia, a toxic substance formed by the breakdown of amino acids, by converting it to urea. Urea is a relatively non-toxic substance eliminated from the bloodstream by the kidneys, which could not deal effectively with ammonia.

The liver also detoxicates drugs so that their concentrations in the bloodstream fall from the time of administration. For example, phenyl-butazone (bute) is converted by the liver into oxyphenbutazone before it can be excreted in the urine.

The same principle applies to nutritional matter absorbed from the gut: the liver deals with this material so that it can be useful to the body cells. For example, protein is changed into carbohydrate, and fat is combined with choline and phosphorus to form the valuable phospholipids, essential components of cell membranes.

Liver also forms the blood proteins albumin and globulin, which give the blood its viscosity (thickness), and fibrinogen and other substances necessary for clotting (see p. 74).

Bile secretion   An adult horse's liver produces about 10 litres of bile a day. Bile contains pigment (bilrubin), salts, protein, cholesterol and certain crystalline substances formed from the breakdown of haemoglobin. Bile pigment is a waste product, but bile starts are useful substances which help in the digestion of fat. Bile also contains many of the hormones produced by the adrenal cortex and the sex gland. The liver alters these hormones so that they are excreted in an inactive form, although some may be excreted unchanged and resorbed from the intestines back into the bloodstream.

The horse is a herbivore and, in the natural state, eats continuously, in contrast to carnivores and man, who eat occasionally. For this reason bile passes continually so that there is no reason for an organ of storage, i.e. a gall bladder.

Conditions of the Liver

There are few diseases of the horse's liver which have a primary origin. Most conditions are the indirect result of infections, toxins or poisons which are absorbed from the gut or arrive, as in focuses of infection, from other parts of the body.

However, because the organ has so many functions it has a corresponding part to play in many disease processes. For example, in the newborn foal suffering from lack of oxygen due to problems of lung function, the liver cells may become damaged and the function of the organ seriously or even fatally compromised.

The diagnosis of liver disease is made on the basis of symptoms and confirmed by tests on blood samples and liver biopsy. Symptoms include jaundice, wasting, diarrhoea and neurological signs such as aimless walking, staggering and running into objects. Oedema of the chest, abdomen and legs may also be present due to disturbances in fluid balances.

Symptoms are the result of liver dysfunction, such as the inability to deal with bilirubin or with the products of digestion.

In severe liver disease blood albumin concentrations fall and globulin rises. Blood enzymes such as sorbitol dehydrogenase (SDH) and aspartate aminotransferase (AST) increase.

Liver function may be tested by injecting a dye, such as bromosulphthalein, and measuring its rate of disappearance from the bloodstream. This will be abnormally slow if the liver cells are damaged.

Liver may be observed directly by obtaining a small piece with a biopsy needle. This specimen is then processed in the laboratory and various features of pathology may be examined.

Pathology of liver disease

A similar pattern of cellular damage is found on microscopic examination whatever the agent causing liver damage. First the cell swells and the nucleus starts to break up. This is followed by cellular death and the laying down of fat. The damaged cells are then replaced by fibrous (scar) tissue. The last phase of fibrosis is also known as cirrhosis of the liver and is a particular feature of poisoning by alcohol and plants, such as ragwort.

Fortunately the liver has remarkable powers of regrowth and it replaces damaged areas by growing new cells. The undamaged parts can take over the function of destroyed areas, and it is only when the damage is widespread that the healthy areas cannot perform the minimal requirements. When this occurs symptoms develop. Symptoms of liver disease are closely associated with the pathology. The following diseases and conditions are predominantly liver-orientated.

THEILER'S DISEASE (SERUM HEPATITIS)

This disease was described first by Theiler in South Africa following the administration of anti-serum against African horse sickness. The condition may also follow the use of any anti-sera. More recently it has been identified in horses that have not received any serum. It is characterized by degeneration of the liver cells and the appearance of jaundice.

Other symptoms include depression, inappetence and an unsteady gait, pressing the head against a wall, sleepiness and violent nervous reactions.

It is not clear whether the condition is caused by a virus or is an allergic response to foreign material, such as that contained in serum.

EQUID HERPESVIRUS 1 (EVH-1, RHINOPNEUMONITIS)

The foetus and newborn foal may suffer liver disease from EHV-1 infection. The virus damages the liver cells, resulting in minute abscess-like areas in the liver (focal necrosis). The disease is not confined to the liver and the virus also affects the lungs, brain and other organs. The cumulative effect is foetal death followed by abortion or, if near to full term, the birth of a foal showing symptoms of jaundice, convulsions and other behavioural abnormalities.

For a detailed account, see p. 339.

PARASCARIS EQUORUM INFECTION

The liver of young horses may be damaged by the migration of roundworm larvae as they pass from the intestine to the lungs through the peritoneum and diaphragm.

For a detailed account, see p. 447.

JAUNDICE

Contrary to popular belief, jaundice is a symptom not a disease in itself. The yellowness of the skin, sclera of the eye and mucous membranes of the mouth, vagina and eyelids is due to the accumulation of bile pigment which the liver normally excretes into the intestines.

If the liver is prevented from clearing the bloodstream of this pigment, its concentration increases until it finally spills into the tissues to stain not only the skin but the muscles, brain and other organs.

There are three types of jaundice: haemolytic, obstructive and that caused by liver damage (hepatitis).

HAEMOLYTIC JAUNDICE

This results from destruction of red cells, i.e. haemolysis. The membrane of the red blood cell ruptures and haemoglobin escapes. Special cells lining the blood channels in the spleen, bone marrow and liver take up the haemoglobin and split it into two parts, globin (containing the iron radical) and bilirubin (the yellow pigment).

This process normally takes place continuously throughout the lifespan of the individual. However, the rate of breakdown of red cells is low; it is only when the breakdown is excessive that we speak of haemolysis and jaundice.

Normally the body retains the iron for the resynthesis of haemoglobin in the bone marrow. It is only the bile pigment that is excreted by the liver.

In haemolytic disease the destruction of red cells is increased to such an extent that the bone marrow fails to keep pace with replacement cells and, importantly so far as the jaundice is concerned, the liver cannot deal with the great quantities of bile pigment.

Haemolytic disease of the newborn foal is an obvious example of jaundice caused in this way. In this case antibodies, absorbed from the colostrum of the mare, destroy the foal's red cells (see p. 393). There is a dramatic fall in the number of circulating red cells from the normal 9×10^9 per litre to sometimes less than 2×10^9 per litre, and a corresponding fall in haemoglobin and haematocrit.

Destruction of red cells on this scale results in severe anaemia, the urine turns red due to haemoglobin passing through the kidneys, and, if left untreated, the foal dies from a shortage of red cells and a consequent insufficiency in the oxygen-carrying capacity of the blood.

Haemolytic disease may also be caused by bacteria, virus or parasites. In these instances the red blood cells are destroyed by the microbes or their toxins. This occurs in conditions such as equine infectious anaemia (see p. 430), leptospirosis (see p. 412) and piroplasmosis (see p. 433). However, jaundice is only caused when the breakdown of red cells is so excessive and rapid that the liver cannot perform its normal function of clearing the blood of bile pigment.

OBSTRUCTIVE JAUNDICE (HEPATIC JAUNDICE)

Jaundice develops when the flow of bile from the liver to the duodenum is obstructed. Pressure in the bile duct rises. This causes a backflow and bile pigment finds its way back to the blood. Its concentration in the bloodstream then increases until it becomes deposited in the tissues and the symptoms of jaundice are seen.

Obstructive jaundice may be caused by inflammation of the duodenum, by bot larvae entering the bile duct or as a result of roundworm (*Parascaris equorum*) migration through the liver. It may also be caused by tumours or be associated with certain conditions of the gut involving obstruction of the large or small intestines (stoppage or impaction).

LIVER DAMAGE (HEPATITIS)

Any process which disrupts the liver cells themselves may lead to jaundice by allowing bile pigment to enter directly into the lymph stream from where it is returned to the blood. It is not always possible to distinguish accurately between obstructive jaundice and that caused by hepatitis. The two conditions often coexist.

The cells may be injured by plant toxins or noxious chemicals. Chemicals include lead, phosphorus, arsenic, copper and carbon tetrachloride. Plants which contain poisons that injure liver cells, include buckthorn, ragwort (*Senecio jacobaea*) and wild pea. The poisonous principles in these plants are alkaloids, some of which, such as morphine, strychnine and hyacine, have medical properties; others are harmful. For further details, see chapter 37.

Viruses and bacteria causing inflammation of the liver cells result in jaundice, for example, the virus causing equine infectious anaemia (see p. 430).

THE PANCREAS

The pancreas is an important gland which lies in the abdomen, nestling against the duodenum and the spleen. It has a dual function both as an exocrine and as an endocrine gland, that is, it produces secretions which pass in ducts to the gut and others which pass directly into the bloodstream in which they are carried to other parts of the body.

The exocrine secretion is collected and delivered by a duct system into the second part of the duodenum. The secretion is alkaline and helps to neutralize the acid stomach contents. It also contains special substances (enzymes) concerned with the digestion of proteins, carbohydrates and fat. The enzymes are not active until they reach the intestine, where they are rendered potent. They help to break down protein into amino acids which can be absorbed through the gut wall. The pancreatic juices contain enzymes that break down starches to sugars or emulsify fat.

The endocrine secretions of the pancreas are formed by cells known as the Islets of Langerhans. These cells are responsible for producing insulin, the hormone that controls levels of blood sugar.

There is increasing interest in conditions in the horse, such as hyperlipaemia (see below), which are associated with the action of insulin.

Metabolic Conditions

DIABETES MELLITUS

This condition is rare in the horse. The symptoms are associated with a lack of insulin production by the pancreas. This results in the body cells being unable to take up glucose from the blood so that an excessive blood glucose level (hyperglycaemia) develops. The excess glucose spills over into the urine, making it smell sweet. The glucosuria (glucose in the urine) is abnormal and takes with it large volumes of water. Consequently the affected horse is seen to drink and urinate more than usual. Weight loss occurs as the animal is unable to utilize absorbed glucose and must rely on the breakdown of body tissue for energy. Metabolic changes occur as a result of this and the animal becomes weak; neurological signs may develop in the long term. Diagnosis is based on demonstration of excessive levels of blood glucose and glucosuria.

DIABETES INSIPIDUS

This is another cause of excessive drinking and urination in the horse. Unlike diabetes mellitus, the urine is very dilute and contains no glucose. This condition is caused by a deficiency in antidiuretic hormone, one of the hormones produced by the posterior pituitary gland and, in the horse, this is usually due to a tumour in the pituitary gland. It is characterized by the excretion of large volumes of pale, thin urine, excessive thirst, weight loss, weakness and exercise intolerance. Confirmation of the diagnosis is made by demonstrating a temporary response to injections of pitressin.

Treatment, if undertaken, involves administration of pitressin, but this is often not practical.

HYPERLIPAEMIA

This condition, caused by an excess of blood lipid (fats), is most often seen in horses with reduced food intake, the consequent breakdown in adipose tissue leading to a build-up of an excessive amount of lipid in the blood. Pony mares are also susceptible. Clinical signs include inappetence, moderate to severe depression, weakness, muscle fasiculation (involuntary twitching) and ataxia. The tongue may have a greyish-white coating and the breath may be malodorous. Mares with a foal at foot may stop producing milk. Most cases can be avoided by ensuring that a horse or pony has an adequate food intake (see chapter 43). In certain cases the administration of insulin and glucose or heparin may be beneficial.

THE SALIVARY GLANDS

There are three glands that produce saliva: the parotid, the submandibular and the sublingual. These glands are paired, one lying on either side of the midline. Saliva contains some cells, but is mainly a thin watery-viscous fluid varying in composition according to the type of stimulus initiating its secretion. It is made up of 99.5 per cent water and 5 per cent salts and organic material consisting of enzymes and mucin.

Saliva provides lubrication and moistens the mouth and lips. It is continuously produced but in much greater quantities when food is taken into the mouth. It aids the process of swallowing and provides a means whereby the mouth is washed clear of debris which might otherwise provide a culture medium for bacteria.

Saliva moistens the food and transforms it to a semi-solid or liquid mass so that it may be swallowed easily. An adult horse secretes over 50 litres of saliva daily.

Salivary enzymes help to break down starch to maltose, and the secretion or lack of secretion of saliva may indirectly aid in the control of water balance in the body.

The parotid glands are found in the space between the back of the lower jaw and the base of the ear. They are well defined with a strong fibrous capsule and each has a duct which opens in the region of the second upper molar tooth.

The submandibular glands lie on the inner surface of the lower jaw and their ducts open into the floor of the mouth. They also have a well-defined capsule.

The sublingual glands do not have a capsule. They are found near the midline below the mucous membrane of the floor of the mouth. Their secretions empty by several ducts.

2
THE RESPIRATORY (BREATHING) SYSTEM

It is convenient for descriptive purposes to divide the upper from the lower respiratory tract. However, the reader should not lose sight of the fact that the two parts of the breathing system are confluent and from a biological point of view they should be considered as one.

In this chapter the term 'respiratory' is used in the sense of breathing rather than to refer to the entire biological system of respiration, namely, the exchange of oxygen and carbon dioxide between the tissues (muscles, organs, etc.) and the air outside the body. The total system consists of the action of the lungs and bloodstream pumped by the action of the heart. These functions are described in chapters 3, 4 and 5.

Editor

THE UPPER RESPIRATORY TRACT

Functional anatomy

The equine upper respiratory tract is a complicated arrangement of mucous-membrane-lined compartments which have the main function of allowing efficient passage of air from the nostrils to the lower respiratory tract.

The nostrils are continuous with the nasal passages, each a rather complicated structure consisting of air channels and delicate bone surrounded by mucous membrane with a rich blood supply (turbinates). The nostrils and nasal passages are divided into two by a partly cartilaginous and partly bony septum.

Beyond the nasal passages is the pharynx, a single muscular cavity separated from the back of the mouth by a horizontal muscular sheet, the soft palate. This sheet divides the nasal part of the pharynx (nasopharynx) from the back of the mouth (oropharynx). It is through a hole in this muscular sheet that the passages of the voicebox or larynx protrude; thus the pharynx is continuous directly with the larynx and trachea (windpipe) and the lower respiratory tract.

Other air-filled cavities communicate with the main airway. The sinuses are a series of intercommunicating air-filled compartments, closely associated with the roots of certain cheek teeth in the upper jaw and other important anatomical structures. The paired guttural pouches are air-filled sacs which sit between the roof of the nasopharynx and the floor of the cranial vault (the bony box which contains the brain). They are out-pouchings of the Eustachian tubes connecting the middle ear to the nasopharynx and are only found in the equine species.

The pouches are closed by cartilaginous flaps on either side of the pharangeal wall and are opened only during swallowing (hence the relief of middle-ear pressure noted by people on aeroplanes). Several important arteries and nerves travel around the walls and roof of these sacs, and diseases affecting the guttural pouch may have profound effects on these structures.

The internal anatomy of the upper respiratory tract varies depending on whether the horse is breathing quietly, galloping or swallowing. The nostrils are extremely distensible and act to funnel air into the nasal passages when the horse is travelling at speed. Similarly the nasal passages become more streamlined by shrinkage of the vascular turbinates and nasal mucous membrane.

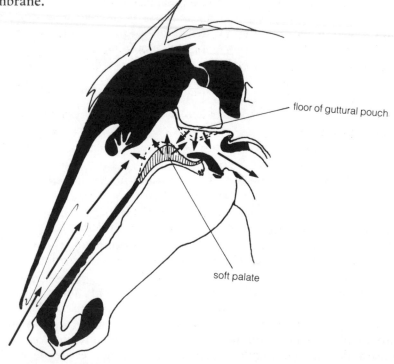

Figure 19   Soft tissue structures of the throat which may produce an abnormal noise or respiratory obstruction with excessive poll flexion

The larynx can be considered as a biological valve which, when opened fully, allows the maximum flow of air to the lower respiratory tract during galloping. It also acts to prevent the aspiration of food material during swallowing, when the laryngeal opening is completely closed. During resting respiration, the valve is open in an intermediate position.

The other significant alteration in upper respiratory architecture occurs during swallowing. At the exact moment of swallowing the muscular soft palate is elevated to block off the back of the nose, and the larynx moves forward and becomes closed (see Figures 12 and 13). This allows the passage of food material from the back of the mouth into the oesophagus (gullet) without leakage into the respiratory tract.

Thus the upper respiratory tract is a marvellously designed aerodynamic system which permits the passage of large volumes of air to the lower respiratory tract during fast exercise. The horse is frequently used as a competitive animal and it is obvious that diseases which result in the narrowing of any part of the upper airway can produce serious impairment of airflow and therefore of performance.

Methods of examining the upper respiratory tract

Diseases of the upper airway have been recognized for hundreds of years The clinical symptoms of such diseases have been recorded since the beginning of veterinary literature. However, the recent introduction of more advanced radiographic techniques and fibre-optic endoscopy (using a flexible telescope) has revolutionized our understanding of the anatomy and physiology of the upper airway and of the diseases which affect the respiratory system.

It is important that a horse owner is observant, taking careful notice of even what appear to be rather unimportant details, for it is the recognition of the early signs of a disease which can provide the vet with vital information to help in early diagnosis.

The most common sign of upper airway disease is the presence of a nasal discharge. This may contain mucus, pus, blood or even food material. Identification of the nature of the discharge and of whether it comes from one or both nostrils can provide essential information in the localization of its source.

Similarly, if a horse has a nosebleed, it is important to know whether the quantity of blood loss was large or small, whether the nosebleed occurred down one or both nostrils, and whether it was associated with exercise.

The other common sign of upper airway disease is obstruction to the airflow (see Figure 19). In its most severe form this may produce severe respiratory embarrassment, but more usually it results in reduced tolerance of exercise and/or an abnormal respiratory noise during exercise. There may also be other important signs such as inappetence, raised body temperature, difficulty in swallowing and enlargement of local lymph glands.

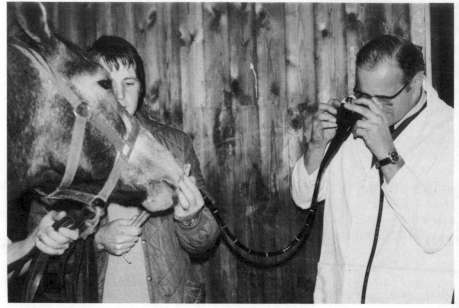

Figure 20   Carrying out an endoscopic examination

The observant owner should be aware of many of these features as they will aid in the rapid diagnosis of the problem. When a vet is called in it is important to supply accurate information about the horse. In particular it is important to divulge whether other animals are affected, whether the horse was kept in or out of doors and its state of fitness.

In addition to carrying out a clinical examination, many vets carry out an endoscopic examination in an attempt to locate the source of a discharge or haemorrhage or to identify the nature of respiratory obstruction.

The modern endoscope is a flexible telescope which, like many other fibre-optic instruments used today, works on the principle of total internal reflection of light. In simple terms this means that light is transmitted from a source down fine glass fibres to the end of the telescope, illuminating even the darkest and most inaccessible regions of the respiratory system. Thus a clear view of the internal anatomy of these areas is transmitted back up optical fibres to the eyepiece.

Most endoscopes flush air and water to keep the distal lens clear of mucus and other debris which are present in the respiratory tract. Although a nasal twitch is usually applied to permit passage of the tube up the nose, the procedure is seldom resented and in most cases can be carried out safely and without complications.

The radiography machine can also be used effectively to investigate the respiratory tract. In many cases the examination is carried out with the patient conscious, but it may be necessary to sedate the horse or to carry out general anaesthesia to obtain special views of certain regions. Although the horse's head is large and bony, the many air-filled cavities inside provide excellent radiographic contrast to the relatively dense structures, such as bone and tooth, and to soft tissues in the throat region.

Nuclear medical technology is developing rapidly and in the not too distant future such techniques as chest scanning will become accepted routine in equine practice.

Conditions of the Upper Respiratory Tract

A large number of diseases related to the upper respiratory tract have been recognized and it is not the purpose of this chapter to catalogue them individually. Instead, the common presenting signs of upper respiratory tract disease will be described because these are usually the symptoms which first bring the problem to the owner's attention and are usually the immediate cause for concern. Brief attention also will be given to veterinary therapy of these conditions, but some mention will be made of appropriate management to be employed by owners in each circumstance.

NASAL DISCHARGE

All normal horses produce a small quantity of mucus which may be seen to discharge from both nostrils on occasions, particularly after exercise. The quantity of this discharge may vary from animal to animal but should not be a cause for concern. The commonest type of abnormal discharge is mucus and pus from both nostrils and this is frequently associated with a cough. A frequent misconception is that the discharge has originated from the sinuses whereas in fact in the vast majority of such cases the horse is affected by chronic obstructive pulmonary (lung) disease (see p. 48).

Sinusitis usually produces a fairly typical discharge of thick pus from one nostril. Often there is a foul smell to the discharge, particularly if a dental problem is involved or if the condition has become chronic. There may be some obstruction to airflow through the affected nostril, and in advanced cases there may be severe blockage with facial swelling. Such horses usually produce a snoring respiratory noise. The lymph gland under the jaw is often swollen on the affected side and occasionally there may be facial pain. A slight discharge from the eye on the affected side may develop.

Under any of these circumstances veterinary attention should be sought immediately. An endoscopic examination may confirm that the nasal discharge has originated from the sinus region and radiographic views may show the presence of pus in the sinuses or even a dental abnormality.

In mild cases antibiotic therapy may be enough to alleviate the problem but in more advanced cases surgical drainage of the sinus is necessary and this is usually carried out under general anaesthesia. At this time the presence of an abnormal tooth can be identified and if necessary removed. (Dental abnormalities are dealt with on pp. 8–10.)

Post-operative treatment involves flushing the sinus and this must be done on a daily basis. Sometimes this procedure is entrusted to the owner or groom but will be carried out under vetterinary advice. As a general rule regular post-operative exercise is also recommended.

A discharge down one nostril also follows infections of the nasal passages, the commonest of these being a **fungal infection of the turbinates**. These usually produce a scanty, foul-smelling discharge which may sometimes be associated with a nosebleed. In such cases veterinary treatment is required and an antifungal drug is usually administered via a facial catheter (a tube for administering drugs or fluids).

Bacterial infections of the nasal passages may be treated by appropriate antibiotic therapy, and the collection of a nasal swab for bacteriological culture to find out which organism is involved and to test its antibiotic sensitivity (that is, to find out which antibiotic will destroy the bacteria) is often of value. Affected horses are not usually ill and there is little reason to suspend normal riding activities.

There are other less common causes of a nasal discharge. **Cystic swellings** associated with the nasal passages and sinuses (for example, **maxillary cysts**) occur, usually in foals and young horses, but they are occasionally seen in older animals. There is often marked facial swelling and nasal obstruction and mucus may be discharged down one nostril. Surgical removal of the cyst is carried out under general anaesthesia.

Nasal tumours (cancer) are relatively uncommon in horses. However, they may be responsible in older animals for a discharge down one nostril which in almost all cases is associated with nasal haemorrhage. The discharge may have a foul smell and frequently there is facial pain and swelling. In advanced cases there may be blindness or other ocular abnormalities. Treatment is only effective if the problem is recognized early enough and comprises radical surgical removal of the growth. This is always carried out under general anaesthesia. In many cases the prognosis is unfavourable.

Rarely **foreign bodies** (usually twigs) may become lodged in the nasal passages, resulting in nasal discharge, haemorrhage and acute headshyness. Removal by a vet usually requires general anaesthesia.

Discharges from both nostrils (bilateral) originate from farther back in the respiratory tract than the nasal septum, that is, in the pharynx or lungs. **Infections of the guttural pouch** usually produce a bilateral discharge, but often this is more profuse down the nostril on the side of the affected pouch. Fungal infections of the guttural pouch are most common in this country. Affected horses usually have severe nosebleeds and there is frequently a foul-smelling nasal discharge. Horses with major nosebleeds should be investigated immediately as fungal infections of the guttural pouch can produce a fatal haemorrhage (see p. 33). In such cases the internal carotid artery may be tied off and the fungal infection treated topically; such treatment may be life-saving.

Abscesses in the throat sometimes burst into a guttural pouch (**guttural pouch empyema**), which then becomes full of pus, and this is usually discharged from both nostrils (sometimes intermittently). There is also swelling of the throat and frequently difficulty in swallowing or breathing. Sometimes the discharge may be foul-smelling. Occasionally horses are very ill, reluctant to raise their heads and display total inappetence. The vet should be consulted immediately; clinical impressions can be confirmed by endoscopic or radiographic examination.

Treatment is usually by flushing the affected pouch using an indwelling catheter. This usually produces fairly rapid relief from symptoms, but affected animals may be sent home for further treatment, which usually involves irrigation of the pouch under veterinary supervision. Nasal swabs may be collected for bacteriological culture and antibiotic sensitivity testing to determine the appropriate antibiotics.

A similar swelling of the guttural pouch is seen in young foals when the pouch becomes distended with air (**guttural pouch tympany**). Affected foals may have difficulty in breathing and sometimes a snoring respiratory noise can be heard. Usually the condition requires surgical treatment. Tympanitic pouches may become secondarily infected and require treatment in the manner described for guttural pouch empyema.

In general, nasal discharges originating from the guttural pouch require irrigation of the affected pouch, but drainage can be encouraged by feeding the horse from the floor or turning it out of doors. The guttural pouch orifice opens during swallowing and if this occurs with the head lowered (as with grazing) efficient drainage of inflammatory exudates is facilitated.

NASAL DISCHARGE OF FOOD

Sometimes a nasal discharge contains food material and such horses may discharge food or water from the nose when they swallow. There are many possible causes for this problem.

In young foals milk may run from both nostrils from birth when there is a defect such as a **cleft of the hard or soft palate**. Such cases usually develop **aspiration pneumonia**. Surgical treatment of the cleft is ineffective and humane destruction should therefore be carried out as soon as diagnosis has been confirmed by clinical or endoscopic examination.

Obstructive problems of the throat, such as guttural pouch empyema or tympany, may produce difficulty in swallowing and nasal return of food material. This may be encountered if abscesses (e.g. strangles – see p. 411) or tumours are present in the pharyngeal region.

Pharyngeal abscesses require immediate veterinary attention otherwise affected horses may suffer from severe respiratory obstruction. However, the condition is generally resolved by appropriate antibiotic therapy.

In younger animals **pharyngeal cysts** may cause difficulty in swallowing and lead to nasal return of food material. These can be diagnosed endoscopically and removed surgically.

One of the most serious causes of nasal return of food material is that of **pharyngeal paralysis** following fungal infection of the guttural pouch. This condition is usually associated with nasal haemorrhage, but some cases only show nasal return of food material and coughing.

Horses with such signs should be examined immediately by a vet and antifungal treatment carried out via an indwelling catheter in the guttural pouch. Anti-inflammatory drugs may also be given. The prognosis is sometimes unfavourable because some cases develop aspiration pneumonia, which necessitates humane destruction.

Probably the commonest cause of the nasal return of food material is choke or oesophagal obstruction. This and other problems associated with the digestive system are described in chapter 1.

NASAL HAEMORRHAGE (EPISTAXIS)

Nasal haemorrhage is surprisingly common in horses. Some of the simple laws which apply to nasal discharge also apply to nasal haemorrhage, namely, if a horse bleeds from one nostril only, the most likely source of the nasal haemorrhage is in the nasal passages on that side. Conversely horses that bleed from both nostrils usually have a problem in the nasopharynx, the guttural pouches or in the lower respiratory tract. In some horses small nosebleeds from one nostril may or may not be associated with exercise and no other clinical signs are noted.

Endoscopic examination may reveal the haemorrhage to have originated in the nasal passages, but in many cases it is impossible to identify the source of haemorrhage accurately. Such haemorrhages usually resolve without the need for treatment. Some cases of acute sinusitis may have slight nasal haemorrhage but this is always associated with a nasal discharge of pus.

Nasal tumours almost invariably induce nasal haemorrhage (usually from one nostril). An endoscopic examination is the most reliable means of confirming this diagnosis. In advanced cases other symptoms, particularly a foul-smelling nasal discharge, may develop. In such cases veterinary attention must be sought and treatment is by radical surgical removal.

Rarely **foreign bodies** may be trapped in the nasal passages, producing epistaxis. These can usually be removed under general anaesthesia. Horses which have bled from one nostril should be examined as soon as possible by a vet; in some cases treatment is unnecessary, but it always important to eliminate more serious causes of the problem.

The commonest cause of bilateral nosebleed is **haemorrhage from the lungs** which occurs, to some extent, in almost all horses at fast exercise (see p. 51).

Horses with a disease affecting both sides of the nasal passages can produce bilateral nosebleeds, but the most important cause of this condition not associated with exercise is **fungal infection of the guttural pouch**. Fungal infection of the guttural pouch can produce a foul-smelling nasal discharge and difficulty in swallowing. However, the most frequent presenting sign is nasal haemorrhage. This may vary in quantity but can be massive and even fatal. Any horse which has a bilateral nasal haemorrhage unassociated with exercise requires immediate veterinary investigation.

Other features of fungal infection of the guttural pouch are pain under the base of the ear, swelling in the throat region, neck stiffness, colic or patchy sweating and, rarely, signs of eye disease. The most useful way of confirming fungal infection of the guttural pouch is by endoscopic examination.

Once the diagnosis has been confirmed an emergency operation should be carried out to tie off the artery producing the haemorrhage. The outlook for horses which cannot swallow is not good, although many cases eventually recover.

There are other causes of bilateral nosebleeds but these are much less common. They include pharyngeal foreign bodies, which are usually associated with paroxysmal coughing and difficulty in swallowing. **Fractures of the skull** usually follow trauma such as a horse rearing over backwards and may be associated with swelling of the head and other signs of facial damage or nervous impairment. In cases in which skull fractures are suspected a radiographic examination is the diagnostic method of choice.

RESPIRATORY OBSTRUCTION

At rest

Many of the conditions described in previous sections will cause some degree of respiratory obstruction at rest. These include sinusitis (p. 29), nasal tumour (p. 30), maxillary cyst (p. 30), guttural pouch tympany and empyema (p. 31), pharyngeal abscess (p. 32) and pharangeal tumour. In most of these cases there are other signs accompanying respiratory obstruction. For obstructions of the trachea (windpipe), see p. 36.

At exercise

The conditions described under this heading are those that will not usually cause obstruction at paces slower than the trot. Most of them do not cause significant obstruction until a horse canters or gallops. The most common of these is the condition which affects young horses, particularly young racehorses, and results from obstruction to airflow in the pharynx by **enlarged tonsular tissue**.

The tonsular tissue of a horse is very much more diffusely located than in man or other domestic animals. In all young horses there are aggregations of lymphatic (tonsular) tissue (**lymphoid hyperplasia**) in the roof of the nasopharynx and these can be readily identified using an endoscope. In the vast majority of cases the condition causes no problem and the tonsils gradually reduce in size as the horse matures. It is thought that they enlarge in response to exposure to infectious agents and allergens in the environment.

In a few horses the lymphatic tissue becomes enlarged to such an extent that it causes obstruction to airflow during exercise. This produces an abnormal inspiratory sound at exercise which may be likened to a whistle or a roar. The problem is exacerbated in unfit animals and will usually disappear as the horse becomes more mature. If such a noise is heard a vet should be asked to examine the horse and to carry out an endoscopic examination in order to eliminate this problem from other more serious complaints. Usually no treatment is necessary.

As mentioned previously, cystic structures occasionally develop in the pharynx of foals and young horses and these may produce signs of respiratory obstruction during exercise. An endoscopic diagnosis is required and treatment is by surgical removal of the cyst.

Another problem occurring most commonly in racehorses, but also in eventers and some hunters, is that of **choking up**; it is also sometimes known as **soft palate disease** or **tongue swallowing**. The condition usually occurs at the end of a race when a horse is apparently galloping easily and the jockey asks it for a last effort. Suddenly there is a rather terrifying gurgling noise and the horse stops within a few strides as if shot. It is then usually able to regain its breath and continue the race, but will have lost all chance of winning. By the time the horse is pulled up and a veterinary examination is requested there are usually no symptoms of respiratory disease.

The problem is thought to be related to a disruption in the anatomical relationship between the larynx and the soft palate. In the normal horse the larynx fits snugly through a hole in the soft palate, forming an air-tight and food-tight seal, and this junction is only disrupted during swallowing.

It is thought that during racing the junction between the larynx and the soft palate is disrupted, breaking the seal and allowing the normally nasal-breathing horse to breathe through its mouth. Thus air passes both above and below the soft palate, producing an effect similar to a sail flapping in the breeze, with considerable turbulence (therefore noise) and severe airway obstruction. The situation is rapidly corrected when the horse swallows and the soft palate and the larynx return to their normal respiratory position.

It is usual when such a noise is identified to ask a veterinarian to carry out a detailed investigation. This is mainly to eliminate other causes of respiratory obstruction. Some abnormalities of the heart may produce similar clinical signs and it is thought that a number of respiratory problems may manifest themselves in the same manner (e.g. **lung disease** or **laryngeal hemiplegia** – see below).

In a significant proportion of horses no primary cause can be found for choking up and under these circumstances surgical treatment is usually advocated. However, a number of managemental aids can be used to help the problem. These include using a dropped noseband in order to keep the mouth closed, tying the tongue forward with a tongue strap, and using a milder bit. Surgical treatment is usually only recommended after trying these aids. The results of surgical treatment are rather variable and if the operation is unsuccessful it may be necessary to insert a tube into the trachea (windpipe) to allow the horse to breathe by bypassing the obstruction (tracheostomy).

Conditions of the Larynx

The larynx (voicebox) is a biological valve which permits an adequate flow of air to the lower respiratory tract during galloping and prevents aspiration of food material during swallowing. Diseases of the larynx, therefore, have considerable importance in relation to the function of the upper respiratory tract. Since the introduction of fibre-optic endoscopy, the larynx is an organ which has received much attention and now a number of different laryngeal problems have been recognized.

The most commonly encountered disease is **laryngeal hemiplegia** (also known as **whistling** or **roaring**): in 90 per cent of cases the left side of the larynx is paralysed, either completely or partly. The cause is a degeneration of the nerve that supplies the muscles which open and close the larynx. Affected horses make abnormal inspiratory noises at exercise, typically a whistle or a roar. The diagnosis can be confirmed endoscopically. Many horses perform satisfactorily without the need for treatment, but if a horse is suffering from exercise intolerance, several types of operation can be performed, including that popularized in this country by Sir Frederick Hobday. In fact, for horses with advanced disease more recent operations – for example, tying back the paralysed side of the larynx – have superseded hobdaying.

Alternatively a tube can be inserted into the trachea, thus bypassing the obstruction and allowing the horse to breathe more freely. Such tubes have to be removed and cleaned at least daily and involve careful management by the owner or trainer. Horses with an unguarded hole in their trachea are prone to inhaling debris and must be kept well away from water (i.e. rivers, lakes or the sea) for obvious reasons.

Several other types of laryngeal obstruction have been recognized since endoscopy has been regularly used and can now be readily differentiated even though their clinical signs are similar to laryngeal hemiplegia. Most of these cases can be treated by surgical means.

Conditions of the Trachea (Windpipe)

Diseases affecting the trachea which produce narrowing, such as **congenital collapse**, development of an **abscess** or other **compressive lesions** or **severe trauma**, will result in obstruction to airflow, an abnormal noise during exercise and severe exercise intolerance. Apart from treatment of infections or excision of accessible masses, the only other method of treatment is to insert a tracheostomy tube below the obstruction. Unfortunately, with a collapsed trachea, this is impossible, as it is with masses at the front of the chest which compress the trachea.

THE LOWER RESPIRATORY TRACT

Functional anatomy

The equine chest is the second largest of the body cavities and is roughly cone-shaped, being narrow and deep anteriorly but wide and flat posteriorly. The shape of the chest is maintained by the ribs, which are well sprung and form the side walls. The posterior wall consists of the diaphragm, which is very oblique and convex. There is a thin membrane running from the top to the bottom of the chest which divides the cavity medially into two halves.

The lungs occupy a large percentage of the chest space, with the heart situated anteriorly and to the left. A number of other important structures are also found within the chest. These include major blood vessels, the oesophagus (foodpipe), lymph glands and tubes carrying lymph. All these organs fit tightly within the chest and the shape of the lungs conforms to them (Figure 22).

Air is conducted to the lungs by means of the trachea (windpipe), which has an average length of 75–80 cm and is approximately 5–6 cm in diameter. The windpipe is situated in the lower aspect of the horse's neck and is held open by rigid C-shaped rings of cartilage.

The trachea divides to form the two bronchi, which enter the lungs and in turn subdivide into numerous smaller tubes which branch throughout the lung tissue. The larger tubes are supported by plates of cartilage which become smaller as the tubes diminish in size. Cartilage is absent in tubes of about 1 mm diameter and these open into regular, roughly circular air cells (alveoli). This meshwork of air cells gives the lungs a soft, spongy consistency.

The function of the respiratory system is to conduct air to and from the air cells of the lungs and to bring about gas exchange, allowing the body to absorb oxygen into the bloodstream and to give off carbon dioxide into the exhaled air. Oxygen is required in order to maintain many of the normal body functions such as the metabolism of food and muscle activity. Carbon dioxide is given off as one of the waste products and has to be removed from the body.

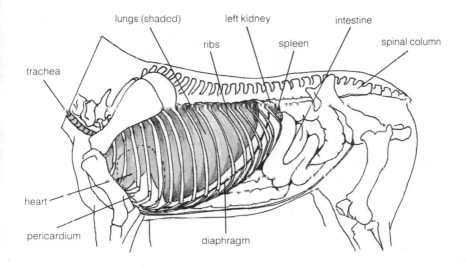

Figure 22   The lower respiratory tract

The mechanics of breathing are complex. Essentially, contraction of the muscle fibres in the diaphragm and in between the ribs causes the chest cavity to expand and air to be drawn into the lungs. Relaxation of these muscles has the opposite effect and air is exhaled.

Capillary blood vessels are situated in very close association with the air cells in the lungs and, in the normal horse, gas exchange occurs readily across the membranes separating these structures (Figure 23). Blood pumped to the lungs from the heart is rich in carbon dioxide, which is given off into the air cells; in exchange oxygen is absorbed into the blood, which then returns to the heart to be circulated around the body.

In the normal horse the airways are lined by a thin film of mucus, which is constantly being moved up the airways towards the throat. This is done by minute hairlike projections (cilia), which also line the airways and which beat anteriorly in a wavelike motion, causing the mucus to move over them. Dust particles and any other foreign material become trapped in the mucus and are removed from the airways in this way. Once reaching the throat this material is swallowed by the horse. In the lining of the airways and alveoli there are many cells whose function is to neutralize and remove any harmful agents which may have penetrated the mucus and gained access to the membrane. These are the basic mechanisms which prevent infections from developing in the lung.

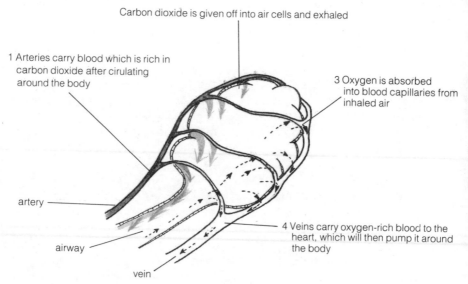

Carbon dioxide is given off into air cells and exhaled

1 Arteries carry blood which is rich in carbon dioxide after cirulating around the body

3 Oxygen is absorbed into blood capillaries from inhaled air

artery

4 Veins carry oxygen-rich blood to the heart, which will then pump it around the body

airway

vein

Figure 23   The process of gas exchanges in the lung

Healthy respiration

In the normal resting horse respiration is a quiet, relaxed process, with inhalation and exhalation of air occurring in a regular, rhythmical fashion. The nostrils are relaxed and clean, although a slight watery nasal discharge is quite normal. There should be no abnormal respiratory sounds such as coughing or wheezing.

The normal respiratory rate of the horse is ten to fourteen breaths per minute and can be counted by watching the breathing movements of the flanks or the nostrils. There are several factors unrelated to disease which can lead to an increase in respiratory rate. These include excitement, exercise, high altitude, high environmental temperature or humidity, and obesity.

The rhythm of respiration is important. In the normal resting horse inspiration and expiration are followed by a pause. The period of expiration is usually slightly longer than that of inspiration, and the length of the pause becomes shorter if the horse is excited or has been exercised preceding examination, or if it has a respiratory problem. The normal horse should be able to undertake exercise in keeping with its degree of fitness and should recover from exertion in five to ten minutes.

Signs of respiration malfunction

In addition to general signs of ill health, conditions which warrant veterinary attention include: (a) coughing or other abnormal respiratory sounds at rest or exercise; (b) increased respiratory rate or deep or laboured breathing in a quiet, resting horse; (c) irregular breathing – that is, spells when a horse appears to stop breathing followed by a spell of rapid breathing; (d) inability to carry out normal amounts of exercise followed by a prolonged recovery period; and (e) abnormal nasal discharge. In the event of any such signs it is advisable to seek veterinary attention at an early stage. This will minimize suffering for the horse, prevent unnecessary advancement of the condition, and hasten recovery. If the condition is infectious, rapid diagnosis, isolation and treatment will minimize spread of infection to other horses.

Factors affecting respiration adversely

The process of respiration may be adversely affected in a number of ways. Broadly speaking, these include interference to the passage of air in and out of the lungs, inability of the lungs to expand normally, interference with the exchange of gas across the walls of the air cells or blood capillaries, abnormal heart function or conduction of blood to and from the lungs. Of these factors, obstruction of the airways appears to be the most common abnormality affecting the equine respiratory system. Obstruction may occur at any level – in the nasal passages or throat (see pp. 31 and 33), or in the windpipe or lungs – and may be mechanical in nature or due to a disease process.

Narrowing of the airways may occur due to pressure being exerted from outside the airway, for example, by a growth or abscess. Spontaneous collapse of the cartilaginous rings supporting the airways may also occur in rare instances, resulting in reduced airway diameter. Narrowing, which in some instances leads to blockage of the airways, may occur in a number of other ways. These include contraction of the muscle layers in the walls, inflammation of the membrane lining the airways, or an increased amount of mucus in the airways. These latter processes are particularly important in the very small airways where such changes may give rise to significant airway obstruction, particularly if the changes are widespread.

At birth the lungs of a foal are collapsed and contain no air, but soon thereafter the foal starts breathing and the lungs become distended with air. In some instances incomplete distention occurs and this gives rise to marked respiratory difficulty in newborn foals. In older foals and adult horses infection may give rise to excess fluid material accumulating in the narrow space between the lungs and the chest wall. This prevents the lungs from expanding to their normal limits and may even compress them. On occasions severe injury to the chest wall may result in the thoracic cavity being penetrated. This allows air to be drawn into the chest cavity, which is normally under negative pressure, resulting in the collapse of a lung.

Any mechanical or chemical irritation to the lower respiratory tract will result in coughing – a highly coordinated reflex action designed to remove such irritants. Sensitive nerve endings or receptors are situated under the lining of the respiratory passages from the throat down to the tiniest airways. Thus irritation at any level will result in coughing. The processes described here and the ways in which they affect horses will be discussed in more detail under the individual conditions.

Methods of examining the lower respiratory tract

The onset of a respiratory problem may be sudden or gradual. The severity may range from mild, with the occasional cough and slightly reduced exercise tolerance, to severe, with the horse coughing frequently and appearing breathless when standing at rest.

Observations made by a groom or owner can be very helpful to a veterinarian. In addition to the rate of onset and effect of exercise, questions will be asked about recent events which may have some bearing on the horse's respiratory problem, such as contact with other horses, either within the stable yard or away from the premises, for example, at competitive events. Inquiries will be made into the health of other horses in the yard, whether there have been any visiting horses, the horse's vaccination status and any previous illness that the horse has had. The circumstances in which the horse developed the respiratory problem may be explored: for example, whether the horse was kept outdoors or stabled and, if the latter, the type and quality of the bedding and forage. More detailed questions will be asked about the horse's wellbeing, such as appetite, thirst and evidence of nasal discharge (amount, colour, consistency, one nostril or both).

When examining a horse with a respiratory problem a veterinarian initially carries out a general examination. Thereafter a visual assessment of the horse's respiratory movements will be made at rest in order to establish the rate, rhythm and depth of breathing. Abnormal respiratory sounds such as wheezing will also be noted. A true reflection will only be gained if the horse is relaxed; thus quiet surroundings and a calm, patient person holding the horse are of utmost importance.

The inspiratory and expiratory effort can be assessed by watching the horse's flanks and nostrils during breathing. Expiration occurs in two phases – a passive relaxation of the chest muscles followed by slight contraction of the flank muscles. In some conditions the latter phase is accentuated in order to force air out of the lungs and contraction of the adominal muscles is increased. This is sometimes referred to as a double lift or heave (Figure 24).

In normal horses the amount of flank movement varies depending on the type of horse and its bodily condition. This is usually considered in conjunction with breathing sounds in the windpipe and chest.

Using a stethoscope, the vet will listen for abnormal respiratory sounds, whether they are present in one or both lungs and, within a lung, whether they are localized or widespread. This provides an indication of the nature of changes within the lung but rarely will establish the cause with any certainty. Another test which may be performed by a veterinarian is percussion. This is the process of tapping the chest in horizontal and vertical directions by means of a percussion hammer or the fingers. This is done in order to establish the area of chest resonance, that is, the extent of the lungs, and to try to locate areas of consolidation. In the horse this technique is generally considered to be of limited value as many deep-seated lesions cannot be detected by this method because of the volume of the chest.

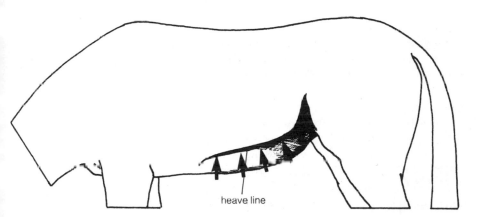

Figure 24   Location of the heave line

An examination of the heart will be carried out in the resting horse. The vet may then ask for the horse to be exercised in order to assess the effects on the heart and lungs.

The diagnosis of respiratory conditions is complex and a vet may wish to take samples for laboratory analysis. These might include samples of blood or swabs taken from the throat area via the nose. The vet may wish to examine the horse's windpipe using a fibre-optic endoscope. This will enable him or her to visualize any changes, particularly the amount and consistency of mucus, and even to collect a sample of mucus if appropriate.

More specialized examinations involving expensive equipment are usually confined to veterinary schools or specialized research centres. They include radiographic examination of the chest and more detailed lung function testing, descriptions of which are beyond the scope of this book.

Conditions of the Lower Respiratory Tract

Lower respiratory conditions may arise due to infectious micro-organisms (viruses and bacteria), parasites (lungworm), hypersensitivity to possible allergens in the environment, and mechanical irritants or abnormalities.

The first signs of lower respiratory malfunction are an increase in respiratory rate (more than fifteen breaths per minute), coughing and reduced exercise tolerance. The signs may increase in severity to include an increase in the depth of respiration up to a state of severe respiratory distress. Clinical signs that warrant veterinary attention are described in more detail on p. 39.

The most common conditions affecting the lower respiratory system fall into five categories: (a) virus infections; (b) bacterial infections; (c) parasitic infections; (d) allergies such as chronic obstructive pulmonary disease; and (e) pulmonary haemorrhage.

Virus Infections

Virus infections are common causes of respiratory illness in horses. The viruses spread rapidly where horses are grouped together in close proximity, for example, in stable yards, and the transporting of horses over long distances may lead to the rapid spread of infections over a wide area. Some outbreaks of respiratory disease are due to mixed infections involving more than one agent, but the majority involve either an influenza virus or a herpesvirus.

EQUINE INFLUENZA (FLU)

Equine influenza is a severe virus respiratory infection which is sudden in onset. The main clinical signs are a high temperature and coughing, with a watery nasal discharge. Most cases recover in two to three weeks but a period of convalescence is desirable. Influenza is prevented by comprehensive vaccination programmes.

For a detailed account, see p. 422.

EQUID HERPESVIRUS 1 (SNOTTY NOSE, STABLE COUGH, VIRUS ABORTION, RHINOPNEUMONITIS)

Equine herpesvirus is a respiratory infection giving rise to outbreaks of illness. Other strains of the virus cause abortion in mares (see p. 339). The clinical signs are a high temperature and increased respiratory rate with listlessness and inappetence. The condition is prevalent in young horses.

For a detailed account, see p. 425.

EQUINE RHINOVIRUS AND ADENOVIRUS (COLD VIRUSES)

These are widespread viruses causing little or no clinical illness. For a more detailed account of the various cold viruses, see p. 429.

Bacterial Infections

Bacteria may enter the body in a number of ways; by mouth, by inhalation, through wounds and, in young foals, via the navel. Bacteria are found commonly in the respiratory passages of healthy horses and, in many instances, will only give rise to disease under conditions of stress or secondary to another illness such as a respiratory virus infection. However, certain bacteria may be the primary cause of respiratory disease, for example, strangles (*Streptococcus equi* – see p. 411). Bacterial infections may affect both upper and lower respiratory tracts and vary in severity according to the type of infection, the age and immune status of the animal. The most severe infections involve the lungs and result in pneumonia.

PNEUMONIA, BRONCHOPNEUMONIA

Pneumonia is a severe respiratory condition in which there is inflammation of the lung tissue caused by infectious organisms or foreign materials in the lungs. Bronchopneumonia is a more extensive condition affecting the airways of the lungs in addition to the lung tissue.

The bacterial organisms which cause pneumonia in the horse most commonly are the *Streptococcus* species. Other organisms, including *Actinobacillus equuli*, *Bordetella bronchiseptica* and *Pasteurella* species, may be involved occasionally. Foreign material such as drenches that have gone down the wrong way, viruses and parasites may also give rise to pneumonia.

Clinical signs

Foals and horses with pneumonia are dull, listless, inappetent, have an inceased respiratory rate and a high temperature. Animals cough and may have a purulent nasal discharge. The condition may increase in severity, indicated by an increase in the depth of breathing and a worsening in the general condition. In a state of severe respiratory distress horses will have flared nostrils, very laboured breathing and a distinct double expiratory effort or heave (Figure 24).

Course of the condition

Bacterial respiratory conditions resulting in pneumonia are contagious. Horses become infected through contact with horses carrying the organisms or with infected nasal discharges or sputum which has been expelled during coughing. Usually infections are acquired by inhalation; however, in newborn foals bacteria may enter the body via the navel, circulate in the blood and, in this way, reach many parts of the body, including the lungs.

Once in the lungs, bacteria multiply and rapidly reach large numbers while continuing to invade the lung tissue. The body's response to infection results in severe inflammation and the formation of pus in the air cells and airways. In addition abscesses can develop and these may involve large areas of lung tissue, take many months to resolve and can result in permanent lung damage.

Pneumonia is a very serious condition and to a certain extent the outcome depends on the body's ability to fight infection. The condition may progress rapidly and prove fatal. In view of this it is imperative that veterinary attention is sought early in the course of the illness.

Adult horses may also suffer from bacterial infections of the respiratory passages without the development of pneumonia. Such cases may have increased respiratory rate, an intermittent cough and poor work performance but a normal appetite and body temperature. These infections may persist for long periods or recur at intervals if untreated.

Diagnosis

A diagnosis of pneumonia or bronchopneumonia can be made on clinical examination. A sample of mucus may be taken from the airways in order to try to identify the organisms involved and to test their sensitivity to antibiotics. This gives an indication of the drug(s) of choice for treating the infection.

Treatment

A course of antibiotics is required to kill or inhibit the growth of bacteria. Expectorant drugs which assist the removal of mucus and pus from the airways are advisable. Bronchodilating agents facilitate breathing and the removal of mucus from the lungs by widening the air passages. Horses which are very ill will benefit from treatment for pain and may require intravenous fluid treatment and oxygen administration.

Nursing is very important. The horse should be kept warm and comfortable on a deep layer of clean bedding and be supported to lie upright rather than flat out. Small, easy-to-eat feeds such as mashes should be offered frequently and water should be available at all times.

Horses with chronic low-grade respiratory infections should be rested, treated with antibiotics, expectorant drugs and/or proprietary cough mixtures.

Prevention

Horses with respiratory infections should be isolated; care should be taken not to spread infection via personnel, tack or utensils to other horses.

PLEURITIS (PLEURISY)

Pleuritis is a severe respiratory condition in which there is inflammation of the membranes lining the chest cavity and covering the lungs. The name of this membrane is the pleura, hence the name pleuritis.

It is usually caused by a bacterial infection and may be secondary to pneumonia. It may also occur following severe stress such as being transported over long distances or experiencing marked temperature changes when moving from a hot to a cold climate or vice versa. Infection may enter the chest cavity by means of penetration wounds.

Clinical signs

In the early stages horses will have increased respiratory rate, shallow breathing, elevated temperature, poor appetite and look generally off colour. As the condition progresses respiration becomes increasingly more difficult and severe cases will be in a state of respiratory distress.

Course of the condition

When certain bacteria gain access to the pleura and multiply, the membrane becomes inflamed and pus is formed. As the chest is an enclosed cavity, the pus accumulates and forms a pool at the bottom of the cavity due to gravity. The amount of pus may increase to such an extent that normal lung expansion during inhalation is impaired and breathing becomes laboured in an attempt to overcome the shortage of oxygen. Toxins from the pus are absorbed and circulate in the bloodstream, causing a deterioration in the horse's general condition. This is a very serious, painful disease and may prove fatal; thus veterinary attention should be sought at an early stage.

As a horse recovers from this condition fibrous strings (adhesions) may form between the lung surface and the chest wall. These are permanent and impair normal collapse of the affected parts of the lung during exhalation, thus interfering with function.

Diagnosis

Pleuritis can be diagnosed on clinical examination, part of which involves percussion of the chest in order to ascertain the extent of the accumulation of pus. If fluid of any type has accumulated at the bottom of the chest cavity, this can be detected as an area of dullness with a horizontal top line or 'fluid line'. Radiographic examination will confirm this. A vet may also take a sample of pus from the chest cavity in an attempt to find out what bacterial organisms are involved and their antibiotic sensitivity pattern.

Treatment

As this is a very serious condition horses are usually hospitalized for intensive care. If much pus and fluid are present in the chest cavity, the vet will draw this material out by means of a needle and syringe and may insert a drain so that this procedure can be carried out as often as required. This will allow the horse to breathe more easily and also help to remove toxins. Antibiotics are needed in order to overcome the infection, and treatment for pain is advisable. Depending on the severity of the condition, intravenous fluids and oxygen administration may be required.

As in the case of pneumonia, good nursing is imperative. The horse should be kept warm and comfortable, in clean surroundings, on light, regular feeds, with water available at all times.

Prevention

As severe stress is a major contributory factor, efforts should be made to avoid or minimize this.

RHODOCOCCUS EQUI INFECTION (SUMMER PNEUMONIA, RATTLES)

This bacterial infection causes pneumonia and abscessation of the lungs, primarily in foals up to the age of six months. For a detailed account, see p. 416.

Parasitic Conditions

LUNGWORM INFECTION

This is a chronic respiratory infection of donkeys and horses caused by lungworm larvae living in the air passages of the lungs. Donkeys seldom show clinical signs of infection, but horses develop intermittent coughing which may persist for many months. General body condition, appetite and temperature are not affected, but the respiratory rate may be elevated, and coughing may become more apparent when the horse is exercised. If the infection is severe the horse may cough more frequently, expel yellow-coloured mucus and show an increased expiratory effort or heave.

The cycle of the lungworm in the horse is such that it is not always possible to find evidence of infection in the dung and a more reliable method of diagnosis is to examine the mucus in the airways for cells and lungworm larvae. Usually a diagnosis of lungworm infestation will be made on a combination of the following factors: association with donkeys, particularly if the donkeys yield positive faecal tests, the horse's clinical signs, the presence of certain cells in the respiratory mucus, and, retrospectively, if a horse responds favourably to treatment.

Both horses and donkeys can be treated successfully with ivermectin. Other anthelmintics, such as fenbendazole and thiabendazole, can be used as alternatives at higher doses than those required for intestinal worms.

For a more detailed account, see p. 449.

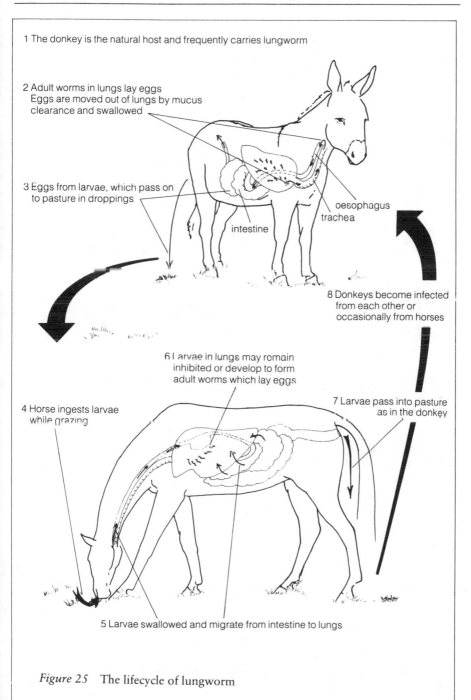

1 The donkey is the natural host and frequently carries lungworm

2 Adult worms in lungs lay eggs
Eggs are moved out of lungs by mucus
clearance and swallowed

3 Eggs from larvae, which pass on
to pasture in droppings

oesophagus
trachea
intestine

8 Donkeys become infected
from each other or
occasionally from horses

6 Larvae in lungs may remain
inhibited or develop to form
adult worms which lay eggs

4 Horse ingests larvae
while grazing

7 Larvae pass into pasture
as in the donkey

5 Larvae swallowed and migrate from intestine to lungs

Figure 25   The lifecycle of lungworm

PARASCARIS EQUORUM INFECTION

This is an intestinal worm infestation caused by the parasite *Parascaris equorum* which affects foals and yearlings. Heavy intestinal infections cause marked loss of weight with possibly fatal consequences due to rupture of the bowel. Respiratory signs occur early in the course of the infection and include coughing, increased respiratory rate and a whitish-yellow nasal discharge. Respiratory signs may persist for two to three weeks. The temperature remains within normal range for the duration of the respiratory signs unless there is secondary bacterial infection.

For a more detailed account, see p. 447.

Allergic Conditions

CHRONIC OBSTRUCTIVE PULMONARY DISEASE (COPD, HEAVES, BROKEN WIND, ALVEOLAR EMPHYSEMA, EQUINE ASTHMA)

This is a chronic respiratory condition due to the horse developing pulmonary hypersensitivity to organic dust antigens in the environment. It is probably the most common cause of chronic coughing in horses in the temperate parts of the northern hemisphere.

The condition is seen most frequently in stabled horses and is associated with a dusty atmosphere and mould in hay and straw. *Micropolyspora faeni* (which causes farmer's lung in man and cattle) and *Aspergillus fumigatus* (a fungus) appear to be the most predominant causative agents in northern Britain but the principle antigens may vary in different parts of the world. Extremely large numbers of such organisms occur in hay and straw with visible spoilage. Baling fodder with a high moisture content results in heat being generated within the bale, which creates optimum conditions for multiplication of these heat-loving organisms.

The problem may be encountered when horses are out of doors during summer months. These cases are thought to be associated with pollen from grass or trees. It is common for horses to show hypersensitivity to more than one agent.

The reason for this hypersensitivty in certain horses is not clear, although a respiratory allergy seems the most likely cause.

Clinical signs

The disease affects horses of two years old and above, becoming more common as horses get older. The clinical signs vary according to the severity of the condition. Early cases of the disease or horses which are mildly affected have an intermittent cough, slight increase in respiratory rate and expiratory effort, and a reduced capacity for exercise. Horses which are more severely affected cough frequently and may cough up thick yellow-coloured mucus. The respiratory rate exceeds twenty breaths per minute and the horse exhibits forceful abdominal respiratory movements with a marked double expiratory effort which gives rise to the so-called heave line (Figure 24). The horse may appear dull and breathless, with flared nostrils. Wheezing can be heard at the nostrils of severely affected cases.

COPD-affected horses have a normal temperature. Appetite is not usually affected unless a horse is suffering severe respiratory embarrassment.

Course of the condition

Initially the onset of the condition is gradual; however, once established, a horse can suffer attacks which develop rapidly. In this respect the disease has been likened to human bronchial asthma. An affected horse may show signs as rapidly as a half to one hour after first being exposed to the causative agent, but usually signs become noticeable from five to ten hours thereafter. Once a horse is showing signs, they may persist at approximately the same severity for the duration of the exposure to the antigen. Alternatively the signs can become progressively worse, with the horse becoming increasingly breathless. Removal of the offending material allows most cases to improve gradually over the course of a few days.

In affected horses exposure to the causative agent brings about widespread changes in the lungs. These include inflammation of the very small airways (less than 2 mm diameter), production of excessive, thick mucus, and spasm of the muscle in the walls of the airways. These changes cause narrowing of the internal diameter of the airways; thus the horse has to make considerably more effort in order to breath its usual volume of air.

The pressure exerted when a horse with this condition exhales causes the small airways to become even narrower, and some collapse completely. This makes exhalation difficult and an increased volume of air is retained in the alveoli. Because these changes are widespread, the lungs have an over-inflated appearance which, for many years, was thought to be the result of irreversible emphysema; hence the term 'broken wind'. However, relatively recent studies have shown that the vast majority of alveoli do not undergo destructive changes. Instead there is a ballooning effect, with the alveoli deflating back to their original size with the remission of clinical signs. The lung changes which occur in affected horses lead to a reduction in the change of air in the alveoli with each breath, and less oxygen is absorbed into the blood, resulting in a general shortage of oxygen in the body.

Changes in the respiratory pattern appear to be reversible in the majority of cases if suitable managemental changes are introduced. If care is taken to maintain these measures a horse can remain free of clinical signs of the disease (asymptomatic) for long periods. However, once a horse becomes affected with COPD, it appears to retain its hypersensitivity for many years if not for life and exposure to the antigen at any time will cause the onset of clinical signs.

Diagnosis

If horses are showing distinct clinical signs of COPD, a veterinary surgeon can make a diagnosis on these grounds. In addition, an injection of a bronchodilating agent brings about a marked though temporary improvement in the horse's condition. The diagnosis can be confirmed retrospectively by assessing the horse's response to a change in the environment.

If horses are asymptomatic or in the early stages of developing the disease, the diagnosis can be very difficult. The veterinary surgeon takes account of the horse's past history of respiratory disease and the clinical signs, and may attempt either to exacerbate or to improve the condition through environmental changes. Such cases may be referred to veterinary schools or equine research centres for assistance with diagnosis.

Treatment and prevention

The most important aspect of treating COPD-affected animals is to introduce environmental control measures (a so-called minimal-dust environment), which can be used in conjunction with drug therapy.

As most cases of COPD are associated with stabling and exposure to hay and straw, the most favourable long-term method of controlling the disease is to use substitutes for hay and straw. Any of the following forms of stable bedding are suitable: shredded paper, hardwood shavings or peat, with soiled material being removed on a daily basis rather than the horse being deep-littered. The horse should be fed on a complete cubed diet and no hay or, alternatively, vacuum-packed hay in combination with a type of cube appropriate to the horse's energy needs. The stable should preferably be at least 50 metres to the windward side of the hay store, according to the direction of the prevailing wind. Dust should be removed from ledges, beams and fitments at regular intervals while the stable is vacated, and time allowed for airing before the horse is brought in. However, it is futile to take these precautions for an individual horse if it is going to be exposed to dust and antigens from the stables of neighbouring horses (via half walls or in barn-type accommodation). All animals sharing airspace with the affected horse should be subject to the same enviroment-control measures.

The alternative method of environmental control is to keep affected horses at grass, provided that they are not hypersensitive to pollen or, if so, that the grasses and trees are not in flower. No supplementary hay should be fed and grazing areas should not be adjacent to hay or straw stores. Simply being out of doors does not alleviate the condition if affected horses are fed hay regularly. Any supplementary feeding should be in the form of a cubed diet.

Even good-quality hay and straw contain large amounts of fungal spores; thus attempts at controlling COPD by using only the 'best' hay and straw will invariably fail. Feeding hay which has been soaked for hours in water is not universally successful. This may be because dust generated in handling the hay (for example, when filling hay nets) blows into the vicinity of the horse, or it may be that wetting the hay does not prevent the effects of exposure to the antigens.

It is never possible to eliminate fungal spores completely from the environment because they can be airborne for many hundreds of miles. However, using environment-control measures, it is possible to reduce the levels of the antigens to below a threshold required to cause clinical disease. Applying these measures allows most COPD-affected horses to become asymptomatic in one to two weeks. However, severely affected horses, in which the illness has been of long duration, may take considerably longer to attain a satisfactory improvement.

There are two approaches to drug therapy of COPD; (a) treatment of horses showing clinical signs of the disease; and (b) preventive medication of asymptomatic horses in anticipation of exposure to the antigens.

When COPD-affected horses are in severe respiratory distress, bronchodilator drugs help to alleviate their condition. In addition drugs which assist in the removal of thick mucus from the airways can be used in the treatment of symptomatic horses. The resulting improvement lasts only for the duration of the treatment; for this reason permanent environment-control measures should be introduced as well. The use of these drugs has no place in the long-term treatment of equine COPD as a substitute for environmental control.

If unavoidable exposure to the antigens is anticipated, horses can be treated with a drug called sodium cromoglycate in an attempt to prevent the onset of clinical signs. Horses should be asymptomatic before treatment commences as it is not intended as a therapy for patients showing clinical signs of disease. A short course of treatment may be useful when there is short-term risk of exposure (for example, a horse stabled away from home for a few days). Alternatively, long-term intermittent sodium cromoglycate treatment could facilitate the management of horses kept at livery or in large stable yards where providing special environmental control measures for a single horse can be difficult.

EXERCISE-INDUCED PULMONARY HAEMORRHAGE (EIPH, LUNG HAEMORRHAGE, EPISTAXIS, NOSEBLEED)

Exercise-induced pulmonary haemorrhage (EIPH) is a condition in which haemorrhage occurs in part of the lungs as a consequence of moderate to strenuous exercise.

The cause(s) are not fully understood but it is considered to be an athletic injury. It is related primarily to mechanical stress in the lungs which occurs with forceful breathing during exertion. This causes the delicate walls of the air cells to rupture, resulting in haemorrhage. It happens in many horses with otherwise normal lungs, but any pre-existing respiratory conditions are believed to increase the risk of EIPH. Any breed or type of horse may be affected and it is recognized worldwide. There is no apparent association with climate, altitude, type of housing, or feeding or bedding materials. Thoroughbreds in training first experience EIPH as two-year-olds with the start of fast work. It can occur in horses of any age.

The amount of haemorrhage varies considerably between horses and episodes. In most cases the quantity is small, and although evidence of haemorrhage can be found on endoscopic examination of the airways, no blood is seen at the nostrils. In more severe cases blood loss will occur from the nostrils in varying quantities and performance can be severely impaired. Haemorrhage occurs in the uppermost posterior part of the lungs and can be seen as an area of increased density on radiographic examination. These changes may resolve within ten days in some cases, but in others it can take months, depending on the degree of the initial changes, repeated exertion with further haemorrhage in the area and subsequent bacterial infection with possible abscess formation in the damaged tissue.

A wide range of drugs has been used in attempts to prevent EIPH, but to date none has proved universally successful. Further studies and a better understanding of the cause(s) of EIPH are required if successful prophylactic measures are to be found.

3
THE HEART AND CIRCULATION

Blood, as discussed in chapter 5, is the fluid that transports around the body all the vital substances and gases on which life depends. It is the transport system *par excellence*, but its many functions depend on its being circulated continuously throughout the body.

Blood is circulated in the arteries, capillaries and veins, a system of branching tubes which convey blood from the heart into the tissues (e.g. the muscles) and back to the heart (Figure 26).

The heart acts as a pump which drives blood through the blood vessels, and it is logical, therefore, to start the description of the heart and circulation with the organ that provides the power that maintains the blood circulating for each second of the individual's lifespan.

The heart

The heart consists of four chambers (Figure 28) with walls composed of muscle. Blood passes from the first to the second chamber, entering from veins and leaving in arteries. The chambers are arranged in two pairs and there are, therefore, a first and second chamber on the left side and a first and second chamber on the right side. There is not normally any communication between the two sides.

The walls of both first chambers (auricles, atria) are comparatively thin, while those of the right second chamber (ventricle) are thicker, with the walls of the left second chamber being thickest of all.

These varying thicknesses are due to the different amounts of power required by each chamber in relation to the pumping action of the heart. For example, the first chambers pump blood into the second chambers and the force required to perform this task is relatively light. The walls are therefore relatively thin.

The second chamber on the right side is responsible for pumping blood via the pulmonary artery through the lungs. The distance involved is small and the resistance in the blood vessels comparatively light. The right-hand

Figure 26 The heart and its circulation

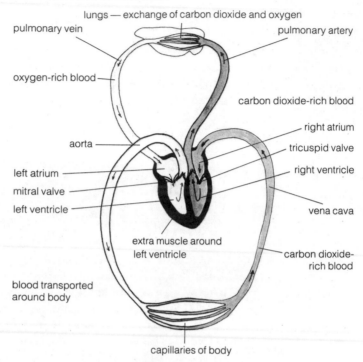

lungs — exchange of carbon dioxide and oxygen

pulmonary vein

pulmonary artery

oxygen-rich blood

carbon dioxide-rich blood

aorta

right atrium

tricuspid valve

left atrium

right ventricle

mitral valve

left ventricle

vena cava

extra muscle around
left ventricle

carbon dioxide-
rich blood

blood transported
around body

capillaries of body

Figure 27 Frontal view
showing the location of the
heart

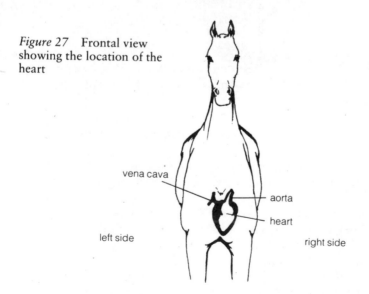

vena cava

aorta

heart

left side

right side

second chamber has a fairly simple task, but nevertheless this requires more power than that of the first chambers. Its walls are therefore moderately thick.

In contrast, the second chamber on the left side has the most onerous task of all, namely, to pump blood to and from the whole body apart from the lungs. It has to drive blood through the arteries to the head and the limbs, providing sufficient force to return it to the heart for recirculation. For this reason the walls of the second chamber on the left side are very thick indeed.

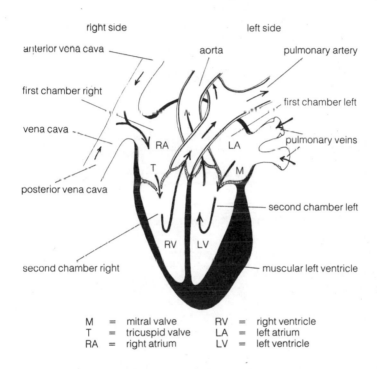

M	=	mitral valve	RV	=	right ventricle
T	=	tricuspid valve	LA	=	left atrium
RA	=	right atrium	LV	=	left ventricle

Figure 28   A section of the heart

The pumping action is supplied by contraction of the muscles in a rhythmic and orderly manner, so that the blood is received from the veins and squeezed through the chambers of the heart into the arteries, which take it to the lungs and to the body. This would not be possible if it were not for the valves which prevent backward flow of blood when the walls of the chambers contract. The reader has only to visualize an attempt to squeeze water from a tube that is open at both ends. Water would, in this instance, escape in both directions on either side of the part that was being squeezed.

There are valves between the first and second chambers on each side which prevent blood from flowing back from the second into the first chamber when the heart muscle contracts. Blood can, therefore, flow only into the arteries; the whole force of the pumping action of the heart is directed onwards rather than backwards.

There are also valves at the point where the second chambers open into the arteries. These valves allow the onward flow of blood into the arteries. The walls of these arteries contain a substance known as elastin, which enables them to expand and contract, and, as pressure mounts within them, it comes to oppose the force being exerted by the contracting chambers of the heart. When the two pressures (in the heart and in the arteries) are equal, the valves shut and prevent blood from passing back into the chambers as their walls relax to accommodate the blood entering from the first chambers to start a fresh pumping action.

Let us now follow a red blood cell as it passes through the heart on its way to the lungs, back to the heart and thence to the body, before returning once more to the heart (see Figures 26 and 28).

The cell enters the first chamber on the right side, that is, the right atrium or auricle. As the walls of this chamber contract, the cell is propelled through the atrio-ventricular tricuspid (i.e. three-cusp) valve. The cell is now in the second chamber, the right ventricle. As this chamber contracts, the cell is ejected through the pulmonary valves into the pulmonary artery. It travels through the lungs, first entering the capillaries and then leaving the lungs in one of the pulmonary veins. These veins take it back to the heart, but now the cell enters the left atrium or first chamber on the left side. From this chamber it passes through the valve guarding the entrance to the second chamber, the mitral (two-cusped) valve, into the left ventricle. From the left ventricle it is pumped through the aortic valves at the entrance to the aorta, the main artery in the body, and from thence through the capillaries back into the veins, eventually returning to the right atrium, the point at which it originally started.

The lining of the chambers of the heart is known as the endocardium and the heart muscle itself the myocardium. The endocardium is a smooth lining composed of special cells that reduce to a minimum the friction between the walls and the blood. The outside of the heart is covered by another fine lining similar to the endocardium and known as the pericardium. This lining is reflected onto a fibrous sac that encloses the heart and thus provides a slippery surface which reduces any friction that might arise from the pumping motion of the heart within the chest.

When blood is squeezed through the chambers of the heart, the pumping action requires an orderly, progressive movement, which can be likened to squeezing a tube of paste by starting at one end and continuing towards the nozzle. The heart muscle starts to contract in the first chambers and the wave of contraction passes towards and into the second chamber, passing from the opening between the chambers towards the arteries, which represent the nozzle of the tube or the exit for the blood.

As each wave of contractions affects one part of the heart, so the part immediately behind it starts to relax and allows blood to enter, thus refilling the chamber for the start of the next contraction. Contraction (systole) is followed by relaxation (diastole). Each beat of the heart consists of a wave of contractions followed by a wave of relaxation.

Two features enable this pumping action to occur. The first of these features is that heart muscle consists of fibres which join with each other in a sheath rather than, as with the fibres of voluntary muscle (the muscles in the arms or back, etc.), being composed of bundles of individual fibres. The special property of heart muscle is its ability to contract in wavelike movements with the inherent rhythmicity that is so characteristic of heart beats.

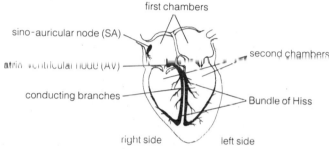

Figure 29   The heart showing the conduction pathways

The second feature is the presence of special conducting pathways which direct the current that stimulates the contraction of the muscles along a given pathway from the first, to and through the second chambers. The wave of excitation of heart muscle starts from a definite site in the right atrium known as the sinus node, spreads throughout the first chambers, activates the atrio-ventricular (AV) node, and passes into the ventricles via a bundle of conducting fibres known as the Bundle of Hiss. From this pathway it spreads throughout both of the second chambers.

It is this electrical activity which stimulates contraction of the heart muscles that can be recorded on an electrocardiograph (ECG). Each beat of the heart produces a definite, discrete pattern on the ECG (see Figure 30c), the associated electrical activity being recorded from the surface of the body. Thus the P wave of the ECG corresponds to the spread of the electrical activity and contraction of the first chambers, the QRS waves to the passage of the electrical activity through the Bundle of Hiss and into the ventricles. The T wave represents the period of relaxation or depolarization. These aspects are discussed more fully below (p. 61).

The pumping movements of the heart are not silent. They can be heard on listening (auscultating) at the chest with a stethoscope. This instrument merely conducts the sounds in a convenient and efficient manner to the ear of the listener. The sounds of the beating heart are a fundamental part of the

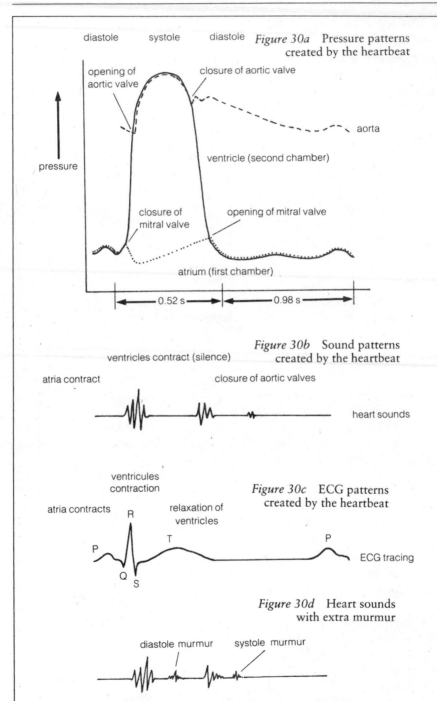

diastole   systole   diastole   *Figure 30a*   Pressure patterns
                                                        created by the heartbeat

opening of   closure of aortic valve
aortic valve

                                                        aorta

pressure   ventricle (second chamber)

          closure of   opening of mitral valve
          mitral valve

              atrium (first chamber)

          ←——— 0.52 s ———→←——— 0.98 s ———→

Figure 30b   Sound patterns
        ventricles contract (silence)   created by the heartbeat

atria contract   closure of aortic valves

                                        heart sounds

        ventricules
        contraction   *Figure 30c*   ECG patterns
                                        created by the heartbeat
atria contracts   R   relaxation of
                            ventricles
        P   T   P
                                                        ECG tracing
              Q
                S

Figure 30d   Heart sounds
        with extra murmur

        diastole murmur   systole murmur

clinical examination of the organ. They originate from contracting muscle, the movement of blood through the chambers and the closing of the valves, which all combine to give the characteristic beat 'lubb-dup' (see below).

Circulation

Blood circulates through the arteries, which branch repeatedly into smaller vessels until they reach their destination in the tissue of muscles, organs, bone, etc. Here their size is so small that they are described as arterioles (very small arteries). However, the walls of arterioles are relatively thick and, in these circumstances, the essential exchange of substances between the tissues cannot take place. It is only when the walls become minutely thinned that this exchange process can occur. At their final destination, therefore, the walls of the arterioles become one cell thick and are called capillaries.

The walls of the vessels which conduct the blood from the aorta or from the pulmonary artery to the arterioles contain an elastic substance known as elastin. This feature has already been mentioned in relation to the blood being pumped into the arteries by the heart. The elasticity smooths the change in pressure as the heart contracts. We can feel this rise in pressure in our arteries if we place a finger on our pulse on the thumb side of our wrist.

This elasticity is responsible for the contours of the pressure wave that occurs during the heart beat (see Figure 30a). The peak of the wave occurs during contraction of the heart (systole) and the lowest pressure at the end of the period of relaxation (diastole). Pulse pressure is therefore referred to as possessing systolic and diastolic pressure; and the normal value for the horse is 120 over 80 mmHg. The value is expressed in millimetres of mercury, which reflects the fact that the top pressure would sustain a column of mercury 120 millimetres high and the lower pressure one of 80 millimetres high.

The pressure in the arteries is due not only to the elasticity of the vessels but to the resistance produced by the ever decreasing size of the vessels, especially that of the arterioles and capillaries. If it were not for this

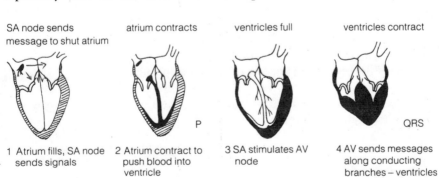

SA node sends message to shut atrium	atrium contracts	ventricles full	ventricles contract
	P		QRS
1 Atrium fills, SA node sends signals	2 Atrium contract to push blood into ventricle	3 SA stimulates AV node	4 AV sends messages along conducting branches – ventricles contract push blood into arteries

Figure 31 The heart in action

resistance, the pressure in the blood vessels would hardly rise at all, and there would be no force to move blood for any distance, let alone to move it round the body.

Blood pressure therefore provides a rough guide to the work that the heart is called upon to meet to overcome the resistance in the blood vessels. The higher the blood pressure the greater the load of work, and this is why, in humans, steps are taken to reduce abnormally high blood pressure (hypertension). There is no evidence that horses suffer from high blood pressure except as a result of exercise, which is a temporary change, or as a result of a disease, such as colic, laminitis or grass sickness, which lasts only as long as the disease itself.

Let us now return to the point at which we left the description of the vessels in which blood circulates. The arterial capillaries lead the blood into the venous capillaries and thence into veins of ever increasing size until they return to the heart. Blood passing back through the heart from parts behind this organ do so in the great vein passing through the chest. This vein is known as the posterior vena cava (see Figure 28). Blood returning from parts of the body in front of the heart do so in a second vein, the anterior vena cava.

The heart has its own special circulation system within the myocardium. It receives its oxygen from blood circulating through the coronary vessels. These arise close to the aortic valve and most drain into the coronary sinus, which opens into the right atrium. A few small cardiac veins drain directly into the right atrium.

Examining the heart

The normality of a horse's heart has always been of major concern to vets and horse owners. The heart is rightly considered to be important in athletic performance and any defect is likely to impose corresponding limits. Horses and ponies used only for riding must also have a healthy heart, but the belief that they might drop dead because of heart disease is not well founded: sudden death in horses is rarely due to heart attacks or coronary disease as experienced in humans; more often it is the result of a rupture of a large artery or from some non-cardiovascular disease.

It is not surprising, therefore, that a clinical examination of the heart has always been an important feature of certification for soundness. In fact, in past times horses might be certified as sound in wind, eye and heart. Unfortunately the interpretation of findings of abnormalities, such as murmurs, has lagged behind the experience and technological capabilities of our profession. We are not alone in this problem: the human cardiologist finds it equally difficult to forecast the future health and performance of the heart from an examination using the most modern medical aids. The reason is that the heart is an organ of amazing adaptability. Its action as a pump may be suspect because of some defect but, unlike a mechanical pump, it has the ability to compensate by growing larger to overcome certain problems. For example, if there is a leaking valve which reduces its efficiency, the heart increases the force of its action to compensate for any reduction in output that may result from the failure of the valve. In doing this it increases the thickness of its muscle in the ventricles and the performance of the horse is maintained as before.

But perhaps the most important limitation facing us is that imposed by the size of the horse, which makes it difficult to complete a full physical examination of the heart by means such as radiography. However, recent developments in ultrasound scanning techniques are likely to overcome this problem because now we can visualize (actually see) the heart and its valves in action.

The heart may be examined clinically by listening (auscultation), electrocardiography (ECG) and ultrasound scanning. Indirectly its action may be assessed by measuring blood pressure and the character of the pulse. Special consideration is given to the state of the horse at the time of examination, especially if it is at rest or excited or if the examination is made during or after exercise.

Auscultation   When we listen to the heart we interpret the sound in four aspects: (a) the rate and sequence in which they occur; (b) their normality or otherwise; (c) their rhythm; (d) the intensity and relationship to other sounds that any abnormal sounds have, should they occur.

When we listen we are, of course, using the human ear and have to accept the limitations that this imposes on the examination. Some sounds may be so faint as to be inaudible to most, if not all, listeners; or they may be made in a sequence which is at so short an interval as to be indistinguishable from one another. If we use sensitive recording devices (phonocardiography) we may more acurately represent all the sounds that are emanating from each heart beat (see Figure 30b).

However, the basic sounds that we can hear are the lubb-dup of a single beat. The lubb is a slow, slurred sound and the dup a sharper, shorter sound. They are referred to as the first and second sounds of the heart beat.

The first sound emanates from the atria as they contract. The interval between the first and second sounds is the period when the ventricles are contracting (see Figure 30b). The second sound comes from the closure or snapping shut of the valves guarding the entrance to the pulmonary artery and aorta. The pause between this event and the next first sound (lubb) is governed by the rate at which the heart is beating. The time intervals involved in the heart beat are shown in Figure 30a. The loudness of these sounds depends to a large extent on the amount of fat and the thickness of the chest wall. In general the sounds are more audible and loudest in thin subjects.

The forward flow of blood through the heart chambers is usually silent.

The same applies to flow through the waterpipes in our homes. Sound only comes from flowing water if some impediment occurs, which causes turbulence. The turbulence or vibrations are transmitted in sound waves that can be heard as such. The nature of the sound depends on the type of turbulence.

Sounds may be evaluated in terms of loudness (intensity), pitch (high or low notes) and quality (tone). This applies to sounds originating from disturbances in the forward flow of the blood. These sounds are called **murmurs**. We may therefore classify murmurs according to their intensity (grades 1–6), pitch (high squeak or low burr) and quality (musical, harsh, metallic, etc.).

The character of the murmur tells us something of the nature of the turbulence and therefore its cause, for example, a leaking or fibrosed valve. It tells us nothing of the location of the problem within the heart itself. More information on this aspect is gained by considering the place that the murmur occupies in the cycle of the heart beat. This may be achieved by placing the sound in the context of the two heart beats (Figure 30d). For example, if the sound occurs after the second sound (i.e. when the heart is relaxing – diastole) this is most likely to be associated with the closure of the aortic or pulmonary valves. It might indicate some insufficiency in their function and, therefore, constitute some problem.

Another example is a murmur occurring between the first and second sounds (Figure 30d). This is during the period when the ventricles are contracting. This might indicate a leaking mitral or tricuspid valve between the first and second chambers.

Other murmurs may be regarded as innocent and merely due to turbulence resulting from a projection in the contour of the heart chamber which is normal but unusual in that it makes the blood eddy and thus cause a sound. This type of murmur is generally referred to as an **ejection murmur**.

The second consideration which may be of help is to designate the area from which the murmur is heard at its loudest. The area of auscultation of the heart ranges from the region of the auricles to the apex formed by the lower part of the ventricles, and on the left and right side of the chest.

Murmurs heard most distinctly on the right side are more likely to originate from the right side of the heart, for example, during the passage of blood between the first and second chambers of this side, whereas murmurs heard loudest on the left side originate on that side.

A defect in the mitral valve, for example, is likely to cause a murmur which is best heard on the left side, whereas one due to tricuspid valve insufficiency will be heard loudest on the right side. By moving the stethoscope over the area of the heart on the left side we may detect loudness in relation to the aortic, pulmonary or tricuspid valves. However, some murmurs can be heard throughout the various regions of the heart and auscultation provides an incomplete indication of their origin.

When we listen to the heart we may also discern its rate and rhythm. The rate depends on whether the horse is at rest or has been exerting itself or is frightened. The rate increases because of stimulation by the sympathetic nerves (see p. 113) and/or by secretion of the hormone adrenaline (see p. 121). The normal rate for an adult horse is forty beats per minute and in very young foals eighty beats per minute.

The output of blood resulting from the pumping action is measured by the volume of blood pumped by the heart at each beat (stroke volume). The amount of blood pumped by the heart per minute is a product of stroke volume × the number of beats per minute. The heart may achieve the same output by halving the output per beat and doubling the number of beats. The heart pump is most efficient at a slow beat and high output per beat. For exercise it increases both the rate and the stroke volume.

Rhythm refers to the way in which beats occur. **Arrhythmia (dysrhythmia)** means that the beat is irregular. There are many reasons for this, some of them significant with regard to the output of the heart (cardiac output) and others with no such effect.

The most common arrythmia is the **dropped beat**. This may be illustrated, as lubb-dup, lubb-dup, lubb-dup, pause, lubb-dup, lubb-dup, pause, lubb-dup, and so on. The dropped beat may, as in this illustration, occur irregularly, or it may be regular, say every fifth beat. This type of arrythmia occurs when the heart is beating at a slow rate. Opinions differ as to its significance but the majority of clinicians attach little importance to its presence.

The dropped beat is in actuality the failure of the second chambers to contract following contraction of the first chambers. Usually when we listen to the heart in these cases we can hear the first sound, which is associated with the contraction of the atria, but not the second sound because the ventricles do not contract. The reason for this failure is that the wave of electrical excitation fails to pass down the Bundle of Hiss to the ventricles in the normal manner. Thus the exact illustration should be lubb-dup, lubb-dup, lubb, lubb-dup, lubb-dup.

The irregularity known as **atrial fibrilation** is a more serious arrythmia. In this the first chambers contract partly and rapidly and the second chambers only occasionally and in a sequence that is in itself irregular. For example, we hear the sounds lubb-dup, lubb-dup, lubb-dup, coming quickly together at a rate of perhaps sixty per minute. These are then followed by quite a long pause before we again hear lubb-dup, lubb-dup; then another pause of, perhaps, greater length than the previous one, followed by a series of perhaps five or six very rapid beats.

Cases of arrythmia may be diagnosed by using the stethoscope, but the definitive diagnosis rests on identifying the electrical disturbances with which they are associated. This technique depends on electrocardiography.

Electrocardiography (ECG)   We have already discussed the way electrical stimulation is involved in the heart beat (see p. 57). The electrocardiogram is a written representation of the wave form that this electrical activity takes. The fact that it is occurring in the heart does not prevent us from picking up signals on the surface of the body. For this purpose electrodes are attached, usually to the limbs, a special conducting jelly is placed between the electrodes and the skin, and the galvanometer within the machine records the electrical activity.

A typical wave form is shown in Figure 30c. Irregular rhythms may be identified and an example is shown in Figure 30d.

The interpretation of the ECG is a technical matter and not within the scope of this book. However, it is hoped that enough has been described to provide the reader with an insight into this valuable technique. ECG not only helps to diagnose the actual cause or reason for arrythmias, but also provides documentary evidence of the state of the heart relative to this electrical activity for future reference should it be needed.

Ultrasound scanning   The use of ultrasound scanning on the heart is known technically as echocardiography (literally, echoes from the heart). This is a relatively new and exciting area of veterinary medicine. By its means we can obtain a graphic picture of the valves and other parts of the heart in action. The use of echocardiography in examing the horse's heart illustrates the need, to which reference has already been made, for means of interpretation. The art of the subject is still young, but it is hoped that with experience the profession may come to be able to pronounce more effectively on the functional effects of apparent defects rather than, as often in the past, on their existence rather than their significance.

Conclusions

The purpose in this chapter has been to provide the reader with a general account of various aspects of the heart, how it functions and how apparent defects may be interpreted. The point has been made that the heart is an amazingly adaptable organ and that its function is to pump blood. A diseased heart is not necessarily incapable of achieving its function, although it may not be able to do so when called upon for maximum performance.

In order to assess function, more sophisticated and elaborate tests are required than are often justified in practice because of time, finance and practicality. The most important means of assessing function is to examine the heart when it is performing at maximum output, that is, when challenged to the extent that it is under pressure in a race, for example. For this reason apparatus has been developed using electronic and radio principles to record heart rate throughout a period of exercise. Unfortunately interpretation of the results is often impossible due to the variables involved, one of which is a feature we have previously discussed, namely, the adaptability of the heart to meet its duties even though it is in some way deficient.

The evaluation of the heart's performance is not the same as evaluating the horse's performance. To say that the heart is not functioning properly requires a test which actually measures cardiac output (amount of blood pumped per beat). This can be achieved under experimental conditions but not, as yet, in clinical practice. It is only with the development of practical methods of measuring the efficiency of the heart under various conditions of stress and exercise that we will be able to claim that we can assess a horse's heart in terms of its ability to support athletic performance. Progress towards this end may eventually come from studies on exercise physiology (see chapter 48).

4
THE LYMPHATIC SYSTEM

The lymphatic system consists of a network of fine tubes or vessels which ramify throughout the body in a similar manner to blood vessels. However, the difference is that the lymph fluid they contain is not driven by a pump, as the heart pumps the blood. The movement of fluid is effected by massage from the extremities as the limbs and their muscles move.

The tubes have blind ends where lymph fluid forms, and these join up with one another to form increasingly larger channels on their way towards the chest. This is identical to the branches of arteries ending as capillaries in the tissues. The difference is that the smallest lymph tubes have blind ends instead of connecting with veins, as is the case with the arteries. For this reason the lymph fluid in the vessels does not circulate in the same way as blood is pumped through the system by the heart.

Lymph drains towards the heart, carried on its way by the massaging action of the movement of muscles and tendons. The flow is aided by valves situated at intervals throughout the system of tubes. These valves prevent backflow and thereby ensure that lymph drains in one direction only. The smaller tubes drain into larger tubes, until eventually the main drainage channel of the lymphatic system discharges into the bloodstream close to the heart.

The lymph vessels have very fine walls, so water can pass easily through them. The channels are thus in close communication with the interstitial fluid, that is, the fluid which bathes the cells of the body tissues such as muscles.

The main function of the lymphatic system is to drain off excess fluid from all parts of the body. The pressure in the blood vessels is greatest in the lower parts of the limbs due to the effect of gravity. The role of the lymphatic system is to facilitate the drainage of fluid from the tissues of the limbs so that they do not become waterlogged.

If the free flow of water into the lymph system is impeded, the tissues become waterlogged and the area becomes swollen or oedematous. The oedema (filling) can be recognized by swellings which pit when firm pressure is applied by the fingers.

Normally there is a balance between water in the bloodstream, in the tissue spaces between the cells and in the lymph stream. This balance depends on the concentration of salts and proteins in the bloodstream on one side of the capillary wall and in the tissue spaces in the other. Any factor which upsets this balance may produce waterlogging of the part unless the lymph can drain away the excess fluid.

More water than normal may pass out of the blood vessels because their walls are affected by toxins. In this instance not only fluid but protein may pass into the interstitial tissues, thus drawing additional water with it. The blood is thinned by the loss of protein and this lowers the osmotic pull across the membrane of the blood capillary walls.

Excess feeding and too little exercise leads to waterlogging because the richness of the food disturbs the delicate protein and electrolyte balance, and the lymph system is unable to carry away the waste material and excess fluid. This occurs in the dependant parts of the limbs because of the particular difficulty of returning water up the limbs against the pull of gravity. If the horse is not exercised, this accentuates the problem due to the fact that movement is necessary to massage the lymph flow back towards the heart.

Lymph also contains lymphocytes and a small number of other white cells. It plays some part in the defence of the body against infection. Thus at various points along the course of the system there are glands (lymph glands) which filter off noxious substances and microbes. The glands also play a part in the production of antibody. This is formed by certain cells in the gland and released into the bloodstream to combat infection.

Conditions of the Lymphatic System

In practice we are not normally aware of the lymphatic system because we cannot recognize the vessels in the same way as we can see veins and arteries. Further, the glands of the system are too small to feel. However, when the system is disturbed, its presence becomes obvious in a number of ways.

The flow of lymph may be reduced by lack of movement as described above. Drainage is then restricted so that water collects and the part becomes filled (**filled leg**). This is an example of **humour** in the horse's limbs which disappears when the individual is exercised and the flow of lymph is increased by the massaging action of the muscles and tendons.

The legs may become filled when the walls of the blood and lymph vessels are damaged by toxins, so that water passes into the tissue spaces at an abnormal rate. The causes of this condition may be an allergy following the eating of substances to which the horse is allergic, the injection of drugs or it may occur as a direct result of a viral or bacterial infection. Diets high in

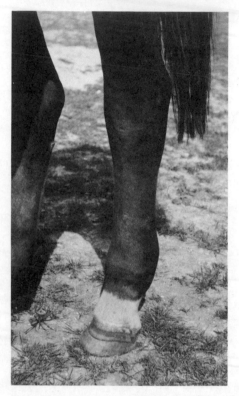

Figure 32   A horse with lymphangitis

protein may aggravate the swellings due to the nutritional element adding to the problem of drainage; lack of exercise may play a further role.

The lymph glands may themselves become swollen due to toxins and microbes carried to them in the lymph stream. One such example of the swellings, occurring between the angles of the lower jaw, is the mandibular gland. This occurs in young horses as a consequence of microbes passing from the lining of the airways of the head into the lymph channels that drain the tissues of the head.

Some bacteria, particularly *Streptococcus equi* (the cause of strangles – see p. 411) and the ordinary streptococcus, may cause pus to form in the glands. An abscess develops which eventually bursts through the skin in foals and yearlings to the outside, discharging pus. These glands may also become infected as the result of bacteria entering the lymph stream from the tissues around newly erupting molar teeth.

The lymphatic system plays an essential role in the repair of injuries by removing debris and excess fluid in the cells brought to the area as a result of inflammation (see chapter 36). If a wound becomes infected, this may spread to the lymphatic vessels and they too become inflamed.

This results in a condition known as **lymphangitis** (Figure 32). In contrast to the ordinary filled legs, in which excess fluid is quickly removed once the cause has been eliminated and proper drainage restored, lymphangitis may lead to a permanently enlarged limb.

In severe cases the inflammation spreads to the tissues surrounding the lymph vessels and drainage becomes so disturbed that excess fluid escapes by breaking through the skin in ulcer-like eruptions.

The hind limbs are most often affected by lymphangitis, as they are by oedematous swellings, by virtue of the increased distance from the heart occupied by the hind compared with the front limbs.

Problems may also arise because of the anatomy of the lymphatic system in the hind limb. As the lymphatic vessels pass over the inside of the hock they are very prone to blockage. It is probable that some cases of lymphangitis are caused by emboli (small clots) lodging in the channels at certain key points as they pass over the bony structures of the hock. This virtually cuts off the drainage of lymph from the lower part of the limb, causing it to become very swollen, hot and painful.

Pain is a feature in lymphangitis. It has the effect of causing the horse to refrain from placing weight on the limb or moving it at all. This accentuates the problem of drainage and creates a vicious circle of fluid and products from damaged tissue, microbes and other matter accumulating to cause further pain from lack of drainage.

Treatment is aimed at combating any infection by the administration of antibiotics and/or other anti-microbial substances, together with pain-relieving drugs such as phenylbutazone or anti-prostaglandins. If the pain can be controlled, the horse starts to put weight on the leg and can then be induced to walk, which helps to restore the circulation of lymph. However, in some cases the tissues under the skin become chronically enlarged and replaced by permanently fibrous tissue.

It is not only the limbs which are affected by oedema due to poor lymphatic drainage. Swellings may appear on the belly of a pregnant mare as the lymphatic vessels become overburdened due to excessive activity associated with mammary development in preparation for the birth of the foal. This oedema usually quickly disperses after foaling.

5
THE BLOOD

Blood is the red fluid pumped by the heart through the arteries and veins, forming the circulation. It is carried to every part and acts thereby as a transportation system, carrying nourishment, vital substances, gases and waste material. Among its many functions it carries oxygen from the lungs to the muscles and other tissues, transports digested food from the gut to the liver and from this organ to all other tissues. It carries the hormones, regulates the water and electrolyte balance, and acts in the defence of the body against infection by mobilizing the body's resources against noxious agents such as microbes, poisons and foreign proteins.

Blood is composed of cells suspended in a fluid known as plasma. There are two types of cell: red and white.

Plasma

Plasma consists of water in which certain mineral salts and proteins are dissolved. It is normally straw-coloured with a slightly yellowish tinge. This can be appreciated when blood is allowed to stand and the red and white cells sediment out, leaving the plasma lying above. This may also be appreciated when the blood is centrifuged. The reading of the percentage by volume of plasma to cells is known as the haematocrit or packed-cell volume (PCV). This is normally 40–50 per cent of the total blood. The percentage is lower in cases of anaemia (see p. 77). It is higher after exercise because red cells contained in the spleen are discharged into the circulation in large quantities when a horse is exerted. The percentage is also higher in horses suffering from dehydration, for example, as a result of diarrhoea.

The plasma contains about 93 per cent water and about 6 per cent protein. Minerals and salts such as sodium, potassium, calcium, magnesium, chlorides, bicarbonates and organic acids comprise the other 1 per cent. The water content passes readily through the capillary walls in either direction. It can thereby enter or leave the tissues of the muscles and organs, and this exchange plays a vital part in fluid balance.

The protein is made up of various components such as albumin and globulin, which have different sized molecules. The larger albumin molecules do not normally pass out of the bloodstream through the capillary membrane into the tissues. They provide the blood with its osmotic gradient, that is, the biological process which pulls water through membranes from an area of lower concentration to that of a higher concentration, until equilibrium is established on both sides.

The protein globulins are divided into alpha, beta and gamma globulins and fibrinogen. The total concentration of these proteins is about 6 g/litre of plasma. In the laboratory proteins are usually measured from the serum, which is the yellow gel formed when blood clots.

The difference between plasma and serum is that plasma contains fibrinogen, which is part of the clotting mechanism that prevents excessive bleeding. The fibrinogen is not activated until exposed to air, which is why, when collecting plasma for analysis, we have to add anti-clotting substances. For further discussion of the clotting mechanism, see below.

The role of plasma proteins is varied. Clotting has already been mentioned. The globulins also contain the immune protective substances known as antibodies. Proteins are also associated with hormones, enzymes and vitamins. Without sufficient protein in the bloodstream, water seeps through the blood vessels into the tissue spaces, a condition known as oedema and recognized in horses as filled legs or soft swelling beneath the skin (see chapter 4). This may occur because the proteins leak through blood vessels, the walls of which have been damaged by toxins or other noxious substances.

The smaller molecules of salts also act in the equation of equilibrium on either side of the capillary membrane. Sodium and potassium are particularly involved in this process and their levels are regulated by the kidneys. The kidneys, as we shall see later (see chapter 6), play a major role in conserving required and eliminating unwanted material from the body.

The acidity of the blood is represented by its pH. The pH is the measure of hydrogen ions associated with organic acids. If there are too many, the blood becomes more acid; if too few, it becomes too alkaline.

Normally blood has a pH of about 7.4 units. The balance between acidity and alkalinity is referred to as base status and is measured in terms of bicarbonate. Bicarbonate acts as a buffer, giving up hydrogen ions when the blood becomes alkaline and absorbing them when it becomes acid.

Bicarbonate levels are usually in the region of 28 mmol/litre of blood. Mmol is a chemical unit by which scientists measure the content of salts dissolved in fluid.

The blood becomes too acid (acidosis, acidemia) in states such as diarrhoea, in which large amounts of alkali are lost in the faeces. A normal acid state develops after exercise when lactic acid is produced in the muscles and passes into the bloodstream. However, this state is only temporary and the mechanisms of balance soon neutralize the lactic acid and restore the base acidity balance to normal.

Excess alkalinity rarely occurs. It may develop when the horse over-breathes at rest. This is because the gas carbon dioxide is then eliminated from the lungs. Carbon dioxide is one of the radicals of organic acids and its elimination leaves an alkaline balance, which is soon restored when the horse stops overbreathing.

The lungs form part of the system of conserving acid, and the kidneys conserve alkaline material. The gut plays a part in regulating both acid and alkaline substances. These organs respond to acidity or alkalinity in the appropriate manner by eliminating acid radicals or, to a lesser extent, alkaline radicals according to the acidity of the blood at any given time.

Blood cells

Red cells (erythrocytes)   The red cells give blood its colour. They are also known as erythrocytes. They consist of a cell membrane or envelope containing a red pigment called haemoglobin. They are extremely small cells whose special characteristic is that they do not have a nucleus, as have all other cells in the body.

Horses have about 7–9 million red cells per cubic millimetre of blood. The modern measurement is the number of cells per litre and this is expressed as $\times 10^9$/litre. In practical terms this means there are about 3200 million red cells per teaspoonful of blood. Red cells, which outnumber white cells by about 1000 to 1, have a characteristic disc shape and are concave on both sides. They consist of about 60 per cent water and 33 per cent haemoglobin.

Red cells carry the gas oxygen. This is essential to life. The blood receives this in the lungs, where it comes into close contact in the capillaries of that organ (see p. 37). The oxygen does not dissolve to any great extent in plasma and, without the red cells, it would therefore not be carried in quantities nearly sufficient to satisfy the body's needs. The haemoglobin in the cells has a much greater affinity for oxygen and also the peculiar property of being able to combine with oxygen when exposed to high concentrations in the lungs. It then forms a product called oxyhaemoglobin.

The blood then passes from the lungs through the heart to the tissues, such as the muscles, and here it is surrounded by tissues containing much less oxygen. In these circumstances the haemoglobin gives up oxygen and becomes what is known as reduced haemoglobin. The muscles are then able to take up the oxygen and use it for burning carbohydrate (sugar) to produce energy. The blood then returns to the lungs, where the reduced haemoglobin takes up oxygen and is again converted to oxyhaemoglobin.

When there is more oxyhaemoglobin than reduced haemoglobin, the blood is bright red; when the reverse is the case, the blood becomes dark or even blue.

Haemoglobin is confined in the red cells and escapes into the plasma only when the cells are destroyed in large quantities (haemolysis). This condition occurs in newborn foals (see p. 393). Haemoglobin is released in large amounts into the plasma and causes jaundice, staining the tissues of the membranes of the mouth, eyes and vagina. It also causes the skin to go yellow but, of course, in animals with hair this cannot be seen as easily as it can in humans.

Red cells have a limited life of approximately thirty days and there is thus a turnover in the population present at any given time. Red cells are produced in the bone marrow. These replace the ones which are old and destroyed in the spleen and liver. The rate of replacement and destruction is normally in balance, so that numbers remain the same. If more cells are eliminated than are produced, anaemia results. This may occur if the rate of destruction is normal but the production in the bone marrow is reduced by disease.

The iron-containing component of haemoglobin is retained in the body when the old red cells are destroyed. The waste content of pigment is excreted in the bile. If the liver is damaged, the bile does not escape and is resorbed into the blood. This may also occur if the channels through which bile is excreted into the gut become blocked. Pigment then accumulates in large quantities in the plasma, a condition called hepatic or obstructive jaundice (see p. 21).

In this condition, in contrast to haemolytic jaundice, the individual is not suffering from haemolysis of red cells and the number of red cells in the bloodstream remains normal. In haemolytic jaundice the red cell count may plummet to less than 4×10^9/litre.

Red cells also carry the gas carbon dioxide from the tissues to the lungs. Carbon dioxide is produced as a waste gas in the burning of sugar for energy. The red cells can easily absorb and release large quantities of carbon dioxide because of their relatively enormous surface area.

The red cell has no nucleus and therefore the whole of its interior is available for haemoglobin. A further attribute is that the cells have rounded edges, which helps them to pass easily through the minute lumen of the capillaries. Further, they have considerable ability to change shape, so that they can squeeze past obstructions or through vessels with narrow diameters.

White cells (leucocytes) There are five kinds of white blood cells or leucocytes. These fall into one of two groups according to whether or not they contain granules. The granules are identified in the laboratory by special staining techniques.

The granular white cells are eosinophils, which take up the red stain because they are acid, basophils, which take up the blue stain because they are alkaline, or neutrophils, which take up neither blue nor red because they are neutral.

The neutrophils are also called polymorphonuclear (PMN) because of the many different shapes into which they can change as they move through the tissues and because of the lobed shape of their nuclei. Neutrophils can engulf microbes and foreign particles.

Two types of white cells which do not contain granules are lymphocytes and monocytes. There are also plasma cells, which may be regarded as modified lymphocytes. All these cells play a fundamental role in the immunity of the body. Monocytes are able to engulf particles. They are the largest of the white cells and gather in large numbers wherever there is chronic infection, such as in lungs affected by pneumonia.

White cells have many functions. Neutrophils and other white cells migrate from the bloodstream whenever tissues are damaged by infection, wounds or foreign bodies such as splinters of wood. They play a fundamental part in the inflammatory process (see chapter 36).

Blood clotting

Blood has the remarkable power of remaining fluid in the blood vessels but clotting as soon as it is shed. This is essential because, although the blood must be fluid to perform its main function of transport and circulation, the risk of excessive bleeding when a vessel breaks is always present.

When blood clots it forms a jelly which, under a microscope, can be seen to consist of a network of gelatinous threads radiating from clumps of disintegrating platelets. The platelets are special blood cells which contain a substance called thrombokinase. Entangled in the threads are red and white cells. After an hour or two the clot gradually separates into a red mass containing cells and a straw-coloured fluid, serum.

By clotting blood blocks any rents in the blood-vessel wall and thereby prevents further bleeding. The exception is when a break occurs in a large artery. In these cases the blood pressure prevents a clot forming or remaining in position to prevent blood loss (haemorrhage). Arterial bleeding is, therefore, much more dangerous than bleeding from veins, where blood pressure is much lower. Bleeding from an artery may cease only if the elastic wall of the artery contracts to seal off the vessel and/or if the bleeding is so severe that blood pressure falls sufficiently to allow a clot to form and stay in position.

Internal bleeding from an artery may eventually stop if the tissues around the broken vessel became sufficiently engorged so as to prevent further blood escaping. This occurs when the pressure formed by the lost blood counteracts the pressure in the artery. However, this may not happen in the case of an artery rupturing in the broad ligament of the uterus at foaling, for example (see p. 363).

Clotting of blood is a result of a series of events, each of which represents a key which must be turned before the next stage can proceed. First, tissue is damaged and platelets release thrombokinase. This reacts with the substance prothrombin to give thrombin. Calcium is required in this step from prothrombin to thrombin. Thrombin acts on fibrinogen, one of the proteins already described as being present in plasma. Fibrinogen is formed by the liver under the influence of vitamin K. The reaction of thrombin and fibrinogen is to form fibrin, which are the threads that can be seen in a clot under the microscope.

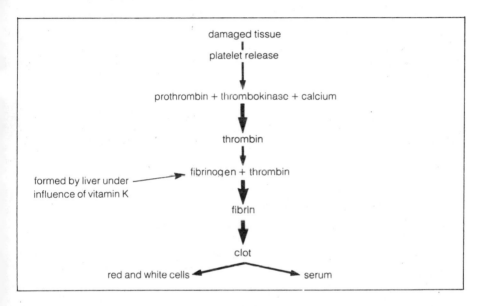

Figure 33   The stages of the clotting process

To prevent clotting we may use anticoagulants, that is, anti-clotting agents. These include substances which precipitate calcium and prevent the step from prothrombin to thrombin occurring.

The essential element in clots is fibrin. This is carried in the inert form fibrinogen in the bloodstream; otherwise the blood would clot in the vessels. Because thrombin is required to convert fibrinogen to fibrin, thrombin is present in the bloodstream only in its inactive form prothrombin. The enzyme thrombokinase, which converts prothrombin to thrombin, is present in the platelets but is locked in unless liberated when tissues become damaged.

There is a further substance, heparin, which is produced by special cells, known as mast cells, distributed throughout the body. It is only present in such quantities as to exert a modifying effect on clotting. When local damage occurs, this overwhelms the heparin present in the bloodstream. However, heparin may be used as an anti-clotting agent in treating heart disease and for keeping blood samples from clotting.

Blood–fluid balance

The fluid balance of the body is a propertyof the bloodstream and the water it contains. Water is the largest single constituent of the body and makes up about 70 per cent of its total weight. A horse weighing 500 kg (1100 lb) contains about 350 litres of water. This water is distributed evenly throughout the body with the exception of bone, which contains only about 20 per cent, and the hoof, the various parts of which contain between 23 and 40 per cent.

The water in the body exists essentially in two compartments. The intra-cellular fluid is the water contained within the cell; the extra-cellular fluid is that outside. The extra-cellular water may be in the bloodstream, i.e. in plasma, or in spaces between the cells. These are usually referred to as the tissue spaces.

Intra-cellular water makes up about 70 per cent of total body water, whereas plasma contains 8 per cent and interstitial fluid (fluid between the cells) about 22 per cent.

The fluid in each compartment is interchangeable. It can thus pass from cells to the tissue spaces to the blood, or in the reverse direction. Water may also be exchanged between the blood and the intestines regulated by the kidneys. These exchanges occur according to the needs of the body at any particular time. Water can also be lost from the skin when the horse sweats or into the air when the horse breathes out. This last process is a natural method of keeping the air moist in the long air tubes leading from the nostrils to the lungs.

We have already discussed the role played by protein, especially albumin, in maintaining the osmotic pressure of the blood within normal limits (see p. 71). In the interstitial fluid sodium forms the major constituent which maintains the concentration, and therefore the osmotic pressure of inter-stitial fluid, in balance with the fluid in cells and in the blood. If, for example, there were too little sodium, water would pass abnormally out of the interstitial fluid and this compartment would shrink. It would pass into the blood or into the cells. In the latter event the cells would swell abnormally.

Water in the cells is maintained by the normal concentration of potassium. Thus the osmotic pressure of the cell is influenced by the amount of potassium it contains. Again, if there is too little of this substance, water will pass out of the cell into the interstitial fluid and the cells will shrink.

There are complex mechanisms whereby potassium and sodium are moved into and out of cells in order to maintain the osmotic pressure and thereby the fluid balance of the body.

Examining the blood

Blood is often examined to help diagnose disease, because it is simple to obtain by inserting a small-size needle into a vein. The sample may be collected using a syringe or a vacutainer.

The examination of blood in the laboratory helps to establish the health status of many parts of the body and to identify abnormal happenings as a result of the indirect changes that occur. We know the normal composition, and if we establish the significance of change we can, with experience, relate our findings to events taking place in various parts of the body. We might liken this approach to recording a sample of traffic using a main road. Using this analogy, we might observe that there are a large number of fire engines on the road and from this we might deduce that there is a fire. Similarly, if we observe an abnormally large number of neutrophils in the bloodstream, we may be sure that this is a response to infection or to stress. If, however, we find the eosinophils in large numbers, we can deduce that a state of allergy or infection with parasites is present.

Of course, we do not rely on these signs alone but read them in conjunction with other signs of clinical and laboratory examination.

Conditions of the Blood

Apart from haemolytic disease of the newborn foal (see p. 393), there are few specific diseases of the blood in the horse. The examination of blood which is so frequently carried out on normal and sick horses is undertaken because changes in the normal constituents of the blood reflect changes in the organs and tissues which may themselves be abnormal. This aspect is discussed below.

Haemophilia is a rare inherited disease of horses. In this condition Factor VIII, which forms part of the clotting mechanism, is missing.

Horses may become anaemic due to infection, for example, equine infectious anaemia (see p. 430). However, this is not really a disease of the blood but a generalized infection by a virus.

Piroplasmosis is a specific disease of blood caused by a parasite (see p. 433).

6
THE URINARY SYSTEM

Functional anatomy

The urinary system consists of the kidneys, ureters, urinary bladder and urethra (Figure 34a).

In the horse the right kidney lies under the cover of the last three ribs, whereas the left is slightly farther back, just opposite the last rib. Both are tightly held up under the lumbar part of the spine. Each kidney is connected via the ureter to the bladder, which lies on the floor of the pelvis when empty. As it fills it expands forwards onto the wall of the ventral abdomen. The bladder empties to the outside via the urethra, which in the male passes through the penis (Figure 36) and in the female exits into the distal vagina and the vulva (Figures 34b and 35).

The function of the urinary system is to maintain water and electrolyte balance within the body, and to excrete from it certain products of metabolism, particularly urea. The kidneys also secrete certain hormones, including those responsible for controlling red blood cell production and

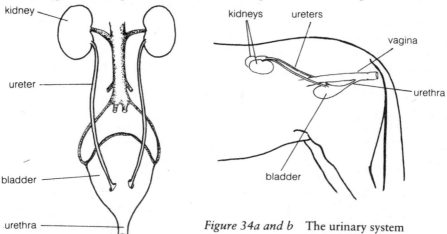

Figure 34a and b The urinary system

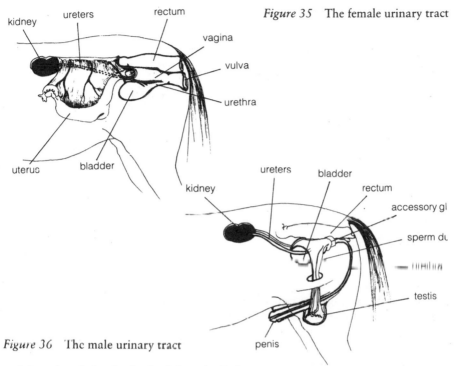

Figure 35 The female urinary tract

Figure 36 The male urinary tract

calcium levels in the body (vitamin D₃).

Symptoms of urinary system disease vary according to which part is affected. Diseases involving the kidneys often upset this organ's control of water and electrolyte balance in the body, as well as decreasing the excretion of waste products. These changes in levels can lead to multiple symptoms, often remote from the urinary system, involving the heart and blood vessels, and the digestive and nervous systems.

Diseases of the lower urinary tract (the bladder and urethra) present mainly as disturbances in the normal flow of urine to the outside (micturition). It is most important to be familiar with the normal act of micturition in order that these disturbances can be observed early on.

Horses usually urinate only at rest, especially when a straw bed is laid down or when they are placed in their stall box. The posture normally adopted by both males and females is with the hind legs separated, the animal leaning slightly forward, and with obvious contraction of the abdominal wall and elevation of the tail. Very often horses grunt and groan and, occasionally, the penis is protruded in the male.

In individual animals bouts of urination may be remarkably regular. The mare in oestrus shows changes in behaviour, including continual winking of the clitoris often associated with frequent squirts of urine, which may be thicker and darker-coloured than usual. Adult horses urinate four to six times a day, producing from 4 to 15 litres/day depending on water intake and diet.

Methods of assessing function

Careful observation and external examination of the horse provides valuable information about the urinary system. Early recognition of abnormal signs by the owner or attendant allows prompt investigation by the vet and limits the possible effects and complications of urinary disease. For example, the presence of dried urine on the tail, vulva and legs of a mare may indicate urinary incontinence.

The act of micturition should be observed and the following assessed:

(a) Normality of position and whether there are continual attempts at adopting this stance. The inability of the horse to adopt the correct position, e.g. as in a recumbent animal, can lead to urine retention.
(b) Frequency of urination and the volume passed at each bout. This will decrease if the horse is unable to drink normally or if fluid intake is restricted.
(c) The nature of the urine passed and, if possible, a sample collected in a clean receptacle.
(d) Signs of pain associated with micturition, i.e. continual straining, excessive grunting and discomfort, and tensing of the abdominal wall muscles. It is important to differentiate these symptoms from those due to colic in other systems. This may require more sophisticated judgements or techniques only available to the veterinarian.

To make a diagnosis in urinary conditions requires an accurate history of the patient, including general information such as the age of the animal, its use, its diet and any previous problems, as well as more specific questions based on the list described above. Having ascertained the history, the following regime may be adopted.

In the mare the external entrance of the urethra can be palpated easily or visualized directly with a vaginal speculum. In the male it is often necessary to tranquillize the animal before the same area can be examined.

Following examination the vet may decide to catheterize the bladder. This involves passing a lubricated flexible rubber or plastic tube up the urethra into the bladder. This technique provides information, including whether the urethra is blocked (for example, by a stone), and allows the collection of a urine sample. It can also be used to introduce treatment.

In the mare it is possible to insert a fibre-optic instrument into the bladder after this organ has been drained of urine. This allows the inside of the bladder to be visualized. Unfortunately this piece of equipment is expensive and not always available. Not all cases require such an examination, however, and the nature of the problem as well as the value of the animal may preclude some of the more sophisticated techniques.

Rectal palpation (insertion of the hand and arm into the rectum) is a useful technique for examination of the urinary system in the adult horse. In the majority of average-sized horses the left kidney is the only one palpable, although the right may be felt if enlarged. In the male the bladder is easy to feel and its size and position identified. In the female the state of the uterus (womb) (i.e., whether the mare is pregnant or not) will affect palpation of the bladder.

Following the physical examination, the vet may decide to take various samples in order further to identify the nature of the problem. Urine can be collected either as it passes from the animal or by catheter. Normal equine urine varies in colour from light yellow to amber and may darken on standing. It can be clear or cloudy, the latter being especially obvious in horses receiving large quantities of calcium in their diet. The pH and specific gravity of the urine vary with diet and environment.

Microscopic and biochemical analysis of urine can be helpful. The presence of blood, as red blood cells or as haemoglobin, may indicate haemorrhage in the urinary system or damage to blood cells elsewhere in the body. Proteins and glucose may also be discovered, the latter increasing in diabetes mellitus. Sediment in urine can be examined for the presence of crystals, blood cells and damaged urinary tract tissue (casts).

Circulatory blood may be analysed usefully in several ways. Most importantly, concentrations of urea and creatinine (waste products) are looked at. These rise in the bloodstream if the kidney filtering system is affected by disease. Other substances in the blood increase or decrease with urinary disease. The creatinine clearance test involves taking a simultaneous urine and blood sample and examining the creatinine, phosphate, sodium and potassium content of each. The results of this test provide useful information about kidney function and some metabolic processes, such as those associated with bone (see pp. 586–8).

Conditions of the Urinary System

Diseases of the urinary system, particularly of the kidney, are uncommon in the horse. To some extent this situation is brought about by the kidney's ability to function even when considerably damaged (up to 75 per cent). Despite this remarkable ability of the kidney to compensate, urinary tract diseases are serious, require prompt veterinary attention and, in some cases, are life-threatening.

Conditions of the Kidney

Damage to the kidney, if severe enough, leads to a situation known as renal failure and this can be separated into two categories: acute and chronic. It is not always true that chronic renal failure follows acute damage, because the onset of renal failure may indicate the sudden failure of chronically diseased kidneys.

ACUTE RENAL FAILURE

Rapid deterioration in kidney function has multiple causes. These can be divided into two basic groups; prerenal, in which the blood supply to the kidney is affected, and postrenal, in which there is physical obstruction of urine flow somewhere in the urinary tract.

Prerenal causes include decreased blood pressure due to severe dehydration or blood loss (haemorrhage) and defects in the circulation such as occur in shock or heart failure. Certain substances also directly damage the kidney tissue (nephrotoxins), including some plants, heavy metals (e.g. mercury) and drugs (e.g. some antibiotics and sulphonamides). Myoglobin, the pigment from muscle, can also cause renal damage when released in large quantities after an attack of setfast or azoturia (see p. 226).

In the young foal renal disease is usually associated with systemic infections (septicaemia). These occur particularly in the colostrum-deprived foal and are caused by a variety of bacteria (see p. 380).

Postrenal forms of acute renal failure are caused by obstruction of the bladder neck or urethra by calculi (stones) and by rupture of the bladder. These conditions are discussed below.

Clinical signs

Symptoms of acute renal failure are similar, whatever the cause, but may be complicated by other symptoms derived from the primary cause. The onset of signs may take up to twenty-four hours to occur, but usually there is a decrease in production of urine which becomes very concentrated. In most cases the kidneys are swollen and tender, and this can be appreciated by the vet on rectal palpation and by manipulation of the lumbar region of the back.

If the animal survives the initial phase, the quantity of urine passed increases dramatically (diuresis) and it becomes very dilute. This may persist for several weeks. Urine and blood samples confirm the diagnosis and also help the vet to arrive at a prognosis.

The urine may contain increased protein, cells and some blood. The blood picture varies, depending on other coexisting disease, but will often show increases in blood urea and creatinine.

Treatment

During the initial phase, when little urine is being passed, treatment is aimed at correcting fluid and electrolyte imbalances (oral and intravenous fluids) by the administering of diuretics and general supportive therapy. If the horse survives the early stages, then it will enter the phase of increased urine production, when measures to maintain the fluid/electrolyte intake and to decrease the nitrogen content of food (grass, hay) are taken. The animal may now be eating and drinking normally, in which case water and salt licks should be available at all times.

Prognosis

The recovery rate for horses suffering from acute renal failure depends largely on the cause and severity of the condition. Laminitis is a possible complication and can be difficult to treat in these animals. The mortality rate can be as high as 50 per cent in some renal failures due to toxic chemicals (oxalates), but diuresis following little urine production is a good sign.

CHRONIC RENAL FAILURE

Although old injuries to equine kidneys are fairly common, they rarely lead to an ill horse. The actual cause of a disease may be difficult to diagnose unless it follows on from an acute attack. One form appears to be more common in horses used for the production of antisera, a valuable product in medicine manufacture. Ingestion over a long period of plants containing high levels of oxalates can also be a factor (see p. 512). Large kidney tumours or calculi (stones) could also be involved, but both conditions are rare.

PYELONEPHRITIS (INFECTION OF THE PELVIS OF THE KIDNEY)

Pyelonephritis occurs more commonly in females, especially after foaling. Infection ascends up the urinary tract and thus the horse presents with symptoms of cystitis (see below). Occasionally infections arrive via the blood (pyaemic nephritis) from an infection source elsewhere in the body, for example, in young foals from an infected stump of the umbilical cord (see pp. 380ff.), although this condition is more likely to present with clinical signs related to conditions of joints (joint ill – see p. 179).

Clinical signs

The majority of affected animals are middle-aged and older, with a prolonged history (months) of lack of appetite, weight loss, depression, weakness and conspicuous oedema (swelling) of the ventral abdomen and legs. Urine production may be decreased or increased, with a larger than normal thirst. Rectal examination can be helpful in the vet's search for a cause, but urine and blood samples are necessary to achieve a diagnosis and arrive at a rational treatment. Frequently there is anaemia, multiple electrolyte imbalances and increased blood urea levels.

Treatment and prognosis

By the time a diagnosis is made, renal failure is often well established and the damage substantial. The prognosis is always unfavourable because the lesions are irreversible and euthanasia may be indicated. Cases involving pyelonephritis may benefit from antibiotic therapy. Supportive therapy (good nursing and management), fluids, electrolytes and a low nitrogen diet can sometimes help.

Conditions of the Bladder

CYSTITIS (INFLAMMATION OF THE BLADDER)

Cystitis is uncommon in the horse. The problem can arise as an ascending bacterial infection up the urethra or secondary to diseases resulting in incomplete emptying of the bladder (e.g. bladder paralysis , urethral calculi) or bladder irritation (e.g. by cystic calculi – bladder stones). These predisposing conditions affect the bladder's ability to protect itself and to prevent multiplication of bacteria, of which it is normally free.

As in the human, the condition is more common in females than in males, for two reasons. First, the female urethra opens into the vagina, which can act as a source of infection in cases of metritis (inflammation of the uterus). Secondly, the urethra in the male is much longer and narrower, and therefore less liable to be a route of ascending infection.

Clinical signs

Acute cystitis occurs rarely and presents as abdominal pain (colic) associated with straining and frequent attempts at passing urine, usually only in small amounts. More often the condition is chronic, with clinical signs which include frequent urination with straining and sometimes urine dribbling, caking of the vulval lips with sediment in the female and urine scalding. In the male the penis may be protruded; in the female excessive clitoral winking occurs. The urine can be discoloured by blood and is more turbid than normal.

Diagnosis

The diagnosis of cystitis is not difficult from the symptoms but has to be confirmed by examination of a urine sample. It is important to suggest a cause for the disease. The urine can be cultured for bacteria and examined microscopically. In a cystitis sample bacterial cells, mineral crystals and red and white blood cells may be present. A rectal examination allows evaluation of the bladder for calculi, paralysis or pain.

Treatment

Treatment of cystitis involves the removal of any predisposing causes and the administration of antibiotics for a considerable period of time based on culture results. Flushing the bladder with antibiotic solutions is not necessary, but using an antibiotic excreted at high levels in the urine is important. The horse is rarely very ill, but full nursing and supportive management are important, including maintaining water intake, keeping the patient warm with rugs and bandages, rest, and preventing urine scalding by applying Vaseline.

Prevention

Preventive measures are limited to ensuring adequate supplies of fresh, clean drinking water at all times, especially in hot, humid environments.

CYSTIC CALCULI

Urinary calculi or stones may form in any part of the equine urinary tract, but the most common site is the bladder (cystic). Calculi are formed by material dissolved in the urine (solutes) being precipitated upon a collection of bladder or other cells, such as red or white blood cells. The factors favouring this precipitation are not well understood but include urine pH – alkalinity increases the formation of carbonate calculi – and the concentration of urine solutes. These can be affected by diet, water intake and loss. The concentration increases when the horse is deprived of water or loses water excessively, as in sweating or diarrhoea. If the diet or water fed to a horse has a high mineral content, this also increases solute concentration, while a high-concentrate, low-roughage ration may allow the deposited solutes to cement together more easily. Usually only one calculus occurs at a time, often composed of calcium carbonate.

Clinical signs

All breeds and both sexes are equally likely to develop calculi, although in mares they become very large before symptoms appear. These are similar to those seen in cases of cystitis, which often is present concurrently. Affected individuals urinate more frequently, with straining and dribbling of urine. Less commonly there may be mild recurrent colic, loss of condition and stilted gait. Occasionally a calculus passes into the male urethra, causing acute obstruction of urine flow.

Diagnosis

Veterinary help should always be sought in cases in which there is obvious difficulty in the passing of urine. Diagnosis of cystic calculi involves urine analysis (the changes are similar to those of cystitis), passage of a urinary catheter, rectal palpation and, occasionally in the mare, passage of an endoscope into the bladder.

Treatment

Surgical removal of the calculus is the only effective method of treatment. The approach and type of surgery is determined by the size of the stone and the sex of the patient.

Some cases may also require treatment for concurrent cystitis.

Prognosis

Prognosis for cases treated successfully by surgery is guarded because the affected horse may remain predisposed to chronic cystitis and calculus formation. Preventive measures are limited to correct dietary management, particularly in regard to mineral and concentrate proportions, adequate sources of drinking water and prompt veterinary attention to any case of suspected cystitis.

BLADDER PARALYSIS

This condition occurs in horses in which there is damage to or disease of the sacral (pelvic) segment of the spinal cord or to local spinal nerves. It also occurs in problems associated with other areas of the nervous system, including injuries to the sacrum, fractures of the vertebrae, infections of the spinal cord (EHV-1 or rhinopneumonitis – see p. 425), spinal abscesses and tumours, poisoning (see chapter 37), and neuritis of the cauda equina (the end of the spinal cord in the sacral and coccygeal regions).

Clinical signs

Symptoms vary according to the cause of the neurological problem. Normal emptying of the bladder does not occur and the collecting of urine distends and stretches it. Eventually the bladder fills to its maximum capacity, and the horse becomes incontinent. The continuous release of urine leads to scalding of the back of the thighs in the mare and some inflammation of the vulva. A secondary cystitis may develop. On rectal examination the bladder will be very distended and displaced ventrally into the abdomen.

Treatment

Treatment of bladder paralysis is designed to control the secondary cystitis and keep the bladder emptied by catheterization and manual palpation. The success of this supportive care and likely prognosis depend on the actual cause of the paralysis.

BLADDER TUMOURS

These are very unusual in horses and present in a similar way to cystitis and cystic calculi. They may be distinguished by rectal palpation and/or endoscopy of the bladder. Treatment by surgery is possible but spread to other areas may have already occurred.

RUPTURED BLADDER (PATENT BLADDER OF FOALS)

A ruptured bladder is a very unusual event in the adult horse, only occurring in association with foaling or obstruction of the urine flow. In the young foal, however, particularly colts, it is fairly common. The bladder usually ruptures near its widest part on the dorsal surface, although occasionally the urachus (a foetal structure connecting the bladder to the umbilicus) tears. The rupture is thought to occur during foaling due to increases in external pressure on the distended bladder. Some cases are due to infection and rotting (necrosis) of the foetal attachment of the bladder to the urachus. Other cases may be the result of the two halves of the bladder not uniting normally during embryological development.

Clinical signs

Symptoms can be quite subtle and, as in all foal diseases, require careful observation over a period of time to detect them. Foaling is usually unremarkable and the foal appears normal for the first twenty-four to forty-eight hours. At this stage it may become lethargic and depressed, suck less and show a distended abdomen

Symptoms of urination are quite variable, but often there will be an increase in the frequency and a decrease in the amount of urine passed. There is often straining and signs of mild colic, which can lead to confusion with meconium colic. The two conditions can be differentiated by observing the position the foal adopts while straining. With a ruptured bladder the foal stands with its back hollowed out, head raised and legs extended out backwards; whereas the foal with meconium impaction tends to have a more humped-up appearance, with tail raised, and occasionally walks backwards. As the condition worsens, more urine collects in the abdomen, leading to difficulties in breathing, an increase in heart rate and greater depression.

Diagnosis

This condition is life-threatening and early recognition of abnormal signs is important. Diagnosis involves several techniques. If ballottement of the abdomen suggests fluid is present, then a needle is placed through the abdominal wall to collect a sample which can be analysed to determine whether it is urine.

Blood samples show increase in blood urea and creatinine content. Other more sophisticated techniques include radiography using radio-dense dyes inserted into the bladder by catheter or retrieving dyes placed in the bladder from the abdomen by needle puncture.

Treatment

Treatment is surgical repair of the rupture as soon as possible. First, urine is drained from the abdomen to decrease complications during anaesthesia. After surgery the foal requires continuous observation, monitoring of its condition, nursing and appropriate therapy. If an abdominal drain and/or urethral catheter is fitted it requires attention.

Prognosis

Prognosis for recovery is good if the diagnosis is made early, but on occasions repair to the bladder or abdominal wall may break down, necessitating further surgery.

PATENT URACHUS

The urachus is the tube connecting the bladder of the unborn foal via the umbilicus to the allantois (see p. 333). Normally the urachus closes at the time of birth and the umbilicus shrivels within hours. When the urachus does not close (i.e. when it becomes patent or pervious), then urine continues to leak from the umbilicus.

The degree of patency varies considerably, ranging from that which allows an occasional drip and a moist navel, to streams of urine appearing from both the umbilicus and the urethra when the foal urinates. Either sex may be affected. The umbilical area becomes scalded and/or infected, causing local abscesses. The infection may spread farther up into the bladder (cystitis), into the bloodstream and via this to the joints (joint ill – see p. 179). It may also be associated with leakage of urine into the peritoneal cavity (see above).

Treatment

A patent urachus may close spontaneously but, in most cases, treatment is necessary. The foal is given antibiotics to reduce the chance of the spread of infection and a barrier cream is applied around the navel to decrease scalding. A cauterizing agent (iodine, formalin or phenol soaked in cotton swab) or silver nitrate styptic may be applied for several days. This produces a localized inflammation within the tube and gradually this closes it. The foal will need to be carefully restrained, manually or chemically, for these procedures. If cautery fails to close the urachus then surgical removal of the structure is indicated. This requires a general anaesthetic and post-operative nursing and care.

Conditions of the Urethra

The urethra is only occasionally affected by disease and almost exclusively in the male.

URETHRAL OBSTRUCTION

The urethra can be obstructed anywhere in its length from diseases within and exterior to it. The main causes include urethral calculi and injuries to or tumours of the penis. Urethral calculi are much less common than their bladder counterparts but their source is almost certainly the same. The calculus is usually trapped at the point where the urethra passes around the posterior part of the pelvis or at the end of the penis (where there is a slight narrowing of the diameter). Even if the stone passes on, the trauma caused to the urethra can cause obstruction.

One way in which the urethra can be obstructed from external sources is following an acute case of paraphymosis (the penis becomes trapped outside the sheath in an erect or semi-erect state).

Clinical signs and diagnosis

Symptoms of urethral obstruction are very similar to those seen in diseases of the bladder and include mild colic, straining and difficulty in passing urine, prolapse of the penis, dribbling of urine and sometimes passage of blood.

The diagnosis of urethral disease is based on physical examination by a vet. A catheter can be passed only to the level of obstruction.

Treatment

Treatment of urethral calculi depends on where they become lodged. If they lodge in the distal part they can be dislodged or removed by catheter or clamp. If this is not possible or if they have lodged higher up, then surgery is indicated. Under general anaesthesia an incision is made over the stone, allowing its removal. In certain circumstances this incision may be left to become a permanent exit for urine.

ULCERATIONS AND URETHRITIS

Damage and inflammation to the urethral lining may occur in male horses. This can follow the passage of a urethral calculus, repeated catheterization, injury to the penis or an ascending bacterial infection.

Clinical signs and diagnosis

Symptoms of urethritis may closely mimic those of urethral obstruction and in the stallion cause pain and, in some cases, a reluctance on the part of the individual to thrust and ejaculate into a mare at mating. The semen and urine may have blood in them and fertility levels may be lowered. Urethral lesions may be identified using a fibre-optic endoscope.

Treatment

Stallions should be stopped from mating until healing takes place. Penile injuries may need specific therapy, and any infection will require local and system antibiotic treatment.

7
THE SKIN AND ITS DISEASES

The skin is the only visible organ of the body and yet it is much more than an inert sheath. Its efficient functioning is essential for health.

It protects against the sun's actinic radiation, prevents trauma and the entry of micro-organisms and is part of the body's immune system. It prevents dehydration, has an excretory function, plays an important part in the control of body temperature, carries sensory nerves for the appreciation of temperature variation, pressure and pain, has a social function in interrelation with other horses, synthesizes vitamin D for subsequent absorption and provides the hooves, which are composed of modified skin on a skeletal framework.

The mammary glands are modified sweat glands of the skin adapted for nourishing the foal, while the eyes (excluding the retina) are also derived from the skin.

The body, in simple terms, can be considered to be encased in a three-layered structure (Figure 37). The outermost layer (the hair) is lifeless and is composed of pure protein (hard keratin) and assists in regulating body temperature. Beneath it is the epidermis, which itself is composed of several layers. The outermost layer of the epidermis (the stratum corneum) is soft keratin and is also lifeless. Thus, all that we see when looking at a horse is a sheath of lifeless hard and soft keratin.

The skin varies in thickness over different parts of the body: it is thickest over the dorsal trunk and thin on the ventral abdomen, lower neck and face. In temperate and cold climates long hair is produced for added insulation during the winter months. The hair follicles then pass into a resting phase. As the duration of daylight increases in springtime, they are stimulated into activity again, and new hairs are produced which grow up through the follicles, dislodging the old hairs. Hair over the body is thereby renewed annually, with the exception of the long hairs of the tail and mane, which may continue to grow for several years.

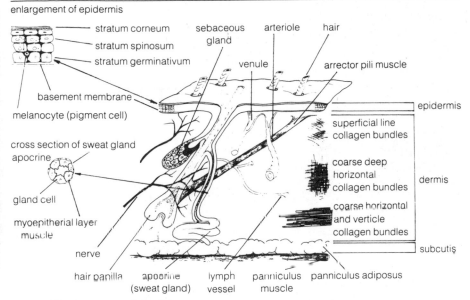

enlargement of epidermis

stratum corneum
stratum spinosum
stratum germinativum

sebaceous gland
arteriole
hair
venule
arrector pili muscle

basement membrane
melanocyte (pigment cell)

cross section of sweat gland
apocrine

gland cell

myoepithelial layer
muscle

nerve

hair panilla
apocrine (sweat gland)
lymph vessel
panniculus muscle
panniculus adiposus

epidermis

superficial line collagen bundles

coarse deep horizontal collagen bundles

coarse horizontal and verticle collagen bundles

dermis

subcutiş

Figure 37 Anatomy of the skin

The epidermis may be greatly modified in various regions for functional adaptations. It rests upon a basement membrane. The first layer of cells resting on the basement membrane is the stratum germinativum where the cells of the epidermis are produced by division.

With time, each cell produced by the stratum germinativum is pushed up to the surface, becoming keratinized and receiving pigment as it does so. It eventually dies and is sloughed off as a dander or scale from the outermost layer of the epidermis, the stratum corneum.

The hair follicles are formed *in utero* from downgrowths of the epidermis. They in turn produce the skin glands, sebaceous and apocrine. The epidermis rests upon the much thicker dermis, which consists of a mass of interwoven collagenous fibres and comparatively few cells. It contains vessels and nerves.

Beneath the dermis is the subcutis, a layer of fatty connective tissue to which the skin is usually loosely attached for its mobility. It contains a sheet of muscle, the panniculus muscle, the function of which is to move the skin to dislodge parasites and to generate heat by persistent contraction (shivering).

The skin is intimately affected by environmental factors and also by systemic factors. Generalized malignancy, liver disease, starvation, dehydration, and heavy parasitic worm burdens, for example, may all have profound effects on the skin. Systemic disease may produce itchiness, loss of hair, decreased elasticity (hidebound), increased scaliness of the skin or photosensitization. Thus an apparent change in the skin condition may not be due to local factors.

Diseases localized to the skin are most usually infectious in origin, the signs presented depending upon the pathogen. Ringworm primarily attacks dead keratin of the hair and epidermis; hair loss results, an allergic reaction may develop and changes in the dermis and epidermis then become apparent.

Skin mites live on or in the epidermis; their activity provokes much itchiness with marked self-excoriation of a particular area. Lice may suck blood or live on skin scale and may also provoke an allergic response; they too are often accompanied by severe excoriation of the body.

Bacterial infections of the skin are not common in the horse: usually they result from poor husbandry, badly fitting and/or dirty tack. Therefore they may be seen on those parts of the body in contact with tack; frank pus with an associated loss of hair may occur.

Breeding may bring together harmful traits which result in imperfect formation of the skin which may be apparent at birth or become obvious shortly afterwards. Areas of ulceration or comparative hairlessness may be seen, as in epitheliogenesis imperfecta.

Examination and diagnostic aids

The veterinarian will seek to determine the previous history of the case before or while making a clinical examination. This will be a general examination to determine if the present skin symptoms are primary to the skin or secondary to a systemic reaction.

The general examination will be followed by a particular examination of the skin. Brushes and combs may be used to isolate any larger parasites; a hand lens may be used during this examination. Fine forceps may be used to pluck hair for detailed examination in the practice laboratory and possible outline for ringworm. Swabs may be collected for microscopic examination and/or culture for bacterial examination. Small pieces of skin may be removed for detailed examination of the tissue after processing and staining at higher magnification under the microscope. Specimens of blood may be collected in various tubes for examination of the haematology, blood enzymes and electrolytes.

Many skin diseases are easily transmitted by contact, though cleaning of tack minimizes the risk. It is foolish to share tack between horses or use clothing belonging to other riders. Pathogens can survive for long periods on clothing and tack.

Conditions of the Skin

VIRAL PAPILLOMATA (WARTS)

These are caused by a virus similar to that causing warts in man, though cross-infectivity rarely occurs. Transmission is often from the dam, the foal being affected during suckling, with slow development over a number of months. Transmission often occurs between foals or from contact with infected material or woodwork.

The disease is almost always confined to young horses less than eighteen months of age. Warts are usually multiple and are most usually found on the relatively hairless parts of the body – the muzzle, nostrils, eyelids and often the front legs – less often elsewhere. They are small, grey, often cauliflower-shaped and firm. They may be very extensive if about the mouth. They may be subject to trauma and bleed or become secondarily infected. The diagnosis is made on the clinical appearance, with confirmation if necessary by biopsy examination.

Treatment

Local therapy is unsatisfactory in unskilled hands. The veterinarian may produce an autogenous vaccine. The warts are self-limiting and regression occurs within four months. If secondary infection occurs, regular antisepsis is advisable, with mild soap and water and an antiseptic dusting powder.

Transmission between young horses easily occurs, therefore affected animals should be isolated from others of the same age group.

EQUINE SARCOID

This is the most common skin tumour of the horse and is viral in origin. Unlike viral papillomata (which is caused by a different virus), it affects adult horses. Sarcoids can be one of three types: verrucae (wartlike), fibroplastic or mixed.

The different characteristics of the warts are determined by histopathological examination. Each type may be squat or stalked. Sarcoids are most often found on the limbs or head – sites commonly subjected to trauma.

The diagnosis of sarcoid is based on the clinical history and clinical signs; it may be confirmed by histopathological examination. They do not regress with age and may return after excision.

Treatment

Treatment should be by surgical excision or cryosurgery (see p. 543). A guarded prognosis is necessary because, although sarcoids do not spread widely through the body, they are generally locally invasive.

ACNE (SADDLE BOILS, HEAT RASH)

Staphylococcus areus is the microbe most commonly associated with acne. It is a common normal resident on the skin surface where it causes no harm. It may enter the skin to provoke a pustular reaction where the skin is abraded and dirty, where there is poor husbandry or lack of grooming. The presence of ectoparasites, dirty or ill-fitting tack and soiled saddle clothing are predisposing factors. Acne is predominantly seen in mild wet winters.

The lesions resemble somewhat those seen in acne in man, though they are not usually pustular in appearance. They are small, multiple, painful raised pimples or boils up to 1 cm in diameter in the saddle, girth or loin region. Occasionally there may be considerable swelling.

The diagnosis is made after a consideration of the history and a clinical examination, with an examination of a skin scrape of a lesion.

Treatment

Acne is caused by poor husbandry and self-abrasion. Standards of husbandry and hygiene must be improved to prevent recurrence. During treatment animals should not be worked. The affected area should be clipped if necessary to ensure adequate cleaning with a mild antiseptic wash. An antibiotic cream or ointment may be prescribed.

DERMATOPHILOSIS (STREPTOTHRICOSIS, MYCOTIC DERMATITIS, RAIN SCALD, MUD FEVER, GREASY HEEL)

The causative organism is *Dermatophilus congolensis* which gains entry into the skin when it is saturated by prolonged rain and self-excoriated due to ectoparasites. It is predominantly seen in mild wet winters. Poor husbandry is a predisposing factor. Lesions are seen on the back, belly and lower limbs.

Horses in poor condition and badly cared for at pasture are at risk and show signs of the condition along the dorsal midline. The hair appears matted and tufted. With gentle pulling some tufts will lift off, revealing grey-green pus stuck to the lower ends. Affected areas may be quite extensive.

Horses kept in small muddy paddocks in prolonged wet weather may develop dermatophilus of the lower limbs and sometimes of the abdomen. Horses with shaggy coats or with feather are particularly at risk. Older texts refer to 'greasy heel'. This is a local dermatophilus infection. Again the hair is tufted, and on the limbs the skin may be cracked and fissured.

Diagnosis is based on the appearance of the lesions and the isolation and microscopic examination of the stained filamentous organisms.

Treatment

The cause of the condition should be considered in treatment. It is favoured by prolonged moisture and poor hygiene; therefore dry conditions and improved hygiene should be the first step in therapy. Affected animals must be housed. Long hair shielding the lesions must be removed by clipping (sterilizing the blades after use). Astringent lotions are beneficial and a systemic antibiotic may be given when the lesions are severe. Fissuring and cracking of the skin may require prolonged careful treatment.

Remove long hair and wash with mild soap and tepid water. Areas must be kept dry after initial washing. Dressing with an antibiotic ointment is helpful. Rest in a dry area for several weeks will be essential.

Prevention is better than cure. The moral therefore is to practise good husbandry, prevent prolonged wetting by providing some shelter, examine regularly for ectoparasites, and *never* subject a horse or groups of horses to confinement in small muddy paddocks without shelter.

STRANGLES (*STREPTOCOCCUS EQUI* INFECTION)

The clinical signs and treatment are discussed elsewhere (see p. 411).

Strangles is a highly infectious disease, predominantly of young horses. It is not primarily a skin infection. However, the skin overlying infected lymph glands may become inflamed too, with swelling, heat, loss of hair and ulceration, particularly in the angle of the lower jaw and upper neck. The abscessed glands rupture and discharge a thick yellow sticky pus. The affected area should be bathed three times a day with warm saline solution and dried with an antibiotic powder. Affected animals must be isolated and care taken to prevent transfer of infected material. Visitors should be discouraged. The location of the abscesses permits easy transfer of the tacky pus to the stable door and thence to visitors' clothing. Normal animals are then at risk when viewed over their stable door. A later sequel to strangles may be the urticarial plaques of purpura haemorrhagica (see p. 411).

GLANDERS

See p. 413. This has long been eradicated from the British Isles.

RINGWORM (GIRTH ITCH, JOCKEY ITCH)

Ringworm of horses in the British Isles is caused by members of two groups of pathogenic fungi, *Trichophyton* and *Microsporum*.

Ringworm fungi are able to survive for at least a year in the crevices of buildings housing horses, in transporting vehicles and in wooden fences. Horses rub themselves on stanchions and woodwork and pick up infected hairs.

Horses may also be infected by other animals, for example, cattle and cats, and by contaminated tack or grooming utensils. Young horses are particularly at risk and may contract infection during transportation, at shows or in sale rings. It is common for such animals to develop the initial signs of ringworm within two weeks of such events.

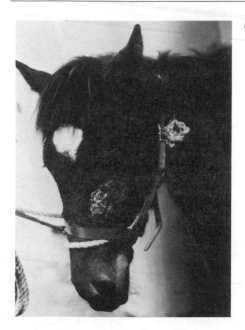

Figure 38　Ringworm

Symptoms

Young horses are particularly at risk but horses of all ages may be affected, although the disease is less common in older horses for immunity develops with increasing age.

The lesions are mainly seen on areas subjected to trauma from tack, clothing and riding boots. The term 'ringworm' is unfortunate: the lesions are rarely ringlike and the disease is not caused by a worm.

The early sign is one or more circular tufted areas (about 1–2 cm in diameter) with a little scale; the hair shortly falls out revealing the scaly skin. These may be abraded and become infected, with pus formation. Itchiness is rarely encountered; scraping a scaly area over with a fingernail may, however, provoke signs of irritation. In foals there may be large, extensive lesions covered by thick grey scale.

Treatment

After isolation, the affected area is clipped with scissors to remove the hair and the lesions treated with a fungicidal dressing for seven days. An antimycotic agent may be prescribed for oral administration.

An attempt should be made to trace the source of the infection. Contaminated woodwork should be cleaned by pressure hosing. All tack that has come into contact with the patient must be treated, first by scrubbing with mild soap and water and then disinfected, preferably by formalin gas. This is a skilled procedure and should be undertaken only under the direction of the veterinarian.

LOUSINESS

Two species of lice parasitize horses: one (the larger) is a blood-sucking parasite, *Haemtoapinus asini*; the smaller is a biting louse, *Damalinia equi*. Lice are small (1.5–3 mm in length), slow-moving, and easily overlooked. They spend their entire life cycle on the host, their eggs (nits) being attached individually to hairs, for there the first immature stage (appearing like a miniature adult) develops. The life cycle is complete within three weeks.

Louse infestation is particularly common in the winter months. Numbers increasing greatly from the end of autumn, with a precipitate numerical decline in the spring. Horse lice may cause a transient itchiness on the skin of humans.

Younger animals are most often infested, but older, debilitated animals may also carry heavy burdens.

Symptoms

Lice are found particularly on the neck, shoulders and on areas where there are opposing skin surfaces, for example, under the base of the tail. However, in heavy infestation the entire body may be parasitized. In young animals louse infestation is associated with marked itchiness. Itchiness provokes self-excoriation with associated hair breakage and loss, so that the body may

Figure 39 Lice

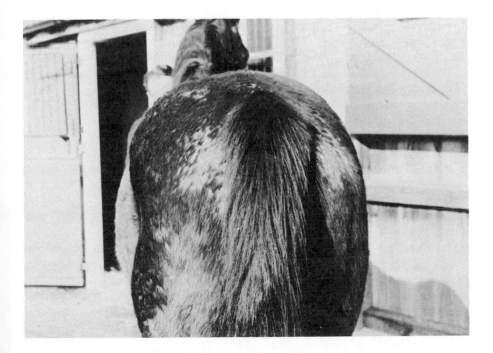

develop a motheaten appearance. The skin may become thickened; persistent itchiness may cause restlessness and debility. Close inspection by parting the hair and examining with a hand lens (though the lice are invisible to the naked eye) reveals the stationary or slow-moving dorsal, ventrally flattened parasites, which are grey-yellow in colour. Nits may be seen too, several being stuck to individual hairs along their length.

Treatment

Several proprietary preparations with an active principle of organophosphorus or synthetic pyrethroids are available as sprays or washes or concentrated pour-on solutions. Therapy should be repeated at least twice. Contact horses should also be treated.

Animals which are regularly inspected and groomed should never be troubled by these parasites. Lice do not survive for long on the host but there is a distinct danger that infestation may be transferred if rugs are shared between horses.

ACARIASIS (MANGE, SCAB, ITCH)

An early edition of this textbook stated that 'Prevalence bears relationship to neglect and filthy conditions – mange is not common in the stabled, groomed and well-cared-for animals in civilian or military employ.' This advice is still true. Mange was common when horses were employed in large numbers by the army. Close confinement during wartime or manoeuvres in horse lines permitted rapid spread.

Sarcoptic mange – scabies, a notifiable disease – was once very common in the British Isles but has now been eradicated for many years. However, mange due to the parasitic mite *Chorioptes equi* is still relatively common.

The mite is small (less than 1 mm in length), active, but barely visible to the naked eye. All stages are parasitic. It lives on the surface of the skin where its burrowing activities promote intense itchiness with consequent self-excoriation.

Symptoms

It is most common in stabled horses during winter. Initially the mite produces irritation on the lower hind limbs, but there may be spread to the upper limb, inguinal areas, belly and forelimbs. The horse nibbles constantly at these areas, which may be denuded of hair, excoriated and exudative. There will be stamping and restlessness. If neglected, the skin may become thickened and ridged.

The disease should be distinguished from infestation with the harvest mite (see below) which occurs in grazing horses during the summer and autumn.

Diagnosis is confirmed by examination of a skin scraping under the microscope. After isolation, the affected areas are clipped and treated with a parasiticide; the dressing is repeated a week later.

A member of the genus *Chorioptes* may live in the ear canal, where it may incite waxy exudation and head shaking (ear mange). Handling of the head may be resented. If suspected, veterinary advice should be sought. The mite can be killed using ear drops containing a parasiticide; the treatment should be repeated a week later.

Forage mites (non-parasitic) can cause extensive skin irritation in horses. Failure to keep mangers clean or allowing fallen food to accumulate may permit massive increase in numbers of non-parasitic mites, which usually are harmless, in confined spaces. However, migration over the body may occur with irritation, loss of hair and self-excoriation. The examination of material taken from affected areas using a fine-tooth comb and subsequent examination under the microscope will reveal forage mites. A parasiticide wash will remove them but the original cause should be dealt with.

NEOTROMBICULOSIS (BERRY BUG, TROMBICULOSIS, HARVEST MITE, HEEL BUG)

Harvest mites, *Neotrombicula autumnalis*, are parasitic only as larvae. Most of the life cycle is spent in the soil. The larvae emerge from the soil from May to late October and are particularly active in warm weather. They are less than 0.5 mm in length. They clamber up herbage and their hooked legs enable them to affix themselves to any passing animal or bird. Horses may therefore pick them up on their legs or about the muzzle. The larvae produce a feeding tube which enables them to feed on tissue fluid. When replete in two to three days they fall off to complete their life cycle.

Symptoms

Close inspection of the skin reveals small mites 3 mm in diameter attached to the skin; a group may crowd together to form an orange patch. Feeding mites cause local irritation, so that there may be shifting of the feet and nibbling of the limbs. Infestation may be suspected when horses at grass show lower-limb irritation (there may be a papular response) or when there is pedal irritation in stabled horses fed fresh hay in mild dry weather during summer.

Treatment

Local antiparasitic dressing is usually sufficient. Control is difficult because of the life cycle of the parasite and the wide availability of potential hosts.

TICK INFESTATION

Ixodes ricinus – the sheep tick – is the only potential tick parasitizing horses in the British Isles. Usually only very small numbers are observed firmly attached to the finer skin of the ventral abdomen.

The sheep tick is easily visible with the naked eye at all stages of its life cycle. The feeding apparatus (hypostome) is armed with backward-pointing barbs. If an attempt is made to remove the tick without making it relax, this is pulled off and a septic focus may result.

Ticks should therefore be removed by applying a pledget of cottonwool soaked in spirit, ether or chloroform to them, waiting a few moments, and then applying gentle traction. The tick can then be pulled off and the triangular hypostome will be seen attached to the tick.

SWEET ITCH (SUMMER SEASONAL RECURRENT DERMATITIS)

This is an allergic reaction to the bites of flies of the genus *Culicoides* – the midges. Horses of all types are affected, particularly ponies. Sweet itch is a common seasonal problem and occurs in all ages other than the first year of life. Midges are active from April to early November, particularly on calm humid days, mostly biting at daybreak and nightfall. Only the females of the genus are bloodsuckers. Moist decaying vegetation is required for development of the immature stages, so that the midges are more common in well-wooded areas, particularly by watercourses and lakes.

Symptoms

The disease is an intensely irritant dermatitis, the lesions of which have a characteristic distribution. They are found along the dorsal midline, mostly in and at the junction of long hair and short hair, forelock, mane, saddle region, trunk and tail base. With time they become more extensive, extending laterally. With continued self-excoriation the hair, particularly of the mane and tail, is broken and lost and the skin thickened and ridged. Severely affected horses are unworkable. The disease recurs during the warmer months of each year throughout the remainder of the animal's life.

Diagnosis

A recurring summer seasonal dermatitis of the dorsal midline with marked self-excoriation is characteristic. The only other diseases which might be confirmable are infestation with the bowel worm *Oxyuris equi* (pinworm) and mange.

With *Oxyuris equi* the female deposits large numbers of creamy-coloured eggs in masses about the anus. There is marked perineal irritation with rubbing of the buttocks against fixed objects. This causes redness of the area and the long tail hairs are broken, making it rat-tailed in appearance. *Oxyuris* infestation is not seasonal, only the buttocks are irritated, and investigation will reveal the eggs, which can be identified by the veterinarian under the microscope.

Figure 40   Sweet itch

M.ange is also irritant. The causal mites can be found in combings and skin scrapings. No mites are isolated from the lesions of sweet itch.

Treatment

Severely abraded areas may be treated with mild astringent lotion (2 per cent zinc sulphate). The availability of pour-on synthetic pyrethroids means that prevention of biting is now possile. These should be diluted according to the manufacturer's instructions and applied at six-day intervals along the animal's dorsal midline. In wet weather this should be more frequent. As midges are particularly active on mild, humid, still days and at daybreak and nightfall, affected animals should then be housed.

FACE FLIES

A number of flies resembling house flies are attracted to the secretions produced by the orifices of the body. The eyes and mouth may be particularly attractive and horses may be severely tormented by the attentions of these pests. Some control of the life cycle is possible if the breeding sites (manure piles) are restricted and cleared regularly.

Synthetic pyrethroid-impregnated tags are available which can be attached to the headcollar. Alternatively the head can be swabbed at weekly intervals with synthetic pyrethroid diluted according to the manufacturer's instructions.

EAR PLAQUES

Raised whitish thickened areas sometimes several centimetres in diameter are very occasionally found on the inner aspects of the ear of adult horses. They may be singular or several in number. The cause is not known. Viruses, mites and biting flies have all been considered but there is no evidence to incriminate either. They apparently cause no pain or irritation. No treatment is necessary.

NEOPLASIA (TUMOURS) (see also chapter 41)

Neoplasms induced by viruses – warts and sarcoids – have been referred to earlier (see pp. 92–3). Exuberant granulation tissue (proud flesh) is an excessive production of normal repair tissue and is relatively common on the limbs where cuts and trauma have occurred. It is to be distinguished from neoplasia and requires veterinary attention.

The aetiology of tumour development is not understood. Some tumours are initiated by viruses, while actinic sunlight may provoke tumours of the skin in relatively unprotected areas. Thus squamous cell carcinomas are more common on the eyelids and in the skin of light-coloured horses. This is so in humans too and emphasizes the dangers of excessive sunbathing. Tumours of pigment cells – melanomas – are common in grey-skinned horses. Sarcoids are commonest on areas subject to trauma – the limbs, head and neck.

Growths should be reported for veterinary examination as soon as they are discovered. Failure to do so may permit them to increase in size, making subsequent removal difficult or impossible, or allowing spread to other organs – a most dangerous development. Early excision is advised for all tumours. Advice about possible recurrence should be sought.

'Neoplasm' literally means new growth in the skin. By definition a neoplasm is uncontrolled cell division in tissue(s) which serves no useful purpose. The result is a visible change in conformation of the skin. Not all such growths are neoplastic: to be distinguished is **nodular necrobiosis**. Here a number of non-painful nodules, usually ovoid, about 2 cm in diameter and slightly elevated, are found in the saddle area of yearlings and older horses. The hair over them is undamaged. Their cause is not known but they may regress with time. Surgical removal may be advised; topical therapy is of no value.

URTICARIA (ALLERGIC REACTIONS, HIVES, NETTLE RASH)

The natural response of the skin to allergic reactions may be the sudden appearance of variable-sized elevations. Allergic dermatitis may follow insect bites, ingestion of substances to which a hypersensitivity has been developed (food, drugs), injection of foreign substances (vaccines, drugs), contact with allergens or following some infections (strangles, for example).

In each case prior exposure to the sensitizing allergen must have occurred at least once. The resulting reaction causes the release of fluid into the dermis and elsewhere, the nature of the response being variable according to the allergen. Allergic reactions to certain midges produce the clinical signs of sweet itch, allergic reaction to the stable fly (*Stomoxy calcitrans*) results in the appearance of flat elevations 1–2 cm in diameter scattered over the trunk.

A fairly common allergic reaction is to animal proteins in concentrates and fresh grass proteins. This is particularly seen in young adults. Numerous papules (small firm elevations) 0.5 cm in diameter appear, scattered over the trunk. There may be severe itchiness and loss of appetite. Earlier texts refer to this condition as surfeit (excessive feeding).

Reactions to injection of foreign substances (earlier vaccines, drugs) may be severe (anaphylaxis), with widespread swelling (oedema). There may be oedema of the eyelids and elsewhere, while released fluid in or about the respiratory tract may cause respiratory distress. The sudden appearance of extensive oedema should be regarded with concern and veterinary advice sought immediately.

PRESSURE SORES (BED SORES (DECUBITUS ULCERATION), SITFASTS, SADDLE GALLS, SADDLE SORES)

Long-lasting pressure in the recumbent animal may result in death of skin tissue (at pressure points) and severe ulceration, while persistent rubbing or pressure (even though light) may cause loss of hair, swelling, thickness of the skin, depigmentation and even ulceration. Common sites for the latter are in the saddle and bridle area and at points of contact with badly fitting harnesses on prominences.

Pressure sores are preventable. Recumbent animals should be regularly turned and well bedded. Their pressure points require gentle massage and washing regularly with soap and water. After drying they should be treated with a silicone cream. Contact points beneath tack should be frequently inspected for early evidence of unnatural pressure, heat, loss of hair and swelling, and the correct adjustments made while the tack itself should also be inspected regularly for wear.

PITYRIASIS (DANDRUFF)

Early texts refer to pityriasis as a disease but this is not correct; it is not a disease but a clinical sign which may occur in several diseases. It may occur in extensive ectoparasitism and in chronically sick or severely debilitated horses. Extensive exfoliative dermatitis with marked pityriasis is a feature of the rare auto-immune disease *periphigus foliaceous.* Mild dandruff may accumulate in neglected, ungroomed, stabled animals on poorly balanced diets.

The cause of pityriasis should be investigated and the primary aetiological factor treated if this is possible.

LEUKODERMA

This is whitening of the previously pigmented skin or hair. Vitiligo is not recorded in the British Isles, but loss of pigmentation of the skin occurs in tropical countries. Acquired leukoderma is a result of trauma to the skin by badly fitting harness or saddlery, the resulting destruction of the pigment cells is permanent with the production of white hairs (adventitial mark).

Loss of pigmentation about the commissures of the mouth may follow the usage of rubber bits. Leukoderma is permanent and there is no treatment. Adventitial marks must be recorded on identification charts (see chapter 54).

PHOTOSENSITIZATION (BLUE NOSE)

Photosensitization results from ingestion of agents which sensitize the skin to actinic rays in sunlight. It can also result from liver damage with subsequent imperfect excretion of the breakdown products of chlorophyll (the green colouring in plants), which in turn sensitize the skin to actinic rays. It may occur in both young and old horses and fortunately is uncommon.

Symptoms

Because the action of the rays is more intense on relatively uncreased skin, the signs are seen in relatively hairless parts of the body – the muzzle and nostrils (particularly if unpigmented) and the tips of the ears. In extensive damage large white-haired areas may be affected. The condition occurs in summer during bright, sunny weather. The first sign may be increased sensitivity – flicking of ears, rubbing of the body. Within a few hours there is reddening and then purplish discoloration and oedema of the underlying skin. The skin of these areas may slough off several days later to reveal the red moist dermis.

Prognosis and treatment

The prognosis for photosensitization must be guarded: if it is due to extensive liver damage, the outcome may be poor to hopeless. However, if it is the result of the ingestion of a photosensitizing plant such as St John's wort (*Hypericum perforatum*), the chances of recovery are quite good. Affected horses should be removed immediately from exposure to bright sunlight and housed in dim light. In the early stages an intravenous injection of an antihistamine may be beneficial. There may be extensive sloughing of the skin, particularly on light-coloured areas and on the extremities. These parts should be lightly dusted with an antiseptic drying powder and regularly inspected for deposited blowfly eggs.

8
SYSTEMS OF COMMUNICATION

The reader has arrived at this page through a series of actions often taken for granted. The recognition of the book, opening the pages, reading and understanding the print, and the decision as to whether or not to proceed with reading it in the context of the time available and motivation are conscious actions. But, awake or asleep, other forms of communication take place in order that the respiratory and metabolic processes of the body are regulated in such a way that we live in comfort with our environment. For example, when the environment is hot the body produces less heat; when we exert ourselves we breathe more deeply and accelerate the circulation of the blood in order to meet the increased oxygen demands. All of these processes depend on communication between one part of the body and another.

In health we are unaware of these processes; it is only in disease when the systems are disordered that recognizable symptoms appear.

If we analyse the systems upon which communication depends, we find that they may be separated roughly into two categories: (a) appreciation of external stimuli and happenings and (b) response. It is possible therefore to recognize an input (i.e. a stimulus) and an appropriate action initiated by the input stimulus (i.e. a response). The means of communication between the input and the response are the messages upon which the body depends for its communication. For example, the stimulus of pinprick causes us to withdraw hurriedly the part pricked. The response to the prick depends on the messages relayed from the skin through the central nervous system to the muscles, which respond by pulling away the affected part in an effort to diminish or avoid the painful stimulus. There is thus an *afferent* (towards) pathway along which the messages are transmitted to the brain and an *efferent* (away) pathway along which messages are carried from the brain to the muscles instructing them to withdraw the part from pain.

In essence all systems of communication within the body are based on these afferent and efferent pathways carrying messages. However, although this analogy is readily understood with regard to nerves, which work in the same way as telephone messages are passed through a central exchange from one house to another, the same applies to messages in the form of hormones which issue from glands and carry chemical messengers to organs, evoking an appropriate response.

These messages are relayed by the following body systems: the central and peripheral nervous systems, the autonomic nervous system, the endocrine (hormonal) system, the neuroendocrine (hormonal) system, and the special senses of sight, hearing and smell. The sensations of touch, pain, heat, cold, etc., will be considered under the central and peripheral nervous systems.

THE CENTRAL AND PERIPHERAL NERVOUS SYSTEMS

The nervous system, as its name implies, is composed of nerve cells and their fibres. The fibres conduct electrical impulses (messages) and are responsible for feeling, consciousness and action. The cells and their fibres are grouped together in the brain and spinal cord. The fibres extend to the periphery, e.g. the skin and muscles, so that the whole system may be likened to the links of a telephone system. The nerve endings in the skin, for example have special properties of being sensitive to pain and touch, pressure and temperature,

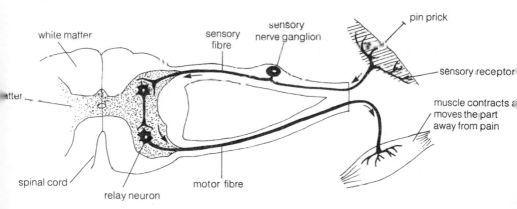

Figure 41 The reflex arc

etc. When these physical stimuli are applied to the skin they set off messages that are conducted along the pathways of the nerves to the cells in the spinal cord. These relay the messages to other cells and their fibres which conduct outward-bound messages to the muscles if the sensation is painful. This reflex arc is illustrated in Figure 41.

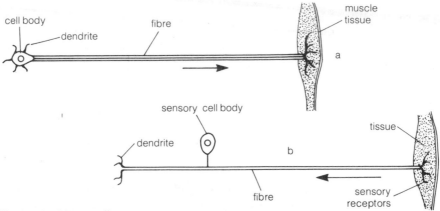

Figure 42 Nerve cells: a) a motor neuron, b) a sensory neuron

The brain is made aware of this nervous activity through nerve fibres that conduct the information up the spinal cord to the brain. In this way the individual has a conscious capacity to modify any action or response and to be aware of what is taking place in the environment.

The response of a nerve cell (Figure 42) is always the same. It conducts a wave of excitation (nervous impulse or message) from one end of the cell to the other. The cell's fibre may be several metres long and can conduct impulses at a very fast rate of up to 100 m/s.

Nervous tissue extends to almost every part of the body, but each segment is connected to form a whole system. This might be likened to the wires and cables of a telephone system connected to the exchange and branching in all directions. The greatest concentration of nervous tissue is in the skull, that is, the brain. The brain and spinal cord are known as the *central nervous system* (CNS) whereas other nervous tissue of the body is described as the *peripheral nervous system* (PNS). Higher functions depend on the CNS and basic functions on the PNS.

The nerve cell

The basic unit of the nervous system is the nerve cell or neuron. Many cells and their fibres are collected together, forming bundles. To the naked eye the nerve fibres appear white and the cell bodies brownish-grey tinged with pink. Nerve tissue is therefore described as white or grey matter. Ganglia (bunches of nerve tissue) are composed of grey matter and are situated on the efferent (sensory) nerve trunks (Figure 42). The nerve trunks are classed according to their connection with the central nervous system as cerebral (cranial), spinal or sympathetic.

The brain and spinal cord are enclosed in three membranes or meninges. The outermost is called the dura mater, the middle the arachnoid mater and the inner the pia mater. The dura mater is attached to the bones of the skull and the bony canal forming the vertebral column.

The brain and spinal cord are surrounded by the cerebral spinal fluid, which is found between the middle and inner layers of the meninges. This fluid buffers the nervous tissue against shockwaves of trauma, as well as acting as a means of nourishment and exchange of fluid and vital substances between the nerve tissue and the surrounding environment.

The spinal cord

The spinal cord occupies the canal running the entire length of the vertebral column, extending from the head, where it emerges from the brain, to the middle of the sacrum (croup). In the horse it is approximately 200 cm long and cylindrical, with slightly flattened sides.

Forty-two pairs of spinal nerves emerge from the cord at intervals between each vertebra. There are eight neck or cervical nerves, eighteen chest or thoracic, six back or lumbar, five croup (sacral) and five tail (coccygeal) nerves. The arrangement of white and grey substance in the cord and the way in which the nerves emerge is illustrated in Figure 43.

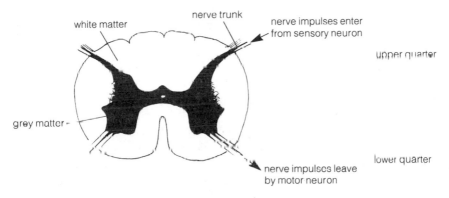

Figure 43   Cross-section of the spinal cord (based on a radiograph)

The brain

The brain is that part of the central nervous system contained in the skull. It weighs about 650 g in an adult horse and forms 1 per cent of the bodyweight. It is composed of various parts, containing white and grey matter and fluid-filled cavities (ventricles) which connect with the space surrounding the spinal cord that contains the cerebral spinal fluid.

The brain has three primary segments – the hind, the mid- and the fore-brain – each associated with specialized functions. The hind brain is formed by the brain stem and contains the centres that regulate breathing. It also contains the pons, which controls emotions and other behavioural activity, and the cerebellum, which controls movement. The midbrain is responsible for sensations of sight and smell and the control of lower centres in the hind brain, e.g. the voluntary control of breathing, behavioural patterns and movement. The forebrain is connected to the pituitary gland and modifies its hormonal secretions (see p. 122).

There are twelve nerves that leave the brain and pass to various parts of the body. Each is responsible for sensory (feeling) or motor activity. These nerves are numbered as follows: I olfactory, II optic, III ocular motor, IV trochlear, V trigeminal, VI abducens, VII facial, VIII acoustic, IX glosso-pharangeal, X vagus, XI spinal accessory, XII hypoglossal. All these nerves except X and XI are concerned with feeling or with muscular movement of the head.

Conditions of the Central and Peripheral Nervous Systems

Diseases and conditions of the nervous system occur when impulses normally passing through the fibres are disturbed. If the impulses are slowed or prevented from passing, this may cause loss of feeling if the nerves affected are sensory or paralysis if they serve motor functions.

Because the central nervous system is concerned with coordination, interference with the passage of nervous impulses may lead to inco-ordination (ataxia).

If the nervous impulses are speeded up or increased in number, they may result in convulsions or hyperirritability, causing spasm, as in lockjaw (see p. 414).

The cause of these conditions may be damage, viral infection, bacterial toxins, haemorrhage or trauma causing disturbance of the pathways.

In the diagnosis of lameness we take advantage of our knowledge of the nerve trunks to cause numbness in certain parts. This technique is known as nerve blocking (see p. 149).

PARALYSIS

Paralysis is usually a sign of an injured nerve which prevents impulses passing from the central nervous system to the muscles. This prevents the horse from using the muscles supplied by the affected nerve. For example, the facial nerve is particularly vulnerable to injury as it passes across the back of the angle of the lower jaw. This nerve supplies the muscles of the lips, nostrils, cheeks, eyelids and ears.

Symptoms of **facial paralysis** are a drooping eyelid and and ear, a partially collapsed nostril and sagging upper and lower lips. Usually only one side is affected and the upper lip tends to be pulled towards the side away from the affected area because the muscles on the opposite side still have normal nervous control.

It is usual to give the paralysis the name of the damaged nerve, e.g. facial paralysis. **Obdurator** is another common form of paralysis in which, following foaling, the obdurator nerve becomes pinched, causing partial paralysis of the hind leg.

Another commonly affected nerve is the suprascapular nerve, which emerges from the chest underneath the shoulder and supplies the muscles of the shoulder. Injury results in wasting of the muscles on the outside of the shoulderblade because of damage to their nerve supply (see Figure 85, p. 229). This condition is known as **sweeny**. It sometimes causes an abnormal gait, best observed when the individual is walked slowly towards the observer.

Radial paralysis is common after surgery, because a horse has to lie on the operating table for a prolonged period, and after collisions. The radial nerve emerges from the chest wall underneath the shoulderblade. It supplies the muscles which advance the leg when the horse moves forward. The muscles also hold the elbow joint in position. Symptoms of radial paralysis therefore include a dropped elbow and difficulty in moving the leg forward (see Figure 86, p 230)

Paralysis is also experienced in conditions caused by equid herpesvirus (see p. 425) and other viral infections. In the human the most well-known example is poliomyelitis. Symptoms displayed by horses suffering from viral infections vary with the nature of the virus and the particular damage that it causes to the central nervous system.

INFECTIONS (see also chapters 28–32)

Infection may affect the lining of the brain and spinal cord (**meningitis**) or the substance of the brain (**encephalitis**). It may also affect peripheral nerves, causing neuritis.

Conditions of nervous disease in horses are Eastern, Western and Venezuelan encephalomyelitis (see p. 430), the nervous form of equid herpesvirus 1 (rhinopneumonitis) infection (see p. 425), rabies (see p. 432) and lockjaw (see p. 414).

LOSS OF SENSATION (see also chapter 18)

Damage to sensory nerves, that is, those taking messages from the periphery to the central nervous system, causes loss of sensation or numbness. Crushing of the spinal cord, as in a **broken neck or back**, causes loss of sensation to large areas of the hindquarters. Because motor nerves are also affected there is associated paralysis.

The loss of sensation may be diagnosed by pricking the skin with a needle or drawing a sharp instrument over the surface of the skin. This normally causes the horse to move the skin or underlying part. However, if the muscles are also paralysed, it may be impossible to be certain that there is also loss of feeling.

Injury to the optic nerve (see p. 128), which conveys messages from the eye to the brain, causes **blindness**. This is often the result of an injury to the head causing haemorrhage and pressure on the nerve. Depending on the severity of the damage, sight may return as the blood clot contracts.

Head injuries may likewise cause paralysis or loss of sensation in any part of the body. Horses suffering from **concussion** or a **fractured skull** may show incoordination, staggering and convulsions. Mild cases recover, but frequently the damage cannot be repaired and the horse dies or has to be destroyed on humane grounds.

LARYNGEAL HEMIPLEGIA (ROARING, WHISTLING)

This condition results from a paralysis of the muscles which control the movement of the larynx. In almost all cases it is the left side that is affected. The muscles are supplied by the recurrent laryngeal nerve and it is damage to this nerve that results in the paralysis.

Paralysis of the movement of the larynx causes the vocal cords and arytenoid cartilage to hang in the airstream when the horse breathes in, and this results in an abnormal sound; hence the popular name of whistling or roaring.

For treatment, see p. 35.

WOBBLER SYNDROME

The wobbler syndrome results from damage to the nerve trunks passing along the spinal cord in the neck. This is usually the result of injury to the bony canal through which the spinal cord passes on its way to the brain. The nerve trunks involved are those carrying messages that enable the horse to be aware of where its limbs are at a particular moment. This sense of proprioception is important in the coordination of movement. If the sense is impaired the affected individual suffers an unusual incoordinated gait. The condition is described in detail on p. 274.

SHIVERING AND STRINGHALT

Symptoms in these conditions are, as their names imply, unusual shivering movements of the hind legs as they are lowered to the ground from a flexed position. Their cause is poorly understood. However, it is probable that they are the result of damage to the nerves at some point in their course from the muscles that control the hind limbs to the higher centre of the brain. For further details, see pp. 258–9.

CEREBELLAR HYPOPLASIA (CEREBELLAR DEGENERATION)

This occurs in Arab horses and is characterized by tremors of the head, incoordination of the legs and a faulty blink response when the eye is 'challenged'. A fine head tremor is usually the first sign and this develops before a foal is four months old. It consists of nodding movements which become more obvious when a purposeful movement is made. In some instances the animal is unable to stand, and in others it lurches or sways when it tries to walk.

There is no treatment. As the disease is thought to be genetically based on a recessive gene, action should be taken to diminish the risk by avoidance of breeding from mares and stallions known to be carriers.

THE AUTONOMIC NERVOUS SYSTEM

The autonomic nervous system can be divided into two parts: the sympathetic and the parasympathetic. The sympathetic nervous system carries impulses to the muscles of the heart and gut and to the secretory glands. It also conducts impulses from the various organs of the chest and abdomen to the central nervous system and thereby serves to control involuntary activity, such as movement of the alimentary tract (peristalsis) and the secretion of the salivary and other glands. It regulates the size of blood vessels by acting on their muscular coat, causing them to constrict or relax and thus influencing the resistance to bloodflow and blood pressure.

The action of the sympathetic system is roughly opposed to that of the parasympathetic system, the nerves of which are carried mainly in the Xth cranial (vagus) nerve. This system decreases gut movement, slows the heart and decreases or changes the character of glandular secretions.

One of the conditions of the autonomic nervous system is grass sickness (see p. 14).

THE ENDOCRINE (HORMONAL) SYSTEM

Hormones are the chemical messengers of the body. They are substances produced by glands, and carried in the bloodstream to control organs at a distance from their source of secretion. For example, the pituitary gland, which is situated just below the brain, secretes the hormone FSH. This is carried in the bloodstream to the ovaries, where it causes follicles to develop.

The hormones of the body, the glands which secrete them, the organs they affect and their action are shown in Table 1.

Table 1 Some Main Hormones of the Body, Their Source and Action

Gland	Hormone	Target organ	Action
Pituitary			
Anterior	FSH	Ovary	Stimulates follicle development
	LH	Ovary	Causes ovulation and yellow body function
	Prolactin	Mammary glands	Causes milk secretion
	GH (growth)	General action on metabolism	Promotes increase in protein, fat, sugar and water in body
	TSH	Thyroid	Causes thyroxine secretion
	ACTH	Adrenal cortex	Causes cortisol secretion
Posterior	Vasopressin, oxytocin	Smooth muscle in arteries/ uterus	Raises blood pressure, contracts uterine muscle
Pancreas	Insulin	General	Controls level of sugar in blood and tissues
Thyroid	Thyroxine	General	Controls general metabolic rate
Adrenal cortex	Cortisone	General	Controls salt, sugar and water content of blood and tissues
Adrenal medulla	Adrenaline		Affects sweating, increases blood flow to muscles
Ovary Yellow body	Progesterone	Uterus and genital tract	Changes of dioestrus and pregnancy
Follicle	Oestrogen	Uterus and genital tract	Causes oestrous behaviour and lubricates genital tract
Uterus	Prostaglandin	Yellow body of ovary	Stops yellow body secreting progesterone
	PMSG	Probably ovary	May protect yellow body of pregnancy and has immune suppressing role
Brain	Releasing factors	Pituitary	Hormones that cause pituitary to release its own hormones such as FSH, LH, ACTH

Measurement of hormones

The reader will probably be more familiar with the subject of hormones in terms of phrases such as 'hormonal imbalance', which is often used of mares that are difficult to get in foal. 'Adrenal exhaustion' is another phrase sometimes used when horses in training perform poorly. These phrases are imprecise and best avoided; they have little relevance to the actual hormonal status of the individual.

Such terms were used in the past, when our knowledge was far from complete. More recently sensitive methods of measuring hormones in the bloodstream have been developed. These have been used to identify the true hormonal status of individuals for diagnostic purposes. However, before describing their application to horses, it is necessary to explain some of the limits of these methods.

The most obvious limitation is that the measurement of the level of a hormone in the blood reflects only its level in transit. It does not necessarily reflect its power of action on the organ which it controls.

There are two main implications behind this statement. First, the hormone being measured in high concentrations in the bloodstream may fail to have a corresponding powerful action because the target organ has a reduced capacity to respond.

For example, ACTH, the hormone stimulating the adrenal cortex to produce cortisone, can only have an effect if the cortex is responsive to the action of ACTH. This action depends on the presence of structures known as receptors.

To put it at its simplest, this means that the ability of ACTH to cause release of cortisone is related to the number of receptors present. The number of receptors varies according to factors which need not concern us here. However, if the number of receptors is small, a large amount of ACTH in the bloodstream will not cause a corresponding increase in secretion. Indeed, the reverse may be true: a large number of receptors will cause a relatively large output despite the presence of only a small amount of ACTH in the bloodstream.

This example reflects the position with regard to all hormones. And it demonstrates the need to be cautious about interpreting the levels of hormones present in the bloodstream at any given time.

The second reason why blood levels do not necessarily reflect the degree of activity resulting from the presence of a hormone is that many hormones are balanced by the action of others. For example, progesterone and oestrogen have contradictory actions and it is the balance of the two that controls uterine contractions at birth.

Notwithstanding the above cautionary remarks, there exists sufficient experience in employing modern methods of measurement for us to comment on selected hormones.

Steroid hormones

Steroid hormones include progesterone, oestrogen, testosterone and cortisone. They have a chemical structure of four carbon rings and are therefore closely related to one another. The simplest form is cholesterol. The body is able to change one steroid hormone into another.

Progesterone Progesterone in the non-pregnant mare is secreted by the yellow body of the ovary (see p. 320). Its presence in the bloodstream at levels over 1 ng/ml is diagnostic of an active yellow body in one or other of the two ovaries. A detectable level of progesterone in the bloodstream may therefore be taken as a diagnostic sign of dioestrus, that is, the mare is not in heat.

This helps us to confirm the sexual state of the individual as shown when the mare is teased. The test distinguishes between sexual states of heat (oestrus), not in heat (dioestrus), anoestrus (sexually inactive) and prolonged dioestrus (see pp. 326–7).

Pregnant mares have relatively high levels of progesterone for about 120 days after conception. Progesterone is the hormone which maintains pregnancy and it is produced by the ovaries up to this time. From then until the end of pregnancy it is produced by the placenta and does not appear in any quantity in the mare's bloodstream.

Up to 120 days we would expect a pregnant mare to have varying levels over 4 ng/ml. The actual amount is not related to the pregnancy as such but to the activity of the yellow body. We cannot therefore use progesterone as an indication of pregnancy, except in the negative sense that if the value is below 4 ng/ml the mare is unlikely to be pregnant. If it is above 4 ng/ml the mare may be pregnant or merely in a state of dioestrus.

There are divided opinions as to whether progesterone therapy prevents mares from aborting. The problem, as with so many clinical situations, is the absence of objective studies. The facts are that progesterone is indeed required for continuing pregnancy. However, the quantity of progesterone in the bloodstream does not necessarily indicate the effectiveness of the hormone at the target site, i.e. the uterus. For reasons explained above, a small amount of hormone may have a marked effect. Further, because the placenta is producing progesterone from about day 50 of the pregnancy, the hormone may be adequate at the level of the interface between the placenta and uterus, even though there are low levels in the mare's bloodstream.

If the level of progesterone in the blood is less than 4 ng/ml, we may assume that the individual is suffering from a deficiency of progesterone, at least up to day 120. After this time we expect very low levels because the progesterone is being produced entirely by the placenta and not by the mare's ovaries. The progesterone does not pass from the placenta into the mare's bloodstream except in very small amounts and the levels of progesterone in the last two thirds of pregnancy is often below 4 ng/ml.

In most cases of abortion progesterone levels fall *because* and not as a cause of the abortion. Most of the claims for the successful use of progesterone as a preventive measure are based on cases in which the drug was given and the mare did not abort, and on mares which were not given progesterone therapy but which did lose their pregnancy. Unfortunately there have been no properly conducted trials using sufficient numbers and containing matched controls, that is, mares given progesterone and those not given progesterone being of identical status with regard to their likelihood of aborting.

It requires 2000 mg of progesterone injected every six days to maintain levels of 4 ng/ml in a mare's bloodstream. This dose rate is far in excess of what is generally administered (and often claimed to be successful). This is a further argument used by those who believe that progesterone therapy is ineffective or, at least, has unproven efficacy.

Progesterone, if given daily, suppresses the output of pituitary hormones (see p. 328) and may be used as a treatment of anoestrus. In these instances the pituitary hormones (FSH and LH — see below) are being produced in insufficient quantity by the pituitary to develop follicles which ovulate. Therefore these individuals are not cycling (see pp. 325–6). The progesterone, by preventing release of FSH and LH from the pituitary, ensures that these hormones are stored. When the progesterone therapy is stopped, the hormones are released in substantial quantities and thus start the mare cycling. This therapy requires daily injections. More recently, the availability of a powerful progesterone-type drug (allyl trenbolone) which can be fed or administered by mouth daily has simplified the approach. However, this therapy will only work in certain individuals that are truly anoestrus and is more likely to be successful if spring follicles are present in the ovaries. The treatment should therefore be given only on veterinary advice, otherwise there may be disappointment and waste of costly drugs.

Oestrogens   Oestrogens are hormones secreted by the lining of the follicles in the ovaries. They are also formed by the placenta from special substances produced by the ovaries of the foetus. They enter the mare's bloodstream and are excreted from her body in the urine. They can be used, therefore, as a means of pregnancy diagnosis from about 120 days of pregnancy until full term. This test is named Cuboni after the scientist who developed the means of analysis (see p. 337).

Oestrogens is a collective term for substances which have varying degrees of activity: oestradiol, oestrone sulphate and oestrone. In the pregnant mare there are two other substances, equenin and equilinin, which are unique to the horse family.

Oestrogens are responsible for signs of heat (oestrus) and for feminine characteristics, and they are essential for the growth and wellbeing of the foetus. At birth they make the uterus more susceptible to the action of oxytocin and prostaglandins, which cause the muscular contractions of uterus.

Various synthetic compounds are available for therapy, the most well known of which is stilboestrol; another that is often employed is oestradiol benzoate. Oestrogens are used to accentuate signs of heat in mares which, although technically in a state of oestrus, may not otherwise accept the stallion.

They are also used as an adjunct to therapy in infections of the uterus in that they improve the blood supply to the mucosal lining and mobilize the action of the white cells (leucocytes) which play a part in the defence against infection.

They may also be used as an adjunct to oxytocin therapy and also at the time of induced foaling in order to soften and relax the cervix.

Therapy should always be applied under veterinary supervision because oestragen therapy can have adverse side effects if not used at a suitable dosage rate or for appropriate conditions in any particular individual.

Testosterone Testosterone is the male sex hormone. It is secreted by the testes (see p. 307) and is responsible for male sexual characteristics. Levels rise when mares are teased or become sexually excited. It is also responsible for engorgement of the penis with blood and the sexual quality or strength known as libido, in which the male mounts the mare and ejaculates.

Testosterone has an anabolic effect, that is, it promotes the development of muscle and the retention of nitrogen in the body. There are similar steroid substances, known as anabolic steroids, which have a similar effect but without the obvious masculinizing features. For this purpose they are nowadays usually employed in preference to testosterone. They may be used because of their supposed benefit on performance but are consequently banned under Jockey Club Rules for racehorses.

Testosterone may be administered to stallions and young colts with poor libido. However, any beneficial effect is temporary and the hormone may, if used over a long period, have a counter-productive effect because it suppresses the individual's own output of testosterone. The use of LH (see below) is therefore preferred.

Cortisone Cortisone is produced by the cortex (outer lining) of the adrenal gland. There are a number of related compounds, some naturally and some synthetically produced. Cortisol (hydrocortisone) is a compound released naturally; cortisone and hydrocortisone are also produced synthetically, as are dexamethasone and betamethasone.

Cortisone stimulates metabolism and is a hormone which prepares for and sustains the individual in athletic performance. It is released when the trophic hormone ACTH is secreted by the pituitary. This is in response to fright or to meet the need for exertion and exercise. High levels in the blood occur when a foal is attempting to get to its feet for the first time. The exception is premature foals, which do not have the ability to secrete cortisone, although they are able to achieve high levels of ACTH; the adrenal cortex in premature foals is unresponsive to the action of ACTH.

Preparations of cortisone are used in therapy in order to enhance the body's response to inflammation and to counter the effects of shock. In general terms cortisone reduces pain and swelling. It is therefore an adjunct to treatment of inflammation due to trauma and, to a lesser extent, of infection.

The disadvantage of therapy in the presence of infection is that cortisone also reduces the response of the inflammatory process that is necessary in countering infection by bacteria. Cortisone may be used in joints and has a dramatic effect on relieving pain and promoting function. Unfortunately it also injures the joint surface and is no longer commonly used in the treatment of damaged joints in racehorses. In the control of inflammation the non-steroidal anti-inflammatory drugs (NSAID) such as phenylbutazone are usually preferred.

Follicle-stimulating hormone (FSH) FSH is produced by the pituitary and stimulates the growth of follicles in the ovary and the secretion of oestrogen. It is also present in pregnant mare's blood from day 40 to about day 120, as pregnant mare's serum gonadotrophin (PMSG) (equine chorionic gonadotrophin or eCG), which is produced by cells in the lining of the mare's uterus (see below). FSH itself is not available as such, largely because it has not yet been synthesized artificially; its only source is the mare's pituitary. Drug therapy depends on the use of releasing factors, such as GnRH (see below).

Luteinizing hormone (LH) LH is secreted by the pituitary gland and causes follicles in the ovary to ovulate. It subsequently promotes the formation of a yellow body in the ovary which secretes progesterone.

LH is produced by the placenta in pregnant women and excreted in urine. Pregnant women's urine can be purified and a drug extracted which contains a substance that acts in a manner similar to LH. This substance is known as human chorionic gonadotrophin (hCG). It is used extensively to cause ovulation in mares which are in oestrus and possess a mature follicle in the ovary. It is claimed to cause ovulation within forty-eight hours of administration.

The hormone is responsible for causing the interstitial cells of the testis to secrete testosterone. It may be used to improve the libido of stallions and young colts. This is a preferable therapy to the use of testosterone itself (see above) because it does not suppress the colt's own output of testosterone or LH.

Pregnant mare's serum gonadotrophin (PMSG)   As already indicated, PMSG contains both FSH and LH. It has been more recently termed equine chorionic gonadotrophin (eCG). The name PMSG is derived from the fact that the hormone is present in large quantities in the bloodstream of pregnant mares from day 40 to about day 120. The term eCG refers to the fact that its source is from cells that originate in the placenta (chorion) of mares.

Because it is present in mares' blood it has been used as the basis of a pregnancy test (see p. 336). Its function in the mare is not clearly established but it is thought to be involved in the protection of the foetus against the immune response which would otherwise be mounted by the mare's uterus. It may also be responsible for causing follicles to ovulate in the ovary and for the maintenance of the yellow bodies of pregnancy (see p. 320).

During the last decade a major advance in our understanding of this hormone was provided by the work of Dr Allen and his colleagues in Cambridge. They showed that the hormone was actually produced by cells that migrated from the developing placenta on the 37th day after conception. At this time the placenta possesses a girdle of cells which comes into contact with the wall of the uterus at the junction of the horn and body (see p. 331). These cells transfer from the placenta and burrow into the wall of the uterus. The girdle thus forms rings of tissue known as the endometrial cups. Here they produce PMSG in large quantities. This forms a sticky secretion between the placenta and the uterine wall and is also absorbed into the mare's bloodstream.

After about sixty days (i.e. about 100 days of pregnancy) the mare mounts an immunological rejection of the cells and they cease to function. One must presume that by this time their function in maintaining pregnancy is at an end. This coincides, of course, with the cessation of activity in the mare's ovaries, and these become quiescent from this time until the foal is ready to be delivered.

PMSG may be harvested from the mare's blood and is available commercially as a drug. It is used extensively in promoting follicular development in sheep and cattle and even in women. However, it is a curious and somewhat frustrating phenomenon that the drug does not have any effect on mares' ovaries. The reason for this is not clear, but it is probably because the ovaries of non-pregnant mares are physiologically resistant to its action, having been exposed to its activity during foetal life.

In order to stimulate mares' ovaries we use GnRH (gonadotrophin releasing hormone).

Gonadotrophin releasing hormone (GnRH)   As described below (see p. 122), there are a number of hormones released in the brain which reach the pituitary and cause this gland to release specific hormones. Thus there is a releasing hormone – gonadotrophin releasing hormone or GnRH – for FSH and LH.

GnRH is available commercially in a synthetic form and has been used successfully for inducing oestrus cycles. However, it must be administered in pulsatile (i.e. several) rather than bolus (single) doses. It is therefore a drug which must be used under strict veterinary control.

Other hormones

Insulin, which regulates levels of sugar (carbohydrate) in the blood, may be used in cases of hyperlipaemia (see p. 23) in conjunction with glucose infusions. Otherwise this hormone does not form part of the equine veterinarian's armoury. Horses rarely suffer from diabetes mellitus (see p. 22) and treatment is not economic or justified on humane grounds.

Adrenaline is a hormone produced by the adrenal medulla (the central part of the gland surrounded by the cortex), which is part of the sympathetic nervous system (see p. 113). It may be used by veterinarians in tests but is not usually used in therapy. It was once used as a stimulant in cases of cardiac arrest but has now been replaced by drugs such as doxapram hydrochloride.

THE NEUROENDOCRINE SYSTEM

The two systems, nerves (pp. 107–13) and hormones (pp. 113–21), which regulate body functions have been known for a very long time. They may be likened to messengers carrying messages of control and feeling around the body. However, in recent years a newer concept has developed of a third system combining both nerves and hormones. This is called the neuro-endocrine system.

This system provides a link between the environment and the mechanisms of internal control represented by the hormonal (endocrine) system. For example, it is the brain – the centre of the nervous system – that receives information about the length of daylight to which a mare is subjected. This information comes from the eye and is relayed to the nervous system by way of the pineal body, a collection of special cells within the brain.

The messages about daylight pass from the back of the eye (the retina), along the optic nerves, enter the brain, and cause the pituitary gland to release follicle-stimulating hormone (FSH) and luteinizing hormone (LH). It is these hormones which control sexual activity (see above). The information about increasing daylight hours in spring and summer is thus translated through the nervous system to the hormonal system, which in turn dictates whether or not a mare undergoes oestrus cycles.

Similarly messages about changes in the outside world, e.g. hot, cold, danger, etc., are conveyed through the nervous system to the hormonal system and evoke an appropriate response.

We have seen that the basic unit of the nervous system is the neuron, i.e. the nerve cell from which nerve fibres originate. The basic unit of the endocrine or hormonal system is the secretory cell, that is, a cell which produces hormones in the hormonal glands.

The concept of the neuroendocrine system is that nerve and hormonal cells have much in common and that nerve cells, as well as possessing the capacity to transmit nerve impulses, can also secrete hormones.

What causes the pituitary gland to release ACTH?

Let us look at some examples to illustrate the subject, starting with ACTH, the hormone which stimulates the production of cortisone (see p. 118). If we address the question as to what causes the release of ACTH, we come to the answer that it is the production of another hormone secreted by nerve cells in the brain. This hormone is one of several releasing hormones (sometimes called releasing factors) which are secreted by cells in that part of the brain known as the hypothalamus.

There are corresponding releasing hormones for other hormones, e.g. for LH, FSH, prolactin, thyroid-stimulating hormone (TSH) and growth hormone (GH).

How do nerves produce hormones?

Nerve cells (neurons) form their own hormone product in the cell under the direction of their ribonucleic acid (RNA), which forms part of the genetic system of the cell. The product is packaged as granules and transported along nerve fibre to its end or terminal. Here the granules are released.

In the case of pituitary hormones, releasing factors are discharged into a special blood supply to the pituitary, thereby regulating the secretion of this gland. The distance is small but the secretion is termed a neurohormone because it enters the circulating blood.

However, similar secretions produced by cells at terminals cross to other cells and have a regulatory impact on these cells. These are termed neuromodulators, i.e. they modulate the activity of other nerve cells.

A third type of secretion from nerves of the hormone system is the hormones released by brain cells connected directly by nerve fibres to the posterior part of the pituitary gland. These cells release the hormones oxytocin (which causes the uterus to contract) and vasopressin (which raises the blood pressure by causing the blood vessels to constrict). Vasopressin is also referred to as antidiuretic hormone because it reduces the output of water from the kidneys.

These two hormones, oxytocin and vasopressin, are synthesized as prohormones in the neurons (nerve cells) in special parts of the brain. They are transported in vesicles (fluid bubbles) through the nerves' fibres to the pituitary, where they are stored. They are then released as hormones when the cells in which they are stored realize the need.

How does the neuroendocrine system function?

To understand how the neuroendocrine system functions, let us consider the example of vasopressin. The cells containing vasopressin are sensitive to changes in the osmolality of blood. Blood osmolality is the measurement of its concentration or thickness. Thus, if blood becomes too thick, antidiuretic hormone is released in order to prevent the kidneys from releasing water. In consequence the urine becomes concentrated and water is retained in the body. The blood is diluted sufficiently for the pituitary to recognize that it is now normal and the output of antidiuretic hormone is therefore decreased.

Similarly, when a foal goes to the udder of a mare, there is a nervous reflex transmitted from nerve endings in the udder. These are conducted through the spinal cord and up to the brain, where they release the hormone oxytocin. This causes contraction of the very small muscles in the udder, thereby releasing milk into the nipple for the foal to suck. This is known as the milk let-down reflex.

Oxytocin is also present when the uterus contracts during first-stage labour. This is the reason why there is a let down of milk at the time of foaling. Sometimes this happens before a mare foals. The stimulus for oxytocin release in these circumstances comes from the placenta and the foetus.

Why do we need to understand the neuroendocrine system?

The subject of endocrinology is complex, but it is necessary to advance the understanding of the subject so that those who are responsible for horses can adjust managerial and veterinary practice. In the past it has been necessary to comprehend the action of hormones such as FSH, LH and prostaglandins in order to grasp the logic of the control of the mare's oestrous cycle. The discovery of each of these hormones, at some time, has been a new development in our knowledge. It is only by such an understanding that we can extend the logic of hormone therapy and thereby our management of barren and foaling mares.

Peptides

Now let us take a further step in this story. I have already indicated that originally the nervous and the endocrine systems were considered to be entirely separate, each made up of their specific cells releasing different messengers.

Curiously, the first indication that this was not really the case came as long ago as 1931, when a discovery was made in horses that a substance known as Substance P could be extracted from the equine brain and gut. It was supposed, at the time, to come from the central nervous system and from cells lining the alimentary tract. It was not until the 1970s that this subject was advanced further. The reason for its advance was that techniques were developed for identifying Substance P in the tissues. This substance was identified as a peptide.

Peptides are substances of low molecular weight composed of organic acids (amino acids). It has been shown that Substance P occurs in nerves in the gut and also in a large number of organs.

The names given to these peptides are technical and some are included here only because the reader may hear them mentioned or read about them and will then be able to place them accordingly. They are vasoactive inhibitory protein (VIP), somatostatin, gastrin, motilin, renin, glucagon and gastrin.

Regulatory peptides are secreted by cells spread throughout the body. It is for this reason that they have not been previously studied in detail, as have organ systems such as nerves and hormone glands. These are so much easier to investigate because they can be removed experimentally to observe the effect. When the secretory cells are spread throughout the body this approach is not possible.

The discovery of these peptide hormones has given rise to the term 'peptidergic nervous system'. Changes in this system have been shown recently to be present in human gut disease and also in the condition of grass sickness (see p. 14). This is a new and expanding subject and we can expect some exciting developments in future knowledge about diseases affecting the gut, kidneys and other organs.

Another group of peptides which has come to light recently are the encephalins and endorphins, sometimes known as 'the brain's own opiates'. These powerful analgesics, similar in structure to the commonly used drugs pethidine and morphine, are secreted by the neuroendocrine cells in the brain in response to severe pain or stress. It is now believed that the sedating effect of applying a nose twitch to a horse occurs because of a release of these opiate-like drugs in response to the pain produced by this action.

9
THE OPTIC SYSTEM

The horse is a creature of the wide open spaces. With its few relatives, it has evolved on the great plains of the world. To escape natural enemies it has acquired the ability to move at great speed. In order to do so, it must be able to recognize its predators. To this end the horse has developed very sophisticated senses of sight, hearing and smell. In this chapter we are concerned with sight.

The eye

The eye of the horse is set high up on the head, towards the side rather than the front. The head in turn is on a long and flexible neck. These two attributes give remarkable all-round vision, even when the horse has its head down to graze. This vision can be both monocular or binocular, that is, the horse can see the same object with both eyes when looking forwards, but also can view a completely different picture on either side with each eye. This vision extends to behind the horse, and it has only to move its head slightly to achieve a complete circle of sight.

The eye lies in the orbit, a cavity formed in the skull. This cavity is encircled by bone which is of particular prominence and strength in front of and above the eye; here the bone is structured into a rigid arch which is called the supraorbital process. Forward of the eye lie the nasal bones and a bony prominence called the facial crest, and below the eye is the mass of the jaw muscles. These complete a circle which is very effective in protecting the eye from injury. Further to this, the orbit contains a large pad of fat. This lies behind the eye and can be felt from behind and above the supraorbital process, where there is an easily seen depression. This fat acts as a flexible, mobile cushion which allows any direct blows that reach the eyeball to be absorbed to a great extent. These, with the facts that the head is on a long neck and the horse has excellent reflexes, explains why the eyes are seldom injured.

Figure 44   Location of the eye

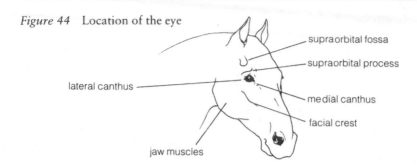

supraorbital fossa

supraorbital process

lateral canthus

medial canthus

facial crest

jaw muscles

The eyelids   The horse possesses two external eyelids and a third, inner, eyelid which arises from the medial canthus of the eye, that is, the lower inner angle between the external eyelids. This third eyelid is formed of mucous membrane and cartilage, and assists in the lubrication of the outside of the eyeball by spreading tears over the surface.

The external eyelids are composed of a sheet of cartilage covered with skin on the outside and the conjunctiva inside. The upper eyelid is the most movable, opening and closing the eye to the greater degree.

At the border, where the skin from the outside meets the membrane from the inside, are the eyelashes – the greater number being on the upper lid.

The tear ducts   The tears, which keep the eye moist, are secreted by the lacrimal gland, which lies beneath the supraorbital process. These tears are discharged onto the surface of the eye and are then collected into the two tear ducts in the inner corner of the eye. The tear ducts unite to run down beneath the bone and cartilage of the nasal bones, forming the naso-lacrimal duct, which eventually discharges on the floor of the nostrils. These openings are easily seen by looking into the nasal aperture while holding the nostril open with the finger. Should these ducts become obstructed, tears overflow the lower eyelid, run down the face and cause scalding with loss of hair.

The conjunctiva   This is a thin, pink, moist, mucous membrane on the inside of the eyelids and covering the third eyelid. From the inside of the eyelids it is turned back to lie over the surface of the eyeball, where it becomes the bulbar conjunctiva. This covers the front of the eye as a layer of transparent cells forming part of the cornea.

The cornea   This is a thick, tough, transparent tissue which forms the anterior portion of the eyeball; it is visible between the lids. At its outer edges it is continuous with the sclera (see below), the junction being called the limbus. The cornea is egg-shaped in outline, with the long axis running across the eye with the broad end to the inside.

The chambers and segments of the eye   (See Figure 46) Behind the cornea lies a cavity, the anterior chamber, bounded by the cornea in front and the iris behind. Between the iris and the lens lies the posterior chamber. These two chambers are joined through the pupil and are filled with a clear fluid known as aqueous humour. Together they are known as the anterior segment. The space between the lens and the retina is the posterior segment, and this is filled with a transparent, jelly-like material known as vitreous humour.

The iris is a pigmented muscular diaphragm situated in front of the lens and visible through the cornea. It contains a central aperture called the pupil, which varies in size and controls the amount of light entering the eye.

When light is bright, the pupil contracts to become narrow and elliptical, with its greatest length in the transverse (crosswise) direction. When dull, the pupil dilates to become more or less round.

The edges of the iris forming the pupil are not regular in outline, but are interrupted by pigmented projections called corpora nigra. These are much larger on the upper edge and may partially occlude (block) the pupil when it is contracted.

The lens is a transparent body, circular in outline, but biconvex when viewed from the side. The front surface is less curved than the back and is in partial contact with the iris. Around the circular periphery of the lens is a series of fine fibres which form the suspensory ligament of the lens, and which attach to the inner surface of the eyeball. The substance of the lens is made up of an outer elastic membrane called the capsule, which encloses layers of transparent tissue centred round a nucleus. These layers can sometimes be seen during examination, not unlike the structure of an onion.

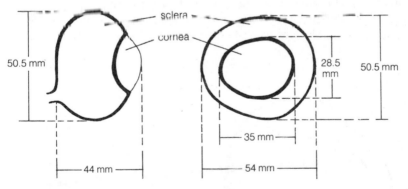

Figure 45   The dimensions of the eyeball and the cornea

The wall of the eyeball   This is made up of three basic layers: the sclera, the choroid and the retina. In the front of the eye the cornea fits into the sclera like a watchglass into a watch.

The sclera is the outside layer of the wall and is often known as the white of the eye as it is the portion showing between the eyelids. It extends all round the eyeball and is formed of thick, tough, white tissue. It gives shape and strength to the eyeball and is lined by the choroid layer.

The inner surface of the sclera, which is nearest to the lens and the iris, carries a pigmented thickening called the ciliary body. From this arise the iris and the lens attachments. It has a muscular component which, when it contracts or slackens, alters the convexity of the lens and thus the horse's ability to focus on objects at different distances. This mechanism is called accommodation.

The choroid is a thin membrane which lies between the sclera and the retina. In general it is pigmented and its inner surface is closely bound to the retina. It extends from the optic nerve to the ciliary body.

The retina is a thin, light-sensitive membrane lying on the inner surface of the choroid; it is in contact with the vitreous humour on its inside surface. It is complex in structure, containing a sophisticated arrangement of nerves and blood vessels. It is this part of the eye which receives the images of the objects seen by the horse and passes them on to the brain via the optic nerve.

The optic nerve   The optic nerve enters the back of the eye, passing through the sclera and the choroid and spreading out filaments to form the retina. It lies below the centre of the back of the eye and towards the outer side.

The anatomy of vision

The eye may be considered similar to a camera, by which small and inverted images are formed on the retina. Rays of light enter the eyeball and are bent by the cornea and lens to converge on the retina. This is called focusing. The lens shape can be altered, as described above, to make rays from objects located at varying distances focus on the retina. The amount of light entering the eye is regulated by the eyelids and the pupil. Light reaching the retina is

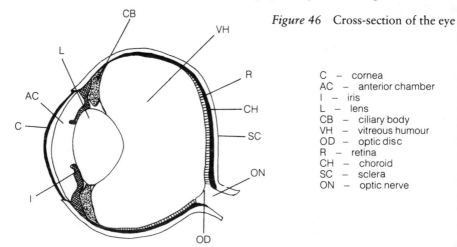

Figure 46   Cross-section of the eye

C – cornea
AC – anterior chamber
I – iris
L – lens
CB – ciliary body
VH – vitreous humour
OD – optic disc
R – retina
CH – choroid
SC – sclera
ON – optic nerve

transmitted as nervous impulses to the optic nerve and then to the brain, where they are translated into visual images.

Examination of the eye

This should be done in two parts. The first – the examination of the outside of the eye – should be done in bright light, preferably outside but otherwise inside with good lighting. The purpose of this is to establish the presence of obvious abnormalities such as tumours, injured eyelids, blocked tear ducts, discrepancies in the size of the eye, and the ability of the pupil to contract in bright light. Infections and injuries to the conjunctiva can be seen at this stage, but the eyelids may have to be opened with the fingers to obtain the best results. To make this examination, place the tips of the thumb and index finger closely together. Apply the tips, held together in this way to the eyelids, which will close when approached by the fingertips. See that the tip of the thumb rests on the lower lid near its margin, and the tip of the index finger on the upper lid. Press gently upon them and slowly draw apart the thumb and finger. This will separate and partly invert the eyelids, thus exposing the conjunctiva to view. Injuries to the cornea are often best seen in bright light.

The second part of the examination is done in the stable with a good pen torch and ophthalmoscope. This may reveal conditions, many of which were previously unknown and which are difficult to interpret; therefore the examination should only be carried out by a veterinarian. The horse should be stood quietly in the dark for several minutes before the examination takes place. The torch can be used to examine the surface of the eye, iris, pupil and anterior chamber, but the inside of the eye can only be examined with an ophthalmoscope, which enables the operator to focus on any part of the interior.

Sometimes, when the eye has a painful condition, the only way that the eye can be properly examined is for the veterinarian to use local anaesthetic to relieve the pain and other drugs to open the pupil, so that the interior of the eye can be seen.

When making a general examination of the eye the vet will note any growth, lumps or wounds to the outside of the eye and its associated structures and whether there is any discharge, either watery or purulent, which may run down the face. The vet observes the eyelids, whether they are free and properly open or closed or partly closed in spasm. The size of the eyeball can be estimated at this stage – sometimes one eye is smaller or deeper in its socket than the other. Some conditions of the head give a droop to the upper eyelid and the horse is unable to lift it in order to open the eye.

The conjunctiva should be pink and moist – not an angry, inflamed deep red colour – with no discharge, and no swelling or puffiness.

The surface of the cornea should be moist, bright and perfectly transparent. It should be free from grey or white spots or streaks or larger opacities, and should not have blood vessels or ulcers present.

The pupil should be regular in outline, and dilate in the dark and contract in bright light. The pupils of both eyes should behave similarly at all times and in all conditions of light.

There should be no deposits in the anterior chamber of the eye, and no strands of fibrous material or adhesions between the back of the cornea and the iris. The lens should be seen through the pupil only as a grey-blue area – cataracts can sometimes be seen as a white area filling the pupil. Occasionally, in certain lighting conditions, a bright fluorescent reflection is seen from the eye. This is a reflection from the back of the eye and is quite normal.

Conditions of the Eye

Some conditions are easily seen by the horse owner, but others can only be diagnosed by a veterinarian, who should always be consulted in any case of doubt or difficulty.

TUMOURS

There are two main tumours affecting the eyelids of the horse. Sarcoids (see chapter 41) are raised, cauliflower-like growths arising usually above and to the side of the eye. These are difficult to treat or remove, and can become a nuisance to the horse because they tend to ulcerate and invade the eyelids. Carcinomas (see chapter 41) occur on the eyelid margins or on the third eyelid. These cause profuse discharge to accumulate, make the eye very sore, and have to be removed surgically.

INJURIES TO THE EYELIDS

These are quite common: the eyelids may be torn by protruding nails, by the horse blundering into objects in the dark or by galloping into hedges or fences. They may become bruised or abraded from external injury such as a blow or a fall.

Whenever an eyelid is torn, seek advice immediately so that it can be repaired surgically. Repair must be carried out, as far as possible, so that healing takes place without contraction or distortion of the eyelid aperture.

ENTROPION

This condition occurs mostly in newborn foals. The eyelids, or one of them, are turned inwards so that the eyelashes and hairs on the outside are in contact with the cornea. This is very irritant, causing pain and discharge, and, if left unattended, the cornea may become inflamed or even ulcerated. Sometimes this condition can be overcome by repeatedly drawing the lid back and uncurling it from the surface of the eye. Often this is enough to make the eyelid regain its correct position, but if not the veterinarian should be asked to attend. He or she will suture the lid in place, or even remove an elliptical piece of skin at the lid margin so that when this heals it will cause sufficient contraction to keep the lid from curling inwards.

CONJUNCTIVITIS

Conjunctivitis is the name given to inflammation of the conjunctival membrane. It is caused by infection or irritation from foreign bodies or substances. It is recognized by a marked congestion of the membranes, which are swollen and turn an angry colour. There is discharge from the eye, often with pus present, and pain, which makes the horse unwilling to have the eye examined.

Treatment is best left to the veterinarian and will depend on the cause. If due to infection, an antibiotic ointment will be prescribed. Any foreign body, such as an oat husk or barley awn, will have to be removed with the help of local anaesthesia. As a first-aid measure, the eye can be washed with lukewarm saline solution made up by adding a teaspoonful of common salt to a pint of tepid water.

BLOCKED LACRIMAL DUCTS

These are indicated by the constant overflow of tears which run down the face. This discharge is clear and watery. The condition requires veterinary attention.

KERATITIS

Keratitis denotes inflammation of the cornea. It is a relatively common condition and may arise from conjunctivitis (see above) or may be due to direct injury or infection. The cornea is very sensitive and when it suffers from inflammatory changes the eyelids are always tightly closed, there is evidence of marked pain and a discharge of tears. This discharge may progress to become purulent after a day or two.

In mild cases the keratitis can settle down to a chronic state. This is when the eye, if examined closely in the light, has grey patches spread across the cornea. These are not always easily seen, but reduce the normal transparent lustre of the cornea and therefore impair vision.

In more severe and acute cases keratitis progresses until the whole of the cornea goes a grey-white colour and often has a fringe of blood vessels growing in from the edges. These appear like twigs and are an attempt by the body to speed the healing of the condition.

Sometimes the eyelids are so tightly closed that not much of this can be seen until local anaesthetic is introduced between the lids. When this is done, if the cause of the condition is injury rather than infection, a ragged ulcer will be seen on the front of the eye. Without proper treatment this can progress until the cornea is perforated and the aqueous humour escapes. Further to that, the iris may be drawn forward inside the eye to stick to the edges of the wound, or the eyeball may steadily collapse, with resultant loss of function and blindness.

If the ulcer is treated adequately, blood vessels will grow across it and it will slowly heal and the pain become less. The horse is best kept in a dark box at this time as light irritates the eye. When healing is complete often there is a small grey scar left on the cornea which can be seen when the eye is inspected closely.

EQUINE RECURRENT UVEITIS (PERIODIC OPHTHALMIA, MOON BLINDNESS)

This is a fairly uncommon disease, characterized by episodes of acute pain and inflammation in usually one or sometimes both eyes. There is apparent recovery after treatment, but the condition will commence again, sometimes in the same and sometimes in the other eye. The interval between these attacks can be as short as a few weeks – hence the old name periodic ophthalmia – or as long as years. There are a few cases in which there has been no apparent recurrence.

The signs of this disease are acute pain with the eye closed, discharge, and an unwillingness to expose the eye to light. There is no apparent reason for these symptoms. Horse owners often say that their animal has had a blow to the eye, but on close questioning it will be found that this is supposition and not fact. If the eye is examined at this stage, the cornea is cloudy and the anterior chamber has a deposit of white, or sometimes red, blood cells collecting in the bottom half. Detailed examination reveals a contracted pupil and deposits of inflammatory debris on the front of the lens. The microfilariae of *Onchocerca cervicalis* have been found in the eye and may be a cause (see p. 454).

After several days of treatment the cornea starts to clear, and the deposit in the anterior chamber becomes a denser white, then gradually becomes absorbed and eventually disappears. Sometimes the pupil will open and the eye return to normal, but occasionally it remains contracted and becomes stuck to the front of the lens, with an irregular and ragged outline instead of the normal smooth oval shape. The lens usually retains some of the debris on the front and examination with the ophthalmoscope often reveals a similar deposit at the back.

Subsequent attacks are similar, but after each one the residual damage to the eye is increased; it may shrink in size, and ultimately the horse is blind in one or both eyes.

Proper treatment modifies the course of the disease, especially if commenced early, and prolongs the horse's usefulness. It does not prevent recurrence and horses that have had one attack will almost invariably have another at some stage. It is important, therefore, to recognize the condition so that treatment can be started as soon as possible.

CATARACT

Any opacity of the lens or its capsule is by definition a cataract. These interfere with the passage of light, the degree of interference ranging from slight to complete obstruction. Therefore the horse's sight may be only slightly affected or it may be completely blind.

Cataracts may be developmental or degenerative. Developmental cataracts result from defects in the eye from birth, and these can vary from a small opacity in the middle of the lens to a total diffuse condition which involves the whole structure and in which the pupil appears as if it were filled with a white marble. It is unusual for congenital cataracts to be progressive.

Degenerative cataracts occur as a result of disease, injury or increasing age. These can be of any size or shape, although they usually radiate in lines out from a central focus, sometimes with a cobweb-like appearance. Often these progress to total dense cataracts and resultant blindness.

The detailed diagnosis of a cataract can only be done with an ophthalmoscope. In some horses layers of the lens reflect the light back to the observer's eye, which gives a fictitious appearance of opacity. Only the vet can really diagnose these cases. There is no effective treatment for cataract.

BLINDNESS

There are several conditions occurring at the back of the eye of which the outcome is usually a serious affect on vision. Such conditions are **inflammation and separation of the retina, degeneration of the vitreous humour** and **optic nerve atrophy**. These are only diagnosable by the veterinarian using specialist equipment. The horse owner will, however, realize that something is amiss with his animal and ask for advice. It is, therefore, necessary to have a working knowledge of how to assess vision.

First, the horse's behaviour and performance will be altered. The owner will notice apprehension when a normally placid horse is subjected to unexpected situations and challenges, such as being startled at the sudden appearance of traffic or not seeing objects that it normally should. If the animal is a performance horse, such as a showjumper, it may see objects on one circle but not on the other. This would indicate a one-sided eye defect. It may not pick up an obstacle which it normally had no difficulty with and so suddenly refuse to take a jump.

A menace response test can be tried: the horse is approached on each side and is suddenly lunged at with an open flat hand towards the eye. Care should be taken not to get too close, so as not to touch the eye or cause air currents that may be felt by the horse. A normal animal will blink and withdraw the head.

An obstacle course can be arranged. The horse is led quietly around an area with which it is familiar and, after one or two circuits, an upturned bucket or horizontal pole is put in its path. Brightly painted cones or drums, which the animal should have no difficulty in seeing can be used. Obviously if it fails to negotiate them, defects in vision must be suspected.

Retinal degeneration is when patches of the back of the eye become ineffective and the images of the objects the horse is seeing are therefore incomplete. This can sometimes be more disturbing to a horse than complete blindness, which it may learn to accept.

The vitreous humour sometimes becomes affected with strands of inflammatory debris which float across the field of vision when the horse makes an eye movement. These can distort vision and disturb the horse by their sudden appearance.

The optic nerve may become injured or degenerate. This condition is called optic atrophy and results in complete and irreversible blindness.

CONGENITAL ABNORMALITIES

There are a number of rare congenital abnormalities which may be genetic in origin. These are listed in chapter 45.

10
THE EAR

The ear consists of three parts – the outer, middle and inner ear – and is the organ of hearing. It is also of vital importance in maintaining balance; in particular the inner ear informs the brain of the position of the head.

Functional anatomy

The outer (external) ear is what most of us are familiar with. It consists of an erect cartilaginous portion (pinna) which can be moved in all directions, enabling the horse to detect sounds from all sides. Each ear moves independently of the other. Thus a horse can scan the area for danger.

The pinna is attached to the head and at its base forms a delicately lined funnel which travels downwards and then makes a right-angled bend inwards until it meets the eardrum within the skull (Figure 47). The eardrum is a membrane which separates the outer from the middle ear and is connected to three small bones, the hammer (malleus), the anvil (incus) and the stirrup (stapes), so called because of their shape, which bridge the middle ear. The middle ear is lined by a mucous membrane and is connected to the pharynx (throat) by a tube (Eustachian tube) which allows equalization of pressure between the middle ear and the atmosphere. The orifice into the pharynx is protected by cartilaginous flap which opens only during swallowing.

The horse has a remarkable structure called a guttural pouch which is a large outpouching of each Eustachian tube. These structures are peculiar to horses and donkeys (and a species of tree shrew) and consist of paired air sacs situated between the pharynx and the floor of the skull. These air sacs are closely associated with very important nerves and arteries, and these may be damaged by diseases affecting the guttural pouch (see chapter 2).

The middle ear is separated from the inner ear by two membranous windows, one of which is attached to the stirrup-shaped bone, the stapes. Thus soundwaves reaching the eardrum are transmitted by the chain of small bones to the inner ear.

Figure 47 The external
ear and its location in
the skull

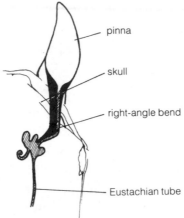

pinna

skull

right-angle bend

Eustachian tube

Figure 48 The internal ear

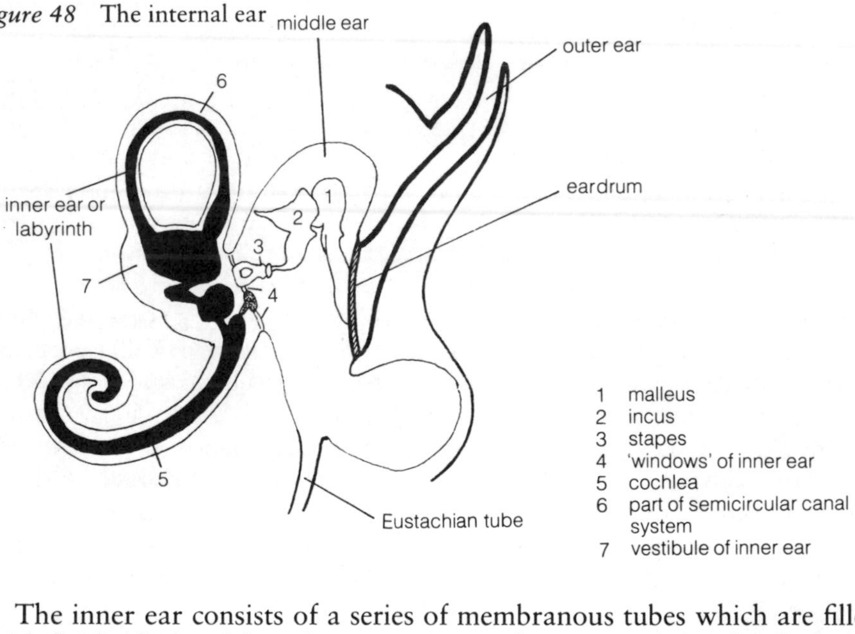

middle ear

outer ear

6

inner ear or
labyrinth

eardrum

1

2

3

7

4

5

Eustachian tube

1   malleus
2   incus
3   stapes
4   'windows' of inner ear
5   cochlea
6   part of semicircular canal
    system
7   vestibule of inner ear

The inner ear consists of a series of membranous tubes which are filled with fluid called endolymph; many nerve endings are contained in the lining of the tubes. The inner ear is called the labyrinth because of its complex shape; it fits into cavities in the bone of the skull. The main cavity is called the vestibule. The complex anatomy of the inner ear can be simplified for descriptive purposes by considering it as two groups of tubular compartments. One, the cochlea, is somewhat like a snail's shell and is responsible for hearing. The other has three semicircular channels, each arranged at right angles to the rest. These semicircular canals are continuous with the main part of the inner ear or vestibule and thus share its endolymph circulation. It is by the movement of the fluid within these canals that positional changes of the head are relayed to the brain. Hearing occurs when the endolymph in the cochlea moves in response to waves transmitted via the small bones in the middle ear.

Conditions of the Ear

EAR MITES (see also p. 470)

Ear mites occur in horses and usually produce no clinical signs. However, they may be responsible for severe irritation, headshyness and an aural discharge (it should be noted that the normal horse ear contains thick, dark grey wax). Some affected horses will rub their ear or side of the head; rarely a haematoma (blood blister) is produced in the pinna as a result of such damage. Treatment with antiparasitic drugs is usually effective.

EAR CANAL INFECTION

Rarely infections may occur in the ear canals, often as a sequel to guttural pouch infections (see pp. 31 and 33). An aural discharge and ear shyness are the usual clinical signs. If guttural pouch infection is the underlying reason for the aural discharge, there is often a concomitant nasal discharge and other signs.

TUMOURS

Malignant tumours of the pinna and canals of the external ear are rare, but when they occur they can be an extremely serious problem. Usually there is a visible growth and often a foul-smelling discharge which may be blood-stained; frequently such horses become extremely earshy. Much more commonly, however, small (often multiple) raised plaques of thickened white skin are visible on the inside of the pinna, but these do not produce clinical signs or require treatment. Other growths such as sarcoids (skin tumours) and dermoid cysts may develop in association with the ear. Usually these can be removed surgically.

DENTIGENOUS CYST

A discharging sinus at the base of the ear or from the edge of the pinna may be associated with a dentigenous cyst. This cyst is a congenital abnormality which may contain an aberrantly situated tooth and can be removed surgically.

NEURAL PARALYSIS

Damage to a branch of the facial nerve which controls movement of the external ear may result in paralysis of the ear, which can no longer be held in an erect position. This is usually associated with other signs of facial paralysis such as a drooping lower lip on the same side or the muzzle twisted away from the affected side.

SWOLLEN PAROTID GLAND

The parotid salivary gland is situated at the base of the ear and may occasionally become swollen when horses or ponies are at grass. Affected animals may look as if they are suffering from mumps. The cause is unknown but is usually considered to be an allergy. The condition spontaneously and rapidly resolves when the horse is brought indoors.

The parotid gland is also a common site for the development of a melanoma – the black-pigmented tumours commonly seen in grey horses (see p. 102).

DEAFNESS

Little is known about deafness in the horse. Profound deafness of both ears is likely to be noticed, but it is difficult to recognize partial deafness or if only one ear is affected.

VERTIGO AND INCOORDINATION

Loss of balance (vertigo) and incoordination of the limbs may result from conditions affecting the inner ear. These fortunately are very rare in the horse. Some cases respond to corticosteroid therapy but in other cases no treatment is effective.

BLEEDING FROM THE EAR

Very rarely horses may bleed from the ear. This is usually caused by severe trauma, such as a fracture, to the skull but can also be caused by fungal infection of the guttural pouch (see p. 33).

The Musculoskeletal System

The musculoskeletal system derives its name from two features of the body concerned with form and movement. The skeleton comprises the bony scaffold to which muscle is attached. Without the skeleton the body would have the flowing form of a jellyfish rather than the exact and circumscribed outline we recognize as a horse. The skeleton is formed of bone, the hard substance of which individual bones are made. These individual bones form joints at one or both ends of their length. It is the joints which provide the supple nature of the skeleton and enable a horse to lie down, stand, trot, canter and gallop. The muscles are the driving power that propels the 1000 lb (500 kg) or so of horse at rates of up to 40 m.p.h.

Sue Dyson describes the anatomy of this system of bones and muscle together with the injuries and ailments that we recognize as stiffness, lameness and unsoundness. Simon Turner contributes on the subject of angular deformities of the limbs of foals and Chris Colles describes shoeing, the protection man gives the horse to prevent wear of the feet when it is being used for human purposes.

At the end of the section is a table, compiled by Sue Dyson, listing some of the common problems of lameness and their possible causes.

11
LAMENESS: AN INTRODUCTION

Lameness is the abnormal movement and/or placement of a limb, due to pain and/or mechanical dysfunction. It is most readily assessed at walk and trot; only rarely will a horse appear lame at canter. Lameness may be sudden or gradual in onset and may affect one or more than one limb.

Normal paces

The normal horse takes equal-length strides with each forelimb and with each hind limb and the feet are placed rhythmically to the ground in a definite sequence. At walk the sequence of foot falls is left hind, left fore, right hind, right fore and the rhythm is four-time. At trot the limbs are moved in a two-time rhythm in diagonal pairs, left hind and right fore

Figure 49   Sequence of limb placement

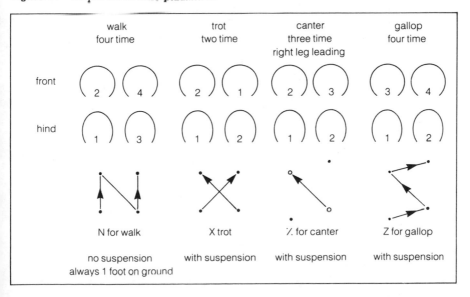

together, followed by right hind and left fore together. Occasionally normal horses pace rather than trot, i.e. the left hind and the left fore move together, followed by the right hind and right fore, in a two-time rhythm. The horse is said to be tracking up at either walk or trot if the hind foot is placed in or beyond the imprint of the forefoot on the same side.

Canter has a three-time rhythm. The sequence of footfalls for canter with the right foreleg leading is left hind followed by right hind and left fore together, and then the right fore. On a circle the horse usually canters with the inside foreleg leading. The sequence is reversed for left canter, i.e. right hind, left hind and right fore together, left fore. The horse is cantering on the wrong leg on a circle if the outside forelimb leads. If the horse changes the sequence of hind-limb movements while maintaining the correct lead in front it is said to be disunited. Some normal horses find it much more difficult to canter with one foreleg leading rather than the other and some tend to become disunited, especially if unbalanced.

Unlevelness

An alteration of the regular rhythmicity of a gait may occur if the horse is unbalanced, is hurrying or is finding a particular movement physically difficult, or it may reflect lameness. The term 'unlevelness' has been used to describe slight irregularities in rhythm. If there is consistent unlevelness, this probably reflects slight lameness. In the early stages of a lameness which is insidious in onset slight irregularities in rhythm may be detectable only when the horse is performing specific manoeuvres. With time these irregularities may become more obvious and frequent.

Gait abnormalities

Ideally the horse should move each leg straight, the left hind and left fore in one plane and the right hind and right fore in another plane. Many normal horses, with either good or faulty conformation, deviate one or more than one leg either to the inside or to the outside as the leg is advanced. This may result in the horse interfering, i.e. striking one leg with another leg. The horse brushes if it strikes the inside of one leg with the inside of the opposite leg. If the point of impact is above the mid-cannon region the horse is said to

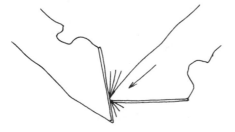

Figure 50   Forging

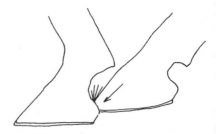

Figure 51   Overreach

speedy-cut. A tread is an injury to the inside of the coronary band of one foot by the contralateral foot. Overreaching is the striking of the back of a forelimb with the toe of the hind foot on the same side and is usually due to asynchronous movement of the limbs because of tiredness, deep going or unbalance. Forging is the noise made by the striking of the hind shoe against the front shoe as the horse is trotting and occurs because the horse is tired or unbalanced or the hind feet are too long. Stumbling may be due to multiple causes including weakness, tiredness, unbalance, poor foot trimming, uneven ground and lameness. Some normal horses drag the toes of one or both hind limbs due to laziness, unbalance, overlong feet or tiredness, but toe dragging may also reflect lameness.

Deviations of limb flight of the forelimb occur more commonly than hind-limb gait abnormalities. However, some normal horses move very closely behind (plaiting), whereas others move very widely behind. When trotting in circles an unschooled or unfit horse will tend to cross the inside hind limb under the body towards the outside fore limb, which makes the hindquarters tend to swing outwards. A well-schooled, balanced, fit horse is more able to flex the inside hind limb and advance it towards the inside forelimb. Many normal horses will appear stiffer when moving in circles to the left than to the right.

It is important to differentiate between gait abnormalities (variations of the normal) and lameness. In the early stages of insidious-onset lameness this may be difficult. In these circumstances it is helpful to know the horse in order to compare how it was with how it is now. This is particularly important in horses with problems which may affect both forelimbs (e.g. navicular syndrome) or both hind limbs (e.g. bone spavin). Initially these conditions cause a slight shortening of the stride or loss of freedom of stride without overt lameness being detectable.

Swellings and lameness

Although the onset of lameness may be associated with the development of an obvious swelling or an area of heat and pain, in many cases there are no detectable visible or palpable abnormalities. The fact that an area looks and feels normal does not preclude it from being the potential site of lameness. Many swellings, for example, distension of the digital flexor tendon sheath (tendinous windgall), which cause a cosmetic defect are unassociated with lameness. Some swellings may cause lameness as they develop, but when fully developed the lameness resolves (for example, periostitis of the second or fourth metacarpal or metatarsal bone, commonly called a splint).

Incidence of lameness

The incidence of forelimb lameness is considerably higher than that of hind-limb lameness. The foot is the most common source of lameness, especially in the forelimb. Lameness originating above the knee or hock is compara-

Figure 52 Sites of some common problems

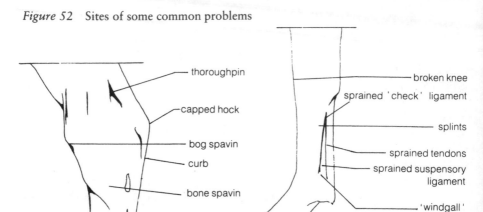

tively rare. The types of problem causing lameness vary considerably depending upon the age, breed, occupation and fitness of the horse. Chip fractures of the small bones of the knee occur not infrequently in Thoroughbred flat-race horses, but are otherwise an uncommon injury. Navicular syndrome is rarely seen in the young racehorse but is a common cause of lameness in the middle-aged riding horse.

Conformational abnormalities and the way in which a horse is trimmed and shod may predispose to lameness. The long-term prognosis for sustained recovery is influenced by the presence of conformational defects. Nevertheless often it is not possible to detect an underlying cause of lameness.

There is minimal reliable information concerning heritability and lameness. There is a disproportionately high incidence of navicular syndrome in American Quarter horses. Osteochondrosis of the tibiotarsal joint of the hock has an unusually high incidence in the Shire horse. Intermittent upward fixation of the patella occurs not uncommonly in the Shetland pony. Thus there are strong indications that there is a heritability factor involved in some types of lameness in some breeds.

Lameness and performance

The fact that a horse is lame does not necessarily mean that the horse is unsuitable for work. Lameness implies pain or mechanical dysfunction. The level of pain which any horse can tolerate is extremely variable. Many horses are able to work satisfactorily despite low-grade lameness, especially hind-limb lameness. This depends not only on the temperament of the horse but also on its occupation. Lameness, however subtle, is unacceptable in the dressage horse. A jumping horse may be able to cope adequately with slight lameness. If a jumping horse starts to stop or to push off unevenly with the hind legs as he takes off, these are indications that his performance is being compromised by the lameness.

Treatment

Treatment is usually aimed at returning the horse to full athletic function; an improvement without soundness is often unsatisfactory unless the horse is destined for breeding. Many kinds of lameness respond to rest. Enforcement of true rest in the horse is difficult. Turning a horse out is not true rest because the majority of horses are inclined to gallop sporadically. Despite this, for many lamenesses this type of rest is adequate. Sometimes it is necessary to confine the horse to a box; most horses adapt to this remarkably well although many owners find it psychologically unacceptable for the horse. Box rest can be combined with controlled exercise at walk and trot, which can provide valuable physiotherapy. With difficult horses it may be easier to ride the horse than lead it. Usually the weight of a rider will not affect the condition deleteriously.

Generally the earlier that a lameness is recognized and treatment is started the better. The quicker the horse starts to respond to treatment the more optimistic is the prognosis. Many slightly lame horses respond well to a few days' box rest and a true diagnosis is never achieved.

After an injury there is often pain, localized heat and swelling, and treatment is aimed at reducing these. Depending upon the age of the injury, local hot or cold treatment or alternating treatments may be beneficial. Local heat will increase the blood supply to the area. Cold treatment tends to reduce soft-tissue swelling, as do anti-inflammatory drugs such as corticosteroids. Many of the non-steroidal anti-inflammatory drugs, e.g. phenylbutazone, are also analgesics.

Local ultrasound treatment produces some heat and helps to dissipate soft-tissue swelling, but care must be taken to use the appropriate current strength and frequency to avoid causing additional damage.

Faradism is the use of an electrical current to produce controlled muscular contractions and is beneficial in the treatment of muscle strains. Electromagnetic therapy is in the embryo stages of development and, although it has potential, there are at present no clear guidelines for its use with horses. Firing is the application of red-hot iron to the skin. It has been widely used for the treatment of a variety of disorders. There is no scientific evidence to support its use, and the author considers it valueless and an unnecessary mutilation of the horse. Blisters are substances rubbed onto the skin which incite local inflammation of variable severity depending on the strength of the blister. The author considers that they have no beneficial effects.

Diagnosis of lameness

The aims of a lameness investigation are to identify the source or sources of pain and then the cause of pain. Only then can a rational treatment be offered and an accurate prognosis given. A systematic examination of the horse should ensure that nothing is overlooked. In many instances the detailed examination described below is unnecessary because the presence of heat, swelling and pain readily identify the site of the problem.

Examination at rest   The horse is observed standing in the box or field. Most normal horses will rest intermittently one or both hind legs, perhaps favouring one more than the other. It is unusual for a horse not to bear full weight on both forelimbs. A horse with navicular syndrome or pain in the back part of a front foot may place one foot in front of the other, with or without the heel slightly raised and the fetlock slightly flexed (pointing). The horse may be observed to stack straw underneath the heels of the front feet. A pony or horse with laminitis of the forefeet tends to stand with the hind legs well underneath the body, with the forelimbs outstretched and its weight rocked back onto the heels.

The conformation of the horse is assessed because conformational abnormalities may have predisposed to the lameness and can influence the long-term prognosis. A racehorse with marked back-at-the-knee conformation is predisposed to small fractures of the carpal (knee) bones. The horse with a small foot relative to body size is predisposed to foot problems.

Figure 53   A horse pointing

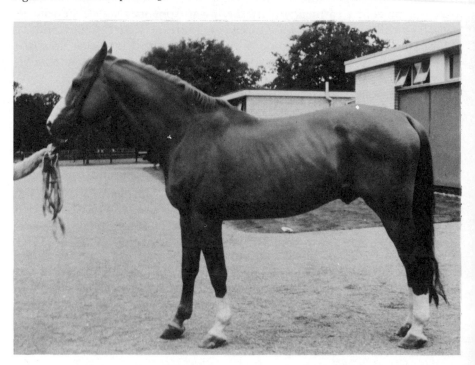

The presence of any abnormal swellings is noted. With the horse standing squarely on a firm, level surface the symmetry of the muscles and bony structures is evaluated. Loss of muscle on one side compared to the other reflects disuse of the muscle but not necessarily injury to that area. For example, a degree of wastage of the muscles of one hindquarter may be associated with problems involving either the foot or the hip region.

The temperament of the horse should be assessed. A highly strung horse is likely to react to palpation much more than a stoical individual, making the identification of pain difficult.

The neck, back and legs are felt carefully, both weightbearing and non-weightbearing. The presence of swellings, unusual consistency of a structure (e.g. increased firmness of a digital flexor tendon), heat and pain on pressure are noted and compared with the contralateral leg. Each joint is flexed to find out whether it has a normal range of motion and if manipulation causes pain. The size and shape of the feet, the way in which they are trimmed and shod, and the wear of the shoes are appraised. Some normal horses have asymmetrically shaped front feet. If one foot is noticeably smaller than the other, it may reflect a current or a previous problem in the smaller foot, but may also be the result of lameness elsewhere in the leg. Hoof testers are used to apply pressure carefully all around the foot. Relatively gentle pressure is applied at first, and if there is no reaction the pressure is increased. A horse with a focus of infection in the foot will react to relatively light pressure applied to that area. Likewise pressure applied to a corn will cause pain. The sole and the hoof wall are also percussed.

Examination at exercise The horse is watched moving on a hard, level surface. On a hard surface the footfalls can be heard as well as seen. It is important that the horse should be moving freely without the head being restricted. It is necessary to watch the horse repeatedly, observing the whole horse first and then watching it from the front, side and back, focusing attention on the forelegs and then the hind legs. There are many things to observe in addition to detecting which is the lame leg. At walk the way in which each foot is placed to the ground should be noted. Is each foot placed to the ground squarely or does one side of the foot land first? If the horse lands consistently on one side of the foot first, this can predispose to problems or reflect a problem. A horse with navicular syndrome may place the foot to the ground toe first. The limb flight of the horse should be assessed. An abnormal limb flight such as swinging the leg outwards as it is advanced may be a reflection of lameness or a predisposing cause. The relative stride lengths of each forelimb and each hind limb should be compared. Subtle hind-limb lameness, when it is difficult to determine which is the lame leg, may be best assessed at walk. The affected leg may have a shorter stride length and bear weight for a shorter time, resulting in an irregular rhythm. The degree to which each fetlock sinks as the leg is weightbearing should be compared. If movement of a fetlock joint causes pain, then that joint may sink less than the contralateral joint. Turning the horse in small circles to right and left is useful to assess the flexibility of the neck and back and the ability to move each leg away from the body or towards the opposite leg. A horse with back pain may hold itself very stiffly when turned. A horse with a slight tendency to delayed release of the patella may hold the hindleg very stiffly and then move it rather jerkily. Pushing the horse backwards is also useful to detect odd limb placement as in shivering.

At trot the above observations should be repeated. In addition, the head carriage should be watched. If the horse has a forelimb lameness, then the head will nod as the sound leg hits the ground and will rise as the lame leg is lifted. If the lameness is severe, this will also be apparent at walk. The horse will land more heavily on the sound foreleg. The length of stride of the lame leg may be shorter than that of the sound leg. Watching the horse from the side and from the front is most useful. If the horse is lame on both forelegs, it may move with a short, pottery stride, occasionally taking lamer steps on one forelimb.

To determine which is the lame hind leg it is most useful to watch the horse from the side and from behind. The lame leg may have a shorter-length stride than the sound leg. This will result in an irregularity of rhythm which can be heard as well as seen. If the lameness involves the hock or upper hind limb, the horse may move the whole leg stiffly, resulting in a lower arc of flight of the foot, and perhaps may also drag the toe. The horse is unable to flex the hock without also flexing the stifle and hip joints. Therefore pain in any of these joints can cause similar stiff-limb flight and toe-drag. Hind-limb lameness will cause asymmetrical movement of the hindquarters. The hindquarter of the lame leg may appear both to rise and to sink more than the sound leg. This is best appreciated from behind. If the hind-limb lameness is severe, the horse may have a head nod as the forelimb on the same side as the lame leg hits the ground; this is because the lame leg is non-weightbearing. This can be confusing, which is why it is important to assess limb flight and stride length too.

Flexion tests   Flexion tests can be useful. A joint is held partly flexed for approximately one minute and the horse is then trotted. Accentuation of lameness or production of lameness when the horse previously appeared sound can indicate pain originating from the stressed joint. It is often difficult to flex only one joint; the hock joint cannot be flexed without also flexing the stifle and hip joints, so the tests are nonspecific but can be very helpful. A normal horse may take two or three slightly lame steps, but sustained lameness is usually significant.

It is helpful to watch the horse move in circles on both soft and hard surfaces. Most horses move more freely on the lunge than when being led. The lameness should be compared on both reins. Although forelimb lameness is often accentuated when the affected leg is on the inside, occasionally it is more obvious when the leg is on the outside. Lameness due to corns may only be apparent when the horse is moving in the direction of the lame leg. If the horse has a short, pottery gait on the straight, obvious lameness may appear on the circle. Lameness associated with concussion, e.g. bruising, corns, etc., is often much worse on a hard than on a soft surface. Hind-limb lameness is sometimes worse with the affected leg on the inside and sometimes the outside. There are no firm rules.

Ridden exercise   Lameness may be exaggerated when the horse is ridden, especially hind-limb lameness. This is sometimes most obvious when the rider is sitting on the diagonal of the affected leg. Bridle lameness is a term which has been used to describe an unlevelness only seen when the horse is ridden. This may be an evasion by the horse which is resisting going forward properly. Alternatively it may be induced by unsteadiness of the rider's hands. If there is doubt about whether a horse is genuinely lame, rather than bridle lame, it should be ridden by an experienced rider and driven forwards in a long, low outline to encourage it to step under more with its hind limbs (i.e. to improve hind-limb impulsion) and to swing its back more freely. If the horse is worked in this manner for several days many rhythm irregularities due to bridle lameness will disappear. Work on the lunge in a Chambon can also be helpful.

Local anaesthesia   At this stage in the examination the lame leg or legs should have been identified and it might be possible to suggest where the pain originates. In many instances it is necessary to use local anaesthesia to define precisely the source of pain. This may be done in several ways. By injecting local anaesthetic over a nerve, transmission of nerve impulses is temporarily stopped and the area innervated by that nerve is desensitized. Therefore if pain originates in the desensitized area the horse should then be sound. This is called nerve blocking. Alternatively local anaesthetic may be infiltrated around a suspect lesion, for example, a splint, and if the horse subsequently goes sound this proves that the splint is the cause of lameness. Pain originating in a joint can be relieved by injecting local anaesthetic directly into the joint. This is called intra-articular anaesthesia. The use of local anaesthesia is important because it allows precise identification of the source of pain. The area might appear normal on radiographic views (X-rays) despite the presence of a significant problem. Not all bony abnormalities which are seen on radiographic examination are necessarily of significance; in other words they do not all cause lameness.

Local anaesthesia may only improve lameness rather than eliminate it. This may indicate that there is more than one problem, or that the cause of the lameness is both painful and mechanical, or it may be due to an inability to desensitize totally the source of pain. In order to appreciate improvement

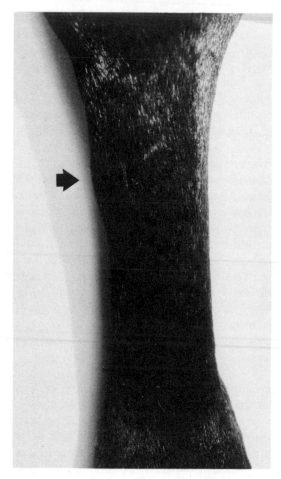

Figure 54　Craniocaudal view of the left metacarpal (cannon) region. There is a swelling on the medial aspect (arrow). Careful palpation reveals that this is an enlargement of the second metacarpal bone, a 'splint'

in lameness it is necessary that the horse shows a reasonable degree of lameness initially. Therefore it may be necessary to work the horse to exaggerate a subtle lameness so that it can be investigated further. Although it may seem contraindicated to work a lame horse because it may exacerbate the problem, in most cases this will not alter the long-term prognosis and, unless the horse is lame enough to be investigated, a diagnosis may never be reached. It is usually impossible to diagnose the cause of a previous lameness unless the horse continues to be lame.

Radiography　Having determined the source of pain, the area is then radiographed. A radiographic picture is a two-dimensional view of a three-dimensional object. It is necessary to obtain views of the object from more than one side to get a complete picture. It is important to recognize the limitations of radiographs and their ability to demonstrate abnormalities.

Little information can be obtained about soft-tissue (muscle, tendon and ligament) problems. Abnormalities of bone are usually readily apparent, but cartilage cannot be seen on a radiographic examination, therefore a picture of a joint may appear normal despite the presence of cartilage damage (as in secondary joint disease or arthritis) unless there is major loss of cartilage with resultant narrowing of the joint space. Interpretation of radiographic views may be complicated by 'false' abnormalities. Dirt on the foot may be misinterpreted as a foreign body within the foot. Therefore interpretation of radiographic views requires a detailed knowledge of normal radiographic anatomy and its variations, which are manifold. 'Normal' abnormalities must be recognized.

Nuclear scintigraphy (bone scanning)

An alternative imaging technique for bone is nuclear scintigraphy or bone scanning. A radioactively labelled bone-seeking substance – for example, technetium – is injected into the jugular vein. After several hours the technetium is distributed in the bones. In the normal mature horse distribution is fairly uniform throughout the body, but if there is an area of increased bone activity or increased blood supply to the bone, technetium accumulates in that place, resulting in a 'hot spot'. This is detected using a gamma camera. The technique is more useful for acute cases of lameness than for chronic cases and is potentially more sensitive than radiography, enabling, for example, the detection of subtle fissure fractures before they can be seen radiographically. Nevertheless, it must be regarded as a complementary technique to radiography, not a substitute.

Muscle enzymes, faradism and ultrasound

Additional techniques are useful for evaluation of soft-tissue problems. Muscle cells contain two enzymes, aspartoamino transferase (AST) and creatine kinase (CK), which are released into the blood if the cells are damaged. An elevation in the concentration of these enzymes in the blood usually reflects muscle damage. Muscle strain may be identified by faradic stimulation. With experience, the type of contraction induced by the electrical stimulation of damaged muscle can be differentiated from that of normal muscle. The horse will usually show resentment of stimulation of damaged muscle. Diagnostic ultrasound is used to create images of soft-tissue structures and allows much better assessment of the structures involved in a soft-tissue swelling than can be detected by palpation (feeling) alone. Extremely subtle areas of damage within tendons and ligaments can be detected and adhesions within a tendon sheath may be identified. By sequential scanning the healing of an injury can be monitored.

Diagnostic medication   It is sometimes useful to know whether or not a lameness responds to treatment with pain-relieving drugs such as phenylbutazone. It is necessary to treat the horse with an adequate dose relative to its bodyweight over a period in order to assess whether or not the drug is effective.

Surgical exploration   Occasionally surgical exploration of an area is indicated to define the nature of the damage more precisely. Exploration of joints has been facilitated by the use of an arthroscope, a narrow viewing tube which is inserted into the joint via a small incision. This has been used in man for many years.

12
CONDITIONS OF BONE

Functional anatomy

Although the individual bones of the horse, such as the humerus, the radius and the metacarpal (cannon) bone, are different in shape, they all have the same basic structure. The long bones have a shaft which consists of a tubular structure with walls of dense, compact, cortical bone surrounding a central medullary (marrow) cavity. The extremities of the bone are cancellous bone, softer bone mixed with marrow, overlain by a thin layer of cortical bone. The cancellous bone is arranged in fine struts or trabeculae, which are orientated in a regular pattern along the lines of stress of the bone. The bone matrix consists of a collagen base in which are deposited bone salts, predominantly calcium phosphate. The matrix contains many bone cells (osteocytes) and is perforated by fine canals containing blood vessels and nerves. The main blood supply is via the nutrient artery of the bone, which enters the bone through the nutrient foramen, passes into the medullary cavity and then radiates to supply the cortical bone. The bone is covered throughout its length by a thin but tough membrane, the periosteum. This is fibrous tissue overlying a layer of connective tissue which has a good blood

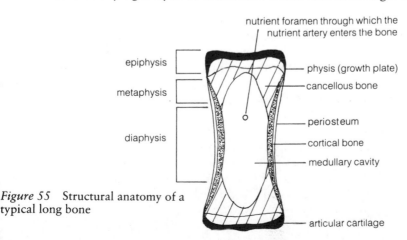

Figure 55 Structural anatomy of a typical long bone

supply and many cells which are capable of becoming active bone-forming cells or osteoblasts. Tendons and ligaments are attached to bone via the periosteum. At the site of attachment of a tendon specialized fibres called Sharpey's fibres penetrate into the bone, providing a strong link. Bone is not a static structure. It is constantly being replaced and, especially in the young animal, has a remarkable capacity to change shape and remodel according to the stresses placed upon it. Therefore if a bony lump develops as a result of trauma to the bone, it is likely that it will subsequently remodel, becoming smoother in outline and smaller. Some residual swelling is likely to persist.

Periostitis

Periostitis is either an inflammation of the periosteum resulting from a direct blow to the periosteum or a lifting of the periosteum away from the underlying bone. The osteoblasts in the connective tissue layer respond by producing new bone. On radiographic views periosteal new bone can be distinguished from cortical bone by its irregular and less opaque appearance. When inflammation has subsided the periosteal new bone remodels, resulting in a smoothly outlined bony lump or exostosis. Common sites of periostitis in the horse are the small metacarpal and metatarsal bones (so-called splints) and the large metacarpal and metatarsal (cannon) bones.

SPLINTS

Functional anatomy

Unlike man, the horse has evolved to stand on one rather than on five digits. Immediately below the knee and hock joints three bones persist, the cannon bone and the splint bones. These bones are correctly called the metacarpal bones in the front leg and metatarsal bones in the hind leg and are numbered sequentially from inside to outside. During evolution the first and fifth metacarpal and metatarsal bones have been lost, leaving the second metacarpal or metatarsal bone (the inside splint bone), the third metacarpal or metatarsal bone (the cannon bone) and the fourth metacarpal or metatarsal bone (the outside splint bone). The splint bones are positioned slightly behind the cannon bone and, in a young horse, are attached to it by an interosseous (between the bones) ligament. In an older horse the attachments become more fibrous and may be bony. Between the two splint bones on the back of the cannon bone lies the suspensory ligament.

In the front leg the splint and cannon bones articulate with the bottom row of bones in the knee, the second, third and fourth carpal bones. The splint bones provide some support to the cannon bone and forces are transmitted through them. The second metacarpal (inside splint) bone articulates with both the second and third carpal bones. This arrangement

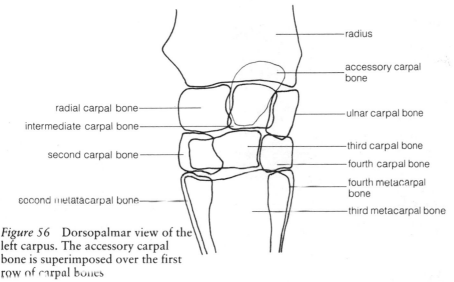

radius

accessory carpal bone

radial carpal bone

intermediate carpal bone

ulnar carpal bone

second carpal bone

third carpal bone

fourth carpal bone

fourth metacarpal bone

second metatacarpal bone

third metacarpal bone

Figure 56 Dorsopalmar view of the left carpus. The accessory carpal bone is superimposed over the first row of carpal bones

tends to result in very slight downward and backward movement of the second metacarpal bone when force is transmitted through the knee during weightbearing. This effect is exaggerated in a horse with bench-knee conformation (i.e. when the leg below the knee is set farther to the outside than usual). The fourth metacarpal (outside splint) bone articulates only with the fourth carpal bone and tends to be displaced only downwards during weightbearing. These functional anatomical differences are important when one considers that splints occur most frequently on the inside in a front leg.

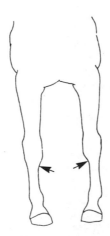

Figure 57 A bench knee

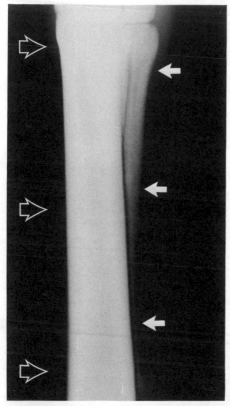

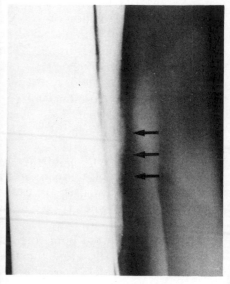

Figure 58 (left)   An oblique radiographic view of the metacarpal region of a normal horse showing the third metacarpal (cannon) bone (open arrows) and the second metacarpal (inside splint) bone (closed arrows). The outline of the latter is smooth and regular

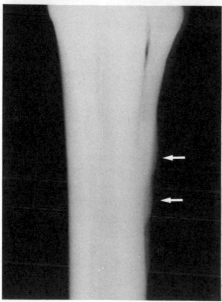

Figure 59 (above)   An oblique radiographic view of the metacarpal region of a horse with periostitis of the second metacarpal bone, i.e. an active splint. The middle third of the bone has a fuzzy irregular outine (arrows)

Figure 60 (left)   An oblique radiographic view of the metacarpal region of a horse after remodelling of the second metacarpal bone, a sequel to active periostitis. There is smoothly outlined new bone around the second metacarpal bone (arrows)

What are splints?

The term 'splint' is the colloquial name for a bony enlargement of one of the small metacarpal or metatarsal bones (see figure 54). A splint may develop for a variety of reasons. In the young horse it most frequently occurs as a sequel to slight tearing of the interosseous ligament between the splint bone and the cannon bone. This also results in lifting of the periosteum to which the interosseous ligament is attached. The damage to the interosseous ligament occurs because of relative movement between the splint and the cannon bones. Thus there is inflammation of the interosseous ligament and the periosteum (periostitis), causing pain and soft-tissue swelling. Some calcification in the interosseous ligament occurs and new bone is produced beneath the elevated periosteum, and ultimately a firmer union between the splint bone and the cannon bone develops. Poor conformation, such as bench knees, and improper trimming of the foot, resulting in the foot being placed to the ground unevenly rather than flatly, predispose to the development of splints. Incorrect proportions of phosphorus and calcium in the diet favour the formation of splints. A splint may also develop as a sequel to trauma to the bone such as a kick. If the horse moves very closely the damage may be self-inflicted, the narrow-chested horse which toes-in being particularly prone. Trauma to the bone results in haemorrhage beneath the periosteum, lifting it away from the bone surface. This stimulates new bone production. There will also be associated soft-tissue inflammation. Although splints occur in both front and hind limbs, the incidence in front limbs is much higher.

Clinical signs

The degree of lameness associated with a splint is variable. The horse usually bears weight fully on the affected leg at rest and is sound at walk. At trot there is mild to moderate lameness, which is most apparent on hard ground. The lameness does not improve with work and may deteriorate. The presence of severe lameness would suggest that there is a cause other than a splint. In the early stages of a splint there is a variable amount of localized swelling, which is predominantly soft-tissue in origin. This swelling may be extremely subtle and may only be apparent by careful palpation of the leg and comparison with its pair. In the acute stages the swelling is usually soft and slight finger pressure may leave a temporary indentation. This is inflammatory oedema. In the later stages the swelling becomes considerably firmer. This swelling is partly bony and partly an overlying fibrous reaction.

Diagnosis

Careful digital palpation of the splint bone with the leg held semi-flexed off the ground usually reveals a focal area of pain. In some horses it is necessary to apply slight pressure on several aspects of the affected splint bone before a painful area can be located. If the reaction appears to be equivocal, then a careful comparison with the other leg should be made.

Pain, and therefore lameness, usually persists until inflammation has fully subsided. Then a firm residual swelling persists. Thus the presence of a discrete swelling on or around a splint bone does not necessarily mean that it is the cause of lameness. It is only likely to be significant if pain can be elicited by palpation of the swelling. Especially in sensitive, hyper-reactive horses, it may be difficult to determine if the horse is really feeling pain; if there is some uncertainty, local anaesthetic may be infiltrated around the swelling. If the swelling is the cause of lameness, this procedure should eliminate the lameness.

Radiography

Radiographs are also useful to determine if a splint is active. The normal splint bone has a regular, smooth outline. It tapers from top to bottom. At the bottom is a slight enlargement, the so-called button of the splint bone. If the periosteum of the bone is inflamed, this will result in alteration of the contour of the bone and the edge will appear roughened rather than smooth. These bony changes take up to ten to fourteen days to occur; therefore at the time of onset of lameness there may be slight soft-tissue swelling but no bony change visible on the radiographs. Subsequent radiographs may demonstrate an active bony reaction. When the inflammation has subsided, when the splint is inactive, a bony lump persists which is smooth in outline. It may be necessary to obtain several radiographic views of the splint bone to identify the bony lesion, which may be localized to one side of the bone. Active new bone formation is most easily seen on an underexposed radiograph and the latter is also useful to eliminate the possibility of a fracture, especially if there was known trauma to the splint bone.

Treatment

The aims of treatment are to reduce inflammation and thus relieve pain. Rest, preferably box rest, is essential. Anti-inflammatory drugs may be of benefit, administered either by mouth (e.g. phenylbutazone) or at the site of the problem. Corticosteroids may be injected around the splint or dimethyl sulphoxide (DMSO) may be applied to the overlying skin and will be absorbed through it. Whether or not anti-inflammatory drugs are used, the horse must be given enough time, and this usually implies at least six weeks' rest; sometimes considerably longer is necessary. A premature resumption of work is likely to reaggravate the problem. Once the acute inflammation has subsided, daily massage may help to reduce the size of the swelling. The ultimate size of the swelling will depend upon the amount of new bone produced. The new bone tends to remodel and eventually decreases in size. One must remember that the visible swelling is not just bony. There is overlying fibrous tissue which contributes to the size of the swelling.

Some individuals seem prone to production of excessive amounts of new bone and occasionally the bony enlargement may interfere with the normal function of the suspensory ligament. In these circumstances surgical removal of the bony swelling may be indicated. It is sometimes desirable for cosmetic reasons to remove the bony swelling and, although this is a relatively straightforward procedure, one must be aware that, however careful the surgeon is, occasionally new bone formation will recur spontaneously post-operatively. Thus a successful cosmetic outcome cannot be guaranteed.

BLIND SPLINTS

The term 'blind splint' is rather nebulous and has been used to describe inflammation of the interosseous ligament which unites the splint and cannon bones. There is no new bone formation visible on radiographs – hence the term 'blind splint'. The clinical signs are more subtle and a definitive diagnosis is usually only possible by infiltrating local anaesthetic into the suspected area. The treatment is identical and the prognosis, as for true splints, is generally good.

PERIOSTITIS OF THE THIRD METACARPAL OR METATARSAL (CANNON) BONES

The third metacarpal and metatarsal (cannon) bones are vulnerable to injury because they are protected by relatively little soft tissue. Above the knee and hock the bones are surrounded by large muscle masses; below the knee and hock only skin, tendons and ligaments surround the bones. A blunt blow to the metacarpal or metatarsal bones may incite inflammation of the periosteum and subsequent formation of periosteal new bone. In the acute stages there is usually overlying soft-tissue swelling. Although the area is painful to touch, this is often unassociated with lameness. The periosteal new bone will gradually remodel and be incorporated into the cortical bone, resulting in a residual thickening of the cortex.

SORE SHINS

Sore shins is a condition almost unique to the young Thoroughbred racehorse. It is poorly understood but results from a skeletally immature horse working on hard ground. The condition involves the forelimbs, is usually bilateral and causes a short, restricted, shuffly gait and/or lameness. There may be some swelling over the front of the bones, resulting in a more convex contour than usual. The exact cause of pain is not known. Pressure applied to the front aspect of the metacarpal bones causes pain. It is not usual in Great Britain to detect any abnormality of the bones, except remodelling of the cortex, on radiographs, although in America small fissure fractures (so-called saucer fractures) of the bone are sometimes seen. Saucer fractures are fatigue or stress fractures, the result of repetitive loading of the bone, and their higher occurrence in America is probably related to the different training and racing conditions. In Great Britain horses are trained predominantly in straight lines and gentle curves, and are both trained and raced on grass, whereas in America horses are trained and raced on oval-shaped, predominantly dirt, tracks, and run consistently anticlockwise. In Great Britain most horses respond well to rest. Additional treatment such as electromagnetic therapy has been tried but is of questionable benefit.

PERIOSTITIS SECONDARY TO MUSCLE OR LIGAMENT STRAIN

Muscles are attached to bones via tendons, which are fibrous structures which are less elastic than muscles. Ligaments are more fibrous and less elastic than tendons and are attached to bones at both ends. They usually cross a joint, their function being to provide support and stability. A strain of a muscle, tendon or ligament may involve its attachment to the bone and induce periostitis. At the site of attachment of the tendon or ligament the periosteum will be lifted and new bone production will be stimulated resulting in an exostosis (bony protuberance). The exostosis will not be seen on radiographs immediately after the injury but will take ten to fourteen days to develop. Lameness is associated with strain of muscles, ligaments and tendons and rest is usually the most efficacious treatment. It may take several months before repair is complete. A smoothly outlined exostosis may persist despite resolution of the lameness, but this is of no consequence.

Osteitis

Osteitis is inflammation of bone. The most common conditions in the horse which are described as osteitis are pedal osteitis and sesamoiditis.

PEDAL OSTEITIS

The distal (third) phalanx or pedal bone is the largest bone in the horse's foot and is supported in the foot by the laminae. The term pedal osteitis implies that there is current inflammation of the bone. This is difficult if not impossible to determine clinically and in the author's opinion the term is misused. The radiographic appearance of the third phalanx of normal horses is extremely variable. The bone may appear more or less porous and may have a relatively smooth or rough outline and narrow or wide vascular channels; it also may have a large or small notch (crena) at the toe. Thus, unless the radiographic appearance of the bone is very abnormal, it probably is a normal variation. A horse with large, flat feet and thin soles is predisposed to bruising, and severe bruising and/or repetitive bruising may incite inflammation of the pedal bone, but, except in a minority of horses, the radiographic appearance of the bone will be within the normal variation. The author believes that pedal osteitis is diagnosed much more frequently than it occurs. Bruising of the foot is discussed in the section on conditions of the foot (see p. 233). The following discussion on pedal osteitis relates to those horses in which major changes can be demonstrated radiographically.

Clinical signs

Both front feet are usually affected, although occasionally the condition is unilateral. The condition may develop secondarily to a distal inter-phalangeal joint flexural deformity (see p. 278). The horse moves with a shortened stride with or without obvious lameness, especially on hard ground. The horse may be lamer on a circle but not invariably so. In contrast to navicular syndrome, the horse does not point when at rest and there is less tendency to place the foot to the ground toe first. Although rest may improve the condition, lameness usually recurs when work is resumed and is worse on hard ground. It is necessary to desensitize the entire foot by a nerve block to improve the action.

Radiography

Radiographic changes include a marked increase in apparent porosity of the bone it appears riddled with holes (seen in the dorsopalmar view) with or without an irregular roughened appearance of the front of the bone (seen in a lateral view).

Treatment

There is no effective treatment and prognosis for future soundness is guarded, although the horse may perform adequately on soft ground.

SESAMOIDITIS

Functional anatomy

The proximal sesamoid bones are two small bones on the back of the fetlock joint which form part of the suspensory apparatus. The suspensory ligament divides into two branches in the lower third of the metacarpal or metatarsal (cannon) region. The inside and outside branches attach to the top of the inside and outside sesamoid bones respectively. Attached to the bottom of the sesamoid bones are three pairs of ligaments – the deep, middle and superficial distal sesamoidean ligaments – which themselves insert on the proximal (first) and middle (second) phalanges (long and short pastern bones). An inter-sesamoidean ligament joins the two sesamoid bones. As the fetlock joint flexes and extends the sesamoid bones move up and down.

Sesamoiditis is a term loosely applied to several conditions involving the sesamoid bones, none of which occurs very frequently. There is limited knowledge of the exact nature of the pathology associated with changes identified on radiographs. Radiographic changes associated with the sesamoid bones include new bone growths on the sesamoid bones (the result of tearing of attachments of the suspensory ligament), variations in the radiopacity of the bone (coarse or mottled bone trabeculation and a change in the number, size and shape of the so-called vascular channels) and areas of mineralization within the sesamoidean ligaments.

Predisposing causes

A long toe, resulting in a broken pastern–foot axis places abnormal stresses on the suspensory apparatus and predisposes to injury. The type of work the horse does influences the incidence of the disease. Injuries to the suspensory apparatus occur in horses racing at speed, especially over fences. Dressage horses and showjumpers place a lot of stress on the suspensory apparatus.

Clinical signs

Lameness is variable in severity and may be sudden or gradual in onset. Forelimb lameness may or may not be accentuated by flexion of the fetlock joint. There may be thickening of either or both of the branches of the suspensory ligaments above the sesamoid bones and pressure applied with the leg non-weightbearing may cause pain. In the acute early stage pressure applied to the sesamoid bone can cause pain if there has been tearing of the attachment of the suspensory ligament.

Diagnosis

Lameness is not affected by desensitization of the foot, but is alleviated by desensitization of the fetlock region. Oblique radiographic views of the fetlock are necessary to highlight the sesamoid bones. The identifiable bony changes have been described.

Treatment

Lameness which is associated with damage to either the suspensory ligament or the distal sesamoidean ligaments resulting in damage of the attachments to the sesamoid bones will resolve with rest, but there is a relatively high incidence of recurrence. Improvement in the pastern–foot axis by appropriate trimming and shoeing is important. If bony abnormalities are present, lameness usually improves with rest but tends to recur with the resumption of hard work. There have been a few reports that isoxsuprine hydrochloride, which dilates peripheral blood vessels, is useful in the treatment of sesamoiditis, but results have been extremely variable.

Osteomyelitis

Osteomyelitis is infection of bone and, in the adult horse, occurs most commonly as a sequel to a deep wound on the metacarpal or metatarsal region. The metacarpal or metatarsal (cannon) bones are particularly susceptible because of their lack of protection by muscles.

Cause

Many different bacteria may infect bone. Infection usually occurs via an open wound but in the young foal may be blood-borne.

Clinical signs

There is soft-tissue swelling and a sinus (hole) through which pus exudes continuously or intermittently. Pressure applied to the area causes pain. The horse may or may not be lame.

Diagnosis

The history of a wound which either failed to heal satisfactorily or healed and then developed a sinus is suggestive of the presence of osteomyelitis or a foreign body. Diagnosis is confirmed by radiographs, with the infected bone having a characteristic fuzzy appearance. Sometimes a piece of bone dies and becomes surrounded by pus and granulation tissue, forming a sequestrum (dead bone) and involucrum (surrounding granulation tissue).

Treatment

Antibiotic treatment is often successful in eliminating infections, provided that there is no dead bone. It is useful to try to culture bacteria from the sinus and find out to which drugs they are sensitive, so that appropriate drugs are administered. If there is dead bone, it is often necessary to remove it surgically.

Prevention

Thorough cleaning of a wound is mandatory. The hair surrounding the wound should be clipped off. All dead and dying tissue should be removed. Hosing the wound is useful, followed by careful cleaning. If the wound is deep, veterinary advice should be sought.

Physitis

Physitis is the term applied to pain associated with abnormal activity in a growth plate (physis), usually the lower growth plate of the radius, just above the knee. It was formerly referred to as epiphysitis. The condition may be related to osteochondrosis (see p. 173).

Clinical signs

The condition occurs in rapidly growing young horses, and most commonly in yearlings. There is usually slight swelling and heat around the lower end of the radius, just above the knee. The horse is not always lame; it may be lame if only one leg is affected or may show a stiff stilted gait if both forelimbs are affected. Pressure applied to the area may cause pain.

Treatment and prognosis

The diet should be restricted and calcium–phosphorus ratios checked to ensure that there is not an imbalance. Dietary supplementation with minerals should only be undertaken with appropriate advice. If the horse is lame, it should be confined to a box or small paddock.

The prognosis is favourable. Given time, the swelling usually subsides.

Figure 61a and b

Bones of the fore- and hind limbs

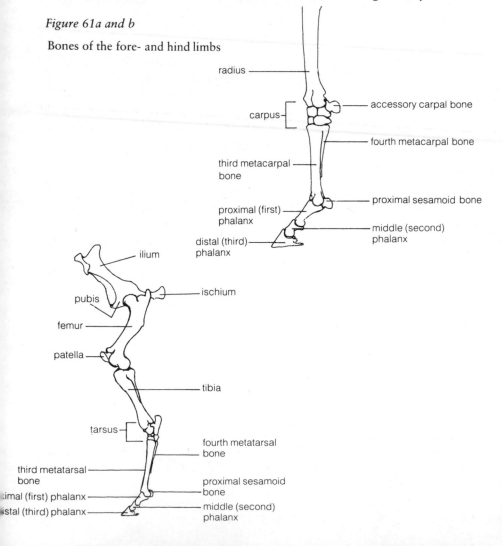

Fractures

It has traditionally been thought that the majority of fractures in the horse are irreparable, but with improving techniques many fractures are potentially treatable either to return the horse to athletic function or to salvage it for breeding purposes. Prognosis depends on many factors, including which bone is involved, the configuration of the fracture, whether or not the overlying skin is damaged, when the fracture occurred, whether or not the fracture involves a joint and, finally but by no means less important, the size, age and temperament of the horse.

Classification

A simple fracture means that there is one fracture which breaks the bone into two pieces. A comminuted fracture has more than two pieces and is more serious. If the bone is not exposed the fracture is closed. If the skin is damaged, exposing the bone, the fracture is compound. The risk of infection is very high and the prognosis is poorer. If the fracture does not extend all the way through the bone, it is incomplete. If it does extend all the way through, it is complete. If the fracture fragments remain in their normal alignment, the fracture is nondisplaced. If the pieces have moved, the fracture is displaced and, depending on the degree of displacement, the pieces will usually require realignment if satisfactory healing is to occur. If the fracture does not involve a joint, it is non-articular. If the fracture extends into a joint it is articular and the prognosis is less good, because there is a significant risk of developing secondary joint disease (arthritis).

Diagnosis

A fracture may often be identified by a careful clinical examination. In some instances it is obvious – the leg is distorted and the fragments are readily felt, and movement between them (crepitus) can be detected, but this is not always the case. In some circumstances it is clear that it is highly unlikely that the fracture can be successfully repaired and the horse should be humanely destroyed. If the fracture is not readily identifiable or if there is a possibility of repair, then radiographs are mandatory. Several different views are necessary to define the configuration of the fracture and the degree of displacement. If the fracture is only a fissure and there is no displacement, it may be extremely difficult to identify. Part of the normal healing process involves bone resorption (removal) along the fracture line, thus on subsequent radiographs the fracture line becomes wider and more readily identified. Therefore, if a fracture is suspected but cannot be seen on radiographs, the horse should be confined to a box and further radiographs taken seven to ten days later.

First aid

In many instances it is necessary to move the horse to suitable radiography facilities. Precautions must be taken to minimize the risks of making the fracture worse. Effective immobilization of the upper forelimb and hind limb is impossible, but below the knee and hock a strong support bandage can be of great benefit. If possible, the joints above and below the fractured bone should be incorporated into the bandage. Sophisticated bandage material is unnecessary, although a proper plaster or synthetic cast is ideal if applied properly. Gamgee, two broomsticks, some pillows and plenty of crepe bandages will suffice in an emergency. Although it is important to provide adequate support, the bandages must not be applied too tightly since they may restrict the blood supply and damage the soft tissues. Plenty of padding (e.g. Gamgee and pillows) should reduce this risk. Although the horse may be in considerable pain, provided that it is not unduly distressed and unmanageable, painkilling drugs should not be administered because it is desirable that the horse should be discouraged from bearing weight on the limb. Most horses are quite adept at walking slowly on three legs. The incline of the ramp of the trailer or lorry should be as slight as possible. A loading bay or a slope against which the ramp is placed is useful. During transport the horse should be supported with straw bales if necessary. If the horse has fractured a forelimb, travelling the animal facing backwards reduces the risks of its inadvertently overloading the fractured limb if a sudden stop is necessary.

Fracture healing

Fracture healing requires adequate alignment and immobilization of the fracture fragments. If the fracture fragments are widely separated or if there is constant movement at the fracture site, then healing will not occur or the pieces will be united by a fibrous rather than a bony union. If the fracture fragments are aligned and kept relatively still, then healing will occur by formation of a bony callus around the bone at the fracture site and direct union between the bone pieces. The more movement there is between the fracture fragments, the greater the amount of callus that will be formed. When healing is complete this callus will remodel and reduce in size to some extent.

In order to achieve adequate stability of the fracture fragments, either external support (a cast) or internal fixation (plates and/or screws) is necessary. Which method is used depends upon the severity of the fracture, its location, the intended use of the horse and financial considerations.

It may be possible to apply a cast with the horse standing, especially if a synthetic casting material which sets rapidly is used. This is satisfactory provided that the fracture fragments are not displaced and obviates the need for general anaesthesia. Major problems can arise during recovery from general anaesthesia: it is difficult to control the movement of a horse and it may take a mis-step while still not properly aware of how it is placing its limbs, resulting in refracture. However, if the fracture fragments are malpositioned, then they must be realigned, and this is only possible under general anaesthesia. Realignment may be achieved by applying traction to the leg. Sometimes it is necessary to expose the bone surgically and in these circumstances a bone plate and/or screws are usually applied. If a fracture fragment is small, surgical removal may be the treatment of choice, particularly if it is within a joint.

FRACTURES OF THE SCAPULA

Fractures of the scapula (shoulderblade) are comparatively rare and are usually the result of direct trauma. There is soft-tissue swelling and considerable pain. The horse is unwilling to move the leg or place weight upon it. The prognosis for most fractures is hopeless.

FRACTURES OF THE HUMERUS

Most fractures of the humerus are non-articular spiral fractures with or without comminution and displacement. There is considerable soft-tissue swelling. Prognosis in the adult horse is usually hopeless. Successful surgical repair has been achieved in foals.

FRACTURES OF THE RADIUS

Fractures of the radius occur in many configurations. There is usually a considerable amount of soft-tissue swelling. The prognosis in the adult horse is poor, although successful surgical treatment has been achieved. Better results are obtained in foals. Occasionally nondisplaced fractures in adult horses have healed spontaneously.

FRACTURES OF THE CARPUS (KNEE)

There are at least seven bones in the knee – the radial, intermediate, ulnar, accessory, second, third and fourth carpal bones – of which five commonly sustain fractures. Fractures occur most often in racehorses and are not usually associated with direct trauma but are the result of repeated stress on the front aspect of the bones, resulting in a small chip fracture of a corner of a bone or a larger slab fracture through the length of a bone. There is usually subtle swelling of the knee and resentment of flexion, with moderate lameness. Chip fractures commonly involve the radial, intermediate or third carpal bone and may be successfully treated by removal of the piece. Slab fractures occur most commonly in the third carpal bone. Thin slab fractures may be removed. Thick slab fractures are treated by inserting a screw through the fragment into the parent bone.

Fractures of the accessory carpal bone occur more often in older horses and are difficult to treat surgically, due to the odd shape of the bone. Prolonged rest renders some horses sound.

Occasionally fractures of several carpal bones occur concurrently; this results in instability of the carpus and merits a poor prognosis.

FRACTURES OF THE THIRD METACARPAL OR METATARSAL (CANNON) BONES

Fractures of these bones are usually the result of direct trauma and, because of the small amount of overlying soft tissue, bone is often exposed through the skin causing a high risk of infection (osteomyelitis – see p. 163). There are often several pieces. If there are not too many pieces and the fracture is not too contaminated and the soft tissues are in reasonable condition, then surgical treatment may be successful. Two bone plates are used, plus additional screws and a bone graft if necessary.

FRACTURES OF THE SECOND AND FOURTH METACARPAL OR METATARSAL (SPLINT) BONES

Fracture of a splint bone may occur spontaneously or associated with inflammation of the suspensory ligament (suspensory desmitis – see p. 221) or be due to trauma. Fractures occur most commonly at the junction between the top two thirds and the bottom one third of the bone, although they may be located anywhere, especially if they are the result of external trauma. In some instances it is possible to palpate a movable fracture fragment, but radiographs are usually necessary to confirm a diagnosis, especially if there is soft-tissue swelling associated with suspensory desmitis.

If the fracture is uncomplicated, that is, if there are only one or two fracture fragments, and the overlying skin is intact, conservative treatment is adequate. Most fractures heal spontaneously by bony union, even if there is some displacement of the fracture fragment. Initially a fairly large bony callus may develop to unite the pieces, but this will remodel and reduce in size. Persistent lameness is unusual, even if the bones do not become united (i.e. even if there is a non-union). Therefore in an uncomplicated fracture surgery is usually not warranted, except for cosmetic reasons, and rest is the treatment of choice. Subsequent radiographs will help to determine when the horse may resume work. If there is associated suspensory desmitis, the prognosis is more guarded.

Surgical treatment may be indicated if there are multiple fracture fragments, if the fracture occurs high up, thus separating the major part of the bone from the top, or if the bone becomes infected secondary to a concurrent skin wound. Infection may usually be managed by removal of infected bone and concomitant antibiotic treatment and a favourable prognosis may be offered. If the fracture has occurred high up, the prognosis must always be guarded. Removal of the fragment may mean that the remaining part of the bone is unstable, and repetitive, slight movement is likely to produce persistent lameness. Attempts have been made to stabilize this piece by inserting a screw through it into the cannon bone and, although this technique is successful in some horses, it is not uniformly so.

FRACTURES OF THE PROXIMAL SESAMOID BONES

Spontaneous fractures of both the sesamoid bones in one or both forelegs occur occasionally in foals and some recover without treatment. Otherwise sesamoid fractures are usually restricted to racehorses but do also occur in other types. There is moderate lameness and pain on pressure over the bone. Fractures of the top (apex) of the bone may be successfully treated by removal of the piece, provided that there is no associated severe suspensory desmitis. Fractures of the middle of the bone are more serious but screwing or the installation of a bone graft is sometimes successful. Fractures of the base warrant a guarded prognosis.

FRACTURES OF THE PROXIMAL (FIRST) PHALANX (LONG PASTERN BONE)

Fractures of the proximal phalanx are not uncommon in all types of horses. If the fracture is displaced and/or comminuted, it is identified readily, but nondisplaced fissure fractures may be difficult to diagnose and multiple radiographic views may be necessary. In young Thoroughbreds with a nondisplaced fissure fracture box rest is sufficient. All other types of fracture require either casting or surgical fixation. The prognosis depends upon whether or not the fracture involves the fetlock and/or the pastern joint and how many pieces there are. Chip fractures of the top of the bone also occur and may be treated by removal of the piece with a good prognosis provided there is no arthritis of the fetlock joint.

FRACTURES OF THE MIDDLE (SECOND) PHALANX (SHORT PASTERN BONE)

Fractures of the second phalanx are rare in Britain but occur more frequently in racing Quarter horses in America.

FRACTURES OF THE DISTAL (THIRD) PHALANX (PEDAL BONE)

Fractures of the third phalanx which do not enter the distal interphalangeal (coffin) joint have a reasonable prognosis following box rest and the application of a bar shoe to immobilize the foot as much as is possible. These fractures often heal by fibrous rather than by bony union and can still be seen on radiographs. Fractures which enter the joint warrant a poor prognosis.

FRACTURES OF THE NAVICULAR BONE

Fractures of the navicular bone cause a sudden onset of moderate to severe lameness and may be the result of the horse kicking a solid object or a mis-step. Without treatment the lameness may improve but usually mild lameness persists. Some horses with recent fractures may be treated successfully by screw fixation.

FRACTURES OF THE PELVIS   See p. 272.

FRACTURES OF THE FEMUR AND TIBIA

Fractures of the femur and tibia in both adult horses and foals warrant a very poor prognosis, although successful surgical repair has been achieved in foals.

FRACTURES OF THE PATELLA (KNEECAP)

Fractures of the patella usually occur as a result of a direct blow; surgical treatment offers the best prognosis.

FRACTURES OF THE FIBULA

Fractures of the fibula are extremely rare. The bone forms as several different pieces which look separate on radiographs and these separations must not be confused with a fracture.

FRACTURES OF THE HOCK

Fractures of the hock usually occur due to trauma and most have a poor prognosis.

Genetic Disorders

HEREDITARY MULTIPLE EXOSTOSIS

This is a rare hereditary condition characterized by numerous growths on the long bones, the ribs and the pelvis. The bony enlargements may rub on soft-tissue structures, causing enlargement of tendon sheaths and joint capsules and mild lameness. There is no known treatment. Affected horses should not be used for breeding.

POLYDACTYLY

Polydactyly is the presence, in the newborn foal, of an extra part of a limb. It can take a variety of forms, for example, an extra lower leg comprising a miniature third metacarpal bone and phalanges growing from the third metacarpal bone. The protuberance, which is hair-covered, can be amputated for cosmetic reasons and to avoid interference with the contralateral leg.

13
THE JOINTS

Joint structure and function

The basic structure and function of all limb joints (articulations) are similar. Articular (joint) cartilage covers the ends of the bones, protects the underlying bone and transmits forces to the underlying subchondral bone. Cartilage has no nerve supply, therefore damage to it does not itself cause pain. It has no blood supply and is dependent on the synovial (joint) fluid for nutrition. If movement of synovial fluid in and out of the articular cartilage is impaired, then the cartilage will receive inadequate nutrition resulting in cell death and a decrease in resistance to stress. Articular cartilage has limited powers of regeneration, therefore damage to it is incompletely repaired.

Figure 62   Structure of a typical joint

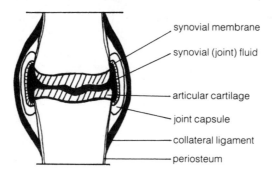

synovial membrane

synovial (joint) fluid

articular cartilage

joint capsule

collateral ligament

periosteum

The synovial membrane controls the composition of the synovial fluid, which consists of some of the constituents of blood plus hyaluronic acid. Hyaluronic acid is produced and secreted by cells of the synovial membrane. Synovial fluid is vital for nutrition of the articular cartilage and has an important role in the lubrication of the synovial membrane and the joint capsule. The synovial membrane has a nerve and a blood supply. Pain is caused by inflammation of both the synovial membrane and the surrounding joint capsule. Distension of these structures due to the presence of excess synovial fluid also causes pain. Damage and inflammation of the synovial membrane and the joint capsule is usually associated with lameness; minor damage of the articular cartilage alone does not always cause lameness.

Both the joint capsule and the collateral ligaments provide stability to the joint and limit its range of motion. The joint capsule and the ligaments are attached to the periosteum, the thin membrane which covers the bone. Tearing of the attachments of the joint capsule or the collateral ligaments will lift the periosteum from the underlying bone, causing pain and subsequent new bone formation. These periosteal proliferative reactions are some distance from the joint surfaces and should not compromise the long-term function of the joint. Thus, when soft-tissue damage has repaired and the periosteal reaction has settled down, lameness should resolve, provided that the articular structures of the joint were not also damaged.

Conditions of Joints

Congenital joint abnormalities in the horse are extremely rare. Occasionally a foal is born with a joint which will not flex. Sometimes parts of a joint are underdeveloped (hypoplastic), predisposing to luxation (dislocation) of the joint.

OSTEOCHONDROSIS (OCD)

Osteochondrosis (OCD) is a developmental abnormality of cartilage and bone which occurs particularly in young, rapidly growing individuals. Direct heritability has not been definitely proved, but probably there is a genetic predisposition to the disease in foals with potential for fast growth. Encouraging a horse to grow quickly using high planes of nutrition may increase the risk of the disease, which in Britain is most common in Thoroughbreds. Although the disease has been identified in most joints, the stifle and hock joints are most commonly affected in the hind leg and the shoulder joint in the front leg. The clinical signs of the disease are usually evident within the first two years of life.

During development of bone, cartilage is converted to bone. Impaired blood supply to the cartilage will delay conversion of cartilage to bone and result in abnormally thick cartilage on the joint surfaces, the lower layers of which may die. Therefore the cartilage on the joint surface is only loosely attached to the underlying bone and may become detached. This causes inflammation within the joint and production of excess synovial fluid, with the result that the joint capsule becomes distended. Therefore the typical clinical signs of osteochondrosis are joint swelling and lameness. The diagnosis is confirmed by radiography. The disease often occurs bilaterally, that is, it involves both stifles, so it is important to take radiographs of both joints even if only one is obviously affected.

Although some joints may have mild osteochondrosis without clinical signs, the majority of lesions cause lameness and deteriorate if not treated. Treatment is by surgery. Abnormal cartilage is stripped off the underlying bone and the bone is scraped until healthy bleeding bone is exposed.

SUBCHONDRAL BONE CYSTS

Subchondral bone cysts are holes in the bone close to the articular (joint) surface. They may or may not communicate with the joint surface via a narrow neck. The holes in the bone are filled with fibrous material and/or joint fluid. There is controversy about whether subchondral bone cysts and osteochondrosis are related conditions. The exact cause of subchondral bone cysts is unknown. Repetitive trauma resulting in tiny fractures in the bone may be important. Cysts occur in most bones, although they are found more commonly in some locations than in others, for example, in the bottom of the femur in the stifle joint. Most cysts which are close to a joint surface cause lameness, although with time this may resolve even though the cyst can still be seen on radiographs. Occasionally cysts fill in and are no longer visible on radiographs. If lameness persists, then surgical treatment may be successful.

DISTENSION AND ENLARGEMENT OF A JOINT CAPSULE

A joint may appear enlarged either due to thickening of the joint capsule or its distension by excessive amounts of synovial fluid. This may occur without lameness. Some horses seem particularly prone. Horses, especially the middle to heavyweight types with upright forelimb conformation, commonly have distension of the fetlock joint capsules, giving a rounded appearance to the joints. This becomes more obvious if the horse does a lot of work on hard ground. The swelling may be controlled by keeping the joints bandaged but this is not essential. These swellings are sometimes called **articular windgalls**.

BOG SPAVIN

Bog spavin is a distension of the joint capsule of the true hock (tarsocrural or tibiotarsal) joint (see Figure 68b). It does not normally cause lameness. One or both hocks may be affected. It is particularly common in young, fast-growing youngsters, and both in these and in older horses usually resolves spontaneously. Distension of the joint capsule may reflect disease within the hock (e.g. osteochondrosis, secondary joint disease or bone spavin), but in

Figure 63 Soft, fluctuant swelling of the tarsocrural joint capsule: bog spavin. The swelling is most obvious on the front and inside of the hock (black arrows). There is also an out-pouching of the joint capsule on the outside of the hock (white arrow). Pressure applied to one swelling causes the other to enlarge

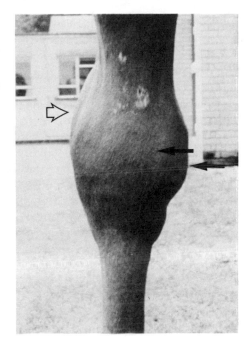

the majority of cases is an innocuous swelling of no clinical significance and no treatment is required. If the swelling is associated with lameness, further investigation including radiography is indicated.

JOINT SPRAIN

Joint disease may be limited to the structures around the joint, that is, to the synovial membrane, the joint capsule and the collateral ligaments. Sprain of these structures is usually the result of the joint suddenly being positioned abnormally, for example, when it is twisted. Not all the structures need be affected simultaneously or to the same degree. Inflammation of the synovial membrane (synovitis) and the joint capsule (capsulitis) alone is less serious than damage to the collateral ligaments, as the latter may impair the stability of the joint and predispose to damage of the joint itself (secondary or degenerative joint disease – see below).

Clinical signs

There is heat around the joint and swelling due to distension of the joint capsule by excess synovial fluid. If the collateral ligaments are sprained, then there is more swelling around the joint. Passive flexion of the joint causes pain and lameness is accentuated by manipulation of the joint. With such obvious clinical signs additional diagnostic tests are frequently unnecessary although it is prudent to examine the joint radiographically to exclude the possibility of a fracture. Radiographs will demonstrate the presence of concurrent bony damage but will often appear normal apart from showing soft-tissue swelling around the joint. Radiographs obtained ten to fourteen days after injury may show periosteal proliferative reactions (new bone formation) at the sites of attachment of the collateral ligaments and joint capsule. Unfortunately it is not always possible to appreciate fully the extent of the damage and to determine whether it is restricted to the soft-tissue structures of the joint or if it involves the articular cartilage, in which case the long-term prognosis is more guarded.

Treatment

Inflammation should be reduced by application of cold to the joint – cold hosing and cold-water bandages. Anti-inflammatory drugs, such as phenylbutazone, may help to relieve pain and minimize the inflammatory reaction. Immediate ultrasound treatment may help to reduce soft-tissue swelling. A firmly applied support bandage may maintain reduction of swelling. The horse is confined to box rest. The duration of rest required depends on the severity of the initial injury and ranges from two to three weeks to several months. Recently a drug called sodium hyaluronate has become available for the treatment of acute joint disorders. It is administered into the joint and permits a more rapid return to normal function. It is extremely expensive and its use has largely been restricted to treatment of valuable racehorses.

SECONDARY (DEGENERATIVE) JOINT DISEASE (OSTEOARTHRITIS)

Despite extensive studies in man and in experimental animals, much controversy still surrounds the exact mechanism of development of secondary (degenerative) joint disease (osteoarthritis). The condition starts as a degradation (breakdown) of the articular cartilage, which may occur secondarily to inflammation of the soft-tissue structures of the joint (synovitis and capsulitis). Loss of substances called proteoglycans from the cartilage into the synovial fluid itself causes synovitis, creating a vicious circle. The structure of the cartilage is altered by loss of proteoglycans and collagens and its function is impaired. This contributes to the vicious circle. Bony changes occur later in the disease and are a response to what is primarily a disease of cartilage. It may develop as a sequel to a traumatic incident such as a severe sprain or it may have a more insidious onset. Conformational abnormalities may result in abnormal stresses on a joint and thereby predispose to development of degenerative joint disease. Back-at-the-knee conformation may result in abnormal stresses on the joints of the knee. This, together with the tendency of the joint to hyperextend when the horse is galloping, causing compression of the front faces of the bones of the knee, results in a high incidence of secondary joint disease of the knee in young racing Thoroughbreds. Although secondary joint disease is predominantly a problem of the mature horse, it is not exclusively so. The lower-limb joints – the knee, hock, fetlock, pastern and coffin joints – are more commonly affected than the upper-limb joints, bone spavin (see p. 193) and ringbone (see p. 182) being common examples.

Clinical signs

Lameness may be sudden or insidious in onset. There may be distension of the joint capsule by increased amounts of synovial fluid. Passive flexion of the affected joint may be resented and may accentuate lameness. The range of motion of the joint may be restricted due to fibrosis of the joint capsule. If there is extensive new bone around the joint, there is firm swelling around the joint.

Diagnosis

It is often necessary to use local anaethesia to determine the source of pain. Radiographs will not always provide enough information because there is often a poor correlation between radiographic abnormalities and clinical signs. The absence of radiographic changes does not preclude a joint as the source of the problem: in early degenerative joint disease no radiographic changes are detectable. Similarly the presence of radiographic abnormalities does not necessarily implicate that joint as the source of pain. There may be fairly extensive bony changes some distance from a joint which may reflect previous tearing of soft-tissue attachments which are currently of no clinical significance. Radiographs cannot demonstrate cartilage damage unless this is extreme with considerable loss of articular cartilage and narrowing of the joint space. Currently there is no reliable means of detection of cartilage damage, but this is commonly present in long-standing joint disorders and is how we define osteoarthritis; it is irreversible and potentially progressive. Radiographic changes diagnostic of secondary joint disease include periarticular bone spurs (osteophytes), narrowing of the joint space and sclerosis of subchondral bone. Their presence indicates a fairly advanced case.

Treatment

Treatment of chronic secondary joint disease is aimed at minimizing soft-tissue inflammation and associated pain, facilitating joint lubrication and maintaining optimal nutrition of the articular cartilage. The precise treatment depends on the joint involved. Prognosis is based on the presence or absence of predisposing causes, for example, conformational abnormalities, the duration of lameness and the severity of changes on radiographs. There is little scientific rationale behind the use of blistering or firing other than enforcing rest. Rest may permit soft-tissue inflammation to subside, but some joint movement is essential for normal cartilage nutrition, therefore complete immobilization of the joint is contraindicated. Rest alone is unlikely to enable the horse to return to full, sustained work. Since the condition is incurable, if the horse is to be functional, analgesic medication such as phenylbutazone, meclofenamic acid or flunixin meglumine is probably indicated. Treatment is performed in the knowledge that the drug is merely alleviating pain and not effecting a cure, and that continual stress of an already damaged joint may accelerate deterioration of the joint. The analgesic drugs mentioned are limited to their ability to control pain and will only permit the horse to work sound provided that the pain is not severe. Hyaluronic acid is less successful in the treatment of chronic joint problems than of acute problems but may facilitate lubrication of the soft tissues of the joint and improve the nutrition of the articular cartilage, and in selected cases can extend the working life of the horse. Other drugs which have been used are orgotein and a glycosaminoglycan polysulphate; on a theoretical basis the latter drug is the most rational choice if bony changes are already present on radiographs. A series of injections into the joint is usually necessary and a successful outcome cannot be guaranteed.

Degenerative joint disease is a common problem which is, as yet, poorly understood. The different postures of man and the horse put different joints at stress; hence the relatively high incidence of hip osteoarthritis in man compared to the horse. In contrast to man, the incidence of rheumatoid arthritis in the horse is extremely rare. There is no firm evidence to suggest that there is a hereditary factor involved in the development of degenerative joint disease in the horse, although both the now obsolete Stallion Licensing Act and the recently introduced National Stallion Approval Scheme preclude recognition of stallions with ringbone. Ultimately the horse has to perform athletically as a sound animal, and at the moment management of degenerative joint disease is a major problem which remains unsatisfactorily answered.

LUXATION (DISLOCATION)

Luxation of a joint means that the bones forming a joint have been displaced relative to one another with resultant extensive damage to the surrounding soft tissues. It is a rare and serious injury in the horse and causes severe lameness. Realignment of the bones may require anaesthetizing the horse in order to get adequate relaxation of the muscles to allow movement of the bones. Early treatment is essential for a successful outcome.

A more common occurrence is subluxation or partial displacement of two bones. Hind pastern joints in young Thoroughbreds are the most commonly involved. The cause is uncertain. It may be related to pain and analgesic medication can be beneficial. It resolves spontaneously in some horses.

JOINT INFECTION (SEPTIC ARTHRITIS, JOINT ILL)

Infection of a joint occurs most commonly in foals, but may be found in adult horses. In foals one or several joints may be infected and the condition is colloquially called 'joint ill'. Infection usually originates from the blood. A foal which is immunologically compromised because of failure to receive colostrum is most at risk. In the adult, infection is usually restricted to one joint and may originate from the blood or be a sequel to a penetration wound.

Clinical signs

There is a sudden onset of severe lameness associated with warm, painful enlargement of the joint capsule. The horse may be depressed and inappetent. Rectal temperature may be elevated.

Diagnosis

The results of infection of a joint are rapidly damaging, so an early diagnosis is essential. Naked-eye examination of the joint fluid may be highly suggestive. The normal yellow, translucent synovial fluid is orange-brown, discoloured and turbid and less viscous than normal. Estimation of the total number and type of white blood cells in the fluid confirms the diagnosis. Although the joint is infected, it is often not possible to isolate the causative organisms. If infection has been present for some time (several days), destructive bony changes may be seen on radiographs. This merits a poor prognosis.

Treatment

The aims of treatment are to kill the infectious microbes and to minimize further damage to the joint by enzymes produced by the bacteria and by the white blood cells which invade the joint cavity in response to infection. This is achieved by aggressive antibiotic treatment maintained for up to several weeks and by flushing the joint to remove debris from within the joint. This may be possible with the horse standing, but sedation or general anaesthesia is often required. A large needle is inserted into the joint and sterile fluid is pumped into the joint and then allowed to escape either via a second needle or through the input needle. This procedure should be done as soon as possible after recognition of infection and sometimes must be repeated.

Prognosis

The prognosis depends on the duration of clinical signs prior to initiation of treatment, and the speed of response to treatment. The longer infection is present the greater likelihood there is of irreversible cartilage damage and development of secondary joint disease. A joint which is suspected of being infected should be treated as such until proven otherwise. Multiple joint infections in foals warrant a guarded prognosis.

Conditions of the Fetlock and Pastern

Functional anatomy

The metacarpophalangeal (fetlock) and proximal interphalangeal (pastern) joints are hinge joints. The joints flex and extend but there is minimal movement from side to side. Side-to-side movement is controlled by the collateral ligaments. On the back of the fetlock joint are two smaller bones, the proximal sesamoid bones. The suspensory ligament attaches to the top of these bones. Three pairs of ligaments – the superficial, middle and deep distal sesamoidean ligaments – attach to the bottom of the sesamoid bones and to the top of the middle (second) phalanx (short pastern bone), to the back of the proximal (first) phalanx (long pastern bone) and to the top of the proximal phalanx respectively. The deep and superficial flexor tendons pass over the back of the sesamoid bones.

Horses with upright conformation of the pastern and fetlock are prone to enlargement of the fetlock joint capsule (**articular windgalls**) and the flexor tendon sheath (**tendinous windgalls**). This is physiological and does not necessarily imply the presence of disease. Horses with a long sloping pastern are likely to stress the suspensory apparatus, i.e. the suspensory ligament, the sesamoid bones and the distal sesamoidean ligaments. Toe-in and toe-

Figure 64 Toe-in and toe-out conformation

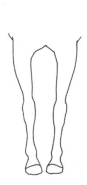
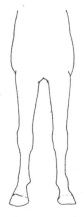

out conformation results in particular stress on the outside and inside of the fetlock and pastern joints respectively.

Fetlock injuries are not uncommon in all types of horses and ponies in both forelimbs and hindlimbs. Injuries and disease of the pastern joints occur less frequently.

SPRAIN OF THE FETLOCK JOINT

Clinical signs

The horse is lame. There is enlargement of the fetlock joint capsule and there may be more diffuse, warm, soft-tissue swelling around the joint. The horse resents flexion of the joint.

Diagnosis

Sudden onset of lameness associated with the development of such swelling is typical. If lameness is severe or fails to improve rapidly with rest, radiographs should be obtained to preclude the possibility of bone damage.

Treatment

The aims of treatment are to reduce pain and soft-tissue inflammation. Cold hosing and cold-water bandages help to reduce swelling and inflammation. Phenylbutazone is beneficial. Ultrasound treatment is also useful in the early stage to reduce swelling but is not essential. Box rest should be continued until all swelling has dissipated.

Prognosis

Provided that there is no major damage of the collateral ligaments of the fetlock joint resulting in instability of the joint, the prognosis is favourable.

SECONDARY (DEGENERATIVE) JOINT DISEASE (OSTEOARTHRITIS) OF THE FETLOCK JOINT

Clinical signs

The horse is lame. Forelimbs are more often affected than hind limbs. There is usually, but not always, slight to moderate distension of the fetlock joint capsule and resentment of passive flexion of the joint. The fetlock joint may also be abnormally stiff. Lameness is usually accentuated with the affected leg on the inside of a circle or by flexion of the joint.

Diagnosis

Lameness is alleviated by desensitization of the fetlock region by nerve blocks and by intra-articular anaesthesia of the joint. Early disease may be present in the absence of radiographic abnormalities. As the disease becomes more advanced, radiographic changes typical of secondary joint disease develop (see p. 176).

Treatment

In the early stages intra-articular treatment with sodium hyaluronate or a glycosaminoglycan polysulphate can resolve the lameness. When radiographic changes are advanced, the prognosis is poor.

SECONDARY (DEGENERATIVE) JOINT DISEASE (OSTEOARTHRITIS) OF THE PROXIMAL INTERPHALANGEAL (PASTERN) JOINT (RINGBONE)

Secondary (degenerative) joint disease of the pastern joint is known as high articular ringbone. It may arise spontaneously or be secondary to an injury.

Clinical signs

Both fore- and hind limbs can be affected. The horse shows a variable degree of lameness. If more than one leg is affected, the lameness may be difficult to pinpoint. There is firm swelling in the pastern region and there may be resentment of manipulation of the joint and/or limitation of its range of motion.

Diagnosis

In the early stages it is necessary to use local anaesthesia to confirm the site of pain. In more advanced cases radiographs confirm the clinical diagnosis. There is loss of joint space and production of new bone around the joint.

Treatment

The condition is incurable. The horse may be enabled to work sound by treatment with phenylbutazone. Some horses fuse the joint spontaneously and, provided that there is not an excessive production of new bone, may become sound. If there is excessive new bone production lameness may persist despite fusion of the joint. If only one joint is affected, surgical fusion can be performed. The prognosis is better for hind limbs than for forelimbs.

FLEXURAL DEFORMITY OF THE METACARPOPHALANGEAL (FETLOCK) JOINT (CONTRACTED TENDONS) See p. 279.

ANGULAR DEFORMITY OF THE FETLOCK JOINT See p. 280.

CHIP FRACTURES IN THE FETLOCK JOINT

It is not particularly unusual to see on radiographs a small bony piece on the top front aspect of the proximal phalanx (long pastern bone). If smooth,

Figure 65 An oblique radiographic view of the metacarpophalangeal (fetlock) joint showing a small chip fracture or separate centre of ossification (arrow). Such abnormalities can be seen in both lame and sound horses and must be interpreted with care

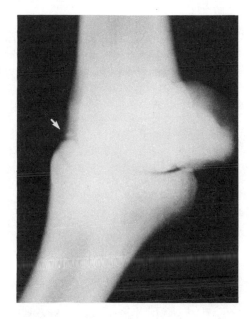

small and well rounded, this may be an insignificant radiographic abnormality and can be present in more than one leg. It may represent a separate centre of ossification or an old chip fracture. It can be present without causing lameness. If seen in a lame horse, its significance must be proven. It should not be assumed that it is the cause of lameness.

Diagnosis and treatment

The horse is sound after intra-articular anaesthesia of the joint. If the bony piece is slightly irregularly shaped or if some abnormality in the contour of the top edge of the proximal phalanx can be identified, the piece is likely to be significant.

Treatment is by surgical removal.

Prognosis

Provided that there are not major radiographic changes indicative of secondary joint disease, the prognosis is good.

CONDYLAR FRACTURES

Condylar fractures are fractures of the bottom end of the cannon bone which enter the fetlock joint and extend obliquely upwards. They occur almost exclusively in young racing Thoroughbreds and Standardbreds when working at speed. They usually occur in forelegs, but sometimes in the hind legs.

Clinical signs and diagnosis

The horse is very lame and may be non-weightbearing on the limb. At the time of injury there may be little to see, but within twelve to twenty-four hours some swelling in the fetlock region usually occurs. There is pain on movement of the joint.

Diagnosis is confirmed by radiographs.

Treatment and prognosis

The fracture is stabilized surgically using screws and the lower leg is temporarily immobilized in a cast, which is then replaced by a heavy support bandage.

Provided that the fracture is nondisplaced and is treated early, the prognosis is good.

FRACTURES OF THE PROXIMAL (FIRST) AND MIDDLE (SECOND) PHALANGES See p. 169.

FRACTURES OF THE PROXIMAL SESAMOID BONES See p. 169.

SESAMOIDITIS See p. 161.

WINDGALLS See pp. 174 and 208.

STRAIN OF THE DIGITAL FLEXOR TENDON SHEATH See p. 209.

CONSTRICTION OF A TENDON SHEATH BY AN ANNULAR LIGAMENT See p. 210.

Conditions of the Carpus (Knee)

Functional anatomy

The carpus consists of two rows of small bones. Three bones of the top row, the radial, intermediate and ulnar carpal bones articulate with the bottom of the radius. On the back of the knee is the accessory carpal bone. The top row of bones articulate with the lower row, the second, third and fourth carpal bones. The small first and fifth carpal bones may be present or absent. The lower row of bones articulate with the metacarpal (cannon and splint) bones. Most of the flexion in the carpus occurs in the top two joints, the

Figure 66 Anatomy of the carpus (knee); a) craniocaudal view, b) flexed lateral view

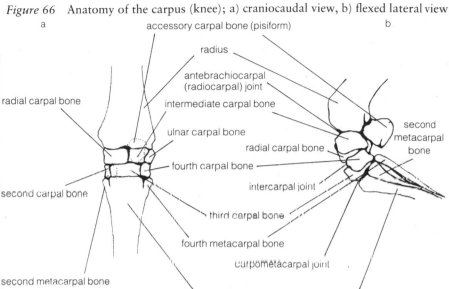

a

accessory carpal bone (pisiform)

b

radius

antebrachiocarpal (radiocarpal) joint

radial carpal bone

intermediate carpal bone

ulnar carpal bone

radial carpal bone

second metacarpal bone

fourth carpal bone

second carpal bone

intercarpal joint

third carpal bone

fourth metacarpal bone

carpometacarpal joint

second metacarpal bone

third metacarpal bone

antebrachiocarpal (radiocarpal) and intercarpal joints. The small bones in each row of carpal bones are connected to each other by short ligaments.

When the carpus is hyperextended, as in the galloping horse, the front edges of the bones of the carpus move closer together. This effect is exaggerated in a horse with back-at-the-knee conformation. Bony carpal problems and degenerative joint disease are most common in racehorses, but are found in other types of horses as well.

Over the front aspect of the knee pass several tendons, the largest of which, the tendons of the extensor carpi radialis muscle and the common digital extensor muscle, are enclosed in tendon sheaths. On the back of the knee, on the inside of the accessory carpal bone, run the digital flexor tendons within a synovial structure, the carpal canal.

SECONDARY (DEGENERATIVE) JOINT DISEASE (OSTEOARTHRITIS) OF THE CARPUS

This is a common condition in racehorses but occurs occasionally in other types of horses. Either or both the intercarpal and antebrachiocarpal (radiocarpal) joints are affected.

Clinical signs

The horse is lame. The leg may be swung outwards as the limb is advanced to minimize flexion of the carpal joints. There is slight palpable distension of the joint capsule of the affected joint. The horse may resent full flexion of the carpus and lameness may be exaggerated by flexion.

Diagnosis

In some cases the diagnosis can be based on the clinical signs and radiographs. The correlation between radiographic abnormalities and the degree of lameness is not very good. In particular, bony proliferation on the front face of the small carpal bones at the site of attachment of the intercarpal ligaments does not necessarily cause lameness. The diagnosis is confirmed by intra-articular anaesthesia. This is mandatory in early cases when there may be no radiographic abnormalities.

Treatment

In the early stages in young Thoroughbreds the condition may resolve with rest. A more rapid return to soundness is achieved by intra-articular treatment with sodium hyaluronate. If there are advanced changes seen on radiographs the long-term prognosis is poor. In older horses sodium hyaluronate or a glycosaminoglycan polysulphate is sometimes useful. Flexion of the carpus many times daily helps to maintain full mobility of the joints. This is especially important in a jumping horse.

BROKEN KNEES　See p. 261.

FRACTURES OF THE CARPUS　See p. 167.

PHYSITIS　See p. 163.

HYPOPLASIA OF THE CARPAL BONES　See p. 289.

HYGROMA (see also Acquired or False Bursae, p. 207)

A hygroma is an acquired bursa on the front of the knee as a result of repetitive trauma, such as banging the knee on the stable door. It results in a cosmetic blemish. If the swelling is very large, flexibility of the knee may be restricted. The swelling may be variable in size and a blow to the knee will cause temporary enlargement of the swelling and inflammation. Occasionally there is slight lameness.

If a horse with a 'big knee' is kept in work the swelling will usually persist, although it may fluctuate in size. If the horse is rested for several months the swelling usually diminishes and becomes firmer.

Treatment

If the swelling is small, no treatment is required. If the swelling is large, drainage and injection of a corticosteroid can be helpful if the limb is then bandaged and the horse confined to box rest for seven to fourteen days, but the results are not uniformly successful. Surgical removal of the false bursa gives the best cosmetic result.

Prevention

If possible, the cause should be removed. Lining the stable door with coconut matting is sometimes helpful.

DISTENSION OF THE TENDON SHEATHS OF THE EXTENSOR CARPI RADIALIS, THE COMMON DIGITAL EXTENSOR AND THE LATERAL DIGITAL EXTENSOR TENDONS

The tendons of the extensor carpi radialis, the common digital extensor and the lateral digital extensor muscles pass over the front of the knee. These tendons are each enclosed in a tendon sheath. Inflammation of the tendon sheath (tenosynovitis) causes production of excess synovial fluid and long tubular swellings around the tendon. Inflammation is usually the result of direct trauma. These swellings must be differentiated from the more diffuse swelling of a hygroma. Lameness can occur but is rare unless there is tendon damage or adhesions develop within the sheath. Treatment is usually unnecessary but some swelling is likely to persist.

Conditions of the Elbow

With the exclusion of capped elbow (a cosmetic blemish which does not cause lameness), fractures of the olecranon and radial nerve paralysis, problems involving the elbow are extremely rare. Lameness associated with the elbow causes a similar type of lameness to shoulder lameness and the two are difficult to differentiate.

Functional anatomy

The elbow joint is a simple ginglymus or hinge joint. The main part of the joint is the articulation of the humerus with the radius. The ulna in the horse is not exactly similar to that in man. It lies on the back of the elbow joint and its upward projection, the olecranon, forms the point of elbow. The ulna fuses with the back of the radius and does not extend beyond the top half of the radius although a separate vestigial lower remnant is sometimes seen. The joint is supported on the inside and outside by the medial and lateral collateral ligaments.

CAPPED ELBOW (see also p. 207)

Capped elbow is the name applied to an acquired bursa on the point of the elbow. It develops due to repetitive trauma, such as the heel of the front shoe

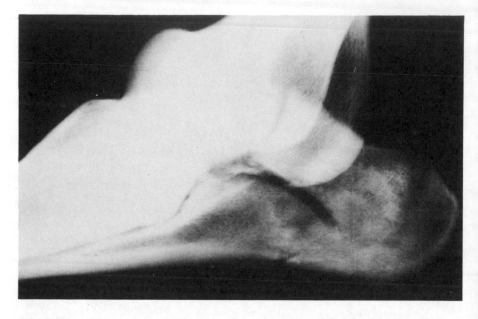

Figure 67   A simple displaced fracture of the olecranon of the ulna involving the elbow joint, sustained as the result of a kick. The fracture was treated successfully by reduction and internal fixation using a contoured bone plate

pressing on the elbow when the horse is lying down. Although it may be unsightly, it is of no real clinical significance.

Application of a sausage boot around the pastern should prevent the heel of the shoe and the elbow coming into contact.

FRACTURE OF THE OLECRANON

Fractures of the olecranon of the ulna usually occur as the result of direct trauma, such as a kick or a fall, but sometimes occur spontaneously.

Clinical signs

One of the principal extensor muscles of the upper forelimb is the triceps muscle which attaches to the top of the olecranon. If the olecranon is fractured, the function of this muscle is compromised and the horse will tend to stand with the limb semi-flexed and the elbow dropped. The limb is advanced with difficulty. There may be audible or palpable crepitus (grating of the bones), and manipulation of the elbow causes pain.

Diagnosis and treatment

Diagnosis is confirmed by radiographic examination.

Although some simple, nondisplaced fractures of the olecranon heal spontaneously with box rest, surgical stabilization of the fracture is the treatment of choice. Single fractures warrant an optimistic prognosis. If there are many bone fragments, the prognosis is poor.

RADIAL NERVE PARALYSIS   See p. 230.

Conditions of the Shoulder

Although, in the absence of any obvious swellings or areas of heat or pain in the lower leg, the shoulder is often incriminated as the cause of lameness, genuine shoulder lameness in the horse is comparatively rare.

Functional anatomy

The scapula (shoulderblade) and the humerus form the shoulder joint, which is a ball and socket joint, which principally flexes and extends but can also rotate. Unlike other joints, the shoulder joint has no collateral ligaments and support is provided by muscles which cross the inside and outside of the joint. In contrast to man, the horse does not have a collarbone. The foreleg is attached to the rest of the body by the serratus muscles, which attach to the lower neck and side of the chest and to the inside of the scapula.

SHOULDER LAMENESS

Most horses with a genuine shoulder lameness exhibit a gait with certain characteristics. The horse tries to limit the amount of movement of the joint by taking a much shorter stride. The flight of the foot is lower than normal to avoid flexion of the shoulder and the horse may drag the toe as the leg is advanced. There is a marked lift of the head as the lame leg is advanced, resulting in a very obvious head lift and nod. The horse is often lamer with the affected leg to the outside of a circle, especially in soft going. Because the horse is not using the leg normally, the muscles over the shoulderblade may become atrophied (wasted).

OSTEOCHONDROSIS (see also p. 173)

Osteochondrosis is a developmental abnormality of cartilage and bone and one of the most common sites is the shoulder joint. The condition affects either the scapula or the humerus or both.

Clinical signs

The disease is most often seen in young (six months to two years of age), rapidly growing horses, especially, in Great Britain, in Thoroughbreds. In the early stages the lameness is often intermittent and variable in severity.

When the lameness is moderate to severe the gait abnormality is characteristic of shoulder lameness. The muscles over the affected shoulder tend to atrophy.

Diagnosis

In some instances it is necessary to use local anaesthesia to confirm the source of pain, but in most young horses the history and clinical signs are suggestive of the condition, which is confirmed by radiography. Although using very powerful equipment, radiographs of the shoulder may be obtained with the horse standing, it is sometimes necessary to anaesthetize horses to obtain good-quality pictures. The condition may be bilateral and both shoulders should be radiographed routinely.

Treatment

Without treatment the disease usually deteriorates and secondary joint disease develops, resulting in permanent lameness. A small number of horses have been treated surgically with encouraging results.

FRACTURE OF THE SUPRAGLENOID TUBERCLE

The supraglenoid tubercle is a large bony projection on the front of the lower end of the scapula, to which is attached the biceps brachii muscle. This muscle is a powerful flexor muscle of the elbow and its downward pull tends to displace fractures of the supraglenoid tubercle. The fractures are usually the result of a fall on the shoulder or a collision with either another horse or a solid object such as a gatepost.

Clinical signs

There is usually considerable soft-tissue swelling over the front of the shoulder and typical shoulder lameness. The swelling dissipates fairly rapidly and the lameness often improves significantly within seven to ten days so that a fracture is not suspected. Muscle atrophy over the shoulderblade may develop rapidly due to concurrent damage of the suprascapular nerve.

Diagnosis and treatment

Diagnosis is confirmed by radiographic examination.

These fractures have a poor prognosis because the fracture usually enters the joint surface of the scapula, and the fracture fragment becomes displaced forwards and downwards because of the strong pull of the biceps muscle. Conservative treatment of box rest usually produces improvement, but the horse rarely becomes sound. Surgical treatment by stabilization of the fracture has had poor results.

FRACTURE OF THE SCAPULA See p. 167.

FRACTURE OF THE HUMERUS See p. 167.

BRUISING OF THE SHOULDER REGION

Because of its prominent position the shoulder region is extremely prone to severe bruising due to a kick or a fall or a similar accident.

Clinical signs

The clinical signs can be extremely difficult to differentiate from those of a fracture of the supraglenoid tubercle (i.e. a severe shoulder-type lameness) and it is often necessary to obtain radiographs to exclude the possibility of the latter. The horse often remains very lame for weeks and then starts to make a rapid improvement.

Treatment

Ultrasound treatment is useful in the early stages, together with anti-inflammatory analgesic drugs to help to reduce the swelling and pain. Subsequent faradic treatment can help to prevent muscle atrophy due to disuse. Muscle atrophy may occur due to concurrent damage to the suprascapular nerve (sweeny).

The long-term prognosis is usually good.

INERTUBERCULAR (BICIPITAL) BURSITIS See p. 207.

MUSCLE STRAIN

Due to an abnormal step or exertion, a horse can strain muscles in the shoulder region, principally the triceps muscles, the brachiocephalicus muscle (a muscle at the base of the neck) and the pectoral muscles.

Clinical signs

Depending on the severity of the muscle strain, the horse will show a variable degree of lameness, which is often worse as the horse moves on uneven ground, on soft surfaces or up or down a gradient.

Diagnosis and treatment

Palpation and manipulation of the forelimb may enable a painful focus to be detected. Faradic stimulation is helpful.

Treatment consisting of rest and faradism, followed by a controlled exercise programme, usually results in a successful outcome.

SWEENY   See p. 229.

INSTABILITY OF THE SHOULDER JOINT   See p. 230.

NECK INJURIES (see also p. 266)

Occasionally injuries to the lower neck can cause forelimb lameness.

Conditions of the Hock

Functional anatomy

The tarsus or hock is not a simple joint, but consists of several joints. The largest joint, the tarsocrural (tibiotarsal) or true hock joint, is the top joint and is the articulation between the tibia and the talus (tibiotarsal bone). This is where most of the flexion of the hock occurs. Adjacent to the talus is the

Figure 68a/b   The bones, joints and principal ligaments of the tarsus (hock)

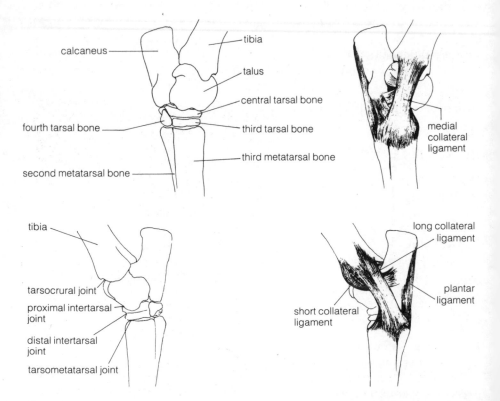

calcaneus (fibular tarsal bone). It is this bone which forms the point of the hock. There are two layers of small hock bones. The joint between the talus and calcaneus and the first row of small hock bones is the proximal intertarsal joint. The next joint, between the two rows of small hock bones, is the centrodistal (distal intertarsal) joint. The bottom row of hock bones articulates with the cannon and splint (metatarsal) bones at the tarso-metatarsal joint. Even in the normal horse little movement occurs in the three lower joints, the proximal and distal intertarsal and the tarsometa-tarsal joints. There are several strong collateral ligaments on the inside and outside of the hock which attach to the tibia and the next row of bones, the talus and calcaneus. There is a broad plantar ligament which attaches to the back of the fibular tarsal bone. There are several small ligaments which attach to the small hock bones.

SECONDARY (DEGENERATIVE) JOINT DISEASE (OSTEOARTHRITIS) OF THE HOCK (BONE SPAVIN)

Bone spavin is the colloquial term for degenerative joint disease or osteoarthritis of the hock. It is one of the most common causes of hind-limb lameness in the horse. Just as the hip joint of man is prone to development of osteoarthritis, the hock of the horse is similarly predisposed. That there are different predilection sites is probably attributable to the upright posture of man and the four-legged position of the horse. Bone spavin commonly affects the centrodistal (distal intertarsal) and tarsometatarsal joints and only occasionally involves the proximal intertarsal joint.

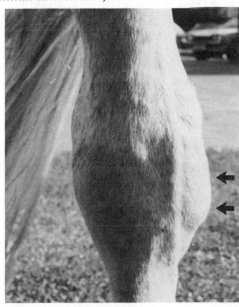

Figure 69 Firm swelling (arrow) on the inside of the right hock associated with bone spavin

Clinical signs

Because the disease is often bilateral, that is, affects both hind legs, one of the common presenting signs is a generalized hind-limb stiffness which is often worse when the horse first comes out of the stable and then improves with exercise. It is usually more obvious in horses that do some form of dressage or flat work, because lack of hind-limb impulsion is more readily apparent under these circumstances than when hacking. The horse may take a few unlevel steps, especially when moving in small circles. He may find it difficult to maintain a regular rhythm in lateral work, tending to hop. Frequently when working in medium and extended paces, the horse may lose rhythm or take obvious lame steps or break stride. There are many reasons for these symptoms – inadequate training, lack of suppleness, insufficient preparation for the movement – but if there is no good explanation, slight lameness may be the cause. If the horse is a jumper, he may start to stop uncharacteristic-ally. Sometimes, because the horse is not pushing properly from behind, he appears rather restricted overall and the problem is wrongly attributed to back trouble. Many horses with a hind-limb lameness will develop back muscle soreness secondarily to an abnormal way of moving.

If the problem is unilateral or one leg is affected worse than the other, then the first sign may be obvious hind-limb lameness. This can be gradual or sudden in onset. If it develops gradually, the hindquarters may appear asymmetrical with the muscles on the affected side less well developed because the horse has been favouring the leg.

Although not characteristic of all horses with spavin, the limb flight may be altered so that, as the affected leg is brought forward in trot, it deviates in underneath the body and is then stabbed outwards as it comes to the ground. This results in excessive wear of the outside branch of the shoe. The stiff-legged horse tends to drag the toes, which causes abnormal wear of the toes of the feet and shoes. Toe-dragging is a feature not only of spavin: lameness associated with the stifle or hip joints can cause a toe-drag; many young horses drag the hind toes, particularly if unfit; and toe-dragging may just reflect laziness. With spavin, restricted flexibility of the hind limb or resentment of flexion may be noticed first by the farrier. The horse may be reluctant to hold the leg hyperflexed for a long time.

Some horses develop a swelling on the inside of the hock at the so-called seat of spavin. This is at the level of the distal intertarsal and tarsometatarsal joints. Although the swelling feels very hard, it is not bony, but is a fibrous reaction around the joints.

Diagnosis

A history of hind-limb stiffness improving to an extent with exercise, or of hind-limb lameness characterized by stiffness and dragging of the toe is suggestive of bone spavin. Spavin is one of the most frequent cases of a hind-limb disability in the horse. Swelling on the inside of the hock and abnormal wear of the shoes are useful indicators. Careful observation of the horse moving may give additional clues. It is useful to watch the horse on a hard surface such as a driveway or road. Then subtle abnormalities in the limb flight and unevenness in stride length may be detected. It is easiest to appreciate slight irregularities in rhythm by listening to the horse, as well as looking at him. A slight, intermittent toe-drag may be heard more easily than seen. In some instances lameness may be more apparent when the horse moves in circles rather than in straight lines – either with the affected leg on the outside or on the inside. This is particularly so in deep going.

Lameness associated with spavin is accentuated by prolonged flexion of the leg in most horses, although failure to react to the spavin test does not preclude this diagnosis. The spavin test is performed by holding the leg in maximal flexion underneath the body for at least a minute, and then trotting the horse and reassessing the lameness. Although called the spavin test, it is nonspecific because it is impossible to flex the hock without also flexing the stifle and hip joints. Prolonged hyperflexion of the leg will stress all these joints and can accentuate the lameness associated with any of them. Whenever doing the spavin test, it is important to assess the reaction of both legs. It is best to test the sounder leg first because, if the lame leg is flexed first, lameness may be accentuated to such an extent and for so long a time that it is then difficult to interpret the reaction to flexion of the sounder leg. Occasionally, after prolonged flexion of one leg, the horse will show increased lameness on the other leg, due to having borne more weight than usual on that leg.

Radiographic examination

Because the disease is often bilateral, although obvious lameness may only be seen in one leg, it is advisable to have a radiographic examination of both hocks.

Degenerative joint disease starts as a disease of the articular cartilage and only later progresses to involve the underlying bone. Cartilage cannot be seen on radiographs. It appears as a black line between adjacent bones – the joint space. In the early stages of bone spavin radiographs of the affected hock may look normal, but this does not necessarily mean that the joints are normal. In the normal horse the joint spaces are readily seen as black lines. The bones have a clear outline with no fuzziness. The corners of the bones are square or slightly rounded. The bones are of fairly uniform whiteness.

As the disease progresses the joint spaces may become narrower or even completely obliterated, due to destruction of the articular cartilage which normally fills the space between adjacent bones. Nature appears to try to stabilize the affected joints by producing new bone to bridge the joints. This can be seen either as bone spurs (osteophytes), which are smoothly outlined projections of bone, or as irregularly outlined, fuzzy periosteal new bone. The destructive part of the disease may progress to involve the bones as well

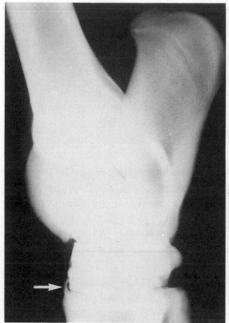 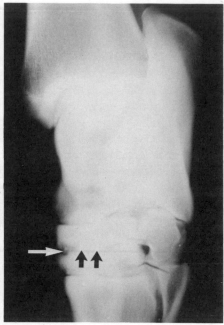

Figure 70 A side radiographic view of a hock with degenerative joint disease of the tarsometatarsal joint (bone spavin). There is a large bone spur (arrow) on the top of the third metatarsal (cannon) bone, bridging the joint. The radiograph has been deliberately underexposed to highlight the bone spur which is less dense than the normal bone. Therefore the joint spaces cannot be seen

Figure 71 An oblique radiographic view of a hock with degenerative joint disease of the distal intertarsal joint (bone spavin). The distal intertarsal joint is partly fused (black arrows). There is some bone destruction (white arrow)

as the cartilage, and black areas become apparent in the normally white bone. All these changes are typical of degenerative joint disease (bone spavin). In some horses an end stage is reached. The joint spaces are completely obliterated and the bones look fused. At this stage the horse is usually sound again. Nature, by fusing the bones, has removed the source of pain.

The correlation between clinical signs and radiographic changes is often poor. The horse may be very lame but show minimal radiographic changes. Similarly radiographic changes may be very extensive but be associated with only slight lameness.

Nerve blocks

In some horses the history and clinical signs do not clearly indicate a hock problem. In other horses with typical clinical signs the radiographs may not confirm the suspected diagnosis. In these situations it is necessary to use local anaesthesia to define the source of pain. This can be done in one of two ways. Either local anaesthetic may be infiltrated over the nerves which convey sensation from the hock region, effectively numbing the area, or local anaesthetic may be placed directly into the suspected joints. The latter is more specific but much more difficult.

In most cases the lameness is improved but only rarely can it be eliminated totally by nerve blocks. It is therefore important that the horse is showing a sufficient degree of lameness, so that improvement can be appreciated. If the horse is only marginally lame, interpretation of the nerve block is extremely difficult. Therefore, although superficially it may seem contraindicated to work a lame horse, in some instances it is necessary to do so in order to accentuate or maintain the same level of lameness, so that a diagnosis may be reached.

Treatment

The end stage of the disease is functional fusion of the affected joints. In some horses this occurs spontaneously, but it is impossible to tell in which horses it will happen or how long it might take. If an affected horse is rested, the clinical signs usually subside, but they tend to recur when work is resumed. The degenerative changes progress fairly slowly. Treatment aims to accelerate the degenerative changes in order to achieve effective stabilization of the joints. Fortunately most of the flexion of the hock occurs in the tarsocrural joint, which is unaffected in this condition. Therefore, even if the affected joints do fuse, the ultimate flexibility of the leg should not be compromised unduly.

One method of accelerating the degenerative changes is to maintain the horse in work, while judiciously treating it with a painkilling drug, such as phenylbutazone, to enable it to work sound. This is satisfactory provided that the horse is not too lame. It is not possible to predict for how long medication will be required – it may be for years. The toxic effects of phenylbutazone in the horse are much less than in man and many horses have been maintained on continuous treatment with phenylbutazone for months or even years without any untoward effects. A few horses do not tolerate the drug and develop soft faeces or diarrhoea quite quickly. Other horses will not eat the drug. It can be disguised by mixing it with milk of magnesia and injecting it into the mouth by syringe, but some horses become wise to this trick.

Many horses are helped additionally by appropriate shoeing. The foot should be trimmed as short as possible and the toe of the shoe rolled in order to help the foot break over. Shoeing the horse with a flat shoe, with an extension on the outside heel, an outside trailer, helps to widen the gait of affected horses and improve the lameness.

The type of work which the horse does can be important. Excessive hill work or deep going may aggravate the problem. Controlled exercise may be better than turning out. An over-exuberant horse which bucks and races round and stops suddenly in the field may twist the joints and accentuate the lameness. A careful, slow, progressive warm-up programme is probably important. Thus if treatment by work and painkilling (analgesic) medication is adopted, then the work programme should be planned carefully and corrective shoeing performed concurrently.

An alternative treatment is to inject the affected joints with an anti-inflammatory corticosteroid drug. The use of corticosteroids in joints is usually contraindicated, because these drugs accelerate cartilage degradation, and thus in other locations will aggravate the disease long term, but in this instance destruction of the cartilage is beneficial. There are several problems associated with this treatment. The joint spaces are very small, and it is not at all easy to insert a needle accurately into the joints in order to administer the drug. The effects of the treatment are usually temporary and repeated injections may be necessary several times each year. Nevertheless this can be a useful method of treatment.

If the horse fails to respond to conservative treatment or is very lame, then surgical treatment may help. Again the aim of treatment is to destroy some of the articular cartilage to try to accelerate fusion of the joint. In practice it seems that removal of approximately 40 per cent of the articular cartilage is optimal. This is achieved by inserting a drill into each of the affected joints and drilling out several tracks of cartilage. Like most orthopaedic operations in the horse, it is not uniformly successful. Approximately 60 per cent of treated horses respond favourably, becoming sound within six to twelve months of surgery. Some exercise post-operatively is beneficial, and again phenylbutazone is a useful painkiller to use in the interim period, before the horse becomes sound.

In association with degenerative joint disease the pressure within the bones on either side of the joint may be elevated and this can cause pain. Recently a new surgical technique has been developed which involves drilling holes into the bones in order to reduce the raised subchondral bone pressure. Early results have been encouraging.

Occasionally the proximal intertarsal joint is involved. This warrants a very poor prognosis regardless of treatment because this joint communicates with the tarsocrural or true hock joint, where most flexion occurs. Inflammation in the proximal intertarsal joint induces inflammation in the tarsocrural joint, causing persistent lameness.

ENLARGEMENT OF THE TARSOCRURAL (TIBIOTARSAL) JOINT CAPSULE (BOG SPAVIN)

Distension of the joint capsule of the tarsocrural (tibiotarsal, true hock) joint is colloquially called 'bog spavin'. It results in a soft, fluctuant swelling on the inside front aspect of the hock and another swelling, slightly higher, on the outside of the hock. If pressure is applied to one of these swellings, the other one is seen to enlarge because they represent outpouchings of a single joint capsule. The condition is often seen, either unilaterally or bilaterally, in big-jointed young horses. It does not cause lameness and usually resolves spontaneously. It is also seen in older horses and rarely causes lameness.

If the horse is lame in association with a bog spavin, then the hock should be radiographed. Horses with osteochondrosis (see pp. 173 and 200) usually develop distension of the tarsocrural joint capsule and there may or may not be associated lameness. Horses with degenerative joint disease (bone spavin) of the proximal intertarsal joint (see p. 199) can have a bog spavin. The proximal intertarsal and tarsocrural joints communicate, and degenerative joint disease in the former can incite inflammation in the latter and therefore distension of the joint capsule.

If the hock is severely twisted and sprained there is usually not only distension of the tarsocrural joint capsule but also more extensive soft-tissue swelling.

SPRAIN OF THE HOCK JOINT

Clinical signs

There is a sudden onset of lameness associated with soft-tissue swelling and usually some heat around the hock. Flexion of the hock may be resented and will accentuate the lameness. Lameness may be very severe.

Diagnosis

The clinical signs are fairly typical and, especially if there is a known history of trauma, further diagnostic tests are unnecessary unless the horse is very lame. Then the possibilities of a fracture or infection of the joint must be excluded by radiographs and by analysis of a sample of synovial (joint) fluid.

Treatment

Rest is mandatory. Initially anti-inflammatory analgesic drugs and ultra-sound treatment can be beneficial. When the horse starts to improve, controlled exercise is useful. If marked lameness persists, then follow-up radiographs should be obtained at intervals to see whether any bony proliferations have developed at the site of ligamentous attachments. This would indicate severe ligamentous damage requiring a more prolonged recovery time. If the joint has been very severely sprained, secondary degenerative joint disease (bone spavin) may supervene.

Prognosis

The prognosis depends on the severity of the initial injury. Frequently a degree of swelling persists, due to some thickening and fibrosis of the joint capsule.

CURB See p. 223.

DISPLACEMENT (LUXATION) OF THE SUPERFICIAL DIGITAL FLEXOR TENDON   See p. 220.

THOROUGHPIN See p. 210.

FRACTURES

Clinical signs

There is a sudden onset of severe hind-limb lameness. The horse is reluctant to bear weight on the leg and resents flexion of the hock. There is usually some soft-tissue swelling.

Diagnosis

Because of the complex structure of the normal hock joint, multiple, high-quality radiographs may be necessary to identify a fracture.

Treatment

Most fractures warrant a guarded prognosis for future soundness. Small fractures originating from the bottom outside and inside parts (lateral malleolus and medial malleolus) of the tibia usually have a fair prognosis and, depending on the size of the fracture and its degree of displacement, can be treated either by rest alone or by surgical removal of the fragment. Slab fracture of the central or third tarsal bone can sometimes be treated successfully by internal fixation.

OSTEOCHONDROSIS (see also p. 173)

The tarsocrural (true hock) joint is a common site for osteochondrosis in the horse.

Clinical signs

There is usually moderate to marked distension of the tarsocrural joint capsule (bog spavin). The horse may be lame or sound. If lame, the lameness can be accentuated by flexion of the joint. The condition may be unilateral or bilateral.

Diagnosis

Diagnosis is by radiographic examination. There are several sites at which osteochondrosis occurs in the hock – at the lower end of the tibia and on the trochlear ridges of the talus (tibiotarsal bone).

Treatment

Osteochondrosis of the lower end of the tibia can be an incidental radiographic abnormality, unassociated with lameness, in which case no treatment is indicated. Even if the separated bone fragment is removed, a bog spavin usually persists, causing a cosmetic blemish. Osteochondrosis of the trochlear ridges of the talus often causes lameness. Surgical treatment offers a fair prognosis for future soundness although a bog spavin may remain.

COLLAPSE OF THE THIRD AND/OR CENTRAL TARSAL BONES See p. 291.

Conditions of the Stifle

Functional anatomy

Four bones form the stifle joint: the femur, the tibia, the fibula and the patella (kneecap). The major bones of this hinge joint are the femur and the tibia. In the middle of this joint and attached to these two bones are the cruciate ligaments. Two small cartilages, the menisci, are also interposed between the joint surfaces of the two bones. The fibula is a small bone situated on the outside of the tibia and has little function. It is often formed from two or more separate ossification centres which sometimes never unite and this should not be confused with a fracture. The patella slides up and down the bottom end of the femur over the trochlear ridges. It is a sesamoid bone in the quadriceps muscle and its smooth movement depends upon normal function and strength of the muscle. Attached to the inside of the patella is a large cartilaginous extension. Three ligaments, the medial, middle and lateral patellar ligaments, run from the bottom of the patella to

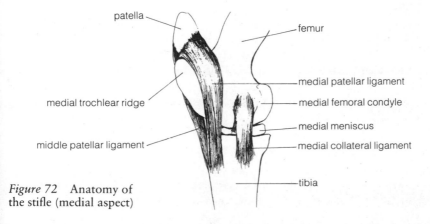

Figure 72 Anatomy of the stifle (medial aspect)

the tibia. This unique arrangement of the patellar cartilage and ligaments allows the horse to hook the patella over the top of the trochlear ridges of the femur and fix the stifle in extension. This means that the horse can stand with little muscular effort, so can sleep standing up. The stifle joint cannot flex independently of the hock because of another unique arrangement of muscles and tendons, the reciprocal apparatus, so stifle and hock lameness can appear similar.

INTERMITTENT UPWARD FIXATION OR DELAYED RELEASE OF THE PATELLA

Clinical signs

The clinical signs depend on the severity of the condition, which occurs most often in young horses and ponies, especially those which are unfit and poorly muscled. In the most severe cases the leg becomes stuck in extension and the patella is 'locked'. The horse may hop on three legs, dragging the affected leg behind it. The horse may release itself spontaneously. Some horses remain unable to flex the leg and it may be necessary to force the horse either to back or to jump forward in order to release the patella, which has become effectively stuck on the upper part of the trochlear ridges of the femur. This may happen intermittently several times a day, especially if the horse is kept in. One or both hind legs may be affected.

In less severe cases the patella moves jerkily and its release from the position when the leg is extended is slightly delayed. This may be most obvious as the horse walks up or down a slope or when pushed sideways. If moved over in the box, the horse may move the leg very stiffly. It may find it difficult to make smooth downward transitions from trot to walk and the back legs may appear slightly uncoordinated and jerky.

It is usually not a painful condition and the horse is not as such lame.

Treatment

In many horses and ponies the condition appears to be related to poor muscular tone of the quadriceps muscles. If the horse is kept in work and got fitter, the condition frequently improves and with enough time disappears completely. Hill work is particularly beneficial, as are long, slow canters. Work in straight lines is often preferable to work in circles. Some people feel that elevation of the heels of the hind feet with special wedge-heeled shoes is helpful, but the author has not found this to be particularly useful.

In horses and ponies which fail to respond to conservative treatment a simple surgical procedure, cutting the medial patellar ligament, usually effects a cure. There are potential complications of this procedure and the author feels that it should be reserved for those horses for whom regular work has failed to produce adequate improvement.

CONGENITAL LUXATION OF THE PATELLA

This is a rare condition in which the patella slips sideways (usually outwards). In some cases the lateral trochlear ridge of the femur is unusually small and this predisposes to abnormal movement of the patella. The signs are usually present at birth. The foal finds extreme difficulty in standing because it is unable to straighten the hind limb(s) and squats with all the joints of the hind limb(s) flexed. The patella can be felt unusually positioned towards the outside of the joint.

If the lateral trochlear ridge is unusually small, the prognosis is poor. If there is no identifiable underlying bony abnormality surgery may be successful. A tuck is placed in the joint capsule of the femoropatellar joint to stabilize the patella.

OSTEOCHONDROSIS (see also p. 173)

The lateral trochlear ridge of the femur is one of the most common sites for osteochondrosis.

Clinical signs

The condition is usually seen in young horses (six months to three years old) but is occasionally identified in older horses. There is marked distension of the femoropatellar (stifle) joint capsule and slight to moderate lameness characterized by a stiff limb flight, lowered arc of flight of the foot with or without an intermittent toe-drag. Lameness may be accentuated by flexion of the limb. The condition may be unilateral or bilateral. Young horses with both stifles affected may become slightly roach-backed and have difficulties in getting up after lying down.

Diagnosis

Diagnosis is confirmed by radiographic examination.

Treatment

Without treatment lameness usually persists. Provided that the lesions are not too severe, surgery is generally successful.

SUBCHONDRAL BONE CYST (see also p. 174)

The stifle joint is a common location for subchondral bone cysts, which almost invariably occur at the point of maximum weightbearing in the lower end of the inside of the femur, the medial femoral condyle. They occur most often in young horses when first starting serious work, but are also found in older horses.

Clinical signs

The horse shows a sudden onset of a variable degree of lameness. The lameness may be extremely subtle or very severe. The horse usually improves with box rest but the lameness recurs when work is resumed. There is only slight distension of the stifle joint capsule, if any.

Diagnosis

It is often necessary to exclude other potential sites of lameness first by nerve blocks. Diagnosis is confirmed by radiographs.

Treatment

Prolonged rest (six to nine months) results in soundness in approximately 60 per cent of horses. In horses which fail to respond to rest surgery can be performed with a fair prognosis.

SPRAIN OF THE STIFLE JOINT

Clinical signs

There is a sudden onset of lameness associated with some swelling of the stifle joint capsule.

Diagnosis and treatment

Diagnosis is based on the clinical signs.

Treatment consisting of rest usually resolves the lameness. The duration of rest depends on the severity of the initial injury. If lameness persists, the stifle should be radiographed. If there has been severe ligamentous damage, there may be detached bony fragments at the site of ligamentous attachment or a bone spur. These warrant a poor prognosis.

FRACTURE   See p. 170.

BRUISING OF THE STIFLE REGION

Bruising of the stifle region is a common injury either as a result of a kick or hitting a fixed fence when jumping. The latter is a common injury of event horses.

Clinical signs

There is a variable degree of swelling and lameness.

Treatment

Anti-inflammatory analgesic drugs are extremely helpful in reducing swelling and removing pain. Plenty of slow exercise prevents the horse from becoming excessively stiff, so if it can be turned out in a small paddock or walked in hand regularly, this is helpful.

Provided that there is no underlying bony damage the prognosis is good. If the horse does not improve rapidly the stifle should be examined radiographically. A fracture of the patella or other bony damage might otherwise be missed.

14
BURSAE, TENDONS AND LIGAMENTS

BURSAE (TRUE BURSAE) AND TENDON SHEATHS

Bursae

Bursae are sacs lined by a synovial membrane. They contain synovial fluid. They are found over bony prominences and facilitate the movement of tendons or muscles over the bony protrusion. These are the so-called true bursae; they have standard anatomical locations and are present in all horses. They may become enlarged and/or inflamed, resulting in swelling with or without pain and lameness.

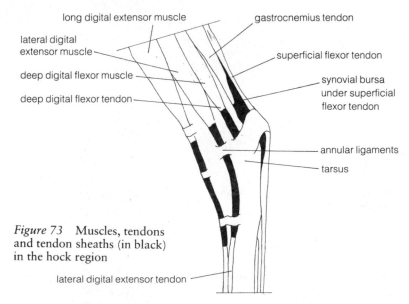

long digital extensor muscle

gastrocnemius tendon

lateral digital extensor muscle

superficial flexor tendon

deep digital flexor muscle

synovial bursa under superficial flexor tendon

deep digital flexor tendon

annular ligaments

tarsus

Figure 73 Muscles, tendons and tendon sheaths (in black) in the hock region

lateral digital extensor tendon

Conditions of Bursae

INTERTUBERCULAR (BICIPITAL) BURSITIS

There is a bursa over the front of the top of the humerus through which passes the tendon of origin of the biceps muscle. This bursa may become inflamed, resulting in severe lameness and a reluctance to advance the limb. Rest and administration of an anti-inflammatory drug is usually successful, but sometimes lameness persists despite treatment.

TROCHANTERIC BURSITIS

There is a bursa over the greater trochanter of the femur, a bony protuberance close to the hip joint. Inflammation of the bursa may cause hind-limb lameness. In the author's experience the condition is very difficult to diagnose and occurs rarely. There is said to be a high incidence in Standardbred trotters and pacers.

ACQUIRED OR FALSE BURSAE

Acquired or false bursae are synovia-filled sacs which develop as a result of repetitive low-grade trauma. They are not present in all horses and usually result in a cosmetic blemish but rarely cause lameness. Common examples are a capped hock, a capped elbow and a hygroma (an acquired bursa over the front of the knee). Once acquired, these swellings persist and may become increasingly firm and fibrous, especially if the inciting cause remains.

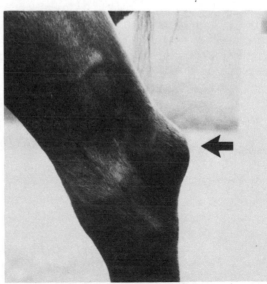

Figure 74 A capped hock (arrow). This is an acquired bursa which develops as a result of repetitive trauma to the point of hock. It is a cosmetic blemish which does not cause lameness

Treatment

There is no uniformly successful treatment and unless the horse is to be used for show purposes treatment is unnecessary. Removing fluid from the bursa, injection of a corticosteroid and application of a pressure bandage may result in temporary resolution of the swelling. Most of the acquired bursae occur in places which are either difficult to bandage or where repeated bandaging is likely to result in rub sores. Elasticated support bandages (Pressage bandages) are now available and are particularly good for the knee and hock. Some swellings remain permanently reduced but others recur. There are potential complications with injection of a long-acting corticosteroid. The drug is a potent anti-inflammatory agent and can depress the body's response to infection, thus, to minimize risk of infection, it is of paramount importance that strict aseptic techniques are employed when injecting this drug into a synovial structure. Calcification within the soft tissues may occur as a result of injection of a corticosteroid.

Irritating solutions such as concentrated iodine have been injected into false bursae, the aim being to destroy the lining membrane which produces synovial fluid and to encourage fibrosis and fusion of the walls of the sac. The results are unreliable. Surgical removal gives the best long-term result for a large false bursa.

Tendon Sheaths

Tendon sheaths are long sacs which are lined by a synovial membrane which secretes synovial fluid. They enclose part or all of a tendon. The fluid provides lubrication for the movement of the tendon. Inflammation of the synovial membrane may result in excessive accumulation of synovial fluid and swelling of the sheath. Tendinous windgalls and thoroughpin are common examples. The sheath may become permanently stretched so that the swelling persists, although there is no longer inflammation. The sheath itself can become thickened.

Conditions of Tendon Sheaths

TENDINOUS WINDGALLS

Tendinous windgalls are enlargements of the digital flexor tendon sheath. Although the sheath extends above and below the fetlock joint, swelling is usually confined to above the fetlock and does not cause lameness. The swelling occurs between the suspensory ligament and the flexor tendons and should be distinguished from distension of the fetlock joint capsule (articular windgall – see p. 174) which occurs between the back of the cannon

Figure 75 Normal forelimbs demonstrating clear demarcation between the cannon bone, suspensory ligament and the deep and superficial digital flexor tendons. The site of distension of the metacarpophalangeal (fetlock) joint capsule (an articular windgall) (closed arrow) between the cannon bone and the suspensory ligament and the site of distension of the digital flexor tendon sheath (a tendinous windgall) (open arrow) between the suspensory ligament and the digital flexor tendons are indicated

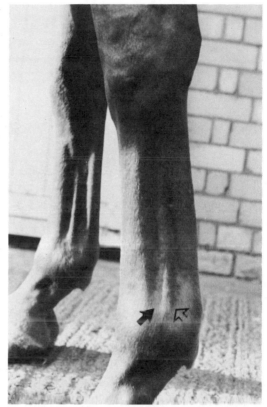

bone and the suspensory ligament. Windgalls occur in both front and hind legs and are often larger behind, especially in heavier types of horses. Although unsightly, these swellings rarely cause problems.

STRAIN OF THE DIGITAL FLEXOR TENDON SHEATH

Occasionally the digital flexor tendon sheath becomes suddenly very swollen and the horse is lame. The swelling occurs above the back of the fetlock, behind the suspensory ligament. This is due to an acute strain and inflammation of the tendon sheath, which can occur without damage to the flexor tendons contained within it. If the sheath is very swollen it may not be possible initially to detect whether or not one or both tendons have been damaged. This assessment can only be made when some of the swelling has subsided or by use of diagnostic ultrasound.

Treatment
Anti-inflammatory analgesic drugs, such as phenylbutazone, help to reduce the acute inflammation. Cold hosing for short periods is beneficial. The leg

should be kept bandaged and the horse box-rested for a minimum of ten to fourteen days. Although slight swelling of the sheath may persist, the horse may slowly resume work. Some horses have recurring problems if excessive pressure is applied to the sheath by an overtight bandage or boot. Occasionally fibrous adhesions develop within the sheath causing chronic lameness.

CONSTRICTION OF A TENDON SHEATH BY AN ANNULAR LIGAMENT

The annular ligament which passes around the back of the fetlock area can constrict the tendon sheath, resulting in a characteristic notching of the contour of the back of the fetlock. Fibrous adhesions may also form within the sheath, and both of these can cause lameness, which has to be treated surgically. If adhesions are present the prognosis is guarded.

THOROUGHPIN

A thoroughpin is an enlargement of the deep digital flexor tendon sheath above the hock and must be distinguished from distension of the hock (tarsocrural) joint capsule (bog spavin – see p. 198). The swelling of a thoroughpin is higher up and farther back and may be pressed from inside to

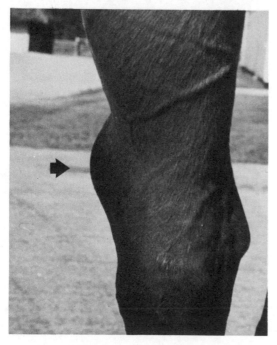

Figure 76 Soft, fluctuant swelling on the upper, outside aspect of the right hock (arrow). This is distension of the deep digital flexor tendon sheath: thoroughpin. The swelling is higher than a bog spavin

outside and vice versa. The swelling is usually innocuous and may resolve spontaneously. Topical application of a corticosteroid, dimethyl sulphoxide mixture, may speed its resolution. Drainage of excess synovial fluid and placement of corticosteroids within the sheath has proved successful for cosmetic results in more chronic cases. Occasionally lameness is associated with a thoroughpin. Radiograph views of the hock may show bony changes on the sustentaculum tali, over which the deep digital flexor tendon passes. This warrants a poor prognosis.

INFECTION OF A BURSA OR TENDON SHEATH

Infection of a bursa or tendon sheath is usually the result of a penetration wound, and, like an infection of a joint, is extremely difficult to treat unless recognized early. It can be helpful to clip in the region to identify the puncture wound. There is a hot, painful swelling and the synovial fluid is turbid. Treatment consists of the aggressive use of antibiotics combined with flushing the bursa or tendon sheath.

TENDONS AND LIGAMENTS
Tendons

Functional anatomy

Tendons attach muscles to bones and, in comparison to muscles, are relatively inelastic. The evolution of the horse has resulted in an animal which stands on its toes, with slender lower limbs. The bellies of the muscles which flex the lower joints of the legs are confined to the upper limbs, that is, above the knee and hock. The superficial and deep digital flexor tendons are long flattened cords of tissue, approximately oval in cross-section, which connect these muscle bellies to the middle (second) and distal (third) phalanges (short pastern bone and coffin bone). These tendons are covered only by skin and therefore are extremely susceptible to damage by a direct injury to the lower leg.

The structure of tendons is fairly complex (see Figure 79). Surrounding the tendon is a loose connective tissue sheath, the paratenon, and it is from this that blood vessels extend into the substance of the tendon itself. Contrary to popular belief, the tendon has a relatively good blood supply. It is subdivided into groups of fibres called fascicles, which are orientated in a longitudinal fashion, that is, in the direction of stress on the tendon. Within each fascicle the tendon fibres are arranged in parallel in a helical spiral. The fibres also exhibit 'crimp': rather than being straight, they bend in a regular zigzag pattern. This arrangement confers a degree of elasticity to the tendon. When the tendon is stretched, the crimp straightens, but it can resume its

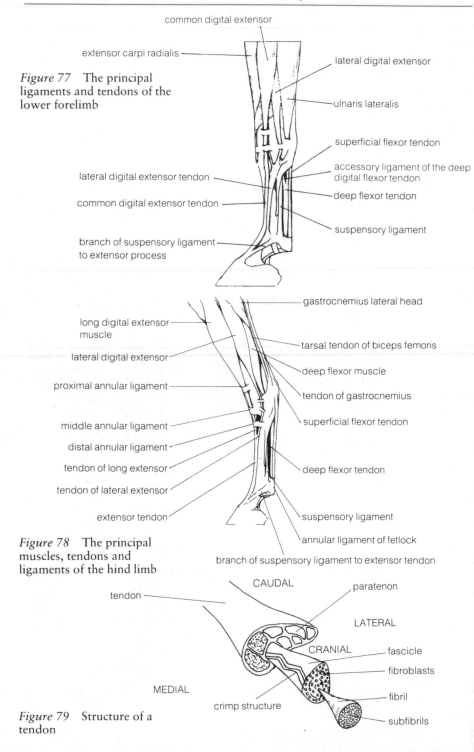

Figure 77 The principal ligaments and tendons of the lower forelimb

common digital extensor

extensor carpi radialis

lateral digital extensor

ulnaris lateralis

superficial flexor tendon

accessory ligament of the deep digital flexor tendon

deep flexor tendon

lateral digital extensor tendon

common digital extensor tendon

suspensory ligament

branch of suspensory ligament to extensor process

Figure 78 The principal muscles, tendons and ligaments of the hind limb

gastrocnemius lateral head

long digital extensor muscle

tarsal tendon of biceps femoris

lateral digital extensor

deep flexor muscle

proximal annular ligament

tendon of gastrocnemius

middle annular ligament

superficial flexor tendon

distal annular ligament

tendon of long extensor

deep flexor tendon

tendon of lateral extensor

extensor tendon

suspensory ligament

annular ligament of fetlock

branch of suspensory ligament to extensor tendon

Figure 79 Structure of a tendon

CAUDAL

paratenon

tendon

LATERAL

CRANIAL

fascicle

fibroblasts

MEDIAL

fibril

crimp structure

subfibrils

original form provided that the maximum safe load is not exceeded. The fibres can further be subdivided into bundles of collagen fibrils. Collagen is a protein produced by special cells, tendon fibroblasts. These cells are arranged in long columns, parallel to the fibrils. There are several types of collagen which are found in different tissues in the body. Normal tendon is composed of type 1 collagen, which is relatively elastic. Unfortunately, if the tendon is damaged, repair tissue is formed from relatively less strong type 3 collagen, thus creating a mechanically inferior structure which is susceptible to re-injury. It is the complex arrangement of the fibres within the tendon which confers strength and elasticity, and disruption of this arrangement compromises the function of the tendon.

Conditions of Tendons

There are a number of types of tendon injury, and they vary in their severity and the long-term consequences for the horse. Constriction of the tendon by an overtight bandage causes the classical 'bandage bow' – localized inflammation around and within the superficial digital flexor tendon.

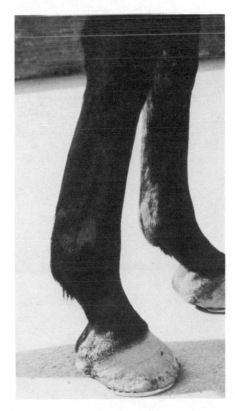

Figure 80 Typical appearance of an old, severely 'bowed', i.e. strained, superficial digital flexor tendon. The back of the leg above the fetlock has a convex contour instead of being straight

Inflammation results in the accumulation of fluid, causing swelling and distortion of the normal anatomical arrangement of fibrils within the tendon. Usually the fibrils are not themselves damaged, thus the long-term consequences for the horse are not serious, although a small, subtle swelling often persists at the site of injury.

A direct blow to the tendon is more serious because, although it is a relatively localized injury, there is usually rupture of some of the tendon fibrils and associated bleeding into the tendon. The fibrils will be repaired by mechanically inferior collagen, thus there is some potential for re-injury, although the prognosis is more favourable for this type of injury than for tendon strain.

In a strained tendon the normal pattern of fibrils and fibres is disturbed and some of the fibrils rupture. In more serious cases fibres or complete fascicles of fibres may be damaged. Occasionally the entire tendon is completely separated. There is bleeding into the tendon and accumulation of inflammatory fluid, which contains enzymes which may cause further damage to the collagen fibrils.

Incidence of tendon strain

The flexor tendons of the forelegs are strained much more often than those of the hind legs. In the forelegs the superficial digital flexor tendon is much more frequently injured than the deep digital flexor tendon. The most common site of injury is the middle of the superficial digital flexor tendon. The tendon has its smallest area of cross-section in this region, therefore the stress on the tendon per unit area is highest. Back-at-the-knee conformation and hyperextension of the fetlock joint associated with a long sloping pastern probably place additional stresses on the tendon, predisposing to injury.

Tendon strain is definitely an occupational hazard of moving at speed, especially if combined with jumping. Thus hunter-chasers, point-to-pointers and event horses are particularly prone. When a muscle becomes fatigued it contracts and relaxes less efficiently. Lack of complete muscular co-ordination means that the forces applied to the tendon may be more sudden in onset than usual and may not be transmitted evenly through the tendon, resulting in injury. Similarly a sudden change in the going or placing the foot on uneven ground can put abnormal stresses on the tendon.

Clinical signs

Haemorrhage into the tendon and accumulation of inflammatory fluid cause considerable swelling and pain. In the acute stage the degree and extent of swelling usually reflect accurately the severity of the injury. Careful palpation of the tendon with the leg both weightbearing and non-weightbearing enables an experienced clinician to determine the amount of damage. When non-weightbearing, the normal tendon feels firm; damaged tendon feels slightly softer. Once the initial acute reaction has subsided, it is very much more difficult to assess the nature and extent of damage; therefore veterinary advice should be sought as soon as possible in order to obtain an accurate prognosis. It is important to differentiate between minor tendon strain and damage due to localized trauma. Sometimes the swelling associated with a tendon injury is very extensive and it is not possible to define precisely which structures are involved. It is necessary to initiate treatment in order to reduce the swelling before an accurate diagnosis can be made unless diagnostic ultrasound is available.

Significant tendon damage can be present *without* lameness. In the early stage of tendon injury the amount of swelling may be slight. Usually the vein on the inside of the leg is enlarged. A few days' rest and application of cold may resolve these clinical signs temporarily, but when work is resumed the problem is likely to recur and deteriorate. These early signs must not be ignored. It is important to know exactly what your horse's legs look and feel like, and subtle changes must be noticed and appropriate action taken if more serious damage is to be avoided. The most accurate method of assessing whether or not there is damage to a tendon is by an ultrasound scan. This produces images of the tendons and even very small areas of damage can be detected. The extent of the injury and its severity can be assessed and, by sequential scanning, healing can be monitored. If there is any doubt about the significance of slight swelling in the region of a tendon the author strongly recommends that an ultrasound scan should be performed. It must be remembered that tendon strains often do not cause lameness unless very severe, therefore small swellings should not be ignored just because the horse appears sound.

Treatment of an acute injury

Treatment of an acute tendon injury aims to relieve swelling as soon as possible in order to restore normal alignment of the tendon fibrils, to minimize the inflammatory reaction and to relieve pain. Movement should be limited to prevent further injury. Cold compresses, in the form of ice packs bandaged to the leg, should be reset at frequent intervals. Intravenous injection of the anti-inflammatory analgesic drug phenylbutazone will help both to minimize inflammation and to relieve pain. The more rapidly the soft-tissue swelling is resolved the better the final functional and cosmetic results are likely to be. Careful use of therapeutic ultrasound can be very effective in dispersal of inflammatory fluid and is thus useful in the acute stage of the injury.

Tendon repair

Following the subsidence of the acute inflammatory reaction, fibroblasts, the cells that synthesize collagen, migrate into the damaged area in a fairly random fashion. It is important that the cells are arranged longitudinally if the repair fibrils are to be correctly aligned. Slight longitudinal tension applied to the tendon is important. Therefore, once the acute inflammatory reaction has subsided, short periods of controlled exercise by walking in hand are beneficial. This also helps to prevent the development of adhesions between the tendon and surrounding structures. Obviously an adequate blood supply to the area is necessary for repair tissue to be formed, but it is likely that this is not a limiting factor in tendon repair, therefore it is unnecessary to promote blood supply to the area artificially.

Complete repair of tendon tissue takes a long time. After significant damage to collagen fibrils, a minimum of fifteen months is necessary before the tendon has achieved its maximum healing. Rest, combined with controlled exercise, is probably the optimal treatment currently available. The author usually recommends total box rest until the acute inflammation reaction has subsided, with the leg being kept under bandage. Small periods of in-hand walking exercise are then commenced and gradually increased in duration until, after eight weeks, the horse is walking for up to an hour twice daily. At this stage ridden walking exercise is quite acceptable and short periods of trotting can start. The amount of trotting is progressively increased, up to a maximum of thirty minutes after three to four months. The horse is then turned out for a further convalescence until at least nine months after the initial injury. Slow ridden work is then recommended. Horses become sound long before repair of the damaged tissue is sufficient to withstand stresses of normal work, therefore the temptation to return the horse to work prematurely must be resisted strongly. Ideally, healing of the tendons should be monitored using diagnostic ultrasound because it seems that some horses heal more slowly than others. A premature resumption of work is likely to result in re-injury.

Firing

Much controversy surrounds the practice of either pin or line firing. There is no scientific evidence that either of these procedures is at all beneficial, although there is plenty of anecdotal support. A recent study by Professor Silver and his colleagues from the University of Bristol indicated that neither line nor pin firing accelerated tendon repair. Pin firing actually caused additional damage and prolonged the healing process. Scar collagen in pin-fired tendons was not aligned along lines of stress and remained a cause of permanent weakness. Firing tended to be associated with development of peritendinous adhesions, thus compromising the normal function of the tendon. The study was performed on experimental animals, and the tendon injuries were artificially created and cannot be regarded as exact replicas of naturally occurring injuries. However, the basic results are irrefutable and, in the author's opinion, firing is contraindicated in the treatment of tendon injury.

Tendon splitting

Tendon splitting involves the insertion of a small knife into the tendon at several sites and the creation of multiple small cuts within the tendon. Various rationales for this treatment have been proposed, including drainage of inflammatory oedema from an acutely strained tendon and stimulation of an increased blood supply, especially in a chronically damaged tendon. It has also been suggested that tendon splitting can help to create better interdigitation of normal tendon and repair tissue, making re-injury less likely. Professor Silver concluded from his studies* that tendon splitting delayed repair and reachievement of a normal gait when compared to horses treated by rest alone.

Currently there is work being undertaken at Ohio State University by Dr Larry Bramlage and his colleagues, who are investigating the beneficial effects of cutting the superior check ligament. The theory behind this approach is that it relieves strain on the superficial flexor tendon to which the ligament is attached, thereby allowing it to heal and also to reduce the chances of strain recurring. This is an interesting approach, but it is too early to assess the results at the time this work goes to press.

Carbon fibre implants

Implantation of carbon fibres into damaged tendons has been used in people and horses. The carbon fibres are placed longitudinally in the tendon to form a scaffolding along which the fibroblasts, the cells which produce the collagen fibrils, can align. This encourages the fibrils to be laid down along the lines of stress. It is obviously an invasive procedure which inevitably causes additional damage to the tendon. Therefore, unless the strain is extremely severe, resulting in almost total disruption of the tendon, or the tendon has been badly lacerated, this procedure is not warranted. In the latter circumstances carbon fibres may offer the best chance of recovery, although a recent study in America indicated that the use of carbon fibres was in no way superior to stitching a tendon which was lacerated.

Laser therapy

There are anecdotal reports of low-output lasers being used successfully for the treatment of tendon injuries. Although one cannot disprove the reports, there is no scientific evidence to indicate that such treatment is at all efficacious in accelerating tendon healing although unquestionably soft-tissue swelling is rapidly reduced and this may be beneficial in the long term.

---

*I. A. Silver and P. D. Rossdale, 'A clinical and experimental study of tendon injury, healing and treatment in the horse', *Equine Veterinary Journal, Supplement I*, 1983.

Pulsating electromagnetic field (PEMF) therapy

A lot of interest has recently surrounded the use of pulsating electromagnetic field therapy (PEMF) and a number of products have been available, e.g. the Blue Boot, Magnetopulse. There is evidence that this treatment can accelerate the healing of delayed unions of bone fractures in people. Although there is anecdotal information concerning this treatment for various problems in the horse, one must be extremely sceptical about its interpretation. Unquestionably, if the current is applied at a specific frequency and strength, the behaviour of certain cells may be influenced, but the signal characteristics required to affect tendon cells is different from that for bone cells. The signal characteristics of the currently available devices are probably not ideal and much more experimental work is necessary before we can assess properly whether or not tendon repair can be accelerated or improved. At present we can say that probably there are no deleterious effects of PEMF on tendon healing, but with the present equipment one must be sceptical about any benefits.

Practical implications of tendon strain

From the preceding discussion it should be clear that optimal repair of a strained tendon requires time – at least nine months. The repaired tendon is functionally less efficient than a normal tendon, therefore there is a real danger of re-injury. The horse with poor conformation is particularly susceptible. The future work programme of the horse must be adapted accordingly. The horse should be as fit as possible for the intended job. Many horses which are unable to withstand the rigours of racing are able to perform in other activities such as hunting.

Prevention of tendon injury

The use of boots and/or bandages can provide some protection to the flexor tendons from injury due to direct trauma. They cannot prevent tendon strain and can, incorrectly applied, actually cause damage to the tendon. Early detection of subtle abnormalities of the tendon is very important. Careful daily observation and palpation of the lower legs should enable an astute manager to detect early changes in the contour of the superficial digital flexor tendon or localized increases in temperature. Care must be taken not to confuse swelling of the tendon with the vein which runs down the inside of the leg just in front of the superficial digital flexor tendon; it is particularly obvious just below the knee. Compare like with like, one leg with another leg. If there is a suspect area, pick up the leg and gently squeeze each tendon between finger and thumb, starting at the top and working slowly down. Assess the consistency of the tendon and the reaction of the horse to gentle pressure. Is there any area of abnormal softness? Does the horse flinch? Is there a similar reaction in the same area of the normal leg? Recognition of the early-warning signs is most important. A few days' rest and moderation of the training programme may prevent more serious damage. Initially there may be just localized inflammation without damage to the fibrils and, once the inflammation has subsided, the tendon is restored to normality. Assessment of this can only be done objectively using diagnostic ultrasound, therefore, if in any doubt, rest the horse and seek veterinary advice. It is helpful for the vet if the leg is not bandaged during the twelve hours prior to his examination. This helps him to assess the problem most accurately. If swelling increases without a bandage, this bodes ill.

Should one buy a horse with an old tendon injury?

Inevitably after any tendon injury there is always some slight conformational abnormality of the tendon, and careful palpation of the tendon with the leg non-weightbearing should confirm the presence of an old injury. The length of the tendon affected, the presence or absence of adhesions of the tendons to the surrounding tissues, and whether the deep or the superficial digital flexor tendon is involved must all be assessed. Generally speaking, injury to the deep digital flexor tendon is more serious than a similar degree of damage to the superficial digital flexor tendon, but deep digital flexor tendon injury is rare. The conformation of the horse and its intended use will also determine whether or not it is likely to stand up to work. If there is a known history of blunt trauma to the tendon, the prognosis is better than for a true tendon strain.

TENDON RUPTURE (BREAKDOWN)

Complete rupture of either or both of the superficial and deep digital flexor tendons occurs occasionally. Division of the superficial digital flexor tendon results in sinking of the fetlock. If the deep digital flexor tendon is disrupted, the toe of the foot tips up. The prognosis for either injury is poor.

TENDON LACERATIONS

Lacerations may partially or completely sever the superficial digital flexor tendon and the deep digital flexor tendon and are serious injuries. The wound must be very thoroughly cleaned and all badly damaged, dying tissue removed. This is best achieved under general anaesthesia. If the tendon has been severed completely, it may be possible to stitch it back together, provided that the ends are not too widely separated. Carbon fibre implants have been used to facilitate healing. Whichever of these techniques is used, the limb is then immobilized in a plaster cast. It is usually necessary to raise the heel of the foot so that the ends of the tendon are not pulled apart. The height of the heel is gradually reduced to avoid excessive contraction of the tendon during healing. The horse is box-rested. Although the horse may be pasture sound, recovery cannot be completely guaranteed. A few horses are able to resume work twelve to eighteen months after the injury, especially if it involves a hind leg. If the laceration occurs within a tendon sheath, the prognosis is less favourable. Lacerations of extensor tendons are less important and surgical repair is often unnecessary.

DISPLACEMENT OF THE SUPERFICIAL DIGITAL FLEXOR TENDON OF THE HIND LIMB

The superficial digital flexor tendon is a flattened fibrous band as it passes over the tuber calcanei (point of hock). Here two fibrous bands detach on either side and insert on the calcaneus and help to keep the tendon in position. If either or both of these bands is damaged, the tendon may be displaced either to the outside or, more rarely, to the inside. The injury usually occurs while the horse is cantering or galloping. The tendon may move on and off the tuber calcanei and the horse shows great distress and is unwilling to bear weight on the leg. Initially there is minimal soft-tissue swelling and careful palpation reveals the diagnosis. Within twenty-four hours considerable soft-tissue swelling may develop making accurate palpation more difficult.

Treatment

If the tendon has been displaced and remains displaced, a prolonged period of rest results in considerable improvement; some horses are able to resume work, although there may be some mechanical impairment of the gait. The prognosis is less favourable if the tendon is displaced medially or continues to move on and off the tuber calcanei. Anti-inflammatory medication may be contraindicated, as some inflammation and subsequent fibrosis may help to stabilize the tendon in a displaced position.

Numerous surgical techniques have been attempted to stabilize the tendon, with limited success.

Ligaments

Functional anatomy

Ligaments are fibrous bands which attach to bone. They are similar in structure to tendons but are more fibrous and less elastic. Damage to collateral ligaments is discussed under joint injuries (see pp. 173 and 175).

The suspensory apparatus

The suspensory ligament attaches to the top of the back of the third metacarpal (cannon) bone. Two thirds of the way down the metacarpal region it divides into two branches, the medial and lateral branches, which

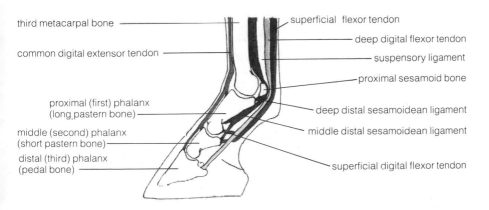

third metacarpal bone

common digital extensor tendon

proximal (first) phalanx (long pastern bone)

middle (second) phalanx (short pastern bone)

distal (third) phalanx (pedal bone)

superficial flexor tendon

deep digital flexor tendon

suspensory ligament

proximal sesamoid bone

deep distal sesamoidean ligament

middle distal sesamoidean ligament

superficial digital flexor tendon

Figure 81   The ligaments and tendons of a lower limb

attach to the proximal sesamoid bones. There are also branches which cross onto the front of the pastern region. Attached to the bottom of the sesamoid bones are the distal sesamoidean ligaments, which insert on the proximal (first) and middle (second) phalanges (long and short pastern bones). These structures are important for support of the fetlock joint.

The normal suspensory ligament is uniform in width throughout its length and has a firm consistency. Pressure applied to it does not cause pain, although some hypersensitive horses may show some reaction to its palpation, as may horses doing a lot of fast work.

Conditions of Ligaments

SPRAIN OF THE SUSPENSORY LIGAMENT (SUSPENSORY DESMITIS)

Clinical signs

The suspensory ligament may be sprained anywhere along its length. The top of the ligament is hidden beneath the digital flexor tendons and between the splint bones and cannot be seen or felt directly. Damage in this area may cause localized heat and/or enlargement of the medial palmar vein on the inside of the limb. Lameness may be extremely slight and only evident after fast work or very long periods of exercise. The most common site of injury is lower down, above and at the site of the division into two branches. Either of the two branches alone may also be damaged. An acutely damaged ligament is thicker and of softer consistency than a normal ligament. Pressure applied to the damaged area with the limb non-weightbearing causes pain. If one of the branches of the suspensory ligaments is damaged, there may be concurrent damage to the sesamoid bone to which it is attached.

Predisposing factors

Poor foot balance and pronounced toe-in and toe-out conformation may predispose to injury of the suspensory ligament. Horses which work at speed are most prone.

Diagnosis

Although sprain of the lower two thirds of the suspensory ligament is usually readily diagnosed due to obvious thickening of the ligament and pain on palpation, the top of the ligament may be damaged without overt clinical signs other than lameness. The horse is often more lame on a circle than on a straight line, especially with the affected leg on the outside of the circle. Lameness is alleviated by infiltration of local anaesthetic in this area. Radiographic examination of the third metacarpal bone may show abnormalities at the site of attachment of the suspensory ligament. An ultrasound scan may be the only method of reaching a definitive diagnosis. Ultrasound scans are also useful for assessing the extent of damage of lesions involving the body or branches of the ligaments.

Treatment

The principles of treatment are the same as those for tendon strain (see p. 215).

Prognosis

The prognosis depends upon the severity of the initial injury, the conformation of the leg and use of the horse. Re-injury occurs not infrequently.

Concurrent suspensory desmitis and fracture of a splint bone are a not uncommon injury in point-to-point horses and steeplechasers. Prognosis depends largely on the severity of the suspensory desmitis.

SPRAIN OF THE DISTAL SESAMOIDEAN LIGAMENTS

Clinical signs

The distal sesamoidean ligaments are not easy to feel. The middle pair of ligaments which attach to the back of the proximal (first) phalanx (the long pastern bone) are most frequently injured. This causes swelling on the back of the pastern region and lameness.

Diagnosis

This injury is most accurately diagnosed using diagnostic ultrasound. If the injury occurred some weeks previously, oblique radiographic views highlighting the areas of insertion of the middle distal sesamoidean ligaments may show periosteal proliferative reactions. In chronic cases there may be calcification in the ligaments.

Treatment

Rest is the best treatment. There is a relatively high rate of recurrence.

SPRAIN OF THE ACCESSORY LIGAMENT OF THE DEEP DIGITAL FLEXOR TENDON (THE INFERIOR CHECK LIGAMENT)

Functional anatomy

On the back of the knee are palmar carpal ligaments which connect the second and third carpal bones with the metacarpus. The accessory ligament of the deep digital flexor tendon is a direct continuation of these and lies between the suspensory ligament and the deep digital flexor tendon. It merges with the deep digital flexor tendon in the middle of the metacarpal region.

Clinical signs

Sprain of this ligament results in a variable degree of lameness. There is usually palpable enlargement of the accessory ligament of the deep digital flexor tendon, but it is vitally important to be sure that swelling is limited only to this structure and that the damage is not more extensive. Lesions are best identified using diagnostic ultrasound.

Treatment and prognosis

The principles of treatment are the same as those for tendon strain (see p. 215), although generally a shorter period of rest (three to six months) is adequate. Ideally, healing should be monitored using diagnostic ultrasound.

The incidence of recurrent injury of this ligament is less than for strain of the deep digital flexor tendon itself and for sprain of the suspensory ligament.

SPRAIN OF THE PLANTAR TARSAL LIGAMENT (CURB)

The plantar tarsal ligament is a long flat band which runs down the back of the hock and is attached to the back of the top of the tuber calcanei (point of hock) proximally and to the calcaneus, the fourth tarsal bone and the head of the fourth metatarsal (outside splint) bone.

Clinical signs

Sprain of this ligament results in a swelling, usually at its insertion on the lower part of the back of the hock. This swelling must be differentiated from the head of the fourth metatarsal bone, which can be very prominent. Strain of the ligament may cause mild lameness.

Figure 82   A hock showing the location of a curb

Treatment

Rest usually results in rapid resolution of lameness, although a mild swelling may persist. This swelling is difficult to eradicate. Swelling may occur without lameness. Although curbs can be a recurrent problem in Standard-bred trotters and pacers, they are rarely a significant injury in other types of horses.

15
MUSCLE PROBLEMS

MUSCLE ATROPHY

Muscles control movement of the body. They are attached to bone via tendons. An adequate blood and nerve supply is essential for normal function. Muscles waste (atrophy) either due to lack of use or due to damage to the nerve supply. If a horse has a severe hind-limb lameness due to pain in the foot, the muscles of the hindquarters on that side may atrophy. The site of muscle atrophy does not necessarily imply that the problem is in that area.

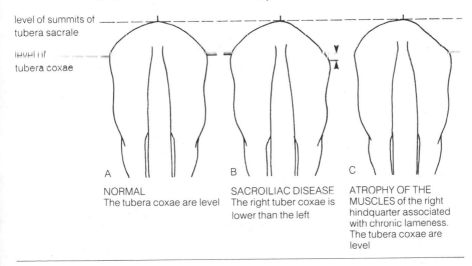

level of summits of
tubera sacrale

level of
tubera coxae

A

NORMAL
The tubera coxae are level

B

SACROILIAC DISEASE
The right tuber coxae is
lower than the left

C

ATROPHY OF THE
MUSCLES of the right
hindquarter associated
with chronic lameness.
The tubera coxae are
level

Figure 83   An assessment of muscle atrophy and pelvic symmetry

Although the lameness may resolve, it may only be when the horse is returned to regular work that the muscle mass is restored. If a nerve is damaged irreversibly, then associated muscle atrophy will not recover unless the muscle receives innervation from more than one source.

MUSCLE STRAIN AND MYOSITIS (MUSCLE INFLAMMATION)

Muscle strain may be the result of a sudden incoordinate muscle contraction or overstretching of a fatigued muscle. The degree of lameness is variable. Muscle inflammation (myositis) is also present.

Diagnosis

Pressure applied to a strained muscle or manipulation of that muscle may cause pain. Faradic stimulation of a damaged muscle causes pain. A skilled operator can detect differences in the way a damaged muscle contracts in response to faradic stimulation compared with a normal muscle.

Treatment

Rest or a controlled exercise programme is required. Treatment with ultrasound or faradism aids resolution of inflammation and facilitates return to normal athletic function. Some muscles may go into spasm and this contributes to pain. Muscle spasm can be relieved by faradic treatment or, in some circumstances, by manipulation. The period of rest required depends on the severity of the initial injury.

AZOTURIA (TYING UP, SETFAST, EXERTIONAL RHABDOMYOLYSIS)

Clinical signs

Azoturia is a relatively poorly understood disease, resulting in a variable degree of muscle stiffness and pain, which occurs under a number of different circumstances. Traditionally the problem occurs relatively soon after the start of exercise, particularly in fit horses receiving high-concentrate rations on a day following a rest day. The clinical signs vary from mild hind-limb stiffness to a total reluctance to move, sweating and obvious severe pain. The muscles of the back and hindquarters may feel unusually firm. Identical symptoms may develop part way through a three-day event, typically at the ten-minute halt prior to phase D. The exact cause of the condition is unknown. Some horses seem prone to recurrent attacks. Highly strung individuals, especially mares, seem particularly susceptible. Vitamin E and/or selenium deficiency has been suggested as a possible cause, but there is little data to support this hypothesis and it is probably a multifactorial condition. A similar condition occurs in some wild ungulates and is known as capture myopathy; the clinical signs are usually associated with exercise and stress while being caught.

What actually happens? Whatever the actual cause, it results in damage of the muscle cells (myopathy). Their outer membranes become more leaky, permitting loss from the cells of two enzymes, creatine kinase and aspartate aminotransferase. As a result the concentration of these enzymes increases in the blood. This rise in concentration reflects accurately the severity of muscle damage. Within minutes of the onset of clinical signs a measurable increase in the concentration of these enzymes may occur, and their concentration continues to rise for the following twenty-four hours. Thus there is a reliable blood test which can confirm a clinical diagnosis of azoturia.

If the damage to the cells is severe, a muscle pigment, myoglobin, may be released into the blood. This is a large molecule which is excreted via the kidneys causing dark discolouration of the urine. The name azoturia refers to this. Because of their large size, myoglobin molecules may impair the filtration mechanism of the kidney and, in extremely severe cases, cause irreparable kidney damage.

The muscle damage causes release of lactic acid (a substance responsible for muscle cramp) and pain. Continuing to work a mildly affected horse may exacerbate considerably the degree of muscle damage and pain, therefore, if azoturia is suspected, work should stop immediately and the horse returned carefully to his box. If some distance from home, the horse should be transported back if at all possible.

Treatment

In the acute case the main aim of treatment is to moderate pain and the anti inflammatory analgesic phenylbutazone is the drug of choice. For rapid onset of action it is administered intravenously. If the horse is very distressed, it may be necessary to tranquillize it. The tranquillizer aceprom-azine also dilates peripheral blood vessels and may enhance the blood supply to the damaged muscles. Fluid therapy is beneficial to maintain adequate kidney function. The concentrate ration should be severely reduced. Adding salt will encourage the horse to drink adequately. The time taken for complete recovery is variable and depends upon the initial severity of damage. Some horses make a complete recovery and never have another attack. A minority of horses appear to recover, only to have repeated episodes.

Prevention

Prevention is all-important, and careful attention to diet and management is effective in the majority of horses. If the horse has a day off, the concentrate ration should be restricted. Problem horses often appear better if fed cubes rather than oats. In some horses with a recurrent problem selected blood and urine tests (creatinine clearance test) indicate a deficiency of sodium, potassium and/or calcium, and appropriate supplementation of the diet with these minerals has been most effective. Severely restricting the protein intake by the substitution of bran may be a complicating factor, because bran contains a substance called phytate which can bind dietary calcium and prevent its absorption by the gut, thus effectively limiting the body's supply of calcium. It is probably best just to reduce the total amount of food fed if the horse is to be rested confined to the box. Most commercially produced horse and pony cubes fed with hay provide a nutritionally balanced ration. In problem horses the addition of approximately 15 g (1 oz) sodium chloride (common salt) a day to this diet controls the condition. Oral aspirin treatment has apparently successfully prevented the problem in some young Thoroughbreds, but the reason for this is unclear. A drug called Dantrolene is helpful in some horses with recurrent problems.

When work is resumed after a day off, it seems important in susceptible individuals to increase slowly the amount and type of work done, i.e. walk for up to thirty minutes before starting slow trotting, and trot for fifteen to twenty minutes before doing any fast work.

RUPTURE OF THE FIBULARIS TERTIUS MUSCLE

The fibularis tertius muscle, one of the muscles of the hind leg, is part of the reciprocal apparatus which prevents the horse from flexing the stifle without simultaneously flexing the hock. It is largely tendinous. Spontaneous rupture of the muscle can occur and is usually the result of the horse getting the leg stuck or left behind in for example, a ditch. The horse is lame and has an odd hind-limb gait because the stifle may be flexed without flexing the hock. If the leg is picked up and extended behind the horse, there is a characteristic dimple in the contour of the back of the leg above the hock.

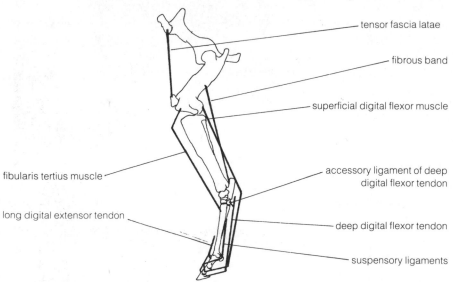

tensor fascia latae

fibrous band

superficial digital flexor muscle

accessory ligament of deep digital flexor tendon

deep digital flexor tendon

suspensory ligaments

fibularis tertius muscle

long digital extensor tendon

Figure 84   The 'stay apparatus' of the hind limb. These structures allow the horse to sleep standing up

Treatment

Rest is the only treatment. Most horses become permanently sound.

Abnormal Muscle Function Secondary to Nerve Injury

SWEENY

Sweeny is atrophy of the supraspinatus and infraspinatus muscles, which cover the scapula (shoulderblade). It is a result of damage to the supra-scapular nerve, the nerve which innervates these muscles. This nerve passes over the front of the scapula and is liable to damage if the horse falls on the shoulder or runs into a solid object. If the nerve is damaged irreversibly, muscle atrophy will be permanent. Nerve damage takes a long time to recover and, after severe bruising of the nerve, it may take several months for normal muscle mass to return.

Some horses recover spontaneously. If there is no improvement, isolation of the nerve surgically and removal of a piece of bone over which the nerve passes can relieve pressure on the nerve and muscle mass may ultimately be restored.

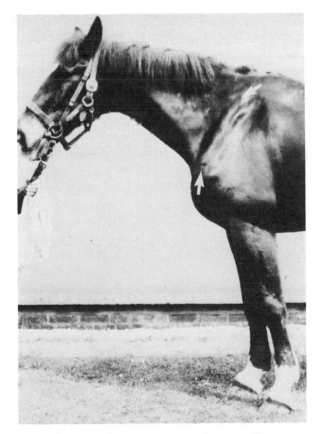

Figure 85 A horse with sweeny. Atrophy of the supraspinatus and infraspinatus muscles which cover the scapula results in abnormal prominence of the ridge on the shoulderblade, the scapular spine (arrows)

INSTABILITY OF THE SHOULDER JOINT

If the nerve supply to the muscles on the inside and outside of the scapula is damaged, then the shoulder joint can move much more than normal because these muscles normally provide stability to the shoulder joint. As the horse starts to take weight on the leg, the shoulder will appear to slip sideways. This injury is usually the result of the horse colliding with something and stretching or rupturing the nerves of the branchial plexus on the inside of the shoulder.

If the nerve damage is not too severe, the horse will slowly improve, but it may take many months. If the damage is severe, the horse will not recover.

RADIAL NERVE PARALYSIS

The radial nerve innervates the muscles which extend the elbow, carpus (knee) and digits. Damage to the radial nerve results in inability to use these muscles properly. Damage to the nerve usually occurs where it passes around the humerus and can be the result of a knock or a fall.

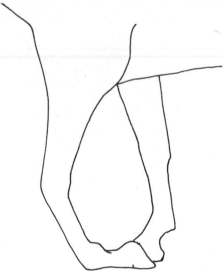

Figure 86   Radial nerve paralysis – the muscles which extend the elbow, carpus and digits are non-functional, therefore all these joints are held flexed, with the elbow 'dropped'

Clinical signs

The horse adopts a typical stance with the elbow dropped and sometimes with the fetlock knuckled forwards. It is unable to move the leg forward properly and may drag the toe, and is unable to walk over small obstacles. It may compensate to a degree by swinging the leg outwards as it is advanced. The muscles innervated by the nerve rapidly atrophy.

Treatment

The lower leg should be bandaged to prevent damage to the skin if the horse tends to knuckle over. Faradic stimulation of the affected muscles helps to retain muscle mass. Prolonged rest to allow time for nerve damage to recover is essential. This may take many months. If the damage is severe, the horse will remain permanently incapacitated.

16
THE FEET

Functional anatomy

There are three bones in the foot: the middle (second) and distal (third) phalanges (the short pastern bone and the pedal or coffin bone) and the navicular or distal sesamoid bone. The middle and distal phalanges articulate via the distal interphalangeal or coffin joint. The navicular bone lies on the back of this joint. The deep digital flexor tendon passes over the back of the navicular bone and inserts on the distal phalanx. Attached to the sides of the distal phalanx are the cartilages of the foot, which may become ossified from one or more ossification sites (sidebone). The distal phalanx is supported in the foot by the laminae. The sensitive laminae are attached to the distal phalanx and interdigitate with the insensitive laminae, which line the inside of the hoof wall. The division between the sensitive and insensitive laminae can be seen on the sole of the foot as a white line. The wall of the foot is horny tissue secreted by the coronary band. The horn is produced at the rate of approximately 1 centimetre per month. The walls of the foot are infolded at the heels, forming the bars of the foot. The walls are covered by a thin membrane which controls the movement of moisture into and out of the wall. The frog is a thick horny cushion on the sole of the foot. There is considerable controversy about its true function and whether it should make contact with the ground.

Most horses have symmetrically shaped and equally sized front and hind feet. The hind feet have more sloping walls than the front feet. The soles are usually slightly concave and only the wall makes contact with the ground. The soles are of variable thickness. A horse with relatively flat soles which are readily compressible by firm thumb pressure is more prone to bruising and sore feet than a horse with firmer, more domed soles. In the wild, constant roaming by the horse wears down the feet, so trimming is not required. With domestication it is necessary to trim the feet regularly every four to six weeks to maintain correct shape, size and balance. Correct trimming is essential for normal function. Shoeing is not essential but helps

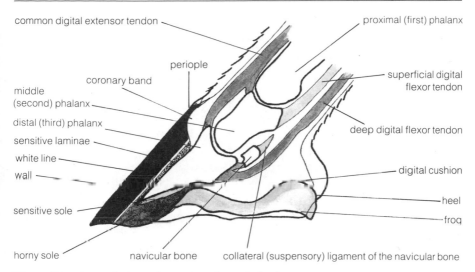

Figure 87a Lateral view of a section through the foot

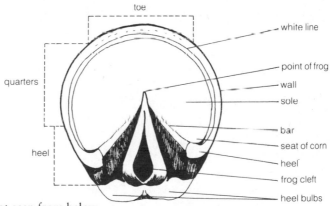

Figure 87b The foot seen from below

to prevent excessive wear of the feet and provides some protection and grip. However, bad shoeing can create problems (see chapter 20).

The foot is the most common site of lameness in the horse. The incidence of lameness of front feet far exceeds that of back feet.

Conditions of the Foot

BRUISED SOLE, SORE FEET AND CORNS

The flat-footed, thin-soled horse is most prone to bruising. Bruising is usually the result of standing on a solid object such as a stone or repetitive trauma to the sole by a poorly fitting shoe or excessive work on hard ground.

A corn is a bruise which occurs between the wall and bar of the foot at the so-called seat of corn.

Having trodden on a stone, the horse may become suddenly lame and remain so. Alternatively after a few lame steps the horse may recover, only for lameness to recur the following day. Lameness associated with corns may only be obvious as the horse turns, especially with the affected foot to the inside. Generalized bruising or sore feet may be manifest merely as a slightly restricted, pottery, shuffling gait with shorter strides on corners, a reluctance to demonstrate medium and extended paces and a slight hesitation to jump. The horse usually shows more willingness and fluidity in the paces on soft ground.

Hard ground results in a greater concussive force being transmitted through the foot than does soft ground. If the foot is placed flat to the ground, the force is dissipated over the entire hoof wall. If the initial impact is concentrated on a smaller area, the force transmitted through that area will be greater. If the branches of the shoe are too small, the effective surface area making contact with the ground is reduced. If the foot starts to overgrow the shoe, especially at the heels, this predisposes to bruising at the heels. If one part of the foot is slightly higher than the other, that part will make contact with the ground fractionally earlier, concentrating stress on that area. This is a common trimming error. The same unbalancing effect is created by the use of studs, especially if a single stud is used on one branch of the shoe.

Diagnosis

The area of pain can usually be located by the careful use of hoof testers to apply pressure to discrete areas of the sole. Particularly in a white foot it may be easy to identify red areas which reflect subsolar haemorrhage. It may be necessary to remove several superficial layers of horn before an area of bruising can be found. The absence of visible subsolar haemorrhage does not preclude the existence of severe bruising. It is often necessary to remove the shoe before the bruised area can be found. If the horse is just footy or jarred, there may be neither visible bruising nor a discrete area of pain. The digital blood vessels may feel fuller and the pulse in the digital arteries may be more intense than in the normal horse. The diagnosis may be reached only by a careful evaluation of the way in which the horse moves and by exclusion of other potential causes of lameness.

Treatment

If there is a discrete area of bruising, some of the overlying horn is pared off to relieve pressure. Poulticing the foot for a couple of days is of benefit and is essential if a corn has become infected (a suppurating corn). Once the horse has significantly improved, the affected area of the sole must be rapidly hardened so that it can withstand pressure. Application of aureomycin (purple) spray is effective. Direct pressure to the affected area should be avoided. The shoe should be fitted accordingly. If the sole has been severely damaged, it may be helpful to place a rigid metal plate over the affected area, provided the sole is reasonably domed so that the plate does not press directly onto it. The plate must be rigid to avoid any distortion. A horse with a narrow wall and flat sole should be shod with a wide-webbed shoe with a concave solar surface (a seated-out shoe). This provides some protection to the sole without the potential complications of pads. If the sole is thin and soft, the application of sole paint (a mixture of equal parts of phenol, 7 per cent iodine solution and 10 per cent formalin) has proved useful. If possible, studs should be avoided on hard ground. A relatively new fullered shoe with rough-headed nails should provide adequate grip.

There is some controversy over the use of pads, particularly over the type of pad used and the way in which it is fitted. A simple leather pad may protect the site from direct bruising on stony ground and may be of definite temporary value on flinty terrain or for a horse with a recently bruised foot. These pads do little to alter the concussive force transmitted through the foot and at the same time encourage the foot to sweat. It is much more difficult to fit the shoe so that force is transmitted evenly over the wall. So a leather pad may protect against direct trauma but will do little to moderate concussion. There are a number of commercially available pads which are claimed to absorb concussion, although there is little scientific evidence to support this; indeed, there is some evidence that pads may actually increase the forces accepted by the sole of the foot, a structure not designed to bear weight. It is important that, if a pad is used, it should not alter the balance and angle of the foot.

PEDAL OSTEITIS

The term pedal osteitis implies that there is active inflammation of the pedal bone or distal phalanx. Traditionally the diagnosis has been based on clinical signs (lameness associated with pain in the foot) and radiographic abnormalities of the distal phalanx. However, there is tremendous variation in the radiographic appearance of the distal phalanx in normal horses. Many horses have distal phalanges with fuzzy outlines, especially at the heels, prominent vascular channels, which appear as broad black lines radiating through the bones or a large notched area at the toe. Therefore it is extremely difficult, in the author's opinion, to assess what radiographic abnormalities are clinically significant. The author reserves the term pedal osteitis for those horses with severe radiographic abnormalities in which other potential causes of lameness have been eliminated. It is often possible to localize pain to the foot and not be able to reach a definitive diagnosis, despite good-quality radiographic views. Many of these horses are diagnosed as having pedal osteitis, thus implying a specific condition. The author believes that this is incorrect and that veterinary surgeons and owners should acknowledge that it is not possible, with the current diagnostic techniques available, to give a name to every lameness. Often we just do not know.

If there are major radiographic abnormalities of the distal phalanx, e.g. periosteal proliferative changes (new bone) on the front of the bone and a marked reduction in the overall density of the bone, this is pedal osteitis and warrants a poor prognosis for future soundness. The bony abnormalities are permanent. A horse with this condition will always be inclined to be footy, especially on hard ground.

LAMINITIS

Laminitis is inflammation of the sensitive laminae of the foot. In Great Britain it occurs most commonly in overweight ponies and horses kept at grass, especially when the grass is growing rapidly. Small ponies are particularly susceptible. It is also associated with excessive consumption of carbohydrates (grain overload) or with generalized toxaemia (e.g. severe diarrhoea). Excessive weightbearing on one leg may induce laminitis, as can excessive work on hard ground.

Clinical signs

Usually only the forefeet are involved, although sometimes the hind feet are as well. Initially the pony shows extreme reluctance to move and stands with the hind legs well underneath the body, rocking back on the heels of the forefeet to take some weight off the toes. The feet feel hot and the pulses in the blood vessels which supply the foot are pounding. The pulse in the digital arteries is most readily felt at the level of the fetlock joint. Here the arteries supplying the foot are relatively close to the skin surface on the inside and outside of the fetlock.

What causes the pain?

The normal blood flow to the foot is disturbed so that some areas, notably the sensitive laminae, receive an inadequate blood supply, especially in the toe region. The blood supply brings oxygen and nutrients to the tissues, without which the cells become damaged and ultimately die. Damage to the cells induces inflammation (laminitis) and chemical mediators are released (e.g. prostaglandins), which cause pain. The inflammation also causes swelling, which within the close confines of the rigid hoof wall, contributes to pain.

Treatment

The aims of treatment are to eliminate the cause and to alleviate pain. The cause – overconsumption of lush grass – is removed by confining the pony to a box or a 'starvation square' where there is no grass. The diet should be severely restricted and limited solely to hay and water. It is vitally important not to overfeed and constant access to hay is not necessary. Half a slice in the morning and a slice in the evening are plenty. Pain is alleviated by the use of drugs such as phenylbutazone or flunixin meglumine. These may initially be administered by injection in order to achieve rapid onset of action; subsequently they may be mixed in water or milk of magnesia and squirted into the mouth by syringe.

Walking is important for blood flow within the foot, but excessive exercise carries with it a risk. The sensitive laminae, which clothe the distal phalanx (pedal bone), interlock with the insensitive laminae and thus suspend the pedal bone in the foot. If the laminae are damaged, the

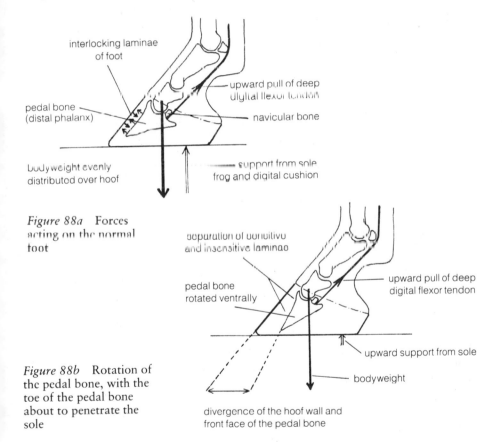

interlocking laminae of foot

upward pull of deep digital flexor tendon

pedal bone (distal phalanx)

navicular bone

Body weight evenly distributed over hoof

support from sole frog and digital cushion

Figure 88a Forces acting on the normal foot

separation of sensitive and insensitive laminae

pedal bone rotated ventrally

upward pull of deep digital flexor tendon

upward support from sole

Figure 88b Rotation of the pedal bone, with the toe of the pedal bone about to penetrate the sole

bodyweight

divergence of the hoof wall and front face of the pedal bone

interlocking is liable to break down. The deep digital flexor tendon attaches to the back of the pedal bone, and if it pulls upwards and the interlocking mechanism is no longer holding the pedal bone firmly, the pedal bone is likely to rotate so that its toe drops. This can ultimately result in the tip of the bone penetrating through the sole. Therefore, although moderate exercise (for example, ten minutes everyone or two hours) may be beneficial, overexercise may have dire consequences. Rotation may occur very rapidly and is difficult to control. It may be beneficial to bed the pony on peat, which will pack up into the foot and provide some support to the sole.

Within the first twenty-four to thirty-six hours of treatment most affected ponies show improvement, but treatment usually has to be continued for considerably longer to avoid recurrence of clinical signs. Any pony which has once had an attack of laminitis must be regarded as a prime candidate for future attacks and therefore must be managed accordingly: access to pasture must be severely limited and bodyweight carefully controlled.

Chronic laminitis

Regardless of the initial treatment, some acute cases of laminitis become chronic, so that there is persistent lameness of variable severity. It is usually associated with some rotation of the pedal bone. Often the toe of the foot is excessively long and the sole appears remarkably flat or even convex. Successful treatment can sometimes be achieved by appropriate trimming of the foot and concurrent starvation. Trimming necessitates cooperation between the vet and the farrier. Radiographs of the foot can reveal the amount of rotation of the pedal bone and its position relative to the hoof wall. Based upon these observations the vet can advise how much of the toe of the foot can be safely removed. Careful, regular trimming is the key to success and a normal shape of the foot and alignment of the pedal bone can slowly be re-achieved.

In severe cases of laminitis which do not respond to more conventional treatment removal of the entire hoof wall from the coronary band to the ground around the front half of the foot can provide some relief. The hoof must be kept scrupulously clean and under a bandage until firm protective tissues redevelop. Provided that the coronary band is not damaged then the wall will slowly regrow.

In selected cases application of a heart-bar shoe can produce considerable relief. The shoe provides some support over the frog; it is essential that it is fitted correctly or the problem may be compounded.

In any horse with laminitis as a result of poor blood supply to the hoof wall, development of new wall may be impaired, especially in the toe region. Rings on the hoof wall reflect varied hoof growth. In a horse with chronic laminitis these rings may be very prominent and may diverge at the heel because the heel has grown faster relative to the toe. Biotin and methionine are amino acids required for the manufacture of keratin, one of the essential components of the hoof wall. Supplementation of the diet with these amino acids may be beneficial to the chronic laminitic pony.

In a minority of cases these measures do not achieve complete resolution of the problem and blood tests are performed to determine if fatty liver syndrome may be an underlying predisposing problem. Additionally the diet of some ponies is deficient in certain materials (e.g. potassium) and blood and urine tests help to establish this so that appropriate dietary supplementation can be recommended.

Treatment of chronic laminitis is a long-term project. It may be a year or more after the initial onset of clinical signs before the pony is able to resume work.

PROBLEMS ASSOCIATED WITH TRIMMING AND SHOEING

The importance of correct shoeing and trimming cannot be overemphasized. Each foot should be symmetrically shaped with equal-height heels, so that the foot lands on the ground squarely. However well a shoe fits, unless the foot is prepared properly first, the end result may cause uneven distribution of forces through the foot and predispose to lameness either in the foot or in the lower joints of the limb.

The foot should be trimmed so that there is a straight pastern–foot axis to which the heels of the foot are parallel. The medial and lateral halves of the foot should be symmetrical, with the heels of equal height, so that when the horse is standing the foot is in the same plane as the rest of the limb. If one heel is higher than the other, this may predispose to bruising of the foot, damage to the sensitive laminae, disease of the lower limb joints and sprain of the suspensory ligament. Collapse and contraction of the heel may predispose to the navicular syndrome. Poor trimming and its relationship to bruising are discussed above (see p. 233).

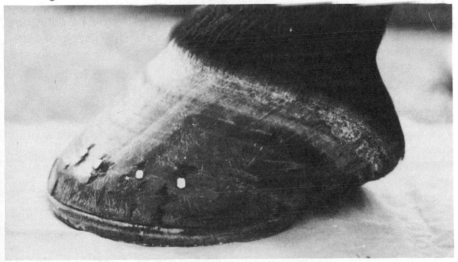

Figure 89 Poor foot conformation typical of many horses with the navicular syndrome. The toe is over long and the heels are low and collapsed and are no longer parallel with the front of the foot. The shoe is too small and gives no support to the heels

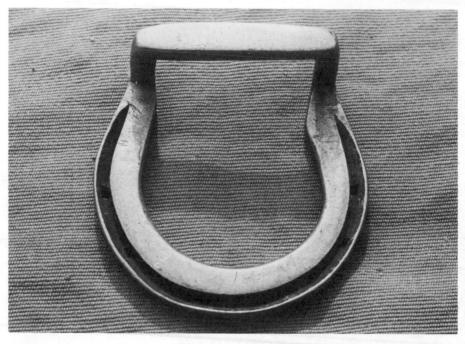

Figure 90 A
raised-heel shoe used for
horses with traumatic
disruption of the
superficial and/or deep
digital flexor tendons

Figure 91 A bar shoe
used to provide stability
to the foot. It is useful
for the treatment of
fractures of the distal
(third) phalanx (pedal
bone), for sheared heels,
and for cases of severe
imbalance of the heights
of the heels

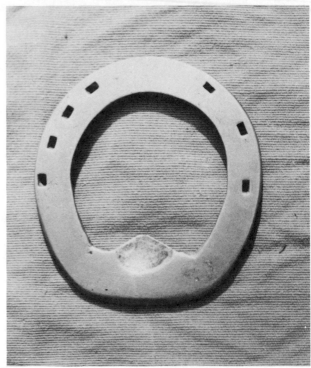

The concept that the shoe must be made to fit the foot and not vice versa is not strictly correct. The shape of a foot can be improved by fitting the shoe to an ideal shape (for example, wide or long at the heels) to encourage the foot to grow to that shape. If the shoe conforms exactly to the shape of the foot when the horse is shod, then the foot will soon overgrow the shoe and the shoe will tend to migrate inwards, predisposing to bruising at the seat of corn. Fitting the shoe wide at the heels does not cause problems with brushing or losing the shoe provided the horse does not move excessively closely and the shoe is properly finished with the inside edge bevelled.

If the horse is shod with shoes that are too small, this will encourage the heels to become more contracted and to collapse, especially if the toes are left too long. The area through which forces are tramsitted is also artificially reduced. This may be compounded by the use of pads. All these factors can cause the horse to move less freely.

NAIL BIND

The shape of a horseshoe nail is designed so that, as the nail is driven into the hoof wall, it is directed upwards and outwards, rather than inwards towards the sensitive laminae. If the nail is placed too close to the white line, it will put pressure on the sensitive laminae causing pain. This is more likely to occur if the wall is very thin. Lameness is evident soon after the horse has

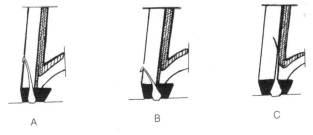

Figure 92   Nail problems: a) correct position of a nail; b) nail angle too great so that nail emerges too low; c) pricked foot – nail penetrates sensitive laminae

been shod. If the wall is struck with a hammer over the offending nail, then the horse will flinch. Removal of the nail usually provides adequate relief, but it is sometimes necessary to remove the shoe and poultice the foot for a couple of days.

NAIL PRICK

If a nail is driven into the sensitive tissues of the foot, the horse is said to have been pricked. This is more serious than a nail bind and usually causes more severe lameness. There may be a trace of blood when the nail is removed.

Provided that the nail prick is recognized immediately and the nail withdrawn and the hole flushed with a strong antiseptic solution such as iodine solution, then complications should not ensue. If the nail is left, infection is likely to develop.

INFECTION IN THE FOOT, PUS IN THE FOOT, UNDERRUN SOLE

This is the most common cause of lameness in the horse.

Infection in the foot may develop following a puncture wound (e.g. nail prick) or as a sequel to a crack in the white line. In some cases, particularly in the early stages of the infection, when lameness is only slight, it is not always possible to identify the site of infection. Infection in the foot causes inflammation and the production of pus. Because the hoof wall is rigid, pressure rises within the foot, causing extreme pain.

Clinical signs

Although only slight lameness may be evident initially, this may develop so that the horse is reluctant to bear any weight on the limb, sweats profusely, blows and refuses to eat. The foot feels warm and the digital blood vessels have a bounding pulse. The site of infection can usually be identified by applying light pressure with hoof testers to the sole. A discrete area of pain can be located, surrounded by less sensitive areas. Even finger pressure may cause pain and pus may be heard squeaking beneath the sole. The sole may be thinner at this area and a small amount of pus (usually black) may exude through it. The pus will tend to track along paths of least resistance and will migrate beneath the sole (underrun sole) and up between the laminae, eventually to burst out at the coronary band. Before this happens an area of sensitivity and swelling at the coronary band may be identified. There may be diffuse soft-tissue swelling above the foot extending as far as the knee which may make the horse reluctant to flex the fetlock joint.

Treatment

The aims of treatment are to relieve pressure within the foot by draining the abscess and to eliminate infection. If a discrete area of pain is identified by pressure on the sole, then removal of the overlying sole will allow drainage of pus and this will produce considerable relief of pain. Although a large hole may facilitate drainage, it is likely to result in exposure of sensitive tissues, which can itself cause pain. Therefore it is best to create a medium-sized hole and then encourage further drainage by poulticing the foot with hot Animalintex for several days. Provided that drainage is established, the horse usually resolves the infection spontaneously. Tubbing the foot, that is, standing the horse in a tub or bucket of warm water and Epsom salts, also helps to draw infection. The bacteria which cause infection in the foot usually thrive in an environment with small or negligible amounts of oxygen (anaerobic bacteria). Flushing the hole with an oxidizing agent such as hydrogen peroxide creates an unfavourable environment for the bacteria, helping resolution of the infection. In very severe cases the use of a special antibiotic, metronidazole, which is effective against anaerobic bacteria, is extremely helpful. The drug is injected directly into the drainage hole daily for two to four days. The use of other antibiotics injected intravenously or intramuscularly is usually unnecessary and, unless adequate drainage is established, may prolong infection in the foot.

Once the infection is resolved, any sensitive tissues that have been exposed must harden and some new protective horn must develop before the horse is likely to be completely sound. If infection bursts out at the coronary band, horn production in the area will be temporarily impaired. This will result in a horizontal defect in the hoof wall which will gradually grow out.

Puncture wounds create ideal conditions for the multiplication of the bacteria which cause tetanus, so it is essential that if the horse has not been vaccinated against tetanus it should receive tetanus antitoxin.

Any soft-tissue swelling above the foot will resolve spontaneously if the foot is treated appropriately.

Complications

Occasionally a deep puncture wound in the region of the frog can result in infection of the pedal bone and/or the navicular bursa. This is a very serious condition and early surgical treatment is essential. All infected and dead tissues must be removed. This inevitably causes damage to vital structures of the foot such as the deep digital flexor tendon, but without such radical treatment the horse will remain permanently lame.

Prevention

Horses which are turned out unshod and develop hoof wall cracks are particularly prone to pus in the foot. The hoof walls should be regularly trimmed, and if they are inclined to break up excessively the feet should be kept shod.

THRUSH

Thrush is a degenerative condition of the frog which results in the accumulation of black, foul-smelling, moist material in the frog clefts. In the early stages the horse is sound. If the condition is allowed to progress and extends into the sensitive tissues, the horse may become lame. The condition usually develops due to poor hygiene, failure to clean the feet regularly and leaving the horse standing in dirty, moist conditions. A horse with deep clefts is particularly susceptible. Horses with long toes and contracted heels will tend to develop deep frog clefts.

Treatment

Treatment aims to eliminate the cause, to clean the foot thoroughly and to control any infection. The frog and frog clefts must be aggressively trimmed to remove all loose dead tissue. The foot should be thoroughly scrubbed with a dilute iodine solution. An antibiotic spray should be applied to the affected tissues. This will help to dry and harden them. Alternatively the clefts may be packed with sulphanimalide powder. The feet must be cleaned and treated daily until the condition is resolved. The horse should stand on a clean dry bed.

Prevention

The condition is easily prevented by good hygiene – daily, thorough cleaning of the feet and a clean dry bed. Foot shape is important: the toes should be kept short.

SEEDY TOE OR SEPARATION OF THE WALL

Separation may occur at the white line. The separation is usually greatest at the sole and becomes progressively less higher up the wall. If the separation occurs at the toe, it is called seedy toe. The zone of separation is filled with dry, dead, cheesy-type material. It is often seen in horses whose toes have been allowed to become too long. It does not cause lameness unless infection occurs or there is severe instability of the attachment of the wall to the foot, resulting in inflammation of the sensitive laminae.

The cause of seedy toe is not properly understood.

Provided that the horse is not lame, then the condition can be managed by the farrier by careful trimming of the foot. Gradually the defect should grow out. The toes should be kept short because the tip of the toe tends to act as a lever and may increase separation between the laminae.

HOOF-WALL CRACKS (SANDCRACKS)

Vertical cracks in the hoof wall either develop from the lower, bearing surface of the wall and extend upwards (grasscrack) or develop at the coronary band and extend downwards (sandcrack). The latter develop as a result of injury to the coronary band so that the secretory function of the horn-producing cells is impaired either temporarily or permanently. The length of crack which develops reflects the severity of the injury. If the cells permanently lose function, there will be a permanent crack down the length of the wall. If the cells recover function, then the crack will grow out slowly, at a rate of approximately 1 centimetre per month. Cracks which develop at the bearing surface of the wall are usually the result of the foot being overgrown and splitting. Some feet seem particularly prone.

Clinical signs

The clinical signs depend on the depth of the crack. If the crack is only superficial, then the horse is sound, but if the crack extends deeper into the sensitive tissues, the horse may be lame either due to the edges of the crack moving, which causes inflammation of the sensitive laminae, or due to infection.

Treatment

Cracks which are only superficial usually require no treatment other than regular careful trimming of the foot. Applying a shoe helps to stabilize the crack. If a deep crack becomes infected, then the infection must be controlled before an attempt is made to stabilize the crack. Immobilization of the edges of a deep crack is not easy and the method used depends on the location and depth of the crack and the proposed use of the horse. Cooperation between the vet and farrier is essential. A well-fitting shoe with a clip on either side of the crack is sometimes satisfactory. In some horses the edges of the crack can be laced together or bonded using an acrylic resin. When the resin is applied, it often incites inflammation and temporarily accentuates the lameness.

BRITTLE FEET

Some normal horses develop multiple splits around the bottom of the hoof wall, especially during the summer months. In the unshod horse this predisposes to infection. The shod horse becomes prone to losing shoes. The cause of brittle feet has not been properly established.

The moisture content of the hoof wall is probably controlled by the membrane which overlies the wall, the periople. This permits moisture both to enter and to leave the wall. It has been suggested that damage to the periople can lead to excessive desiccation of the wall, making it prone to cracking. If the horse's feet are allowed to become too long and overgrow the shoes, this also encourages the walls to crack. If the shoe becomes slightly loose, there will be more movement of the nails within the wall, predisposing to cracking.

Treatment

Regular trimming and shoeing are extremely important. Some horses seem to benefit from hot shoeing rather than cold shoeing. If the horse is turned out on hard ground, a shoe will help to protect the wall. Horn growth requires certain amino acids, including methionine and biotin, and although there is no scientific evidence proving their efficacy as dietary supplements in the horse, their use is recommended. The application of a mild blister to the coronary band seems to improve the hoof growth in some horses. Hoof oil is of doubtful benefit and may impair normal movement of moisture through the wall.

NAVICULAR SYNDROME

Navicular disease is most accurately described as a syndrome rather than a single disease, as the term 'disease' implies that there is one specific condition with a single cause. There are probably multiple causes of pain in the navicular bone giving rise to a variety of pathological changes which result in similar clinical signs.

Functional anatomy

The navicular bone lies on the back of the distal interphalangeal (coffin) joint. It is supported by suspensory ligaments which attach to its top border. The deep digital flexor tendon passes over the back surface of the navicular bone and, interposed between it and the bone, is the navicular bursa, a small fluid-filled sac which communicates with the coffin joint. Infoldings of the synovial membrane project upwards into the lower margin of the navicular bone, forming synovial fossae.

Many theories have been postulated as to why navicular disease occurs. These include impaired blood flow in the back part of the foot due to poor venous return from the foot, perhaps related to the conformation of the foot. As a result the pressure within the bone may be elevated, causing pain. Thickening of the walls of the blood vessels within the navicular bone have been reported, as have bloodclots (thrombi) in the blood vessels. An alteration in blood flow through the bone may alter bone cell metabolism.

In some horses with the navicular syndrome there is evidence of increased bone turnover within the bone. This may represent a regenerative process. In some cases the primary problem may involve the navicular bursa or the distal interphalangeal joint. At present the cause or causes of pain associated with the navicular syndrome are poorly understood.

Clinical signs

Navicular disease occurs almost exclusively in the front feet of horses. Ponies are rarely affected. It occurs in all breeds of horse, although there is a higher incidence in some breeds, for example, the Quarter horse. Usually both front feet are affected, resulting initially in an insidious shortening of the stride and slight unlevelness on turns rather than obvious lameness. The condition appears worse on hard ground. In the early stages the horse may appear reluctant to go forward properly or to lengthen the stride. The horse is described as 'footy'. The horse may show slight, intermittent lameness on one or both legs, especially when working in circles. In some horses more obvious lameness develops in one or both legs. The horse may point one or both feet when standing at rest. Horses with all types of foot conformation develop the disease. Many affected horses have poor foot balance, long toes and low, collapsed heels. The disease is also seen in horses with upright narrow feet. In some horses with navicular disease the feet appear to become more contracted at the heels.

Diagnosis

The horse with navicular syndrome tends to place the foot to the ground slightly toe first. This is most readily appreciated when the horse is on a hard, flat surface. The stride length is shortened. Lameness may be accentuated by flexion of the fetlock and lower joints. Obvious lameness may become apparent when the horse is lunged on a hard surface, left forelimb lameness on the left rein and right forelimb lameness on the right rein.

The pulses in the digital arteries may be stronger than usual although the feet are of normal temperature. Hoof testers rarely cause pain.

Desensitization of the back part of the foot should make the horse sound on that leg. If the horse is affected in both legs and previously demonstrated a shortness of stride without obvious lameness, lameness may become obvious in the leg which has not been nerve-blocked. This lameness should be eliminated by desensitization of the back of the foot and the horse should then move more freely.

Diagnosis is confirmed by radiography but cannot be based on radiographic examination alone. There is a large variation in appearance of navicular bones in normal horses. Along the lower border of the navicular bone are a variable number of black triangular areas which represent the synovial fossae previously described and vascular channels (nutrient foramina). In some horses with navicular disease these areas are increased in number and size and are more variable in shape. It can be difficult to delineate strictly between what is normal and what is abnormal and the radiographs must be interpreted in the light of clinical observations. In some horses black radiolucent areas develop in the middle of the navicular bone and these are considered diagnostic of navicular syndrome. Erosion of the back (flexor) aspect of the navicular bone is also diagnostic. There is controversy regarding the significance of bone spurs on the upper edge of the navicular bone, especially those which occur on the top corners. Occasionally horses with typical clinical signs of navicular syndrome have small chip fractures along the lower border of the bone. Some horses with clinical signs typical of the navicular syndrome have no radiographic abnormalities.

Treatment

No single treatment alone is uniformly successful. A number of the treatments outlined below can together produce marked improvement provided that there are no erosions on the flexor surface of the bone as these merit a poor prognosis.

Trimming and shoeing   Although some horses show significant improvement if the heels of the feet are artificially raised, either by a wedge-heeled shoe or by the use of a wedge pad, this tends to perpetuate or accentuate abnormalities of the shape of the foot. Pads are also difficult to fit properly.

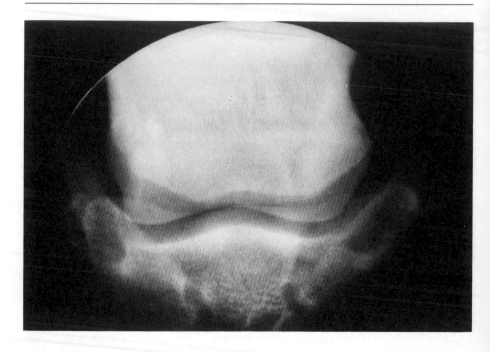

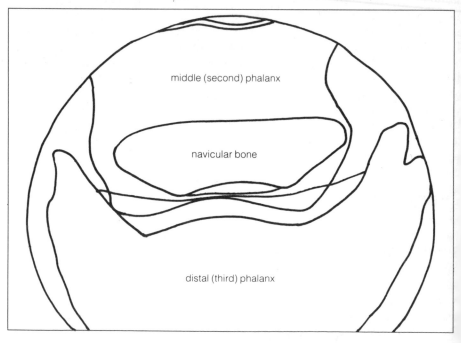

Figure 93a and b Radiograph and diagram of a normal navicular bone

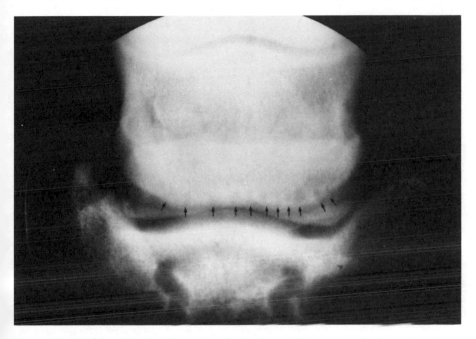

Figure 94   Radiograph of a diseased navicular bone. There are multiple, variously shaped and sized black areas (arrows) along the sloping and lower borders of the navicular bone. Seen in conjunction with typical clinical signs, these abnormalities are consistent with a diagnosis of the navicular syndrome

Correct trimming of the foot is extremely important. The foot must be balanced so that it is placed squarely to the ground. The toes should be kept short. This helps to encourage expansion and growth of the heel.

It is recommended that, after suitable trimming, a flat shoe is used. The branches of the shoe should be long enough to provide support for the heels, and if the heels are badly collapsed and underrun, an egg-bar shoe can be helpful. Grooving the heels has been recommended for horses with contracted heels to allow more expansion of the heels. The author does not advocate this treatment. The shoes should be set wide at the heels to encourage expansion. Nails should not be placed farther back than the quarter of the foot, so that hoof-wall expansion is not restricted.

Exercise   Although rest may produce temporary improvement, lameness usually recurs when work is resumed. Regular exercise is important for normal blood flow through the foot, so any treatment should be combined with exercise to try to maintain normal blood flow. Provided that the horse is not very lame, then work may be done on hard or soft surfaces. The horse should also be turned out daily if possible, so that it is standing in its stable for the minimum possible time.

Analgesics Phenylbutazone and meclofenamic acid are drugs which have both anti-inflammatory and analgesic properties and will relieve lameness in most horses with navicular disease while they are being treated. These drugs merely alleviate the pain and do not treat the disease itself.

Warfarin Warfarin is a drug which prolongs blood clotting time. Some horses with navicular syndrome are improved by the use of this drug, which is administered in the feed. It is a potentially dangerous drug and the horse's blood clotting time must be monitored carefully. Permanent medication is usually necessary, but in some horses which have been treated for two years or more treatment can be withdrawn. Why the drug works is not understood.

Isoxsuprine Isoxsuprine is a drug used to dilate peripheral blood vessels in man. Some horses with the navicular syndrome improve while being treated with this drug, which is given in a feed or as a paste into the mouth. The drug is most helpful in the early stages of the disease and some horses may remain sound after a course of treatment. Results of treatment have been poor in horses in which the disease is more advanced.

Neurectomy The back of the foot can be desensitized by removing a small piece of each of the two nerves which innervate this area (palmar digital neurectomy). This relieves the pain associated with navicular disease. The procedure is successful in some horses but lameness may recur because the nerves regenerate. There are a number of potential complications of a neurectomy, including the development of painful neuromas (fibrous swellings at the cut end of the nerve) and necrosis (death) and rupture of the deep digital flexor tendon. Because the horse cannot feel the back part of the foot, daily foot care is essential so that puncture wounds, etc., are recognized early.

Desmotomy Recently a new procedure involving cutting the collateral (suspensory) ligaments of the navicular bone has been devised. It has produced encouraging results, enabling some horses which had been lame for a long time to return to work. Not enough horses have been followed for long enough after surgery to know whether there are any long-term adverse effects of the operation.

Radiographs and the pre-purchase examination

There is considerable controversy about the interpretation of radiographs of the navicular bone in clinically sound horses. There is an area of overlap between radiographic abnormalities seen in sound horses, which do not necessarily go on to develop the navicular syndrome, and changes seen in horses with this condition. Vets naturally tend to be cautious and may advise against the purchase of a horse with radiographic abnormalities in this category. However, these horses may never have a problem, whereas a horse with apparently normal navicular bones may subsequently develop the navicular syndrome. The author recommends that the feet should be radiographed if they are of unequal size or of abnormal shape; if there is any suspicion of a subtle gait abnormality; if the horse has not been in regular work prior to the examination; or if the horse is being purchased with a view to resale. The horse's shoes should be removed and its feet thoroughly trimmed and cleaned before radiography, and the resulting views must be of excellent quality.

FRACTURE OF THE NAVICULAR BONE

Clinical signs

There is a sudden onset of moderate to severe lameness. The horse may have trodden on a stone or kicked a solid object. Old, non-healed fractures of the navicular bone cause a similar lameness to the navicular syndrome. Fractures of the navicular bone occur both in forefeet and in hind feet.

Diagnosis

The horse is sound after desensitization of the back part of the foot. The fracture is visible on radiographs but must not be confused with a frog shadow, which also appears as a black line crossing the bone.

Treatment

Without treatment a variable degree of lameness persists. A neurectomy can be performed to desensitize the back part of the foot. Similar complications occur as for a neurectomy to treat navicular syndrome (see above). Degenerative joint disease of the proximal interphalangeal joint often develops subsequently. A few horses have been successfully treated surgically by having a screw placed through the bone. If the fracture is displaced or has been present for some time, the prognosis is poor.

ARTHROSIS OF THE DISTAL INTERPHALANGEAL (COFFIN) JOINT

Usually one forefoot is affected and the condition causes a unilateral forelimb lameness, which is worse when the horse is turned towards the affected leg. The lameness is improved by injecting local anaesthetic into the distal interphalangeal joint. No abnormalities of the joint can be identified on radiographs.

The foot must be correctly trimmed and shod. The condition may improve with rest, but often recurs when work is resumed. Some horses are made sound by injecting sodium hyaluronate or a glycosaminoglycan polysulphate into the joint.

SECONDARY (DEGENERATIVE) JOINT DISEASE (OSTEOARTHRITIS) OF THE DISTAL INTERPHALANGEAL (COFFIN) JOINT (LOW ARTICULAR RINGBONE)

The horse is lame. The forefeet are most often affected and the condition may be unilateral or bilateral. Sometimes there is swelling just above the coronary band on the front of the pastern. Lameness is alleviated by desensitization of the foot by nerve blocks. Changes typical of degenerative joint disease are seen on radiographs (see p. 177).

There is no effective treatment, although the use of phenylbutazone may relieve the pain sufficiently to allow the horse to be worked.

FRACTURE OF THE EXTENSOR PROCESS OF THE DISTAL (THIRD) PHALANX (PEDAL BONE)

The horse is lame, with the forefeet most commonly affected. Lameness is alleviated by desensitization of the foot by nerve blocks. The fracture can be seen on a lateral radiographic view of the foot.

Small fractures may be successfully treated by surgical removal. Larger fractures which involve part of the joint surface warrant a poor prognosis.

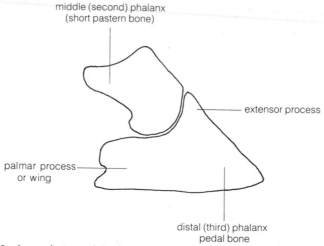

Figure 95　Lateral view of distal phalanges to slow the extensor process or wing of the distal phalanx (pedal bone)

WING FRACTURE OF THE DISTAL (THIRD) PHALANX (PEDAL BONE)

There is a sudden onset of severe lameness. Pressure applied with hoof testers across the affected heel may cause pain. Lameness is alleviated by desensitization of the foot. The fracture is visible on radiographs, although oblique views may be necessary.

If the fracture does not involve the distal interphalangeal (coffin) joint, box rest and application of a bar shoe for three to six months usually produces satisfactory results. If the fracture enters the joint, the prognosis is poor.

SIDEBONE

Sidebone is ossification of the cartilages of the foot. The whole cartilage may ossify from a single centre or from more than one centre. The latter results in two apparently separate bony masses, which should not be confused with a fracture.

Clinical signs

Sidebone occurs most commonly in the front feet of heavier types of horses (hunters, cobs, etc.) The cartilages above the coronary band feel firmer than usual. Many normal horses have sidebone. Both the inside and outside cartilages can be affected equally. In horses which place one heel to the ground momentarily before the other the sidebone may be more obvious on the side hitting the ground first. Only rarely does sidebone cause lameness.

Diagnosis and treatment

The diagnosis is confirmed by radiographic examination.

The condition rarely causes lameness. If one side of the foot is more severely affected than the other, this may reflect poor balance of the foot and the foot should be trimmed to restore correct balance.

QUITTOR

A quittor is a persistent draining sinus on the coronary band towards the heels and is associated with infection of one of the cartilages of the foot.

Clinical signs

The sinus discharges pus. There is associated soft-tissue swelling, pain on pressure to the area and lameness. It used to occur fairly frequently in working draught horses, but rarely in other types.

Treatment

The chronically infected tissue must be removed surgically.

KERATOMA

A keratoma is a tumour of the horn-producing cells of the foot. It is a rare condition. Forefeet and hind feet are affected equally.

Clinical signs

The shape of the foot becomes distorted. There is a variable degree of lameness.

Diagnosis and treatment

The diagnosis is confirmed by radiographs. Although the tumour is usually not radiopaque, and therefore cannot itself be seen, it presses on adjacent structures, such as the distal phalanx (pedal bone), and creates a defect in its outline. This must be differentiated from the radiolucent defect which results from infection.

Surgical removal of tumours is possible, but recurrence is likely.

OVERREACH

An overreach is caused by a horse striking the coronary band or heels of a forelimb by the toe of a hind limb.

Clinical signs

An overreach results in a laceration of variable depth and severity and associated soft-tissue bruising. Depending upon the site and severity of the injury, the horse may be sound or extremely lame – much more lame than would be anticipated from the appearance of the wound itself. This is the result of bruising rather than the wound itself. Although most commonly the back of the foot is injured, the inside or outside coronary band may be damaged. In these lateral locations the horizontal split at the coronary band must be differentiated from that caused by pus, which comes up the white line from a subsolar abscess, bursting out at the coronary band. In both instances pressure applied around the lesion causes pain. If there is bruising due to trauma the surrounding tissues may also be sore. If there is a subsolar abscess, pressure applied to the sole with hoof testers should identify a focus of pain.

Treatment

The wound should be thoroughly cleaned with a suitable antiseptic. If there is a large skin flap, it may be beneficial to cut this off. An antibiotic spray should be applied and this is most easily done by dabbing on the solution using cotton wool. Greasy ointments should be avoided as these tend to attract dirt. Wound powders have poor adherent qualities. The wound should be kept clean and dry and the horse is best kept in until satisfactory healing has occurred. If the horse is lame due to severe bruising, treatment with an anti-inflammatory analgesic such as phenylbutazone may be beneficial. Local laser treatment may accelerate healing of a severe wound.

Complications

Wounds involving the heels may take a long time to heal as repetitive movement in this area pulls the skin edges apart. Sometimes secondary infection may occur, which should be treated by poulticing and, if necessary, the administration of antibiotics. Damage of the horn-producing cells of the coronary band may cause either exuberant horn production or temporary failure of horn production, resulting in a horizontal crack in the hoof wall which will gradually grow out. Occasionally horn production is permanently arrested at the site of injury.

Overreach boots provide some protection.

CRACKED HEELS, MUD FEVER

Mud fever and cracked heels are synonymous terms for an identical condition, which is also referred to as scratches in America.

Clinical signs

The clinical signs are variable in severity, but essentially the underlying disease is the same. The disease is characterized by inflammation of the skin and subcutaneous tissues on the back of the pastern resulting in soft-tissue swelling, stretching of the skin, exudation of serum through the skin and ultimately cracks in the skin. The skin cracks are usually horizontal and may extend deeply. Constant motion of the skin on the back of the pastern encourages the skin cracks to gape. All these factors cause pain, resulting in a stiffness of gait or lameness. Secondarily, there may be diffuse inflammatory oedema of the affected leg(s), resulting in a filled appearance. The fissures in the skin may permit entry of pathogenic bacteria which cause infection and increased severity of the clinical signs. More than one limb may be affected.

Figure 96   A cracked heel

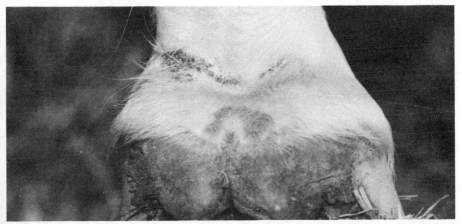

Cause

The condition may occur in stabled horses or horses turned out and is usually associated with wet conditions. Even heavy dew in the autumn may be a predisposing factor. The condition is seen in both heavily feathered horses and those with clipped legs. In grass-kept horses the incidence is higher in horses with a lot of feather, which presumably traps an excessive amount of moisture. Prolonged wetness of the skin may damage it, making it more susceptible to irritation by mud. There is potential for secondary infection. Some horses seem prone to recurrent attacks and in some years there appears to be a higher incidence. Horses may be more severely affected on some soil types. Poor hygiene, combined with a failure to recognize early clinical signs, contributes to development of overt disease.

Treatment

Treatment is aimed at removing the offending cause, reducing inflammation and eliminating infection if present. If at all possible, a grass-kept horse should be brought into drier conditions. Excessive feather should be removed and the area cleaned thoroughly and kept dry. A dilute iodine solution is a most effective cleansing agent. This treatment may be adequate for a mild case, but if there is considerable inflammation, then a soothing ointment containing corticosteroids, with or without antibiotics, should be applied. An oil-based cream will provide a barrier to water and corticosteroids will reduce inflammation. Dermobion is a commercially available ointment containing a corticosteroid (prednisolone), cod-liver oil and an antibiotic (neomycin). The author uses a cheaper, home-made mixture of Cetavlex cream, salphanilamide powder and prednisolone. In a very severe case it may be necessary to administer antibiotics by intra-muscular injection.

Usually clinical signs resolve fairly rapidly, although careful management must be practised to avoid a re-exacerbation. The skin must not dry out excessively, as this in itself will predispose to further cracking. Once the acute inflammation has resolved, a lanoline-based ointment may help to keep the skin supple as well as providing a barrier to water.

Prevention

Careful management of the stable-kept horse, including thorough cleaning and drying of the legs after exercise, usually prevents occurrence of the disease. Excessive feather should be removed, but clipping the legs is not recommended. Much controversy surrounds whether or not horses' legs should be washed clean and then dried or should be allowed to dry and then brushed clean. It has been suggested that washing legs while the pores are open permits the entry of dirt through the skin pores. The author has had no problems associated with washing, provided that the legs are dried properly afterwards. Many horses tolerate this better than having dried mud brushed off. Leaving the legs wet will not necessarily create a problem in a normal horse, but in a susceptible horse drying is important. Bandaging the legs is the best way to dry them effectively. Prevention in the grass-kept animal is more difficult, due to the ubiquitous mud. Excessive feather should be removed and the horse examined daily.

DISTAL INTERPHALANGEAL JOINT FLEXURAL DEFORMITY (CONTRACTED TENDONS, CLUB FOOT) See p. 278.

17

MISCELLANEOUS CONDITIONS
OF LAMENESS

STRINGHALT

Traditional stringhalt is a poorly understood condition in which the horse hyperflexes one or both hocks. It usually occurs in adult horses, is gradual in onset, and may be slowly progressive. In Australia a different type of stringhalt has been recognized, occurring mostly in pasture-kept horses in certain geographic locations, especially after periods of drought, often affecting several of a group of horses. Australian stringhalt is rapid in onset and invariably affects both hind limbs and sometimes the forelimbs as well. The majority of horses recover completely, but a few deteriorate progressively. The condition may be caused by ingestion of a plant toxin. The following discussion refers to traditional stringhalt.

Clinical signs

The horse exaggeratedly flexes one or both hind limbs when in motion. The abnormality is sometimes evident at all paces, but it is usually most apparent at walk, especially if the horse is turned or backed, and may disappear at trot. The condition may be intermittent and remain static or deteriorate.

Treatment

The cause of the condition is unknown. Some horses are successfully treated by the removal of a piece of the lateral digital extensor tendon at the level of the hock.

Prognosis

Unless the gait abnormality is extremely severe, affected horses are usually able to perform adequately, including jumping, but are unsuitable for dressage. A guarded to fair prognosis is warranted after surgery. Some horses improve initially but subsequently relapse.

SHIVERING

Shivering rarely results in a horse being unridable unless it cannot be shod. Therefore very few horses with this condition are humanely destroyed, so opportunities for post-mortem examination of affected horses are rare. As a result very little is known about the cause or causes of shivering.

Clinical signs

The horse involuntarily picks up a hind leg and holds it partly flexed, slightly away from the body. The leg shakes. Usually both hind legs are affected. The tail may be raised and quiver simultaneously. It is a rare condition seen most often in big horses, especially draught type. The symptoms are intermittent and are most reliably provoked by making the horse move backwards.

Treatment and prognosis

The cause of the condition is unknown, and there is no known treatment. Mildly affected horses are still able to work, but the condition is usually progressive, and may result in the farrier being unable to hold the affected limb in the shoeing position in order to shoe the horse.

LYMPHANGITIS

Widespread swelling of a limb below the knee or hock occurs for many reasons, including lymphangitis. A careful clinical examination of both the foot and the swollen region of the leg is necessary to establish the cause of the swelling.

Clinical signs

One or more legs are diffusely swollen. Hind legs are more commonly affected than forelegs, and usually the entire leg is swollen up to the level of the stifle, resulting in moderate to severe lameness. Surface lymph vessels are prominent and local lymph nodes are enlarged. Serum may exude through the skin. The rectal temperature may be raised. Heavy-hunter types seem especially prone.

Diagnosis

The clinical signs are fairly typical. The inflammation is often secondary to a chronic low-grade infection of the leg and careful inspection usually reveals an old wound or wounds. The condition must be differentiated from other causes of filled legs (see below).

Treatment

Treatment aims to eliminate the primary infection and reduce the soft-tissue swelling. Relatively long-term treatment with appropriate antibiotics is combined with cold hosing of the leg, bandaging and exercise.

Prognosis

Vigorous treatment can produce rewarding results, although the leg may remain permanently thickened. The problem may be recurrent, especially in hind limbs, and careful vigilance is necessary to detect and treat small wounds as early as possible.

FILLED LEGS

Filled legs are usually a managemental and cosmetic problem rather than one causing lameness.

Clinical signs

The condition is usually confined to the stabled horse. Heavy-hunter types are especially prone. There is diffuse swelling of the lower legs if the horse is kept in for more than twenty-four hours without exercise. The swelling is usually restricted to the areas below the knees and hocks and results in loss of definition of the tendons and suspensory ligaments. The hind legs are more commonly affected than the forelimbs, although all four may be affected simultaneously. Usually both hind legs are involved, and although the presence of soft-tissue swelling may impede mobility and cause stiffness, this resolves with exercise.

Diagnosis

The clinical signs are fairly typical but the condition must be differentiated from other problems which cause diffuse swelling of the legs. These include purpura haemorrhagica, congestive heart failure, recurrent lymphangitis (see above) and excessively low blood protein levels due to malnutrition or chronic liver disease.

   If there is only one hind limb or forelimb affected, it is more likely that there is a more serious underlying reason for the filling, such as cracked heels, pus in the foot, a puncture wound or a chronic low-grade infection.

Treatment

The condition usually resolves with exercise. Keeping the legs bandaged helps to prevent recurrence. If the horse has a day off it should be turned out for a few hours if possible.

BROKEN KNEES

Broken knees is the colloquial term used to describe lacerations on the front of the carpi (knees), caused by a fall onto the knees. It does not imply that any of the bones of the knee have been fractured. Because the horse is usually moving when the accident occurs, the knees tend to scrape along the ground for a short distance, resulting in tearing of the skin and underlying structures and bruising.

Clinical signs

There is usually an area of complete skin loss and moderate haemorrhage (bleeding). The severity of damage is extremely variable. Sometimes only the skin is torn, but in more serious cases the underlying soft tissues may be stripped off to reveal the bones. The sheath of one of the tendons which passes over the front of the knee (extensor carpi radialis, common digital extensor, lateral digital extensor) may be torn so that there is leakage of synovial fluid. Very occasionally the joint capsule of one of the knee joints may be disrupted.

Treatment

The extent of the damage must be assessed carefully and this is only possible after thorough cleaning of the wounds. The hair in the area immediately around the wound should be trimmed and each knee hosed for at least five minutes to remove any debris which may have accumulated in the wound. Any pieces of tissue which have been severely damaged and are likely to die due to disruption of their blood supply should be trimmed off. This is called débridement of the wound. The wound should be further cleaned using an antiseptic such as a dilute iodine solution. At this stage it should be possible to evaluate which structures have been damaged. Thorough cleaning is essential to minimize the risks of secondary infection. Administration of a short course of antibiotics may also help to reduce the likelihood of infection occurring.

Unlike a cut, where the two skin edges remain close together and heal by so-called first intention, with minimal scar formation, broken knees must heal by second intention. This is the ingrowth of skin epithelial cells from the edges of the wound. The skin defect is first filled by granulation tissue. Constant movement of the edges of the wound and the granulation bed will delay healing, therefore comparative immobility is important. For this reason it is necessary to restrict the horse to a box and ideally he should be tied up for twenty-four hours a day to prevent him from lying down until healing is well established.

Bruising usually causes swelling and this will tend to draw the skin edges farther apart. To minimize swelling it can be beneficial to administer an anti-inflammatory drug such as phenylbutazone as soon as possible after the injury. Application of a light bandage over the knees is also helpful. A non-adherent dressing (e.g. Melolin) is placed over the open wounds, followed by Gamgee and a crepe bandage, held in place by either Elastoplast or a Pressage bandage.

Bandaging the knees until healing is progressing satisfactorily helps to keep the wounds clean. Granulation tissue tends to dry and crack if left exposed; keeping the wounds covered helps to keep them moist, which probably aids healing. Bandaging may also reduce the likelihood of production of exuberant granulation tissue (proud flesh). Horses are particularly prone to development of excessive granulation tissue, especially in wounds on the limbs. This must either be cut off, a pain-free procedure since granulation tissue has no nerve supply, or controlled using a suitable substance applied directly onto the tissue. There are many such preparations, including corticosteroid creams, copper sulphate solution and lead lotion.

Normal wound healing may be accelerated by laser therapy and this treatment can be extremely helpful, although it needs to be repeated. Under normal conditions the wounds may take four to six weeks to heal completely. The horse may need to be kept tied up for at least two weeks but may be given small amounts of walking exercise in hand. Wound healing may be delayed if the horse is permitted to move about or, especially, if it is allowed to lie down.

Tetanus prophylaxis is mandatory. The horse should be fed maintenance rations only.

Complications

If a tendon sheath has been damaged, it is occasionally possible to repair it surgically. However, often it is too badly torn and must be left to heal spontaneously. Sometimes a synovial sinus develops: there is a small hole in the skin through which synovial fluid drains. This will close eventually, although it may take considerably longer to heal than the original skin wounds.

Prognosis

The wounds will ultimately heal satisfactorily but some residual fibrous swelling may persist. The amount of scar tissue which develops is related to the size and severity of the initial injury and the speed of healing. White hairs may grow at the sites of injury and there may be small areas of permanent hair loss.

Prevention

If a horse is prone to stumbling, then knee boots should be worn when it is worked on roads or hard tracks. The toes of the feet should be kept short. Rolling the toes of the shoes may facilitate breakover, thus reducing the chances of stumbling.

GENERAL TRAUMA WITH SECONDARY INFECTION

One of the most common causes of lameness is trauma causing bruising and laceration, with secondary infection, or a puncture wound. Infection may develop due to failure to recognize and treat the wound or due to inappropriate treatment. The horse is generally found with a so-called big leg.

Clinical signs

There is diffuse, warm, painful swelling. A wound which exudes pus may be readily identifiable. Alternatively it may be necessary to clip the hair to identify the nature and extent of the wounds. Lameness is moderate to severe and the horse may be depressed and inappetent and have an elevated rectal temperature.

Treatment

The hair around the wound should be clipped and thoroughly cleaned with a suitable antiseptic. If the wound is severely contaminated, preliminary hosing may be helpful. If the wound is of puncture type, a hot poultice may help to draw the infection. The poultice should be replaced twice daily. Depending on the nature and extent of the wound, a dry, non-adherent dressing may be applied if the area is accessible to bandaging.

If infection is severe, then appropriate antibiotic therapy is required for at least five days. Tetanus prophylaxis is essential. If the horse has received regular tetanus vaccinations, no further preventive treatment is required. However, if the vaccination history of the horse is uncertain, tetanus antitoxin should be administered and a course of tetanus vaccination started. If possible the horse should be confined to a box or covered yard. If infection is not resolved completely within five days or if no improvement is observed after three days of treatment, then swabs should be collected from the wound for bacterial culture and antibiotic-sensitivity testing to check which antibiotics are effective against the bacteria causing the infection.

If appropriate antibiotic treatment fails to resolve the infection, then radiography should be performed to identify bony changes, if any, typical of infectious osteitis or osteomylitis and to preclude the presence of a radiopaque foreign body. Diagnostic ultrasonography can be used to identify a non-radiopaque foreign body. Surgical exploration is indicated if neither is identified.

HEREDITARY MULTIPLE EXOSTOSIS See p. 170.

18
THE NECK, BACK AND PELVIS; INCOORDINATION

Functional anatomy

The horse's neck consists of seven cervical vertebrae. The back comprises eighteen thoracic vertebrae, five or six lumbar vertebrae, the sacrum and the coccygeal vertebrae. The vertebrae are complex in their structure and lock firmly together. The bones are held together by ligaments and muscles which attach to them. The back is a relatively rigid structure capable of only limited movement and it is the author's opinion that vertebrae cannot become displaced relative to each other. Each vertebra has a large hole in it, the vertebral canal, through which passes the spinal cord. On the top surface of each vertebrae is a bony projection of variable size, the dorsal spinous process. These are longest in the withers region. The tops of the dorsal spinous processes can be felt in poorly muscled horses. Particularly in the cranial lumbar region (the area behind the saddle, in front of the 'jumper's bump') prominence of the dorsal spinous processes due to muscle wastage may make the back appear 'roached' (i.e. an upward, convex curvature). Attached to the top of the dorsal spinous processes is the supraspinous ligament (Figure 101). On either side of the dorsal spinous processes are the paired longissimus dorsi muscles.

The pelvis, consisting on each side of the fused ilium, ischium and pubis, is attached to the sacrum via the sacroiliac joints. The pelvis is bound tightly to the sacrum and lumbar vertebrae by the sacroiliac ligaments. The so-called jumper's bump is the tubera sacrale (part of the ilium). These are more or less prominent depending on the horse's conformation and degree of muscling. The tubera sacrale are normally level when viewed from behind (see Figure 83, p. 225). The tubera coxae are also normally level.

There is considerable variation in the normal conformation of the horse's back. Long-backed horses seem more prone to muscular injuries. Short-backed horses are more likely to have impingement (rubbing together) of the dorsal spinous processes.

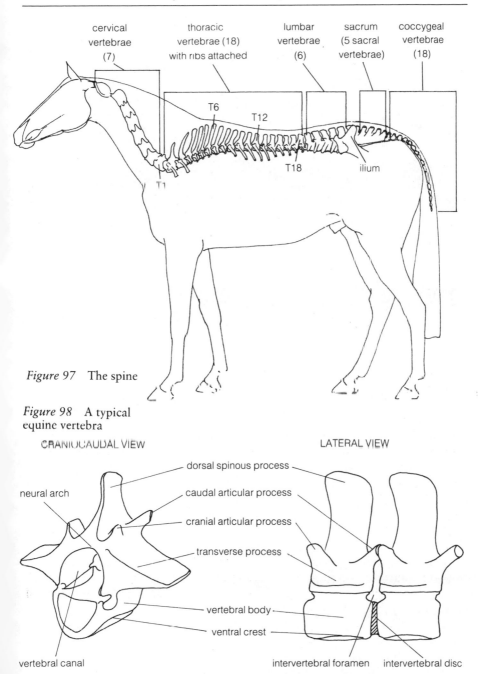

cervical vertebrae (7)

thoracic vertebrae (18) with ribs attached

lumbar vertebrae (6)

sacrum (5 sacral vertebrae)

coccygeal vertebrae (18)

T6

T12

T18

ilium

T1

Figure 97 The spine

Figure 98 A typical equine vertebra

CRANIOCAUDAL VIEW

LATERAL VIEW

neural arch

dorsal spinous process

caudal articular process

cranial articular process

transverse process

vertebral body

ventral crest

vertebral canal

intervertebral foramen

intervertebral disc

Firm palpation of the back in the area behind the saddle induces the horse to dip its back. This is a normal reaction. Firm palpation of the top of the hindquarters stimulates the horse to arch its back. The normal horse should

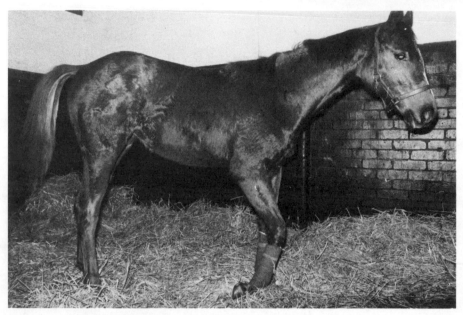

Figure 99   A roached back

be able to dip and arch the back repeatedly without showing resentment and without the back muscles going into spasm. If the horse has back pain, it may be reluctant to dip and arch the back; the back muscles may feel firm and may fasiculate – that is, show small, localized muscle contractions – and the horse may demonstrate resistance to palpation of the back. It may initially sink exaggeratedly and then the muscles become tense. Some hypersensitive horses show an exaggerated response to palpation of the back in the absence of pain. It is therefore important to judge the horse's temperament and the way it reacts to handling before making a conclusive judgement about the presence or absence of back pain.

Back pain may be a primary problem or may develop secondarily to an altered way of moving due to lameness. A careful assessment of the whole animal is essential when examining a horse with suspected back pain.

It is the author's opinion that certain methods of palpating the back can relieve muscle spasm and associated pain, thus producing clinical improvement. The author does not believe that any method of manipulation can move vertebrae or move the pelvis relative to the back.

Conditions of the Neck

Many normal horses are slightly less well muscled on one side of the neck compared with the other and are stiffer to the right than to the left or vice versa. A horse with neck pain usually shows stiffness of the neck – it is unable to flex the neck from side to side and may find it difficult to raise and lower its head. The neck may be held abnormally low at rest. In order to graze the horse may need to straddle the forelimbs or even go down on one knee. With the exception of the wobbler syndrome (see p. 274) and congenital malformations of the cervical vertebrae (see p. 275), most neck problems are the result of a fall or other traumatic incident.

MUSCLE DAMAGE

Clinical signs

There is neck stiffness and pain on manipulation of the neck. Faradism may help to identify the affected muscles.

Treatment

Treatment is aimed at relieving pain and facilitating muscle repair. Non-steroidal anti-inflammatory drugs such as phenylbutazone alleviate pain. Treatment with faradism or ultrasound facilitates muscle repair. The horse should be rested until the clinical signs have resolved. The prognosis is usually good.

FRACTURES OF THE CERVICAL VERTEBRAE

Clinical signs

Fractures of the cervical vertebrae cause neck stiffness and pain. There may be an area of localized sweating and some of the neck muscles may atrophy. The horse may also show signs of incoordination (see p. 274). The diagnosis is confirmed by radiography.

Figure 100 Anatomy of the neck and withers region

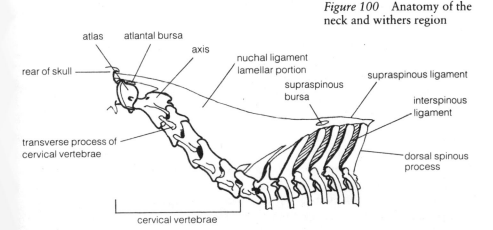

Treatment

Most fractures are not amenable to surgical treatment and must be allowed to heal spontaneously. The horse should be confined to a restricted area. It should be fed at chest height if unable to raise or lower its head. If there are signs of incoordination, treatment with corticosteroids or dimethyl sulphoxide may be beneficial during the first forty-eight hours after the accident. If signs of incoordination persist the prognosis is guarded. Some fractures heal spontaneously with excellent results; sometimes there is a degree of permanent neck stiffness.

NECK ABSCESS

An abscess in the neck can be the result of an intramuscular injection, a penetrating foreign body or, rarely, a blood-borne infection.

Clinical signs

There is localized heat, swelling and pain, and neck stiffness.

Treatment

Hot compresses applied to the area may resolve the problem if it is the result of a reaction to an intramuscular injection. Oral administration of phenylbutazone will resolve pain. In more serious cases antibiotic therapy, preferably administered orally, may be necessary. If the abscess does not resolve then an ultrasound scan may be used to define better its extent, before surgical drainage is performed.

TORTICOLLIS (WRYNECK)　See p. 628.

Conditions of the Thoracolumbar Spine

BACK PAIN

The clinical signs of back pain are often subtle and result in a reduced standard of performance. The horse may move in a restricted fashion with limited hind-limb impulsion with or without intermittent dragging of the toes. Obvious unilateral hind-limb lameness is rarely associated with a primary problem involving the thoracolumbar spine. The horse may be stiff and reluctant to work on a circle. It may also be difficult to keep on the bit. A horse which formerly made a well-shaped bascule over fences may start to hollow the back, find combination fences difficult and rush on the approach or refuse. The horse may be difficult to turn. The clinical signs can be more obvious when the horse is ridden rather than moving freely on the lunge. The horse is often poorly muscled over the back.

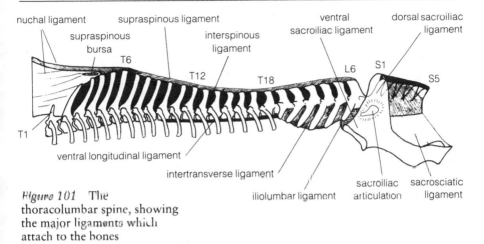

nuchal ligament   supraspinous ligament   ventral sacroiliac ligament   dorsal sacroiliac ligament
supraspinous bursa   interspinous ligament
T6   T12   T18   L6   S1   S5
T1
ventral longitudinal ligament
intertransverse ligament
iliolumbar ligament   sacroiliac articulation   sacrosciatic ligament

Figure 101 The thoracolumbar spine, showing the major ligaments which attach to the bones

Similar clinical signs are also shown by horses with bilateral forelimb lameness, for example, the navicular syndrome, or bilateral hind-limb lameness, for example, bone spavin. Any horse showing these symptoms must be assessed as a whole. In particular it must be seen working in circles, preferably on a hard surface, which may accentuate lameness and facilitate diagnosis.

IMPINGEMENT AND OVERRIDING OF THE DORSAL SPINOUS PROCESSES (KISSING SPINES)

The dorsal spinous processes of normal horses tend to be closest together in the mid-back region (the caudal thoracic area) and may touch (impinge). This is most common in short-backed horses, especially Thoroughbred types. A moderate degree of impingement is often unassociated with clinical signs. However, severe crowding of the dorsal spinous processes can cause back pain.

Clinical signs

The horse is reluctant to dip the back and will tend to hold it rigidly with the muscles in partial spasm. If the horse is rested, these clinical signs disappear temporarily. Because many normal horses show a degree of impingement, the diagnosis of a clinically significant problem can only be made by the combination of a clinical examination and radiographs, because radiographic examination alone is confusing.

Treatment

In young horses the dorsal spinous processes may remodel and form false joints and the clinical signs improve after approximately six months' rest. If the clinical signs do not resolve completely, then phenylbutazone is helpful.

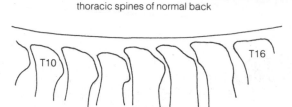

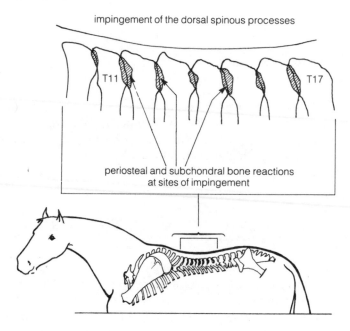

Figure 102   Thoracic spines –
normal and impinged

In selected horses surgical removal of the summits of one or two dorsal
spinous processes is successful.

MUSCLE STRAIN

Muscle strain is usually the result of a fall, an awkward jump or a mis-step.

Clinical signs

Palpation of the back may reveal an area or areas of sensitivity and/or muscle
spasm. Both sides may be similarly affected or one side may be worse. This
can be confirmed using faradism. Damaged muscle cells leak, releasing
creatine kinase and aspartoaminotransferase into the blood; therefore, if
muscle damage is severe, concentrations of these enzymes in the blood may
rise.

Treatment

The aims of treatment are to relieve muscle spasm and to facilitate repair of damaged muscle. Local treatment with faradism or ultrasound, combined with rest and controlled exercise, is beneficial. Muscle spasm can also be relieved by manipulation. The period of rest necessary is extremely variable: sometimes up to three months is required, but in many cases ten to fourteen days is sufficient, followed by a slow resumption of normal work. Premature resumption of work may result in chronic muscle pain, which can be much more difficult to diagnose and treat.

SPRAIN OF THE SUPRASPINOUS LIGAMENT

This usually is the result of a fall when jumping at speed.

Clinical signs

Muscle atrophy over the back develops rapidly. The horse's movement is severely restricted. The history and clinical signs are fairly typical. Sometimes the diagnosis can be confirmed by radiographic examination. Associated with strain of the supraspinous ligament, small flakes of bone are detached from the summits of the dorsal spinous processes in the mid-thoracic region.

Treatment

A prolonged period of rest (six months) usually results in total remission of clinical signs with a favourable prognosis.

OTHER CAUSES OF BACK PAIN

As in man, the causes of back pain in the horse are poorly understood. Nevertheless the clinical signs of other problems are frequently wrongly attributed to back pain. The horse which is moving poorly should be assessed as a whole; bilateral forelimb lameness or bilateral hind-limb lameness is often confused with a primary back problem.

FRACTURES OF THE BACK

FRACTURES OF THE THORACOLUMBAR SPINE

Fractures of the thoracolumbar spine or the sacrum are rare and are usually the result of an accident such as a fall. The horse exhibits pain and patchy sweating and may show complete or partial paralysis of the hind-limbs due to damage to the spinal cord. Paralysis may not be immediate in onset, but usually develops within twelve to twenty-four hours. There is no treatment and the prognosis is hopeless.

FRACTURES OF THE SACRUM

Fractures of the sacrum may show less severe clinical signs initially because nerve function of the hind-legs remains intact. However, paralysis of the bladder and tail usually result due to damage to the cauda equina, part of the spinal cord. Paralysis of the bladder causes urinary retention and overflow (incontinence) and secondary cystitis. Nerve function is rarely restored, so the prognosis is poor if bladder function is affected. The rare fractures of the sacrum which do not cause nerve dysfunction have a better outlook for recovery.

FRACTURES OF THE WITHERS

Fractures of the dorsal spinous processes in the cranial thoracic (withers) region occur as a result of trauma: for example, a horse rearing up and falling over backwards. There is swelling in the withers region and crepitus may be felt. The horse tends to stand with its forelimbs close together and is reluctant to lower its head and neck to graze. It may move in a restricted manner. The diagnosis is confirmed by radiographic examination. Treatment other than rest is usually unnecessary and the prognosis is favourable, although a specially fitted saddle may be required.

Conditions of the Pelvis

FRACTURES OF THE PELVIS

Fractures of the three bones of the pelvis – the ilium, the ischium and the pubis – occur spontaneously in two- and three-year-old Thoroughbred horses, especially fillies, when galloping. Fractures in foals and yearlings are usually a sequel to rearing up and falling over. Fractures in older horses are less common and are usually the result of a fall or collision with a solid object.

Clinical signs

There is a sudden onset of severe hind-limb lameness. Fractures of the tuber coxae (knocked-down hip) may demonstrate only mild lameness. Careful palpation of the hindquarters and/or an internal examination via the rectum may reveal crepitus. There may be localized patchy sweating over the hindquarters. If the ilium has been fractured, the pelvis may appear asymmetrical when viewed from behind.

Diagnosis

A fracture can usually be suspected based on the clinical signs. The exact configuration of the fracture can only be determined by radiographic examination, which necessitates placing the horse on its back under general anaesthesia. The prognosis depends on the location and configuration of the fracture.

Treatment and prognosis

There is usually no treatment other than box rest. Some horses become sound, especially if the fracture involves the tuber coxae or the ischium.

Many horses with pelvic fractures will be suitable for breeding, although permanently lame. If the fracture involves the hip joint, the prognosis is generally guarded because secondary degenerative joint disease (arthritis) is an inevitable sequel. Young horses have a better prognosis than older ones.

SECONDARY (DEGENERATIVE) JOINT DISEASE (OSTEOARTHRITIS) OF THE COXOFEMORAL (HIP) JOINT

Unlike in man, this is a rare condition in the horse and is usually the result of getting a hind leg trapped and severely wrenching the joint or an awkward fall, or it may develop secondary to a fracture. There is severe wastage of the muscles of the hindquarter and moderate to severe lameness. The horse may swing the leg outwards as it is advanced to avoid flexion of the joint, or may move on three tracks with the hindquarters deviating from the lame limb, so that the lame leg is placed between the imprints of the two forelimbs. The lameness may be accentuated by hyperflexion of the hind leg or by pulling the hind leg outwards or forwards. Diagnosis is confirmed by radiographic examination, but this is only possible with the horse lying on its back under general anaesthesia. There is no treatment and the prognosis is hopeless.

SACROILIAC DISEASE

Clinical signs

Slight unilateral or bilateral hind-limb lameness or poor hind-limb impulsion is associated with asymmetry of the bony prominences of the pelvis, the tubera sacrale and the tubera coxae (see Figure 83, p. 225). Symmetry or levelness can only be assessed with the horse standing perfectly squarely on level ground. Muscle wastage may give a false impression of asymmetry (unlevelness) of the tubera sacrale and tubera coxae. There may be muscle wastage in association with the unlevelness. A marked disparity in height of the tubera sacrale is suggestive of disease of the sacroiliac joints, although many clinically normal horses show slight asymmetry.

Diagnosis

All other possible causes of hind-limb lameness must be eliminated before chronic sacroiliac disease is suggested as the diagnosis. Occasionally changes involving the sacroiliac joints can be seen on radiographs. This merits a poor prognosis.

Treatment

Some horses respond to rest. Slight hind-limb unlevelness may persist, though this is thought to be related to mechanical instability of the sacroiliac joints, rather than to pain.

Prognosis

Many horses are able to perform adequately despite slight unlevelness especially if they are kept fit. A few horses have recurrent problems. Big horses seem especially prone. The condition is rarely seen in ponies.

SPRAIN OF THE SACROILIAC LIGAMENTS

There is a sudden onset of hind-limb lameness which may be associated with a fall or a mis-step. Palpation of the hindquarters in the region of the tubera sacrale and tubera coxae causes pain. Manipulation of the leg may be resented.

Rest is the most important treatment. Faradism and ultrasound may be helpful. The prognosis is usually fair, although some horses may develop signs of chronic sacroiliac disease.

INCOORDINATION

Incoordination is a general term used to describe abnormal placement of a limb or limbs due to lack of awareness of the precise position of the limb. In some cases there may also be motor dysfunction due to an inability to use certain muscles. There are many potential causes of incoordination, the most common of which is the wobbler syndrome.

WOBBLER SYNDROME

The wobbler syndrome describes a number of conditions which result in compression of the spinal cord in the neck and cause a typical incoordinate gait. Hind limbs are more severely affected than forelimbs and, because the horse lacks awareness of where it is placing its limbs and often has some hind-limb weakness, it has a loose, wobbly gait – hence the name wobbler syndrome.

Clinical signs

The syndrome occurs most commonly in young, rapidly growing Thoroughbreds. The incidence in colts is higher than in fillies. The syndrome can also occur in older horses of all types. Ponies are rarely affected.

The clinical signs may be sudden and severe or subtle and insidious in onset, and may remain static or progress. If the syndrome develops gradually, at first the horse may show slight, intermittent, shifting hind-limb lameness. The toes may be dragged. When turned in small circles, the horse may place the hind-legs abnormally and may swing one leg outwards (circumduction). As the condition progresses the horse will tend to stand with the hind legs in odd positions. When the horse walks and trots the legs may be placed very deliberately to the ground. The hindquarters may look bouncy. The forelimbs are usually much less severely affected, but may show a stiff, stilted, spastic gait. If the clinical signs are sudden and severe in onset, the horse may appear normal one day and have little control over limb placement the next. If it has to stop or turn suddenly, it may fall over.

Diagnosis

The clinical signs are typical. The reason for compression of the spinal cord can sometimes be determined by radiographs of the neck. It is important to try to establish the cause of the problem if breeding is being considered.

Treatment

The condition is incurable, and may or may not be progressive. Some horses learn to accommodate to an extent but are not safe to ride, although they are suitable for breeding. However, in some forms of the syndrome there is probably a hereditary predisposition for development of the disease, so these horses should not be used for breeding. In the United States surgery has been performed on selected cases, resulting in some improvement in the clinical signs, but rarely are treated horses completely normal.

Prevention

One form of the syndrome is related to osteochondrosis (see p. 173), for which there is a hereditary predisposition. High planes of nutrition which encourage rapid growth may encourage manifestation of the condition; therefore young animals should be restricted in their plane of nutrition and growth rate.

CONGENITAL MALFORMATION OF THE CERVICAL (NECK) VERTEBRAE

Congenital malformations of the cervical vertebrae may cause abnormal pressure on the spinal cord resulting in incoordination. Although the bony abnormality is present at birth, the clinical signs of incoordination are sometimes nor apparent until the foal is several months old. The most common condition is called occipito-atlanto-axial malformation, which occurs most frequently in Arabs and in this breed is an inheritable disease (see p. 628). There is no evidence that other congenital malformations are inherited.

NEUROAXONAL DYSTROPHY OR EQUINE DEGENERATIVE MYELOENCEPHALOPATHY

Equine degenerative myeloencephalopathy is a primary degenerative condition of the spinal cord, the cause of which is uncertain. It occurs most commonly in Arabs and Morgans suggesting a familial incidence, but is not directly heritable. Clinical signs usually develop within the first year of life and may be slowly progressive. As in the wobbler syndrome, the hind limbs are usually more severely affected than the forelimbs. The disease cannot be diagnosed definitively except at post-mortem examination. There is no treatment.

FRACTURES

A fracture of a cervical vertebrae is usually the result of a fall and may cause compression of the spinal cord resulting in incoordination. There is usually associated neck stiffness and pain. The diagnosis is confirmed by radiography. In some horses, depending on the site and configuration of the fracture, incoordination persists. In a few horses the signs of incoordination resolve rapidly, suggesting that there is not permanent pressure on the spinal cord. Some fractures heal spontaneously, and although the horse may have some permanent neck stiffness, it may otherwise be normal. However, if a large amount of callus is produced during fracture healing, the callus itself may press on the spinal cord and cause incoordination. It may be impossible at the time of the accident to predict the eventual outcome for the horse; it may be necessary to monitor its progress for several weeks or months.

BRUISING OF THE SPINAL CORD

The spinal cord may be severely bruised following a fall. Inflammation around the cord results in the formation of oedema, causing pressure on the spinal cord. Either of these conditions will result in incoordination. Treatment with anti-inflammatory agents such as corticosteroids or with the drug dimethyl sulphoxide may facilitate recovery. Signs of improvement are usually apparent within twenty-four hours although it may take considerably longer before the horse appears completely normal. Persistence of severe incoordination for more than forty-eight hours warrants a guarded prognosis and usually indicates that there is additional, irreversible, damage.

MIGRATING PARASITES

Parasites which migrate through the spinal cord causing damage are a rare cause of incoordination. In contrast to the wobbler syndrome, the clinical signs are usually asymmetrical – one hind limb may be much more severely affected than the other. There is often muscle wastage. The diagnosis is usually based upon the clinical signs, lack of significant radiographic abnormalities and the progression of the disease. Most cases are not amenable to treatment but some early presumed cases of equine protozoal myelitis have been treated successfully.

CEREBELLAR HYPOPLASIA   See pp. 113 and 627

OTHER BRAIN LESIONS

Conditions of the brain are rare in the horse but can cause incoordination together with other clinical signs involving the head: for example, a head tilt, drooping of an ear or one side of the lips, blindness, abnormal position of the eyes or patchy sweating. Treatment is usually unsuccessful.

19
FLEXURAL AND ANGULAR LIMB DEFORMITIES IN FOALS

Limb deformities in foals are quite common and can be divided into flexural deformities and angular limb deformities. Some foals may have both types of deformity.

FLEXURAL DEFORMITIES

Flexural deformities of the limbs (so-called contracted tendons) may be congenital, i.e. present at birth, or acquired, i.e. develop after birth.

Congenital Flexural Deformities

A number of foals are born unable to straighten one or more limbs. If the limbs are manipulated passively they can usually be straightened. This condition is thought to be in part related to the position of the foetus in the uterus (windswept deformity). The majority of these foals show progressive improvement over the first few days of life and no treatment is required. Occasionally it is not possible to straighten the affected limbs passively, and this warrants a more guarded prognosis. Similarly many foals are born with apparently lax flexor tendons, so that the fetlocks are overextended and drop towards the ground. This condition usually improves spontaneously (see p. 290).

Acquired Flexural Deformities

DISTAL INTERPHALANGEAL (COFFIN) JOINT FLEXURAL DEFORMITY

Although this has been called contracture of the deep digital flexor tendon, there is no evidence to support the hypothesis that the tendon is contracted.

Clinical signs

Rapidly growing foals between six weeks and six months old are most commonly affected, the condition appearing in one or both forelimbs. The position of the limb becomes more upright and affected foals have been called toe dancers, as the foot becomes upright and boxy. The condition may occur apparently spontaneously or secondarily to a painful condition such as pus in the foot.

Diagnosis

The clinical signs are typical. Any underlying primary condition must be identified and treated accordingly. If the condition has been present for longer than two to three weeks the foot should be radiographed to establish whether any secondary problems have developed.

Treatment

Any primary problem must be treated and appropriate analgesics administered. If the condition has occurred spontaneously, the diet must be severely restricted. The feet should be carefully trimmed to lower the heels as much as possible. The toes should be kept well rounded to facilitate breakover. If the disease is recognized early and treated quickly, the condition may resolve. If no improvement is observed or if the condition deteriorates, surgical treatment (cutting the accessory ligament of the deep digital flexor tendon the inferior check ligament) is indicated.

Prognosis

The prognosis is usually favourable unless secondary changes (for example, degenerative joint disease of the distal interphalangeal joint) have supervened. Pedal osteitis may be a sequel.

METACARPOPHALANGEAL (FETLOCK) JOINT FLEXURAL DEFORMITY

This condition has also been incorrectly called contracted tendon.

Clinical signs

The condition occurs mostly in the forelimbs, and one or both legs may be affected. It is usually seen in well-grown yearlings. The fetlock and pastern joints become more upright and the fetlock starts to knuckle over and may be held permanently so.

Diagnosis

The clinical signs are typical. In contrast to distal interphalangeal joint flexural deformity (see above), the foot shape is not usually deformed.

Treatment

In mild cases conservative treatment may be successful. The diet must be restricted and analgesics administered. Corrective shoeing is sometimes helpful. A toe extension can be placed on the shoe to delay breakover. Slight elevation of the heels may also help. Keeping the leg in gutter splints may be beneficial.

If conservative treatment fails, surgical treatment is indicated. Some cases are improved by cutting the accessory ligament of the deep digital flexor tendon (the inferior check ligament). If this fails desmotomy of the accessory ligament of the superficial digital flexor tendon (superior check desmotomy) may help.

Prognosis

The prognosis is more guarded than for distal interphalangeal joint flexural deformities, especially if surgical treatment is required.

ANGULAR LIMB DEFORMITIES

Many foals are born with legs that are not completely straight: for example, the knees may deviate inwards (knock knees) or the fetlocks deviate outwards. Such foals usually show progressive and fairly rapid improvement. The condition usually affects both front legs and less frequently the hind legs. One leg may be more severely affected than the other. There is cause for concern if the deformity is severe or if no improvement occurs.

There are many causes. If a foal is born prematurely or is one of a twin, the small bones of the knee or hock may not be properly formed and may be unable to withstand the stresses of weightbearing, which tends to compress and distort the bones. In other foals the bones are completely formed but, for various reasons, growth may occur more rapidly on one side of the leg compared with the other (imbalance of metaphyseal or epiphyseal growth – see below), so that the leg is crooked. If one of the physes (growth plates) of a bone is injured, the growth in that area will be decreased.

IMBALANCE OF METAPHYSEAL OR EPIPHYSEAL GROWTH

In this condition one side of the growth plate is growing faster than the other due to the imbalance of growth in the metaphysis or the epiphysis (Figure 103). This imbalance causes the limb to deviate away from the side of fastest growth.

Precise nomenclature is necessary to describe accurately the direction of angulation of the affected leg. This is accomplished by using a line bisecting the leg (Figure 104). The term 'carpus valgus' is used when the leg below the

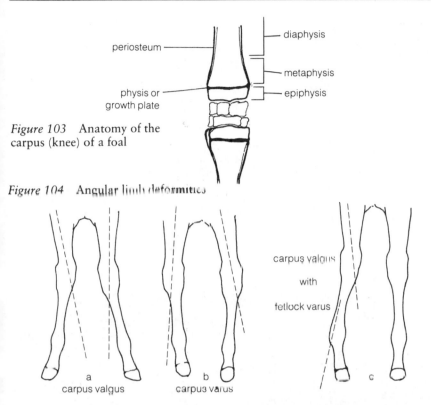

periosteum

diaphysis

metaphysis

physis or
growth plate

epiphysis

Figure 103 Anatomy of the
carpus (knee) of a foal

Figure 104 Angular limb deformities

carpus valgus

with

fetlock varus

a
carpus valgus

b
carpus varus

c

carpus (knee) falls outside this line (Figure 104a). The term 'carpus varus' is used when the leg falls inside this line (Figure 104b). In these cases the direction of the fetlock follows the line of the third metacarpal (cannon) bone. However, there may be a combined situation in which the third metacarpal deviates to the outside of the line bisecting the carpus but the fetlock deviates towards the midline (Figure 104c). This is described as 'carpus valgus with fetlock varus'. In addition, some degree of rotation of the third metacarpal bone usually occurs with a valgus deformity.

Location

These deformities are seen in a variety of locations:

(a) the carpus (valgus more commonly than varus);
(b) the fetlock (varus more commonly than valgus);
(c) the distal tibia (valgus more commonly than varus);
(d) other locations (very rare).

Cause

The cause of angular limb deformities in foals due to asynchronous longitudinal growth is complex. Certain factors that contribute to this

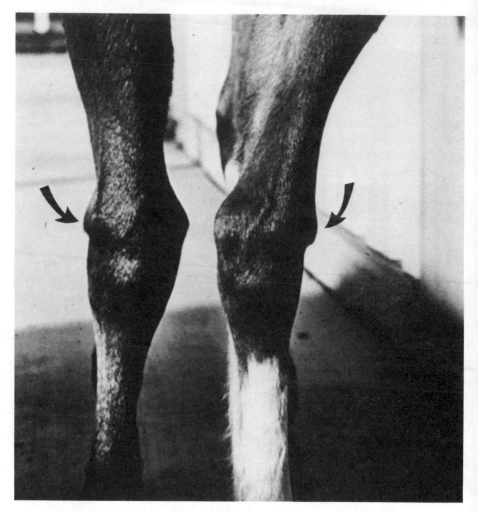

Figure 105   A case of angular limb deformity (carpus valgus) with physitis (arrows)

condition also contribute to the syndrome of physitis (see p. 163). Both physitis and angular limb deformities can be seen in the same individual, although physitis is generally seen in older animals (Figure 105).

Trauma   Trauma in the form of abnormal pressure on the growth plate is believed to be one of the main underlying causes of angular deformities in foals. This pressure can cause cartilage cells within the growth plate to die and bone growth at this site to cease. If the pressure is asymmetrical, the growth plate damage is uneven and this leads to retarded longitudinal growth on the side of excessive pressure (the concave side of the joint). If the asymmetric loading is not severe, nature responds by increasing growth on the concave side to achieve normality. If the loading is excessive and nature cannot respond adequately, a vicious circle ensues with the resulting angulation leading to an even greater asymmetry of load. Virtually all forms of treatment (surgery, casting, etc.) are directed at interrupting this cycle (Figure 107). Factors which can cause asymmetrical loading on the growth plate include joint laxity, malpositioning in the uterus (windswept deformity), poor foot trimming, heavy muscling, overactivity or lameness in the opposite limb.

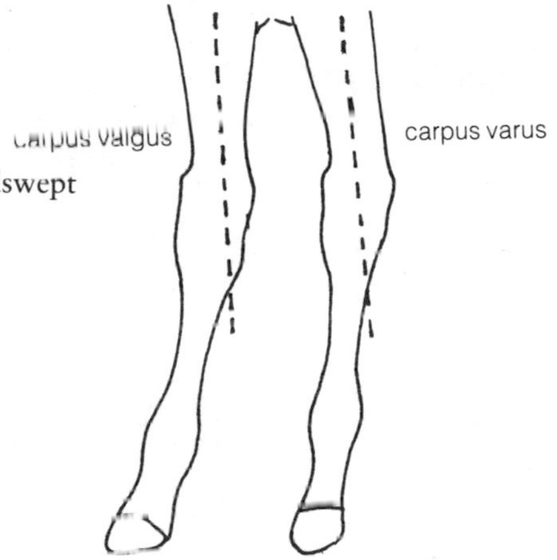

carpus valgus   carpus varus

Figure 106 Windswept
deformity

Figure 107 The factors involved
in angular limb deformity

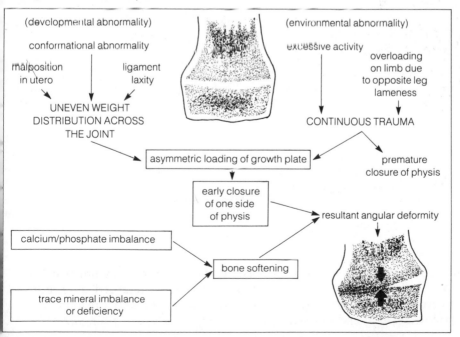

(developmental abnormality) (environmental abnormality)

conformational abnormality excessive activity

malposition ligament overloading
in utero laxity on limb due
  to opposite leg
  lameness

UNEVEN WEIGHT
DISTRIBUTION ACROSS CONTINUOUS TRAUMA
THE JOINT

asymmetric loading of growth plate premature
  closure of physis

early closure
of one side
of physis resultant angular deformity

calcium/phosphate imbalance

bone softening

trace mineral imbalance
or deficiency

Developmental abnormalities   Hypoplasia (underdevelopment) of the carpal bones can also produce asymmetric loading. The end result in these foals is angular limb deformity due to the collapse of the hypoplastic bones as well as a growth imbalance at the level of the growth plate. Incomplete development of the second and fourth metacarpal (splint bones) can lead to a similar end. These syndromes are discussed in detail below.

Nutrition   The role of nutrition is more complex and poorly understood. Previously deficiencies in calcium, phosphorus, vitamin A, carotene and vitamin D have been suggested and the condition has been erroneously called rickets by horse owners and veterinarians alike.

Rickets is a vitamin D deficiency and, although some features of the disease are seen in angular limb deformities, likening the two conditions is an oversimplification. No experimental evidence has been produced to demonstrate that a deficiency in one of the aforementioned vitamins or minerals leads to angular deformities in foals. Often only one or two foals in a herd are affected and this makes an association with nutrition difficult. Perhaps the sporadic occurrence of angular limb deformity can be attributed to varying levels of calcium, phosphorus or other nutrients in the milk of different mares.

Trace mineral deficiencies, in particular copper, have been incriminated in physitis and angular deformities in cattle and may play a role in horses. Copper is important for bone strength and a deficiency may result in so-called soft bones which angulate easily. Radiographically, the metaphysis appears to flare and overlap the epiphysis. The role of zinc, manganese, molybdenum and other minerals appears unclear, but excessive zinc from industrial pollution may cause a copper deficiency to develop.

Conclusion   Most cases of angular limb deformities are the result of a combination of trauma plus a non-specific nutritional imbalance. Cases in which there is a lameness in one limb resulting in angular limb deformity in the opposite weightbearing limb are obviously trauma-induced, but trauma alone cannot explain all cases of angular limb deformities.

The history of foals with angular limb deformities is variable. Some are normal at birth then begin to deviate, while others are crooked at birth and improve to varying degrees. An attending veterinarian needs to ascertain the rate, if any, of improvement in order to decide if surgery is necessary.

Treatment

With an understanding of the effects of trauma on the growth plate, the rationale behind certain aspects of management of angular limb deformities becomes apparent. The most important factor behind correction of an angular deformity is restriction of exercise.

Foals, by their nature, will do everything possible to stay near their dams early in life, and overactivity in this regard produces increased trauma to the growth plate. Trauma should be minimized by restricting the foal's exercise by confining it to a loosebox. This must be done until the limb has straightened.

Foot trimming (or balancing) also helps correct conformation and subsequent asymmetrical loading. Frequent evaluation, including radiographic examination by a veterinarian, is necessary to monitor the progress of conservative therapy.

These two factors can correct a large proportion of angular limb deformities and should always be used as a first step in correction, provided there is no evidence of hypoplasia or immaturity of the carpal bones.

Because of the relatively early closure of the growth plates at the end of the cannon bones, surgery should be attempted as soon as the deformity is noted in these areas. Surgical treatment for such angulations after sixty to eighty days of age is unsuccessful.

Casting and braces have often been regarded as conservative methods, but these have no scientific basis and are fraught with pressure-sore problems because of the thinness of young foals' skin.

In cases in which there is another orthopaedic problem that causes excessive loading on the 'good' limb the solution is not as clear-cut. Sometimes the resultant lameness is so severe or protracted (for example, a healing fracture) that the animal has no option but to take excessive weight on the good limb during convalescence. Clearly the solution is to minimize the convalescent time on the injured limb so that normal weightbearing can resume as soon as possible.

Surgery is indicated in the case of the carpus (knee) and tarsus (hock) if the angular limb deformity is still present at age sixty days or is getting progressively worse. If the limb is nearly straight at this time the veterinarian may wait an additional thirty days before a final decision is made. Occasionally a severe deformity at the carpus will be considered a surgical candidate at forty-five days. Fetlock deformities must be operated on between thirty and sixty days or, preferably, as soon as the deformity is noticed.

Surgical treatment for angular limb deformities has two main objectives: first, to stimulate growth on the retarded side (concave) and, second, to slow down growth on the opposite side (convex).

Stimulation of growth on the concave side

Stimulation of growth on the concave side is achieved by lifting the periosteum away from the bone at the affected site.

There are two explanations as to why this technique is successful: first, the procedure is thought to disrupt the blood supply on the operated side and thus stimulate growth there; second, the periosteum is supposed to have a tethering effect on the growth rate. Thus by surgically incising it, this effect is lost and growth rate increases. This latter explanation is the more likely.

Because periosteal stripping is a stimulation procedure (i.e. it increases bone growth), it is performed on the side of the metaphysis with retarded growth (the concave side). Experimentally it has been shown that making an incision on the inner periosteum *causes* a valgus deformity. Thus, clinically, an incision on the outside (lateral) periosteum is to *correct* a valgus deformity. Therefore, for a valgus deformity of the carpus, the periosteum is transected and lifted on the outside of the lower radius.

Periosteal stripping is the primary surgical technique for angular deformities of the lower (distal) radius and tibia. This technique, in combination with transphyseal bridging (discussed below), is used for angular deformities of the fetlock.

Technique   The surgery for periosteal stripping is performed under a general anaesthetic. The veterinarian makes an inverted T-shaped incision just above the growth plates on the concave side of the deformity and the periosteum is peeled away from the bone at this site. It is then left apart and the subcutaneous tissues and skin are closed. The surgery itself is quite simple.

Post-operative management   The skin incision is covered with a non-adhesive dressing and the entire joint wrapped with adhesive bandaging. Antibiotics are not given prior to surgery unless screws and wires are also to be used (see below).

The wound is kept wrapped for at least ten days with the bandage changed every three or five days. Skin sutures are removed at ten to fourteen days.

During the convalescence (while the limb straightens) the foal must remain relatively confined to minimize concussion to the growth plate. Although complete confinement of the mare and her foal to a loosebox is desirable and recommended, this often meets with resistance from owners. They frequently prefer the mare to be out in sunlight to help induce regular ovulation. As a compromise mare and foal should be placed in a stall that has a small run attached to it. Under no circumstances, however, should the foal be running free with the mare in a large pasture.

The advantages of periosteal stripping over other techniques are that it is relatively straightforward to perform, it does not require expensive implants nor a mandatory second operation to remove screws and wires. The hospitalization period is also slightly shorter and therefore the overall operation is less expensive. It is cosmetically appealing and the surgery can be repeated if necessary. Of interest is the fact that the technique, if used as the sole procedure, has not resulted in *overcorrection* of an angular limb deformity.

Deceleration of growth on the convex side

The second surgical technique used for asymmetrical growth is a retardation by various transphyseal bridging methods. These usually involve the insertion of staples or screws and wires spanning the growth plate on the convex side of the limb. The metal implants create a compressive force causing a change in the blood supply to that side of the growth plate and thus a gradual decline in growth. Continued growth on the opposite side causes the sides of the metaphysis to equalize; thus the leg returns to its normal axis. At this point the implants are removed and normal leg growth continues.

Technique   Metal staples have been used to bridge growth plates in both foals and children. The technique was modified in 1972 and now bone screws are placed on either side of the growth plate, with two wires in a figure of eight connecting the heads. This is the preferred method because the implants are easier to remove and the screws can be inserted independently at convenient sites on either side of the growth plate. In addition, immediate compression is applied across the growth plate, thereby hastening correction. The implants are stronger than staples. There also seems to be less soft-tissue blemish arising from the use of screws and wires compared with staples (Figure 108).

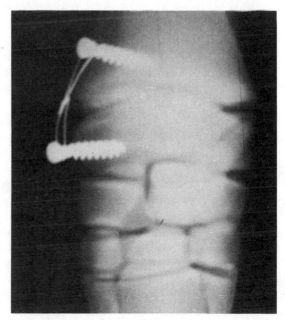

Figure 108   A radiograph of a foal's carpal joint showing two screws bridged by a piece of wire (transphyseal bridging) to retard growth on that side of the limb to correct a carpus valgus deformity

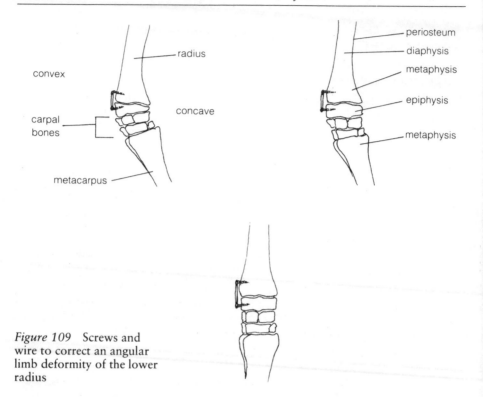

Figure 109   Screws and
wire to correct an angular
limb deformity of the lower
radius

The procedure can be used alone or in combination with hemicircumfer-
ential transection of the periosteum and periosteal stripping for certain
deformities, particularly in the fetlock joint.

Post-operative management   A sterile non-adhesive dressing is placed over
the incision and then the affected joints bandaged. A full-limb bandage using
cotton may be needed, but a light gauze and elastic adhesive bandage
covering only the affected joint may be all that is required if it is carefully
applied. Antibiotics are given before and following surgery because implants
increase the likelihood of infection.

The foal should be confined during convalescence to reduce concussion on
the growth plates. The hooves should receive appropriate trimming.
Frequently foals are fed mineral supplements or given injections of various
vitamins. These are unnecessary in most cases unless a true deficiency can be
identified. Certainly older animals presented for this surgery (e.g. weanlings)
should be fed a ration containing the appropriate calcium–phosphorus
ratio. Analysis of the diet of these older foals frequently reveals a mineral
imbalance. The role of other trace minerals as an adjunct to the treatment of
angular limb deformities in foals is less well understood. A zinc excess and/
or a copper deficiency may exist in isolated instances.

Removal of implants   When the axis of the limb is straight, removal of the implants must be performed to prevent overcorrection of the deformity. Thus owners must observe the leg closely and return the foal to the veterinarian when the limb is straight. Removal of screws and wires can be done with the foal standing under local anaesthesia if it can be adequately restrained.

Wedge osteotomy

If the limb is severely deviated and the growth plate has closed (typically a foal six to nine months old with a severe varus deformity of the fetlock), the only hope of straightening the limb is a wedge osteotomy. Here a wedge of bone is removed with a motorized saw and the limb straightened and held in position with one or two bone plates. It is a radical procedure but has a place with a valuable animal that requires saving for breeding purposes. Wedge osteotomy is performed far more commonly in dogs than in horses but the principles are the same. It is not the type of surgery done routinely in all equine practices and is best referred to a specialized orthopaedic practice.

Occasionally a wedge osteotomy is performed in a foal that has diaphyseal angular limb deformity. Here the bone is bent in the middle of the shaft. Usually the cannon bones are affected. Diaphyseal angular deformities occur in areas of the tubular long bones unrelated to a growth plate. They can be congenital (*in utero* positioning). The only treatment for this is a wedge osteotomy, in which the bone is cut into two. Bone plates are then used to immobilize the bone while it heals. Again, such cases are best left to specialists experienced in orthopaedics.

HYPOPLASIA, NECROSIS OR INCOMPLETE OSSIFICATION (COLLAPSE) OF THE CARPAL BONES

This condition is rare but should be suspected when a foal with carpus valgus or capus varus has not responded to confinement or is becoming progressively worse. It is usually present at birth. Various carpal bones are involved, in most cases at least two, and commonly the ulnar, the fourth and the outer aspect of the third carpal bones. There is usually some distention of the joint capsules due to excess synovial fluid.

The diagnosis is made using radiographs. The affected carpal bones are smaller and more rounded than usual and may be deformed (collapsed) in shape. This is because in this condition the carpal bones are still partly cartilaginous and not completely bony, so they are less well able to withstand the normal forces transmitted through the limb during weight-bearing and therefore are susceptible to being squashed.

The bones in the hock joints of these foals should also be checked for signs of collapse. Advanced cases of collapsed carpal bones will show radiographic signs of arthritis. The cause of the condition is unknown but it is probably asociated with some degree of softness of the cartilage base of the carpal bones during immaturity.

Treatment

Mild cases will respond to conservative therapy as described for growth imbalance (see p. 284 above). Some will be candidates for surgery if there is a concurrent imbalance of metaphyseal growth. Severe cases will not respond simply to temporary transphyseal bridging (screws and wires). In severe cases of hypoplasia or collapse of the carpal bones the only hope is casting to remove pressure from the bones to allow normal bone formation (ossification) to proceed.

This is done by the use of tube or cylinder casts. These extend from the top of the radius to the top of the sesamoid bones and prevent the tendon laxity and osteoporosis (breakdown of bone cells) seen with casts that encase the entire foot. Foals with casts should be hospitalized and the casts changed every two to fourteen days under general anaesthesia.

Cast application in foals and adults is difficult and must be performed by a veterinarian. After three to four weeks' casting, ossification and the natural formation of the carpal bones should have been completed and usually the bones can then withstand the strength of normal loading without collapsing. Even after ten to fourteen days some improvement will be found. The key to success is early recognition of the problem before complete collapse and arthritis has occurred.

INCOMPLETE DEVELOPMENT OF THE SMALL METACARPAL (SPLINT) BONES

This is a relatively uncommon cause of any limb deformity and is manifest by a less than normal degree of attachment of the splint bones to the carpus.

LIGAMENT LAXITY

This is present to some degree in *all* foals at birth and can be manifested as laxity of the flexor tendons.

Laxity will appear as an angular limb deformity of one kind or another (usually a valgus deformity of the carpus). Some foals with ligament laxity show carpus valgus in one front leg and carpus varus in the other (windswept deformity – see Figure 106). Windswept deformities can also occur in the rear limbs.

Treatment

Nature will usually correct these, so box rest (perhaps with access to a small run) is indicated to reduce the trauma of asymmetric loading on the growth plates. Occasionally in very young foals splinting is required, but care must be taken to avoid pressure sores and the splinting should be done by a vet.

Casting is contraindicated and will usually exacerbate the condition by preventing exercise, which has a physiotherapeutic effect. Everything loses strength and mass in a cast, not only muscles but tendons, joint cartilage and ligaments. Thus casts are not recommended.

TRAUMATIC LUXATION AND FRACTURE OF THE CARPAL BONES

This dislocation is a rare cause of carpal deviations. These foals usually have a history of severe trauma, such as being caught under a fence or stepped on by the mare. The prognosis for future soundness is grave because of irreversible damage (structural change) in the affected bones.

COLLAPSE OF THE THIRD AND/OR CENTRAL TARSAL BONES OF THE HOCK

This has also been called necrosis (cellular death) of the third and/or central tarsal bones.

It is a condition in which, early in postnatal life, the third and sometimes the central tarsal bones of the foal's hock begins to collapse. The end result is a severe and crippling arthritis of the distal rows of tarsal joints. The condition generally occurs in both hocks but is worse in one. It is found most commonly in foals born prematurely or as one of a twin. As in hypoplasia of the carpal bones (see above), the tarsal bones are not completely bony (incompletely ossified) at birth and are therefore susceptible to being squashed. An affected foal shows sickle and slightly curby hock conformation (see Figure 179, p. 614). If examined early (within the first fourteen days of life) the tarsal bones are found to be smaller and more rounded than usual and treatment at this stage can prevent the more debilitating secondary changes. If left untreated the condition progresses and an affected foal usually develops signs of a stiff, stilted gait in the first two months of life. It lies down a lot and is less active than other foals. It will have a cow-hocked and/or sickle-hocked conformation. Such foals eventually develop a severe degenerative tarsitis (arthritis) of the hock resembling bone spavin. Usually an enlargement can be felt in the inner fore aspect of the lower hock because, as the bone collapses, a piece of bone becomes pushed forward. Treatment of collapsed tarsal bones is usually unsuccessful.

Casting in very early cases can be successful but foals are usually presented to the veterinarian when collapse has already occurred, in which case there is no effective treatment. Eventually severe bone spavin (arthritis) and chronic lameness result and the prognosis for future athletic soundness is poor. Obviously more work is needed to establish the exact cause of this condition.

20
SHOEING

Unshod horses can do light work without causing undue wear and damage to their feet, particularly in countries with a dry climate or on light or sandy soils. Where the soil is heavy or moist, however, or on hard surfaces such as roads, work for any length of time will cause undue wear and damage to the hooves. Wet or moist conditions result in softening of the hoof and the foot will wear down more quickly than in dry conditions.

Shoeing is carried out for two basic reasons: first, to prevent undue wear of the hoof as this can result in damage to the foot, leading to pain and lameness; and, second, to spread the load around the hoof wall so that small segments of the horn do not come under high pressure, which could result in damage to that segment.

Horses' hooves, like the nails in a human's hand and feet, grow continually and need constant trimming if they are to remain properly balanced and shaped. Thus shoeing inevitably necessitates regular trimming of the feet. The feet of young horses, even before the time of shoeing, should be inspected and, if necessary, trimmed at least once a month. This practice pays dividends in the long run by ensuring the growth of well-shaped feet; it also enables corrective trimming to be carried out at an early age to encourage formation of straight limbs.

Horses working on the road almost invariably need shoeing. However, depending on the degree of work, shoeing of the hind feet may sometimes not be necessary. Horses working predominantly on a soft surface or in indoor schools may not, in fact, require shoeing at all, although regular trimming is essential.

The period between shoeing varies with the type of shoe and the work carried out by the horse. Reshoeing may be required for two reasons. First, the shoe may be so worn that it is liable to break, causing damage to the horse, or the position of the shoe on the foot may have altered so that the branches are putting pressure on the sole. Secondly, the foot is continuously growing and, although some wear occurs at the heels as they rub against the shoe, no wear occurs at the toes. This means that the foot gets gradually longer, and the toe becomes disproportionately long compared with the heels. Thus the foot needs trimming in order to keep it in good order, and the shoes should be removed or replaced at least once every four to six weeks. In exceptional cases reshoeing may be needed as frequently as every two to three weeks.

Traditionally shoes are made of iron, and this has the advantage that the farrier can shape the shoes with a high degree of precision to fit the vagaries of individual feet. It has one disadvantage, however: on hard road surfaces shoes become polished and horses are apt to slip. Various devices have been introduced to combat this, ranging from the use of Carborundum on the ground surface of the shoe to small cogs or hardened heads on the horseshoe nails. Recently experiments have been carried out with different materials including rubber and plastic as alternatives to the traditional iron shoe but, to date, none of these has proved very satisfactory.

Growth and function of the hoof

In the natural state the hoof grows at a rate that compensates for the natural forces of attrition. In the average horse it takes between eight and twelve months for new horn formed at the coronary band to grow down to the lower border of the foot. The rate of growth varies in different animals depending on the work carried out and the wear on the foot.

The quality of the horn is a reflection of the bodily condition of the animal, and a sick horse or one in poor condition will produce poor horn at the coronary band. Frequently this will not be noticed until this region of horn has grown to the bearing surface of the foot some eight to twelve months later.

There is a theory that black horn is stronger than white. However, it has now been proved that the mechanical properties of horn of both colours are identical, the colour being due purely to pigment granules in the horn which do not affect its strength although they may reduce the rate of wear.

The horn of the hoof wall is composed of a large number of tubules of horn growing down from the coronary band, and these are bound together by intertubular horn. The wall itself is formed entirely at the coronary band and grows downwards to the bearing surface of the foot. It is attached to the pedal bone by the sensitive laminae; under normal circumstances the laminae do not form horn themselves. The sole and the frog are formed separately by a layer of young cells which form a sheet across the sole of the foot. In the normal foot the sole is not a prime weightbearing area, only coming into contact with the ground on very soft surfaces. The bulk of the horse's weight is carried by the hoof wall, with some weight being taken by the frog.

There are many theories about the function and movement of the foot. At the present time, however, many of these are considered unreliable and it is not possible, therefore, to give a detailed description of foot function. It is well recognized that the heels of the foot normally expand during weightbearing and that the hoof wall itself distorts as it takes weight.

The process of weightbearing is also responsible for pumping blood from the foot back towards the heart, and this may play a dual role, the vascular pressure acting as a hydraulic cushion to absorb concussion as the foot takes weight. It is suggested that, as the foot is brought to the ground, veins within the foot (probably across the sole and in the bulb of the heel) come under pressure. The pressure forces the blood along the vessels and through the digital veins up the limb. At the same time the resistance of the blood being forced through the veins may help to absorb pressure as the foot is placed on the ground.

The movement of the limbs and feet are affected and controlled by the action of muscles. These muscles and their tendons are attached to appropriate sites on the skeletal framework, so that when a muscle contracts (works) precise movements take place and the joints are flexed or extended. There are no muscles present below the knee or hock of the horse, all the actions in the lower limb being transmitted by the long tendons.

The principle movements in the limb are those of flexion and extension. The flexor muscles and tendons lie behind the skeletal column of bones and the extensors in the front. When the horse is standing at rest, the flexor tendon to the foot is under tension, pulling on the pedal bone and around the back of the fetlock in order to maintain the horse in a standing position. When the horse moves, the muscle attached to the flexor tendon shortens, increasing the pull on the tendon and thus flexing the pastern and fetlock joints as the heel is raised from the ground.

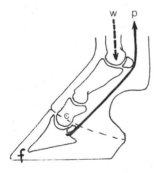

Figure 110 The mechanics of the foot

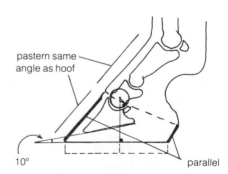

Figure 111 Normal hoof conformation

This can be considered in mechanical terms (Figure 110). In effect the pull of the tendon P supports the weight of the horse bearing down on the fetlock W. At the end of the stride the pull P lifts the heels, the toe of the foot F acting as a fulcrum. Hence it is evident that the longer the toe grows the greater the leverage it exerts and the greater the strain put on the tendons.

Strain on the tendons is also increased by lowering the heels of the foot to excess. The ideal angle for the front of the hoof varies from one horse to another, depending on the individual's conformation. The angle of the hoof, however, should be the same as that of the pastern (and this in turn is the same as the angle described by the shoulder). Thus a line drawn from the front of the fetlock to the coronary band and then on down the front of the hoof should be straight, with no deflection forwards or backwards at the coronary band (Figure 111).

In the natural state the length of the hoof is determined by the rate of wear and the rate of growth of horn. In the shod horse length is determined by the farrier trimming the feet when the horse is shod. There is no simple guideline as to how long a foot should be; one simply has to rely on the experience of an expert farrier for the foot to be trimmed correctly.

Weightbearing surfaces of the foot

The horn of the foot is not sensitive, being formed in a similar manner to the human fingernail. The hoof wall is formed exclusively from the coronary band, but the sole and frog are derived from the solar corium, a membrane which covers the bottom of the pedal bone. This membrane is very sensitive, and the foot is designed with an arch to the sole in such a manner that weight is not normally carried on the sole itself. The arch of the sole is greater in hind feet than in front feet, and if it is flattened (as in dropped soles), the foot and deeper structures become more liable to bruising, which may result in lameness.

When standing normally on a hard surface the weight of the horse is supported on the ground surface of the wall and on the immediately adjacent rim of the sole, the bulk of the sole remaining clear of the ground. The bars, which are an inturned continuation of the wall at the heel of the foot, may also be weightbearing in unshod horses. The frog is normally just clear of the ground in the standing animal, but may be responsible for a degree of weightbearing when the horse is in motion, particularly on softer ground.

When a horse is shod the weight-supporting function of all the parts should be utilized as fully as possible. The shoe should normally not only put pressure on the wall of the foot but also cover the white line and the immediately adjacent part of the sole. In the shod horse, however, the bars of the feet seldom play their full role in weightbearing.

The wall of the foot is thickest at the toe, becoming relatively narrower at the quarters of the foot. However, it is normal practice to make the shoe of an equal width around the entire foot. The portion of sole which lies in the angle formed by the wall and the bar at the heel of the foot (the so-called seat of corn) should not bear any weight in a well-shod horse as this area is very prone to bruising. If the shoe is poorly fitted, it may put pressure on this area, with resulting bruising.

Because is is generally not weightbearing, the sole is not subject to much wear, and in the normal horse there is a continuous exfoliation of the superficial layers of horn over the sole to prevent a massive build-up and thickening of horn. In some circumstances, for example, in dry conditions, exfoliation may not take place and it may be necessary for the farrier to trim excessive horn away from the sole.

Similarly the size of the frog is normally regulated by wear, and a well-balanced, well-shaped foot shows a healthy frog. When trimming the foot, any excessive growth of the frog should be trimmed away in order to prevent moisture and infection collecting around the loose leaves of horn that can sometimes form in the frog and in the frog clefts.

Preparing the foot for shoeing

The shoe is applied to the foot in order to protect the hoof from excessive wear. When the foot is prepared for reshoeing it is trimmed, taking great care to maintain the normal slope and contour of the hoof. The heels, quarters and toes grow at approximately the same rate. When the animal is shod the shoe protects the toe from wear, but the branches of the shoe are not fixed to the heels and therefore there is a degree of movement and attrition of horn as the heels expand and contract as the horse moves. When the shoe has been on for some time the toe will need shortening rather more than the heels in order to maintain the balance of the foot. For this reason it is common practice amongst farriers to shorten the toe with hoof cutters, but to trim the heels only with a hoof rasp.

Some confusion exists with regard to the meaning of the terms 'lowering the toe' and 'shortening the toe'. In lowering the toe the horn is removed from the ground surface of the foot, reducing the toe horizontally. In shortening the toe the long anteroposterior (front to rear) axis of the hoof is reduced by vertical removal of the horn of the hoof wall at the toe.

Although it is generally accepted that the shoe should be fitted to the hoof and not the hoof to the shoe, the advantage to be gained by judicious manicuring of the toe of the foot should not be overlooked. Long toes affect the balance of the foot and increase the stress on the flexor tendons. There is also evidence that a long-toed, low-heeled foot increases the loading on the heels and may interfere with blood flow through the foot as a whole. Shortening the toe in these cases is an essential practice. In some circumstances the shoe may be set back under the toe of the foot and the projecting superfluous portion of horn rasped off. This is common practice in the shoeing of the hind feet in order to avoid the dangers of overreaching.

When the hoof is being prepared for shoeing, the bearing surface (the portion of the foot against the ground) should be perfectly level. When the limb is viewed from in front, the bearing surface from medial to lateral sides should be at right angles to the long axis of the limb. When viewed from the side, the angle the wall at the toe makes with the ground should be the same as the angle of the pastern. Some trimming of the sole and frog may be necessary to remove flakes of horn from the sole and remove any ragged portions of the frog, and the bars may be trimmed to prevent them from growing across the sole of the foot. Undue thinning of the sole or paring of the frog or the bars should be avoided; thinning should be just sufficient to maintain the shape of the foot.

Trimming and balancing the foot are probably the most important and skilled aspects of shoeing a horse. Unfortunately the significance of trimming is not immediately obvious to the casual observer; it is far less impressive than the working of red-hot iron. For this reason, in recent years, probably insufficient attention has been paid to trimming, balancing and, in particular, maintaining the shape of the heel.

The horn at the heels of the foot should grow down in a line parallel to the horn at the toe, and the quarters of the foot should not be allowed to spread. If the heels are overlowered or the shoe is placed rather short under the heels, there is a tendency for the heels to collapse forwards and inwards, and this has been incriminated as one contributory cause of foot disease.

Evidence of hoof function currently suggests that the continual expansion and contraction of the heels as the horse moves are necessary for healthy normal horn growth and also for normal blood flow through the foot as a whole. Contraction of the heels may result in the horn losing much of its elasticity and the frog and the horn tending to waste. There is no doubt that regular exercise and careful trimming to maintain correct balance of the foot play an important part in maintaining the health and function of the hoof itself.

The shoe

Modern economic constraints have resulted in the majority of farriers now using machine-made shoes. There is little doubt, however, that the farrier who still makes his own shoes from straight iron has an expertise and ability to fit the shoe accurately to the foot which is unlikely to be equalled by the farrier using ready-made shoes. There is nothing inherently wrong with a

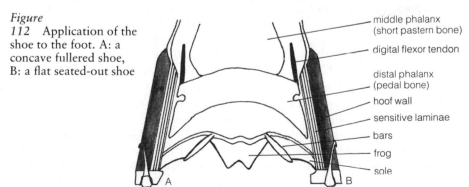

Figure 112 Application of the shoe to the foot. A: a concave fullered shoe, B: a flat seated-out shoe

middle phalanx (short pastern bone)

digital flexor tendon

distal phalanx (pedal bone)

hoof wall

sensitive laminae

bars

frog

sole

machine-made shoe, providing the shoe is the correct size for the animal. However, this entails keeping a large selection of ready-made shoes available, considerably more than if each shoe is purpose made from the straight iron stock.

In Britain the majority of horses are shod with concave fullered shoes (Figure 112). The iron has a ground surface with a deep groove (the fuller) around its entire length, which gives additional grip. Many shoes used in continental Europe are flat and do not have this groove.

The foot surface of the shoe, whatever type it may be, should be flat and level. The weight should be distributed evenly around the foot, and no pressure points should be caused by twisted or unlevel shoes.

The width of iron should be adequate to cover the entire wall and a small portion of sole inside the white line. In some horses a slightly wider shoe may be used in order to give a degree of protection to the sole. In such cases the inner portion of the solar surface should be bevelled so that it does not come in contact with the sole of the foot; this process is called 'seating out' (Figure 112). In theory the use of seated-out shoes may increase the likelihood of stones getting caught between the sole and the shoe, which is almost impossible with a concave fullered shoe. However, many competition horses have a large bodyweight and comparatively weak feet, making the use of a flat, seated- out shoe essential in order to give additional support to the foot by taking a small amount of pressure on the periphery of the sole.

In order for the frog to bear weight in a relatively normal fashion, and to prevent the shoe from being too heavy, which may interfere with the horse's gait, the shoe should be as thin as practicable. However, this reduces the life of the shoe and may result in it becoming distorted if it wears too thin. For this reason the farrier must compromise by choosing a shoe which has adequate width to give the support needed and adequate thickness to give good wear, but which at the same time is not too heavy for the horse's foot. The fullered shoe serves this purpose well in that it is relatively light for its thickness; however, the very act of fullering reduces the area of shoe in contact with the ground and thus increases the rate of wear. A flat shoe will show better wear for its thickness, although it is relatively heavier.

A normal shoe is of uniform thickness from the toe through the quarters to the heels. Thus, when fitted, it does not disturb the trim and balance of a foot that has been correctly prepared. Some shoes are made with varying thickness from toe to heel, but these are only used in special cases to correct abnormalities of the hoof. The width of the shoe should also be uniform from the toe to the heels; the pactice of narrowing the inner branch of the shoe should be discouraged as this tends to allow the shoe to press on the seat of corn.

In shape the shoe should follow the general form of the weightbearing surface of the wall of the foot. It should be the same dimension at the widest point of the quarters as it is from the middle of the toe to the ends of the branches at the heel (Figure 113); if two shoes are superimposed they should form a smooth elliptical shape. (A horse's hind feet are slightly narrower and longer than the front feet.) The outline of the shoes should follow a smooth curve and should not have sharp inturnings of the heels. Shoes are normally fitted a little wide at the heels. As they are not fixed there by nails the heels are able to expand and contract as the horse moves. Thus it is important that sufficient margin should be left so that the heels do not slip over the edge of the shoe as they expand.

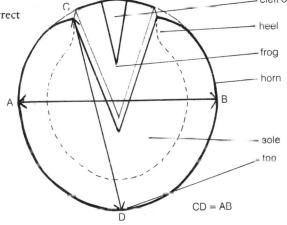

Figure 113   The correct shape of a shoe

Front shoes frequently have a clip at the toe and hind shoes a clip either side of the toe. Side clips help prevent lateral rotation of the shoe, and side slips and toe clips tend to stop the shoe moving backwards on the foot as the shoe comes into contact with the ground. Some people consider that clips on shoes are unnecessary; indeed, in India many of the army horses were shod without such clips and showed no resulting problems. Many horses are shod with a rolled toe, in which instance no clip is provided, but no ill effects appear to result.

The shoes should be made to project slightly beyond the ends of the heel (any risk of a fore shoe getting caught by a hind foot is obviated if the toe of the hind foot is dressed well back). As the foot grows, the horn growing down at an angle tends to pull the shoe forwards, and it is important that the heels should remain on the shoe. If the heels of the shoe terminate slightly in front of the heels of the foot, then they will soon become embedded in the hoof wall and the hoof will not be maintained at the correct angle, the heels gradually collapsing inwards and forwards.

With wear, the toe of the shoe (or an unshod foot) is generally worn more than the rest of the foot. This can be imitated by thinning the toe of the shoe from the ground surface (rolled-toe shoe) or even turning up the entire shoe at the toe (Blenkinsop shoe). Whereas the rolled-toe shoe is quite commonly used nowadays, particularly for animals that tend to stumble, Blenkinsop shoes are seldom used because of the difficulty and time involved in making and fitting them.

Heavy shoes change a horse's action slightly and they are sometimes deliberately used to encourage a hackney action. One disadvantage of heavy shoes is that they require larger nails to fix them, increasing the amount of damage to the wall.

Calkins, studs, cogs, etc., which are supposed to increase the grip of the shoe, should only be used after careful consideration. If used they should be fitted on both branches of the shoe, rather than on one alone, because they interfere with the normal balance of the foot. The use of a single calkin or road stud in just one heel on hard ground can seriously affect the growth of the horn and the action of the foot, and in some cases will result in lameness. Their use on soft ground, where the protuberance can dig into the surface, is much more acceptable.

Traditionally many hunters and driving horses are shod behind with a calk and wedge shoe, and this is a satisfactory practice for increasing the grip. The calk and wedge are relatively small, and balance each other, one on each branch of the shoe, so there is a minimum of interference with the balance of the hoof. Many heavy draught horses are shod with high calkins on the inner and outer heels, the theory being that this will reduce slip on the roads. In some cases this is coupled with a toe piece and in others the toe of the foot is simply left excessively long. This practice is greatly to be deprecated as it frequently results in bad balancing of the feet and it is questionable whether the horse gains any increased security from it. If the foot is balanced and trimmed in the normal way, after an initial period of sliding many horses will regain their previous degree of grip after the calkins have been removed.

Nail holes

With thin fullered shoes it is normal practice to leave the nail, once driven home, slightly proud of the ground surface of the shoe. The taper of the head of the nail is shaped to fit tightly into the fuller of the shoe, and the taper of the shank of the nail is similarly shaped to fit tightly into the hole in the shoe. In this way, as the nail head and shoe wear, the shank of the nail still remains tight in the hole and a loose shoe does not result. If the tapers on nail and shoe do not match, the shoe will rapidly work loose. If the nail head becomes wedged in the taper, then the nail will rapidly work loose with wear. If the shank of the nail binds but the head is left loose, then there is a tendency for the nails to break as they pass through the shoe.

With a flat unfullered shoe the nail hole is stamped to coincide with the shape of the head of the nail. The hole narrows downwards (looking at the shoe from the ground surface). In this manner the nail head lodges securely and solidly in the hole without weakening the shoe.

One advantage with the flat unfullered shoe is that the nail hole can be placed towards the inner or outer margin of the shoe and the angle of the hole altered to suit different shapes of foot. With the fullered shoe the fullering is at an equal distance from the outside edge all around the shoe and the nail holes are punched inside the fullering without reference to the thickness of the horn. Thus, although this method of fullering is labour saving, it may not always result in the ideal positioning of the nail hole or the angle of the nail.

Ideally the nail holes should not be punched through the shoe until the foot is dressed and ready for the shoe to be applied. In this way the farrier can position the nails to avoid driving them through the weak parts of the crust or through areas which may have been chipped, split or pierced by previous nails.

Normally three nails are used on the inner branch of the foot and either three or four on the outer branch. The posterior nail hole should not be more than half to two thirds down the branch from the toe of the shoe. If the last nail is placed too far back in the branch of the shoe, it will either restrict the movement of the heel of the foot or, more commonly, work loose or be torn from the horn.

Fitting the shoe

The outside margin of the shoe should coincide exactly with that of the hoof, unless the hoof wall is being shortened in order to correct the balance of an abnormally shaped foot. The portion of shoe behind the last nail hole should not be set within the outer edge of the hoof wall as, with constant use from being hammered on the ground, it will become embedded in the horn near the heel.

Traditionally the shoe is fitted at a dull red heat and held briefly in contact with the horn of the foot. In this way the shoe can rapidly be altered if its shape does not conform exactly to the foot. Exact juxtaposition of iron and hoof is obtained, with consequent increased security of the shoe. It is also possible to see which areas of foot have not been in contact with the shoe as the horn in those areas is not charred. The shoe can then be adjusted or the foot levelled as necessary.

It has been suggested that burning the hoof wall also renders the bearing surface of the wall and sole impervious to water and the hoof less liable to split when the nails are driven. There is no scientific evidence about this at the present time.

The practice of burning on the shoe is to be deprecated. A shoe which is not quite even is held in contact with the horn for a longer period of time than normal in order that the unlevel areas of hot iron will burn themselves into the horn. This practice, which is an abuse of hot shoeing, can result in severe charring of the hoof wall with subsequent weakening. It allows the poor farrier to bed an inadequate shoe onto a foot, which could not be done with a cold shoe.

The practice of applying shoes cold is spreading, particularly with the increasing tendency for the farrier to visit the horse rather than the horse to visit the forge. The horse can be shod perfectly adequately in this manner, provided the shoe is made flat and the foot is dressed level so that the two surfaces meet. Minor alterations to the shoe, such as spreading or closing the heels to fit the curve on the foot, can be made cold. Although cold shoeing can be carried out perfectly satisfactorily, it is probably more difficult to shoe well cold than to shoe well hot. However, in shoeing a horse with poor or weak heels, hot shoeing may create a problem if the heels are inadvertently burned when the shoe is applied.

Nailing on the shoe

The nails should take a short hold on the wall of the foot, coming up not more than 1 inch from its ground surface. The ends of the nails are then twisted off approximately an eighth of an inch from the hoof wall and the end turned down to form the clenches. After the nails have been driven the rasp should not normally touch the hoof wall, except to file a little horn away from under the end of the nails so that the clenches seat down tight and, if necessary, to shorten the toes slightly. The clenches should all be level at an equal distance from the ground surface of the foot. Nails should be positioned so they do not pass through areas of weak or broken horn and should avoid previous nail holes if possible.

The shoeing nail is made with a bevel on one side of the point only, so that as it is driven into the hoof wall it gradually turns outwards, taking a curved course through the horn prior to breaking out through the wall.

Hoof dressings

There is considerable controversy over the value of hoof oils and dressings. There is little or no evidence that oiling hooves is of value in the normal animal and it is probably far more important that the feet should be kept cleaned out (particularly the sole of the foot) and the horse not left to stand in damp conditions. Dressings applied to the surface of the hoof can have little effect on horn quality.

There is evidence that massage to the coronary band may improve the quality of horn. Horn quality also reflects the bodily condition of the horse and its nutritional state. An improved diet may therefore help hoof quality and there is some evidence that in some animals the amino acids methionene and biotin may be beneficial. When assessing dietary supplementation it is important to remember that the hoof wall is formed at the coronary band and so any improvement in the horn is seen first in that area, the new horn gradually growing downwards; improvement in hoof quality throughout the wall will not be seen until some nine to twelve months after supplementation of the diet.

Some Common Problems and Their Causes

There are a number of clinical problems, such as swelling of the metacarpal (cannon) region, which have many different possible causes. The tables below aim to direct the reader towards the primary cause of some clinical complaints. The tables are not complete but include the most common causes.

'Filled leg' – swelling of the metacarpal or metatarsal (cannon) region

Bruising
Cellulitis (e.g. secondary to puncture wound)
Secondary infection following a cut
Subsolar abscess
Lymphangitis
Purpura haemorrhagica
Fractured splint bone
Cracked heels or mud fever
Enlarged blood vessels
Strained tendon or ligament (superficial digital flexor tendon, deep digital flexor tendon, accessory ligament of the deep digital flexor tendon, suspensory ligament)

Swelling of the carpus (knee)

Distension of the tendon sheath of extensor carpi radialis, common digital extensor tendon or lateral digital extensor tendon
Hygroma – false bursa
Enlarged joint capsule (antebrachiocarpal or intercarpal joint) due to degenerative joint disease, fracture or infection
Periarticular soft-tissue swelling due to trauma (bruising or sprain)
Cellulitis
Distension of the carpal canal

Swelling of the hock region

Thoroughpin
Bog spavin (idiopathic, secondary to osteochondrosis, degenerative joint disease, fracture or infection)
Periarticular swelling due to trauma (bruising or sprain)
Cellulitis
Curb
Fracture
Bone spavin

Swelling of the fetlock region

Suspensory ligament desmitis
Sprained fetlock
Enlarged joint capsule of the metacarpophalangeal joint due to degenerative joint disease, infection or fracture
Distension of tendon sheath (windgall) with or without constriction by the palmar annular ligament
Fracture of the metacarpal bone, proximal sesamoid bone or proximal phalanx
Distal sesmoidean ligament strain
'Low' strain of the superficial or deep digital flexor tendons

Forelimb lameness with no obvious focus of pain or swelling
Foot pain (corns, navicular syndrome, degenerative joint disease of the distal interphalangeal joint, pedal osteitis, poor trimming and shoeing)
Early degenerative joint disease of the proximal interphalangeal joint
High suspensory desmitis
Desmitis of the accessory ligament of the deep digital flexor tendon
Subchondral bone cyst – any location
Osteochondrosis of the shoulder

Stumbling
Tiredness; bad riding; rough ground
Excessively long feet
Navicular syndrome
Ringbone
Incoordination

Hind-limb toe drag
Laziness; unfitness
Young, unbalanced horse
Excessively long toes
Hind-limb lameness (e.g. bone spavin)
Incoordination
Scirrous cord (infection at castration site)

Hind-limb lameness with no obvious site of pain or swelling
Bone spavin
Subchondral bone cyst – any location (particularly the stifle)
High suspensory desmitis
Early degenerative joint disease of the proximal and distal interphalangeal joints

Very severe lameness
Joint infection (infectious arthritis)
Fracture
Subsolar abscess
Blood in joint (haemarthrosis)
Nerve damage resulting in inability to bear weight
Myopathy

Poor performance
Rider problem; sourness and/or overfacing
Bilateral forelimb lameness (e.g. navicular syndrome)
Bilateral hind-limb lameness (e.g. bone spavin)
Subclinical forelimb or hind-limb lameness
Excessive concussion ('jarred up')
Back pain
Medical problem (e.g. low-grade respiratory infection)
Temperamental problem (e.g. marishness)

The Reproductive System

Reproduction is based on the female and male genital organs and glands. These have special functions which determine sexual behaviour leading to mating and fertilization of the egg. The foetus is housed in the genital tract of the mare, specifically in her uterus. Here it is nurtured for eleven months until expelled at the time of foaling. The newborn foal must adjust to the new environment and then start the two-year or so development to maturity before puberty is reached and the reproductive cycle starts over again in the new generation.

The process of reproduction is described in the chapters of this section against the background of anatomical features on the one hand and the function of sexual organs on the other. John Cox describes reproduction from the stallion's viewpoint, whereas I have contributed chapters on the female. Donald Steven describes his particular area of special interest regarding the placenta and certain aspects of pregnancy.

An understanding of the reproductive process is essential to good stud management and as a basis for the management and care of the stallion, barren mare, pregnant mare and newborn foal. It should be possible for the reader to use the chapters for reference or for reading about the subject as a whole, starting with the male and passing to the female, through pregnancy, foaling and the development of the newborn foal.

21
THE MALE GENITAL ORGANS AND THEIR ENDOCRINE GLANDS

Functional anatomy of the testis and adnexa

The reproductive organs of the male consist of the testes, situated within the scrotum, the epididymis, the spermatic cord, the accessory glands and the penis within its sheath. The functioning of these organs depends on both nervous and hormonal stimuli. The hormones control the way the organs develop and the substances or cells they produce and the nervous stimuli control the response of the stallion to the presence of a mare in oestrus.

Hormonal control

Stimuli from the outside affect that part of the brain known as the hypothalamus through nervous pathways leading from the sense organs. In particular, lengthening periods of daylight stimulate the hypothalamus to produce increasing amounts of a hormone called gonadotrophin releasing hormone (GnRH).

GnRH is carried in the bloodstream to the anterior pituitary causing this gland to release follicle-stimulating hormone (FSH) and luteinizing hormone (LH). These hormones are identical to those secreted in the female but in the male FSH stimulates the tubules in the testes to form sperm, whereas LH stimulates the Leydig cells (specialized interstitial cells which lie between the tubules which produce the sperm) to produce testosterone.

Testosterone is responsible for the development of the male genitalia in the foetus, the growth of the male genitalia at puberty, the final stages of sperm maturation, and the growth, maintenance and function of the accessory glands. It stimulates the central nervous system in producing libido (sexual drive) and male sexual responses, and is responsible for the secondary sexual characteristics such as muscular development and the crest of the neck.

Thus significant increases in semen volume, sperm density, total sperm per ejaculate (and a reduction in reaction time of the stallion to mating) occur during spring and summer compared with autumn and winter.

Figure 114   The male reproductive organs

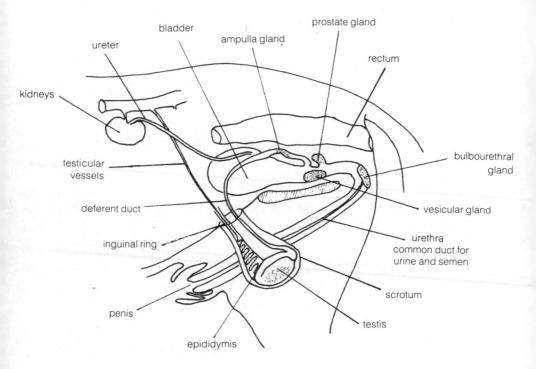

TESTES

Normal descent and growth

In the foetal foal the testis develops near the kidney, but it moves into the scrotum during the last month of gestation. Newborn foals, therefore, usually have both testes in their scrotum. The testes are quite small at this stage and grow very little during the ensuing twelve months. The gubernacular structures, which help to move the testes out of the abdomen, are quite large at birth, shrinking afterwards as their function is completed. The contents of the scrotum can therefore actually become smaller during the first few weeks of life.

In rapidly maturing breeds the testes begin to grow significantly in the second summer and autumn while the animal is a yearling; most growth, however, occurs over the next winter. By the spring of the year in which the horse is a two-year-old, the testes are almost fully grown. This growth is controlled by hormones from the brain (see above), and these hormones are also responsible for sperm production; most testes weighing over 70 g are capable of producing fertile sperm. In particular, the male hormone testosterone appears at this time.

The testes continue to grow after two years of age, but the rate of growth is much slower. By three years of age the horse is also producing large quantities of the female hormone oestrone sulphate, which can be used as the basis of a blood test for cryptorchidism (retained testicle – see p. 311).

The mature testes hang horizontally in the scrotum at the front of the pelvis. Normally they measure 6–12 cm long, 4–7 cm high and 5 cm wide. The testis consists of very small tubules lined by cells which divide and change into spermatozoa – the sperm cells are nursed during their development by specialized cells called Sertoli cells. When the spermatozoa are formed, they are shed into the tubules and pass into the epididymis.

Each epididymis lies just above its testis, to which it is attached by a sheet of tissue. The epididymis (Figure 115) can be divided into three parts – head, body and tail – but it is in fact one very long, much-coiled tube, and the spermatozoa enter the epididymis at one end and pass along it, maturing as they go. The mature sperm are stored in the tail of the epididymis prior to ejaculation and this tail can be seen as a discrete swelling at the back of the testis. (Some horses have the tail of the epididymis at the front of the testis but this is unusual.)

At ejaculation (see p. 316) the sperm leave the epididymal tail and enter the vas deferens, which is part of the spermatic cord. This cord (which is actually a triangular sheet of tissue with its base at the testicle and its apex high up in the groin) contains not only the vas deferens but also the blood vessels and nerves which supply the testis and epididymis. The cord is severed when a horse is castrated (see p. 539).

Figure 115   A detail of the testis

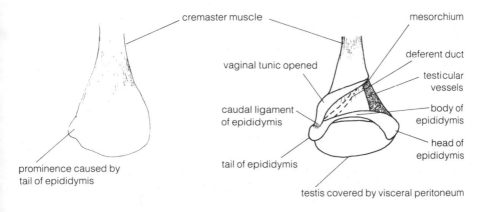

cremaster muscle — mesorchium
vaginal tunic opened — deferent duct
testicular vessels
caudal ligament of epididymis — body of epididymis
head of epididymis
prominence caused by tail of epididymis
tail of epididymis
testis covered by visceral peritoneum

Each testis lies enveloped in a sac called the vaginal tunic, and attached to this tunic is a powerful muscle, the cremaster muscle. This is quite capable of pulling the vaginal tunic and its enclosed testis up into the groin and will do so in response to fear, sometimes to excitement and invariably to the touch of cold hands.

Conditions of the Testis

For castration and related conditions see p. 539. Disorders of the testis are relatively rare in horses but they include the following:

ORCHITIS

This disease is characterized in the acute phase by pain and swelling of one or both testes and can be caused by a kick, by migrating strongyle larvae or by infectious agents. The horse will be infertile. Treatment is aimed at keeping the testis cool with a spray of cold water, and includes systemic antibiotics and painkillers. As the condition resolves the pain abates and the testis often shrinks and degenerates, no longer producing sperm.

TESTICULAR TUMOURS

Various types of tumour can be found in the testis but differentiation depends ultimately on histological examination. The commonest and most striking are seminomas, which produce gross distortion of the testes and eventually degeneration, often preceded by a high proportion of abnormal sperm. Other types are Sertoli cell tumours and interstitial cell tumours, the latter (which are not always large) having been incriminated as a cause of viciousness. Spread to other organs is rare but not impossible and unilateral castration is the treatment of choice. Teratomas occur more commonly in cryptorchid testes (see below) and can be enormous if cystic tissue develops in them; others contain bone and teeth.

TESTICULAR TORSION

Occasionally a testis and its vaginal tunic twist through 360 degrees, producing symptoms of acute colic and a markedly swollen, oedematous scrotum. As the testis gets cut off from its blood supply, it dies (undergoes necrosis) and the pain may ease, though the swelling remains for longer, resolving only to reveal a shrunken testis. In the early acute phase testicular torsion needs to be differentiated from strangulated inguinal hernia (see pp. 536–7), though both are serious and require surgical intervention.

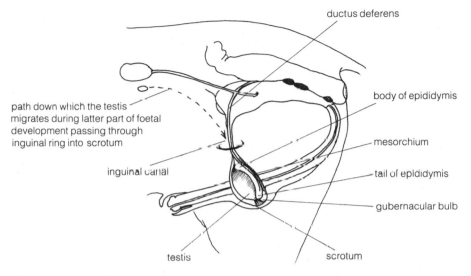

Figure 116 The descent of the testis. It has passed through the inguinal canal but is not fully in the scrotum

CRYPTORCHIDISM (RIG, RIDGELING)

Most testes reach the scrotum in the last months of gestation but some fail to pass out of the abdomen, resulting in abdominal cryptorchidism; or fail to descend from the abdominal opening to the scrotum, resulting in inguinal cryptorchidism. Cryptorchidism may be unilateral, the other testis reaching the scrotum normally and sometimes being much larger than expected, or (in about 10–20 per cent of cases only) bilateral, both testes then usually being retained in the same place.

Any testis which does not reach the scrotum will not produce sperm and will be infertile; a unilateral cryptorchid, however, will be fertile from his scrotal testis. All testes, however, whatever their location, produce hormones in the usual way and any mature animal, even those with only one testis, will behave like a stallion.

A testis which is retained in the abdomen will never descend to the scrotum after the first few weeks of life – the opening through which it passes becomes too small.

Most of these testes are quite small and flabby, weighing about 20 g. Others may be teratomas (i.e. tumorous, see above).

Some testes retained in the inguinal region are simply late developers which grow in size and descend into the scrotum during the transition from two-year-old to three-year-old. Removal of the contralateral testis will *not* make it descend. Some inguinally retained testes, however, never descend. These are often high up in the groin and are difficult to feel, even with the animal anaesthetized and on its back.

Unilateral cryptorchids should *never* have the one scrotal testis removed and the other one left. Bilateral cryptorchids should never be passed off as geldings – such action could lay the vendor open to a charge of criminal fraud.

In my opinion, cryptorchid horses should not be used in a breeding programme because there is evidence that the condition is inherited. Surgical castration and the removal of both testes are the only suitable management approach. Today cryptorchid castration is one of the safest and most successful operations.

FALSE RIG

The false rig is defined as an animal which has been completely castrated but is demonstrating some masculine behaviour. The male behaviour shown may vary from simply attempting to round up mares or being attracted to a mare on heat, to a full erection and intromission (see below) and, occasionally, ejaculation.

A male horse whose castration history is uncertain and which has no visible or palpable testes but which is exhibiting stallion-like behaviour should first be subjected to a blood test. This will determine whether it is in fact a cryptorchid horse, with one or both testes retained (see above), or whether it is a false rig. If the animal is less than three years of age or is a donkey, it is necessary to take two blood samples, one before and a second sample thirty to 120 minutes after the intravenous injection of human chorionic gonadotrophin (hCG) (see p. 119). A reputable laboratory used to analysing samples from horses should be asked to measure testosterone in both samples. If the horse in question is aged three years or older, then a single sample will suffice, but the concentration of oestrone sulphate must be determined. Most laboratories have a range of values for this hormone which helps the vet to make a diagnosis of whether a particular individual is a false rig.

Masculine behaviour in castrated horses is *not* due to the animals having been improperly castrated – recent scientific investigation has totally discredited the idea of false rigs being 'cut proud'. Rather, most horses behave the way described because such behaviour patterns are part of normal social interaction between horses meeting and living together for the first time; the unpleasant and unwelcome aspects of that behaviour usually wane with time.

Geldings which are simply difficult to handle or ride and show no sexual behaviour usually behave so because of a failure of discipline. Sometimes the rider and horse may just be incompatible.

No treatment is likely to be effective for a false rig, but if a blood test has been performed and a diagnosis has been made, you will know exactly where you are and will have to decide whether the individual's behaviour is acceptable or not.

ACCESSORY SEX GLANDS

The spermatozoa which are ready to achieve fertilization leave the tail of epididymis and pass along the vas deferens (ductus deferens). This tube passes through the inguinal canal, the opening in the body wall through which the testes descend, and opens into the urethra at the neck of the bladder (see Figure 116). The watery products (secretions) of four sets of glands are added to the spermatozoa to make up the semen, which is eventually ejaculated into the mare.

These four glands (Figure 114) are:

1 The ampulla of the ductus deferens (paired)
2 The vesicular gland, often wrongly called the seminal vesicles as it was believed they stored semen (paired)
3 The prostate gland (bilobed)
4 The bulbourethral gland (paired)

The first three lie around the neck of the bladder where it opens into the urethra. Complex mechanisms come into play to prevent urine becoming mixed into the semen. The bulbourethral glands lie farther back, just underneath the anus.

It is very uncommon for these glands to be affected by disease. Occasionally, however, the vesicular gland becomes infected (**vesiculitis**) and pus cells are added to semen, rendering the stallion infertile. Some horses with vesiculitis have their vesicular glands removed but fertility does not always return.

In castrated horses these glands become very small and insignificant.

PENIS

The horse's penis normally lives inside its sheath, out of sight. It is held in position by muscles within the body of the penis and is extruded initially by relaxation of those muscles, producing a flaccid penis. The horse can then fill the spaces between the muscles with blood and he may do this at two different pressures, a low one producing a turgid penis, and the second a very high pressure producing the erect penis necessary for entering the mare (intromission). On erection the penis doubles its length and thickness. After ejaculation the rose at the end of the penis enlarges to three times its resting size.

Besides the muscles and blood spaces, the penis also has passing along all its length the tube that carries urine at urination and semen at ejaculation. This tube is called the urethra and is housed on the lower aspect of the penis.

The penis begins just below the anus, but the only part which is seen is that which lies within the sheath, covered by a special fold of skin called the preputial fold. When the penis drops out of the sheath, the fold of skin unrolls over it. The very end of the penis has an opening for the urethra, which protrudes slightly beyond the end, forming the urethral process and surrounded by a cavity called the urethral sinus. Occasionally debris may accumulate in the cavity causing obstruction to the passage of urine, but its major significance today is that this fossa may harbour potential venereal-disease-producing bacteria, e.g. the contagious equine metritis organism or *Klebsiella* or *Pseudomonas* (see p 419).

The sheath is quite voluminous and movement of the penis within it may cause a sucking noise when the horse is trotting. Deep inside the cavity of the sheath, debris from the glands and skin lining the cavity accumulates. This accumulation is called smegma. Occasionally so much smegma can accumulate, or it can turn so hard, that it causes the horse discomfort.

A number of bacteria normally live on the skin covering a horse's penis and it is not a good idea to wash them away with strong antiseptics or antibiotics because this may actually encourage the development of serious infections. In order to clean a horse's penis the penis should be caught at staling and washed gently with soap and water.

Conditions of the Penis

PROLAPSE

Most horses will drop at least part of their penis out to stale (urinate), but usually withdraw it quite readily. Occasionally, however, the penis hangs out of the sheath and the horse seems unable to retract it. Thus, prolapse can occur in an exhausted horse, but usually recovery takes places readily. Similarly, the horse prolapses his penis under the influence of many sedatives but the effect usually wears off.

Overdosage, however, or certain types of tranquillizers in stallions may result in prolonged relaxation, and persisting prolapse may occur in certain systemic diseases such as rabies and in some debilitating diseases like parasitism, malabsorption or enteritis. In such cases the paralysis can be reversed if the disease causing the prolapse is also reversible. Paralysis is also seen as a sequel to a painful kick or, accompanied by swelling, to a sadistically inflicted whip wound.

A prolapsed penis is in greater danger from kicks and bruising, either of which may produce such swelling as will make it impossible for the horse to pull his penis back in. In addition the free end of the penis is susceptible to drying and cracking, and if this is prolonged it will lead to further swelling and a worsening of the prolapse.

In the early stages cold-water hosing may help to reduce the swelling, but the most important part of treating a prolapsed penis is to support it. This can be done most effectively by padding the inner surface of an appropriate length of plastic guttering and holding it against the penis with bandages. The padding must be changed every day and the penis should be washed and smeared with a bland ointment such as petroleum jelly before the clean gutter is replaced.

Your veterinarian should be involved in giving advice on this, as well as in providing supportive therapy *and* a diagnosis of the cause.

TUMOURS

Two sorts of tumour may be associated with the horse's penis.

Skin tumours generally occur only on the outside of the sheath and the outer layer of the preputial fold. These tumours can be any of the various types of skin tumours, including sarcoids (see chapters 7 and 41).

Cancerous growths usually occur on the free end of the penis of aged horses. They look like angry cauliflowers. Although cancerous, these tumours usually grow slowly and do not spread throughout the body. They can be dealt with by amputation of the free end.

EQUINE COITAL EXANTHEMA (HORSE POX)

This is a contagious disease transmitted naturally at coitus and characterized by vesicular or pustular lesions of the external genitalia. It is caused by an equid herpesvirus (see p. 428), but not the same type as is responsible for rhinopneumonitis or abortion. Mechanical transfer may occur, for example, by nuzzling, by direct contact with mares or teasers, or by handling the part.

The incubation period varies from three to six days, but in many instances it may be from twelve to twenty-four hours. The disease is most commonly observed during the spring months, this being the time at which mares are sent to the stallion. It is widespread throughout the world, but is often not noticed unless there is routine veterinary inspection of the stallion prior to mating.

In the mare the eruption occurs on the inner surface of the lips (labia) of the vulva, on the vaginal mucosa (especially in the vicinity of the clitoris), and to a lesser extent on the external surface of the vulva and undersurface of the tail. Dark red spots the size of a pin head first appear; these become papules which develop into vesicles (sacs containing fluid) or pustules (collection of pus within or beneath the epidermis).

The vesicles are transparent in the early stages, then change to various tints of yellow, then darken to a brown colour; in some cases the contents are of a red colour, due to the presence of blood. The pustules develop into flat ulcers with a deep red base and discharge a yellowish glutinous fluid.

Frequently two or more ulcers become confluent and are covered by a brown scab. When healing takes place, smooth white scars or depigmented areas remain. As a rule fever and constitutional disturbances are absent, but discomfort may be displayed by apparent sexual excitement, frequent attempts at staling and rubbing of the tail.

In the stallion the penis is rarely affected, but vesicles and pustules develop, which later form ulcers. When healing occurs, depigmented scars are left. Occasionally the outer surface of the sheath and scrotum may be affected, also the inside of the thighs and undersurface of the abdomen, extending to the inside of the fore limbs, probably due to contact with infected secretions. A urethral discharge may be present in some cases and frequent attempts at staling may be observed. The affected stallion may be unwilling to mate mares because of the discomfort.

The eruptions in both sexes generally heal spontaneously in from three to four weeks, and sometimes in fifteen days if mating is prevented.

Severe secondary infection with bacteria can occur occasionally and the animal may then be systemically ill, discharges may be gross, and swelling due to oedema extensive. Fertility, however, is not usually affected, although the stallion may be unwilling to serve due to discomfort. It has been suggested that the virus can cause short cycles (i.e. oestrus cycles that are less than the usual twenty-one day cycle) in mares.

Preventive measures

These consist of strict isolation of the affected animals; they should not be used for breeding until perfectly cured. It is important not to overlook such simple measures as wearing disposable gloves when handling infected animals. A careful examination should be made of all mares before mating. It is probably best not to attempt to treat infected animals, as handling can spread the disease; isolation is more important. If secondary infection with bacteria has occurred, then spraying the affected parts with an antibiotic or weak antiseptic, perhaps incorporating a bland oil, can be beneficial in accelerating healing. Animals may be bred again when the lesions are no longer infective; that usually means when a scab has formed.

DOURINE

This venereal infection of the horse's penis is discussed on p. 435. It does not occur in the UK, Australia, South Africa or Argentina.

SEMEN

At ejaculation spermatozoa leave the epididymal tail and pass along the vas deferens, entering the pelvic urethra near the neck of the bladder. The secretions of the accessory glands are added to the spermatozoa, so producing the semen. This passes along the pelvic urethra by muscle action and then along the penile part of the urethra by a hydraulic system involving muscle pumping and bloodflow.

The stallion is believed to engage his urethral process in the cervix of the mare on heat and so deposit the semen within the uterus. The semen is deposited in four to seven spurts and this process is often accompanied by flagging of the tail by the stallion.

Examination of semen

The penis can be diverted into an artificial vagina into which the stallion can then be persuaded to ejaculate and so allow the semen to be collected and examined.

Semen has a white, opaque appearance and usually consists of three fractions. The first fraction is watery and contains little or no sperm; the second is also thin and watery and contains the sperm; the third is viscous, contains gel and comes mainly from the vesicular gland.

Semen is usually examined as soon as possible after ejaculation for volume (often divided into gel volume and gel-free volume), for sperm numbers and for motility and for the proportion of dead or abnormal cells.

Stallions vary enormously in all these characteristics and different collections from the same stallion also vary considerably. Therefore stallions with poor fertility may need to have several semen collections made before a positive diagnosis can be reached, though some with specific sperm abnormalities can be identified on a single examination.

There is general agreement now that for a stallion to approach normal fertility he should have the following minimum values:

total volume	35 ml
gel-free volume	25 ml
sperm concentration	$20 \times 10,000,000$ml
total number of sperm	$1.5 \times 10,000,000,000$
total number of live sperm	$1 \times 10,000,000,000$

However, fertility also depends on the number of mares to be mated and the frequency with which they are mated. Examination of semen, therefore, is *not* a fertility examination.

Problems arise with young horses in their first season and this may be because they have been discouraged in training from displaying interest in mares; or it may be due to overuse early in the year before the advent of spring and summer when sperm output is at its highest.

22
THE FEMALE GENITAL ORGANS AND THEIR ENDOCRINE GLANDS

The female genital tract consists of the ovaries, the Fallopian tubes, the uterus, the cervix and the vagina. It extends from the vulval orifice to the ovaries, receives the male organ, forms a pathway up which the spermatozoa travel to meet the ovum, houses the developing embryo and provides a passage for expulsion of the foetus to the exterior.

Functional anatomy

Ovaries The two ovaries contain the female gametes (ova or eggs). Many thousands of eggs are present in the two ovaries at birth and no more develop during the animal's lifetime. After puberty ova are extruded from the ovaries at intervals determined by secretions of anterior pituitary hormones.

The ovaries are typically bean-shaped and vary in size, depending on age and season of the year. Individual variations also occur. The ovaries of maiden mares in winter are usually about 2–4 cm long and 2–3 cm wide. The ovaries increase in spring to 5–8 × 3–4 cm in size. In winter they may feel hard, and in spring or during sexual activity they usually feel soft.

The size of older mares' ovaries varies considerably, irrespective of the season of the year. During sexual quiescence (anoestrus) their size is minimal, i.e. 3–6 cm long. During seasons of sexual activity they grow, but do not normally become larger than about 10 × 5 cm. In many cases the ovaries lose their typical bean shape and become rounded or irregular in contour and one ovary may be much larger than the other.

Typically the ovary has a convex border (hilus) to which the broad ligament containing blood vessels and nerves is attached. The opposite or free border has a narrow depression (the ovulation fossa) through which the ova are shed. The ovary is covered by peritoneum except at the hilus where the nerves and vessels enter.

The ovarian stroma is composed of spindle-shaped connective tissue cells and intercellular substance. Bundles of cells and fibres run in various

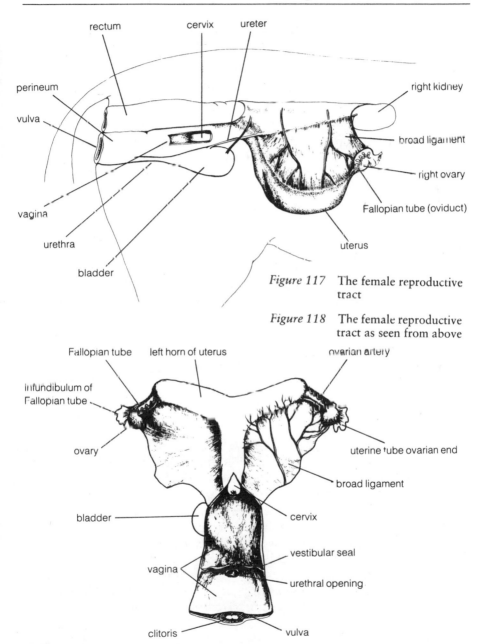

Figure 117 The female reproductive tract

Figure 118 The female reproductive tract as seen from above

directions giving a swirly appearance. The stroma is organized into a tough fibrous capsule which encloses the ovary except at a point opposite the hilus, the ovulation fossa.

The ovaries are situated in the sublumbar region beneath the fourth or fifth lumbar vertebrae. The average distance from the ovaries to the vulva is

50–55 cm in a mare of medium size. The clinician can easily pick up the ovaries on rectal examination and identify by palpation the rounded extremities.

Follicles   The stroma contains small bodies consisting of a central cell (primordial germ cell) enclosed by a single layer of epithelial cells (primordial follicle). There are several hundred thousand of these structures in the two ovaries at birth. In the immature ovary the germ cell (oogonium) is surrounded by a layer of follicular epithelial cells (granulosa). At puberty some of the oogonia develop into larger cells (primary oocytes) which undergo the first stage of meiosis (division). They do not complete meiosis until after puberty when the follicle is mature.

Of the many primary follicles present in the two ovaries at birth only a fraction reach maturity and liberate ova. Most of the follicles degenerate or undergo partial development followed by regression (atresia).

The primary follicle about 45 mm in diameter. As it develops the epithelial cells surrounding the oocyte change from a flat to a stratified columnar shape. The oocyte increases in size and develops a thick outer membrane, the zona pellucida.

Fluid accumulates among the follicular epithelial cells and eventually fills a central cavity lined by follicular cells. The oocyte is attached to one side of the cavity on a mount of follicular cells known as the cumulus oophorus (*cumulus* = heap; *oon* = egg; *phorus* = bearer).

The stroma immediately adjacent to the follicle becomes organized into a membrane (theca), the inner lining of which is vascular and the outer lining non-vascular.

Yellow body   Follicular development continues until the follicle reaches about 3–5 cm in diameter. It then bursts at the ovulation fossa and discharges its contents towards the open end of the Fallopian tube. After the ovum and part of the follicular wall have been extruded, the follicle collapses and the thecal lining and remaining epithelial cells are thrown into folds. Bleeding occurs into the centre of the follicle and a clot forms.

The follicular or granulosa cells grow into the clot and, together with thecal cells, constitute the yellow body (YB) or corpus luteum. The yellow body is the gland which produces progesterone. It has a variable life span. While it is functional it produces progesterone, but at the end of its life it becomes non-functional and ceases to produce this hormone. The diagnosis of the presence of the functional yellow body can be made by measuring progesterone in the mare's bloodstream (see p. 116). Blood vessels and fibroblasts (connective-tissue cells) enter the yellow body, which changes from a soft consistency and a reddish-purple colour to a firm consistency and reddish-brown. As the yellow body becomes non-functional it turns yellow and eventually brown or white as the active cells are replaced by scar tissue.

Figure 119 Events in the ovary during the oestrous cycle

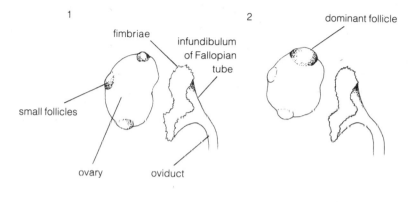

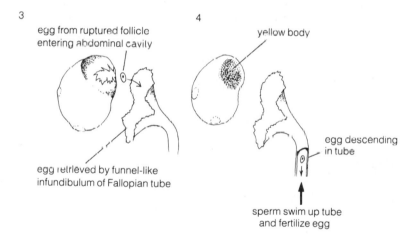

Histologically the granulosa and thecal cells are at first arranged loosely, but soon develop into a compact homogeneous mass, which subsequently degenerates.

If an ovary is cut into sections some or all of the structures described may be present. The follicles are distributed throughout the stroma; they may have thick non-vascular or thin vascular walls. Yellow bodies of varying ages and colour may be found. Recent yellow bodies are usually wedge-shaped with the base on the far side of the ovulation fossa. They do not project from the surface of the ovary, as in the cow and pig, but are embedded in the ovarian stroma.

In addition to its role of ovum producer, the ovary acts as an endocrine gland forming the hormones oestrogen and progesterone (see p. 326).

Fallopian tubes (oviducts)   The oviducts or Fallopian tubes are two tortuous tubes 20–30 cm long, extending from the uterine horns to the ovaries. They are 2–3 mm in diameter at their uterine end and 4–8 mm in diameter at their ovarian end. Each tube is enclosed in a peritoneal fold (mesosalpinx); the ovarian extremity is funnel-shaped and its edge irregular with projections (fimbriae) attached to the ovulation fossa. The tube communicates with the peritoneal cavity via a small opening through which the ovum can pass at ovulation.

The tube itself consists of three layers: an outer fibrous and serous coat, a middle muscular coat of circular and longitudinal fibres, and an inner mucous membrane composed of single-layer, columnar, ciliated secretory cells.

Cysts and embryological remnants are sometimes present in the fimbriae and mesosalpinx. For example parovarian cysts may be present and palpated rectally as small fluctuant cysts, often at one pole of the ovary.

Uterus and cervix   The uterus is a hollow muscular organ continuous with the Fallopian tubes anteriorly and opening posteriorly through the cervix into the vagina. It is attached to the sublumbar region by two folds of peritoneum (the broad ligament) and consists of two horns, a body and neck (cervix). The horns are about 25 cm long, and the body 18–20 cm in length and 10 cm in diameter.

The wall of the uterus consists of three coats: an outer serous layer continuous with the broad ligaments; a muscular layer (myometrium) containing an external layer of longitudinal fibres and an internal layer of circular fibres; and a mucous membrane (endometrium) comprising luminal epithelium (lining cells), stroma of connective tissue, glands and their ducts.

The uterus is supplied by the uterine artery and the uterine branch of the utero-ovarian artery, and its nerves are derived from the uterine and pelvic

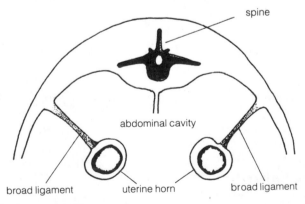

Figure 120   Location of the broad ligament and the uterine horn in the abdominal cavity

sympathetic plexuses (ganglia bodies containing accumulations of nerve cells).

The cervix is the constricted posterior part of the uterus. It is about 7 cm long and 4 cm in diameter in the sexually inactive phase and projects into the anterior vagina.

Vagina The vagina extends horizontally through the pelvic cavity from the cervix to the vulva. It is about 20 cm long and up to 12 cm in diameter but its walls are normally in apposition. Most of the vagina is uncovered by peritoneum and it is surrounded by loose connective tissue, veins and fat. Its wall is composed of muscular and mucous coats. The mucous coat is very elastic and covered with stratified epithelium.

The vagina is divided into anterior and posterior parts by a transverse fold (hymen) which is usually patent (open). The arterial supply comes from the pubic arteries and the nerves are derived from the sympathetic pelvic plexus.

The vulva is covered by mucous membrane and is continuous in front with the vagina and opens externally about 7 cm below the anus. It consists of two lips connected by a dorsal and ventral commissure. Immediately inside the ventral commissure is the glans clitoridis. The vulval lips are covered by thin pigmented skin which is supplied with sebaceous and sweat glands. Beneath the skin are muscles that fuse above with the anal sphincter.

Perineum The perineum (Greek *perineas* = space between anus and scrotum) is a loosely defined region in the mare, including the anus, vulva and adjacent skin. Its conformation is of clinical importance because of the part it plays in protecting the genital tract from the entrance of air (pneumo-vagina – see p. 534) and bacteria through the vulva. It is also subject to lacerations, wounds and bruising during birth or from kicks by other horses.

The entrance to the anterior vagina is protected by the arrangement of the vulva, posterior vagina and hymen, which form a valve preventing air from entering the vagina. The valve may be defective because of malconformation or breached by introducing a speculum into the anterior vagina.

The optimal conformation is one in which the vulval labiae are in the vertical plane and 80 per cent below the pelvic floor or ischium. If the pelvic floor is low relative to the labiae, there is a tendency for the anus to retract anteriorly and the upper part of the vulva to fall into the horizontal plane.

23

THE OESTROUS CYCLE

The oestrous cycle is a pattern of physiological and behavioural events under hormonal control, forming the basis of sexual activity and conception. The cycle has two components: oestrus (heat), in which the mare is receptive to the stallion and the ovum is shed, and dioestrus, which is a period of sexual quiescence.

The cycle typically lasts twenty-one days (five days of oestrus and sixteen of dioestrus) and may recur throughout the year, although in the horse sexual activity is characteristically confined to a restricted breeding season and outside this period the cycles cease (anoestrus).

There is considerable individual variation in cycle length and character. Oestrous periods are longer and less intense in behavioural terms at the start and end of the season than in the middle. The cycle starts at pubery (about one and a half years) and continues throughout the mare's lifetime.

It is convenient to discuss the cycle under the separate headings of its physiological and behavioural components.

Pituitary gland

The pituitary gland lies immediately below the base of the brain, to which it is attached, and rests in a depression in the upper surface of the sphenoid bone. From a functional viewpoint the pituitary is divided into the posterior lobe, which is innervated by nerve tracts originating in the hypothalamus, and the anterior lobe, which has no direct nerve supply.

The posterior lobe secretes the hormones oxytocin and vasopressin, and the anterior lobe secretes the gonad-stimulating (gonadotrophic) hormones, follicle-stimulating hormone (FSH), luteinizing hormone (LH) and prolactin. The character and actions of these hormones are discussed below.

The anterior pituitary also secretes adrenocorticotrophic hormones (ACTH) and thyroid-stimulating hormone (TSH), which influence the reproductive system indirectly but are not usually considered true reproductive hormones.

1   DAY 0–5 OESTRUS   tail up, winking, relaxed cervix, moist tract

FSH and OEST dominant

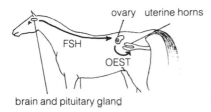

brain and pituitary gland

2   DAY 5 OVULATION   tail up, winking, relaxed cervix, moist tract

LH dominant

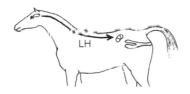

FSH = follicle stimulating hormone
LH = luteinizing hormone
PROG = progesterone
OEST = oestrogen
PROST = prostaglandin

3   DAY 7 DIOESTRUS   ear back, kicking, closed cervix, dry tract

PROG dominant

4   DAY 13 DIOESTRUS   midcycle surge

FSH and PROG dominant

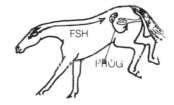

5   DAY 20 start of NEW OESTRUS

FSH and PROST dominant

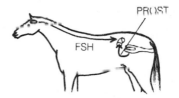

Figure 121   Hormone changes in the oestrous cycle

The posterior pituitary develops from a ventral outgrowth of the forebrain and is composed of nerve tissue. The nerve cells are situated in the supra-optic and paraventricular nuclei of the hypothalamus. Besides conducting nerve impulses, these cells manufacture the polypeptide hormones vasopressin and oxytocin. The hormones travel down the axons of the nerve cells to the posterior lobe, where they are stored until release by appropriate nervous stimuli. For example, oxytocin is released by reflexes initiated during parturition by the stretching of the vaginal wall and, later, when the foal approaches the mammary region (milk-ejection reflex).

The anterior pituitary develops from the ectoderm of the roof of the buccal cavity and has no direct nervous control. It is, however, connected indirectly to the hypothalamus by a portal system of blood vessels which conveys releasing and inhibiting factors secreted by hypothalamic cells.

There are about ten of these factors. The FSH- and LH-releasing factors and prolactin-inhibiting factor are of particular interest because of their effects on the oestrous cycle and mammary secretions respectively. Although work on the practical application of these substances is in its infancy, future development could have far-reaching significance in equine medicine and the management of the reproductive process.

Physiology

The classic view of the endocrinology of the oestrous cycle is as follows:

1. Follicle-stimulating hormone (FSH) stimulates the development of ovarian follicles which secrete oestrogen. These hormones are responsible for oestrous signs and changes in the genital tract.
2. Rising blood levels of oestrogen stimulate the anterior pituitary to produce luteinizing hormone (LH) and reduce the secretion of FSH. Ovulation occurs and a yellow body forms (see p. 320) which produces progesterone.
3. Falling oestrogen and rising progesterone levels in the blood are responsible for dioestrous signs and changes in the genital tract.
4. The secretion of a luteolytic hormone (now identified as prostaglandin) from the uterus ends dioestrus by arresting the functional life of the yellow body and causing blood progesterone levels to fall to zero.
5. Falling progesterone levels stimulate the anterior pituitary to secrete FSH and restart the cycle.

This account is a simplified one for ease of understanding and, as with all simplifications, it represents but part of the truth. There are many facets to the interaction of hormones on their target organs (see chapter 8) and it is usually the net effect or balance which determines the outcome in any given instance. For example, oestrus represents a dominance, rather than an absolute status, of FSH and oestrogen relative to LH and progesterone. The activation of endocrine glands may also be based on their sensitivity to changing levels of hormones and the rapidity with which these occur. Many hormones leave their endocrine gland in an inert form and become potentiated by the target cells. In the mare oestrous cycles are promoted by outside factors such as daylight and nutrition.

Controlling the oestrous cycle

Before discussing how we may control the oestrous cycle of mares we must be clear as to the states which require treatment.

Oestrus is the period of heat in which ovulation occurs. This normally takes place twenty-four hours before the mare goes out of heat, that is, enters dioestrus. Typically oestrus lasts five days. However, it may last for much longer, especially in spring. In February, March and maybe the beginning of April heats may last for one, two or even four weeks. In some of these prolonged oestrous periods ovulation may occur at the end in the normal fashion. However, in other instances no ovulation occurs at all.

Prolonged dioestrus is a condition in which the normal dioestrous period of fourteen to sixteen days is prolonged by the abnormally continuing function of the yellow body (producing progesterone). This may last several weeks or even months in some cases.

Anoestrus is the condition of inactivity of the ovaries and sexual organs during winter.

Controlling the oestrous cycle therefore implies that treatment is used to bring mares from anoestrus into full fertile oestrous cycles combining five days oestrus and fifteen days dioestrus. Let us now consider how this may be done in our present state of knowledge.

Our aims at controlling the oestrous cycle are, essentially, to manipulate events so that one ovum is shed at a particular time, convenient to the interests of owner and manager in arranging a mating for the mare on a given day in a given month during an arbitrarily selected breeding season. Various therapies involving the administration of follicle-stimulating hormone (FSH), luteinizing hormone (LH), pregnant mare's serum gonadotrophin (PMSG), prostaglandin, gonadotrophin releasing hormone (GnRH), progesterone and/or oestrogen have all been tried with varying degrees of success at different points of the oestrous cycle. The most successful of these appears to be prostaglandin for inducing oestrus and luteinizing hormone for inducing ovulation. The effect of artificial light in promoting oestrous cycles during the early part of the breeding season is well known, as is the efficacy of intra-uterine irrigation of mares in dioestrus.

However, many therapies fail for reasons which are unclear or because they are based on insufficient knowledge of the physiological state of the individual at the time of application, or, indeed, because they are fundamentally incapable of action for reasons at present unclear. An example of the last category is the failure of PMSG (see p. 120) to stimulate follicular development or to cause ovulation, a fact which is peculiar considering that it is composed of FSH and LH. The refractory state of the mare's ovaries to exogenous administration of this hormone remains a physiological mystery.

Advancing the onset of the cycle The onset of the breeding season can be advanced artificially by exposing mares to artificial light. Temperature, nutrition and other environmental factors appear to play a secondary part, and prolonged periods of oestrus without ovulation occur commonly in mares during transition from deep anoestrus to complete sexual function.

There are a number of differing regimens. One researcher found that 200- and 400-watt lamps caused mares to come into oestrus sixty-five to eighty days earlier than anticipated. Another used 15-watt bulbs three and four months prior to the beginning of the breeding season and 200–400-watt bulbs one and two months before the season, gradually increasing the length of artificial daylight until the mares were in light for sixteen out of twenty-four hours. There was a time lag of forty to a hundred days before the onset of oestrous behaviour in light-exposed anoestrous mares.

A practical disadvantage to light stimulation is the need to continue the programme until spring conditions occur. It is useful, therefore, only for mares that are resident on one stud during the whole period in which they are being treated; should the mare be moved from one stud to another, the programme on the second stud should be phased to meet the protocol under which the mare has started her treatment.

If a mare is in anoestrus or prolonged spring oestrus, progesterone may be given for about ten consecutive days. This may be injected, but nowadays potent progesterone-like substances are available (e.g. allyl trenbolone) may be given by mouth for about ten days. Progesterone therapy used in this manner causes accumulations of FSH and LH in the pituitary gland. When the treatment is stopped there is a rebound effect and the hormones are released from the pituitary in more substantial quantities than would otherwise have been the case. This causes the mare to come into heat and for a follicle to mature. This occurs at about seven to ten days following ceasing the treatment.

The incidence of ovulation   The oestrous cycle of the mare represents a coordinated sequence of events in which ovulation occurs at the end of a limited period of behavioural receptivity. In this way the ovum and spermatozoa are able to meet under optimal conditions for fertilization to take place. From a practical point of view this shedding of the egg from the mare's ovary provides an opportunity for conception; once the egg has been shed and remains unfertilized, a further opportunity for conception does not appear until the next oestrus, some twenty days later. Under ideal conditions, in which dioestrus lasts for two weeks and oestrus for one week, there are four opportunities during three calendar months. And within the Thoroughbred breeding season there is a maximum of six opportunities.

There are unfortunately a number of reasons why this number is reduced in many cases. The breeding season is arbitrarily arranged so that two thirds of it occur during the winter or early spring, when the oestrous cycle in many individuals is naturally absent or contains prolonged oestrus often without ovulation. Then there are mares which undergo prolonged periods of dioestrus which, if mating has taken place, resemble pregnancy; and by prolonging the cycle they cause a corresponding decrease in the number of ovulations that can occur during the breeding season. There are also foaling mares that cannot start their post-foaling oestrous cycle for some weeks or even months after the start of the breeding season.

We have to accept, therefore, that under average conditions of stud management there may be only three or four ovulations, i.e. eggs or opportunities for conception, per individual mare per breeding season. In most circumstances this is a more than sufficient number for the purpose of obtaining annual conception in a herd of broodmares. Indeed, the 60–70 per cent conception rates obtained on average bear witness to this claim. However, when we, as veterinarians, are considering our contribution to the problem, we must, of necessity, concentrate on the substantial incidence of non-conceptions, i.e. barrenness and foetal loss. In this context, the more ovulations that occur the greater the chance that a satisfactory outcome can be achieved.

For example, in an individual suffering from endometritis (inflamed lining of the uterus) and therefore presenting a particularly hostile environment to the spermatozoa, repeated attempts to achieve fertilization may be required. Nor can we dismiss the importance of semen quality and the libido of the stallion from the equation in establishing the balance for or against individual success.

Inducing oestrus The need to induce oestrus occurs in the following circumstances:

1. When a mare has either been found to be not in foal at a pregnancy examination or is in a state of prolonged dioestrus without having visited the stallion.
2. When mating has to be arranged to suit managerial requirements as, for example, in synchronizing oestrus in a herd, reducing the length of the cycle in cases that have, inadvertantly or deliberately, been missed in a previous oestrus (e.g. when ovulation has occurred before mating or when foaling or other heats have been avoided for reasons of infection, etc.), and, out of the breeding season, to promote oestrus for bacteriological tests of the genital tract.

Essentially there are two methods of inducing oestrus: uterine infusion with saline and the injection of a natural or a synthetic prostaglandin. However, it must be stressed that in both cases treatment can only be successful if the failure to show oestrus is due to the presence of an active yellow body. Prostaglandin acts directly with a luteolytic effect to dissolve the yellow body and this causes the mare to come in heat within two to five days. Uterine infusion acts indirectly, probably by stimulating the release of prostaglandin from the uterus. Mares do not respond in either instance if treated within about five days of a new yellow body forming, presumably because the yellow body is refractory to the action of prostaglandin during this period. The judgement of when to inject the mare is, of course, a veterinary decision.

Inducing follicle development Two drugs, gonadotrophin releasing hormone and progesterone, are currently used to promote the development of mature follicles in the ovary. The use of gonadotrophin releasing hormone has exciting possibilities. However, this hormone acts by causing the pituitary gland to release FSH and LH. It does so only if administered in a pulsatile (rhythmic) manner and not if given in a single bolus dose. Implants releasing small doses over a period of days or a programme of injecting doses two or three times a day has been found to be most effective.

If a mature follicle is present in the ovary it may be assisted to ovulate by administering the luteinizing hormone hCG (human chorionic gonado-trophin). This treatment brings oestrus to an end and enables mating to be arranged just before ovulation occurs.

Use of treatments   As with abnormal mares, the treatment of normal mares is very much a matter for veterinary judgement in the context of the particular individual that requires treatment. It is not therefore in the scope of this book to argue the various methods that may be used and how these should be applied. However, there are some fundamental points which should be made in order for mare owners to appreciate the advantages and disadvantages of therapy aimed at altering a mare's sexual activity.

The reality of the changing hormonal concentrations in the body of a mare relative to changes in her sexual behaviour during the oestrous cycle is a complex interaction, not just a simple relationship of cause and effect. For example, although we know that follicles mature under the influence of FSH, they do so in relation to other hormones such as LH, progesterone and oestrogen.

Changing the level of hormones in the body by artificial means can never, therefore, be simplistic. Administering one hormone at any given time may be likened to increasing one ingredient of a cake without reference to the other ingredients. The outcome may, in effect, be the same type of cake as the one we started to make but its balance depends on the quantity of each ingredient. There may, therefore, be too much fruit or too little flour depending on the ingredients with which we started. And when we give hormones to a mare much of the effect depends on the makeup or state of the mare at the start of the treatment.

Unfortunately we do not have very precise means of diagnosing the exact state of a mare at any given time. We may say that she is aneostrus but we cannot determine the finer details which lie behind this state. We cannot measure directly the activity or inactivity of the pituitary gland and identify the control of this gland being exerted by cells in the brain producing GnRH. This inability to make a precise detailed diagnosis is one reason why our treatment works in only a proportion of cases, even if this proportion is sometimes as high as 70 per cent. The failure of the 30 per cent may be ascribed to a lack of current methods of distinguishing differences between individuals.

It is no coincidence that the most successful means of changing the mare's sexual state from one of inactivity (anoestrus) to one of activity (oestrous cycling) is by increasing the length of daylight artificially over a period of six to eight weeks. This mimics the natural stimulus more effectively than any combination of drugs can achieve in a shorter period of time.

24
PREGNANCY

PLACENTATION

The foal, unlike the young of smaller nesting mammals such as the rat, mouse, rabbit, cat or dog, is born at an extremely advanced state of development. It can stand within minutes after birth and is capable of highly coordinated movement within a matter of hours. The preparations for this dramatic entry into the world take place unseen in the mother's uterus, which is part of the female reproductive tract (see chapter 22).

Attachment of the blastocyst and the development of the foetal membrane

After mating, sperm meets the egg (ovum) within the Fallopian tube, and the single cell of the egg begins to divide. The fertilized ovum enters the uterus as a hollow ball of cells, the blastocyst.

The blastocyst of the horse, like those of the other large domestic mammals, does not erode the endometrial lining of the uterus but remains within its central cavity. It comes to lie at the base of one or other uterine horn, where, on or about the thirtieth day of gestation, certain specialized cells on its outer surface begin to invade the endometrium. The cells form the structures known as endometrial cups which secrete the hormone eCG into the maternal bloodstream. The hormone is also excreted in the mother's urine and detection of its presence is the basis for one of the methods of the early diagnosis of pregnancy. The concentrations of eCG in the serum rise until about the seventieth day and then begin to decline. This pattern is reflected in the development and regression of the endometrial cups, which seldom persist longer than the 120th day of gestation. The endometrial cups have nothing whatever to do with the development of the placenta, which does not become fully established before the 100th day.

From its original position at the base of the uterine horn, the spherical conceptus expands to fill the whole of the cavity of the uterus, extending through the body and into the non-gravid horn. Nevertheless the foetus itself remains in its original position at the base of the gravid horn. By forty days it has become enclosed by three membranes, which together form two concentric fluid-filled sacs (Figure 122). The inner sac, the amnion, contains a slimy fluid. The outer sac, the allantois, not only wraps itself completely round the amnion, but also forms an inner lining to the outer limiting membrane, the chorion. The space between the two double membranes, the allanto-amnion and the chorio-allantois, is filled with watery allantoic fluid. The chorion, the outermost component of the chorio-allantois, forms the foetal side of the placenta.

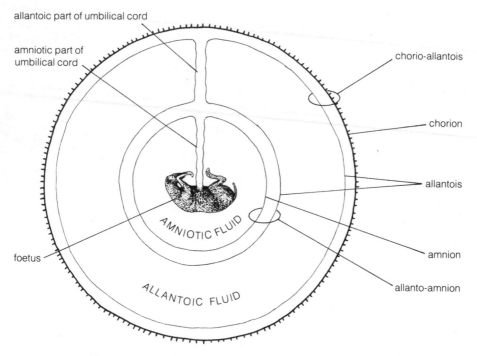

Figure 122   The placental membranes in the uterus

Flattened, oval, leathery bodies known as hippomanes float free in the allantoic fluid. They are aggregations of cell debris which have no known function, though they feature prominently in horse-related folklore. Tales may still be told of hippomanes lodging in the mouth of the foal and shaping its tongue, or of dried and powdered hippomanes having aphrodisiac properties. Unfortunately for the romance of folklore, neither of these tales is true.

The embryo is connected to the placenta by the umbilical cord, which passes first through the amnion and then crosses the space between amnion and chorion. Thus, unlike the situation in many other mammals, the umbilical cord has two distinct divisions: these are known as the amniotic part and allantoic part respectively. The umbilical cord carries blood from the foetus to the placenta in paired umbilical arteries, and oxygenated blood is returned to the foetus in a single umbilical vein. Foetal and maternal circulations are entirely separate, but they come into very close apposition within the placenta. It is within the placenta that oxygen and nutrients are transferred to the foetus, while carbon dioxide and the majority of waste products are passed in the opposite direction.

The development and structure of the placenta

The chorion is at first avascular, but blood vessels from the embryo spread across its inner surface shortly after the primitive circulation of the foetus becomes established. Along the course of these blood vessels tiny fingerlike outpocketings of the chorion push into corresponding depressions which form in the lining of the uterus. The outpocketings of the chorion are known as foetal villi, and the depressions in the endometrial lining of the uterus as maternal crypts. The original villous outpocketings branch repeatedly to form very small tufts which, together with the correspondingly more complex maternal crypts, form minute globular structures known as microcotyledons. These are the functional units of the equine placenta; they number many thousands and are found in all parts of the uterus except the cervix and the points of entry of the Fallopian tubes.

The tiny tufts of foetal villi can be seen on the red side of the afterbirth after delivery. If a small piece of afterbirth is immersed in water, the villi float out like miniature sea anemones closely packed together on the surface of the membrane.

Placentae in twin pregnancy

The birth of live twin foals is a newsworthy event, but the conception of twin embryos is hardly a cause for celebration. The reason is that twin foals are usually aborted; survival seems to depend on the placenta of each foal occupying exactly half of the surface area of the uterus (Figure 123).

If the placentae are asymmetrically distributed, the foal attached to the smaller placenta will die (Figure 124). If this happens early in pregnancy, the embryo may mummify and the placenta of the living twin may expand its territory and enclose the mummified embryo (Figure 125). The result is the birth of a single living foal, and the evidence of twinning may never be suspected or discovered. More tragically, and usually not later than the ninth month of pregnancy, the death of one foal results in the abortion of both.

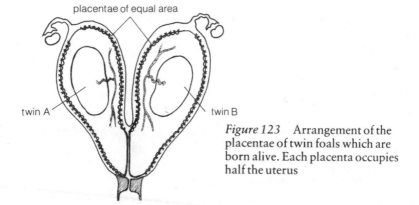

placentae of equal area

twin A   twin B

Figure 123   Arrangement of the placentae of twin foals which are born alive. Each placenta occupies half the uterus

Placenta of B occupies less than half the uterus, it will *not* survive

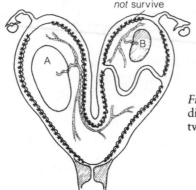

A   B

Figure 124   Asymmetrical distribution of the placentae in twin foals

3

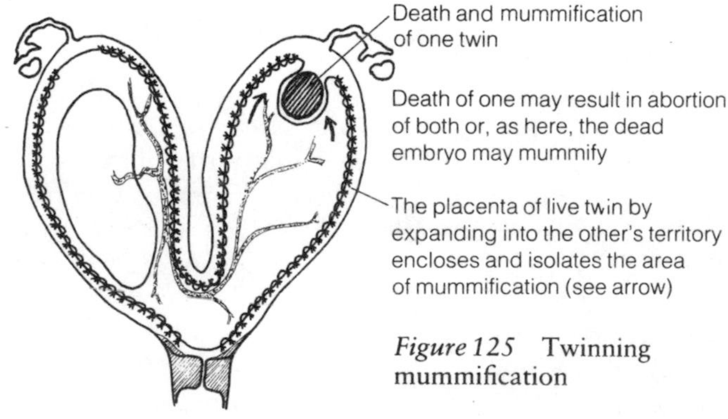

Death and mummification of one twin

Death of one may result in abortion of both or, as here, the dead embryo may mummify

The placenta of live twin by expanding into the other's territory encloses and isolates the area of mummification (see arrow)

Figure 125   Twinning mummification

PREGNANCY

Length of pregnancy

Pregnancy lasts, on average, 340 days in the Thoroughbred and larger breeds. In ponies and other small breeds pregnancy is shorter by up to twenty days. However, individuals within all breeds vary quite considerably. The range for a Thoroughbred is some 320–65 days or even longer.

Pregnancy lasts about 365 days in donkeys and about 350 days in a horse mare carrying a foal by a donkey stallion. These differences illustrate that the genetic makeup of the foetus determines in part, at least, the length of pregnancy and that this may be influenced by the genetic contribution of individual stallions and mares.

The length of pregnancy is also influenced by nutrition, for well-fed mares tend to have shorter pregnancies than poorly fed ones. The time of year is also important: mares delivering in winter have longer pregnancies than those delivering in summer.

Pregnancy diagnosis

Pregnancy diagnosis is important to those who manage broodmares for a number of reasons. First, during the breeding season an early (seventeen to twenty days) diagnosis enables management to make a decision as to whether or not a mare requires further mating or whether measures should be employed to bring her into oestrus so that she is given a further chance of conceiving. Second, mares that are pregnant may be identified for purposes of sale, insurance or in continuing plans for the subsequent mating season. Third, it is important to determine whether or not twins are present and, if so, the measures to be taken to eliminate one or both members. Finally, it is helpful to be able to confirm barrenness in cases where diagnosis of conditions or treatment of the uterus is being considered at some stage following mating.

Rectal examination   The traditional method of pregnancy diagnosis in the mare is rectal examination. The operator places a gloved and lubricated arm in the rectum and feels the uterus. This method is accurate from about forty days after mating, depending on the individual. Experienced operators can achieve an accurate diagnosis earlier than this, even at twenty days.

Echography (ultrasound scanning)   More recently the advent of ultrasound has enabled operators to make accurate diagnosis as early as fifteen days after conception. In practice the seventeen-to twenty-one-day period is usually the first routine examination made with scanning (Figure 126a).

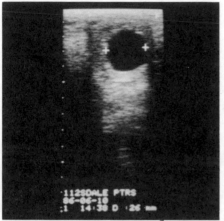 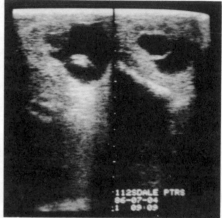

Figure 126a/b   Ultrasound scans at (left) 21 days and (right) 29 days (two views)

At this time the fluid sac representing the foetus and its membranes may be visualized. By Day 24 the foetus itself may be identified and progressively, with time, further structures may be seen (see Figure 126b).

After about Day 80 the foetus may be visualized by an external examination placing the probe in the region of the udder.

Scanning has the advantage of very much improved accuracy in early pregnancy, while at the same time providing the means of diagnosing twins. Twins may be contained one in each horn of the uterus (see Figure 123) or together in one horn. In the first instance a diagnosis can lead to squeezing of one of the two members of the twins and its elimination with the probable normal continuation of the other one. This procedure is best performed before about Day 25. After this time the chances of successfully eliminating one without the other member are markedly reduced.

If twins are in the same horn, i.e. adjacent to one another, the usual approach is to abort them with prostaglandin. The importance of eliminating twins by one means or another (i.e. by removing one or both) are discussed on p. 338.

Detection of eCG   As discussed on p. 120, eCG is a hormone present in the bloodstream of pregnant mares between about Day 45 and Day 100. A blood sample taken during this period and tested for the presence of eCG is used as a pregnancy test.

More recently an immunological test has been developed. This is based on the fact that the hormone acts as an antigen and, when mixed with an antibody, a reaction occurs. This reaction can be identified when red blood cells are incorporated into the test system . This is usually referred to as the MIP test (mare immunological pregnancy test).

The MIP test has certain limitations. For example, once the endometrial cups (see p. 331) from which the hormone eCG is secreted are established in the uterus, the hormone is produced until about Day 100 irrespective of whether or not the foetus lives. In other words, we may have a situation in which the foetus has died at, say, Day 45 and, when the test is performed at perhaps Day 80, the test is positive despite the mare having lost her pregnancy. The accuracy of the test is high, probably over 95 per cent, apart from this one proviso. It is possible to rely on the test almost to a 100 per cent if the result is negative but only to about 90 per cent if it is positive.

The test is favoured by those who believe that the rectal examination may in itself cause abortion. It cannot be denied that such an examination may cause abortion, but in mares used to being handled for examination the chances of abortion are very small.

Cuboni test   The Cuboni test is based on a chemical test-tube reaction in the laboratory. Urine from the mare is mixed with hydrochloric acid and heated for ten minutes. After cooling, the hydrolysed urine is removed with benzene and transferred to a test tube. Concentrated sulphuric acid is poured down the side of the tube to lie under the benzene. The tube is stoppered, inverted once and heated. Under an ultra-violet lamp in reflected daylight a positive result shows as a green fluorescence.

Conditions of Pregnancy

ABORTION

Abortion means the expulsion of the foetus before it has any chance of living, that is, while it is non-viable. Thus abortion may occur at any time before Day 300 of pregnancy. After this time it is more usual to describe an abnormal termination of pregnancy as prematurity, dysmaturity or stillbirth (see p. 391).

It should, however, be appreciated that these terms are arbitrary definitions and do not represent different disease conditions. It is necessary to use the terms so that we have some convenient headings under which to discuss these conditions.

When abortion occurs early (before about Day 100) it may be described as foetal loss, embryonic death or resorption. Again, these descriptions are largely technical and need not concern the reader except, in so far as they may be used by vets, some understanding is necessary. For the purpose of description here the term 'abortion' is used to describe abnormal loss of pregnancy at any stage of pregnancy up to about Day 300.

Abortion concerns two beings, the mare and her foetus. It is the mare that expels the foetus but the cause of this may be the foetus itself dying. On the other hand, the foetus may be expelled in a relatively healthy state and it is the mare that is responsible for the event. An obvious example of this type of abortion is if a drug such as oxytocin is given to the mare.

The distinction as to whether the abortion is of maternal or foetal origin is a technical matter and outside the scope of this book. However, the expression of this difference is of interest practically because, when the foetus and placenta are failing, the mare springs an udder and may run milk. When no such development is present, this implies that the foetus has died suddenly or that the mare herself has been responsible for initiating the expulsion of her foetus.

The causes of abortion

Infection Any microbe which is found in the genital tract of the barren mare may be responsible for abortion at any stage of pregnancy. The most common bacterial infections are streptococci, staphylococci, *Escherichia coli* and *Klebsiella* (see chapters 28 and 29).

Fungus (mycosis – see chapter 28) is responsible for abortions occurring in the second half of pregnancy. These microbes usually infect the placenta and cause substantial thickening of and damage to this membrane. Eventually the microbes may enter the foetus itself where they cause lesions in the liver and lungs.

Viruses, especially equid herpesvirus 1 (EHV-1, rhinopneumonitis), cause abortion typically from about the seventh month onwards. However, cases can occur as early as five months and frequently in mares that are near to or at full term. The condition may be epidemic and it has an especial place in veterinary and stud management practice (see p. 340).

Arteritis virus may cause abortion, particularly in the first half of pregnancy. The abortion is, however, usually a secondary event associated with general infection of a pregnant mare. For a description of this condition, see pp. 428–9.

Non-infectious causes **Twin conception** leads to abortion. The reason for this is the nature of the horse's placenta (see p. 333). In all other species twins can be carried successfully because there is space on the uterine wall for the attachment of more than one placenta. In the horse, however, the area of placental attachment in single pregnancy normally involves the whole of the uterine wall. Thus, in twin pregnancy there is an inevitable reduction of the placental area available to each foetus, usually to the detriment of both. In most cases one twin dies and both are aborted. If twins *are* born alive, they are often smaller than usual, are especially susceptible to infectious disease, and may be subject to deficiencies in normal skeletal development.

Twisting of the umbilical cord around the hind limb sometimes results in abortion because of strangulation of the blood supply to the foetus. This may also occur, less commonly, because of abnormal twisting, which has the same effect. Many of these cases are probably due to abnormally long cords.

In other species it has been established that early abortions are due to **chromosomal abnormality** in the foetus. This is nature's way of ensuring that defective individuals do not survive pregnancy. This type of abortion has not been proved to occur in the horse but probably accounts for a number of the early abortions, i.e. those occurring before Day 100.

It is often difficult if not impossible to diagnose the cause of every abortion. This is because it may be the result of failure in the relationship between the uterus and the placenta, e.g. bloodflow or immunological and hormonal failure. States of incompatability may develop between the uterus and the placenta. In making a diagnosis of the cause of any particular case of abortion the pathologist is presented with material that provides evidence only of death, that is, the pathology of shortage or absence of oxygen.

If a mare aborts up to about Day 150 it is probable that the foetus itself will not be found. The reasons for this are either that it is too small or it has been resorbed. The abortion is only established by the fact that the mare comes into heat or suffers a vaginal discharge. However, in other cases the event will be recognized only because the mare is found, at a subsequent examination, not to be pregnant. These abortions require veterinary interpretation of the cause and treatment of the mare if required.

EQUID HERPESVIRUS 1 (EHV-1, RHINOPNEUMONITIS, VIRUS ABORTION)

After Day 150 of pregnancy the abortion will probably be evident in the form of the expelled foetus and its membranes. The same approach as to earlier abortions should be made, namely, a veterinarian should be called to decide whether the mare requires treatment. However, whereas early abortions are almost certainly the result of causes which are not a threat to other mares, later abortions may, if they are caused by a virus, be a threat to other mares. For this reason all abortions after Day 150 should be regarded as being potentially cases of equid herpesvirus 1 (EHV-1) infection unless demonstrated otherwise by post-mortem examination of the foetus.

Herpesvirus causing abortion in mares is essentially a respiratory virus, causing the snotty-nose condition of foals and yearlings. The virus can be transmitted from one individual to another by two means and in both cases the mare inhales the virus. The virus may either be exhaled from the lungs of another infected mare in the vicinity, or it may be spread from an aborted foetus. At the time of an abortion a large amount of virus is spread into the atmosphere; any pregnant mare in contact with the abortion can inhale the virus and herself become infected.

The herpesvirus may be present in many individuals, especially foals and yearlings. There are two strains: subtype 1, which is usually associated with abortion, although it may cause the respiratory (snotty-nose) type of infection; and subtype 2, which is almost entirely respiratory and rarely causes abortion (see p. 425).

Following infection, immunity to either strain is short-lived and lasts only about two or three months. Further, infection with one strain does not necessarily confer immunity to the other. This presents a problem when we use vaccines. Most vaccines against herpesviruses are relatively ineffective and have to be administered frequently, say, every two months.

When any mare aborts, it is prudent to place the foetus and all its membranes in a leak-proof plastic container or bin. These should then be taken for post mortem at an appropriate veterinary establishment. Here the possibility of the case being one of herpes infection will be established. The diagnosis depends on histological examination of the liver and lungs for typical lesions and by growing the virus in tissue culture. It may take only twenty-four to forty-eight hours for a positive diagnosis to be made, but up to a week for a negative diagnosis to be confirmed.

The precautions that should be taken on a stud where other pregnant mares are stabled should be applied until a definite diagnosis has been achieved. These precautions are as follows:

1. A mare that has aborted should be confined to the loosebox in which she aborted. If she aborted in a paddock she should be brought in and placed in her own loosebox or in one which is isolated from any other pregnant mare. All areas which have been contaminated by the fluids of the foetus and placenta should be thoroughly disinfected.
2. All pregnant mares that have been in contact with the aborting mare for at least the previous three weeks should be regarded as being potentially infected. These mares should therefore be isolated as a group and not brought into contact with any other pregnant mare.
3. All other mares on the premises should be isolated as a potentially non-infected group. And all traffic of horses into or out of the studfarm concerned should be stopped.

If the abortion is subsequently diagnosed as being not due to herpesvirus, these restrictions can then be lifted. However, it cannot be overemphasized that the measures taken immediately after an abortion may mean the difference between a simple case, the condition spreading to only a very few other mares and a widespread epidemic affecting more than one studfarm.

The immediate measures described above should be followed in every case of abortion. However, some cases of virus infection may occur at full term, and foals which are born sick should also be considered as possible cases of virus infection. In these circumstances they too may be a threat to other mares that have not yet foaled.

If a case of abortion or a foal dying in the first week of life is confirmed as being the result of virus infection, the long-term precautions have been stated by the Thoroughbred Breeders Association in their code of practice. The following is abstracted from the 1986 code of practice.

RHINOPNEUMONITIS VIRUS ABORTION

Prevention and Control of Equine Rhinopneumonitis

It must be remembered that any recommendations for the control of virus abortion are inevitably a compromise between procedures that are scientifically desirable and those that are practicable for the industry.

a. Management

(i)   Where practicable, mares should be foaled at home and sent to a stallion with a healthy foal at foot.

(ii)   When this is not possible, the mare should be sent to the stallion stud at least one month before foaling is due and put into group isolation. Ideally these groups should be as small as possible. Mares in late pregnancy which have come from sales yards or from abroad constitute a particular risk and should be separately isolated.

(iii)   Pregnant mares should be segregated as far as possible from weaned foals, yearlings, horses out of training, hunters and competition horses. If handled by the same attendant, the work schedule should be arranged to allow the mares to be handled first.

(iv)   There is a risk in transporting mares in late pregnancy with other stock. In particular they should not be travelled with recently aborted mares.

(v)   If a *foster mother* has to be brought on to a stud where pregnant mares reside, she should be strictly isolated until the possibility of her own foal's death being due to rhinopneumonitis is excluded.

b.   Isolation Facilities

Isolation facilities should be provided at all studs to prevent the spread of rhinopneumonitis and other infections. The design and construction should be undertaken in consultation with the stud's veterinary surgeon, who should also be consulted about the precautions to be taken to prevent the spread of infection by the attendant.

c.   Disinfection

It is essential that routine and regular cleansing of horse conveyances is carried out in accordance with regulations of the respective Ministries of Agriculture, Fisheries and Food.

d.   Vaccination

An inactivated rhinopneumonitis vaccine is presently available for the control of the disease and mare owners should consult their veterinarian about its use and a suitable vaccination programme. Vaccination programmes formulated to provide protection against rhinopneumonitis virus abortion should not, by themselves, be allowed to engender a false sense of security. It must be stressed that vaccination cannot replace sound management practices, which should be arranged in consultation with the stud farm vet.

Action to be taken when Abortion, Stillbirth or Birth of a Sick Foal occurs

(i)   Action should be taken in the case of any abortion, stillbirth or foal death within 7 days of birth, even if the mare concerned is believed to have been vaccinated against rhinopneumonitis. The stud's veterinary surgeon must be notified immediately and arrangements made, on his advice, for appropriate investigations to be undertaken. The foetus or foal and its membranes should be sent to a recognised centre for post-mortem examination. The possibility of virus infection should also be considered when the foal is ill at birth. If the foal is alive but possibly infected, a diagnosis may be made by virological examination of nasopharyngeal swabs taken from the foal. These should be submitted to an appropriate laboratory as soon as possible.

(ii)   The mare should be put in strict isolation pending results of the examinations. All bedding should be sprayed in the box with disinfectant and left for 48 hours; it can be removed and burned at a later date. The box should then be washed and liberally soaked with a disinfectant such as one of the Iodophor group and the box thoroughly cleansed with water under pressure or steam according to the instructions of the stud's veterinary surgeon.

(iii)   No horse should be removed from the stud premises until the possibility of rhinopneumonitis abortion has been excluded.

(iv)   If preliminary laboratory investigations are indicative of rhinopneumonitis infection, close-contact pregnant mares should be divided into small groups as soon as possible to minimise the spread of infection. Despite these precautions some of these mares may still abort.

(v)   If rhinopneumonitis abortion is subsequently confirmed at a stud, the appropriate Breeders' Association should be notified immediately. At the same time owners or their agents with mares at the stud or due to send mares there should be informed. Those studs to which mares from the infected premises have been or are to be sent should also be informed.

(vi)   Notification of cases to the Breeders' Association is of the utmost importance to the long-term interests of all owners of mares. No stigma is attached to an abortion attributable to rhinopneumonitis on a stud, but failure to notify the disease leads directly to the spread of infection to the detriment of all owners and their horses, especially mare owners.

(vii)   Any foal which is ill at birth or becomes unwell within seven days of birth should be carefully examined by a veterinary surgeon.

Subsequent Action

(i)   Providing there is no sign of infection at home, barren and maiden mares and mares which have foaled at home and produced normal healthy foals can be accepted on the stud on which a confirmed virus abortion has occurred.

(ii)   These mares (enumerated in (i) above) can leave the stud at which the abortion has occurred after one month from the date of the last mare to abort at the stud, provided they are subsequently isolated from in-foal mares for at least two months.

(iii)   The infected stud's own non-pregnant mares can visit other premises after one month from the date of the last abortion, provided they can be isolated for at least two months from heavily pregnant (more than 5 months) mares at the stud they are visiting. Full agreement on these arrangements should be reached between the home stud and the receiving stud and their respective veterinarians. Pregnant mares must remain on the infected stud until they foal.

(iv)   Present evidence indicates that there is little risk of spread of infection if a mare is covered on her second heat cycle after abortion. It is emphasized that she must be isolated from mares in late pregnancy for 8 weeks after abortion.

(v)   Mares that have returned from studs where rhinopneumonitis virus abortion has occurred during the previous season should be foaled *in isolation* at home.

Check List for Action

1.   When an abortion occurs or a foal is born dead or shows signs of illness within 7 days of birth *veterinary advice should be sought immediately.*

2.   The foetus and its membranes or the foal carcase for post-mortem examination should be sent to a laboratory as instructed by the veterinarian. All material should be placed in leakproof containers.

3.   Put the mare in strict isolation.

4.   Do not move any horse off the stud until rhinopneumonitis has been excluded as a cause of the abortion.

5.   If the foal is alive but possibly infected, isolate the mare and foal. The attendant should have no contact with pregnant mares.

6.   Destroy bedding, clean, disinfect premises and vehicles under veterinary supervision.

7.   Notify owners (or their agents) due to send mares to the stud.

If rhinopneumonitis infection is confirmed, notify:

1.   The appropriate Thoroughbred Breeders' Association.
    (i) by telephone
    (ii) in writing

2.   Owners (or their agents)
    (i) all those with mares already at the stud
    (ii) those due to send mares to the stud

3.   Other studs
    (i) those to which mares from the infected premises have been sent
    (ii) those to which mares from the infected premises are to be sent.

25
PARTURITION

Birth marks the end of pregnancy and the beginning of life as we know it outside the security of the womb. It is, as the name 'parturition' implies, a bringing forth of the offspring or foaling, the delivery of a foal. Birth is, in fact, a partnership between mare and foetal foal, as we will discuss shortly. Because birth is a dramatic event and sometimes hazardous, man plays some part in the partnership and foaling is often supervised. However, we must not forget that the event is natural and that problems arise only in a small percentage of cases.

Maternal preparation for birth

The first external sign that the mare is preparing for the event is the development of the udder or mammary glands. These start to enlarge about three weeks before foaling. However, there is quite a marked variation, and movement in mammary size occurs earlier in some mares and later than average in others. Younger mares tend to have a longer preparation time and this often occurs in two distinct stages: an earlier period, perhaps four to five weeks prior to foaling, followed by a pause of about two weeks, then a final preparatory enlargement terminating as a full udder a week or ten days prior to the event.

Secretions within the gland also change, becoming thicker in consistency and changing colour from gold to white. The calcium content rises sharply within four or five days of foaling, sodium levels fall and potassium levels rise.

We can estimate the date of foaling from changes in mammary size and from an analysis of the content of the pre-foaling milk. Traditionally, mammary size and the appearance of wax on the teats has been used for this purpose. Wax is the beads of milk that ooze from and dry at the end of the teats about twenty-four hours prior to foaling (see Figure 135, p. 352). However, some mares do not form wax, while others run milk, i.e. squirt milk from the teats hours, days or even weeks prior to foaling.

Most mares foal during the hours of darkness, but the prediction as to which night the event will take place has always been a problem to those responsible for supervising foaling. More recently studies in the changes in the milk composition have enabled us to make predictions more scientific and accurate. By measuring the calcium, sodium and potassium levels in pre-foaling secretions we can determine that foaling is not likely to occur on a particular night.

Measurements are less reliable for predicting the actual night of foaling, although they can be used to indicate foaling within two or three days once calcium content has increased (above 10 mmol/litre) and sodium levels are higher than potassium levels.

A strip test has been devised by Robert Cash and Jenny Ousey, based on a test for water hardness. There are four squares on the strip and these change colour according to the ionic level in the secretions with which the strip is brought into contact. This test is most appropriate for people who have a limited number of mares and therefore find it inconvenient or uneconomical to have someone present each night in case a mare foals. The test can predict that a mare will not foal (less than two squares changing colour) or that she is likely to foal (three or four squares changing colour). However, as with all tests of this nature, exceptions can occur. The test strips are available from Beaufort Cottage Laboratories, High Street, Newmarket.

Colostrum The milk in the udder at birth is called colostrum, sometimes referred to as first milk because it is the first milk of the foal once it is born. It contains antibodies or protective substances which provide the foal with protection against infection (see p. 372). These protective substances do not appear suddenly in the mammary secretions before birth, but increase slowly to a peak during the preceding two to three weeks.

Foetal preparation for birth

People do not always realize that the foetus plays its own substantial part in preparing for and initiating the birth process. The foetal foal and its placenta produce hormones such as oestrogen, progesterone, prostaglandin, cortisol, etc. It is these hormones which start and control the birth process.

Readiness for birth The foetal foal develops during the pregnancy to a state of maturity. Maturity means that its organs and the cells and tissues of which they are composed are ready to function normally after birth and thereby sustain the foal in the world outside the uterus – a very different environment from that it has experienced previously. Maturity has, therefore, two components.

First, there is a structural development in which organs become shaped and formed so that we recognize them as the kidneys, the lungs, the liver, etc. For example, the lungs are at first solid, but by two thirds of the way through pregnancy potential air sacs (spaces)and a branching system of air tubes have formed, albeit, at that stage, they are filled with fluid. At the end of pregnancy these potential airways are fully formed and ready for the first breath, in which the fluid they contain will be replaced by air.

The other component to maturity is a functional one. The organ cells and tissues are able to function because of a complex system of enzymes, hormones and other substances which control and regulate their activity. These systems do not appear suddenly but are evolved during pregnancy, and it is only when the foal is ready for birth (functionally mature) that their potential is fully realized.

For example, the lungs may have the structure (airways and alveoli) of maturity but lack that vital function which enables them to stay inflated when breathing air. This depends on the system known as surfactant.

Surfactant is a chemical substance secreted by cells lining the air sacs (alveoli) and small air tubes. It forms the lining of the air sac and reduces the surface tension. If surfactant is not present in sufficient quantities, the surface tension causes the air sacs to collapse, just as a bubble of water collapses unless lined by soap which is itself a surface-tension-lowering substance.

Unreadiness for birth or prematurity may involve a surfactant deficiency which makes the lungs unable to stay expanded although structurally they appear normal. This is discussed further on pp. 389–91.

Initiation of birth

In the previous chapter the average length of pregnancy was said to be 340 days with variation of about fifteen days. Each individual has, therefore, a selected date for foaling varying between 325 and 355 days. Some individuals may foal outside this range and the foals still be normal.

From this we may assume that each individual has a selected length of pregnancy which is normal for that individual in that particular year. The actual date is determined more by the foetal foal rather than by the mare herself. It is probable, if we assume the mare is similar to other mammals which have been studied more closely by scientists, that the foetus triggers the process of hormonal events leading to birth.

However, because most foalings occur at night it would seem that mares have some control over the timing of birth and they may be able to hold up the event until darkness arrives. They may also be able to delay the event because of threats in their own environment. This control was probably evolved in order to allow mares to foal at times when predators were less active; and it may be one reason why today some mares appear to be able to foal only when people are not present.

In summary, it seems probable that the foetus determines the overall length of pregnancy and that the mare has some fine-tuning capacity which determines the actual hour, or even night, of delivery.

The exact hierarchy of changes that precipitate birth is unknown in the horse. The mechanism on which all mammalian birth depends is the contraction of the uterine muscle. This is largely under hormonal control, and any hormone which stimulates contraction or which increases the contractability of the muscles contributes to the initiation of the birth process.

The hormones most associated with this are oxytocin and prostaglandin, which cause contractions to occur, and oestrogens and cortisol, which make the muscle more susceptible to their action. However, progesterone prevents contractions and can override the action of the others, depending on the amount available. A decrease in progesterone levels is therefore a pre-requisite for normal birth.

The way in which these hormones play their part need not concern us here; it is a process not as yet fully understood and quite complex. What is important for the reader is to recognize that these hormones play a part in contractions of the uterus and that they are produced from the foetus and the placenta as well as by the mare's pituitary gland.

Once contractions start the mare goes into first-stage labour. When the contractions are strong enough, the cervix dilates and the foal is pushed through the birth canal during second-stage labour.

Forces of birth

The foal is pushed through the birth canal by the forces brought to bear on it from contractions of the uterus and the abdominal muscles. During the first stage of labour increasingly powerful contractions of the uterus cause

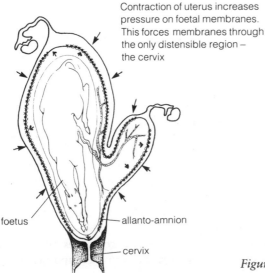

Contraction of uterus increases pressure on foetal membranes. This forces membranes through the only distensible region – the cervix

foetus

allanto-amnion

cervix

Figure 127 The first stages of labour

Figure 128   The rupture of the chorio-allantoic membrane

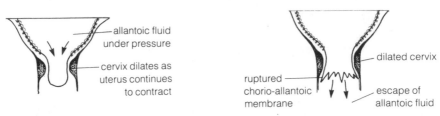

pressure to rise in the fluids surrounding the foetus and these press against the placenta. So long as the cervix remains closed these pressures are contained, but as the cervix dilates it leaves a weak spot through which the placental membrane (the chorio-allantois) bulges, forced by the pressure of the foetal fluids into the birth canal. This action has often been likened to that of a hydraulic wedge.

The end of the first stage of labour is normally marked by the rupture of the chorio-allantois and the escape of allantoic fluid. The cervix, now fully dilated, is prepared for the second stage of labour, and delivery of the foal. The pressure of the contracting uterine muscle, supplemented by the powerful straining action of the abdominal muscles and the diaphragm, propels the foetus through the opening in the cervix and the ruptured part of the placenta, and through the birth canal. Because the contours of the foal are relatively smooth, birth is usually a fairly rapid process.

Positioning of the foal for delivery

At the start of birth the foetal foal is typically lying on its back with its legs, head and neck flexed (Figure 130). As uterine contractions begin, so the foetus extends its forelimbs and head, turning into the upright position (Figure 131). Its forelegs and muzzle press against the cervix and may play some part in causing this to open. By the time the second stage is under way the foal lies in the most advantageous manner, namely with its head resting above its outstretched front legs and the body lying slightly to one side of the midline of the mare's pelvis (Figure 132).

If we examine the pelvis of the mare (Figures 136–7, p. 353), we can see the optimal alignment by which the foal negotiates the birth canal with least risk of impediment.

Definitions of alignment   It is usual for vets to refer to the manner of presentation at the pelvis in terms of the parts that appear or present first in the birth canal. The only normal presentation is anterior, i.e. head and feet first. Posterior presentation (hind legs), breach (tail) and transverse (body) are comparatively rare and all abnormal.

The term 'posture' refers to the way the limbs, head and neck are arranged. They should be extended for normal delivery. Flexed posture is abnormal and obstructs the foal's delivery (dystocia).

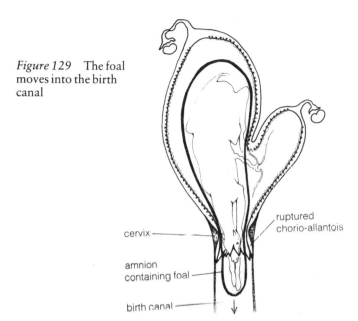

Figure 129 The foal moves into the birth canal

cervix

ruptured
chorio-allantois

amnion
containing foal

birth canal

'Position' describes the relative proximity of the foal's backbone to that of the mare. For example, the normal position is with the foal's backbone to the uppermost, i.e. in the dorsal position. During pregnancy and in the first stage of labour the foal's backbone is lowermost, i.e. in the ventral position.

Delivery of the afterbirth

The afterbirth consists of the outer membrane, the chorio-allantois, the long allantoic part of the umbilical cord, the amnion and the shorter amniotic part of the cord. After the foal has been born, the weight of the amnion hanging from the vagina pulls on the allantoic part of the cord and thus on its attachment to the inner surface of the chorio-allantois. As a result the chorio-allantois is usually delivered inside (or white side) out, with the placental (or red side) hidden within the inverted sac. Sometimes the afterbirth is delivered red side out, but this is less usual.

The afterbirth, covered in straw on the stable floor, is not a prepossessing sight. Nevertheless it should not be thrown away without examination, for if any of it has been left behind in the uterus, professional help is required to remove it and avert the danger of infection.

When spread out on a clean concrete floor, the chorio-allantoic part of the afterbirth looks like a baggy pair of trousers. The legs are the parts which lie within uterine horns, and the hole at the waist is the tear at the cervix through which the foal was born (Figure 133). The umbilical cord is attached near the top of one of the legs; the amnion is the separate membrane which surrounds the severed end. Apart from the tear at the cervix, the chorio-

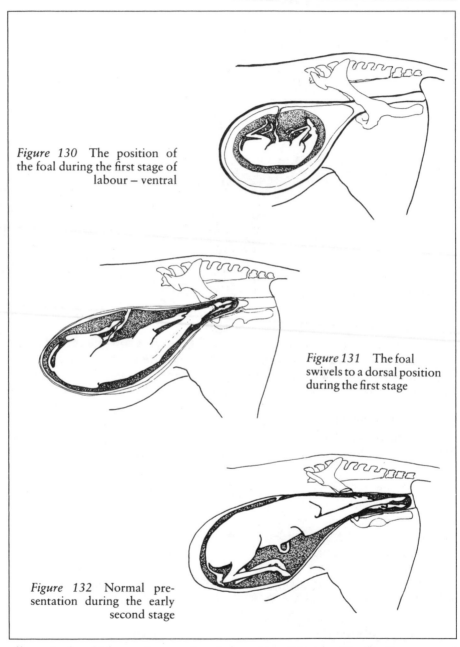

Figure 130 The position of the foal during the first stage of labour – ventral

Figure 131 The foal swivels to a dorsal position during the first stage

Figure 132 Normal presentation during the early second stage

allantois should be undamaged and complete. Fortunately missing parts of the membrane are relatively rare (see p. 356).

Mares, unlike cattle, sheep and goats, do not usually eat the afterbirth. The one reported case which came to my notice could not be substantiated.

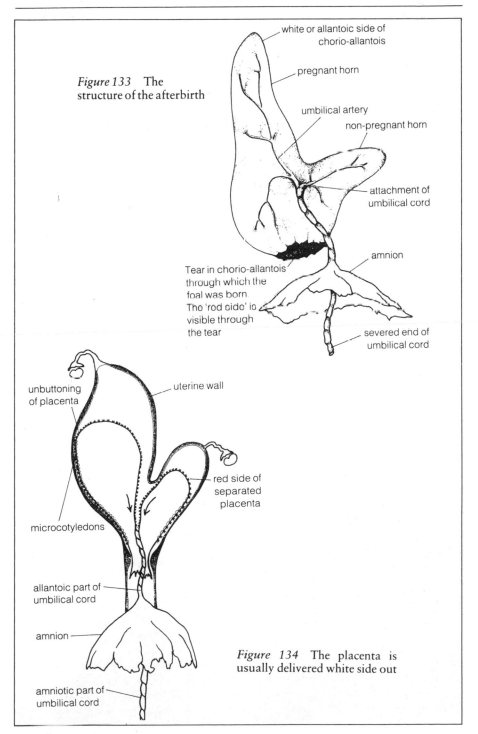

white or allantoic side of
chorio-allantois

pregnant horn

Figure 133 The
structure of the afterbirth

umbilical artery

non-pregnant horn

attachment of
umbilical cord

amnion

Tear in chorio-allantois
through which the
foal was born.
The 'red side' is
visible through
the tear

severed end of
umbilical cord

unbuttoning
of placenta

uterine wall

red side of
separated
placenta

microcotyledons

allantoic part of
umbilical cord

amnion

Figure 134 The placenta is
usually delivered white side out

amniotic part of
umbilical cord

DESCRIPTION OF FOALING

When we attend a foaling we must appreciate those matters described above, many of which we cannot see. We must appreciate them because this helps us to understand the normal birth process and, more particularly, to diagnose and correct matters when they are abnormal. This description is therefore an explanation of those points considered to be important in this process of understanding.

First stage

Mares become uneasy, pace the box, paw the ground, look round at their flanks and sweat. These are all signs of first-stage labour arising for the simple reason that contractions of the uterus are painful. The signs may vary according to the degree of pain caused and the appreciation of the individual. There is, therefore, considerable variation as to the length of the period and severity of first stage according to each individual.

The contractions of the uterus are caused largely because of the release of oxytocin from the pituitary and its effect on the uterine muscle. However, it also has an effect on the muscle of the mammary gland and may cause milk to spurt from the gland (milk-ejection reflex). This is another sign of first stage. Other signs include lengthening of the vulva and slight puffiness of the vulva labiae (lips).

Figure 135   Waxed teats

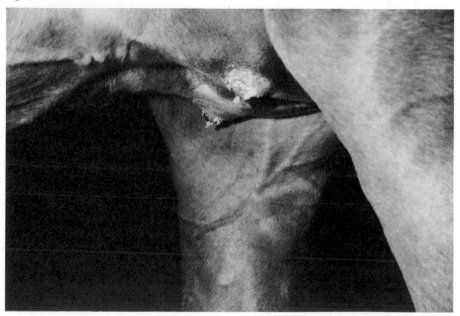

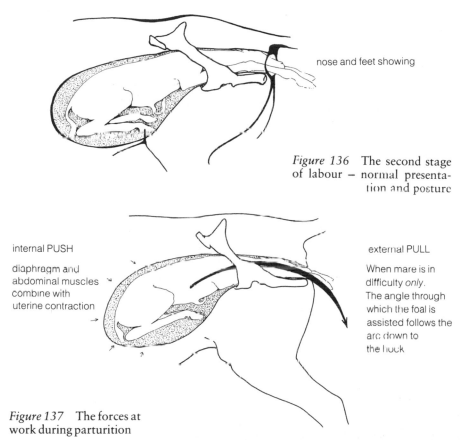

Figure 136 The second stage of labour – normal presentation and posture

internal PUSH

diaphragm and abdominal muscles combine with uterine contraction

nose and feet showing

external PULL

When mare is in difficulty *only*. The angle through which the foal is assisted follows the arc down to the hock

Figure 137 The forces at work during parturition

First-stage signs may be apparent long before a mare actually foals. The reason for this is that the contractions may not be strong enough to open the cervix. This remains closed and first-stage signs diminish as contractions cease. This is usually referred to as cooling off. It is not unusual for a mare to show first-stage signs one night or for several nights prior to actually foaling.

Second stage

Second-stage labour follows the first stage when the cervix relaxes and the placenta ruptures. This allows escape of allantoic (placental) fluid. This marks the start of the second stage; from this point there is, for the mare, no turning back from the act of foaling.

The escaping fluid is the first evidence that foaling is to take place and the foal will necessarily be delivered within the next hour at most. If the foal is in normal presentation and posture, the next landmark is for the shiny white membrane, the amnion, to appear between the vulval lips.

Next we can observe the feet and then the muzzle as delivery proceeds. These should be evident within five to ten minutes following rupture of the placental membrane (breaking water). Failure of the amnion to appear suggests that the foal may be in the wrong posture and not able to enter properly into the birth canal.

The mare may lie down during first stage but it is more usual for her to go through this in the standing position. However, the opposite is the case in second stage. The mare lies down, perhaps first on one side and then on the other. Occasionally she may roll.

It is tempting to suppose that this behaviour is an attempt to help the foal lie in the correct position. There is, of course, no way of proving that the mare has this intention, but those who have attended many births agree that the action of a mare appears to be purposeful. In many instances it is certainly helpful.

One aspect is obvious; lying down helps the propulsive force as the foal does not have to be pushed upwards over the brim of the pelvis against the force of gravity (see Figure 136). If the mare is lying on her side, the arc through which the foal is pushed through the pelvic canal lies in the same plane as the mare's forces are directing it. The drag of gravity is thereby avoided.

The foal is presented and its posture and position are such that it forms the minimum cross-sectional area. This is why one foreleg is usually delivered in advance of the other. The bulk of the elbows thereby pass through the pelvic outlet of the mare with the least risk of impediment. Sometimes one of the elbows may become lodged against the pelvic brim, and it is helpful in these cases to ease it forward so that the forelegs come together rather than have a marked discrepancy between the two.

Pulling on the forelimbs during second stage introduces a different force to that applied by nature, which, as we have seen, is from behind the foal – a push not a pull. We must bear this in mind when we apply traction to assist the foal and recognize that it is an unnatural force. This is not to suggest that such a pull may not be helpful or even necessary in certain instances.

When the foal's chest is delivered, the hind legs become, probably passively, extended. At this stage the umbilical cord is being dragged across the pelvic floor and may suffer pressure. Once the foal's chest has been delivered it is important that delivery is completed as quickly as possible, within a few minutes. The chest is then freed for respiratory movements and the foal can breathe air instead of relying on the blood circulation in the cord, which may at this time be compromised.

The final stages of delivery are illustrated in Figures 138a-b. It will be noted that the direction of delivery completes the arc towards the hocks of the mare. The important matter to emphasize here is that any pull applied to the foal should follow the line of this arc if it is to be helpful and successful.

In 96 per cent of cases final delivery is completed with the mare lying on her side. Few individuals foal completely in the standing position and those

Figure 138　The final stages of labour

that do are usually nervous and become disturbed by the presence of people. Second stage lasts sometimes as little as five or ten minutes and seldom as long as an hour.

Mares foaling for the first time generally take longer than those that have had a number of foals. However, old mares may appear to be lazy and lie in the recumbent position without straining for long periods unless someone activates them by pulling on the forelegs of the foal.

Third stage

Third stage is the expulsion of the placenta or afterbirth. Although, so far as the foal is concerned, it is not strictly speaking part of delivery, it is an essential element of maternal function.

The placenta, as explained in chapter 24, is held to the uterine surface by the interlocking of the small button-like structures known as micro-cotyledons. Successful expulsion of the membrane depends, therefore, on the unbuttoning of this arrangement. This seems to occur as the placental circulation ceases and blood is transferred from the placental circulation to the foal.

The circulation within the placenta, through the cord into the foal gradually diminishes in the minutes during which the foal, completely delivered, lies close to the mare, who usually remains lying down for up to twenty minutes after delivery. If this process is allowed to occur and the mare does not get up, thus breaking the cord, the microcotyledonary buttons on the placenta shrink and become detached, thus releasing the whole of the uterus from the placental membrane.

Other factors may play a part: for example, the contractions of the uterine muscle and the weight of the membranes hanging behind the mare help to pull the placenta through the cervix.

Expulsion of the placenta normally occurs within half to one hour of foaling. It may take considerably longer and, in this case, may only be shed as the placental tissue (the microcotyledonary buttons) shears and is left *in situ*. This may have a somewhat harmful effect on the resolution of the uterus back to the barren state after foaling and thus make a mare more difficult to get in foal at the foaling heat.

DUTIES OF PERSONNEL PRESENT AT FOALING

Those present should be quiet and discrete, especially if the mare is of a nervous disposition. They should observe rather than interfere.

They should know whether the mare has had a previous Caslick (sutured vulva) operation (see p. 534) and whether she has run milk and thereby lost colostrum (see p. 344). They should know whether the mare has suffered any problems in the past (such as a fractured pelvis or a difficult foaling) which might complicate the present birth.

Someone should note the exact time of the breaking of water. This is obvious in most cases but sometimes only a trickle of water appears. If there is any doubt the vulval lips should be parted to observe whether or not the amnion is in the vagina.

Soon after second stage has started any part of the vulva which has been previously stitched should be cut. This can be performed with the mare in the standing position or when she is lying down. The cut should be made with a pair of straight scissors with the blade about 12 cm long. The cut should be in the midline and carried out in one or two strokes.

It is usual for the vulva to lose feeling at this stage but some individuals retain sensation, so care should be taken when making the cut with the mare standing. It may be best to leave attempts to cut the vulva until the mare is lying down. However, this may not be possible in all cases because some individuals get to their feet on any approach to the hindquarters.

The safety of the operator is, of course, paramount and, if necessary, the mare's foreleg should be raised or the procedure carried out by a vet. Although it is preferable to make the cut at the time of foaling, those who are not experienced yet have responsibility for foaling may prefer the cutting to be carried out professionally some days prior to the event. In these circumstances a local anaesthetic is administered.

Early in the second stage an examination should be made to ascertain that the foetal foal is normally presented and in the extended posture. This examination may be conducted with the mare either standing or lying down. A washed or gloved hand should be inserted into the vagina and the presence of two feet and a muzzle confirmed. If the mare is standing, it will be necessary to reach farther into the birth canal than if she is lying down.

If one or more of the three appendages are not felt to be present in the birth canal, the person concerned should consider whether or not his/her experience is sufficient to correct any abnormality. If not, someone of experience should be called immediately.

If attempts at correction are to be made, these should be performed with the mare standing because its weight pulls the foetal foal back into the uterus and away from the pelvic inlet. This action allows more room for the operator to correct an abnormal posture. Sufficient room for manoeuvre is essential if corrections are to be made.

Straining and contractions of the uterus force the foal into the birth canal, and these may have to be reduced or suppressed in some cases before posture can be changed. The vet may inject drugs (beta adrenergic) to reduce uterine contractions and/or spinal anaesthesia to abolish them completely.

The responsibility of those attending birth is to decide whether they have the experience to correct the malposture or whether to call for professional assistance. It is better to err on the side of caution in this respect because the earlier a vet is called to the case the more chance of success.

Vets do not mind being called to a case only to find that the foal has been successfully delivered between the call and their arrival. But, conversely, it is disappointing for them to arrive too late and leave feeling that they might have achieved a happy outcome had they been called earlier.

Although there is considerable variation in the manner in which mares deliver – for example, the time they take, the effort they make and their individual behaviour, such as rolling or getting up and down frequently – there are certain signs that the onlooker may discern which indicate that all is not normal.

In the early stages of the delivery a mare that fails to strain and does not get on with the job may be reflecting a difficulty in passing her foal – a leg back or wrong positioning. On the other hand, a mare may show the opposite behaviour, getting up and down repeatedly or lying first on one side and then the other, especially when the foal's position is incorrect.

Positive, firm yet gentle assistance may be all that is required to help delivery in these instances. A forelimb may be pulled level with the other or traction on both limbs may be applied, provided the attendant bears in mind the fact that the forces of pulling are unnatural, as explained above. Inexperienced people may feel a compulsion to speed delivery, and this should be resisted.

These decisions and the approach to foaling are largely matters of experience, and instruction cannot be given in a text. The best advice is that those who have to be responsible for foaling should attend as many births as possible in the company of those that already have experience.

A moment of risk of which those present should be aware comes when the front feet have entered the vagina but not yet cleared the vulva. At this point the front legs and body of the foetal foal are pointing upwards, arrowlike, when the mare is standing. As she becomes recumbent she may, inadvertently, drive the outstretched forelimbs of the foal into the roof of the vagina. In most cases the feet, with their soft covering of horn, slide along the roof and out of the vagina so that no harm befalls the mare. But if the feet become caught in the roof of the vagina, as will occur if they are trapped by the suturing of the vulva, they may be driven through the roof of the vagina, into the rectum and appear from the anus. Thus creates a serious fistula (opening) between the rectum and the vagina.

If those present are aware of the risk, they can take quick action to guide the feet out of the vulva at this stage. However, the damage may already have been done by the time that they get to the mare and the feet may already be coming through the anus. In these circumstances it is essential to push them back into the vagina and redirect them through the vulva. In this event professional assistance should, of course, be called immediately.

There comes a moment in delivery (Figure 138b) when the foetal chest has been delivered through the vagina and only the back and hindquarters remain. This is the moment of no return, when delivery needs to be completed as quickly as possible so as to avoid pressure on the umbilical cord, which is being dragged across the floor of the mare's pelvis.

Although this is usually achieved through a combination of uterine contractions pushing from behind and the weight of the foal's body dragging it down and out of the vagina, there are some instances in which the hips of the foal lock against the pelvic inlet surrounding the birth canal.

This leaves the foal in a situation in which its umbilical cord is being squeezed and its source of oxygen from the placenta being compromised, while it cannot start respiratory movements in an unrestricted way because the chest is still in part surrounded by the vagina. It is therefore in danger of being asphyxiated.

The contraction at this stage may not be sufficient to unlock the engagement of the foal's hips and it is necessary to release them by pushing the hindquarters of the foal first one way and then the other until they slip easily from the mare. Here, it should be emphasized, the problem may be due to the direction in which we are pulling the foal. If, at this stage, we pull on the foal's forelimbs and body in a line which is a direct continuation of the axis of the vagina, we may be compounding the problem. If we change the line of direction of pull so that it is towards the hocks of the mare, this simulates the natural arc of delivery referred to above. This change of direction may in itself release the hindquarters of the foal for delivery.

A word of warning is required: any twisting of the forelegs of the foal in order to rotate the hind parts of the body may inadvertently fracture ribs or cause undue pressure on the heart. Twisting movements should be carried out only when essential. If possible, the body should be grasped behind the thorax and this should be supported gently as the rotational movements are conducted.

Again, it is prudent to remember that these manoeuvres are best learned by practice with others more experienced than oneself and are not really within the province of instruction in a text or classroom.

When dealing with the afterbirth it is good practice to tie the amnion to the cord as it hangs from the mare to prevent her from trampling on or kicking it. The weight of the amnion (about 2 kg, 5 lb) may help to pull on the placenta, thus aiding its expulsion from the uterus. The amnion may be knotted and then tied by string to the cord.

Some mares, especially those of heavy breeds, are susceptible to infection of the uterus and to laminitis if the placenta is not expelled soon after foaling. How soon, depends on the mare's susceptibility to the breakdown products of the foreign protein contained in the placenta.

In Thoroughbred practice the usual veterinary advice is that assistance should be called after about ten hours from foaling if the placenta has not come away. This gives ample time for the placenta to come away naturally while, at the same time, allows a reasonable time for it to remain *in situ*. As already described, most afterbirths are evacuated within about an hour of foaling.

In larger breeds it may be advisable to seek veterinary assistance before ten hours, while in ponies it may not be necessary for considerably longer. However, because it is abnormal for the membranes to remain *in situ* for longer than about two hours, some understanding with the veterinarian in advance of the event should be established. This gives an opportunity for the vet to give guidelines according to the circumstances of the client and the interest of the patient. For example, if the mare is prone to laminitis, special arrangements may have to be made for earlier removal of the placenta.

It is general practice to administer small doses of the hormone oxytocin and, if this does not achieve the desired evacuation, to remove the majority of the offending membrane manually. The remainder may then be removed hours, even days, later. Again, the manner of approach is a veterinary matter and may differ somewhat from one clinician to another.

The afterbirth, once it has been voided, should be checked to ensure that all of it has been discharged. In particular the horns should be examined to make sure they are intact (Figure 133) and no fragments have been left in the uterus. If there is any reason to suspect that some have been left behind, veterinary advice should be sought.

The surface of the placenta should be examined for any abnormal thickening or discolouration. The normal appearance depends to some extent on the length of time the membrane has been held in the uterus. It may go brown and have a parchment-like appearance the longer it remains attached.

The fresh appearance is of a velvet-like nature, dark to light red in colour. Blotching may be apparent, but areas of brown discoloration with a sticky surface may indicate that the placenta was diseased. These observations are important should the newborn foal suffer any illness. The placenta, cord and amnion, together with the fluids they contain, are valuable evidence in these cases (see p. 380).

Having checked the membrane and, if necessary, reported abnormalities to the vet, they should be placed immediately in a leakproof plastic sack and tied securely. They may then be placed in an isolated area until such time as the foal is diagnosed as being quite normal, for example, after twelve hours.

They should then be disposed of by burying, burning or in some other manner which avoids any possibility that, should they be contaminated with infection, this will not come in contact with other pregnant mares. This is a particularly important part of good management in the event of an outbreak of viral infection (for example viral arteritis, p. 428; equid herpesvirus 1, p. 339).

Abnormal Birth (Dystocia, Bad Birth)

Birth is a partnership between the mare and her foetus. Abnormal birth encompasses any untoward happening to either or both participants.

Foetal contribution

We have already discussed the problems arising from the malpositioning, malpresentation or malposture of the foetal foal and how this may result in

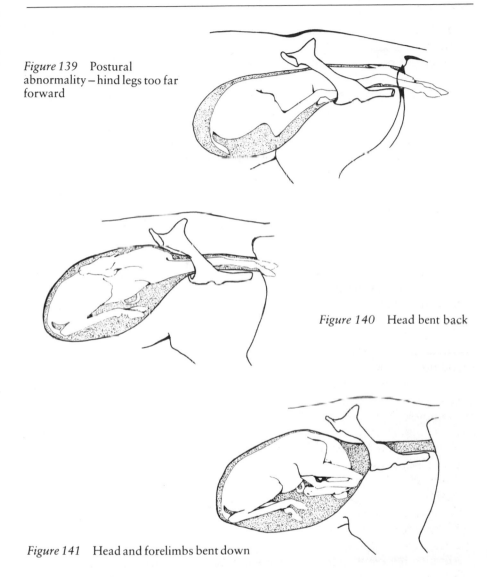

Figure 139 Postural abnormality – hind legs too far forward

Figure 140 Head bent back

Figure 141 Head and forelimbs bent down

an impeded passage through the bony ring formed by the mare's pelvis around the birth canal (see Figures 139, 140 and 141). **Foetal abnormalities** are, broadly speaking, either the result of a normally formed foetal foal lying incorrectly or consist of abnormal conformation of the limbs or body. The most common cause of malposture is a depressed reflex state of the foetus, often the result of infection or malfunction of the placenta; in other words, some disease process of pregnancy has diminished the normal activity of the foetal foal. The foetal body and/or limbs with abnormal conformation, may result from the way in which the foal has been lying in the uterus or because the development has been affected by infection and other forms of stress.

Compression on the umbilical cord restricts oxygen supply to the foetus and may result in death or in cerebral damage causing the newborn foal to be seriously ill (see pp. 389–91). This compression may be caused by the cord becoming entangled around the foal's hind leg or prolapsed in front of the chest as it passes through the birth canal, or it may be the result of the weight of the foal's belly in the final stages of delivery but prior to the foal being able to establish a normal respiratory rhythm.

Maternal contribution

Difficult birth may be the result of imperfect straining or uterine contractions. This condition is often described as **uterine inertia**. We have already considered this condition in relation to the age of the mare and the apparently instinctive reluctance of mares to strain if the foal is lying incorrectly. However, there may be cases in which uterine inertia has hormonal origins and needs to be treated.

The usual therapy is to administer oxytocin. However, this is obviously a professional decision and needs to be backed by an assessment that the foetus is normally aligned, otherwise the extra stimulus provided by the oxytocin may be dangerous.

Rupture of the uterus may occur due to the powerful contractions against an obstructed passage, as a result of a weakness in the uterine wall or from vigorous movement of the foetal limbs. Rupture may be associated with lack of straining efforts or the tear may only be found after the foal has been delivered normally.

Rupture of the large intestine may sometimes occur and is associated with signs of pain (sweating and rolling, getting up and down) that may be indistinguishable from the normal signs of foaling, except they are more severe and prolonged. Rupture of the intestines is rare but when it occurs it is usually fatal and may prevent the mare from delivering her foal normally.

Uterine torsion is a condition well recognized in breeds heavier than the Thoroughbred, but is probably less common in smaller breeds. In this condition the uterus twists on its long axis, thus preventing any chance of the foal being delivered through the cervix and birth canal.

The condition is very painful and the mare shows signs of severe colic before any chance of going into first- and second-stage labour. In practice, delivery cannot start and it is essential to have veterinary assistance if this condition is suspected. The uterus can then be returned to the normal position under general anaesthesia followed by a laparotomy (an incision through the abdominal wall).

Uterine haemorrhage is of two types. Haemorrhage from the lining of the uterus is less common and certainly less severe in the horse than that experienced by women. The essential difference is that, in the mare, the placenta does not erode the tissue of the uterus as it does in its human counterpart (see p. 333).

At the end of foaling the uterus may contain fluid tinged with blood and this may give the erroneous impression of bleeding on a large scale. This may occur in cases of delayed uterine involution (see below).

The dangerous type of bleeding associated with birth is haemorrhage into the broad ligament, which suspends the uterus (see p. 322). An artery may rupture during second stage or following delivery.

The initial symptom is acute pain: the mare may roll violently, sweat and tremble. Pain is caused by stretching of the peritoneum as the membrane of the broad ligament is dissected by the haemorrhage. Eventually the pressure of the ligament restrains the bleeding or, if the haemorrhage bursts through into the peritoneal cavity, the mare literally bleeds to death, her membranes becoming white, as she collapses gasping in her final death throes.

If the haemorrhage is contained within the membrane it causes symptoms of shock. The mare, besides showing signs of pain, develops a rapid heart beat, a cold clammy sweat, pale membranes turning to jaundice colour and, as the haemorrhage tracks back towards the vagina, a swelling may appear to one side of the vulva and anus.

The outlook for these cases is usually good, although it may take several weeks for the mare to recover fully. Symptoms of pain usually subside within a few days but the mare remains anaemic and slightly jaundiced for much longer.

The haemorrhage into the ligament may be felt per rectum as a large firm swelling in the wall of the uterus. The vet may advise against having the mare mated in the following breeding season. The swelling usually subsides and disappears completely within about nine months.

The bleeding may occur into the wall of the vagina. **Haematomas**, as these sacs of blood are called, bulge into the vagina and may burst, releasing considerable quantities of blood. If the bleeding comes from one of the major branches of the uterine artery, the haemorrhage can be fatal.

Mares foaling for the first time or those that deliver oversized foals or experience difficult delivery for other reasons may suffer **bruising of the vagina** and perineum (the area of the vulva and anus). A complication of haematomas and bruising is infection; in these cases it may be advisable to administer antibiotics for several days following foaling. Those responsible are advised to consult their vets if any signs of these untoward happenings develop following foaling.

A further complication, especially if infection is present, is the development of **laminitis** (see p. 236). This results from the combination of the products of dead tissue and bacterial infection. The products are toxic and, together with the proteins released into the circulation, cause severe vascular changes with constriction of the blood supply to the foot and consequent laminitic disease. Mares which suffer lameness after foaling, especially if reluctant to move, and stand with their feet bunched under the body and show excessive heat in one or more hooves should be suspected as suffering the acute stage of laminitis. In such cases professional advice should be sought.

Delayed uterine involution is the term used to describe a failure in the normal process of contraction of the uterus following foaling. It is not a specific condition but reflects differences in the degree and rate of elimination of the residual products of pregnancy.

These include foetal fluids which may have escaped through tears in the placenta, debris from the placenta itself and blood, fluid and cells which may have come from the uterine lining. Usually the accumulation (lochia) is expelled or absorbed following birth.

The lochia is normally a brown, somewhat sticky material. The fluid passes from the uterus through the cervix into the vagina and thence is voided to the outside, partly as a result of the uterus contracting and partly as a result of movement by the mare, e.g. walking, trotting, coughing, etc. This is the reason why it is important to turn mares out in a paddock or exercise them in hand in the first few days after foaling.

Normal involution also entails the uterine wall becoming less oedematous (waterlogged) and regaining the tone which is consistent with the barren state, i.e. ready for receiving the stallion's sperm and, after the egg is fertilized, the new conceptus at the start of another pregnancy.

The uterine lining must also be restored to a healthy and receptive state. Thus normal involution is a process involving the voiding of extraneous material and the resolution of the uterine lining into the condition required for successful reconception.

This situation may be achieved by the first heat (foal heat) at seven to fourteen days following birth. However, satisfactory resolution at this early stage is probably the exception rather than the rule and in many individuals it takes much longer for the uterus to be ready for reconception to take place.

Uterine prolapse sometimes occurs following delivery. The ligaments of the uterus are stretched by the weight of the foetus and the enormously enlarged uterus during pregnancy. However, they normally retain the organ, but in some instances the restraining mechanism fails and the organ turns inside out, being inverted through the cervix, vagina and vulva.

If this should occur, those present should call immediately for veterinary assistance and, if possible, keep the mare standing until help arrives. This position keeps the organ off the ground but increases the problem of gravitational effects. It is therefore helpful if the organ is supported, employing a moistened pillowcase or sheet.

If the mare is allowed to lie down this removes the gravitational effects but increases the risk of damage from straw bedding. When the mare is lying down it is therefore helpful gently to introduce a sheet under the organ to protect it from the straw.

Prior to the vet's arrival the protruding uterus should be kept wet by washing with normal saline. This may be prepared by adding a level teaspoonful of common salt to every 600 ml (1 pint) of warm water. Sluicing the saline frequently over the surface will keep the surface moist and remove debris.

The vet will replace the organ, probably employing spinal anaesthesia. This technique involves placing a needle between the vertebrae at the base of the tail and injecting an appropriate amount of local anaesthetic. Further measures may include injection of oxytocin to reduce the size of the uterus, anti-inflammatory drugs and antibiotics. Laminitis is always a risk following prolapse.

26
THE NEWBORN FOAL IN HEALTH

This chapter is intended to provide the reader with an understanding of the healthy foal in terms that lead to an appreciation of ill health. It is only by a knowledge of the normal that we can interpret the abnormal state. For example, the manner in which foals get to their feet is dictated by a nervous reflex action inherent in the species.

Horses raise their foreparts before their hind parts, in contrast to cattle, which use the reverse sequence. Foals instinctively adopt the adult pattern almost from their first efforts to stand and certainly when an hour or two old. Both the manner and the ease with which they achieve the standing position provide a general impression of the health of the foal. If it displays lethargy or difficulty in accomplishing the standing position, we may suspect illness.

Adaptive period
Behaviour of a newborn foal is dictated largely by the urge to seek and suck from the udder. The learning period is remarkably short, considering that the foal has spent all its previous life without either the need for feeding in this manner or the means of coordinating the reflexes of standing and the movement involved in sucking from the mare. Thus, within the space of about two hours, the foal has stood and sucked for the first time, a remarkable achievement of nervous coordination.

This change from a way of life in the uterus to one of independent existence outside requires a period of adaptation in respect of all the organs and functions of the body. This change has to be appreciated if we are to understand the difference between normal and abnormal changes. In the older animal changes occur as a result of outside stimuli rather than as an internal need for adjustment.

For example, the independent individual takes food into its alimentary canal and digests it. The changes which occur in this process do not alter fundamentally; the only variations are related to the type and quality of the food and the demand for energy and growth dictated by age and status.

However, the change from feeding *in utero* to that outside is profound. *In utero* the foal's supply of nourishment comes indirectly from the mare through the placenta. The mare digests food and the products of digestion (amino acids, carbohydrate, fatty acids) cross passively by diffusion or actively by selection through the placenta into the umbilical vein.

Thus the foetal foal has a continuous supply of nourishment in an already digested form. The substances it requires enter its body and are received directly by the liver through the umbilical vein.

After birth food is imbibed and swallowed; it is digested in the stomach, small and large intestines, absorbed through their walls into the blood-stream, and transported through the portal vein to the liver. Unlike the continuous supply present in the umbilical vein, food is taken at intervals, so that peak levels of nutritive material (amino acids, etc.) may occur. Although these are dealt with adequately by the organs and systems of the body when in health, there may be problems in a premature or otherwise impaired newborn foal.

We may contrast the needs of the newborn with the foetal situation by reference to Table 2 (p. 368).

Dealing with the newborn foal

The essential basis of dealing with a newborn foal is, as with a foaling mare, patience and observation rather than interference, unless there are definite reasons for taking action. Those responsible for foals should therefore make themselves familiar with the normal patterns of behaviour so that they can judge when action is required or when veterinary assistance should be called.

Once the foal has been delivered completely there are a number of duties which those present should perform. The first is to avoid any sudden movement or disturbance within the loosebox which might cause the mare to rise to her feet prematurely.

Most mares, even with several people present in the foaling box, remain lying down for up to twenty minutes after the end of their exertions. During this time the foal turns onto its brisket and withdraws its hind legs from the vagina. The cord remains intact and the circulation of blood between the placenta and the foal gradually diminishes. This means that a substantial quantity of blood is drained from the placenta and received by the foal over the period of two or three minutes.

Premature rupture of the cord may deprive the foal of as much as a third of its circulating blood volume. It is for this reason that mares should be left, as far as possible, undisturbed and encouraged to remain lying down after they have delivered their foal.

Although every effort should be made not to disturb this relationship, it is usual, and probably good practice, for someone to be present during the final stages of the delivery in order to assist the foal should this be necessary.

Table 2 Essential Differences between Intrauterine (Inside) and Extrauterine (Outside) Life of the Foal

System	Foetal	Newly born
Respiration	Oxygen and carbon dioxide exchange in mare's lungs and transported in maternal bloodstream; exchange at the level of the utero-placental junction	Gases exchanged in foal's lungs, used for first time
Digestive	Mare eats and digests food; products circulate in bloodstream; pass between uterus and placenta into foetal bloodstream. Metabolism controlled by mare	Food taken into alimentary tract and digested; products absorbed into bloodstream. Independent metabolism
Alimentary excretion	Faecal matter stored in caecum, colon and rectum as meconium. Foetus swallows amniotic fluid into stomach but does not defaecate	Meconium (first dung) evacuated within the first 48–72 hours after birth. Subsequently waste material eliminated as dung in the usual independent manner
Urinary	Waste products filtered by kidneys and passed by urine through urachus into placenta (i.e. mixes with allantoic fluid). Kidney function minimal; most waste products pass across placenta into mare's bloodstream to be eliminated in urine of mare	Enormously increased output of kidneys to match increased metabolism and waste products of digestion; volume of urine output correspondingly increased; bladder filled under tension for the first time as urachus closes after birth
Senses (hearing, sight, feeling)	The foetus may hear and certainly has feeling but acuity and response are much reduced	Sight, hearing and feeling are present almost immediately after birth
Temperature control	Body temperature controlled by mare	Balance of heat established by metabolic rate, activity and, in the first six hours, by shivering matched by heat loss through conduction, evaporation and radiation

System	Foetal	Newly born
Neurological function	Nervous system becomes increasingly mature throughout pregnancy. By full term reflex activity is established in preparation for post-natal adaptation but activity while *in utero* is reduced	Neurological basis of reflex activity for getting up, sucking, following the mare and galloping are activated and well established by 12 hours
Coat	In the uterus saturated with fluid; fine hair becoming coarser towards full term	Dry coat and sweating may form part of heat balance

Peeling the amniotic membrane from the foal's head and raising this above any pool of amniotic fluid in which it might take its first breath is unnecessary in a healthy foal but may be life-saving in one that is experiencing breathing difficulties. Because the diagnosis of a sick foal is often only possible in retrospect, assistance for all foals may be justified.

Foals should start regular breathing movements almost as soon as they are delivered. Gasping or delayed onset of a breathing rhythm is indicative that the foal has suffered some problem before or during birth that makes it less healthy than normal. We discuss in the next chapter what measures should be taken in these circumstances.

A further check on the foal's normality is to record the heart rate immediately after the foal is born. This may be accomplished by placing the hand gently on the left (or right) side of the chest over the heart just behind the elbows and counting the number of beats in 15 seconds. If we then multiply that number by 4 we obtain the number of beats per minute; this should be in the range of 50–100 beats per minute.

If the number of beats is outside this range, especially if the heart rate is slowed, some form of stress is indicated and the foal may not be entirely healthy. An arrhythmic (irregular) heart beat may also denote a problem, although this may be of a temporary nature only.

In performing these duties, as the delivery is completed, anyone present should crouch behind the mare and make slow movements, keeping his/her voice down and trying to be as quiet and unobtrusive as possible. Literally keeping a low profile is recommended for anyone moving round the box, and crouching behind the mare is preferable to standing, particularly if the mare is nervous or inclined to get to her feet. People should avoid walking past the front end of the mare because this may cause her to jump to her feet.

The next duty is to wait discreetly, observing both mare and foal to make sure their behaviour is normal. It is good practice to record on a sheet of paper the time at which the water broke and the time of complete delivery.

The next landmark is the time at which the cord breaks. This may be the result of the mare getting to her feet or the foal struggling in its attempts to stand. In both instances the cord breaks because of a tug.

It should be appreciated that cord thickness varies from relatively thin to quite thick and strong. Very thin ones may rupture as the mare makes her final expulsive effort and shoots the hips of the foal clear of her vagina. This will depend to some extent on the length of the cord itself.

Whatever the method or time of rupture, the cord breaks at a point about 3 cm (1 inch) from the abdominal wall. It will be remembered from chapter 24 that the cord contains two arteries and a vein. These rupture in such a way that the arteries are immediately sealed and retract into the stump left at the umbilicus (navel).

This describes the usual happenings. However, a number of exceptions may occur. Some cords are quite thick, but they become brittle at the point of rupture providing the cord is left intact and the circulation of blood diminishes with time as already described. However, if the mare gets to her feet prematurely, separation in these cases may be abnormal and the arteries may not contract but may continue to spurt blood.

Pinching the stump between the finger and thumb for a minute or so will usually be sufficient to stop the bleeding completely. If this is not the case a ligature of tape should be applied; it is prudent to have such an item in one's foaling kit (see below).

It is usual to dress the stump of the navel with iodine or antibiotic powder. Before deciding on the approach, those responsible should consider the following points of view. Iodine dries the stump but also damages tissue and causes a hard scab to form. This may seem, therefore, to be an overharsh approach to the delicate tissues.

Antibiotic powder does no such harm, but it is probable that the mare will lick the foal's coat and the navel, thus removing most of the powder. In any case, the stump seals naturally and the powder will not penetrate into the stump where infection, if it is to occur, will develop.

Because the stump seals on its own, the risk of infection is slight and probably depends more on the condition of the foaling box and on the particular circumstances of the stables. A clean foaling box and allowing the navel stump to form naturally (i.e. without cutting the cord, as used to be common practice) should be sufficient to avoid infection.

If there is a particular problem in the stables, as might result from contamination with a specific virulent microbe, some extra precautions may be necessary. But in these circumstances it is best to obtain veterinary advice. Changing management (for example, using different boxes) and/or the administration of antibiotics by injection in the first few days of life, together with checking on the immune status of the foal (see p. 379), will probably be recommended.

This last precaution may also apply to foals born with abnormally large cords which bleed from the navel or whose navel stump looks abnormal in any way. In addition, if the mare has run milk and the foal has been deprived of its protective antibodies, extra veterinary precautions will be required (see p. 384).

Once the cord has broken, the foal can be left to get to its feet, which it will do after numerous unsuccessful attempts. The duty of those present is to ensure that there is sufficient bedding on which the foal can rest. It will tend to push straw to one side in its struggles and thus allow its hocks to rub on the bare floor below. This may cause sores on the outside of the hocks. Someone should, from time to time, enter the box and rearrange the straw bedding to avoid this happening.

There is little point in trying to help the foal because it has to learn how to coordinate its actions in getting to its feet unaided. However, once on its feet it may be steadied for a minute or two by gently holding the tail. But it should be appreciated that any manipulation of foals at this stage may be resented and be counterproductive in attempts to help rather than hinder its actions.

Helping the foal find the mammary gland and suck requires considerable patience. The adage that you can lead a horse to water but you can't make it drink certainly applies to foals. The temptation to hurry completion of foaling by seeing that the foal sucks from the mare and thus confirms its wellbeing naturally influences those present, especially as foaling takes place mostly at night and the prospect of returning to bed depends on the mare's and foal's cooperation to this end.

The bonding of mare to foal and foal to mare takes place through a combination of sight and smell. Whatever help we give the foal towards obtaining its objective of finding and sucking from the udder, we must be careful not to break or delay this bonding process. The mare smells and tastes her amniotic fluid in which the foal's coat is saturated at birth. This fixes its identity in the mare's memory, eliciting maternal instincts towards the foal and evoking antagonism towards other, foreign, foals.

The foal is much less sophisticated in its instinctive powers of recognition. For the first week or two after birth the bonding of the foal to the mare depends almost entirely on recognition of the udder as a source of food, and it is not particular about whose gland the milk is coming from. It is, however, aware of the shape and movement of its dam and will follow and keep close to her instinctively.

If it strays away and tries to suck from another mare, it is the mare that shows antagonism and rejects the approach. This rejection is the negative aspect of the bonding process and is complemented, in the positive sense, by the foal's own instincts of being attracted to its own dam.

If mares foal outside with other mares present crossing over of one foal for another can occur. This is most likely to happen if foaling takes place on the same night and the mares have not bonded each to her own progeny.

The pedigrees of two Thoroughbreds were shown to be incorrect by blood typing. On tracing back their history it was found that they had been foaled on the same night on a studfarm in Newmarket and had been turned out together in a paddock soon after foaling.

It appears that the foals had switched dams without anyone realizing it. This is a rare happening in Thoroughbreds because it is more usual for foaling mares to be segregated for sufficient time to prevent switching because bonding occurs soon after birth. Where mares foal in herds in the open this type of switching may be more common.

The foal should stand on its own for the first time within about an hour of birth. There is considerable variation in this period, depending on the size and strength of the individual. Some foals may get to their feet within fifteen minutes of being delivered and others take ninety to 120 minutes. However, at the longer end we are entering a period that may indicate that the foal is abnormal and that professional assistance is required.

Once the foal is on its feet the next objective is to have it sucking from the mare as soon as possible. The average time from birth to sucking for the first time is about two and a half hours. However, foals vary quite considerably in the time taken to find and suck from the udder. It is important that they imbibe a substantial quantity of colostrum at their first suck and that this should occur within the first five or six hours after foaling.

The protective substances (antibodies) in the colostrum are absorbed from the small intestines of the foal, providing it is under about twelve hours of age, but probably the younger it is at the first suck, the more efficient the transfer into the bloodstream. But even more important is the fact that, once protein has been swallowed, the pathway is blocked to further transfer. Thus, if the foal sucks only small amounts over several hours, less antibody is transferred than if a large amount is sucked at first and then the foal does not feed for several hours.

This principle is particularly important if a foal has to be fed by bottle or through a stomach tube for its first feed. However, it should be appreciated that giving ordinary milk before the foal receives colostrum will block the pathway and this must if possible be avoided.

A foal is attracted towards its dam's udder by inborn instincts that depend on certain visual and olfactory (smell) senses. In the first place it is attracted towards dark undersurfaces. Thus it may be seen seeking the brisket, belly and finally the region of the udder. Here it is undoubtedly attracted by the odours emanating from the mammary glands of the mare and also from the milk.

The suck reflex is stimulated by contact with warm soft surfaces, as can be appreciated when the foal's muzzle comes in contact with the mare's skin or tongue in the period after birth before the foal has even got to its feet. It may then be seen with its lips and tongue curled in the manner characteristic of sucking from a teat.

Anyone who has been present at birth and watched a foal getting to its feet and sucking from the mare cannot but help to be impressed with this miracle of nature. We should now turn to how we may help or hinder the foal in this natural process of bonding.

We may use the information of natural behaviour and the instinctive basis on which it is built to avoid some of the pitfalls that may present in helping a foal to establish the sucking relationship with its dam.

Perhaps the simplest basis of help is to mimic the assistance given by the mare. A good dam will stand still while the foal is attempting to reach the mammary glands. However, she will stand in such a way that the udder is tilted towards the foal. To do this the mare flexes the opposite hind leg and straightens the nearside one. Individuals differ in their degree of cooperation with the foal, younger mares being less cooperative than older ones. Some mares are quite ticklish and this is the reason for their non-cooperation.

In other cases the maternal instincts may be such that, especially at first, the mare moves around and even resents the approach of the foal. Holding such a mare by a headcollar and manoeuvring her into a suitable position may be helpful to the foal. If a mare is ticklish and/or resentful, a tranquillizer may be administered under veterinary supervision. Some Thoroughbred studfarms routinely inject every mare foaling for the first time with a tranquillizer after the birth.

We may also mimic the help of the mare by gently pushing the hindquarters of the foal when it is attempting to suck. This support is often displayed by mares: they will turn their heads and lick or nudge the hindquarters of the foal.

Figure 142 A mare nudging her foal

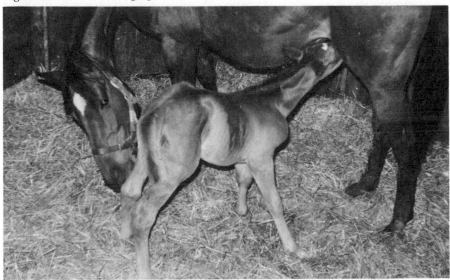

Assistance in which the front part of the foal is held, as, for example, the head being supported and the lips applied to the teats, may be less helpful or even counterproductive if the foal fights against the restraint. The judgement here must be whether the foal has been given time to attach itself or whether it really requires some assistance because the first suck has been delayed beyond the normal period of, say, three hours.

If this is the case, we should identify the reasons before giving assistance. For example, if the foal is weak, veterinary assistance should be called because the foal may have an underlying disease. The veterinarian will usually administer colostrum through a stomach tube in this instance.

In other cases the foal may be dazed. This may be because it has been frightened – for example, by the mare being antagonistic – or confused as a result of an innate dysfunction of neurological coordination, or because happenings in its environment have interfered with the natural process of bonding.

The innate dysfunction may be due to the foal's having suffered oxygen lack or to some circulatory disturbance which is causing pressure in the brain and interfering with the pathways of nervous coordination. This is a veterinary matter and the foal should be treated accordingly. The vet will probably administer drugs that reduce the pressure in the brain at the same time as giving the foal its first feed through a stomach tube.

If the foal has been confused by environmental factors, patience is required, but it may be advisable for the vet to feed the foal through a stomach tube in order to make sure that it receives a full dose of colostrum. An alternative approach is to use a bottle and artificial teat. The foal is fed either standing up or lying on the floor and is then allowed to establish its own relationship with the mare during the course of the next few hours.

The one disadvantage of this approach is that it may cause the foal to seek the artificial teat rather than that of the mare. However, one feed with a bottle is unlikely to lead to this type of misconception.

Perhaps the most important advice in respect of preventing a foal from becoming confused is to be aware of the possibility that human interference may in itself cause this confusion. Because the foal is attracted to dark undersurfaces, it is preferable for attendants to wear light-coloured clothes – white rather than brown overalls, for example. Some foals have become attached to attendants wearing dark overalls, and in the New Forest a pony foal is on record as having become attached to a tree rather than to its mother.

Sounds may also be important to the foal's appreciation of its environment and for this reason any extraneous noise, especially loud sounds, should be avoided in the foaling box.

Finally, the environment of the foaling box should be controlled to avoid dust, too much humidity or undue warmth. The ideal conditions are a minimum amount of dust, especially that emanating from straw and hay, a humidity of 60–90 per cent and an air temperature of 20° C (68° F) plus or minus 3° C (6° F).

The passing of meconium is essential to the wellbeing of the foal. Some individuals have problems in expelling all of this material and may suffer discomfort and colic as a result.

Measures to aid evacuation of meconium are therefore usually routine. Some people like to give castor oil or some other preparation by mouth soon after birth; others may give a concentrated oily solution of vitamins A and D. There is no harm in any of these procedures providing the medicaments are administered in a scrupulously clean condition. However, care should be taken when selecting a drug to be given in the first forty-eight hours, because during this period the gut is particularly permeable and substances which are not harmful to older foals may be absorbed and cause problems. This has occurred in the USA where administration of an iron preparation to newborn foals was found to be the cause of illness and death.

Enemas and injections of oil into the rectum are also common practices to assist the evacuation of meconium. More recently phosphate buffered solutions (phosphate enema, sodium acid phosphate, sodium phosphate) used for infants have found favour.

The enemas may be administered at any time after birth, although I suggest that they should not be given until the foal has sucked from the mare. At this time it is more tolerant of handling, and there is the added advantage that the enema will coincide with the gastrocolic reflex that stimulates the hind part of the gut when food enters the stomach.

It is important to appreciate that the method of giving enemas and the frequency at which they are given may cause problems. If the nozzle of the tube inserted into the rectum contains any firm or sharp edges or if the instrument is used roughly, this may cause bruising of the anus or even in exceptional circumstances rupture of the rectum. Application requires very gentle handling and the instrument must have a soft, non-abrasive nozzle.

If enemas are given too frequently or in too great a quantity they may cause the rectum to balloon and in itself delay successful evacuation of the meconium.

The loosebox in which the foal is kept should be maintained as free from dust as possible at all times. Straw bedding should be mucked out or rearranged when the foal is at grass or, if this is not possible, it should be moved with the mare temporarily to another box. Foals are particularly susceptible to inhaling dust and this initiates infection of the lungs.

The loosebox should be kept at about 10° C (50° F). Temperatures above or below this are not harmful but cold environments challenge the foal and it has to burn more food just to keep its body temperature normal. At higher temperatures the foal may suffer problems of metabolism associated with keeping its body cool.

Figure 143   How to pick up and carry a foal correctly

The foal's ability to maintain the balance of heat produced and heat lost (thermoregulation) is compromised if the atmosphere is humid. Humidity may be measured or guessed because there is condensation on the wall. This condensation is most likely to be due to poor insulation of the walls so that the walls are cold relative to the warm, moist atmosphere in the box. Incidentally, condensation may make the foal more susceptible to infection of the lungs.

Steps should be taken to avoid placing the foal in draughts because this may cause excessive heat loss and chilling.

Exercise is as important to the young foal as it is to the mare. Foals and their dams should be confined to their looseboxes for minimum periods. The mare should be exercised up to the time of foaling and, together with her foal, allowed out in a paddock or placed in a large yard or barn when the foal is two days old.

Although facilities and weather conditions may combine to make this impracticable, the problem of restricting a foal to a loosebox and then allowing it freedom may cause it to gallop, and the unaccustomed stress may result in a fractured sesamoid or other injury to the limbs.

In these unfavourable circumstances, therefore, special measures should be taken when the foal is first turned out after several days or weeks of confinement. These measures may include giving the mare her freedom for fifteen to thirty minutes prior to letting her foal join her. This is intended to take the steam out of the mare so that she does not gallop with her foal on first experiencing freedom.

Another approach which might be combined with this is to walk the mare in the paddock for some time prior to letting her loose with her foal. It is the mare and not the foal which usually causes the problem when first freed after a long confinement.

Care of the feet should start at about age two months. If there is abnormal conformation, attention should be paid prior to this but under veterinary supervision (see chapter 19).

27
CONDITIONS OF THE NEWBORN FOAL

In considering conditions of the foal it is helpful to take account of age, whether or not the condition is infective, and to recognize that although newborn foals are growing they may still be affected by the in between status of life within and outside the uterus. All these considerations apply to conditions which are unique to the age and status of the individual; they also modify those conditions experienced in older and adult horses.

For example, meconium colic is unique in that it is related to the passage of the first dung; once this is passed by about the end of the second day after foaling, the individual will never suffer this particular form of colic again. It is, therefore, a condition peculiar to the first few days of newborn life. Further, it is a non-infective condition, that is, it is not related to microbes and may be distinguished therefore from septicaemic or infective diseases.

Meconium colic is one of a category of conditions with their origins in foetal life or arising from abnormal happenings of birth. One of the major characteristics of these conditions is that the first symptoms appear during the first three or four days after foaling, and often within the first twenty-four hours.

There is logic, therefore, in describing these conditions separately to those developing later. We may also distinguish conditions which are peculiar to the period up to four or five months, that is, up to the time of weaning. These conditions, such as summer pneumonia caused by the microbe *Rhodococcus equi* (p. 416), do not affect older foals or adults, nor are they found in the first few days after foaling.

However, infections do not fit exactly into the categories of the newborn period, the older foal or adulthood. They are ubiquitous and cross the boundaries of definition. For example, infectious disease of the newly born may start *in utero* with symptoms appearing in the first day or two, or even as early as a few hours after birth. However, the same microbe may be present in the environment of the newborn and enter the body through the umbilical stump. Here they grow in the blood clot formed in the remnants of the umbilical arteries and vein, thus acting as a focus for infection at an older age. This is a classic route for the spread of microbes causing joint ill (infective arthritis) that occurs in foals aged one to three months.

Another route of infection is inhalation of microbes into the lungs or swallowing them in feed. These may result respectively in pneumonia or diarrhoea. These infections occur in both the very early and the later periods and are also responsible for infectious disease in weaned and older foals, yearlings and adults.

A very important consideration in the young foal is its immune status. We discuss in chapter 26 the way in which immunity is transferred passively to the foal by way of the protective substances (antibodies) in the colostrum. Some individuals do not receive sufficient quantities due to the mare's running milk or for other reasons described above (see p. 372). These individuals are at risk because microbes gaining entrance to the body are not killed by the protective substances and are therefore capable of setting up infection.

This is an example of a failure related to events of the first twelve hours after foaling being the prime cause of diseases which do not appear until the foal is older.

The passive immunity lasts for about six weeks and is then replaced by active immunity gained by the foal's responding to the challenge of infecting microbes in the same manner as an adult responds to infection. However, in the interval between the waning resistance afforded by the antibodies supplied from the mare and the acquisition of new antibodies produced by the foal, infection is more likely to occur. This is one reason why foals aged about six weeks commonly suffer from infectious disease.

Notwithstanding the blurring of definitions, especially of infectious disease, it is convenient to describe conditions of the foal as those occurring in the neonatal or newborn period and those suffered beyond this period and up to the time of weaning.

Conditions of the Newborn (Adaptive) Period (the First Four Days)

The relationship between neonatal conditions and the pre- and intra-natal environment of the foetus is complex. Before birth the foetus may be affected by viral or bacterial infection – e.g. equid herpesvirus 1 (rhinopneumonitis) or *Actinobacillus equuli* – by developmental abnormality, or by placentitis due to hypoxia (shortage of oxygen) or unknown causes. These factors may cause retarded growth, malnourishment or functional immaturity of foetal organs. In these cases the stresses normally imposed by birth and the newborn environment may become disproportionately great. Alternatively, the birth may be abnormal and cause chemical or physical damage to a previously normal, well-developed foetus.

Pre- and intra-natal disturbances account for non-infective conditions such as stillbirth, prematurity and immaturity, developmental abnormalities and states which we will describe under the neonatal maladjustment syndrome (i.e. barkers, wanderers, dummies and convulsive foals).

The term 'stress' applies to abnormal changes in the environment of the foetus at any stage of gestation or birth. It may be acute or chronic, according to the degree of interference produced in the physiological stability of the foetus. Acute stress early in gestation produces foetal death and abortion; in late gestation or during birth it causes stillbirth, delayed onset of respiration, convulsions and other behavioural abnormalities.

Once delivered, the foetus is subjected to extrinsic factors, the most challenging of which are an air environment, gravity, relatively low surrounding temperature, the presence of micro-organisms and the need for alimentation (digestion) and excretion unassisted by the placenta.

No set of conditions which have such diverse, yet interrelated, causes can be classified in other than a broad framework into which further definitions may be introduced as knowledge becomes available. Such a framework is shown in Table 3.

Table 3   Classification of Neonatal Conditions

Infective conditions
    Group I: Fever, lethargy and reduced strength of the suck reflex

Non-infective conditions
    Group II: Gross disturbances in behaviour
    Group III: Developmental abnormalities
    Group IV: Immunological reactions between maternal and foetal tissues

Group I: Infective Conditions (Sleepy Foal Disease, Septicaemia, Meningitis)

This group comprises infective conditions characterized by fever, lethargy and reduced strength of suck reflex.

Cause and incidence

Causal organisms include *Streptococcus pyogenes* var. *equi* (*Streptococcus zooepidemicus*), *Escherichia coli*, *Actinobacillus equuli* (*Bacterium viscosum equi*, *Shigella equirulus*), *Staphylococcus aureus*, *Salmonella typhimurium*, *Klebsiella pneumoniae*, equid herpesvirus 1 (EHV-1) and cytomegalovirus, in approximate order of incidence. About 1 per cent of foals are affected, but incidence varies according to geographical area, climate, management and the type and virulence of infecting organisms. In any particular locality the predominant challenging organisms may change from year to year. About 50 per cent of all foal deaths are due to infection.

Predisposing causes

Predisposing factors are chronic uterine endometritis, overcrowding and continual use of foaling boxes, prematurity, artificial severance and ligation of the cord, loss of colostrum before birth and failure to absorb specific antibodies.

Transmission

Prenatal infection may occur by haematogenous spread (i.e. through the blood) or through the amniotic fluid; postnatal infection occurs via the umbilicus or the alimentary tract. It is not usually possible to determine in any particular case whether infection occurred pre- or postnatally. Most of the causal organisms inhabit the alimentary or genital tract of the mare and are a cause of abortion and/or infection of the placenta.

Acute signs of septicaemia may be present within twelve hours of birth and in these cases it is difficult to see how overwhelming infection could begin postnatally. However, to establish a prenatal origin of infection the organism must be recovered from the placenta and/or genital tract of the mare immediately after birth.

Sources of postnatal infection are faeces, contaminated bedding, soil, the mammary region of the mare, feeding utensils, and the hands and clothes of the attendants. Equine infectious anaemia (EIA) may be transmitted through colostrum.

Manner of spread

Localization in various tissues depends on the nature of the causal organism. *Actinobacillus equuli* has a predilection for kidneys, adrenal glands and brain, and *Sta. aureus* and *S. typhimurium* for articular and periarticular structures including epiphyses. *Str. pyogenes*, *E. coli* and *Klebseilla pneumoniae* are ubiquitous, occurring in lungs, peritoneum, pleura, joints and umbilicus. EHV-1 and cytomegalovirus infect primarily liver and lung tissues.

In practice it is rare to find complete localization and most cases are partly septicaemic (i.e. blood-borne) and generalized. Traditional classifications have, however, been based on clinical signs and these are often related to the organs most severely affected, for example, joint ill, meningitis, diarrhoea and sleepy foal disease (nephritis). For this reason a summary of the predilections of causal organisms is presented in Table 4, together with a summary of predominant signs, but none of these subdivisions is likely to be found alone in any particular instance.

Table 4 Causes and Symptoms of Infective Conditions

Condition	Synonyms	Characteristics	Aetiology
Generalized infection	Diarrhoea Scours Pleurisy Pneumonia Peritonitis	Fever at 39° C and persisting Diarrhoea Increased respiratory rate, with rales Dehydration, retraction of eyeballs	*Escherichia coli* *Streptococcus* species
Hepatitis	Virus abortion Rhinopneumonitis	Convulsions Lethargy Mild jaundice Leucopenia	Equid herpesvirus 1 Cytomegalovirus
Nephritis	Viscosum Shigellosis Sleepy foal disease Sleeper	Initial fever to 39° C, becoming subnormal Sleepiness Diminished strength of suck Diarrhoea, mild colic Convulsions Uraemia; protein cells in urine Variable leucocytosis	*Actinobacillus equuli*
Meningitis	Convulsions	Fever to 39° C and persisting Convulsions	*Streptococcus* species *Escherichia coli* *Actinobacillus equuli*
Encephalitis		Gross disturbances of behaviour Leucocytosis	
Infective arthritis	Joint ill Navel ill	Fever to 39° C and persisting Lameness	*Streptococcus* species *Salmonella typhimurium*
Tenosynovitis		Painful swelling round joints Increasing leucocytosis	*Staphylococcus* species *Escherichia coli*

Symptoms

Although many signs are related directly to the site of infection, in most cases foals show lethargy, reduced strength of the suck reflex and inability to stand and hold the sucking position. Symptoms may appear at any time up to the end of the fourth day after birth but are most common on the second day. They start as slight dullness and a reluctance to feed.

The reduced amount sucked from the mammary glands leaves the udder distended, and milk may drip from the teats so that it stains the face and muzzle of the foal as it makes half-hearted attempts to suck. The rectal temperature at this stage may be normal or slightly raised to 38.9° C (102° F).

After several hours, depending on the severity of the condition, the foal becomes increasingly lethargic, disinclined to suck and exhibits definite signs of illness. Rectal temperature may rise to 41° C (106° F), although in many cases it remains below 38.9° C (102° F), especially if the foal becomes comatose; terminally the temperature may become subnormal.

Temperature should be recorded at least every six hours to establish the presence of transitory rises which have diagnostic significance and may be missed by less frequent recordings.

Buccal mucous membranes may become pale, injected or greyish. The conjunctiva may be pale or injected (livid) and the sclera (white of the eye) tinged with jaundice.

Increasing heart and respiratory rates may be present and signs of dehydration include loss of mobility of the skin and retracted eyeballs. Convulsions and extensor rigidity (stiffness) are common neurological signs. A foetid, evil-smelling diarrhoea may develop and be associated with signs of colic, such as rolling or lying in awkward attitudes, such as on the back with the head turned backwards or with a foreleg hung over the poll.

Lameness and painful swelling around the joints are associated with periarticular or articular infections, and rales or dullness over the lung area can be detected in bronchitis and pneumonia.

It is possible to distinguish peracute, acute and chronic cases, but premonitory signs are usually noted by watching carefully. In some instances, however, death occurs suddenly.

Diagnosis

Septicaemia should be suspected if a foal makes half-hearted attempts to suck and after a few swallows of milk lets its head fall down and, with eyelids half closed, allows milk to dribble from its mouth. The foal may also go lame, suffer from diarrhoea or show signs of dehydration. The rectal temperature is greater than 38.8° C (102° F). Increasing white blood cell and blood urea counts and the presence of protein in the urine confirm the diagnosis, but a complete diagnosis can only be made when an organism is isolated from body tissues or fluids.

Treatment

Antibiotics should be given immediately infection is suspected, because delay may make this condition less amenable to treatment. For this reason all newborn foals should be observed hourly if managerial conditions allow.

In the absence of laboratory isolation of the causal organism, the choice of a therapeutic agent is subjective (e.g. neomycin sulphate, amikacin, ampicillin, cloxacillin or trimethoprim and sulphadiazine in chloromycetin or amoxycillin). Therapy must be evaluated against the response obtained and treatment continued for at least forty-eight hours after symptoms have subsided.

Dam's plasma or whole blood, cross-matched against the foal's red cells, may be injected into one of the foal's jugular veins using a syringe or transfusion apparatus.

Prevention

Antibiotics can be given during the first few days after birth. The choice of drug and the length of time it should be given is subjective. A regimen of trimethoprim and sulphadiazine, intramuscular neomycin and oral framycetin represent approaches used in practice, but the decision to introduce a preventive programme and the choice of drug are matters for veterinary advice, taking into account local circumstances.

Antibiotic therapy may be supplemented by about 400 ml of donor colostrum fed from a bottle and artificial teat or by stomach tube if gammaglobulin blood levels are below an arbitrarily defined level of 4 g/litre.

Group II: Gross Behavioural Disturbances

This consists of non-infective conditions characterized by gross disturbances in behaviour. We recognize three categories: neonatal maladjustment syndrome (NMS), prematurity and dysmaturity (immaturity) and meconium retention (Table 5).

NEONATAL MALADJUSTMENT SYNDROME (NMS) (BARKER, WANDERER, DUMMY OR CONVULSIVE SYNDROME)

The term neonatal maladjustment syndrome (NMS) has been coined to include all the conditions listed above. Future research will undoubtedly require the classification to be modified further, but for the present it appears appropriate.

Cause and incidence

The cause of this condition is not fully understood but it is essentially the result of brain haemorrhage or swelling around the nerve cells of the brain due to waterlogging (oedema). The haemorrhages may result from low oxygen concentrations (hypoxia) in the blood and episodes of low and/or high blood pressure surges in the blood circulating through the brain.

Such combinations (hypoxia and alternating low and high blood pressure) may result from exaggeration of the normal effects of the birth

Table 5 Causes and Symptoms of Gross Behavioural Disturbances

Conditions	Synonyms	Characteristics	Aetiology
Neonatal maladjustment syndrome (NMS)	Barkers Wanderers Dummies Convulsions	Full-term gestation Onset within first 24 hours: often normal until onset Complete loss of suck reflex and ability to nurse Apparent blindness Convulsions, hypertonus, spasms Coma Hypothermia Acidaemia, hypercapnia	Asphyxia Birth trauma Foetal stress
	Respiratory distress	Low PaO_2 breathing air and 100% oxygen Respiratory rate and minute volume increased Tidal volume decreased	
Prematurity		300–320 days gestation Signs apparent at birth Weakness, delay in first standing Low birth weight Reduced strength of sucking, ability to suck and ability to maintain body temperature Tendency to colic after feeding 'Bedsores' Discoloured tongue, silky skin PaO_2 low breathing air; increased breathing 100% oxygen	Foetal stress
Dysmaturity	Immaturity	More than 320 days gestation but appearance and signs of prematurity Emaciation, dehydration Diarrhoea Susceptibility to infection	Foetal stress Placentitis
Meconium retention	Stoppage Ileus	Signs from birth to third day Straining, colic, lying in awkward postures Generally not off suck and in good health Abdominal tympany	Unknown

PaO_2 = arterial oxygen pressure.

process and also from damage to the chest (e.g. fractured ribs), leading to damage of the heart muscle and consequent impairment of the circulation.

Damage to the brain causes convulsions and severe behavioural problems, which in turn lead to disturbances in the balance of organ function on which stability of fluid electrolyte and gaseous exchange is based. These disturbances lead in turn to further neurological problems as they cause further bleeding and waterlogging of the brain.

Symptoms

Behavioural signs usually occur during the first twenty-four hours of life, most commonly during the first hours. The foal may appear normal at first, but becomes affected by convulsions of a jerky (clonic) or general type.

There is a complete loss of the suck reflex and the ability to nurse, although both faculties were present originally. The foal may be unable to stand or may make violent and aimless galloping movements with its limbs; at the same time it may dash its head against the floor. Head and neck and increased extensor tone may be present, the limbs extended and the tail held upright.

Convulsions may be followed by or may alternate with periods of coma. Signs of irritability are manifest by continual chewing, grinding the teeth, sneezing and wandering aimlessly round the box. When able to stand, the foal may appear blind and walk into or press against walls or other objects.

The affected foal may show exaggerated response to handling and restraint. Normal reflex behaviour may continue after stimulation has been removed and certain patterns of behaviour may become displaced.

For example, a foal may suck a teat on a bottle whether or not it is receiving milk, and continue to suck until the teat is removed from its mouth, when it goes into a deep sleep. Some foals exhibit determined sucking motions with the head extended and directed downwards, but seem unable to adopt a sucking attitude under the mare and fight violently against being held in that position. Affected foals often lie in awkward positions and have a tendency to go into a deep sleep when laid on the ground.

Not every case is affected by all the behavioural signs described. Some foals do not convulse, but show loss of suck reflex and wandering; others may be able to suck at a bottle but lose the ability to suck from or even recognize their mothers.

The rectal temperature depends on the activity of the foal. It rises to 41.1° C (106° F) and is accompanied by profuse sweating during convulsions, and falls during coma to 35° C (95° F), remaining within normal limits in mild cases or during convalescence.

Prominent symptoms of respiratory distress (rapid breathing rate) and circulatory failure (jugular pulse and venous engorgement) are commonly associated with this condition.

Course of condition

Signs of NMS may continue for several hours or it may take up to thirty days for the foal to be capable of sucking and following its mother. When recovery occurs it is usually complete. Convulsive foals recover in a definite sequence, first exhibiting coma and then the ability to get up and stand. Auditory and visual awareness return before the ability to suck and recognize the mare.

Diagnosis

Pathognomic (diagnostic) signs of NMS are sudden. There is complete loss of the suck reflex and of visual and other senses, including the ability to seek or follow the mare. Respiratory distress is defined by an increase in the respiratory rate, small amounts of air being inhaled at each breath, and low levels of oxygen in the blood.

Treatment

Symptomatic and supportive treatment is required, aimed at allowing time for the foal to re-establish its bodily means of adapting to the newborn environment. For example, if it is unable to suck, it must be fed through a stomach tube until it learns and is able to do so in the normal manner.

Behaviour and convulsions A foal unable to get up or stand unaided should be kept under close observation with, if practicable, an attendant always in the box to prevent it from exhausting itself in its attempts to stand.

The attendant should sit with the foal's head resting on his/her lap, the animal being restrained in the recumbent position by placing a hand on the undersurface of its head, so that in periods of struggling the muzzle can be raised. At the same time the upper foreleg is held so that the attendant can lean back and avoid being kicked by the hind legs.

It is helpful for a second person to grasp the tail of a foal which is convulsing or struggling violently, to keep the foal's body at right angles to the person at the head. The legs should not be held together since this may

Figure
144 Handling a convulsed foal

exacerbate the foal's struggles. If the foal is on its own, a soft surface such as a rug should be provided.

Convulsions can be controlled by various types of anticonvulsant drugs including barbiturate and diazapines.

Once the convulsions have been brought under control, the foal accepts restraint and sleeps on a rug or the lap of an attendant with only an occasional movement. It is helpful to reduce the usual stable noises. Vigorous restraint should be avoided wherever possible to minimize the risk of cardiac failure.

Feeding   In the absence of a suck reflex the foal should be fed through a rubber or plastic stomach tube with an outer diameter of about 1 cm and a blunt distal end. The tube should be lubricated with water or liquid paraffin and may be passed with the foal either standing or recumbent.

The end of the tube should not be passed beyond the entrance to the thorax. Before withdrawal it should be flushed with normal saline to prevent milk being deposited in the nasal passages. If the suck reflex is present, a bottle with an artificial lamb's or calf's teat may be used if the foal has lost the ability to suck from the mare.

Clinical experience suggests that a foal up to one week old should be fed according to the following principles:

1. In the first three days after birth the quantity and frequency of feeding are important.
2. Where a normal suck reflex is present, the foal's appetite is a rough guide to the quantity of fluid necessary. If adequate quantities are given, the foal should sleep readily after feeding and yet appear hungry at a subsequent feed.
3. Mare's milk or reconstituted dried milk may be fed at the rate of 150–200 ml/kg bodyweight/day, divided into a minimum of ten equal feeds. A foal of 50 kg bodyweight would then be fed 7–10 litres/day.

   Digestive upsets associated with the explosive growth of pathological coliform bacteria are less serious when small feeds are given frequently. The dry matter of liquid diets should be somewhere between 15 and 20 per cent, which is approximately double that of skimmed cow's milk. A number of proprietary dried milk preparations are available and these should be reconstituted using sufficient powder to provide a 50-kg foal with about 4000 kilocalories a day.
4. Strict hygiene should be practised and it is important to feed at 38° C (100° F) or below, but never above.

The advice given here provides a rough guide to the approach to feeding foals that cannot feed for themselves from the mare. However, it should be emphasized that the proper course for the reader is to seek the advice of his/her veterinarian whenever a sick foal is encountered. Cases differ both in the terms of diagnosis and their requirements, so general advice does not necessarily hold good for the particular.

Hypothermia Body temperature represents the balance of heat produced by metabolism and heat loss by radiation, conduction, convection and evaporation. In the foal the basis of heat production is shivering and muscular activity in movement. A normal foal can maintain its temperature against very low surrounding temperatures, but one suffering from coma and hypoxia, which prevent normal oxygen metabolism, requires special measures.

Mildly affected cases of NMS can be kept warm by fitting a woollen pullover over the body. Severely affected foals require ambient temperatures of 26.6–32.2° C (80–90° F). Radiant heat sources are the most effective, but if these are not available the foal may be covered with a washable electric blanket or rug. Hot-air blowers have some effect, but they create draughts and thereby increase heat loss by evaporation.

As a general measure box walls, ceilings and windows should be adequately insulated to reduce loss of radiation. It has been estimated that most heat is lost in other species by this route.

Homeostasis (blood content stability) For clinical purposes it may be assumed that foals affected by convulsions, severe diarrhoea or those that fail to establish a normal respiratory rhythm suffer from acidic blood.

Cardiac failure Cardiac embarrassment can be recognized by a heart rate greater than 120 beats/minute at rest, a marked jugular pulse and evidence of venous engorgement.

Prevention

There are no specific measures which can be taken to prevent NMS. As far as possible the cord should be left intact after birth until the placental circulation has ceased and a respiratory rhythm is established. Any action liable to place increased stress on the foal when it is getting to its feet and sucking for the first time should be avoided. During the first two hours after birth, the foal should be handled as little as possible.

ASPHYXIA NEONATORUM (FAILURE TO BREATHE AFTER BIRTH)

There is evidence in several species that the foetus makes episodic breathing movements *in utero* associated with rapid eye movement sleep (REMS). The significance of this activity is unknown at the present time, but it may form part of neuromuscular preparation for extra-uterine existence.

The stimuli for the first breath and subsequent rhythmic respiratory movements following delivery are tactile, cold and chemical, that is, decreasing arterial oxygen pressure (PaO_2) and increasing arterial carbon dioxide pressure (PaO_2).

The foal may gasp as the chest is being delivered, but the onset of respiration and the establishment of rhythmic movements of the chest and abdomen usually occur within 30 seconds of the hips passing out of the birth canal.

Alterations in blood gases may assume pathological proportions because of undue pressure on the umbilical cord during second-stage labour before the thorax has been completely delivered. Pressure may be caused by the cord being squeezed by the abdomen as it passes through the maternal pelvis, by posterior presentation or by an unusually large chest relative to the maternal pelvis. Other causes of pathological asphyxia are prematurity, inflammation of the placenta or prolonged manipulation to correct abnormal labour (dystocia). In theory changes in maternal uterine blood-flow during birth may affect gaseous placental exchange to the detriment of the foetus, but as yet there is no evidence to support this. A further aspect which must be considered is that a foetus which has already been subjected to stress during development may be detrimentally affected by the usual asphyxial processes. These are physiological to a normal foetus.

Resuscitation

The newborn foal may be delivered with no signs of breathing (primary apnoea) but the gasping which follows will expand the lungs and, provided the airways are clear, spontaneous rhythmic breathing will be established. Respiratory stimulants are therefore unnecessary and all that is required is to ensure that the nostrils are not obstructed. In terminal apnoea (prolonged shortness of breath) the respiratory centre does not respond to stimulants and resuscitation is essential.

Since it is not possible to distinguish primary from secondary apnoea in a newly delivered foal, any individual that fails to establish a respiratory rhythm within 30–60 seconds should be resuscitated in the following manner. The foal's head should be extended and the nostrils cleared of amnion and mucus. The operator should kneel between the foal's head and forelegs, placing the right hand under the foal's muzzle, and inflate the lungs either by inserting a rubber tube attached to an oxygen cylinder into the upper nostril and allowing gas to flow at a rate of approximately 5 litres/minute, or by applying the mouth to the upper nostril.

In both these methods the under nostril is closed with the right hand while the left hand is free to seal the upper nostril around the rubber tube or mouth. The lungs are inflated by positive pressure, but care must be taken not to overinflate. It is necessary to move the chest only a perceptible amount to cause a substantial rise in arterial oxygen pressure. After inflating by either method both nostrils are released to allow exhalation of carbon dioxide. This inflating should be maintained at the rate of about twenty-five a minute until a spontaneous rhythm is established.

Endotracheal intubation provides a more efficient means of lung inflation because it avoids accidental inflation of the stomach, but once the foal is conscious the tube must be withdrawn to prevent excessive struggling.

Depending on the course of the condition, which is related to the amount of hypoxia, acidity of the blood and consequent cerebral damage, the foal should be further sedated and any convulsions controlled by phenytoin and by gentle restraint.

STILLBIRTH

Many cases of stillbirth are presumably the consequence of cord obstruction or placental disturbance during second-stage labour, causing the foal to be born without any signs of breathing. In the absence of adequate measures of resuscitation, death is recorded as a stillbirth.

PREMATURITY, IMMATURITY AND DYSMATURITY

Considerable confusion surrounds the terms 'prematurity', 'immaturity' and 'dysmaturity'. In human medicine the term 'small for dates' has been used to acknowledge the fact that maturity is a relative state and that quality rather than length of gestation is the major factor. A pregnancy ending close to the average length may, in any species, result in an undersize, weak and at-risk individual. The term 'prematurity' signifies a shortened pregnancy, usually taken as a foal born within 320 days of the last mating. 'Immaturity' and 'dysmaturity' are interchangeable terms. 'Dysmaturity' describes foals that are small for dates and suffering from deprivation due to placental dysfunction or insufficiency. Newborn maturity implies the ability to adapt to the extra-uterine environment, but the definition must be qualified by the extent to which the environment nowadays can be artificially altered.

In horses, the wide size variation between breeds – even within a breed – makes birthweight a somewhat unreliable parameter against which to measure maturity.

Group III: Developmental Abnormalities

These are composed of developmental deformities. Hyperflexion (contracture) of the forelimbs is the most common abnormality and this condition is described in chapter 19.

Table 6   Developmental Abnormalities Seen in the First Weeks of Life

Conditions	Synonyms	Characteristics
Hyperflexion of limbs	Contracted tendons	Range from uprightness or fore- or hind legs to knuckling over at the fetlock and/or inability to extend knee joints
Hypoflexion of limbs	Weakness Down on pasterns	Laxity of ligaments Muscle hypotonia
Parrot jaw	Overshot jaw Parrot mouth	Upper and lower incisors overlapping by degrees varying from 1 mm to 3 cm, molars also overshoot at front and back
Umbilical urachal fistula	Pervious urachus	Wet cord stump, maybe dripping Often necrotic tissue present on both sides of abdominal wall
Congenital abnormalities of genito-urinary tract		
Patent bladder	Ruptured bladder	Signs appear two to three days after birth: may be confused with meconium colic
Deviation and shortening of the maxillary bones and asymmetry of the mandibles	Squiffy face	Often the tongue is held to one side and the foal has difficulty in sucking
Atresia coli Anal agenesis	Incomplete alimentary tract	Signs of meconium colic becoming increasingly severe and unremitting
Cleft palate		Regurgitation of milk down nostrils soon after or during feeding
Microphthalmia	Button eyes	Blindness
Scrotal hernia		Soft swelling in scrotum due to descent of abdominal contents. Appears in first few days or immediately following birth; often resolves spontaneously but may become strangulated

Cardiac septal defects Persistent truncus		Sudden death, fainting and/or respiratory embarrassment with rapid heart rate and murmurs
Hare lip		
Hydrocephalus		Excessively dome-shaped forehead
Omphalocele	Hernia	Open abdominal floor
Absence of urachus Megavesica		Dystocia due to size of bladder. If delivered, foal may suffer from acute maladjustment, usually fatal
Ectopic lung		Respiratory embarrassment if in chest and swelling if on ventral aspect of neck

Inherited abnormalities (e.g. **parrot jaw**) are the result of dominant or recessive genes in the individual's makeup or are caused by damage to chromosomes at the time of fertilization of the egg. Many defective individuals are aborted early in pregnancy, as is the case in other mammals.

Drugs given to the mare, especially in the period of the first month or two following conception when the foetus is developing rapidly, may be the cause of deformities such as **cleft palate**.

Later in pregnancy, illness of the mare, the administration of drugs, infection and damage to the placenta may cause deformities such as hyperflexion or hypoflexion (weakness) of the fore- and hind limbs, absence of parts of the gut or other faults in development.

The position in which the foal lies in the uterus may cause some deformities, especially those affecting the skeleton (e.g. skewing of the spine and deviation from the midline in the limbs).

The developmental abnormalities commonly encountered in foals in the first week of life are shown in Table 6.

Group IV: Immunological Reactions between Maternal and Foetal Tissues

This group is composed of immunological conditions, such as haemolytic disease or combined immunodeficiency of Arabian horses (see p. 625).

HAEMOLYTIC DISEASE

Haemolytic disease is the result of differences in inherited structure of foetal and maternal red blood cells. The foetal cells contain antigens not present in maternal cells. That is, the mother has not inherited these blood cell types from her parents, whereas the foetus has inherited them from its father.

Red cells cross from the foetal into the maternal bloodstream and provoke an antibody response in the mare similar to that stimulated by the administration of vaccine. The antibodies become concentrated in the colostrum and absorbed from the foal's stomach after it has sucked for the first time. They circulate in the foal's bloodstream, attach themselves to the surface of the foal's red cells and cause them to clump and break down (haemolysis).

The ability of these antibodies to be absorbed through the lining of the gut is limited to the first twelve to twenty-four hours after birth. This enables us to prevent the occurrence of haemolytic disease if we can diagnose that a mare is likely to give birth to an affected foal. This can be achieved by testing blood samples two to three times over a period of weeks prior to the expected date of foaling.

Symptoms

Affected foals become sleepy and may yawn repeatedly. If exerted or excited, their breathing and heart rates increase very markedly and the pulse may be observed in the jugular furrow of the neck.

Jaundice develops in the whites of the eyes and on the visible mucous membranes of the mouth and vagina in the case of fillies. Urine becomes red in colour.

Symptoms may appear on the first, but more often on the second, day after foaling. The severity of the case varies depending on the number of red cells destroyed.

If the case is very acute the first symptoms may be collapse and the foal becomes moribund. Less severe cases show symptoms described above.

Diagnosis

The diagnosis is made on symptoms and laboratory examination of the blood. Profound anaemia and haemolysis, together with the detection of antibodies, confirms the diagnosis.

Treatment

The damaged red cells must be replaced and this is achieved by administering a blood transfusion. The best source of red cells is the mare's blood, but these have to be washed free of the mare's serum so as not to introduce further antibody into the foal. This is, of course, a veterinary decision and treatment.

When a mare has been diagnosed as having been sensitized to her foetal foal's red cells, the foal should be muzzled for up to thirty-six hours after birth and the mare's udder stripped of colostrum. It is important that the foal should receive another mare's colostrum in the first feed (see p. 372) and then reconstituted dried milk and subsequent feeds until it is aged about thirty-six hours.

Infectious Diseases

Infection is a subject with which all readers will be familiar because it affects both themselves and their horse. In this section Mary Mackintosh contributes a description of the bacteria, viruses and other microbes that infect horses. Then Michael Roberts describes in detail the main bacterial diseases, and Jenny Mumford the diseases caused by viruses. Finally Sheelagh Lloyd discusses the various parasites that infest horses.

The story of infection is one of a battle between two sides, the microbes or parasite and the horse. The reactions of the horse to the presence of the infecting agent are the symptoms of the disease. These symptoms are typical of diseases such as influenza, metritis (infection of the uterus) and virus abortion. The chapters are written to enable the reader to associate a particular disease with a particular microbe. Causes and symptoms are described and the reader may thereby gain an understanding of each condition likely to be encountered. Recognition of symptoms is important at the early stages of disease so that professional advice may be sought in time for treatment to be effective.

An understanding of the way in which infectious disease develops is also important for the practice of good management to ensure that logical and effective control measures are established. The same principles of control apply to parasitism. It is important therefore for the reader to understand how microbes and parasites spread from one individual to another, how they spread throughout the body and, finally, the manner in which they leave the body to infect others.

28
THE CAUSES OF
INFECTIOUS DISEASES

Infectious diseases are caused by living organisms, most of which are very small. In fact, they are so small that individually they cannot be seen by the human eye unaided. We call them micro-organisms or microbes because we need a microscope in order to see them. There are many different kinds of micro-organisms, which are grouped according to how they grow and reproduce. These groups are called viruses, bacteria, mycoplasma, chlamydia, rickettsia and fungi.

Two other groups of organisms must also be included when considering the causes of infectious disease, and these are protozoa and parasites. They are not always quite as small as micro-organisms.

Infection implies that a micro-organism has become established in the body's tissues or on its surface and reproduces itself at the body's expense. It may live outside (extracellular) or inside (intracellular) the body's cells. Its presence causes damage (alteration of function) and death (necrosis) of the cells, and this results in the symptoms of disease usually characteristic of the particular organism involved.

The terms 'virulence' and 'pathogenecity' are used to describe the ability of an organism to enter the body, set up disease and cause symptoms. A pathogen is an organism capable of causing disease; a virulent pathogen is one which readily sets up infection and produces severe symptoms. A venereal pathogen is one transmitted at coitus from male to female or the reverse.

Such organisms enter the body by way of one of several routes: through the mouth (by being swallowed); through the nostrils (by being inhaled); through the skin (by way of wounds, injected by insects, or directly, for example, certain worms burrow through the skin); through the urinogenital tract; or through the conjunctiva of the eyelids.

Identification of the organism causing an infectious disease determines the treatment and prognosis of the disease and the likelihood of spread to other horses.

Bacteria

Bacteria, probably the best-studied group of infective agents, are usually single-celled organisms which occur in a wide variety of forms. They are distinguished from other unicellular organisms such as protozoa in that they contain no nucleus, but they have a special nuclear apparatus with only a single strand of the genetic material DNA (deoxyribonucleic acid). They can be found free-living in soil and water or within a host – a plant or an animal. They have a rigid cell wall which supports and protects them, and most can be cultured on laboratory media.

Bacteria were observed directly as early as 1683 by a Dutch lens maker, Antonine van Leeuwenhoek, but problems of isolation and cultivation took another two hundred years to solve, despite suggestions by von Plenciz, in 1762, that these very small organisms might be the specific cause of certain diseases.

Louis Pasteur is the person whom everyone thinks of as the founder of bacteriology and this claim is certainly true, but there were many others working in the field between 1870 and 1885 who are remembered every day as names of bacteria: Neisser, Loeffler, Welch, Klebs and Shiga, to name but a few.

Pasteur studied the infectious nature of disease and how it was passed from host to host, which were not necessarily of the same species. He demonstrated the cause of anthrax and how to protect against the disease by vaccination. However, this principle had already been demonstrated by Jenner who, in 1796, showed that infection with the mild disease called cowpox conferred a high degree of protection against the virulent smallpox infection.

Pasteur also showed that there were some infective particles much smaller than those which could be seen by the new magnifying instrument, the microscope. When passed through the filters which retained bacteria these particles were able to produce disease. These filterable agents were called viruses.

A further important discovery was made by Joseph Lister, who was Professor of Surgery at Glasgow Royal Infirmary. He was both interested and concerned in post-operative sepsis, which caused high fatality in hospital patients at that time. He applied Pasteur's observations to the problem and showed that sepsis could be prevented by the use of carbolic acid, which killed bacteria in the wounds and in the air. Antiseptic techniques were introduced in 1867.

Normal flora

In the healthy horse (and man) bacteria live on the skin, in the mouth, around the teeth, in the upper respiratory tract, in the genital tract of the female, and on the external genitalia of the male; they also exist in very large numbers in the gut, particularly in the large intestine. These bacteria

Table 7 Bacteria Associated with the Normal Flora

Site	Bacteria
Mouth, nose and respiratory tract	*Acinetobacter* species *Bacillus* species *Bacteroides* species *Fusobacterium* species *Micrococcus* species *Moraxella* species *Pasteurella* species *Staphylococcus* species *Streptococcus* species *Veillonella* species
Gastro-intestinal tract	Anaerobic cocci *Bacteroides* species *Clostridium* species Enterobacter species *Escherichia coli* *Klebsiella* species *Proteus* species *Pseudomonas aeruginosa* *Rhodococcus (Corynebacterium) equi* *Streptococcus faecalis*
Mare's genital tract	*Bacteroides fragilis* *Micrococcus* species *Staphylococcus* species *Streptococcus* species
External clitoris	*Bacteroides* species *Bacillus* species *Clostridium* species *Corynebacterium* species Fusobacterium species *Proteus* species *Pseudomonas* species *Veillonella* species

constitute what is called the normal flora. They play an important role in the gut in helping to break down food, especially in herbivores, forming a finely balanced, mutually advantageous relationship with the host.

The bacteria in the normal flora do not, on the whole, produce disease in the host, except under special circumstances (see below), but it is common to find potential pathogens among them. If these bacteria are present and the horse is not showing symptoms of the disease, such an organism is said to be 'carried' and the host is called the 'carrier'.

The normal flora are established soon after birth and certainly within the first few days of life, transmitted from the mother and the surroundings. It is thought that the normal flora are able to protect the host to a certain extent from infection by pathogens. For example, the bacteria present on the horse's external genitalia may protect the individual from becoming infected with venereal microbes (for example, *Klebsiella* or *Pseudomonas* – see p. 413).

Types of bacterial infections

Bacterial infections can be divided into three groups, according to the manner in which the organism gains entry to the host, in this case the horse. Group I includes infections caused by physical breakdown of the skin, which then allows bacteria from the outside to gain entry to the body. Group II includes infections caused by access of bacteria to sensitive tissue within the body, for example, via the respiratory, alimentary or genital tract or the conjunctiva. Group III consists of infections caused by bacteria present within the normal flora.

Having entered the host, bacteria seek out a site or situation where they are able to grow and produce substances called toxins and other metabolites responsible for the clinical symptoms that characterize the particular disease.

Group I: Infections caused by the physical breakdown of the skin Skin is an efficient barrier to infection, but once it is breached, bacteria invade susceptible tissue. For example, streptococci and staphylococci may be present in eczematous sores on the skin following abrasions from harness or wounds caused by splinters or other foreign bodies. Minor skin infections are an everyday occurrence.

Wound infections usually result from an accident, but occasionally surgical wounds break down and allow infection to become established. The microbes which infect wounds are opportunist: they are those which happen to be there at the time. Organisms of faecal origin and those which live or survive in the soil are prevalent in infections of the foot and cuts and wounds on the legs.

This is particularly important if wounds are deep and dirty. Dirt represents dust, soil and faecal material, all rich in microbial flora. Many of these organisms grow in the absence of oxygen. One such organism is the bacterium which causes tetanus, *Clostridium tetani* (see p. 414). This microbe is present in soil and faeces but is normally unable to penetrate the skin. However, when in a deep or dirty wound, it can grow in the absence of oxygen, producing its toxin with often fatal results.

When one considers the origin of this type of infection it is unlikely that only one bacterial species is causing the infection; many different types of organisms are normally involved. For example, twelve different bacterial species have been identified from an equine foot abscess. This is very important when treatment is being considered because different organisms require different treatment.

Another source of infection is the skin itself. Bacteria which live on the skin can cause infection if the skin is broken and they are able to penetrate the underlying tissue. Abscesses are a very important form of sepsis because they often form deep in the body and are walled off by a barrier of inflammatory reaction (see chapter 36). This often makes them difficult to treat by antibiotics alone and surgical drainage may be necessary.

Table 8   Bacteria Associated with Wounds and Abscesses

Aerobes	*Escherichia coli*
	Proteus species
	Pseudomonas aeruginosa
	Staphylococcus aureus
	Streptococcus zooepidemicus
Anaerobes	*Bacteroides fragilis*
	B. melaninogenicus
	Clostridium perfringens
	C. septicum
	C. tetani
	Peptococcus species
	Peptostreptococcus species

A list of bacteria which might be expected to be isolated from wound infections is given in Table 8. The terms 'aerobe' and 'anaerobe' refer to the ability of the bacteria to grow in conditions where oxygen is present (aerobe) and where it is absent (anaerobe).

Animal bites are another source of wound infection. Here the bacteria associated with the teeth of the biting animal are the chief source of infection, plus those on the skin of the bitten horse as shown in Table 9.

Burns may also become infected and, again, it is the opportunist microbes which get in first. The bacterium *Pseudomonas aeruginosa* is often associated with burns.

Table 9   Bacteria Associated with Bites and Burns

Bacteroides species
Escherichia coli
Fusobacterium species
Pasteurella species
Pseudomonas aeruginosa
Staphylococcus species
Streptococcus zooepidemicus

Group II: Infections caused by access of bacteria to sensitive tissue within the body   In this group microbes are transmitted from one infected individual to another healthy animal, either directly or indirectly. A common method of host-to-host transmission is by aerosol. Very fine droplets of water or particles of dust containing microbes are inhaled and, because they are so small, they penetrate to the nasopharynx and even to the lungs.

Aerosol transmission is most common with viruses. However, certain bacteria, such as *Bordetella bronciseptica* and *Rhodococcus equi* (formerly called *Corynebacterium equi* – see p. 416), which cause respiratory infection, and *Streptococcus equi*, the causative agent of strangles (see p. 411), can be transmitted by aerosol. Strangles can also be transmitted by direct contact, horse to horse, or by indirect contact, that is, a horse can be infected from a contaminated stable, horsebox or even paddock which has recently been used by an infected animal.

Whether infection is by inhalation of contaminated dust particles or by ingestion by licking or using contaminated water buckets, etc., is irrelevant to the disease process (see Table 10).

The best example of transmission of bacteria by direct contact is venereal disease. The bacterium which causes contagious equine metritis (CEM – see p. 420) is a true venereal pathogen – in the natural environment it is only transmitted from mare to stallion and stallion to mare at coitus, or from an infected mare to her foal at birth or to her foal at foot.

The bacterium, formerly called *Haemophilus equigenitalis* and now called *Taylorella equigenitalis*, but usually referred to as CEM or CEMO, does not survive outside the host for any length of time, probably not more than an hour or so. The stallion does not become infected in the sense of suffering from a disease (as in venereal disease in humans), but if he mates an infected mare and picks up the microbe, it can become established as part of the normal genital flora, where it can survive for years. It only becomes a problem when the stallion subsequently infects a mare at mating.

Both colt and filly foals can be contaminated by an infected dam at birth or soon after; and the microbe may be carried in the normal flora until the animal goes to stud. It is then that the colt foal, now a stallion, infects his mares at mating and the filly, now a mare, passes the organism she has been carrying to the stallion who mates her. He may then infect the next mare which he mates.

Fortunately this cycle can be broken because, although the bacterium can be carried for years, most carriers clear themselves in time. But to control this serious disease any animal thought to be infected, or which has been on stud premises where there has been an infection, should be examined by a vet and, if found to be a carrier, should be treated.

It should be remembered that, although the most serious outbreaks of CEM have been in the Thoroughbred, it can infect all breeds of horses, ponies and donkeys. It will only be kept under control by identification of infected animals. Veterinary treatment of those infected and all possible carriers is important and meticulous stud hygiene on infected premises should be followed (see chapter 38).

The bacteria *Streptococcus zooepidemicus*, *Klebsiella pneumoniae* and *Pseudomonas aeruginosa* cause other diseases in the horse but can be

Table 10   Aerosol and Indirectly Transmitted Respiratory Bacterial Pathogens

Bordetella bronchiseptica
Enterobacter agglomerans
Klebsiella pneumoniae
Mycobacterium avium
M. bovis
M. tuberculosis
Pasteurella pneumotropica
Streptococcus equi
S. pneumoniae
S. zooepidemicus

Table 11   Bacteria Responsible for Venereal and Venereally Transmitted Disease

Klebsiella pneumoniae (certain capsule types only)
Pseudomonas aeruginosa
Streptococcus zooepidemicus
Taylorella equigenitalis (CEMO)

Table 12   Directly and Indirectly Transmitted Bacterial Diseases

Bacteria	Disease
Actinobacillus equuli	Shigellosis
Bacillus anthracis	Anthrax
Brucella species	Brucellosis
Corynebacterium pseudotuberculosis	Ulcerative lymphangitis
Dermatophilus species	Rain scald
Mycobacterium avium ⎫	
M. bovis ⎬	Tuberculosis
M. tuberculosis ⎭	
Pseudomonas mallei	Glanders
Rhodococcus (Corynebacterium) equi	Pneumonia in foals
Salmonella abortus equi	Septicaemia in foals; abortion in mares
Streptococcus equi	Strangles
S. zooepidemicus	Common cause of inflammatory infection

transmitted from stallion to mare or mare to mare via the stallion at mating. They are important because they cause metritis in the mare and, unlike CEM, can infect the accessory glands of the stallion.

Two other bacteria, *Rhodococcus Corynebacterium equi* and *Actinobacillus equuli*, cause disease in foals, but the route of infection is uncertain. The organisms can be isolated from soil but also from the gut of normal, healthy animals, and the dam may be the source of infection.

Rhodococcus equi is the cause of pneumonia in foals, sometimes called summer pneumonia (see p. 416). The bacteria can survive for years in the soil and can be isolated from garden soil which has had no known contact with horses. *Actinobacillus equuli* is the causative organism of shigellosis or sleepy foal disease (see p. 380), a highly fatal septicaemia of newborn foals. Postnatal infection is thought to be via the navel. The foal may be infected *in utero*, though the mare is not clinically infected.

The diseases caused by *Brucella abortus*, brucellosis, and *Mycobacterium bovis*, tuberculosis, are now rare in horses in this country but both can be transmitted from cattle to the horse. Man can also infect horses with tuberculosis caused by *Mycobacterium tuberculosis*, which is very similar to *M. bovis*; the disease is indistinguishable. There is also tuberculosis in birds caused by *M. avium*, but transmission to horses is thought to be very rare. Glanders is another bacterial disease of historic interest. It was identified by Loeffler in 1882 and is caused by an organism now called *Pseudomonas mallei*. The last reported case in the United Kingdom occurred in 1928.

Group III: Infections caused by bacteria present within the normal flora This type of infection is called endogenous. It is not really an infection as such, because the bacteria are already present in the body, but the outcome is a disease which has to be resolved. It is not caused by a change in pathogenicity of the organism but by a change in the condition of the host. Such changes may be caused by stress, trauma or infection by other agents.

Stress covers many situations, from malnutrition, overwork and heavy worm burden to being transported; and what stresses one animal may have no effect on another. Stress causes the natural defence mechanisms of the host to be impaired, resistance is said to be lowered, and pathogenic bacteria already present are able to outgrow the normal flora and disease follows.

Table 13 Endogenous Infections – potential pathogens which, when present in the normal gut flora, may be responsible for diarrhoea

---

Campylobacter jejuni (formerly called *Vibrio jejuni*)
Clostridium perfringens
Escherichia coli
Salmonella species
Yersinia enterocolitica

Diarrhoea is a common clinical symptom of such a situation. Species of *Salmonella*, *Campylobacter* and *Clostridia* and *Escherichia coli* are the most common bacteria responsible. Diarrhoeic diseases can be caused for many other reasons, and viruses and even protozoa can be the causative agents. Disturbance of the normal gut flora by the indiscriminate use of antibiotics can have a similar effect, caused by the overgrowth of undesirable bacteria present within the gut flora.

Familiarity breeds contempt. Because antibiotics are so freely available it is sometimes forgotten how powerful they can be. Antibiotics cannot distinguish between pathogen and normal flora and they kill all bacteria sensitive to them. Upsetting the gut flora of a horse can be fatal.

Antibiotics may have other adverse side effects. Some cause serious damage to nerves, kidney function and so on, and dosage is critical. They should never be used on any animal without veterinary advice.

Another group of endogenous infections are those associated with internal injuries and deep-seated pathological changes such as tumours. The bacteria associated with such conditions are as secondary invaders and usually originate from the gut.

There are also examples of endogenous abscesses. These include dental abscesses originating from the normal flora of the mouth, peritonitis and intra-abdominal abscesses where the bacteria originate from the gut, and pelvic abscesses where the bacteria may be of gut or genital origin.

Yet another way in which bacteria carried in the normal flora are able to cause infection is if tissue is damaged by another infective agent, such as a virus, allowing the bacteria access. Bacteria present in the respiratory tract do not penetrate the epithelial lining cells, although they may attach to the outside, but viruses are able to damage the integrity of the cell wall, and are usually followed by secondary bacterial infections. *Streptococcus pneumoniae*, as the name suggests, can cause serious respiratory disease but is carried in the normal flora of horses, especially in young horses, and has only been shown to cause problems after virus infection.

Table 14   Bacteria Associated with Dental Abscesses

Aerobes	*Staphylococcus* species
	Streptococcus species
Anaerobes	*Bacteroides* species
	Fusobacterium species
	Peptococcus species
	Peptostreptococcus species

Table 15   Bacteria Associated with Deep-Seated Abscesses

Anaerobic cocci
Bacteroides species
Clostridium species
Escherichia coli
Fusobacterium species
Staphylococcus aureus
Streptococcus species

There are two diseases of horses which are not caused directly by a bacterium but by its product (toxin). These are botulism (see p. 415) and tetanus (see p. 414). Both microbes are inhabitants of soil and plant material. As organisms grow, toxin is produced. It is the ingestion of preformed toxin in one (botulism) and the production of toxin from the microbe in an abscess within the body in the other (tetanus) that cause fatal disease.

Viruses
Viruses are sub-microscopic organisms. This means that they cannot be seen when under an ordinary light microscope but require the even higher magnification that can only be achieved by using an electron microscope.

They have a central core of a single strand of genetic material, either DNA or RNA (ribonucleic acid), which is surrounded by a protein coat. They have the basic material required to replicate themselves but can only do so inside a living cell. They require tissue culture or animal inoculation for culture in the laboratory. They are described in detail in chapter 30.

Many viral conditions – influenza, arteritis, rhinopneumonitis (equid herpesvirus) are caused by viruses being inhaled into the respiratory tract and setting up infection by that route.

Mycoplasma, rickettsia and chlamydia

Mycoplasma, rickettsia and chlamydia are organisms which are neither bacteria nor viruses but come somewhere in between the two.

Mycoplasma are the smallest free-living organisms. They do not have a rigid cell wall and are therefore very vulnerable to environmental changes. They can be grown in the laboratory on special media. They have been shown to be pathogenic in animals and are responsible for bovine pneumonia. They have been isolated from the respiratory tract of horses and may be involved in mixed viral-bacterial-type infection.

Rickettsia and chlamydia can only live and grow in an animal host cell. They require tissue culture or animal inoculations for culture in the laboratory. Rickettsia are only found associated with lice, fleas, ticks and mites, which are responsible for their spread. Chlamydia are pathogenic for man and other animals, causing serious diseases such as trachoma and psittacosis. They have been isolated from the eye and nose of the horse, but have not, as yet, been proved to be associated with infective disease.

Fungi

Fungi are physically larger than bacteria. Most can be grown on laboratory media. The organisms come in two forms: single-celled round or oval yeasts and the multicellular, mycelial forms. A mycelium is just like a plant's rooting system with lots of branches.

Fungi are very important in the environment. They are responsible for much of the breakdown of decaying plant material because, unlike bacteria, they produce an enzyme which is able to digest cellulose. Of the many fungi which have been identified, only a few cause disease. The majority live in the soil or on plant material. They reproduce themselves by spores. These are very small water-resistant structures which are dispersed into the atmosphere in very large numbers. The mould found on cheese and bread is a fungal growth caused by spores carried in the air.

Fungi are not only larger than bacteria but have one fundamental difference in the cell nucleus. Together with all animals and plants except bacteria and viruses, fungi have two strands of DNA forming their genetic material (chromosomes).

Because fungal spores are so widespread in nature their isolation from clinical material is not always significant, and to be certain that a fungus is causing a disease it is necessary to establish that the fungus is present within the tissue.

Fungal spores penetrate into the tissues of the host where they germinate and form a seat of infection. *Aspergillus* is the most common pathogenic species in the horse, causing infection of mucous membrane and serious infections in the guttural pouch (see p. 33). Spores can cause an allergic reaction, as in chronic obstructive pulmonary disease (see p. 48), without causing an infection.

Some fungi, particularly yeasts, are present in the normal gut flora, where they can become a problem if the flora are upset, particularly by the use of antibiotics. Yeasts are not sensitive to bacterial antibiotics and can overgrow the bacterial populations in the gut.

Yeast infections are not common in the horse, although species of *Candida* can cause infection of the oral and intestinal mucosa in foals and have occasionally caused genital infections in both mares and stallions. *Cryptococcus neoformans* infection is more serious. It starts as a subacute or chronic infection, usually in the form of a nasal granuloma, but may extend to other parts of the body.

The most important and common fungal infections in the horse are the dermatophyte skin infections and ringworm (see p. 95). There are many different fungal species which cause ringworm in the horse but the two most important are *Trichophyton* and *Microsporum*. *Microsporum canis* infects not only the horse but humans, dogs, cats and many other animals. This is important when considering transmission, which is by contact. *Trichophyton equinum* is the common cause of ringworm in horses and donkeys, occasionally in dogs and rarely in humans.

Protozoa

Protozoa are much larger than bacteria. They have two strands of DNA genetic material, and although they are only single-celled, the cell has a very complex structure. Protozoa are grouped according to their shape and life style. One group has a tail-like projection or a form of membrane which provides mobility. In this group are found trypanosomes and leishmania. Another group comprises those protozoa with a complex life cycle which includes two different hosts, such as an arthropod (e.g. a tick) and a vertebrate (e.g. a horse). One example is the piroplasm which causes tick-borne babesia (see p. 433).

Parasites

A parasite is an animal or plant that lives in or on another (the host) from which it obtains nourishment. Therefore bacteria, viruses, fungi, etc., can all be referred to as parasites and often are, but the parasites to be considered here are much bigger and more complex than any micro-organism.

The most successful parasites live at the expense of the individual host but do not kill it. The degree of dependence and the degree of harm inflicted vary widely with different parasites, a pathogenic parasite being one which damages the tissues of the host to cause disease.

Parasites can be divided into three categories: helminths, (worms), arthropods, (joint-limbed parasites), and protozoa (see above).

Helminths can be subdivided into trematodes (flukes), which are usually dorsoventrally flattened and often leaf-like in outline; cestodes (tapeworms), which are also dorsoventrally flattened, but which have a ribbon-like body made up of segments; and nematodes (roundworms), which are elongated and cylindrical in shape, and taper at each extremity.

Arthropods consist of insects and arachnids. Insects (lice and flies) have a body which is divided into a head, a thorax and an abdomen, three pairs of legs and usually one pair of wings, although lice, which belong to this category, are wingless. Arachnids (ticks and mites) often have a sac-like body with mouthparts at the anterior end and four pairs of legs in the adult stage. Ticks may reach 1 cm or so in length, but mites are usually microscopic and cannot be seen by the naked eye.

The life cycle of a parasite is said to be either direct or indirect. In the direct life cycle the parasite is transferred from horse to horse without the intervention of another organism. However, there may be a period during which the parasite exists as a free-living stage outside the host in the environment, on pasture, for example, while being transferred from horse to horse. In the indirect life cycle the parasite requires two or more different hosts. One host acts as the definitive host, in which the sexually mature, egg-producing stages of the parasite are found. The other acts as the intermediate host, in which the parasite develops but does not reach sexual maturity. The intermediate host is essential to the parasite's life cycle. The most common intermediate hosts are flies and ticks, although for some parasites the horse itself will act as an intermediate host.

Having experienced a first infection with a parasite, the horse may develop the ability to kill all or some of the parasites invading in a second or subsequent infection. This is known as the protective immune response and it is the main reason why adult horses tend to be less susceptible to infection than foals or yearlings. However, sometimes an exaggerated, allergic type of immune response can occur and the horse becomes hypersensitive to the parasitic infection. This hypersensitivity may itself cause lesions and disease.

A variety of drugs are used to kill or suppress the development of parasites. These are called anthelmintics, insecticides, acaricides and antiprotozoals and are used to treat helminths, insects, arachnids and protozoa respectively. The same drugs often kill both insects and arachnids.

A few parasites have developed resistance to the effects of the specific parasiticide used to control them. This means that the population of parasites which previously was killed by a certain dose of that particular drug is no longer killed by that dose and the parasites remain alive in or on the horse after treatment with the drug.

29
DISEASES CAUSED BY BACTERIA

Large populations of different micro-organisms are normal inhabitants of the external (skin) and internal (e.g. upper respiratory tract, alimentary tract) surfaces of all animal species. The body's natural defence mechanisms (components of the immune system) prevent these organisms from exerting deleterious effects and becoming pathogenic. In horses, diverse micro-organisms contribute to natural fermentation processes in the large intestine enabling the animal to utilize insoluble fibrous material for energy and protein needs. If the active defence mechanisms are compromised, suppressed, do not develop, or passive immunity is deficient as in newborn foals receiving inadequate colostral protection, then opportunistic bacteria in the immediate environment may multiply, invade tissues and produce pathogenic effects (disease). The requirements for optimum growth vary with different bacterial species. For instance, the ubiquitous *Streptococci* of the horse require air (aerobic) as on the skin surface and in the oral cavity. *Taylorella equigenitalis*, the cause of contagious equine metritis, needs a low oxygen tension (micro-aerophilic) whereas *Clostridium tetani* grows in the absence of air (anaerobic) in deep wound penetrations of the foot or muscle.

Under favourable conditions bacteria can cause infection in any tissues and body systems. Such infections, which are not classified as distinct disease entities, may be attributable to a single bacterial species, but are more likely to involve a mixed population of organisms. Newborn foals are susceptible to a wide range of organisms and, when maternal antibody protection (through the colostrum) is inadequate, may develop systemic illnesses (septicaemia) with clinical signs referable to the respiratory, alimentary or nervous systems and joints, for example. One particular organism, *Actinobacillus equuli*, can cause a neurological condition known as sleepy foal disease (see p. 380), although this cannot be considered a specific disease syndrome as other organisms can produce similar clinical signs.

However, several infectious diseases of horses which are distinct conditions are attributable to, and can be induced by, specific bacteria.

Examples include strangles, which is caused by *Streptococcus equi*, and tetanus, which results from a toxin produced by *Clostridium tetani*. An extensive list of infectious diseases of horses caused by specific bacteria and of particular significance in the UK is provided in Table 16. This chapter highlights several of the most important distinct bacterial disorders under the heading of the specific micro-organism.

STREPTOCOCCUS EQUI (STRANGLES)

Strangles is a disease of the upper respiratory tract primarily of younger horses, although animals of any age can be affected. It is characterized by an acute pharyngitis and rhinitis followed by abscessation of the regional lymph nodes (glands), which may rupture and discharge thick, creamy pus. The disease can be sporadic or may become a severe problem in some areas, for example, when young stock are mixed at a sale or an infected animal goes to a show or pony club event.

Although *Streptococcus equi* is isolated usually in pure culture from nasal discharges or pus from affected animals, the development of the disease may require concurrent or prior involvement of other upper respiratory pathogens (e.g. viruses).

Clinical signs

Affected animals have a fever, a nasal discharge at first watery but which becomes mucopurulent, and a poor appetite. Incubation period can be three to six days. Head carriage may be stiffer than normal, swallowing may be difficult and a soft cough heard. Fever decreases until the lymph nodes beneath and behind the lower jaw enlarge. These swellings, which are hard and painful, can impair breathing (hence strangles) by compressing the pharynx. The animal may be depressed and off its feed. The lymph nodes may rupture in ten to fourteen days (or require lancing), releasing thick, creamy pus. The nasal discharge and pus can contaminate the environment, increasing the risk to other horses. Usually animals recover rapidly once the swellings rupture.

Occasionally the regional lymph nodes are unable to filter (block) the organisms, which spread down the lymphatic chain producing internal abscesses in the thorax or abdomen ('bastard strangles'). Subsequent rupture could have grave consequences. Other complications include empyema (pus) of the guttural pouches, aspiration pneumonia, respiratory distress and pleuritis. **Purpura haemorrhagica** can be a sequel, characterized by progressive swellings of the lower limbs, ventrally along the body wall and even of the throat and head. This appears to be an immunological reaction and is not restricted to strangles.

Diagnosis of strangles is presumed on clinical grounds and should be confirmed on bacteriological culture. The presence of swollen lymph nodes

Table 16 Infectious Diseases of Horses Caused by Bacteria

Disease (synonyms)	Micro-organism	Presence in UK	Age range	Features
Strangles	*Streptococcus equi*	Frequent	Generally young (after weaning)	Respiratory disease; lymph node abscesses. Favourable response to therapy or abscess evacuation. Isolate. Vaccine (not UK).
Tetanus (lockjaw)	*Clostridium tetani*	Uncommon	All	Neuromuscular disease; therapy unrewarding unless recognized early. Vaccination effective in prevention.
Botulism (forage poisoning – adults; shaker foal syndrome)	*Clostridium botulinum*	Rare	Suckling foals to adults	Neuromuscular disease: weakness and paralysis. Avoid feeding silage. Antiserum available in USA.
Summer pneumonia (rattles)	*Rhodococcus equi* (*Corynebacterium equi*)	Rare, single or sporadic cases	Foals 2 to 6 months; occasional adult	Respiratory disease ± alimentary tract involvement. Insidious course, therapy difficult.
Salmonellosis	*Salmonella* serotypes esp. *S. typhimurium*	Sporadic outbreaks can occur	All; primarily young, old, debilitated	Enteric disease (many syndromes: diarrhoea, shock, septicaemia in young foals). Favourable response to vigorous fluid and electrolyte replacement. Isolation – sanitation, hygiene. Zoonosis.
Tyzzer's disease	*Bacillus piliformis*	Rare	Foals under 2 months	Acute hepatic disease; sudden death.
Leptospirosis	*Leptospira interrogans* serovars	Infrequent	All	Multisystem; association with abortion, renal disease in foals and adults, and periodic ophthalmia (probably immunological).

Disease	Organism	Frequency	Age group	Comments
Brucellosis	*Brucella abortus*	Infrequent	Adult	Musculoskeletal problems; serological evidence in certain lamenesses: may be involved with other bacteria in fistulous withers. Contact with infected cattle.
Tuberculosis	*Mycobacterium bovis* *Mycobacterium avium*	Very rare	Mature	Multisystem: infection of the cervical vertebrae, internal abscesses, chronic wasting; possible association with inflammatory bowel disease.
Anthrax Glanders	*Bacillus anthracis* *Pseudomonas mallei*	Extremely rare Notifiable Eradicated	Mature	Septicaemia; sudden death.
Contagious equine metritis (CEM)	*Taylorella equigenitalis*	Notifiable Sporadic recovery of organism	Breeding females; mares and fillies	Venereal disease; genital discharge, mares return to heat; stallions not affected. Therapy effective, sexual rest. Control: improved stud hygiene.
Klebsiella metritis	*Klebsiella pneumoniae* Capsule types 1 and 5	Occasional case or outbreak	Breeding mares	Venereal disease: mares affected, may infect accessory glands of stallion. Specific antibiotic therapy.
Pseudomonas metritis	*Pseudomonas aeruginosa*	Can become endemic	Breeding mares; newly introduced, aged mares – prior fertility problems	Venereal disease: depressed fertility, can be difficult to eliminate with treatment. Clitoral infection – removal or sinusectomy. Overzealous antiseptic or antibiotic washing of stallion's penis.

under the jaw is not definitive for strangles, and can be a feature of many viral respiratory diseases, particularly EHV-1 (rhinopneumonitis) infection in foals and young horses (see p. 425).

Treatment

Nursing care is important. The nostrils should be cleaned, hot pads applied to the swellings, and soft, easily swallowed feed provided. Strict hygienic measures should be adopted as the organism can be transmitted on hands and clothes. Antibiotics are used in severe cases and particularly when bastard strangles is suspected. Penicillin is the drug of choice. Antibiotics are not indicated when mature abscesses are close to rupture or ready to be lanced. Tracheostomy may be required to alleviate acute respiratory distress.

Preventive measures

The organism can be shed from draining abscesses for up to four weeks and can remain viable in the environment for another month or longer. Contamination is a problem unless isolation measures are implemented. Ideally, in-contact animals should be quarantined and observed for clinical signs. Antibiotic therapy may be justified. A vaccine (cell free M protein) is available in some countries but not in the UK. Unfortunately the immunity conferred is not long-lasting, although the incidence and severity of the disease may be reduced in the face of an outbreak.

CLOSTRIDIUM TETANI (TETANUS, LOCKJAW)

Tetanus is a highly fatal infectious disease of all domestic animals produced by the toxin of *Clostridium tetani*. It is characterized by hypersensitivity to noise or touch, provoking painful (tetanic) muscular spasms and progressive muscle stiffness. Horses are the most susceptible species. The organism enters through puncture wounds, the umbilicus in the newborn foal, or via the alimentary tract where it is a normal inhabitant. A puncture wound in the foot is a common portal of entry. The bacterium is unable to survive in normal tissue and devitalized (damaged) tissue is a prerequisite for development of tetanus. The organism is ubiquitous in the soil.

Clinical signs

The incubation period varies between one and three weeks, although it can be much longer. There is a general increase in muscle stiffness, accompanied by spasms and paralysis of the voluntary muscles. Jaw movement is restricted (hence lockjaw). All four limbs are stiff and the animal may adopt a 'saw-horse' posture with the tail held out stiffly behind. The third eyelid is prolapsed (across the medial half of the eye), and the expression is anxious and alert due to pricking of the ears, eyelid retraction and nostril dilation. Responses to stimuli are exaggerated.

Initially the animal may continue to eat and drink but spasm of the muscles of mastication and swallowing make this more difficult. Saliva drools from the mouth, and water or food may be regurgitated from the nostrils. Signs are progressive and tetany increases. Eventually the animal may fall down and be unable to rise. The head is drawn back and the limbs are held in extension. Sweating can be profuse and the body temperature rises. Spontaneous convulsions may occur and death follows respiratory arrest. The disease may progress over ten days and can end fatally, although mild cases may recover over a period of weeks or months. Diagnosis is based on the classic clinical signs and history.

Treatment

Therapy should be directed at preventing further toxin absorption by aggressive wound care (if this can be located), neutralizing circulating toxin, control of muscle spasms and supportive care. Administration of tetanus antitoxin will not reverse clinical signs. It is unable to cross the blood–brain barrier or penetrate nervous tissue to combine with toxin already in transit to the central nervous system. The purpose is to neutralize circulating toxin outside the nervous system. Some success has been claimed for injecting antitoxin into the fluid space around the spinal cord and brain stem.

High doses of penicillin should be administered. The animal should be kept in a quiet, dark environment. Hyperexcitability, muscle spasms and convulsions may be controlled by tranquillizers, sedatives and/or muscle relaxants. Attention to feed and water intake is vital. A recumbent animal has a poor prognosis.

Preventive measures

Tetanus can be prevented by vaccination. Toxoid, a converted form of toxin with immune stimulating properties, is administered intramuscularly in two doses four to six weeks apart, followed by revaccination after one year, and subsequently every one to three years. Previously immunized mares should receive a booster one month before foaling to ensure colostral antibody protection against tetanus in the newborn foal. The foal should then be inoculated with tetanus toxoid at approximately two, three and six months of age and boosted after one year. If the vaccination history of a horse which has been injured or had surgery is unknown or nonexistent, tetanus antitoxin should be administered together with the toxoid at a separate site. Subsequent vaccinations should follow the established schedule.

CLOSTRIDIUM BOTULINUM (BOTULISM, FORAGE POISONING, SHAKER FOAL SYNDROME)

Botulism is caused by the toxin of *Clostridium botulinum*. Horses are among the most susceptible species. The toxin may be produced in food, such as silage or vacuum-packed moist hay, which has been contaminated by decaying matter containing the organism.

Clostridium botulinum is a spore-forming anaerobic bacterium which reproduces in decaying animal or plant matter. Under favourable conditions of warmth and humidity spores multiply and produce a highly lethal toxin. There are at least five different toxin types: A, B, C, D and E. Ingestion of the preformed toxin is the major route of infection in adults. The foal disorder is believed to result from ingestion of spores which vegetate and produce toxin within the alimentary tract.

Clinical signs

The rapidity of onset, in addition to the severity of clinical signs, is toxin-dose related. Affected foals usually are less than eight months and often less than two months old. Presenting signs include impaired suckling, inability to swallow, decreased eyelid and tail tone and dilated pupils. There is progressive muscular weakness and tremors, leading to collapse, recumbency and an inability to rise. Adults may exhibit mild motor weakness to nearly total paralysis of the entire voluntary and much of the involuntary musculature. Muscle tremors over the shoulders and flanks are evident after exertion. Tongue tone, mastication and swallowing are all affected. Saliva drools from the mouth. The gait is weak, shuffling and unsteady. The animal may fall and have difficulty rising. Death results from respiratory paralysis.

Treatment

The availability of polyvalent equine antitoxin in the USA has improved the prognosis for survival, particularly if the condition is recognized in the early stages. Optimal nursing care and nutrition are critical. Recumbency carries a poor prognosis. Parenteral but not oral antibiotic therapy may be advantageous.

Preventive measures

Despite the availability of a vaccine, it is rarely used owing to the sporadic nature of the disease. Feed subjected to fermentation processes such as silage or exposed to damp, moist, warm conditions should be avoided.

RHODOCOCCUS (CORYNEBACTERIUM) EQUI (SUMMER PNEUMONIA, RATTLES)

This condition usually affects foals aged two to six months. The respiratory problem is the most common disorder although there may be alimentary tract involvement to a greater or lesser extent. Abscesses form in the lungs accompanied by progressive signs of pneumonia. Abscesses in the abdominal lymph nodes, together with invasion of the large bowel lining producing deeply fissuring ulcers are associated with signs of abdominal pain and/or diarrhoea.

Rhodococcus equi gains entry to the body through inhalation or ingestion. The disease appears in most countries and is endemic in certain regions of the USA and Australia. In the UK it is sporadic and usually affects only a single animal, although it can be a problem on some farms. Occasionally adult horses are affected.

Clinical signs

The condition is insidious. Foals rarely show definitive signs until abscesses and attendant bronchopneumonia are well established. Signs include rapid and laboured breathing, cough, nasal discharge, a persistent, slightly elevated temperature, poor appetite and weight loss as the disease progresses. Loud, moist rales or rattles may be audible with a stethoscope as respiratory embarrassment increases. Diagnosis can be difficult especially in an isolated case. The organism can be cultured from washings obtained from the trachea or, in fatal cases, from post-mortem samples of lung, lymph node or bowel. If available, radiography or ultrasound scanning can be used to identify lung abscesses. The prognosis is grave in cases with multiple lung abscesses and particularly with abdominal involvement.

Treatment

R. equi is an intracellular organism which provokes an inflammatory reaction characterized by thick-walled abscesses containing caseous (cheese-like) pus. Treatment is difficult. The organism is sensitive to several antibiotics in the laboratory, but achieving high enough concentrations in abscesses within diseased tissues is a problem. Antibiotic penetration into cells and through thick, fibrous tissue is vital. A combination of erythromycin and rifampin, an anti-leprosy agent, has proved successful in some cases. Such therapy should be aggressive, may need to be maintained for a prolonged period and is expensive.

Preventive measures

R. equi is a ubiquitous organism found wherever horses are kept. Thus isolation of the bacterium from faeces is not indicative of infection. Specific factors which may precipitate the disease on some studs are not clearly understood. A dry, dusty atmosphere may be important, is difficult to moderate, and may explain the extremely low incidence in the UK. There is no vaccine.

SALMONELLOSIS

Salmonellosis is a comon cause of acute enterocolitis and diarrhoea in the horse. However, equine diarrhoea is a multifactorial problem and *Salmonella* infection accounts for relatively few cases. Horses of all ages and under all conditions of management may be affected although the young, old and debilitated are the most susceptible. There are over 2000 *Salmonella* serotypes, not all of which are pathogenic for animals. A small number have been isolated from horses, and *Salmonella typhimurium* is by far the most common serotype identified from clinical disease.

Salmonella infection in horses is manifest as a variety of clinical syndromes. These range from acute diarrhoea in young horses; a peracute shock-like condition often without diarrhoea; mild to severe abdominal pain mimicking colic episodes where diarrhoea may or may not develop; protracted diarrhoea; to septicaemia in very young foals and enteric disease in older foals.

Equine salmonellosis is commonly associated with stressful conditions such as transport, exhaustion, general anaesthesia, surgery, antibiotic or deworming medication, changes in feed or management and weaning. These events may precipitate changes in food intake, intestinal motility and in the normal intestinal microbial flora allowing overgrowths of opportunistic *Salmonella* which are present in the intestinal tract of many healthy horses. The development of disease depends on the immune status of the host, the serotype involved, the challenge dose and the presence and nature of inciting factors. Furthermore, specific epidemiological features must be implicated as salmonellosis is much less of a problem in the UK than it is in the USA.

Clinical signs

Acute diarrhoea can occur at any age but is most prevalent in young performance horses. Presenting signs include fever, depression, abdominal pain and dark red mucous membranes. Diarrhoea, which may not appear for two to four days, is watery, projectile, foul-smelling, and may persist for up to four weeks despite therapy. The peracute shock-like syndrome is more likely to occur in adult horses. Death can ensue six to twelve hours after the first appearance of abdominal signs. Very young foals may develop an acute generalized infection (septicaemia). Older foals may have severe enteritis followed by localization of the organism in joints, the growth region of bones, the lungs, kidneys or central nervous system. Chronic diarrhoea is rarely attributed to *Salmonella* infection but can represent the recovery phase after an acute episode.

Those cases presenting with mild to severe abdominal pain can be confused with an impaction colic or even an acute abdominal crisis. Diarrhoea may not be evident for several hours. However, the horse is depressed and may have a fever. If laboratory facilities are available, the white blood cell count will be found to be reduced markedly. This is a feature of other forms of salmonellosis. Complications arising from the types of clinical syndrome encountered can include laminitis, thrombosed veins, liver and kidney failure, some of which can be reversed.

Confirmation of *Salmonella* infection depends upon isolating the organism from the faeces of affected animals. At least five consecutive faecal samples should be cultured as salmonellae are shed inconsistently even during the acute phase. In animals that have died the intestinal wall and the contents should be cultured. As many normal horses can shed salmonellae, isolation *per se* is not indicative of clinical disease. Selected blood and clinical chemistry tests can aid the diagnosis.

Treatment

The major objective in treating diarrhoeal disease in the horse (whatever the age) is to restore and maintain fluid and electrolyte balance. In the acute stage this may require administration of large volumes of fluid intravenously over twelve to twenty-four hours or longer. Plasma transfusions may even be indicated in very severe cases. If the animal's condition stabilizes, further fluids can be given orally by stomach tube or by allowing access to water containing electrolyte solutions (fresh water must be available). Normal faecal consistency will be restored in the vast majority of cases without recourse to other medications including antidiarrhoeal agents. Use of antibiotics is questionable in diarrhoeal disease attributable to *Salmonella*. Foals with septicaemia or the enteric disease should receive a course of intravenous antibiotics to counter seeding in other tissues. Oral antibiotics should not be used.

Preventive measures

Salmonellosis is a highly infectious disease, and the build-up of contamination in the environment of an affected horse can place susceptible in-contact animals at risk. Ideally, suspected or confirmed cases should be isolated, and strict hygiene and sanitation measures observed. Many serotypes including *Salmonella typhimurium* are pathogenic for humans. As some normal animals excrete the organism intermittently, screening of all animals potentially in contact at a stud or farm would be unsatisfactory (and expensive) as a control measure. Such positive shedders are not true carriers. The most effective prevention involves good management practices to reduce stressful situations and sanitation. Vaccination using a killed bacterium has not been successful.

Venereal Disease (VD)

A venereal disease is one that is sexually transmitted and may affect both males and females. In horses, apart from the herpesvirus disease equine coital exanthema, the stallion is usually a carrier of the causal organism while the mare exhibits clinical signs. Bacteria causing equine VD include *Taylorella equigenitalis*, certain strains of *Klebsiella pneumoniae* and *Pseudomonas aeruginosa*.

These organisms can induce disease in the mare's genital tract. *Taylorella equigenitalis* is a true venereal pathogen causing disease only in the genital tract, whereas *Klebsiella* and *Pseudomonas* can cause infection at other sites including joints, the respiratory tract, skin and wounds. Other bacteria such as *Streptococcus* and *Escherichia coli* may be transmitted sexually but do not assume the same clinical significance and are not considered to be venereal pathogens. Venereal diseases are usually transmitted at coitus but infection can be spread from mare to mare by contaminated speculae, other utensils, by the handlers or by veterinarians during examinations if strict hygiene is not practised.

TAYLORELLA EQUIGENITALIS (CONTAGIOUS EQUINE METRITIS, CEM, CEMO)

CEM is a highly infectious venereal disease of mares caused by *Taylorella equigenitalis* (formerly *Haemophilus equigenitalis*) first identified following an epidemic of metritis (uterine infection) in the mid 1970s. The bacterium had not been recognized previously. The organism is carried on the external genitalia of stallions and transmitted at mating to mares, most of which are highly susceptible. The disease is self-limiting and usually clears with sexual rest after about three months. Some individuals may take longer to recover and require treatment, and others remain as carriers (harbouring the organism but showing no symptoms) for years. Colt foals born to infected mares may be carriers (the organism residing on the sheath and penis) until bred and thus are capable of starting an epidemic by infecting mares during mating.

Clinical signs

As with most uterine infections, irrespective of the cause, there is genital inflammation, vaginal discharge and lowered fertility. The exudate is seen at the vulval lips and on the hairs of the tail, buttocks and the inside of the hocks. Affected mares may return to heat unexpectedly, often with shortened interheat periods, but usually breed successfully once the infection has been eliminated. Stallions do not exhibit clinical signs. Diagnosis is made on culturing the organism from swabs taken from the mare's genital tract or from the penis and sheath of the stallion.

Treatment

Most cases appear to resolve spontaneously without treatment. However, infection appears to persist longer in older mares and recently foaled mares. Infected mares may be treated with antibiotics (especially penicillin and synthetic penicillins) by intrauterine infusion and/or intramuscular injection over a seven to ten day period.

In a small proportion of cases unresponsive to therapy, the organism has been found to persist in smegma in the clitoral sinuses. Although the clitoris and sinuses can be cleansed by antibiotics or disinfectant washes, complete elimination of the organism is not always possible. Surgical procedures to remove the sinuses of the clitoris have been developed to overcome the problem. The operation may be required if brood mares or fillies at stud are exported to the USA. Apart from this, surgery is rarely performed in the UK. Washing the sheath and penis of stallions with disinfectants and applying antibiotic cream over a prescribed period will eliminate the presence of the organism. The stallion is not returned to breeding until several sets of swabs have been taken over a set time period and are clean.

Preventive measures

Efforts by veterinarians and the Thoroughbred industry in the major horse-breeding countries culminated in control of this disease. A code of practice for the control of CEM has been in operation since 1976 and has been acceded to in France, Ireland and the UK for most of that time. The organism is rarely isolated from horses in the UK, where the disease is notifiable.

30
DISEASES CAUSED BY VIRUSES

Viruses usually cause specific diseases such as influenza. Unfortunately the diagnosis of viral disease is complicated in practice because there may be evidence of the presence of a virus but no symptoms. Further, viruses may affect the body in an almost symptomless way and be followed by a bacterial infection which develops as a direct result of the virus, as, for example, when young horses are affected by one of a variety of viruses (herpes-, rhino- or picornavirus) and subsequently develop a cough or catarrhal nasal discharge (snotty nose). The following viral diseases are therefore described from the clinical viewpoint, that is, based on the typical symptoms displayed in each case.

EQUINE INFLUENZA (FLU)

This is a highly infectious disease associated with high fever and a severe dry cough which lasts one or two weeks.

Symptoms

A harsh dry cough is the particular feature, spreading rapidly to most if not all individuals in a stabled population if unvaccinated. High fever, inappetence and depression are features at the height of the illness, which usually lasts for one to two weeks, although some individuals may suffer for a longer time. A watery discharge from the nose may be present and, in some cases, this may become thick and pus-like, although this is not a common consequence of influenza as it is in herpesvirus infection (see p. 425). There may be stiffness of gait and constipation.

Most cases recover completely, but complications of pneumonia, pleurisy and/or damage to heart muscle sometimes occur, especially if precautions to minimize the effects of the disease are not taken (see below).

Foals, particularly those aged one to five months, may be severely affected by a typical pneumonia causing proliferation of cells and restriction of air spaces. This condition is seen usually when a strain of the virus challenges a population which has hitherto not been exposed to this particular type.

For example, when the Miami strain of the virus appeared in the UK in the 1960s, the population of horses had not had previous exposure to the strain and mares and foals on studfarms were affected by an epidemic. A number of foals died of pneumonia at this time, but a similar happening has not occurred since then partly due to the absence of a completely new strain causing a similar episode and partly because most animals are now vaccinated.

Treatment

There is no direct means of combatting the virus by drugs, although anti-influenza compounds are available for use in humans. However, these have not been used extensively in horses and expense does not justify such therapy, especially because protection by vaccines is practical.

The most important contribution to recovery of affected cases is the provision of fresh air and rest. The avoidance of dust helps to minimize the risks of bacterial infections of the upper airways and lungs following a bout of flu. An affected horse should be confined to a loosebox and walked for short periods in order to maintain proper circulation of blood and lymph through the limbs. This approach should be adopted for at least the period of fever and coughing, followed by a period of gradually increasing exercise, rather than a sudden return to fast or strenuous work.

Preventive measures

Vaccines containing killed whole subtypes of the virus are available to protect against both types (1 and 2) of influenza infection in horses. Although there may be some variation in recommendations between manufacturers in the use of their particular product, the basic programme of use is an initial injection, followed by a booster at about four to six weeks and a further booster at six months, followed by annual injections. This type of programme serves to protect horses absolutely or to a large degree and thus prevent epidemics.

In racing establishments vaccination programmes should start when foals are aged about three months. However, programmes should take account of Jockey Club Rules and be arranged so that annual boosters are not required during the flat racing season from March to December. The Rules are as follows:

Rule 35

(i) No horse shall enter property owned, used or controlled by the Managing Executive of a racecourse unless it is certified by a veterinary surgeon to be correctly vaccinated against equine influenza in accordance with the general requirements of Sub-Rule (ii) and (iii) of this Rule, but this Rule will not apply to horses crossing land used or controlled by the

Managing Executive where such land is common ground or is subject to statutory rights for public access for air and exercise, or to any foal which is less than three months old and whose dam was, prior to foaling, vaccinated in accordance with the general requirements of Sub-Rule (ii) or (iii) of this Rule.

(ii) No horse for which a passport has been issued shall enter property owned, used or controlled by the Managing Executive of a racecourse unless the vaccination section of its passport is endorsed by a veterinary surgeon who is neither the owner or trainer of the horse, nor a person whose name is included in the Register of Stable Employees as being employed by the trainer of the horse at that time or by a recognised Turf Authority, that it has received two injections for primary vaccination given no less than 21 days apart and no more than 92 days apart. In addition, where sufficient time has elapsed subsequent to the primary vaccination the passport must be similarly endorsed to show that:—

(a) A horse foaled on or after January 1st, 1980 has received a first booster injection given no less than 150 days and no more than 215 days after the second injection of the primary vaccination, and

(b) A horse has received booster injections at intervals of not more than a year apart (commencing after the second injection of the primary vaccination or the booster injection required under (a) above) or such lesser time as the Stewards of the Jockey Club may, in an emergency, decide, except that for horses foaled before January 1st 1980, the intervals between booster injections given before March 16th, 1981, may have been not more than 14 months

and that none of these injections has been given within the previous ten days including the day of entry into racecourse property.

(iii) In the case of horses trained in countries where passports are not issued vaccination certificates may be accepted, provided that the horse is correctly identified and that the certificates have been signed by a veterinary surgeon, who is neither the owner or trainer of the horse nor a person whose name is included in the Register of Stable Employees as being employed by the trainer of the horse at that time, stating that it has received the vaccinations required under Sub-Rule (ii) of this Rule.

Rule 36

Except in those cases where Sub-Rule 35 (i) does not apply, the trainer or the owner of any horse which enters property owned, used or controlled by the Managing Executive of a racecourse when that horse has not been vaccinated as required under Rule 35 or the passport for which is not endorsed as required under Rule 35 (ii) or the passport is not available for inspection as required under Rule 35 (ii) shall be guilty of an offence.

EQUID HERPESVIRUS 1 (EHV-1) (SNOTTY NOSE, STABLE COUGH, VIRUS ABORTION, RHINOPNEUMONITIS)

Herpesvirus causes respiratory infection and is an incidental cause of abortion in pregnant mares, the abortion characteristically occurring between seven months and full term. In horses under the age of two years herpesvirus infections are characterized by catarrh or nasal discharge (snotty or dirty nose) and an intermittent cough infrequently associated with fever. In older individuals a mild watery nasal discharge may be the only sign of infection.

Cause

Equid herpesvirus 1 (EHV-1) has two subtypes (strains); subtype 1, the abortive strains; and subtype 2, the respiratory strain. Both types are essentially infections of the respiratory system, causing bronchilitis and inflammation of the lungs (pneumonitis); the passage of the virus into the foetus, thereby causing abortion, is a comparatively infrequent happening and the virus cannot be considered to be primarily of an aborting nature. However, the subtype 1 abortion strain appears to have a special ability to cross the placenta and affect the foetus, whereas the respiratory strain rarely has this capacity.

Paralysis of the hind limbs and sometimes the front limbs is another incidental form of infection with subtype 1, affecting horses of all ages, but is less common than the abortion form

Symptoms

EHV-1, subtype 1, abortive strain The abortion form of the disease starts with the virus being inhaled, entering the body of the mare and crossing from the uterus and placenta into the body of the foetus. Here it causes death with characteristic signs of damage (lesions) in the liver, lungs and other organs of the foetal foal. As the foetus becomes ill and dies, the mare expels the contents of the uterus (i.e. her foetus and its membranes) in a sudden, unheralded event.

The incubation period between infection of the mare and abortion is very variable. It may be as little as seven days or as much as a hundred days. The explanation for this variation is unknown although it may depend on the immune status of the mare and the stage of pregnancy when the virus enters her body.

For a fuller description of the disease, see p. 339.

The foetus and foetal fluids are heavily contaminated with virus and are a source of infection to in-contact animals, unless removed quickly and the local environment disinfected.

Depending on the time of the initial infection, a mare may remain infectious for several weeks after the abortion, shedding virus from the respiratory tract or harbouring virus in the blood.

There is no effective treatment. Control of the infection must be based on sensible management practices and vaccination. An inactivated vaccine (Pneumabort K) for use in the prevention of abortion is available.

Pregnant mares should be vaccinated in the fifth, seventh and ninth months of pregnancy, and it is recommended that young stock on studfarms should also be vaccinated because they are a potential source of infection. Although vaccination may not protect the individual from abortion, it reduces the amount of virus shed if an animal does become infected and thereby reduces the spread of the infection and the likelihood of abortion storms occurring.

EHV-1, subtype 2, respiratory strain   A watery discharge from the nose starts about three days after infection. It may cause a sore tract to appear at the junction of the nose and muzzle where the nasal discharge runs over the area. At this stage the affected individual may suffer a slight fever and an occasional cough. After about a week a secondary bacterial infection occurs and the nasal discharge becomes pus-like (purulent), the cough may increase and pneumonic signs develop (i.e. increased rate and effort of breathing). Rales and moist crackling sounds may be heard on listening to the lungs through a stethoscope.

Pharyngitis develops and an increase in the lymphoid (tonsular) tissue in the pharynx may be seen by means of an endoscope. These symptoms (lymphoid hyperplasia) are particularly prevalent in horses of two years old or less.

Diagnosis can be achieved only by recovering the virus in material collected from the windpipe or pharynx during the early stages of the disease. Once the secondary infection has developed it is probable that the virus can no longer be obtained by these means.

Confirmation of the disease can be made by serological tests on blood serum. This consists of measuring antibody levels (titres) at the onset of the symptoms (acute phase) and again two to three weeks later (convalescent phase). A fourfold increase or more in antibody levels indicates that the individual has been challenged by the virus.

It is possible by both these means of diagnosis (growth of virus and serology) to establish whether the infection is caused by subtype 1 or subtype 2 of the virus.

Course of condition

Affected horses show symptoms to a greater or lesser extent according to the age of and the degree of immunity possessed by the particular individual. Immunity is short-lived, so repeated attacks may occur, although the older the animal the less likely that severe secondary infection occurs.

A four-year-old or older animal will probably only present the initial signs of increased nasal watery discharge rather than suffering the snotty-nose condition. However, younger individuals may suffer the secondary effects for weeks or months following an initial infection.

The infection may be *latent* (i.e. no symptoms) for long periods and subsequently episodes of symptoms occur following stress or other precipitating factors many of which are as yet poorly understood.

Treatment

The principles for treatment and management of virus respiratory infections outlined under equine influenza also apply for equid herpesvirus 1 infection (see above).

Preventive measures

Vaccination against equid herpesvirus 1 is undertaken principally to prevent the potentially large economic loss due to abortion in mares. The value of vaccines in the prevention of respiratory infections is not fully known and booster vaccinations may be required at three to six monthly intervals in order to maintain effective immunity against the disease. On account of this many vets doubt the value of vaccination against EHV–1 infection other than in pregnant mares. It is best to discuss this with your own vet, who will advise you according to the horse's age, the type of work for which it is required and the risk of infection.

HIND LIMB INCOORDINATION AND PARALYSIS

The paralytic form of this disease is capricious in onset. It is not clear why some individuals suffer this debilitating condition whereas most do not. However, the paralytic form often occurs in several individuals, but as yet it has not been shown that there is a subtype which has a special attraction for the nervous system. Current opinion is that the nervous form is due to the virus (EHV–1, subtype 1) indirectly affecting the blood vessels supplying nervous tissue, possibly as the result of some immunological or allergic response of the individual.

Symptoms include loss of coordination and paralysis of the hind limbs (sometimes also of the forelimbs). Incontinence (failure to hold urine in the bladder) may be a feature. Cases of the paralytic form show symptoms similar to horses which have broken backs or suffered other major skeletal injuries (see chapter 18).

Recovery occurs providing sufficient time is given and the paralysis is not such as to leave the individual unable to get to its feet or otherwise so disadvantaged that survival is virtually impossible.

Treatment

Injection of corticosteroids and supportive measures, such as suspending an individual in a sling or supporting it with straw bales in the standing position to avoid the risk of its lying down and being unable to get to its feet.

EQUID HERPESVIRUS 3 (EHV-3) (COITAL EXANTHEMA, SPOTS)

This venereal disease is characterized by small blisters which develop on the vulva of mares and penis of stallions and break to form small deep ulcers. It is caused by equid herpesvirus 3, a virus distinct from equid herpesvirus 1 (see above).

Symptoms

The vesicles (blisters) are not usually visible before they burst, and the first symptoms seen are the ulcers, with their distinctive circular outline and craters varying up to about 0.5 cm in diameter. In the mare the ulcers occur on the vulval lips and sometimes on the vulva itself.

In the stallion the ulcers may occur on any part of the penis. Usually the infection can be identified on both the stallion and one or more of the mares with which he has mated during the previous ten days.

However, the condition can occur in mares without any recent history of mating. It seems that mares may be infected either by the virus remaining dormant in the body for long periods until activated by some unknown trigger or that infection occurs through ingestion or inhalation without any sexual contact.

Treatment

Treatment is not really necessary, although mild antiseptic lotions or cortisone and antibiotic ointments may be applied. Healing of the ulcers takes about ten days and mares and stallions are not usually infectious after a lapse of about two weeks. Sexual rest is therefore important because, if mating is continued, the ulcers may fail to heal and become wider and deeper and fresh crops of blisters and ulcers develop.

EQUINE ARTERITIS (PINKEYE)

This disease is caused by a togavirus which can be transmitted via the respiratory tract, by venereal contact or by contamination with infected urine. The virus may be present in blood and in the semen of stallions.

Symptoms

An incubation period of about six days is followed by fever, watery nasal discharge, which may become pus-like, accompanied by redness of the eyes and oedema of the eyelids and the dependent parts of the body. There may be loss of appetite, depression, conjunctivitis (runny eyes) and swelling of the limbs, sheath and scrotum.

A cough and difficulty in breathing may develop, although the severity of the symptoms varies with the strain of virus involved and the resistance of the particular population of horses affected. In the USA the disease is present in Standardbreds without severe symptoms, whereas in the 1984 outbreak among Thoroughbreds in that country symptoms were more severe.

Virulent strains of the virus can cause heavy losses in breeding establishments, and abortion rates of 50–80 per cent have been recorded in some outbreaks. Both the illness of the mare and the infection of the foetus may contribute to the abortion.

It has been proposed there are virulent and avirulent strains of the virus because some populations of horses which have no history of disease have evidence of infection (from blood serum tests).

If the virus is found on a breeding establishment, all mating should cease immediately. If stallions are infected, they may become persistent shedders and excrete the virus in their semen, passing on the infection to mated mares. A live attenuated vaccine has been used in the USA in areas where the infection has been active. The vaccine is not licensed for use in the UK.

EQUINE RHINOVIRUS 1 (ERV-1, COLD VIRUS)

ERV-1 can cause upper respiratory tract disease, characterized by an increase in temperature (pyrexia), copious nasal discharge and enlarged submaxillary lymph glands. It can also infect individuals without causing any overt clinical signs of disease. Infection normally results in long-term immunity.

OTHER EQUINE PICORNAVIRUSES (COLD VIRUSES)

Equine rhinovirus 2 and 3 and acid stable picornavirus have occasionally been recovered from cases of mild respiratory disease but are generally regarded as apathogenic. Picornaviruses can often be recovered from the oral cavity of apparently healthy horses.

There are no vaccines available for prevention of equine picornavirus infections.

ADENOVIRUS (COLD VIRUS)

Adenovirus has been recovered from the respiratory tract of horses affected by mild respiratory disease. Soft faeces are sometimes a characteristic of adenovirus infections. This virus is generally regarded as apathogenic except in Arab foals with combined immunodeficiency disease (see p. 625). In these individuals the virus produces a generalized infection which alone or in association with other micro-organisms leads to death.

EQUINE INFECTIOUS ANAEMIA (SWAMP FEVER)

Cause

The virus is present in the blood and is transmitted from an affected to a non-infected individual by way of insect bites or by the use of contaminated hypodermic needles or other implements with which blood may be involved, for example, tooth rasps. The virus may also be transmitted from a mare to her foal in milk, and under certain conditions ingestion of the virus may be responsible for spread of infection.

Symptoms

Symptoms include fever, which may be constant or intermittent, anaemia accompanied by depression, profound weakness to the point of inco-ordination and marked loss of condition. Fever rises and falls precipitately and may vary considerably within the space of an hour. Jaundice and soft swellings of the abdomen, prepuce (in colts and geldings) and legs develop, and there are small pinhead-sized haemorrhages on the lining of the tongue and on the mucous membrane of the nose.

Symptoms vary in intensity and there may be periods of remission when the individual appears quite healthy. A definitive diagnosis is made using a blood test named after Dr Coggins.

No specific treatment is available, although supportive measures, including blood transfusions and iron therapy, may be used. In the UK the disease is notifiable and, apart from an outbreak in the 1970s, the condition is not known to be present here. The disease is found in certain areas of the USA, Canada, France, West Germany and South America, as well as in numerous other countries.

Preventive measures

Use of the Coggins blood test to identify affected individuals and carriers of the virus enables measures of control to be introduced whereby healthy horses are segregated from indirect contact with affected individuals.

Because the chief means of spread is through biting flies, the spread of the disease is seasonal, and measures to reduce the fly population may help. However, the optimal means of eradication of the disease is the slaughter of affected animals or confining them to premises at some distance from unaffected horses. The greater the seasonal or climatic risk of biting flies being present, the greater the distance that must be introduced between healthy and affected animals.

VIRAL ENCEPHALOMYELITIS (EASTERN, WESTERN AND VENEZUELAN ENCEPHALOMYELITIS – EE, WE AND VE)

An infectious disease affecting horses and communicable to man and characterized by symptoms of paralysis, incoordination and loss of consciousness.

Cause

The disease is caused by an arbovirus, of which three strains are known, Eastern, Western and Venezuelan. These are distinct and vary in their ability to cause disease, although the symptoms are similar with all three viruses.

Symptoms

The disease is restricted mainly to North and South America. The incubation period is one to three weeks. Initially there is fever accompanied by loss of appetite and depression. However, the reaction may be so mild that it goes unobserved. Nervous signs develop later and include exaggerated response to sound and touch, and transient periods of excitement and restlessness with apparent blindness.

An affected individual may stand with the head low and appear to be asleep, perhaps with a half-chewed mouthful of food hanging from the lips. This dummy-like effect is illustrated by the reaction of some individuals if food is placed in their mouth but not otherwise.

Paralysis follows these initial symptoms. There is an inability to hold up the head, the lower lip becomes pendulous and the tongue may hang out. Unnatural postures are adopted, such as standing with the weight balanced on the forelegs and with the legs crossed. Head pressing or leaning back on the halter is often seen.

The course of the condition is progressive and affected horses do not recover, usually becoming recumbent and completely paralysed before death ensues.

Treatment

There is no specific treatment although supportive measures may be undertaken to enable the affected individual to survive sufficiently long for recovery to take place.

Preventive measures

Control is based on a programme of identifying and destroying or segregating affected individuals, taking steps to avoid contact with mosquitoes, which spread the virus.

Vaccination may be practised in areas where the disease is likely to occur. Vaccination should take place well before the anticipated season of infection occurs – the summer months. Two doses of vaccine are given ten days apart, followed by annual revaccination, which is necessary because effective immunity in response to the vaccine does not appear to last beyond a year in all individuals.

ROTAVIRUS INFECTION

Rotavirus infection in young foals (four days to five months) causes diarrhoea. Infections are rarely lethal unless they occur in association with bacterial pathogens such as *Salmonella typhimurium* and toxinogenic strains of *Escherichia coli*.

The virus damages the lining of the intestinal tract. The villi (minute folds) on the surface of the lining become damaged, sometimes irrevocably. Thus a foal which has suffered from rotavirus may fail to absorb nutrients satisfactorily, a problem which may sometimes last for the rest of the individual's life.

In severe cases affected foals go off suck and develop a profuse diarrhoea. They become depressed, lose condition and experience temperatures up to 41°C (105°F). Duration of diarrhoea can vary between two and twelve days.

Rotavirus can be detected in scours shortly after the onset of the disease and occasionally has been detected in the faeces of healthy individuals, indicating that the inapparent-carrier state exists and is likely to be important in the spread of this infection. There are no vaccines available for foal rotavirus although products have been developed for use in calves.

RABIES

A highly fatal viral infection of the central nervous system affecting all warm-blooded animals and transmitted by bites from affected individuals.

Cause

A rhabdovirus which has an affinity for nerve cells. However, it is susceptible to most standard disinfectants and is killed in dried saliva in a few hours.

Symptoms

Horses show excitement and mania. Their uncontrolled actions may be violent and include galloping blindly, sudden falling and rolling. They may chew at their skin. Death usually ensues within days.

The disease is notifiable but it occurs infrequently in horses even in countries where the disease is prevalent. The disease is not present in the UK or Eire. If cases occurred, they would be destroyed on humane grounds and to prevent serious risks to man and other animals.

31
DISEASES CAUSED BY PROTOZOA

A number of different protozoa infect horses. Some of these are very important causes of disease in tropical and subtropical countries. On the whole they affect horses less in temperate countries. Although protozoa have a simple, single-celled structure, their life cycles can be exceedingly complex and can differ markedly from one species to the next.

BABESIA CABALLI, BABESIA EQUI (BABESIOSIS, BILIARY FEVER, PIROPLASMOSIS)

Both B. caballi and B. equi are parasites of the red blood cells in horses, causing babesiosis or biliary fever. The infection is widespread in Asia, the USSR, Southern Europe, Africa, the southern United States, Central and South America, and occasionally is seen in imported horses in other countries, such as Australia.

Life cycle

Ticks act as the intermediate host transmitting the *Babesia* parasites from one horse to another. The tick picks up the infection when it sucks blood. The *Babesia* then multiplies in the tissues of the tick as it develops on the ground to its next life-cycle stage. When in its next stage of development the tick feeds on a new horse, the *Babesia* move to the mouthparts and are injected into the horse. The *Babesia* parasites then infect and multiply in the red blood cells in the circulation of the horse.

In addition to *Babesia* being transmitted by ticks, a horse can become infected if it is injected with blood containing the *Babesia* parasites. It is very important, therefore, in areas where *Babesia* is common that the same needle is not used to inject different horses.

Clinical signs

Babesiosis can be quite severe in horses and 10 per cent or more of those infected may die. About ten to twenty days after the horse has become infected the first clinical signs are seen. Initially there is marked depression, with fever and loss of appetite. This is followed by a massive destruction of the red blood cells so that the horse becomes anaemic, showing very pale mucous membranes in the mouth and eyes. The mucous membranes later become yellow with jaundice. The urine may be stained red with the contents of red blood cells. The animal is constipated and passes very hard, small balls of faeces, which may be covered with yellow, sticky mucus. Colic may be seen. In some horses oedematous, fluid swelling of the head, legs, lower abdomen and chest occurs, and in a few cases the central nervous system is affected so there may be paralysis of the hind legs. Severely affected horses may die within one or two days of the onset of symptoms. The disease may also run a longer course lasting several weeks in which the horse rapidly loses condition; subsequent recovery can take months.

After the horse has recovered from the illness the parasite remains in its red blood cells, although at very low levels so that no illness is seen. The parasite may remain in the horse in this way for years and sometimes relapses occur, most commonly after some form of stress, such as travelling to shows or competing in three-day events, etc.

Diagnosis

The infection is usually diagnosed on a smear of the horse's blood. When this smear is stained and examined microscopically in a laboratory the very small dark-stained, pear-shaped bodies of the *Babesia* parasites can be seen in the red blood cells. If the diagnosis is not made early in the course of the infection, only a few cells may contain *Babesia* and it may be necessary to examine the blood by serological tests in the laboratory. These tests indirectly demonstrate that the horse has been infected rather than directly demonstrate the presence of the parasite itself.

Treatment

One of the several different drugs available can be injected into horses to treat babesiosis. These include phenamidine, amicarbalide, imidicarb and pirevan. These drugs have some side effects and so must be used with care. To aid its recovery, an acutely ill animal may be given a blood transfusion to replace the red blood cells being destroyed by the parasite.

Preventive measures

It is very difficult to control infection with *Babesia* in horses. The possibility of transmission can be reduced by reducing the population of the tick intermediate hosts. Regular spraying or dipping in acaricide will reduce the number of ticks considerably but will not eliminate them. If the horses are stabled and groomed, then daily removal of the ticks ensures that they will not have been on the horse long enough either to pick up the infection from or to inject the *Babesia* parasites into the horse. Unfortunately the tick can transmit *Babesia* at all stages of its life cycle, and some of these, particularly the larvae, can be less than 1 mm long and attach anywhere on the body. It is unlikely that these ticks would be noticed. Nevertheless regular removal of all visible ticks will help reduce the overall incidence and hence the incidence of the *Babesia* parasites. It may be necessary for horses to be tested and declared free from *Babesia* before they can be imported into certain countries.

Trypanosomes

These leaf shaped protozoan parasites live in the plasma of horses and cause a variety of serious diseases – dourine, surra, mal de caderas, nagana. Most of these trypanosomes are transmitted from horse to horse by biting flies. *Trypanosoma equiperdum* (dourine), however, is a venereal disease transmitted at service.

TRYPANOSOMA EQUIPERDUM (DOURINE)

T. equiperdum occurs in Africa, Central and South America, the Middle East and parts of Asia. The first sign of dourine is a swelling of the genitalia two to four weeks or longer after a mare has been served by an infected stallion or vice versa. In the stallion the scrotum and sheath become filled with fluid and swollen, and the swelling may extend along the belly. In the mare the vulva becomes swollen and reddened, and there may be a discharge. This phase is followed by the appearance of circular areas of swelling, 2–10 cm in diameter, in the skin on the body. These are called 'dollar spots' as they often look as if a coin has been inserted under the skin. These appear, last a few hours to days, and then disappear, frequently to reappear. Dollar spots, however, are not seen in every infected horse. The final stage in the disease is the development of paralysis. The majority of the horses which show signs of dourine will die if untreated. There are some animals, however, in which the course of the disease will take several years or in which few signs of disease are ever seen.

Infected horses can be treated with injections of suramin or quinapyramine, but these drugs have side effects; also in some countries where dourine has been eradicated treatment is not allowed as it interferes with the eradication programmes. Horses may have to be tested and declared free from *T. equiperdum* before they can be imported into a number of countries.

TRYPANOSOMA EVANSI (SURRA)

T. evansi causes a highly fatal disease of horses in parts of Asia, North Africa and Central and South America. The organism is carried between horses by biting flies. The trypanosome contaminates the mouthparts of the fly as it sucks blood and is then carried to be injected into the next horse.

Surra is nearly always fatal to horses if left untreated, death occurring within a few days to months, depending on the severity of the infection. The affected horse may have a temperature, will lose weight very rapidly and develop fluid, oedematous swelling on the legs, belly, chest and neck. The drugs used for dourine can be used to treat surra.

TRYPANOSOMA EQUINUM (MAL DE CADERAS)

This trypanosome occurs in Central and South America and is also transmitted mechanically by biting flies. Again, if untreated, it will cause death in the majority of horses infected with it. Mal de caderas runs a much slower course than surra, with the horse dying within weeks up to as long as six months after infection. The horse has a temperature, and swellings followed by scabs form on the body. It will rapidly lose weight, becoming very weak and staggering, and eventually collapse.

TRYPANOSOMA BRUCEI, TRYPANOSOMA CONGOLENSE (NAGANA)

These cause nagana, which is an African word meaning 'to be in low or depressed spirits', in all types of animals, including horses. The infection is confined to tropical Africa, as the intermediate host, the tsetse fly, which is a required part of the life cycle for the development of the parasite, occurs only in Africa. The infections are severe in horses, with progressive loss of weight, fluid swelling of the lower part of the body, weakness, depression and sometimes nervous signs. The disease will last for a few weeks to months, until the horse dies.

SARCOCYSTIS FAYERI, SARCOCYSTIS BERTRAMI

The life cycle of these protozoa and the fact that they cause disease in horses has been discovered only recently by experimental studies. Now that the disease-causing potential of *Sarcocystis* has been demonstrated experimentally, cases of naturally occurring disease have been diagnosed. Since the parasite occurs in horses throughout the world, it is possible now that disease also may be seen in horses throughout the world. Nevertheless, while a large proportion of horses seem to be infected with *Sarcocystis*, in fact only a very few ever show any signs of disease and these perhaps may be very heavily infected animals.

The life cycle of *Sarcocystis* uses the dog as the definitive host, and the dog shows no signs of being infected but passes cysts in its faeces. When these cysts are eaten by horses the parasite multiplies in a number of organs, including the brain and spinal cord. At this point signs of neurological disease (trembling, shaking of the head, staggering gait, etc.) may be seen in a few horses.

The *Sarcocystis* then moves to the muscles, where it multiplies slowly in white cysts. These, when eaten by dogs, complete the life cycle to infect the dogs. The infection is seen therefore only in dogs fed raw horsemeat. It is usually hounds (foxhounds and beagles) which pass the cysts in their faeces, and horses grazing land where hounds are exercised have the highest risk of infection.

As yet there are no tests available with which to make a diagnosis of *Sarcocystis* infection or to differentiate it from other neurological diseases caused by viruses and bacteria. Nor is there any effective treatment for infected horses.

BESNOITIA BENNETTI

This protozoan has been reported in the skin of horses in southern France, Africa and Central America. Over a period of months cysts, like those of *Sarcocystis*, develop in the skin. The skin becomes thickened, looks scurfy and loses its hair. Gradually the horse loses weight and becomes weak. Little more is known about this parasite, although it is assumed that, like *Sarcocystis*, it requires a wild or domestic carnivore to transmit the infection.

32

PARASITIC CONDITIONS

HELMINTHS

Helminths, the large class of parasitic worms, include the various forms of roundworms (nematodes), tapeworms (cestodes) and flukes (trematodes).

Nematodes (Roundworms)

Life cycle

The life cycles of the different nematodes have several similar features. The simplest life cycles are seen of nematodes which live in the gastrointestinal tract. In general, eggs are passed in the faeces of horses and then three life stages take place outside the host.

A first-stage larva develops inside the egg shell and then escapes by hatching. It develops in the manure to a second- and then a third-stage larva, and only this third-stage larva can infect horses, usually by ingestion with grass. All these stages are microscopic and not visible to the naked eye.

A variation with some nematodes is that the first-, second- and third-stage larvae all remain within the egg shell, and the horse becomes infected by eating the egg containing the infective larva. The infective larva then hatches from the egg inside the host. The advantage for the parasite is that, while in the egg shell, it is relatively protected from adverse environmental conditions so that the larva within the egg can remain alive for months and even years.

An additional variation is that these three life-cycle stages can take place within an intermediate host, i.e. within the bodies of flies. The third-stage larva is then eaten with the fly or injected through the skin of the horse by the fly.

When the infective larva has been eaten, two more life-cycle stages take place in the horse. The third-stage larva develops to the fourth stage, which

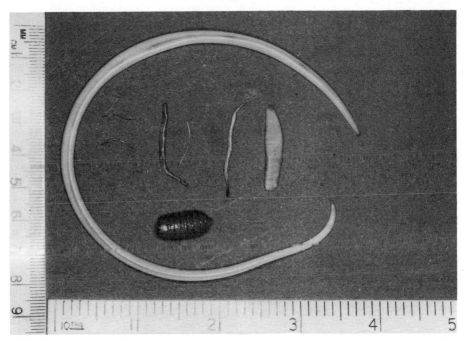

Figure 146   Parasitic worms

then becomes the fifth and final stage; these latter are the immature and then the sexually mature adult males and females.

Once in the host, the larvae of the gastro-intestinal nematodes may develop to adults without leaving the intestine, or they may penetrate through the intestinal wall and migrate quite extensively in the horse's body before they return to the intestine to develop into adults.

STRONGYLES

These are very important parasites of horses and are found in horses throughout the world. For ease of description they can be divided into two groups: the large strongyles, which are the *Strongylus* species (*S. vulgaris*, *S. edentatus*, *S. equinus*), adults of which are 1.5–4.5 cm long, and a large number of different species of small strongyles (i.e. *Cylicodontophorus*, *Cylicostephanus*, *Cylicocyclus*, *Cyathostomum* species), all 1–1.5 cm long in the adult stage. Both the large and small strongyles cause disease in horses but in different ways.

Life cycle on pasture

The life cycle of all the strongyles outside the horse is similar. Eggs are passed in the faeces of infected horses, and the greatest numbers of eggs are passed in the spring and autumn months. In warm, moist conditions the first-, second- and third-stage larvae develop in the manure. To infect horses the infective larvae must migrate from the manure out onto the grass so that they can be eaten. This migration occurs in wet, warm weather, particularly after rain. If the weather stays dry the larvae will remain in the manure where they are relatively protected from adverse conditions.

For the purposes of control of strongyle infections in horses, it is important to understand both the rate at which the parasites develop to the infective third stage and the ability of the free-living stages to survive on the grass. The development of the eggs to infective larvae requires a degree of moisture as well as temperatures of over 8°–10° C (46°–50° F) but under 35°–39° C (95°–102° F). The rate of development is slowest at the lower temperatures, taking several weeks, but once developed, the infective larvae can remain alive and available to infect horses for weeks or months. At the higher temperatures infective larvae develop in a few days, but they remain alive for only a few days in very hot weather. The parasites are killed by prolonged freezing, by very high temperatures, and by dry conditions.

Some examples of the development of the strongyles and the times of the year at which the horses are infected follow. In temperate climates such as Great Britain the most important factor in the infection of horses with strongyles is the increased number of eggs passed in the faeces of horses in the spring and the continued passage of eggs in early summer. As spring and summer progress the rate of development of these eggs to infective larvae increases, taking several weeks in the spring to a few days in midsummer. So large numbers of larvae are present from mid-July onwards, and after rain these larvae will migrate from the manure onto the grass to be eaten by horses. Where the summer is longer, as in the eastern USA, large numbers of larvae are present on the grass as early as June. These do not survive long in the heat of midsummer, but increased numbers will be present again in the autumn. In climates where the winters are less severe some development of parasites can occur throughout the year, but again most parasites will be present in early summer. In tropical climates rapid development will occur throughout the year, but this and the survival of larvae will depend on adequate rain. Very few or no larvae will survive the dry season.

Life cycle in the horse

When the large strongyle larvae are eaten, the immature stages migrate quite extensively in the horse's body before they return to the large intestine to mature to egg-laying adults. *S. vulgaris* larvae migrate through the intestinal wall and in the wall of the main artery supplying blood to the intestine, until they reach the junction of this artery and the aorta, the main artery in the body. Here the larvae remain for three to four months before they return to nodules in the wall of the large intestine, emerging six weeks later to mature to adults in the large intestine. The adult worms begin to lay eggs six months after the horse became infected. *S. edentatus* migrate in the liver and then the inner wall of the flank before they return to the intestine. *S. equinus* migrates in the liver, pancreas and abdominal cavity.

The life cycles of the small strongyles in horses are much simpler. When eaten these larvae migrate no farther than the wall of the large intestine. After about six weeks they break out of the wall of the intestine into the lumen and begin to lay eggs two to three months after infection. However, the small strongyles also can prolong the time they spend in the wall of the intestine, so that larvae eaten in the autumn do not emerge to become egg-laying adults until the following spring. In this way the small strongyles survive the adverse outside winter conditions by being inside the horse. The same probably is true in hot, tropical climates, where the larvae may prolong their development in the horse in the dry season and probably recommence their development when the rainy season begins.

Clinical signs

It is the immature stages of the large strongyles parasites that cause damage and disease while they are migrating in the body. The presence of *S. vulgaris* in the arteries causes damage and thickening of the arterial wall and clots within the artery. This can cause acute, severe colic and sometimes death, particularly in young animals, or depression and unthriftiness in less acute cases. The artery will heal considerably when the larvae leave a few months later but a degree of damage will always remain. Also the repeated infections that horses acquire over years of grazing in the field can produce permanent damage, with thickening and hardening of the arterial wall. This will cause intermittent bouts of colic, probably with some loss of weight. Repeated infections with *S. edentatus* and *S. equinus* can cause hardening of the liver, adhesions of the intestines to each other and to the abdominal wall, and clinical signs of colic and unthriftiness.

The small strongyles can cause disease when they are present in large numbers, either as the immature larval stages or as adult parasites. Very large numbers of the adult small strongyles present in the lumen of the intestine can cause soft or diarrhoeic faeces and loss of condition in animals of all ages, but particularly in foals and yearlings. This problem is seen mainly in late summer. The horses will have picked up large numbers of infective larvae from the pasture over the summer and all these are now present as adults causing damage to the intestinal wall.

Disease due to the immature larval stages of the small strongyles is seen particularly in the spring. At this time the infective larvae eaten the previous autumn, which had slowed their development and overwintered in the horse, emerge to continue development to adults. They all emerge simult-aneously from the wall of the large intestine and, if a very large number of worms are present, this massive emergence breaks down the intestinal wall. Young animals can be acutely ill with colic and severe diarrhoea, and sometimes the faeces comprise only blood. Less severely affected animals, usually the adult horses, may show a longer course of diarrhoea, loss of appetite and loss of weight.

Diagnosis

Heavy infections with adult small strongyles causing diarrhoea, loss of condition and even death in horses in the late summer and autumn can be diagnosed by counting the numbers of eggs in the faeces. The numbers of eggs present in the faeces relates to the number of adult worms producing eggs in the intestine, and a high faecal egg count will show the presence of sufficient worms to cause disease.

Unfortunately most of the clinical signs of the disease (colic, poor condition, diarrhoea, etc.) due to the large strongyles or in spring due to the small strongyles are caused by the immature stages migrating in the horse's body or emerging from the intestine. These worms are not yet laying eggs, and so a diagnosis cannot be made directly by a faecal egg count. Indeed, there is no certain method with which to diagnose these infections. However, two tests can be helpful aids to diagnosis if they are interpreted carefully. The first of these is faecal egg counts. Large numbers of eggs in the faeces will not directly demonstrate the presence of immature strongyles, but indirectly they show that the horse has been exposed to large numbers of parasites and may well be infected with the immature stages also. However, interpretation is important, since very low faecal egg counts may be seen in infected horses. The second type of test looks for high levels of certain blood constituents: eosinophils, globulins, IgG(T) (a class of immunoglobulins), etc. While the levels of these constituents will rise in horses infected with a number of other parasites, and while the levels will not necessarily be high in horses infected with larvae of *S. vulgaris* in their arteries, high levels in a horse with colic could suggest that it is infected with a variety of parasites, and in turn these probably would include the immature, migrating strongyles. The correct interpretation of high faecal egg counts and high levels of the blood constituents, taken together with information on how frequently the horses had been wormed and on the type of grazing, could lead to a diagnosis of the infection. However, since the tests are not specific for the disease the accuracy of diagnosis is not great.

Treatment

It is far more satisfactory to institute a regular anthelmintic treatment and/or management programme to control infection and prevent disease due to the large and small strongyles than it is to treat the disease after the damage has already been done. Also, while the adult worms are killed readily by anthelmintics, the larval stages actually causing the disease are much less susceptible to being killed. Nevertheless, there are a few anthelmintics that can kill the migrating larval stages. Horses showing signs of disease can be treated with ivermectin or oxfendazole at the normal dose rate (see Table 17) or with fenbendazole at an increased dose rate (30–60 mg/kg).

Diarrhoea and poor condition in horses in the late summer and autumn due to the effects of large numbers of adult small strongyles can be treated with any of the drugs listed in Table 17.

Preventive measures

The control programmes are designed to prevent the pastures becoming infected with the infective stages of the strongyles and so consequently to prevent infection in horses.

The first, and certainly most effective although labour-intensive, programme is purely managemental and consists simply of regular removal of the manure from the paddocks either manually or by vacuum machines. The manure must be removed twice a week during the warm summer months when the parasites are developing very rapidly, but slightly less frequent removal would suffice in the colder months. Horses will avoid grazing near areas of grass contaminated with manure so that the grass tends to grow roughly and rankly in these areas (the zone of repugnance), so removing the manure also has the advantage of increasing the amount of grazing and improving the pastures.

The second method of control is designed to reduce greatly the number of eggs being passed in the faeces of horses out onto the grass. The adult worms are killed with an anthelmintic. This will greatly reduce the number of eggs being excreted for a period of four to eight weeks and in turn will markedly reduce the number of infective stages available to develop on the pasture. The programme consists of regular anthelmintic treatment given to the horse every four to six weeks throughout the year using any one of the variety of drugs available (see Table 17). Whether the treatments should be given every four or six weeks will depend partly on the particular drug being used, and advice from your veterinarian should be sought.

The third method of control is known as strategic treatment as the horses are treated with anthelmintics at a time that is very important in the life cycle of the strongyles. Thus, in climates with a cold winter and warm summer (e.g. the UK, the northern USA) it is the increased number of eggs passed in the spring and early summer which is the most important part of the life cycle, providing the major proportion of the infection for horses from early to midsummer onwards. The horses are treated every four to six weeks (depending on the drug) from just before turn-out in the spring until after midsummer (August in the northern hemisphere). This will reduce the number of eggs and consequently the number of infective larvae available on grass to infect the horses and the horses will be protected from dangerous levels of infection. This strategic treatment programme is more economical, but not quite as effective as the conventional, year-long treatment programme since the infective stages can build up on the grass in late summer and autumn. These are less important as a cause of disease. In areas with hot, dry midsummers strategic treatment during the hot, dry weather is effective.

Table 17   Drugs Available for the Treatment of Parasites in Horses

Drug name	Commercial name	Form	Dose rate (mg/kg)	Bots Gaster-ophilus	Large strongyles	Small strongyles
Piperazine	Citrazine Piperazine	Powder Tablets	200	−	+ (400 mg/kg)*	++ (400 mg/kg)
Oxfendazole	Systamex Synthatic	Paste	10	−	++	++
Mebendazole	Telmin	Paste	5–10	−	++	++
Fenbendazole	Panacur	Liquid Paste Granules	7.5	−	++	++
Thiabendazole	Thibenzole Equizole	Paste Powder	44	−	++	++
Febantel	Bayverm	Paste	6	−	++	++
Oxibendazole	Equitac Equidin Rycovet Wormer	Paste	10	−	++	++
Dichlorvos	Astrobot Equigard	Pellets	36.5	++	++	++
Haloxon	Equilox	Paste Pellets	50–70	++	++	++
Metriphonate Trichlorphon	Neguvon	Paste	35	++	−	−
Pyrantel	Strongid P	Granules	19	−	++	++
Ivermectin	Eqvalan	Paste	0.2	++	++	++

++   A highly effective drug killing 90 per cent of the worms.
+   A moderately effective drug
−   Not tested against this parasite (although some drugs may have effect) or has insignificant effects.
*   A higher dose of the drug needs to be used for effect against certain parasites.

Note: The information on the leaflet enclosed with the drugs should be read before the drug is used as there may be contra-indications against the use of a drug in some animals, i.e. not for use in young foals; in early pregnancy; in horses with broken wind, diarrhoea, constipation, colic.

This table is not a complete list of all the anthelmintics available to treat worms in horses. The availability and the approval of drugs for use in horses will vary in different countries.

Large roundworm P. equorum	Pinworm O. equi	Threadworm S. westeri	Habronema	Lungworm D. arnfieldi	
++	++	-	-	-	Benzimidazole drugs. If worms develop resistance
++	++	-	++	-	to one of these drugs then cross-resistance also occurs
++	++	-	-	++ (15–20 mg/kg) for 5 days)*	(i.e. the worms will be resistant to the effects of all the drugs in this group).
++	++	++ (50 mg/kg)*	-	++ (15–30 mg/kg)*	
++ (88 mg/kg)*	++	++	-	-	
++	++			-	
++	++	++ (15 mg/kg)*	-	-	Worms resistant to the effects of the other benzimidazole drugs are not resistant to this drug.
++	++		-	-	Organophosphate drugs. These drugs are not suitable for use in every animal.
++	++	-	-	-	
++	++	-	-	-	
++	++	-	-	-	
++	++	++	++	++	

Other measures which are helpful in reducing the number of infective strongyle larvae on pasture include: avoidance of overcrowding on pasture; not grazing young animals with older horses; ideally using reseeded pastures or pastures that have not been grazed by horses the previous year; using either mixed grazing with sheep and cattle or allowing sheep and cattle to follow the horses into a paddock – the sheep and cattle will eat the infective stages and therefore reduce the number available for the horses (if mixed grazing is carried out, the horses will become infected with *Trichostrongylus axei*, which is a stomach worm shared by sheep, cattle and horses – see below); not spreading manure directly from stables onto the grass as this will create infection on the grass; treating any newly arrived horses with ivermectin, pyrantel or dichlorvos (Table 17) and keeping them indoors for forty-eight hours after arrival. It should be borne in mind that when horses are taken to areas frequented by other horses (other stables, showgrounds, even roadside verges on which horses are ridden) they are at risk of becoming infected even by eating small amounts of grass.

Whichever method is used to control the strongyles, particular attention must be paid to the foals and yearlings. Young animals are highly susceptible to infection and can pass very large numbers of eggs in their faeces. Also, anthelmintic treatment does not produce as big a reduction in the number of eggs passed by foals and yearlings compared with older horses. Managemental control by twice weekly removal of manure is the method of choice for paddocks grazed by foals and yearlings.

It is vital that, whatever the control programme used, it is monitored regularly. Faecal samples should be taken by your vet from selected animals and examined for strongyle egg numbers, preferably once a year in the autumn. The levels of globulins or IgG(T) in the blood of groups of horses also can be monitored, either in a laboratory or with the test kit Agglutinade-Strongyle. Starting from the beginning of a control programme, the levels of these blood constituents should decrease and then remain low if the programme is successful.

Resistance of strongyles to anthelmintics

One problem does arise in the anthelmintic treatment control programmes. The worms are capable of developing resistance to the effects of the anthelmintics. This means that a dose of drug which was effective in killing the worms no longer is able to do so as the worms resist its effects and are still present in the horse after treatment. Resistance to the benzimidazole anthelmintics (see Table 17) has been detected periodically in horses in all countries of the world. This is because these drugs have been used very frequently, but in fact, the worms have the ability to develop resistance to any anthelmintic if it is used frequently enough. It is essential that, before an anthelmintic treatment programme is begun, your vet should examine the worms for resistance. If the worms are resistant to a drug, then it is pointless to use this drug or any related drug to treat the horses. Advice of which drugs are suitable for use should be obtained from your vet.

If anthelmintic treatment control programmes are used, care must be taken to ensure that the worms do not develop resistance to the drugs used. To prevent the development of drug-resistant worms, one anthelmintic is used for a year and then a completely different and unrelated drug the next year. Obtain the advice of your veterinarian as to which drugs can be used in rotation.

PARASCARIS EQUORUM (LARGE ROUNDWORM)

These long, robust roundworms, up to 50 cm long, are found in the small intestine. Large numbers may be found in foals, yearlings are infected to a lesser extent, while adult horses carry only a few or no worms.

Life cycle

Eggs passed in the faeces develop on the ground to infective larvae retained within the egg's shell. This takes two to three weeks or much longer, depending on the weather, development being the most rapid in the summer. When foals eat infective eggs, the microscopic larvae hatch and migrate through the intestinal wall and via the blood to the liver and lungs. In the lungs the larvae break out into the air spaces, migrate up the trachea to be swallowed and develop to adults in the small intestine. The mature adult worms start laying very thick-shelled eggs two to three months after infection.

Young foals can become infected with several hundred to a thousand adult *P. equorum* in their intestines, but these worms are lost gradually over six to nine months. The foal then gradually develops a protective immune response so that, on reinfection, an increasing proportion of the invading larvae are killed and cannot develop to adult worms. Therefore the infection · is most common in young suckling and weanling foals up to six to nine months of age and to a lesser extent in yearlings. Occasionally adult horses will be infected with a few adult ascarids but these infections normally are unimportant.

Because the majority of worms are found in foals, *P. equorum* infection is passed from the foals born and infected in one year to the foals of the next year. The infective eggs, protected by their thick shells, are very long-lived and remain alive at least a year and probably two or three. The eggs of *P. equorum* have a very sticky coat and will attach to various objects. Thus, the eggs passed by foals in one year will stick to and remain alive on the walls, floors and equipment in stables and also on the pastures. They act as the source of infection for the foals born in the next year's foaling season.

Clinical signs

Occasionally, if a foal is exposed to a large number of eggs over a short period of time, then coughing and respiratory distress can result one to three weeks later as the larvae migrate through the lungs. More usually the foal eats eggs over a longer period of time, and then the adult worms in the intestines cause loss of appetite, dullness, unthriftiness and diarrhoea. The foal will not grow as well as expected and may have a pot-belly and a staring coat. Very occasionally large numbers of worms coiled and tangled in the intestines can block it physically.

Diagnosis

The characteristic, thick-shelled eggs can be detected on faecal examination. As the female worms are prolific egg layers, only very large numbers of eggs will be significant.

Treatment

The majority of anthelmintics developed to treat the strongyle nematodes of horses are effective against *P. equorum* (see Table 17).

Control

Since the thick-shelled eggs are very long-lived on pastures and in stables, as well as being very resistant to disinfectants, etc., control of *P. equorum* infections by good hygiene is almost impossible. The use of different stables and pastures for the foals each year will reduce levels of infection substantially, but some of the eggs will survive more than a year in temperate climates, so this procedure is not absolute in practice. The best method of control is to eliminate the infection from the foal by anthelmintic treatment. This can be achieved by treating the foals with an anthelmintic at intervals of one to two months until they reach six to nine months of age.

OXYURIS EQUI (PINWORM)

These nematodes occur in the large intestine of horses throughout the world. The males are small, but the females may reach 10 cm long and are white-grey in colour, with a long tail tapering to a point, hence the name pinworm.

Life cycle

The female worms live in the large intestine, but when mature and filled with eggs they move down the gut and crawl out of the anus to lay clusters of eggs which the female attaches in a gelatinous mass onto the skin around the anus under the tail. The eggs develop to an infective larva within the egg in a few days. The eggs will fall off onto bedding, into feeding troughs, and so on, and horses are reinfected when they eat eggs with fodder and bedding. If the eggs fall off in the paddocks they dehydrate and die quite rapidly, so pinworm infections are seen mainly in stabled horses.

Clinical signs

The presence of the female worms laying their eggs and particularly the presence of the eggs themselves stuck in a gelatinous mass around the anus are irritating, so affected horses will rub their tails. This rubbing will break the hairs at the base of the tail and produce an unkempt appearance (rat-tailed). If the horse rubs its tail on rough or protruding objects within the stable it can break the skin and cause sores on and around the top of the tail.

Diagnosis

Sometimes the characteristic female pinworms with their tapering, pointed tails are passed in the faeces. A rubbed tail will also suggest an infection with O. equi. This can be confirmed by examination of the anal region for eggs. These can be seen microscopically on a piece of clear sticky tape which has been applied to the skin around the anus and then pulled off. The horse should be restrained properly during this procedure.

Treatment

All the drugs listed in Table 17 are effective for the treatment of pinworms.

Preventive measures

Measures are not usually applied specifically for the control of pinworms. Any programme of treatment to control the strongyles will control infection with O. equi also. In fact, the presence of O. equi may suggest that a strongyle control programme is not being applied or applied properly and the complete worming programme should be reviewed. However, if the strongyle worms are being controlled by twice weekly removal of manure from the paddocks, then O. equi could develop in horses stabled for all or part of the day. In this case the horse should be treated for pinworms twice a year.

DICTYOCAULUS ARNFIELDI (LUNGWORM)

These white, 3.5-cm-long, slender worms live in the air passages (bronchi and bronchioles) of the lungs. Although lungworms are probably found throughout the world, usually only a small proportion of horses are infected or show signs of disease.

Life cycle

Eggs containing a larva are laid in the air passage, coughed up and swallowed and passed in the faeces. In the summer months the larvae hatch and develop quite rapidly to the infective stage. When eaten with grass by horses, the larvae migrate through the intestinal wall and via the circulation to the lungs, where they break out into the air passages to develop to adults. In many horses, particularly adult horses, the development of the worms is stopped when they reach the stage of immature adults. Consequently the worms never actually lay eggs.

Most commonly horses become infected from donkeys when they graze land in common with donkeys. Some 70 per cent of donkeys are infected with lungworms, but show no clinical signs of disease. However, donkeys are not essential to the life cycle as the parasites can be transmitted from one horse to another, although less efficiently.

Clinical signs

It is not known how many horses are infected with lungworm nor what proportion of those infected actually show any clinical signs of disease. Infected foals usually show no signs of disease, but certainly some infected adult horses will have a chronic cough, particularly during exercise, and an increased respiratory rate, and these signs can persist for a long time.

Diagnosis

Diagnosis is difficult since usually, in horses infected with lungworm and displaying a chronic cough, the parasites have developed only to immature adults. Therefore eggs will not be passed in the faeces and no other satisfactory diagnostic test is available. It is possible, using an endoscope tube, for a veterinarian to obtain cells from the horse's trachea. The presence of certain cells (the eosinophils) in the washings of the trachea suggests lungworm infection. However, this diagnosis is not absolute since equally well these cells could be present in a horse without lungworm but with an asthmatic, allergic bronchitis. Perhaps more satisfactory is the fact that lungworm eggs may be passed in the faeces of other horses, particularly foals, or donkeys grazing the same pasture. This would be sufficient indication to warrant treatment for lungworm.

Treatment

The horses can be treated with the normal dose of ivermectin or with increased doses of mebendazole or fenbendazole (Table 17).

Preventive measures

All the horses (and donkeys) in the stable should be treated to prevent continued transmission of the infection. Horses should not be grazed with donkeys, nor should they be grazed near paddocks where donkeys are grazed as the infective larvae can be transferred quite a distance.

STRONGYLOIDES WESTERI (THREADWORM)

This is a very small, fine worm found in the intestine of foals. It occurs throughout the world.

Life cycle

S. westeri has a very complicated life cycle. The mare passes the infection in her milk to her foal when the foal is only a few days old. The worms develop very rapidly in the foal and eggs will be passed in its faeces by the time it is ten days old. In warm, moist conditions these eggs develop in as little as twenty-four hours to infective third-stage larvae to reinfect the foal. In addition, in very warm, damp conditions, in the wet bedding of dirty stables, for example, the parasites can multiply their numbers outside the host in a non-parasitic form of the life cycle to free-living males and females, which in turn produce eggs and infective larvae, thereby increasing greatly the number of parasites available to infect the foal. Horses become infected either by eating the infective larvae or, alternatively, the larvae can penetrate through the horses' skin. In foals the larvae migrate via the circulation through the liver and lungs, are coughed up and swallowed and develop as adults in the intestine. In adult horses, in contrast, the larvae usually migrate into the body tissues, where they remain without any further development to adult worms. Only in the mare do these larvae reactivate, and when she begins to produce milk the larvae migrate to the udder to be transferred in the milk to her foal.

Clinical signs
S. westeri used to be considered a relatively common and important cause of diarrhoea in very young foals. Much of this diarrhoea now is thought to be due to overconsumption of milk (nine-days scours) and to bacterial or viral infection, so that the importance of *S. westeri* has fallen. Nevertheless in some heavily infected foals, particularly those kept in relatively unhygienic conditions, damage to the intestine caused by the worms will result in yellowish to bloody, fluid faeces.

Diagnosis
Thousands of thin-shelled eggs already containing a first-stage larva will be present in the faeces. Only very large numbers of eggs will be significant.

Treatment
The foals can be treated with the normal dose of ivermectin or thiabendazole or with increased doses of oxibendazole or fenbendazole (Table 17).

Preventive measures
Control usually is not attempted, but on stud farms, where heavy infections in foals occasionally can be encountered, the mares can be treated with ivermectin just before they foal to reduce the number of larvae passed in their milk to the foal. Clean, very dry bedding will prevent the parasites increasing their numbers by the free-living part of the life cycle.

HABRONEMA AND DRASCHIA (SUMMER SORES)

These worms, *H. muscae*, *H. majus* and *D. megastoma*, all 1–2 cm long, are found in the stomach of horses. The infective third-stage larvae can be deposited on wounds in the skin, where they cause summer sores.

Life cycle
The life cycle is indirect, using flies (the house fly and stable fly) as

intermediate hosts. Infection of horses therefore takes place in the warm summer months when the flies abound. The *Habronema* and *Draschia* larval stages in horse manure are eaten by the larval (maggot) stages of the fly, which also are growing in the manure. When the adult fly develops it contains the infective third-stage worm larvae, and these move to the fly's mouthparts. When the fly imbibes fluid from the lips and nostrils of the horse, the larvae crawl out of the fly's mouthparts and are swallowed by the horse. Horses can also eat dead infected flies in food and water. The adult worms then grow to maturity in the stomach. The flies feed on other moist surfaces such as wounds, and in response to the moisture the larvae again will crawl out of the fly's mouthparts and infect the wound. The *Habronema* or *Draschia* larvae cannot develop any further in the wound but they do cause summer sores.

Clinical signs

The adult worms in the stomach of the horse generally cause no problems. Summer sores in contrast are more serious.

The presence of the *Habronema* larvae in the wound causes the formation of soft, yellowish or reddish brown material, which protrudes from the wound. Continual reinfection of the sore can cause a quite extensive lesion. The summer sore is very irritating to the horse, which rubs it, causing it to bleed.

The sores are seen in the summer months when the flies are active and carrying the worm larvae. The sores are much more common in warm climates and relatively rare in temperate climates. The lesions occur on those parts of the body most likely to be injured (legs, head, withers) and on the sheath in males and on the inner corner of the eye. The wounds attract the flies, but, for some reason, although many horses are exposed to infected flies, only a few develop summer sores. This predisposition of certain animals may be related to their developing a hypersensitivity reaction to the *Habronema* larvae, and often the condition will recur annually in these horses.

Diagnosis

Usually a diagnosis of the presence of adult worms in the stomach of horses is never made, because very few eggs or larvae are passed in the faeces and they are very difficult to see. The lesions of summer sores are fairly characteristic. A small piece of tissue, a biopsy, or an extensive scraping of the wound must be taken by a veterinarian to confirm the diagnosis and to differentiate summer sores from other conditions (particularly fungal infections and skin tumours). These conditions are identified by the type of cells invading the lesion. Occasionally a *Habronema* or *Draschia* larva may be seen.

Treatment

The drugs listed in Table 17 as effective against *Habronema* are able to kill only the adult worms in the stomach of horses. Summer sores are much more difficult to treat. A form of ivermectin which is not normally used in horses can be injected by a vet. It will kill the larvae in the wound and is effective in about 70 per cent of uncomplicated cases, but sometimes causes side effects. Occasionally pain or swelling at the site of injection or oedema and pruritis possibly due to the response of the horse to the death of *Onchocerca* microfilariae are seen. Alternatively the lesions can be treated by surgery to clean the wound of diseased tissue. The wound must be covered after treatment to prevent renewed fly attack and reinfection.

Preventive measures

No measures are taken to prevent infection with the adult worms in the stomach of horses. However, measures should be taken to prevent summer sores, particularly in horses which have developed them in previous years. The intermediate fly hosts should be killed in manure piles where they breed (see p 463) and fly repellent should be applied to all wounds in the fly season. This also will help to prevent myiasis caused by blowflies (see p. 466).

ONCHOCERCA CERVICALIS (FILARIAL WORMS, ONCHOCERCIASIS)

O. cervicalis infects the neck, skin and occasionally the eyes of horses. It is found throughout the world. Another species, *O. reticulata*, infects the tendons and suspensory ligaments, usually of the front legs

Life cycle

Adult *O. cervicalis* live in the ligamentum nuchae, which is the main ligament in the neck. The adult female worms lay first-stage larvae (called microfilariae) which migrate to the skin. The microfilariae congregate in the skin on the lower abdomen and chest. From here they are picked up by a biting *Culicoides* midge when it feeds on the horse. The first-stage larvae or microfilariae develop to the infective third-stage larvae in the body of the midge. When the midge bites another horse the larvae are injected, and they migrate to the ligament in the horse's neck, where they complete their development to adults.

Clinical signs

Adult *O. reticulata* in nodules, tendons or suspensory ligaments sometimes cause swelling or lameness in the front legs. Adult *O. cervicalis* are usually not considered to cause problems. Previously *O. cervicalis* adults were thought to be a cause of fistulous withers, a discharging sinus in the area of the withers. This now appears to be unlikely, although the point still remains somewhat controversial.

The microfilariae of *O. cervicalis* can cause skin lesions. A high proportion of horses carry O. *cervicalis* microfilariae in their skin, but most of them never show any signs of the infection. It is only in a small proportion of animals that the skin lesions are seen, and their presence is thought to be associated with the horse's hypersensitive immune reaction to the microfilariae dying in the skin. The skin becomes roughened and the hair is lost along the ventral part of the belly and chest and sometimes on the head and other parts of the body. The lesions are very irritating and itchy, and the horse will bite, kick and scratch at itself, causing further damage. The microfilariae also are thought to be one of the causes of periodic ophthalmia (see p. 132) in horses, and even though there is no conclusive proof of this, the microfilariae can be found in the eye.

Diagnosis

A number of other parasites cause skin lesions in the horse, so a positive diagnosis of O. *cervicalis* microfilariae as the causative agent is difficult to make. Another reason for this difficulty is the fact that the majority of horses which are infected with O. *cervicalis* never develop skin lesions; it is only a few animals that become hypersensitive to the parasite. This means that simple identification of the microfilariae in the skin of affected horses is not sufficient to make a diagnosis, since these microfilariae will be present in normal horses also. However, a small piece of skin can be taken as a biopsy and examined in the laboratory. A microscopic examination of the tissues may suggest that the horse is hypersensitive to the microfilariae. Also useful is a count of the number of microfilariae per gramme of skin. This number tends to be very high in horses showing skin lesions compared with unaffected animals.

Treatment

No drug is available to kill the adults of O. *reticulata* in the tendons of the foreleg or the adults of O. *cervicalis* in the neck. Those few horses which develop the skin lesions can be treated with ivermectin, preferably early in the course of the disease, to kill the microfilariae in the skin. However, since the skin lesions seem to be associated with the reaction of certain horses to the natural death of microfilariae in the skin, anthelmintic treatment which will kill a large number of microfilariae at a time could make the lesions temporarily more severe. A fluid oedematous swelling may appear ventrally along the belly, chest and neck, with swelling of the face. To prevent this increased reaction, and also to protect the eyes of the horse, it should be injected with anti-inflammatory agents to dampen the host's response to the dying microfilariae at the same time as it is treated with the anthelmintic.

Animals which have been suffering from the skin lesions for a long period of time may never fully recover their hair coat. Also, once animals have been affected by the skin lesions, these are liable to recur, and this may happen seasonally, often in the summer and autumn months.

Preventive measures

Control is not usually attempted as it is very difficult to prevent the horses becoming infected with the *Onchocerca* parasites. Attempts can be made to prevent the horse being bitten by *Culicoides* midges, which transmit the infection to horses (see p. 462).

TRICHOSTRONGYLUS AXEI

These very small, 6-mm-long, slender worms occur in sheep, cattle and goats in every country of the world. They can also be found in the stomach of horses. Horses usually become infected when they graze with sheep and cattle, but once infected they may transmit the infection among themselves.

The life cycle of *T. axei* on the ground is similar to that of the horse strongyles, infection of horses occurring mainly in midsummer. Once eaten, the larvae become adult, egg-laying females in three weeks. Usually *T. axei* is not pathogenic in horses and causes no disease, so no measures need be applied to control the infection. Occasionally in extremely heavy infections the horse may develop diarrhoea and lose weight.

Diagnosis is difficult since the eggs laid by *T. axei* are virtually identical to those produced by the horse strongyles. The faecal sample has to be taken to a laboratory and the third-stage larvae grown so that *T. axei* can be differentiated from the horse strongyle larvae by their structure.

PARAFILARIA MULTIPAPILLOSA (BLOODY SWEAT)

This parasite is found in Russia, Asia, Eastern Europe, the Mediterranean area, North Africa and South America. A blood-sucking fly acts as the intermediate host and injects the larvae into the skin of horses. The adult female worm grows in a nodule under the skin. In the warm summer months the female worm pierces through the skin and lays her eggs on the surface to be picked up by the flies. A bloody fluid also exudes from the nodule and drips down the skin, attracting flies. The nodules usually appear suddenly, break open, bleed and then heal up, but a succession of female worms may pierce the skin at different times over the spring, summer and autumn. The nodules may reappear the following summer. The worms usually cause no major problem unless they interfere with the saddlery. Little is known about treatment, although ivermectin or high and repeated doses of fenbendazole may be tried by veterinarians.

Cestodes (Tapeworms)

The cestodes (or tapeworms) all have an indirect life cycle which requires two hosts. The adult, sexually mature tapeworm lives in the intestines of animals. These are the definitive host. In the intestines the adult tapeworm grows continuously from its head, producing a ribbon-like body made up of a large number of segments. The segments at the end of the tapeworm contain the eggs, and break off and are shed daily in the faeces of the definitive host. The eggs do not need to undergo any further development once they have been passed in the faeces onto the ground. They are immediately infective for and are eaten by the second host in the life cycle, called the intermediate host. A fluid-filled cyst is formed in the internal organs of the intermediate host, and one or more future head(s) of the tapeworm develop in the cyst. The life cycle is completed when the definitive host eats the intermediate host containing the cyst. The tapeworm head(s) in the cyst attach to the wall of the definitive host's intestines and from them the adult tapeworms grow.

Horses may act as the definitive host for some species of tapeworms and carry the adult tapeworm in their intestines. Horses also can act as the intermediate host for other species of tapeworms and carry the cysts in their body.

ANOPLOCEPHALA PERFOLIATA, ANOPLOCEPHALA MAGNA (TAPEWORM)

These greyish-white, flat, segmented worms are found in the intestines of horses of all ages and throughout the world. *A. perfoliata* is the most common of these species. It lives as an adult tapeworm in the lower part of the small intestine and in the large intestine of horses. The adult worms are wedge-shaped in outline, finely segmented and up to 8 cm long and 4 cm wide. *A. magna* is ribbon-like, up to 80 cm long, and is found in the small intestine of horses. Other species of tapeworm are reported from some countries.

Life cycle

The adult tapeworms in the horse continually grow segments containing eggs. These are passed in the faeces onto the pasture. The eggs are eaten by free-living oribatid mites which live in the matt of the grass. The tapeworm develops as a microscopic cyst in the body of the mite. Horses become infected when they eat the mites containing cysts while grazing.

Clinical signs

Generally adult tapeworms are of little significance to the horse. In fairly large numbers *A. magna* may cause some damage to the small intestine and perhaps diarrhoea and unthriftiness. Very occasionally rupture of the small intestine has been attributed to *A. magna* but perhaps sometimes erroneously. *A. perfoliata* can produce small ulcers and inflammatory tissue at the site where their heads are attached in the caecum. Frequently the tapeworms cluster around the ileo-caecal valve which divides the small and large intestines. Very occasionally their physical presence here, plus the granular tissue produced in response to them, can interfere with the passage of food or cause an intussusception with colic. It has not been shown but it is probable that large numbers of tapeworms in the intestines could affect the performance of a horse.

Diagnosis

These worms usually are noted only on a routine post-mortem examination carried out for other reasons. Sometimes eggs will be seen when the faeces are examined for the detection of strongyle eggs, but usually eggs will not be seen even if the horse is known to be infected. Therefore a positive diagnosis of tapeworm infection can be difficult to make.

Treatment

Tapeworms themselves are rarely treated specifically. Should a heavy infection cause problems in a horse, then it can be treated with pyrantel embonate at 38 mg/kg, which is double the normal dose rate, or with a drug used to treat tapeworm in cattle, sheep and dogs, namely niclosamide, which can be prescribed at a dose rate of 200–300 mg/kg. Ivermectin does not kill tapeworms and treatment specifically for tapeworms might be considered if ivermectin only is being used in a treatment programme.

Preventive measures

Because the life cycle of the tapeworms involves a free-living mite which is ubiquitous on pastures, control of the infection is not attempted.

ECHINOCOCCUS GRANULOSUS (HYDATID CYST)

The tapeworm *E. granulosus* uses the horse as its intermediate host and the dog as its definitive host. The tapeworm is quite common in horses in Great Britain and Ireland but rare in the USA and Australia except in imported horses. The very small, 2–6-mm-long adult tapeworms live in the intestines of dogs and eggs are passed in dog faeces. Dogs show no signs of the infection. Horses become infected by eating the eggs, and a cyst, called a hydatid cyst, develops, most commonly in the horse's liver. Dogs become infected with adult tapeworms when they are fed raw horsemeat. This life cycle makes the infection common in packs of foxhounds and beagles which are fed raw horsemeat in the kennels. These dogs then contaminate fields with the eggs in their faeces, with the result that hydatid cysts are most common in horses grazing fields where the hounds are exercised regularly. Fields over which the hounds hunt can also become contaminated with faeces containing eggs.

Even though the cyst(s) can grow to a large size in the horse's liver and contain several litres of fluid, they usually cause no clinical problems and are noted only incidently on a post-mortem examination carried out for another reason or in a knacker's yard. Occasionally cysts may occur in other body sites and produce clinical signs, but this is rare and the signs diverse depending on the organ infected.

There is no treatment for the cysts in horses. The only way they can be prevented is to prevent the infection in the dogs. These should be fed only well-cooked horsemeat (heat kills the cyst); alternatively they can be treated every six weeks with the anti-tapeworm drug praziquantel to kill the tapeworms.

A second type or strain of *E. granulosus* exists. This tapeworm again infects dogs, particularly sheepdogs or any dog that is fed or can scavenge raw sheep meat, as the main intermediate host for this strain of *E. granulosus* is sheep, in which the cysts are found in the liver and lungs. This strain of *E. granulosus* is far more important than the horse strain as man can become infected by it. A human who accidently ingests eggs develops one or more hydatid cysts in the body (in the liver, lungs, brain, bone, etc.). The infection in man can have serious consequences and government-sponsored schemes to control and eradicate the sheep strain of *E. granulosus* from sheep and dogs are in operation in several countries. The strain which has a dog–sheep (or man) cycle does not seem to infect horses; nor do humans seem to become infected with the dog–horse *E. granulosus* tapeworm. Thus the infection in horses is not of significance to human health.

Trematodes (Flukes)

Flukes have a complicated life cycle involving an intermediate host which is a snail. Eggs passed in the faeces of the host develop in a warm, moist environment and the larval stage, called a miracidium, hatches into water. The miracidium swims in the water until it finds and penetrates the tissues of a snail. The miracidium multiplies asexually in the snail and eventually the next free-living life-cycle stage, the cercariae, are released from the snail. These produce a thick cyst wall around themselves for protection and encyst on plants or in the mud. Horses become infected by eating the cercariae with herbage.

GASTRODISCUS AEGYPTIACUS

This fluke is found in the large intestine of horses, but also of pigs and warthogs, and mainly in Africa. It has a typical trematode life cycle involving a water snail. Horses become heavily infected in the dry season. This is because the snails congregate in and around permanent water, so the greatest concentration of the infective cercariae occurs there. The most palatable grazing is also in these areas, so the horses will gather near the water and become infected.

Heavy infections can cause a bloody diarrhoea and rapid loss of weight. Diagnosis can be a problem since it is the immature stages developing in the intestine and before they become egg-laying adults that cause the most harm. The clinical signs, season of the year, type of grazing with suitable habitats for the snails and knowledge of previous outbreaks of disease due to *Gastrodiscus* in the area would warrant treatment. Chronic, long-lived cases will show large, clear *Gastrodiscus* eggs in their faeces.

Although the effective drugs are usually approved only for use in cattle and not in horses, a veterinarian can prescribe resorantel or oxyclozanide to treat horses infected with *Gastrodiscus*. Permanent control would be to supply water in clean troughs and to fence off permanent water inhabited by the snails, or to kill the snails with molluscicides. Since this is usually impracticable, the number of parasites can be reduced by treating the horses to eliminate any infection they might be carrying just before the dry season. This will reduce the number of eggs being passed in the faeces and therefore reduce multiplication of *Gastrodiscus* in the snail population.

FASCIOLA HEPATICA (LIVER FLUKE)

F. hepatica is an important infection in cattle and sheep in areas throughout the world where the geographical conditions are suitable for multiplication of the amphibious (mud) snail, the intermediate host of the parasite. Horses sometimes become infected when they are grazing poorly drained or marshy pastures in common with infected sheep or cattle. The snails and the parasite can also develop in irrigation ditches to infect animals grazing irrigated pastures. This infection can cause abdominal pain, anaemia and poor performance in horses.

Diagnosis requires the detection of the yellow-stained *F. hepatica* eggs in the faeces of the horse. No drugs have been approved to treat *F. hepatica* in horses but veterinarians can prescribe oxyclozanide or rafoxanide.

ARTHROPODS

This large group of organisms includes flies, lice, ticks and mites. A number of these cause disease, particularly lesions on the skin of horses producing worry, irritation and loss of condition.

Biting and Nuisance Flies

A number of different flies will attack horses. The flies breed in the warm, hot summer months, and this is the time when fly attack occurs. They are more prominent in tropical and subtropical countries than in countries with a temperate climate, although even in temperate climates fly attack can be severe. Some flies, the nuisance flies, have mouthparts for lapping fluids and feed on the secretions around the eyes, nose, etc. Other flies, the biting flies, have mouthparts which can penetrate through the skin of the animal for the fly to feed on blood. The bites of the flies can be painful, but also, while feeding, the fly injects into the skin saliva and other substances which, for example, stop the blood from clotting as the fly feeds. Some horses can develop allergic or hypersensitivity reactions to the injected materials and develop skin lesions, although why only a few and not all horses react in this way is not known. Flies also will transmit other diseases either mechanically, simply by physically carrying the organism on their mouthparts from horse to horse, or as an intermediate host in the life cycle of the transmitted parasite.

There are four stages in the life cycle of flies. The adult female flies lay hundreds of eggs, usually about 0.5–1 mm in length. From these hatch larvae. The fly larvae are maggots, usually white, segmented and somewhat circular, increasing in breadth from front to back. They grow from about 1 mm to 10 mm in length. The larvae then pupate, frequently inside a hardened, protective pupal case. During the pupal stage the tissues of the larva dissolve and are re-formed to produce the adult fly. Once developed, the adult fly emerges from the pupa and is on the wing to attack horses.

Different types of flies have preferred places (manure, water, etc.) in which they breed for the development of the larval stages. Therefore, to control flies adequately in a stable, it is important to know which types of flies are present. Most flies can be readily differentiated by a veterinarian from their size, colour, patterns on their wings and structure of their mouthparts.

MUSCA DOMESTICA, MUSCA SORBENS, ETC. (HOUSE FLIES)

These are yellow-grey nuisance flies which feed on the secretions around horses' eyes, nose, vulva and prepuce, and on wounds. They are common in stables as they prefer to breed in horse manure. The flies irritate the horse when they are present in any numbers, causing it to shake its head and swish its tail. Their irritation to the eye can cause excess tear formation, attracting other flies, which further damage the eye. In addition to the general control measures described below, fly veils attached to the browband can help to protect horses' eyes. The flies can transmit *Habronema* or summer sores (see p. 451) to horses.

STOMOXYS CALCITRANS (STABLE FLIES)

These greyish-coloured biting flies also are common in stables as they prefer to breed in wet bedding contaminated with horse urine and manure. During the day they can be seen resting on sunny walls and windows. Their bites can be quite painful and they will bite a horse several times or switch between horses to complete their feeding. They can be extremely annoying to the horse, which will stamp, kick and switch its tail. The bite often leaves a small nodule and scab and may bleed after the fly has fed, attracting other flies such as the house fly. Some horses can develop crusts on the back, chest and neck when bitten by many flies. The flies also will bite humans, and dogs which frequent stables may have crusts, particularly around the edge and on the bends of their ears, from the bites of stable flies. Stable flies also transmit a number of diseases – for example, *Trypanosoma* (see chapter 31) and *Habronema* or summer sores (see p. 451) – to horses.

HAEMATOBIA IRRITANS, HAEMATOBIA STIMULANS (HORN FLIES)

These small, dark grey flies are normally found biting cattle as they prefer to breed in fresh cow manure, but they can be very irritating to horses grazing with or near cattle. The flies often cluster on the horse's ventral abdomen. Their bites are painful, and they often stay in the same area for quite some time after feeding, causing the horse to become very agitated and repeatedly stamp its feet and kick at its belly. In some horses the flies cause discrete areas of crusts, perhaps ulcers, on the belly and the hair is lost. Apart from the general measures for fly control described below, often a thick coat of Vaseline over the lesion will provide a barrier to prevent more flies biting.

TABANUS, HAEMATOBIA, HYBOMITRA, CHRYSOPS (HORSE, DEER AND BUFFALO FLIES)

The flies are recognized easily by their painful bite, their large size (ranging from 0.5 to 2.5 cm) and brownish colour; they often have brightly coloured eyes. They breed in mud and water, and are most commonly seen flying near water on hot, sultry days, although some species can be active in woodlands. Their bites make horses restless, and they rub and bite at themselves to remove the flies, which will then repeatedly return to the same horse or to one very close by to finish feeding. The horses will try to move away from the flies or even stampede. They will stop feeding and lose weight if continually attacked.

The horse flies transmit equine infectious anaemia (EIA – see p. 430) between horses, carrying the virus mechanically on their mouthparts. Since the flies will not move far to complete their feeding, separation of horses and separation of paddocks to prevent the flies feeding in quick succession on different horses will prevent transmission of EIA.

SIMULIUM (BLACK FLIES)

These are small, black, hump-backed flies which breed in fairly fast-running water in streams and rivers. They emerge to attack animals, particularly those grazing near water on warm, sultry days. Their bite is painful and they also inject a toxic substance, leaving behind a small, painful, fluid-filled blister or nodule. Only small numbers of these flies are present in the UK but swarms of them occur in hotter climates near rivers. If the flies swarm and hundreds of them bite a horse, they can inject enough toxin to kill the animal.

CULICOIDES (MIDGES, PUNKIES, NO-SEE-UMS – SWEET ITCH, QUEENSLAND ITCH, SUMMER ECZEMA)

Midges are minute flies, perhaps most important for their transmission of horse sickness in Africa. They breed in wet, muddy areas in marshes, along the estuaries of rivers and around lakes or in wet, decaying vegetable material. The flies are active, usually as swarms, biting horses principally in the early morning and late afternoon; if it is humid and cool they may remain active through the day. When the flies are biting the horses will be very uneasy and restless with tail-swishing and rubbing, and they may huddle together to escape the flies. A proportion of horses, particularly but not only those that are outdoors all the time, develop an allergic, hypersensitivity reaction to the midge bites.

This condition is given a variety of names – Queensland itch, sweet itch, summer eczema, etc. The midges which cause sweet itch usually are those that feed along the dorsal surface (forehead, withers, back, rump, base of tail) and these are the areas where the lesions are seen. The allergic reaction to the fly bites starts as very small, itchy nodules, and the horse will rub and bite at itself. Initially the hair is lost and crusts are seen on the ears and the base of the tail. Eventually the whole dorsal area of the horse can become reddened, with crusts and scaly material over the surface and no hair. Because of the irritation the horse may rub itself for prolonged periods against trees or posts, and may mutilate itself. Some of the *Culicoides* midges bite along the ventral abdomen and, although less common, the allergic reaction and skin damage can occur along the belly.

The time of the year (summer) and the distribution of the skin lesions on the horse (dorsal) suggest that the damage is caused by an allergic reaction to the bites of the midges. However, diagnosis is difficult since other allergies and other skin parasites cause similar types of lesion. A veterinarian may be able to obtain an extract of the midges, although this is not easy. If the horse reacts to a small injection of this extract over twenty-four hours with an irritating lesion and nodule, then it is allergic to the fly bites.

Application of ointments containing corticosteroids will reduce the severity of the lesions by reducing the itchiness of the reaction. However, this will only alleviate the problem temporarily. The only way to prevent the lesions in hypersensitive horses is to protect them from the bites of *Culicoides* midges each year.

Table 18 Some Examples of Insecticides and Acaricides Used to Treat Horses

Drug name	Trade name	Form	Use
Organochlorine derivatives			
Bromocyclen	Alugan	Spray Dust	Lice, mange
Camphechlor	Toxaphene Coopertox	Spray	Mange, ticks
Gamma HCH	Lindane Gamma-BHC Cooper's Lice and Mange Dressing Skin Dressing No. 3	Spray Dust Wash	Lice, mange, ticks
Organophosphate derivatives			
Dioxathion	Tick Dip Liquid Bercotox	Spray Wash	Ticks
Ethion	Cooperthion Diethion	Spray	Ticks

Fenithrothion	Durakill
	Cooper's Residual
	  Spray
		Dust
		Liquid
			Treatment of fly
			  breeding areas and
			  buildings

Iodofenphos	Nuvanol	Spray	Treatment of fly
			  breeding areas and
			  buildings

Pyrethroids			

Pyrethrin	Flyban
	Cooper's Veterinary
	  Insecticide
		Spray
		Spray
			Fly repellent on
			  horses

Permethrin	Stomoxin
	Coopex
		Spray
		Spray
			Fly repellent on
			  horses, treatment
			  of buildings

Cypermethrin	Rycopel Cyperkill	Spray	Fly repellent on horses

Prevention of Fly Irritation

Various managemental changes can markedly reduce the number of flies and the type of flies.

The house fly and stable fly both breed in piles of horse manure. Their breeding and numbers can be reduced greatly by the construction of a three-sided, concrete-based manure pit. The manure and soiled bedding is then packed tightly into this and the heat generated by the wet, fermenting manure and bedding will kill any flies developing in the manure. The surface of the pile, where it is cooler, can be sprayed with an insecticide (Table 18) to kill the flies. A channel around the pit filled with insecticide will kill the larval stages as they crawl out of the manure to complete their development as pupae in the surrounding soil. Unfortunately it is more difficult to control the breeding and reduce the number of the other types of flies by managemental practices because their breeding sites are so diverse.

Other general control measures can be used to reduce the number of flies and to protect horses from fly attack. The walls and partitions of barns and stables can be sprayed (every few days to weeks, depending on the length of activity of the insecticide used). This will kill the flies when they rest on the walls. The horses can be also sprayed with an insecticide, usually every few days, again depending on the level of fly attack and the insecticide used, to repel and/or kill the flies. More recently browbands of a synthetic plastic impregnated with an insecticide have become available. These can be attached to halters and bridles and worn permanently by the horse. The insecticide rapidly spreads over the surface of the horse's body to repel and kill flies. Each band will remain active, releasing insecticide and repelling flies, for several weeks. If horse browbands are not available some cattle ear tags have a similar effect. With the advice of a veterinarian a suitable type of cattle ear tag can be chosen and sewn to the halter.

If black flies and horse flies are a problem, in addition to using insecticide sprays, horses can be kept indoors on hot, sultry days, or at least away from water where the flies are breeding, to prevent attack. In paddocks horses will congregate in the fumes from burning smudge pots to protect themselves from biting flies. To protect them from the midges, which is particularly important if the horse is allergic to midge bites, horses can be stabled in the morning and the evening or all day if the weather is cool. The midges tend not to enter the darkness of stables. Burning smudge pots around the stables in the morning and particularly in the evening will reduce the numbers of midges.

GASTROPHILUS INTESTINALIS, GASTROPHILUS NASALIS (BOT FLIES)

The larval stages (bots) of these flies are found throughout the world in the stomach of horses. The majority of horses are infected. Usually *G. intestinalis* is the most common of the bots. In some countries *G. nasalis* is the more abundant but it is not found in the colder climates, such as central and northern England and Scotland. *G. haemorrhoidalis* can be found occasionally in many countries but is common in the USSR and parts of Asia.

The adult flies have yellow and dark bands on their bodies and look like bees except they have only one pair of wings. The female bot fly has an ovipositer curving down from her abdomen with which she attaches her eggs to the horse, and this can be mistaken for a sting. The larval bots are yellow to pink in colour, reach 1–2 cm in length and are made up of broad segments. They have a pair of large black hooks at their anterior end with which they attach to the wall of the horse's stomach.

Life cycle

G. intestinalis female flies attach their yellow eggs to the hairs on the forelegs, shoulders, neck and mane. After a few days the first-stage larvae are ready to hatch and they are stimulated to do so by the moisture, warmth and friction of the horse's tongue and lips when biting itself. On stimulation the larvae escape from the eggs and penetrate into the horse's mouth. Here they burrow into the tissues of the tongue and into the gums around the molar teeth for a month before they are swallowed. The second- and third-stage larvae then attach to the stomach wall. In all the larvae spend nine months in the horse. At the end of this time they release their hold and are passed in the faeces to develop for one month in the soil to the adult stage.

The life cycles of *G. nasalis* and *G. haemorrhoidalis* are similar to that of *G. intestinalis* except that their yellow and black eggs respectively are laid on hairs of the head. These eggs do not require stimulation to hatch; instead the larvae hatch spontaneously and then enter the horse's mouth. Again, the larvae spend a month in the mouth and about eight months in the stomach. *G. haemorrhoidalis* and *G. intestinalis* larvae as they leave the horse sometimes reattach by their hooks to the wall of the rectum for a short period of time.

The adult flies lay their eggs on horses in late summer and autumn in temperate climates, but the flies are active for longer – during spring, summer and autumn – in warmer climates. The adult flies are killed by cold and frost, so in winter the entire population of bots is present as larvae inside the horse. This is important for the institution of control measures.

Clinical signs

Generally bots are not of major importance. Egg-laying female flies, especially those laying eggs on the head, may annoy and upset the horse as they hover near the animal and dart in to lay their eggs. Larvae migrating in the tongue and gums may temporarily put the horse off its food and occasionally cause sores. The larvae in the stomach make circular, crater-like depressions where they are attached to the wall. Although never studied, large numbers of larvae in the stomach and their lesions over a large part of the stomach must cause some discomfort, which could be very important in performance horses. Occasionally the larvae cause ulcers in the stomach wall and rarely fatalities if these perforate through the stomach wall. Clusters of larvae may also interfere with the pyloric sphincter valve between the stomach and the small intestine and affect passage of food. If the larvae temporarily attach to the wall of the rectum, they can cause discomfort and sometimes straining, as if the horse is trying to pass faeces.

Diagnosis

There are no tests to diagnose the presence of the larvae in horses. If eggs have been seen on the horses in the summer and autumn, this will indicate that the animals are infected.

Treatment

A number of drugs are available to kill the larvae in the stomach. In particular, ivermectin and organophosphates (i.e. dichlorvos) (Table 17) are highly effective. The horses should be treated in early winter after the flies have been killed by the first frost of the autumn. It is important at this time to cut all the eggs of *G. intestinalis* from the hairs as the larvae which have not yet been stimulated to hatch can remain alive in the eggs on the hairs for several months and so continue to infect the horse after treatment.

Preventive measures

The only certain means of preventing the infection is to cut or shave off all the eggs from the hairs every two to three days. Bathing the horse with warm water or insecticidal compounds to remove eggs or larvae and the use of fly repellents to deter female flies from laying eggs tend to be ineffective.

MYIASIS (BLOWFLIES, SCREW-WORM FLIES)

Myiasis is a condition found throughout the world where blowflies (which include the green-bottle, blue-bottle and flesh flies) and screw-worm flies are attracted to and lay their eggs in wounds. The immature larval stages (maggots), hatch from the eggs, invade the living tissues in the wound and grow to about 1 cm long, feeding by dissolving the tissues.

Clinical signs

The maggots growing, moving and tunnelling into the wound are irritating, and the horse will stamp, kick and swish its tail. The wound will begin to ooze a foul-smelling cream or reddish-stained fluid. The screw-worm fly, found in Africa, Central and South America and Southern Asia, is particularly unpleasant; its larvae cause very serious lesions and untreated cases may die.

Diagnosis

A horse affected by these larvae often can be recognized by its restlessness. Close examination will reveal the infected wound in which maggots can be seen.

Treatment

The wound must be cleaned thoroughly and as many maggots as possible removed manually. The wound must then be treated with an insecticide to kill any remaining larvae which either cannot be reached, are too small to be easily visible or are hidden in pockets and tunnels. Commonly used insecticides for this purpose are gamma-HCH, fenchlorphos and coumaphos. The surface of the wound then must be covered or treated with a fly repellent to stop the adult flies being reattracted to the wound.

Preventive measures

All wounds found on horses in the warm summer months when blowflies are active should be treated with a fly repellent to prevent the adult flies laying their eggs on the wound. In hotter climates, where numerous flies are present, it may be useful to spray groups of horses routinely with an insecticide or repellent every few days to weeks. The frequency of treatment will depend on the length of activity of the insecticide used and the number of flies present. This is particularly true where the screw-worm fly exists because of the severity of the lesions its larvae produce. The importance of screw-worm fly myiasis, particularly in cattle, is such that in some countries tremendous efforts have or are being made to eradicate the fly or to prevent it from entering the country. In these areas screw-worm fly myiasis is notifiable and any suspect maggots must be preserved in alcohol and sent to government laboratories for identification.

HAEMATOPINUS ASINI, DAMALINIA EQUI (LICE – LOUSINESS)

Horses are affected with both sucking and chewing lice, *H. asini* and *D. equi* respectively. These are flattened, wingless, six-legged insects which live on the surface of the horse's skin. Sucking lice have pointed heads and penetrate the skin with their mouthparts to suck blood and tissue fluids. They are most common on the long-haired parts of the body such as the mane, tail and fetlocks but can spread over the whole body. They are 3–5 mm long and normally yellowish-brown in colour, although they become bluish when they have just fed on blood. The chewing lice are slightly smaller, 2 mm long, very light yellowish-brown in colour, and feed on scurf and surface cells. They are found most commonly along the back and flanks but may spread over the whole body.

Life cycle

The whole life cycle takes place on the horse. The lice attach eggs (nits) to the hairs. Immature lice (nymphs), which closely resemble the adults, emerge from the eggs in about ten days and gradually develop to mature adults in about three weeks. The lice are transmitted from horse to horse by direct contact, but, if warm and damp, they will survive hours to a few days on inanimate objects, and so can be transferred from horse to horse on saddlery and stable equipment.

Clinical signs

Louse populations build up in the cold months under the protection of the horse's long coat; they can be found in very large numbers on ill-kempt, poorly fed horses, often those out on pasture. There is dandruff in the coat, and as the lice are very irritating, the horse will bite and rub itself, pulling out the hair and even causing self-mutilation. The horse will feed poorly and its condition will deteriorate. A very large number of sucking lice can remove a significant amount of blood so that the mucous membranes of the horse may become pale.

Diagnosis

The poor condition and ragged, ill-kempt coat are highly suggestive of lice infection. The brown- or blue-coloured sucking lice are easily visible to the naked eye. The chewing lice live close to the skin and may be very difficult to see amongst the dandruff, but close scrutiny will reveal the tiny lice moving away from light.

Treatment

A variety of insecticides are available to treat lice on horses (see Table 18). These are usually in the form of dusts, sprays or washes and they must be applied thoroughly. Treatment should be repeated in two weeks to kill those lice which were present as eggs at the time of the first treatment and so not affected by the insecticide. These lice will have hatched out and will be killed by the second treatment.

All the horses in a stable should be treated at the same time as they probably are infected with at least a few lice even if they are not showing the clinical signs of a heavy infection.

Mange Mites

Mange mites are microscopic parasites of the skin. They all have an essentially similar life cycle. A six-legged larva hatches from an egg and develops to an eight-legged, sexually immature nymph. Finally the sexually mature male and female mites are formed. The whole life cycle takes about ten days to two weeks from egg to adult laying eggs. Transmission of the mites from one horse to another is by close contact, whereupon the mites are transferred directly from the skin of the infected horse to the skin of the uninfected horse. However, the mites also can survive a short time (hours to a few days) off the horse if the environment is warm and damp, and so can be transferred between horses on saddlery and equipment.

CHORIOPTES EQUI (LEG MANGE)

This still is a common form of mange of horses throughout the world. The mites live on the surface of the skin and are found mainly on the fetlocks and back of the pasterns, although they can spread up the legs even to the belly and groin.

Clinical signs

The mites puncture the skin to feed on tissue fluid, which also accumulates in the skin in response to the mites and oozes to the surface to dry and form crusts over reddened, inflamed skin. The lesions are itchy, so the horse will stamp and kick at itself, and the hair is lost.

Diagnosis

A skin scraping taken from a lesion by a veterinarian will reveal the mites with their characteristic structure when examined microscopically after the skin tissues have been digested.

Treatment

A variety of acaricide washes are available (see Table 18). These are applied as a leg bath and to any other affected part of the body. The horse is treated twice at a ten-day interval. This second treatment is necessary to make certain that any parasites which were present as eggs and hence not susceptible to the first treatment and which have hatched are killed. There are reports that *C. equi* has developed resistance to some acaricides and that these are no longer effective. If a marked improvement is not apparent within a week of the first treatment, the treatment should be started again using a different type of acaricide.

SARCOPTES SCABIEI (SARCOPTIC MANGE, SCABIES)

These mites burrow in tunnels in the surface layers of the skin and the lesions they produce can be quite severe in horses. The lesions usually begin on the head and neck but spread over the body if the horse remains untreated.

Clinical signs

The infected horse develops a hypersensitivity reaction to the mites and their waste products in the skin. This hypersensitivity reaction takes some time to develop and the lesions are first seen some two to five weeks after the horse contracted the infection. Initially, small, highly irritating nodules appear on the head and neck and the skin may be reddened. The horse will begin to rub and scratch itself on objects to relieve the irritation. The skin damage progresses, with loss of hair and crust formation, and later thickened, often very thickened, scaly skin develops, and the mites and the lesions gradually spread over the body. The irritation is intense so that the horse may actually create sores while rubbing and scratching itself, and will lose condition. Sarcoptic mange in horses has public health significance, as humans handling infected horses can pick up the mites on their skin and develop the highly irritating lesions of scabies; the infection on humans will die out once contact with infected horses ceases.

Diagnosis

As with the other mites, diagnosis is made by identification of the mites in a skin scraping. In this case the scraping must be deep (sufficient to cause bleeding, as the mites burrow into the skin) and extensive enough to find the mites as sometimes only very few seem to be present.

Treatment

The presence of the mites in tunnels burrowed into the skin makes treatment difficult. The acaricide creams or washes (see Table 18) must be rubbed or scrubbed in well and at least two treatments at a ten-day interval are required. It helps to wash the lesions first with Tetmosol soap. This will remove surface grease and soften the skin, allowing better penetration of the acaricide down into the skin to the mites. As the infection can be transferred readily to man, any humans handling or treating infected horses should wear protective gloves.

Preventive measures

Any horses that have been in contact with infected horses, and communal saddlery and stable equipment should be treated at the same time as the animals with mange. Even if in-contact horses are showing no signs of the infection, they may be incubating the infection as it takes two to five weeks from contact for the lesions to appear. In some countries sarcoptic mange in horses is a notifiable infection.

PSOROPTES CUNICULI, PSOROPTES EQUI (PSOROPTIC MANGE, EAR MITES)

Psoroptic mange can be seen in two forms. The mites may either be confined to the ears or cause lesions on the body.

Clinical signs

In the UK and Australia *Psoroptes* mites have been reported only occasionally in the ears of horses, although it is probable that they may occur elsewhere in the world. The mites occasionally cause an excessive production of wax in the ear, sometimes in the form of a thick brown exudate. The horse can become very sensitive around its ears, resent bridling or become a head-shaker. The infected ear may droop.

Psoroptic mange on the body is more severe. The lesions can be quite extensive and the infection can spread rapidly from horse to horse. Like the *Chorioptes* mites, the *Psoroptes* mites live on the surface of the skin, which they puncture to suck fluid. Lesions first form at the base of the mane and tail and under the forelock, but then spread over the body. The skin becomes very reddened and inflamed, and fluid oozes out to form crusts on the surface. The hair is lost and the horse will constantly rub, scratch and bite itself, even to the extent of self-mutilation.

Diagnosis

In a quiet or sedated horse a veterinarian may be able to examine the ear. When magnified, the small white mites will be visible deep in the ear moving about on the surface of the wax. Alternatively a swab of the secretions in the ear can be taken and examined for mites under a microscope in the laboratory. A skin scraping is taken from the edge of a lesion to diagnose body mange.

Treatment

All horses in the stables or herd should be treated twice with an acaricide wash or spray.

DEMODEX EQUI (DEMODECTIC MANGE, NODULAR MANGE)

This form of mange is uncommon in horses; only rarely are cases seen. The mites live deep in the hair follicle at the root of the hair and are transferred from the mare to her nursing foal. Probably all horses are infected with the mites but only a few ever show any signs of the infection.

Two types of lesion can be seen. In the first the skin becomes thickened and scaly and the hair is lost over the head, neck and withers. In the second the horse develops pea-sized or larger nodules over the neck, shoulder and face. If the nodules are squeezed, a creamy, cheesy material can be extruded. Diagnosis is made on a deep scraping of the skin or on the cheesy material extracted from the nodules. Thousands of the cigar-shaped mites will be seen microscopically in this material.

There is really no effective treatment. Some animals may recover spontaneously without any treatment. Various washes such as fenchlorphos can be scrubbed in well at frequent intervals. This must be done under veterinary supervision as there can be side effects. Nodules in the saddle area can be cut out surgically.

TROMBICULA (HEEL BUG)

The *Trombicula* species mites, commonly known as harvest mites, scrub itch mites or chiggers, live in the soil on low-lying pasture, scrub land or arable land. They are most common on sandy or chalky soils. The mites are normally parasites of small, wild mammals, but they may attack horses, particularly in the late summer and autumn after the corn harvest. The larval stages attach around the heel and pasterns, hence the name heel bug. The mites attach to the skin to suck fluid and a crust forms over the reddened skin. The mites are extremely irritating and the horse may damage itself by kicking at itself and stamping. When the crusts are removed the mites can be seen as very small orange or red dots embedded in the skin.

The mites are easily killed using a leg bath of one of the acaricides.

Preventive measures

The infection can be prevented only by keeping horses away from the land where the harvest mites are common in the autumn. Benzyl benzoate can be applied to the heels and pasterns as a possible repellent. If the stable, sand roll or bedding are infected with mites, these areas can be sprayed with an acaricide, e.g. chlorpyrifos or camphechlor. In parts of Southeast Asia where these mites transmit scrub typhus to man, large areas of ground can be dusted or sprayed with acaricide.

Ticks

Ticks have round bodies with, at the anterior end, some simple mouthparts and three or four pairs of legs. There are four life-cycle stages. The adult female tick lays eggs from which hatch six-legged larvae, 1–2 mm long. The next stage is the eight-legged nymph, which is slightly larger than the larva. The nymphs in turn develop into the adult males or females, which again have eight legs but which are now sexually mature. Each life-cycle stage feeds once. With some ticks all the stages (larva, nymph, adult) feed on one host and it is only the adult female tick which, when fed, drops to the ground to lay eggs in protected places (in cracks and crevices or under stones). Alternatively, each life-cycle stage can feed on a host and then drop off; however it has then to find another host for its next life-cycle stage.

The tick pushes its mouthparts through the skin and anchors itself for about five to ten days, or occasionally much longer, and sucks blood. As it feeds, the tick swells and becomes a blood-filled, leathery bag, usually grey or yellow-brown in colour. A few species of ticks may be ornate, with white, green or other coloured enamelled markings on the dorsal or anterior-dorsal surface.

OTOBIUS MEGNINI (SPINOSE EAR TICK)

This is a pink or blue-grey, leathery tick found in America, Southern Africa and Asia. It will infect the ears of many different animals including the horse.

Life cycle

Only the larval and nymphal stages will infect animals. The larvae attach themselves onto a horse, climb to the ears, inside which they feed. The larvae and nymphs feed from one month up to seven months and, when feeding, become almost spherical. Eventually the nymphs drop off the horse. The adult ticks are not parasitic but live and lay eggs in sheltered spots such as cracks in poles, crevices in walls, under mangers and under the bark of trees. Because the females need this type of shelter, spinose ear ticks are found only on stabled and corralled horses where parasite and host are in close proximity. They are not found on horses on open range.

Clinical signs

The ticks feeding in the ears may make the horses sensitive about the head, shaking their heads and rubbing their ears. The ear may droop.

Diagnosis

A large number of ticks in the ear are easily visible. If only a few are present, then a swab can be rubbed firmly over the skin in the ear canal; some ticks will be dislodged and can be seen on the swab.

Treatment and preventive measures

Infected ears should be treated with a few drops of acaricide (see Table 18).

Horses' ears should be treated with an acaricide once a month to kill the ticks and reduce the number leaving the horse to lay eggs in stables and paddocks. Where horses are becoming heavily infected, the wood and walls of the stable, etc., should be sprayed with an acaricide.

OTHER TICKS AND TICK PARALYSIS

A large number of other species of tick will feed on horses, attaching themselves to the body, in the ears and under the tail. The ticks suck blood and may leave sores and scabs. Heavily infected animals are irritated and will lose condition. The occasional tick on a horse can be removed manually or treated individually with an acaricide so that it will drop off when it dies. In heavy infections in tropical countries horses can be sprayed with an acaricide or, if possible, dipped like cattle.

There are a few ticks that cause **tick paralysis** in animals, including horses. Foals are the most susceptible, but even adult horses can be affected by the presence of forty or more female ticks. Tick paralysis is brought about by a toxin injected into the animal by the adult female tick as she is feeding. It usually starts as a paralysis of the hind legs which moves progressively forward until paralysis of the muscles of respiration and the heart cause death. A case of tick paralysis can be treated by searching the horse for and removing all the ticks. If the paralysis has not progressed too far, it will reverse itself when the ticks are removed.

The most important ticks which cause paralysis and the areas where tick paralysis is most common are: *Ixodes holocyclus* in eastern Australia; *Ixodes rubicundus* in Southern Africa, particularly the Karoo; and *Dermacentor andersoni* in northwestern USA and western Canada.

There are other ticks which cause paralysis and occasionally the condition is found in other countries including Western Europe. Ticks are most important, however, for their transmission of parasites to horses, particularly the protozoan *Babesia* (see chapter 31).

Medical and Surgical Matters

This section contains chapters on various aspects of medical and surgical matters. Deidre Carson describes how medicines are administered and summarizes those which are currently available and Neil Steven's chapter covers the causes, course, treatment and prevention of inflammation.

Poisoning is a risk and worry for owners and those responsible for horses. The chapter by David Frape is therefore appropriate to this section. Preventive medicine is a most important subject on the grounds that prevention is better than cure. Nicholas Wingfield Digby puts forward some ideas regarding this subject particularly in relation to the studfarm.

Casting and anaesthesia, described by Deidre Carson, are a very necessary adjunct nowadays to surgery, a subject dealt with by Neil Steven, while John Cox describes castration and the conditions arising from it.

Wounds, their nature and management are discussed by Deidre Carson and the advice on the first-aid kit is contributed by Jennifer Dykes. Finally in this section I have described growths or, as they are often known, tumours or neoplasias.

The reading of this section should provide the reader with the basic concepts of veterinary practice. As with previous sections, it may be used as a source of reference or individual chapters may be read in order to gain a better understanding of the subjects with which they deal.

33

ROUTES OF ADMINISTRATION
OF MEDICINES

The route of administration of a medicine depends on many factors, including the nature of the disease or injury, the drug being used, the temperament of the patient, the ease of administration of the chosen drug, as well as the nature of the drug itself.

Most drugs can only be administered by certain routes: for example, penicillin is not used orally in horses but may be given intramuscularly or intravenously or applied locally to treat wound infections.

Sometimes different formulations of the same drug are available and each must be administered by a different route. It is important that the person responsible for administering the drug is fully familiar with the chosen route; if not, he or she should use another method of treatment.

The severity of the disease also determines the speed required for the onset of drug action and this influences the choice of drug formulation and the route of administration. For severe infections or other emergency situations it is important to achieve high circulating blood levels of a drug as quickly as possible, and in such cases the intravenous route is often used initially and levels maintained either by further intravenous or by intramuscular or oral treatment. Drugs may be used topically, i.e. applied to the skin, if a local effect is all that is required.

Regardless of the route of administration, the required dose should be calculated accurately before treatment begins.

Oral route

There are several ways to administer drugs to horses by mouth. Powders may be mixed into food or made into a paste, with honey or molasses, which is applied to the tongue. Some drugs are soluble and can be administered in the horse's drinking water.

In these cases the amount of water used to dissolve the drug should be limited and no more given until the dosage is ingested, unless it appears unlikely that the horse will drink any of the medicated water. In the latter instance another method should be used.

Balls or boluses (rounded masses of medication) used to be popular forms of drug presentation but are now seldom used. Prepared pastes are available as vehicles for anthelmintics, antibiotics and anti-inflammatory drugs, as well as for vitamin and mineral preparations. These are often presented in syringes so that the drug can be deposited on the back of the horse's tongue by simply depressing the plunger with the syringe placed well into the horse's mouth.

Drenches or drinks, which are administered by bottle, are occasionally used, but there is a danger of choking the horse if the head is held too high or the medicine given too quickly. The use of a stomach tube overcomes these problems (see below).

Stomach tube

This method of administering drugs is a matter for veterinarians rather than lay people because of the distinct risk of placing the tube in the trachea (windpipe) rather than the oesophagus (gullet).

The use of a rubber or plastic tube allows the administration of a large volume of fluid or medicine directly into the stomach or into the lower part of the oesophagus. It bypasses the mouth, pharynx and much of the oesophagus, so that drugs which may be irritant to these areas can safely be given. It can be used to ensure accurate dosage of drugs such as anthelmintics and anti-inflammatory preparations, for the administration of drugs required to have a local action on the stomach or intestines (e.g. kaolin), or for feeding either debilitated animals or very young or weak foals.

There are many different tube diameter and length combinations available but as a rough guide the following may be used:

	External diameter	Length
Foal	9.5 mm	210 cm
Medium	16 mm	270 cm
Large	19 mm	300 cm

The tube is passed by the veterinarian up the lower part of the nostril, through the pharynx and into the oesophagus. The horse will often have to swallow to allow the tube into the oesophagus. The tip of the tube should be passed to approximately the level of the cardiac sphincter (the opening between the oesophagus and stomach), although it may fall short of this point or actually enter the stomach.

Great care should be taken to ensure that the tube is in the oesophagus and not the trachea because deposition of fluid or drugs into the trachea and lungs can result in severe pneumonia or drowning and death of the horse.

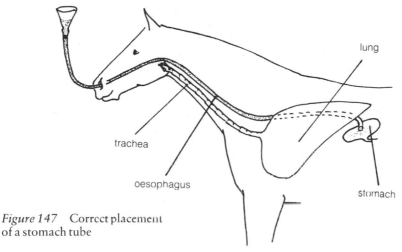

Figure 147 Correct placement
of a stomach tube

There are five ways to check for correct placement of the tube in the oesophagus.

1. The tube can often be seen or felt on the left side of the neck almost in the jugular groove as it passes down the oesophagus.
2. By placing the fingers over the larynx, the tube can be palpated in the very proximal (upper) oesophagus. This may not be possible in horses which are tense or heavily muscled.
3. 'Rattling' the trachea will often result in being able to hear the tube if it has accidentally passed into the trachea.
4. If the tube is in the trachea, it is normally easy to blow down the tube and the horse's breath can be felt at the outer end of the tube when it exhales. If the tube is correctly inserted into the oesophagus there is resistance to the operator's attempts to blow into the tube and a bubble of gas can often be seen passing back up the oesophagus after the tube has been blown down.
5. Air cannot be sucked from the oesophagus.

A funnel or pump can be attached to the free end of the tube to administer the treatment. If a pump is used, do not pump too much too quickly as this may result in overdistension of the stomach and cause pain or rupture.

Parenteral routes

There are several methods for parenteral administration of drugs, that is, other than via the alimentary tract. The main ones are intravenously (IV), intramuscularly (IM) and subcutaneously (SC). No matter which route is chosen, the needle, syringe and drug should be sterile and the skin should be clean and swabbed with alcohol prior to injection.

The needle should be placed in the required site before attaching the syringe or administration set, and its position checked by noting either the presence or the absence of blood in the hub of the needle, the nature and colour of any bloodflow and the depth of needle point. Accidental penetration of an artery or vein when attempting an intramuscular or subcutaneous injection, or correct placement of the needle for intravenous injection, will result in blood entering the needle. If the needle is of wide enough diameter, dark venous blood will either flow freely or drip continuously and steadily from the needle hub when the needle is in a vein. Arterial blood is bright red and either flows in spurts or in a strong stream.

Blood from smaller vessels or through small-diameter needles may only appear in the hub of the needle or come in slow drips. It is important to know whether the drug is suitable for intravenous, intramuscular or subcutaneous administration before proceeding as some drugs which are safe intra-muscularly, for example, may cause severe reactions if given intravenously or subcutaneously.

Intravenous administration This route is used for rapid onset of drug action, for administering large volumes of fluids or drugs either quickly or slowly, or because it is the only safe or convenient route for administration of certain drug formulations. For administration of irritant or large-volume solutions a catheter may be used instead of a needle. A catheter is similar to a needle except that it is made of non-irritant material and is blunt-ended so it can remain in the blood vessel for long periods without causing damage.

The jugular vein is most commonly used because of its large diameter, length and superficial position in the neck. Other veins of the limbs may be used for long-term fluid administration or if the jugular vein is inaccessible for any reason.

Care must be taken to ensure the needle or catheter is placed well *into* and not through the vein. Venous blood should flow from the needle or be able to be aspirated into the syringe to ensure placement is correct before giving the drug.

Accidental intra-arterial or perivascular (around the vein) administration of certain drugs not only reduces their effectiveness but may have severe tissue-damaging or even fatal consequences. Some drugs, if given intra-venously, must be given slowly to avoid side effects, while others must be given very rapidly, as a bolus. It is important to know the properties of the drug before administration.

Intramuscular administration This route is commonly used for administ-ration of drugs as a continuation of therapy and to prolong the action of the drug. The drug usually requires a longer period to take effect than with intravenous treatment.

Such injections may be made into any large muscle mass, the most usual sites being the rump or gluteal region, the neck or the pectoral (chest) region.

Occasionally the back of the thigh (semitendinous, semimembranous muscles) are used.

Proximity to joints, blood vessels or large fat deposits should be avoided because placement of drugs near these structures may result in damage or interference with drug absorption from the site. Always ensure there is no blood coming back down the needle after positioning it in the muscle by withdrawing the plunger on the attached syringe slightly before depressing it to deliver the drug.

Subcutaneous administration   This involves placement of the drug or fluid just under the skin and is achieved by pinching up a fold of loose skin, e.g. on the neck, and placing the needle so that its tip comes to lie in the space created under the fold of skin. This route is used for some vaccines, for fluid administration in certain cases, and for certain drugs which cannot be given by other routes.

Occasionally treatment is given via the intraperitoneal (into abdominal cavity) or intrathoracic (into thoracic cavities) routes, but these are specialized methods of treatment and should not be undertaken by inexperienced persons.

Inhalation

The inhalation of steam or vapours can aid in treatment of respiratory disease. Eucalyptus oil, oil of turpentine or camphor may be added to boiling water in a clean bucket and the horse's head held over the bucket for ten to fifteen minutes. Do not cover the horse's head completely because horses usually resent the resulting interference with respiration.

An alternative method is to use a nosebag or sack in which a sponge or bran soaked in the medicated solution has been placed. Nebulizers, which deliver micro-droplets of drugs, are available for use with drugs cromoglycolate, which is used in the prevention and treatment of allergic respiratory disease (chronic obstructive pulmonary disease or heaves – see p. 48).

Enema

This method allows administration of large volumes of fluids with or without added drugs to aid evacuation of the rectum and colon or to aid in treatment or prevention of dehydration. The rectum should first be cleared of faeces (droppings) using a well-lubricated gloved hand. A lubricated flexible tube is then inserted into the rectum and *gently* passed forward. A pump can be attached to the free end of the tube and the warm fluid slowly pumped into the rectum. No force should be used in an attempt to push the tube farther forward but it may be able to be advanced after the rectum has been distended with fluid. A stomach tube is suitable for this purpose.

Retention of meconium (first faeces) is common in foals and can result in severe pain and signs of colic. Enemas of warm soapy water, paraffin or commercially available solutions which contain sodium phosphate can be used to help lubricate the offending meconium and aid in its evacuation. Extreme care should be taken when positioning the tube in a foal's rectum as the tissues are delicate, often dry and sticky, and the rectum is only small and narrow. Do not use any force but gently advance the tube, if necessary, while pumping the fluid in. A soft tube with no hard or sharp edges is essential for safety.

Intravaginal or intrauterine administration

Treatment of metritis, vaginitis, retention of foetal membranes or induction of luteolysis often requires the administration of fluids into the vagina or uterus. For vaginal or uterine infections and to prevent infection in cases of membrane retention, antibiotics may be added to the fluid. The perineum (the skin around the vulva and anus) is washed and a gloved hand is used to introduce a catheter either through the cervix into the uterus or into the front of the vagina; the fluid is then pumped or poured in. The fluid used must be sterile and preferably warmed to just below body temperature to prevent the introduction of infection and unnecessary irritation.

Pessaries are tablets designed for use in the uterus or vagina which contain antibiotics. Some pessaries foam after contact with the normal tissue fluids to assist the distribution of the contained drug(s).

Topical administration or application

Substances can be applied to surfaces such as the skin, mucous membranes, eyes, hooves, etc., when an effect is only required locally or, in some instances, as a method of administering systemically acting substances, that is, substances which have a general, as opposed to a local, effect. These substances include antibiotics, anti-inflammatory agents, local anaesthetics and astringents, and may be applied as creams, ointments, powders, pastes or solutions. It is important that these preparations are used correctly to be effective.

Some substances, e.g. liniments, have to be rubbed well into the skin to be properly absorbed, whereas others should only be applied lightly. Some should not be used near broken skin as they can be toxic if absorbed into the circulation. To be effective, eye creams and ointments must be placed onto the eye or into the conjunctival sac and not just around the eyelid margins.

34

VETERINARY MEDICINES

There is an enormous number of drugs available to veterinarians, many of which are also easily obtained by owners, for treatment of disease and injury in horses. However although you, as a horse owner, should be familiar with the use and effects of the most commonly used medicines, it is unwise to undertake treatment with unprescribed drugs without consulting your vet.

The following notes are not exhaustive but serve as a guide to the most commonly used and/or readily available medicines.

Acetylpromazine This is one of a group of antihistamines used as tranquillizers and sedatives in the horse. The group also includes chlorpromazine and promethazine. They are useful in fractious horses when proper restraint is necessary for handling when clipping, shoeing or for treatment such as stitching (suturing). The animal must still be handled quietly after tranquillization because overstimulation will result in the horse overcoming the calming effects of the drug.

These drugs also have an analgesic effect and may help to reduce the muscle spasm and pain associated with azoturia. One of the side effects, however, is a decrease in blood pressure, and consequently these drugs should not be used in shocked or debilitated animals.

Acetylpromazine is used orally, intramuscularly or intravenously. Accidental intra-arterial administration results in convulsions and death.

Acridine dyes (acriflavine, aminocrine, proflavine) These dyes have bacteriostatic (microbe-inhibiting) properties and are used in wound powders, solutions or emulsions for skin and wound disinfection and antisepsis. A gel containing acriflavine (0.1 per cent) is often used as a burn treatment; however, it may encourage excessive granulation tissue (proud flesh).

Adrenaline Adrenaline is commonly found in solutions of local anaesthetic agents where it helps to prolong the effect of the anaesthetic. It may be used on its own to control minor haemorrhage when applied topically to a wound. When used systemically, it causes an increase in heart rate and strength, and thus helps to reverse hypotension (low blood pressure) often encountered in anaphylactic shock, i.e. severe allergic reaction.

Aloes (anthracene purgatives)   Aloes is one of a group of substances – the anthracenes – used as purgatives. Other related drugs include Altan and Danthron. They have an irritant and stimulatory effect on the large intestine and aid passage of material through the gut. There is a complex absorption-recirculation cycle associated with the metabolism of the anthracenes and this delays the onset of purgation for up to eighteen hours after administration. The dosage is 8–20 g given by mouth or through a stomach tube.

These substances are most often used as physics (laxatives) or in the treatment of colic associated with impaction of food material or straw in the large intestine. In the latter instance the impacting mass should be lubricated by the administration, by stomach tube, of 2–6 litres of liquid paraffin or faecal softening agents such as dioctyl sodium succinate.

Overdosage or injudicious use of the anthracenes can cause severe diarrhoea (superpurgation) or even death. Purgatives must not be given to any animal with suspected enteritis, peritonitis, intestinal torsion or debilitating conditions.

Ammonia   Ammonia is applied to minor sprains or injuries as a liniment. It is normally available as an emulsion or cream and should be rubbed vigorously into the affected area.

Inhalation of ammonia vapour stimulates respiration and the circulatory system when these are depressed, as, for example, with certain cases of poisoning or after anaesthesia.

Anabolic steroids   This is a group of substances which includes trenbolone, testosterone and nandrolone. Their effects include the acceleration of recovery of weight lost due to debility or undernutrition; an increase in muscular development and tone; the speeding up of tissue regeneration to help the resolution of bone and tissue injuries; assisting in recovery from infectious diseases; and increasing the efficiency of protein utilization. These hormones should not be used without a specific need or for long periods because sudden withdrawal after prolonged administration often results in a marked loss of condition in the treated animal. They may produce male-type behaviour in some fillies and mares.

Anodynes (colic mixtures)   These are medicines which relieve pain in colic. The use of injectable spasmolytics and analgesics such as hyoscine and dipyrone or flunixin meglumine, pethidine and other morphine derivatives has reduced the use of orally administered anodynes. Chloral hydrate is still used orally and/or intravenously. It has a sedative effect and helps in flatulent colic. If given orally, it must be mixed with a large volume of water or oil (paraffin or linseed) to avoid severe irritation to the mouth (if given by bottle) or stomach. Chlorodyne is also given orally in the treatment of colic, either alone or mixed with chloral hydrate.

If no response is seen after dosage or if the colic symptoms become worse, a vet must be called.

The dosage is 15–45 g chloral hydrate given orally in 1–2 litres water or liquid paraffin; or 15 g chloral hydrate and 15 ml chlorodyne with aloes in a vehicle of linseed oil.

Antibacterials and antibiotics These substances are used to destroy (bacteriocidal) or inhibit (bacteriostatic) the growth of bacteria and other disease-causing organisms. There is a large number of these agents and any attempt to cover them all in this book would be impossible and unnecessary. Drugs are constantly being developed and others which were previously only available to doctors are being made available to veterinarians. Many of them are unsuitable for use in the horse because of their side effects, and consequently we often fall back on the basics such as penicillin and sulphonamides.

Briefly, there are several main groups of antibiotics and antibacterial agents.

1. The penicillins, e.g. benzyl penicillin, ampicillin, carbenicillin, cloxacillin and amoxycillin. Penicillin is the most commonly used antibiotic in equine veterinary practice.
2. Aminoglycosides, including gentamycin, streptomycin and neomycin.
3. Tetracyclines.
4. Macrolides, e.g. erythromycin, lincomycin.
5. Cephalosporins.
6. Sulphonamides.

Combinations of drugs are often used either to broaden the range of treatment or to enhance the effectiveness of one or other of the constituents. The effective combinations are fairly standardized, and random mixing should not be undertaken.

The choice of antibiotic or antibacterial agent is essentially based on culturing the infecting organism and observing its susceptibility to various drugs in the laboratory. Veterinary experience, based on recognition of symptoms and the nature of the disease, can enable the most appropriate choice of antibiotic to be made when laboratory facilities are unavailable or can allow treatment to begin before laboratory results are obtained.

Antibiotics can be administered by injection, by mouth or topically, the route depending on the drug used and the nature of the infection (see chapter 33).

Antihistamines This is a class of drugs which interfere with the action of histamine, a substance released in the body which causes pruritis (itchiness), urticaria (rash) and bronchoconstriction (narrowing of the smaller airways). Some antihistamines (see **Acetylpromazine** above) are also used as tranquillizers. The effectiveness of these drugs as antihistamines in the horse is questionable, although they have been suggested for the treatment of conditions including sweet itch, laminitis, azoturia, and allergic skin and respiratory diseases such as chronic obstructive pulmonary disease.

Aspirin This drug is infrequently used as an anti-inflammatory analgesic (pain-relieving) agent in the treatment of muscle or joint injury and arthritis. It is also occasionally used as an antipyretic agent (i.e. to decrease fever) in animals with an elevated temperature. Long-term usage is accompanied by the risk of gastric (stomach) irritation and haemorrhage.

Atropine Atropine is a belladonna alkaloid. It is used topically in eye preparations to relieve pain and spasm of the iris by dilating the pupil. It has a long action of several days. It is occasionally used systemically, being given subcutaneously as a premedicant prior to general anaesthesia and in the treatment of organophosphorous poisoning. It causes a slowing of intestinal motility and reduces the production of saliva and digestive enzymes. Poisoning can occur through overdosage or through ingestion of the belladonna plant from which atropine is derived.

Boric acid (boracic acid) This is used as a wound dressing either alone, as a 4 per cent solution, or combined with zinc oxide and iodoform for application to wounds. It is also often incorporated in poultices.

Camphor This is a volatile oil, like turpentine and mustard oil. All these substances cause mild local irritation and pain relief when applied to areas of inflammation, sprains, etc. They are called rubefacients or mild blisters and are used as liniments. They should be applied with friction.

Catechu Catechu is an intestinal astrigent used to sooth intestinal inflammation in cases of enteritis or diarrhoea. It is usually combined with chalk and kaolin. Dosage is 8–16 g by mouth or stomach tube.

Caustics These are substances which destroy excess granulation tissue and minor superficial tumours. They cause death of cells and precipitation of protein to form a scab, which must be removed prior to reapplication of the caustic agent. This group of substances includes copper sulphate, phenol, antimony trichloride and silver nitrate.

The skin surrounding the excess granulation tissue or tumour should be protected by a covering of Vaseline or other ointment and the caustic carefully applied to the lesion only. The area should be lightly bandaged if possible, and re-examined and cleaned twenty-four to forty-eight hours later. If necessary the caustic can be reapplied at this time.

Chalk (calcium carbonate) Prepared chalk is a valuable antacid and protectant in the treatment of diarrhoea. It is usually combined with kaolin.

Chloral hydrate This drug is less frequently used now than in the past due to the development of modern sedatives and analgesics, although it is still sometimes used for the treatment of colic and prior to induction of general anaesthesia (see **Anodynes** above). Given orally, it produces a sedative effect approximately half an hour after administration and can be useful when clipping or shoeing fractious horses. It must be given well diluted (a dosage of 15–45 g in 1–2 litres water).

Chloral hydrate is also used as a general anaesthetic agent. It is given intravenously, normally in combination with magnesium sulphate and pentobarbitone.

Chlorhexidine Chlorhexidine is a very effective antiseptic agent. It is found in powders or creams at a 1 per cent concentration, and for pre-operative skin preparation as a 0.5 per cent alcoholic or 1 per cent aqueous solution.

Clenbuterol Clenbuterol is used to relieve spasm of the small airways in chronic obstructive pulmonary disease (allergic respiratory disease), chronic bronchitis and influenza. It is available as an injectable solution or as granules which are mixed into feed.

Codeine Codeine is used as a cough suppressant in animals with respiratory disease and as a constipant and analgesic in horses with diarrhoea. It is given orally, either as a solution by stomach tube or drench, or mixed with honey or molasses into a paste to be applied to the tongue.

Copper sulphate This blue salt is used as an astringent and caustic agent in the reduction of granulation tissue (see **Caustics** above). It can be applied as a solution (2–4 per cent) paste or as the dry crystal, care being taken not to damage the epithelium around the edge of the wound.

The area should be covered lightly for twenty-four hours, after which time the scab should be removed and the area washed and dried. Treatment can be repeated, if necessary either immediately or twenty-four hours later.

Copper sulphate solution (1–2 per cent) or ointment/paste (5 per cent) is also useful as an antifungal treatment for ringworm.

Corticosteroids (cortisone) Cortisone is a steroid hormone (see p. 118) produced by the adrenal gland. It and many similar synthetic substances influence metabolism, healing, allergic reactions, kidney function and the body's electrolyte balance. The major application of corticosteroids is in the control and reduction of inflammation associated with skin, muscle and joint conditions. Unfortunately the anti-inflammatory effects cannot be utilized without some of the side effects influencing tissue healing, hormonal balances, and so on. Consequently corticosteroids should only be used as prescribed by a vet.

Commonly used corticosteroids include betamethasone, dexamethasone, prednisolone, triamcinolone and hydrocortisone (cortisol). They may be used intravenously, intramuscularly, intra-articularly (into the joint space), locally or topically (e.g. in the eye or on the skin).

Cough mixtures   A cough is a symptom of disease, not a disease itself. In many cases coughing is due to or worsened by irritants such as dust in the stable. Consequently any horse with a cough should have its feed dampened, its hay soaked, and either paper, shavings or another form of dust-free bedding should be provided. Orally administered preparations usually contain a mixture of expectorants and cough sedatives or suppressants. Potassium iodide, sodium iodide and codeine are common constituents of cough mixtures. Etamiphylline is a stimulant which improves respiratory function; it should only be administered under veterinary supervision.

Dichlorvos   Dichlorvos is used in the treatment of stomach bots (see pp. 464–6).

Dimethyl sulphoxide (DMSO)   Dimethyl sulphoxide is used topically to reduce pain, pruritis (itching) and inflammation and to promote healing. It is rapidly absorbed through the skin and can be used as a carrier to help transport other substances, such as phenylbutazone, through the skin. It is useful in the treatment of musculoskeletal injuries, some skin disorders and joint problems. The area to be treated should be cleaned first and the solution of DMSO applied with a brush. Always use gloves when using any solution of DMSO.

Diuretics   Diuretics are drugs which cause the excretion of larger than normal volumes of urine. They are useful to help in treatment of oedema due to protein loss, as, for example in liver or intestinal disease, and also in cases of parasitism, inflammation, heart disease and allergy. They are also administered in some cases of azoturia and shock to help maintain kidney function. Drugs commonly used include furosemide and hydrochloro-thiazide.

Electrolytes   Electrolytes are salts of various kinds such as sodium chloride (common salt), sodium acetate, sodium bicarbonate (baking soda), potassium chloride and lactate. Combinations of electrolytes in solution are useful in supportive therapy in cases of diarrhoea, excessive sweating, exhaustion and dehydration, when loss of electrolytes from the body may have occurred. Commercially prepared electrolyte mixtures are available as powders or syrups for dilution in drinking water or for administration by drench or stomach tube. Occasionally vitamins, minerals and glucose may also be included in these mixtures. Such preparations must be diluted and administered according to manufacturers' recommendations.

In severe cases of diarrhoea, dehydration or other debilitating conditions, electrolyte solutions can be administered intravenously by a veterinarian. These solutions are specially prepared and sterile and this form of therapy should not be undertaken by unqualified people.

Eucalyptus oil This is used as a liniment and mild counter-irritant for application to sprains and superficial contusions. It may also be used as an inhalant to help relieve catarrh, a few drops of eucalyptus oil being added to boiling water.

Eye lotions In the absence of veterinary advice in cases of conjunctivitis or following a blow to the eye, any of the following can be used with the assurance that, if not beneficial, they will not aggravate the condition:

  10 g boric acid in 250 ml purified, freshly boiled water, which is allowed to cool;
  10 g sodium bicarbonate in 10 ml purified water; *or*
  10 g sodium chloride (regular table salt) in 110 ml purified water.

If no improvement is seen in twenty-four hours, veterinary advice should be sought.

Ferric/ferrous compounds Many iron preparations act as astringents, both internally and externally. Ferrous sulphate is used as an intestinal astringent agent, often with kaolin or chalk. Excessive use may result in gastric irritation, constipation or diarrhoea. Iron compounds are also used as haematinics (substances which stimulate red blood cell formation) in the treatment of anaemias. Ferric chloride is used as a topically applied solution to control minor haemorrhage.

Flunixin meglumine Flunixin meglumine is an anti-inflammatory and antipyretic (temperature-reducing) analgesic used for the treatment of inflammation and pain associated with musculoskeletal disorders and some forms of colic. The recommended dose is 1.1 mg per kilogramme body-weight either orally or by intramuscular or intravenous injection daily for up to five days.

Fomentation   A fomentation is, strictly speaking, the application to the skin of heat and moisture by some vehicle such as flannel. In stable parlance, bathing any part with warm water is called 'fomenting'.

Fomentations over large surfaces are best applied by dipping a blanket or other woollen cloth in hot water, wringing it moderately dry, applying it to the part, and then covering it with a waterproof sheet or dry blanket. When the underneath blanket loses most of its heat, it should be changed for another blanket, care being taken that the animal does not get chilled during the interval. The fomentations should not be hotter than the hand can comfortably bear.

Griseofulvin/antifungal agents   Griseofulvin is most often used as an antifungal agent in the treatment of ringworm. Although administered orally, it accumulates in the layers of the skin. Dosage of 10 mg per kilogramme bodyweight daily should be continued for at least one week.

Other antifungal agents are used topically. These include emilconazade (used as a 0.2 per cent solution) and benzyldazic acid (used as a 0.5 per cent solution). One of these solutions should be applied every two or three days for three or four applications, and then again after an interval of approximately two weeks. Scabs, mud and debris should be removed prior to treatment to ensure total coverage of the affected area(s).

Hyoscine (hyoscine-n-butyl bromide)   This is an antispasmodic with smooth-muscle relaxant properties, used in the treatment of diarrhoea and colic. It is related chemically to atropine (see above) but has more specific actions on the gut with fewer side effects. It is available as an injection for intravenous use.

Iodine   Iodine has antiseptic and irritant actions. Strong iodine solution is used as a rubiefacient and mild blister. Weak solution of iodine contains potassium iodide and iodine, and is used as an antiseptic and mild irritant to help relieve inflammation. Aqueous Solution of Iodine (Lugol's iodine) was frequently used for uterine irrigation but can be very irritant and has lost favour.

Iodine is often found in combination with surface-active agents as iodophors, which are non-irritant, non-staining and have cleansing and antibacterial properties. These are used for pre-surgical skin preparation, the cleansing of wounds and, in very dilute form, for flushing wound cavities or cleansing sites. An example is povidone iodine.

Some iodine salts (sodium iodide, potassium iodide) are used systemically in the treatment of a number of chronic or abscess-forming infections because they appear to reduce or penetrate the fibrous tissue associated with these conditions which often interferes with or prevents adequate penetration of administered drugs.

Magnesium sulphate (Epsom salts) This is commonly used as a laxative and, at higher doses, a purgative in horses. It acts to increase the amount of water in the food material passing through the intestine, thus increasing the fluidity and volume of the intestinal contents. It must not be used in dehydrated animals as it may exacerbate the condition. The normal dose for purgation is 30–60 g in food or administered through a stomach tube.

Mefenamic acid/meclofenamic acid These are related anti-inflammatory agents, with antipyretic and analgesic actions. They are more powerful than phenylbutazone and are used in the treatment of musculoskeletal disorders. Meclofenamic acid is available as granules for administration in feed.

Naproxen Naproxen is an anti-inflammatory agent useful in the treatment of pain and lameness associated with soft-tissue disorders such as muscle sprain and inflammation.

Opium, morphine and related drugs This group includes codeine, pethidine and other morphine derivatives. Their effects on the body are numerous and widespread but they are most valuable for their analgesic, spasmolytic and cough-suppressant actions.

Morphine is commonly used with kaolin in the treatment of diarrhoea. It decreases intestinal mobility and helps reduce pain. Codeine is also useful in diarrhoea.

Pethidine is a commonly used analgesic, although it has only a short duration of action and has been replaced by newer, longer-lasting painkillers such as flunixin meglumine. It is occasionally combined with tranquillizers such as acetylpromazine to enhance the degree of tranquillization.

With all these drugs, central nervous system depression is a major feature. Consequently they must be used with care and are only available to vets.

Peroxide (hydrogen peroxide) Hydrogen peroxide is used as a 10–50 per cent solution for antisepsis and deodorization of tissues. It has a cleansing effect and is useful in deep wounds and abscesses. Its foaming action is associated with the release of oxygen, which has a mechanical cleaning effect and lasts as long as the solution is active.

Phenylbutazone Phenylbutazone is one of the most frequently used and abused drugs available for use in the horse. It is a non-steroidal anti-inflammatory drug (NSAID) which is also an analgesic as a result of its anti-inflammatory action.

It is widely used in horses for reducing pain and inflammation in the treatment of traumatic or inflammatory musculoskeletal disorders, lameness, to prevent or reduce post-operative swelling and pain, and in some infectious conditions such as ulcerative lymphangitis.

It is available as a powder for mixing with feed, as a paste for oral administration, as a solution for intravenous injection, and, in some topically applied medicaments, in combination with dimethyl sulphoxide. The intravenous form is *very* irritant if accidentally administered into muscle or around the vein. If given intra-arterially it causes death.

The recommended dosage for a 450-kg (1000-lb) horse is 2 g both morning and evening on day 1 of treatment, then 1 g morning and evening for four days, then 1 g daily or on alternate days. *Ponies do not tolerate phenylbutazone as well as larger horses and are more susceptible to its toxic effects.* Consequently lower dosages must be used, i.e. 1 g per 225 kg (500 lb) daily for four days, followed by 0.5–1 g every other day.

Long-term use or use in very sensitive horses can cause irritation of the lining of the stomach and intestine and occasionally severe intestinal malfunction. Blood and bone marrow abnormalities may sometimes be associated with phenylbutazone therapy.

Poultices   These are valuable as soothing applications and for cleansing wounds, in which case they should be combined with a mild antiseptic to discourage growth of microbes which would be favoured by the moist warmth of the poultice.

Poultices can be applied to the feet with the aid of a boot or bandage, and can be bandaged or 'plastered' onto limbs or body.

The most commonly used poultices include: antiphlogistine, which is available as a paste; kaolin, which is available as a powder or paste; Animalintex, a proprietary boric-acid-impregnated dressing which should be wetted with warm to hot water before application.

Poultices have a drawing action on wounds and are most useful in cases of puncture or infected wounds. They are also useful in the treatment of bruised sole and in cases of pus in the foot, as they tend to soften the sole and draw the bruise or infection, allowing easier drainage, thus alleviating pain. The hoof should be dry bandaged or otherwise protected after removal of the poultice to allow the horn and wall to dry and harden before the shoe is replaced and the animal put back into work.

Sodium bicarbonate (baking soda)   'Bicarb' is used to reduce gastric acidity following grain engorgement or associated with high intake of soluble carbohydrate. It can be given orally in feed or drinking water. It is believed to help in reducing acidosis associated with exhaustive exercise or azoturia.

Sterile solutions of sodium bicarbonate (usually 1.5 per cent) are used intravenously to treat acidosis associated with colic, respiratory depression or other metabolic disturbances.

Sulphonamides   The sulphonamides are antibacterial compounds used both topically and internally for the prevention and treatment of nonspecific infections. Sulphanilamide is a common constituent of wound powders and dressings. It is also given orally as a powder in the feed, or mixed with honey or molasses to form a paste which can be applied to the back of the tongue. Dosage is 40–60 g daily for a 500-kg adult horse.

The sulphonamides are bacteriostatic, that is, they prevent the multiplication of some bacteria but do not destroy them. Combination with trimethoprim to form potentiated sulphonamides enhances the effectiveness of both sulphonamide and trimethoprim and produces a bacteriocidal (microbe-killing) action for the treatment of established infections.

Sulphur Sulphur has, for many years, been used as a treatment for skin diseases of bacterial and parasitic origin. It is frequently found in shampoos, in some skin lotions and in ointments or combined with talc or kaolin in dusting or dispersable powders.

Tannin/tannic acid This is an astringent used both internally, in cases of diarrhoea, and topically for skin lesions and minor burns. When given orally it helps the formation of a protective coating for irritated or inflamed intestinal lining. Topically, tannic acid may be combined in hydrophilic gels or solutions to sooth minor burns, reduce inflammation and help reduce haemorrhage.

Zinc Commonly used zinc salts include zinc oxide and zinc carbonate. These are used topically in powders, creams, lotions and liniments. They have astringent, antiseptic and protective actions.

Zinc oxide is combined with castor oil to produce a soothing protective dressing (zinc and castor oil cream), and with cod liver oil as a treatment for conjunctivitis. It can also be combined with lard for application to cracked heels.

Wound powders containing zinc oxide or carbonate usually have a chalk, talc or starch base and may contain sulphanilamide and insecticides.

Zinc sulphate is a stronger astringent and promotes scab formation on wounds. White lotion contains zinc sulphate (4 per cent) and lead acetate (5 per cent) in water and is a cooling, soothing lotion for minor superficial inflammation, bruising and itching.

35
METHODS OF RESTRAINT AND HANDLING

Occasionally, just observing a horse loose in its stable or paddock will give enough information to determine if there is anything wrong with it. Most often, however, a degree of restraint is necessary to allow observation, manipulation, palpation and treatment of a part or the whole of the animal. This not only applies to veterinary procedures but also to farriery, dentistry and all aspects of horse handling and education. Restraint can be achieved either by physical or chemical means or by a combination of both.

Physical restraint

For minor procedures in quiet or very ill animals, manual restraint with either a head collar or a bridle is often adequate: most horses can be injected with antibiotics or a vaccine while being held quietly. For firmer control a Chifney (anti-rearing) bit may be useful.

Further restraint can be achieved by grasping or pinching a fold of loose skin on the neck, just in front of the shoulders. The skin should be held tightly in a closed fist. This method is very effective for horses which tend to wriggle or to pull away and is easily achieved by the person holding the horse's head.

For procedures involving one of the limbs or when trying to prevent a horse kicking, a front leg can be held up so that the animal is standing on three legs. This often requires a second person so that whoever is holding the head can concentrate on keeping the head up and the animal still. Obviously no attempt should be made to pick up another of the horse's legs while one is already being held up in case the horse panics or falls over.

The twitch, consisting of a length of smooth wood with a loop of rope or twine through a hole at one end, is a very useful tool when trying to restrain a horse physically. It is normally applied to the upper lip, although occasionally it is used on one of the horse's ears. The loop of the twitch is passed over one of the operator's hands, while the handle of the twitch is held in the other hand or by the person holding the horse's head. The horse's lip or ear is grasped in the hand with the loop. The loop is then passed over the hand and the twitch handle twisted to tighten the loop onto the chosen part. This will result in the animal standing rigidly and any required procedure can then be carried out.

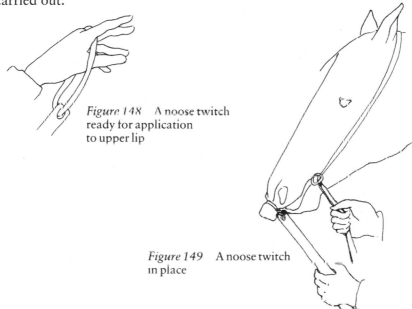

Figure 148   A noose twitch ready for application to upper lip

Figure 149   A noose twitch in place

Veterinary procedures which are made easier and safer to perform with the nose twitch include rectal examination, passing a stomach tube or endoscope up the nostril, and injecting into or around joints and other structures in the legs, procedures for which the horse must be standing absolutely still.

Occasionally you will come across a horse which will fight the twitch and such animals are more dangerous with the twitch on than without.

Casting is an old method of restraint which makes use of ropes and hobbles or a rope and a casting harness. Unfortunately it causes a high degree of anxiety and struggling on the part of the horse as its legs are literally pulled out from under it.

There are basically two types of casting harness, one of which flexes the hind legs and forces the horse into a sitting position before it is cast onto its side. The second consists of hobbles on three or four of the legs, which are drawn together, thereby overbalancing the horse. Once the horse is on the ground, its free leg may be tied or held.

Casting is less widely used nowadays since the development of effective tranquillizers and local and general anaesthetics. Occasionally it is combined with one or a combination of chemical agents which reduce the animal's struggles and thus the risk of injury to horse and humans.

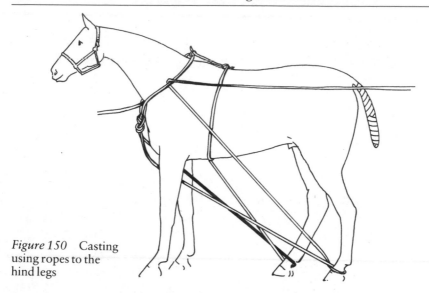

Figure 150 Casting using ropes to the hind legs

Chemical restraint

The use of drugs such as sedatives, tranquillizers, local and general anaesthetics and analgesics makes restraint safer for horse and handler. It also simplifies many procedures by making the animal tractable and helping to minimize pain and anxiety.

Tranquillizers and sedatives are given by injection or by mouth. Their effect can vary from mild tranquillization to profound sedation, depending on the drug being used and the dosage given. Many of these drugs can have a seriously detrimental effect on blood pressure and the central nervous system if given incorrectly or in overdose.

Signs that the drug is taking effect include a dropping of the head, prolapse of the penis in colts and geldings, and a glazed look about the eyes. Profound sedation is marked by a drooping of the upper and lower lips and eyelids, and a rocking motion with the horse occasionally knuckling on one of its fetlocks (the use of certain drugs may result in the horse standing perfectly still without knuckling).

Depending on the drug used, the dosage given, the temperament of the animal and the effects of any other drug or drugs being used, the time for which the animal is effectively tranquillized or sedated will vary greatly, being anything from a few minutes to several hours.

Some drugs have an analgesic (painkilling) action as well as a tranquillizing effect. This property makes them very useful for minor procedures which involve potentially painful steps such as stitching superficial wounds. In most cases, however, such procedures will require the use of an anaesthetic agent, either administered in combination with a tranquillizer or on its own.

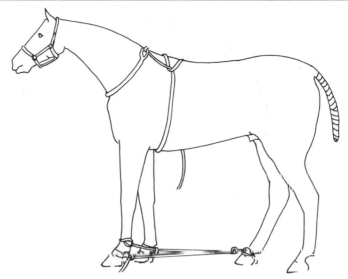

Figure 151   Casting with hobbles

Anaesthetic agents

Anaesthesia may be local, i.e. involving only a small area; regional, i.e. involving a larger region or part of the body; or general, i.e. involving the whole body. Drugs used for regional anaesthesia are called local anaesthetics or local anaesthetic agents. Drugs used for general anaesthesia are called general anaesthetic agents or, more loosely, just anaesthetics.

Local and regional anaesthesia   Local and regional anaesthetics can be used on their own, with the animal twitched, or, if necessary, with the animal tranquillized or sedated. Local anaesthesia is used when stitching wounds, lancing haematomas or removing small lumps of skin. In these cases the local anaesthetic is injected along the edges of the wound or proposed incision. If the wound is extensive, the anaesthetic may be used in an inverted 'L' pattern several centimetres away from the wound and through all affected layers to desensitize the nerves passing to the area to be treated (nerve blocking).

Regional anaesthesia involves desensitizing or numbing the nerve or nerves supplying a particular region which is often distant from the site of injection of the anaesthetic solution. This type of nerve block is most often used in the diagnosis of lameness or when treating limb injuries. The local anaesthetic solution is injected into a specific site around a particular nerve, resulting in the desensitization of part of the limb. Injection over the outer aspect of both sesamoid bones in one limb, for example, will desensitize much of the pastern and foot in that particular limb. If, after desensitization, a lame horse subsequently goes sound it is almost certain that the lesion is below the level of the nerve block.

Local anaesthesia is also used for standing castrations. The solution is injected into the testicle and cord and under the scrotal skin along the line of incision.

Epidural anaesthesia involves the injection of a local anaesthetic agent into the spinal canal around the spinal cord, thus desensitizing the nerves within the spinal canal and where they exit into the surrounding tissues. This type of anaesthesia is most often used for obstetrical procedures and surgery in the region of the perineum or tail.

General anaesthesia   General anaesthesia is anaesthesia of the whole body: the animal becomes recumbent, does not move (except for minor involuntary movements), does not feel pain and does not have any recall of the procedure performed. It is mainly used when the procedure is painful or lengthy, when total immobilization of the patient is necessary, when the temperament of the patient or the site for surgery is not conducive to local or regional anaesthesia, or when the animal has to be positioned unnaturally – for example, on its back. The types of case which require general anaesthesia in the horse include repair of fractures, castration, treating major wounds, surgery for colic and surgery on the head and upper respiratory passages.

General anaesthesia must be induced and then maintained. Induction is the transition from consciousness to the state of anaesthesia; this state must then be maintained for the duration of the procedure. After this the animal is allowed to wake up or recover.

There are a number of anaesthetic drugs available and these can be classified as injectable or inhalable (volatile or gaseous) anaesthetic agents.

Injectable anaesthetics include the barbiturates, the combination of xylazine and ketamine, glyceryl guaiacolate and thiopentone and many others. The drugs are usually injected after premedication of the patient with a tranquillizer and the dose rate depends on the weight of the animal. If the patient is severely ill or depressed, the dose rate is reduced accordingly. Using a combination of different tranquillizers and anaesthetic agents may permit a reduction in the required dosage of all the agents used, thus minimizing the depressant effects on the patient.

Injectable anaesthetics are used for the induction of anaesthesia before maintenance, which is achieved either by giving further incremental doses of the injectable anaesthetic or by transferring the patient to an anaesthetic machine. In the latter case the anaesthetic state is maintained with a volatile or gaseous anaesthetic agent.

Inhalation anaesthesia with volatile liquids or gases is used almost exclusively for maintaining anaesthesia after induction with an intravenous agent. The major exception to this is when inducing anaesthesia in foals. When very young, foals can be masked down, that is, induced by placing an anaesthetic mask over their nostrils or a nasal tube into a nostril to allow the administration of gaseous anaesthetic until unconsciousness is achieved.

After induction in both foals and adults, an endotracheal tube is introduced via the mouth into the trachea and this is connected to an anaesthetic machine which supplies both oxygen and the anaesthetic agent to the patient. The depth of anaesthesia is controlled by altering the concentration of anaesthetic in the oxygen being inhaled by the patient. Once the procedure is completed the concentration of the anaesthetic gas in the mixture is reduced to zero so that the patient is no longer inhaling any anaesthetic, and the horse is allowed to breath pure oxygen via the machine for at least ten minutes. After this time the horse breathes air via the endotracheal tube until it swallows; the tube is then removed and the animal allowed to recover.

The time taken for the horse to recover until it is able to stand varies with the anaesthetic agent or agents used, the duration of the procedure, and the temperament and condition of the horse. Recovery after prolonged intravenous anaesthesia can be long, and the animal may struggle considerably before being able to stand. Horses anaesthetized in the paddock must not be left unattended until standing and able to walk.

Occasionally it is necessary to have an attendant sitting on the horse's head and neck and covering its eyes to try to reduce the animal's struggles and attempts to stand before it is ready. If necessary, the horse should be supported by its head and tail until it is standing steadily on its feet.

Veterinary practices with surgical facilities usually have a special recovery box with padded walls and floor where the horse is anaesthetized and later allowed to recover. In some cases the same room functions as the operating theatre. In others, the anaesthetized horse is moved by hobbles and winch, in a net or on a mobile table or fork lift to the operating theatre and back again.

Although general anaesthesia simplifies many diagnostic, surgical and manipulative procedures in the horse, it is not without its inherent complications. Most of the problems encountered when anaesthetizing horses are associated with its large size and weight. In some cases pressure on the underlying muscles causes muscle cell damage, with associated pain, swelling and release of cell contents, resulting in lameness and in some cases inability to bend or bear weight on one or more of the limbs. This is known as post-operative myopathy. It is most common and most severe in horses held in dorsal recumbency (on their backs) for long periods, although it is not uncommon in horses kept on their sides for a lengthy operation. The affected horse may not be able to stand at all, or may be able to stand but unable to move, or may be able to move only with difficulty after the anaesthetic has worn off. Many of these cases need intensive treatment to recover fully. Occasionally only one or a small group of muscles or nerves is affected and this leads to local paralysis of, for example, the facial nerve or the radial nerve of the forelimb.

Horses are not unlike all other animal species in that some individuals will be particularly sensitive to an anaesthetic agent. All anaesthetic agents cause a drop in blood pressure, respiration and cardiac output. Overdosage in healthy animals or relative overdosage – that is, the administration of normal doses to a sick or otherwise compromised animal or to an animal which is particularly sensitive to a particular drug – will result in severe cardiovascular depression and compromise and in many cases death. On the other hand, there is a very small percentage of horses which, when given an appropriate dosage of an anaesthetic agent, will fail to become anaesthetized or may even go into a stage of excitement. Such animals will usually respond normally to a different drug or combination of drugs.

36

INFLAMMATION

Inflammation is the active response of living tissue to injury and infection. The following description is therefore applicable within the context of this book where diseases caused by infection (pp. 395–474) or injury to parts such as tendons, joints and bone (pp. 153–223) or wounds (pp. 547–56) are discussed. In essence, wherever there is disease or injury suffered by an individual, the inflammatory process is present.

The suffix 'itis' denotes inflammation, e.g. bronchitis = inflammation of the bronchi. It is characterized by the appearance of redness, swelling, heat and pain, and frequently attended by loss of function of the affected part.

The inflammatory process is a non-specific defence mechanism, brought into play by the phagocyte system and initiated in response to chemical messages released by cells and damaged tissues.

The phagocyte system is composed primarily of macrophages and polymorphonuclear leucocytes (types of white blood cell) which ingest and destroy bacteria, particularly foreign material and degenerate cellular tissue. This system is mobilized at the site of injury via the terminal vascular system of capillaries and lymphatic channels.

It should be noted that the inflammatory process may become integrated with the other major body defence – the immune system, which is regarded as a specific defence mechanism.

The immune system attacks invasive bacteria, viruses or toxins with 'killer' lymphocytes and antibodies specifically manufactured to deal with a particular organism which has been recognized as foreign to the host from previous exposure. The phagocyte system primes the immune system with antigens derived from the breakdown of the invasive organisms by the leucocytes.

The inflammatory process occurs in two phases:

1. The immediate response, which is an initial transitory reaction of twenty to thirty minutes' duration induced by any stimulus which damages mast

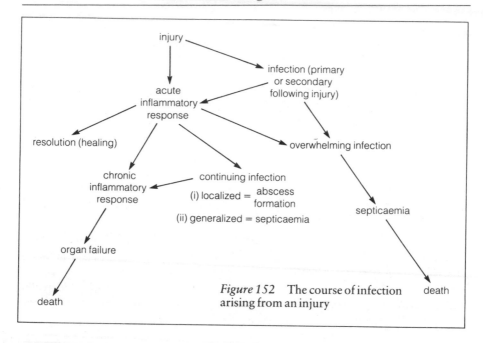

Figure 152   The course of infection arising from an injury

cells (which are found in connective tissue). It is characterized by increased blood flow to the area and leakage of plasma into the surrounding tissues. This is clinically manifested as redness and heat.

2. The delayed response, which is more severe and prolonged, is characterized by persistence of plasma leakage, stasis of blood flow and possible haemorrhage and emigration of leucocytes and macrophages into the tissues. Clinically this is manifested as swelling and pain.

As a consequence of tissue swelling the lymphatic channels open, thereby increasing lymph flow and drainage, with removal of cell debris, bacteria and waste products. Clinically the lymph nodes which drain the area may become reactive and enlarged.

This basic process occurs in all types of tissue injury, from simple skin penetration by a thorn to that of gross tissue damage associated with trauma or in septic states caused by specific bacterial infection, which may affect any tissue or organ system.

Causes

The causes of inflammation are many and varied, but they may be placed in one of four categories:

1. Mechanical – direct trauma or mechanical overload of a tissue, such as overstretching of a tendon resulting in sprain.
2. Thermal – excessive heat or cold, ultraviolet and infrared light and radiation.

3. Chemical – caustic alkali, acids and blisters.
4. Toxic – plant poisons, bacterial and fungal toxins.

Clinical signs

The clinical signs of inflammation are classically defined as redness (rubor), swelling (tumour), heat (calor) and pain (dolour), as well as loss of function – the signs of celsis.

At this stage, if the reader recalls from personal experience the effects of a bee sting, he or she will be able to appreciate the changes described above.

The redness and heat are associated with increased bloodflow to the area, and swelling and pain are associated with the formation of oedema, as well as with the release of enzymes and vasoactive substances which are involved in mediation of the inflammatory response.

The physical signs of inflammation depend on factors such as the nature and severity of the injury or infection, the tissue or organs affected, species susceptibility to particular micro-organisms, and host adaptations of the inflammatory response, as well as the virulence of the invading organisms, the severity of infection and other complicating factors such as loss of blood supply or tissue anoxia (oxygen starvation).

Inflammatory disease of the musculoskeletal system invariably results in lameness, a symptom which is readily appreciated and directly referable to the organ system involved. However, the clinical signs of inflammation may not always be directly attributable to their source. For example, inflammatory disease of the biliary system of the liver may produce clinical symptoms of jaundice in the skin, the membranes or the appearance of bile pigments in the urine. In this instance some of the symptoms of hepatitis are being manifested indirectly via different organ systems.

Pain is another feature frequently associated with inflammatory disease, and appreciation of the source of pain depends on the presence of pain receptor nerve endings in the affected tissue. Some tissues – for example, the myocardium of the heart and the brain itself – are poorly endowed with pain receptors, and injury here may be poorly appreciated. Inflammation of the myocardium or abdominal viscera may result in awareness of 'referred' pain, which the patient may think arises in a part distant from the actual inflamed area.

Frequently when the body mounts an inflammatory response there will be a systemic (general) reaction which may incorporate, in addition to the local signs, a pyrexic episode (an increase in body temperature), rigors and generalized discomfort, dullness and anorexia (lack or loss of appetite).

Course of inflammation

The course of an inflammation depends on several of the above factors, as well as the ability of the horse to mount a vigorous and successful response to the original challenge. A debilitated subject may not be able to muster sufficient reserves to produce an effective response to bacterial challenge which, under normal circumstances, would not be markedly pathogenic. The hope for the outcome of any inflammatory process is for healing of tissues with restoration of function and without undue secondary complications.

The outcome of the acute inflammatory process falls into one of the following categories:

1. Resolution, whereby the injury heals rapidly without complication, as in a surgical wound which heals by first intention with a minimum of scar tissue.
2. Resolution after extensive tissue damage complicated by wound contamination, bacterial infection and resultant exudation. These wounds are characterized by an exudative inflammatory process, followed by the production of granulation tissue and significant end-stage fibrosis (scar formation). Examples of these are suppuration, abscessation, sinus, fistula, cellulitis, ulceration and necrosis.

   Suppuration refers to the formation of pus by massive exudation and accumulation of leucocytes in response to pyogenic bacteria, e.g. staphylococcus, streptococcus and corynebacteria. These organisms produce toxins and are not readily destroyed by white blood cells. Suppuration may occur in any tissue or on any body surface such as the skin and the pleura.

   Abscessation refers to the formation of abscesses, which are localized collections of pus produced by the deep seeding of infectious bacteria, frequently caused by a penetrating foreign body.

   A **sinus** is a blind discharging channel which may form as the drainage tract from an infected vicinity or established abscess. For example, a bony sequestrum (dead bone) will discharge through a sinus. Other examples are fistulous withers and poll evil, often the result of an injury.

   A **fistula** is a channel from a natural cavity or duct to the exterior, for example, a recto-vaginal fistula.

   Cellulitis is a diffuse spreading inflammation in solid tissues – for example, along muscle or tendon sheaths or subcutaneously. It may be purulent.

   Ulceration consists of lesions formed by superficial necrosis of an epithelial surface leading to exposure of underlying tissue; it has little tendency to heal.

   Necrosis means death of a limited portion of tissue and may be a result of anoxia or loss of blood supply secondary to clot formation. Necrosis includes **gangrene**, which is termed dry when it is caused by loss of blood circulation, or moist when it is the result of potent toxins produced by bacterial infection.
3. Non-resolution, which consists of:
   (a) acute inflammation in association with extensive fibrosis;

(b) a proliferative cellular response and induction of the immune system in which a delayed hypersensitivity reaction may occur, as, for example, in tuberculosis; or

(c) infective granulomata. These consist of a particular type of abscess which is produced in response to specific bacterial infections.

Treatment

The general principles of treatment of inflamed areas are as follows:

1. The cause should be identified and removed.
2. Circulation to the affected part should be restored and improved, thereby hastening the removal of waste products and supplying nutrients for tissue repair.
3. Collections of pus should be drained and dead tissue removed as soon as possible.
4. The injured area should be rested in the acute phase and may require immobilization.
5. Local treatment may consist of lavage with antiseptics, saline solution or antibiotic.

If shock or blood loss is apparent, then fluid replacement therapy and administration of corticosteroids may be necessary. Systemic administration of drugs to control pain and inflammation, to reduce oedema and to control bacterial contamination or infection with pyogenic organisms is frequently indicated. Medication with non-steroidal anti inflammatory drugs, diuretics and antibiotics is employed.

Simple acute inflammation of a traumatic nature involving the musculoskeletal system may be treated initially with cold applications to reduce blood supply to the area and control the formation of oedema. The application of pressure with bandages may be helpful to this end. Subsequently application of heat alternating with cold will be beneficial by stimulating the circulation and the healing process. Local application of enzyme preparations, non-steroidal anti-inflammatory drugs or dimethyl sulphoxide (DMSO) with or without cortisone may be employed for treatment of athletic injuries. Articular inflammatory disease is currently treated with the local introduction of hyaluronic acid into the joint space.

Ultrasonic stimulation of inflamed areas may be beneficial. Recently the use of cold lasers has been claimed to control the inflammatory response and significantly improve the healing rate.

Chronic inflammation is more difficult to deal with, and in addition to the above treatments there may also be a place for the use of counter-irritants, whereby an acute inflammation is set up in the hope that this will result in improved repair.

Preventive measures

The therapeutic administration of non-steroidal and steroid drugs, both systemically and topically, is the most important method of controlling inflammation.

It is not recommended that anti-inflammatory drugs be given as a prophylactic measure to healthy horses because, by masking the early signs of inflammation, they may allow a disease process to become well established before it is recognized. This would obviously compromise the prognosis for a complete functional recovery, particularly in the case of injuries of the musculoskeletal system.

Non-steroidal anti-inflammatory drugs are commonly used to enable chronically lame horses to perform, albeit at a reduced capacity. In this way the useful working life of an unsound horse may be prolonged. Steroid drugs may also be beneficial, both prophylactically and therapeutically, in horses with chronic obstructive pulmonary disease; inhibiting or alleviating the inflammatory response in the lungs' airways may render many horses capable of light work.

It is worth stressing the prevention of pulmonary inflammation arising from equine influenza: this may be prevented, or the side effects ameliorated, by prior vaccination.

37
POISONING IN HORSES

A poison is any substance detrimental to health at a specified minimum intake. Poisoning may occur through contact or penetration of the skin, by inhalation or by consumption.

Poisons may be classified as (1) those which are corrosive – these include strong acids and strong alkalis that destroy tissue; (2) irritants, which cause inflammation of tissue; (3) potent fat solvents, which destroy epithelial tissue by dissolving out its fat components; and (4) poisons which interact with metabolism.

In this review those poisons most likely to be encountered by stabled and grazing horses will be discussed.

Routes

Under natural conditions by far the most common route for poisons to gain access to the body is via the gastro-intestinal tract. In comparison with another and larger group of herbivores, the ruminant, the horse seems to suffer a disadvantage. A number of poisons are partly or extensively destroyed by rumen micro-organisms which decrease the extent of subsequent absorption of the poison from the small intestine. In the case of the horse not only is this facility unavailable, but the acid conditions of the stomach may lead to the solution of materials that are insoluble in neutral solutions.

The stomach of a horse under normal feeding conditions contains fairly large quantities of ingesta, so the effect of stomach fill on the toxicity of a poison is not of great significance. However, it is not possible to make any general statement about the effect of the degree of stomach fill on toxicity because for some poisons a full stomach decreases toxicity, but for others it leads to an increase in toxicity.

Toxicity

Although the toxicity of some poisons is increased by their being metabolized in the body, the toxicity of most is decreased. Many organic poisons are processed by the liver into forms which are less harmful and more water-soluble. Most of these poisons are then excreted through the kidneys, although some are passed out with the bile, through the bile duct into the intestinal tract. Much of this is reabsorbed. Many volatile poisons are partly disposed of in the expired air. Some poisons are deposited in a relatively inert form in tissues out of the way of normal metabolic processes. This applies to many elemental poisons such as lead, cadmium and strontium.

Bone is a typical site for such deposition. It can readily be appreciated that horses which have malfunctioning livers and kidneys as a result of malnutrition, parasitic infestation or old age are less able to dispose of certain poisons than are healthy animals, and they therefore succumb to lower intakes. However during periods of stress and malnutrition heavy metals deposited in bone may be mobilized, causing a crisis long after the initial poisoning occurred.

Repeated small doses of a poison may express themselves in a different way from one massive dose, but generally speaking the toxicity in both cases is roughly proportional to the unit of bodyweight (bwt). Because the horse is a large animal, a much bigger dose is required, generally speaking, to kill it than is required by dogs, cats and sheep. However, for many substances the toxic dose is roughly proportional to $bwt^{0.7}$. Thus a dose that was just toxic in a 500 kg horse would be only four times, and not seven to eight times, the dose per animal that was just toxic in a 70 kg sheep. The young and the old may be more susceptible than the healthy adult, so the dose per unit of bodyweight which causes damage may be less in their case than in the case of the healthy adult.

Diagnosis

The differentiation of the great variety of causes of poisoning is extremely difficult because symptoms are similar. The most successful solution to this problem is carefully to examine the environment to determine whether the horse or pony has had access to anything which could do it harm.

For this it is necessary to be fully aware of those substances which are hazardous, and therefore the main purpose of this review is to enlighten the reader of the principal causes of poisoning so that either they may be removed from the environment or measures may be taken to ensure that animals have no access to them.

The most effective way of diagnosing the cause of poisoning is to analyse samples from the stomach contents, faeces, body tissues, feed or other suspected materials which may have been fed to the horse or to which the animal has been exposed. This analysis may have to be performed in specially equipped laboratories, which will have their own requirements as to how the samples should be prepared and dispatched. Certain samples may have to be stored frozen. Advice on these matters should therefore be sought from a vet or other qualified person.

Symptoms

Symptoms of poisoning are numerous and, although they differ between poisons, a number are common and frequently encountered. These include loss of appetite, incoordination of gait and lameness, depression, diarrhoea, irregular and laboured breathing, muscular twitching, discoloured urine and unusual smell of the breath and faeces, salivation, thirst, anaemia, icterus (jaundice), blindness, dilation of pupils, colic, and photosensitization expressed as oedematous swellings around the face, eyes, neck and flanks.

Treatment

Appropriate treatment is not easy to ascertain and normally this should be carried out by a veterinarian. Where damage to the skin has occurred, generally speaking little harm can be done by washing the skin with water. It may not be a good idea to add soap or detergent to the water as this may increase the penetration of the skin by the poison.

Where poisons have been imbibed, the stomach contents may be washed out by gastric lavage, or a substance may be given which absorbs the toxic material, for example, mixtures of activated charcoal, light magnesium oxide, kaolin, tannic acid or charcoal on its own.

Where heavy-metal poisoning has occurred, treatment either orally or by injection with sodium versenate or sodium calcium versenate, sometimes described as sodium calcium EDTA, may be used to chelate the metal, which is subsequently excreted even by the kidney. Demulcents, which are viscid in character, protecting mucous membranes from irritation, are frequently used in the oral treatment of poisoning. These include gum acacia and glycerol.

HEAVY METALS AND OTHER POISONS

Many cases of poisoning by heavy metals and other elements are caused by industrial pollution of grazing areas, often as a result of human carelessness. Others come about through the inquisitive nature of animals themselves, particularly their tendency to chew objects in the environment not intended for eating. There are also some cases of poisoning by elements which, for geographical or geological reasons, have accumulated naturally in the soil.

Selenium   Selenium is found in high natural concentrations in some areas of the world. Parts of the USA are well known for their selenium toxicity, and small areas of marginally toxic concentrations occur in Eire. Selenium is readily absorbed by certain plants and consequently ingested by grazing animals. The chronic disease caused by selenium poisoning has been called **alkali**, owing to the alkaline nature of water that is rich in selenium.

Horses with selenium poisoning suffer loss of hair from the mane and tail, develop rings around the hoof below the coronet, become lame owing to erosion of articular surfaces of leg bones and display a deterioration in appetite.

Where very high concentrations of selenium occur in plants, a condition known as **blind staggers** develops. Horses lose weight dramatically, develop a staring coat and wander aimlessly with impaired vision, salivating and showing signs of paralysis.

Treatment may be unsuccessful. Horses should be removed if possible from the area and given a high-protein, high-quality diet. Some improvement has been achieved by the provision of small amounts of arsenic under veterinary supervision.

Arsenic Somewhat similar clinical signs occur with arsenic poisoning, which is usually caused by an animal inadvertently consuming a product which contains the arsenic. Apart from a staggering gait, paralysis, salivation and thirst, there is severe irritation of the intestinal tract, which develops a rose-red inflammation. Gastric lavage is carried out if the signs are detected early enough.

Fluorine Fluorosis caused by excessive fluorine intake is less frequent in horses than in other grazing stock. Some soils and water courses are naturally rich in this element, and in the past industrial contamination of pasture by aerial deposits has been a typical cause.

Fluorine is deposited in bones and teeth, and if ruminants show pitting and discoloration of the teeth, this may be the cause. Where pasture contains an excess of 50 mg fluorine per kilogramme dry matter, the danger of toxicity exists.

If grazing horses become lame and their forage is shown to contain large amounts of fluorine, it is wise to remove them from the area. Aluminium oxide added to grain-based diets at a level of 0.5 per cent helps to eliminate fluorine from bone.

Molybdenum and sulphur **Induced copper deficiency** arising from excess molybdenum in herbage has been suggested as a possible contributory factor in bone disorders of foals and yearlings. In sheep a condition known as swayback is a characteristic copper deficiency syndrome caused by excessive intakes of molybdenum and sulphur. Symptoms in sheep occur in the so-called teart pastures, which are found in parts of Somerset, Gloucestershire and Warwickshire, where the copper:molybdenum ratio in herbage is less than 6:1.

Induced copper deficiency is caused by copper binding with thiomolybdates either in the gut or in body tissue. The formation of thiomolybdates from sulphur and molybdenum may depend on the presence of rumen micro-organisms and it therefore seems that induced copper deficiency in horses is far less likely than in ruminants.

Nevertheless in areas where grazing sheep and cattle are showing typical signs of induced copper deficiency, it is wise to ensure that young horses in particular receive adequate copper supplementation. This is achieved by injection at regular intervals, a routine and effective therapy. Copper toxicity in horses does not occur until intake greatly exceeds that causing copper toxicity in ruminants.

Lead Lead is one of the commonest causes of poisoning in cattle, sheep and horses. Signs of toxicity are more frequent in young horses and include lack of appetite, muscular stiffness and weakness, diarrhoea and, in an acute form, pharyngeal paralysis and regurgitation of food and water.

Lead accumulates in the bones and as little as 80 mg lead per kilogramme diet may eventually cause toxic signs, which are sometimes brought on by stress. Natural feeds with 1–10 mg of lead per kilogramme cause no problems. However, inquisitive animals will sometimes consume objects in their environment, some of which may be rich in lead. These include putty, linoleum, golf balls, red lead and particularly accumulator battery plates. Lead-based paints are less frequently used today, but they may still be found in old buildings and be ingested by horses which persistently chew wooden objects.

Vegetation in the vicinity of smelter works and highways may contain as much as 500 mg lead per kilogramme dry matter and therefore be a significant cause of damage. Lead shot from shotgun rounds indiscriminantly used on pasture has been found to be a cause of lead toxicity in silage. The acidic conditions which develop in the silage clamp encourage the solution of the metallic lead. Furthermore the acid secreted in a horse's stomach will also contribute to the solution of lead shot.

Unless lead toxicity is suspected it may be somewhat difficult to diagnose, although lead analysis of faeces, stomach contents and blood will help. Lead accumulates in bone and kidney tissue and therefore can be detected post mortem in many cases, but not always. Veterinary treatment includes administration of sodium calcium EDTA (calcium disodium versenate) at a rate of 75 mg per kilogramme bodyweight daily.

Cadmium Pasture may be contaminated by cadmium, which is found in mine workings, waste dumps and sewage sludge, in the form of aerial dust or through water erosion. Cadmium is absorbed by plants to a much greater extent than lead is. Of common pasture species, the daisy (*Bellis*) accumulates 60–80 mg cadmium per kilogramme (thirty times as much as grasses) from contaminated soils.

Symptoms of cadmium toxicity include reduced food intake, diarrhoea, incoordination, icterus and fatty degeneration of the liver.

The only reasonable solution to cadmium toxicity is to remove stock from areas where it may occur. Pastures in the vicinity of factories using zinc ore may be polluted with cadmium.

Mercury   Mercury is highly poisonous and the metal is volatile at normal temperatures. In compounds it occurs as mercuric chloride ($HgCl_2$), mercurous chloride (Hg_2Cl_2), calomel and methyl mercuric chloride (CH_3HgCl). Mercuric chloride is less toxic than methyl mercuric chloride and more toxic than mercurous chloride. However, organic mercury compounds are said to be less toxic than inorganic compounds and therefore they are used more widely. One such use is as seed dressing in agriculture and, despite the lower toxicity, this is a likely source of poisoning in horses.

Symptoms include violent gastroenteritis and diarrhoea, nephritis and inflammation of the mouth. There is a loss of appetite, nervousness and incoordination of gait.

Speedy treatment is essential and includes gastric lavage with saturated sodium bicarbonate solution.

Nitrates, nitrites and oxalates   The rapid growth of pasture after high rainfall and the excessive use of nitrogen fertilizers can lead to high concentrations of nitrates in the herbage and contamination of ground water, ditches and streams through the leeching of soils. Although nitrates are only slightly toxic they can be reduced to nitrites before, or generally after, consumption.

High levels of nitrites may accumulate in plants after herbicide treatment and during the making of oat hay as a result of nitrate reduction encouraged by inclement weather. Where root vegetables such as mangels are boiled and left in the boiling water, nitrite can accumulate and cause poisoning. Sugar-beet tops are frequently fed to cattle after wilting. The purpose of wilting is to allow oxalates present in the leaves to be converted to insoluble salts, which are less toxic, but the leaves can also contain nitrate in lethal quantities – in fact, as potassium nitrate up to 4.5 per cent of dry matter. Sugar-beet tops are less toxic to ruminants as rumen micro-organisms convert oxalates to bicarbonates.

The toxicity of nitrite is due to the conversion of blood haemoglobin to methaemoglobin and also to the formation of dimethylnitrosamine from dimethylamine plus nitrite under the influence of the intestinal flora. These compounds damage the liver.

Some effective treatment of nitrite toxicity is apparently achieved by giving ascorbic acid (vitamin C) or methylene blue intravenously, which brings about the partial reconversion of methaemoglobin to oxyhaemoglobin.

Oxalate toxicity is most likely in domestic livestock in subtropical areas where a number of grass species, either grazed or used as hay, contain high levels of oxalates. Oxalates interfere with calcium deposition in bone and also may cause some kidney damage through the formation of calcium oxalate deposits.

Toxicity has been prevented in horses by supplementing the diet with dicalcium phosphate (CaHPO$_4$). This brings about a deposition of calcium oxalate in the gut, preventing its absorption.

Where there is a large intake of oxalates during grazing, the diet should be supplemented with a cereal concentrate containing 10 per cent dicalcium phosphate at the rate of 1–1.5 kg per day to prevent oxalate poisoning.

Antibiotics   Most antibiotics used for feeding to farm livestock have little ill effect on horses unless given at therapeutic levels, in which case colic might be induced through disruption of the intestinal flora. On the other hand, three antibiotics used agriculturally, and one in particular, are highly toxic in horses.

Monensin, also marketed as Rumensin and Elancoban, can cause death in horses if they mistakingly consume, for more than a very few days, concentrate feed intended for poultry or cattle. Horses present symptoms of posterior weakness, profuse sweating, occasionally muscular tremors and myoglobinuria (dark brown urine). There can be permanent damage to heart muscle, but toxicity may be arrested in the early stages by removing the stomach contents and feeding mineral oil. Generally speaking, confirmation of the cause can be achieved by analysis of stomach contents.

Salinomycin, an anticoccidial ionophore, in higher doses causes somewhat similar symptoms, which may appear immediately or several months after exposure.

Lincomycin is an anti-bacterial drug sometimes included in pig feed. It is less toxic to horses than monensin but can cause liver damage. In both cases the toxic feed should be removed as soon as possible.

Potato poisoning   It is well known that green potatoes contain solanine, which is not destroyed by cooking, although some of it is partly removed by leeching into boiling water. Recent evidence shows that the horse seems to be much more susceptible than ruminants and will succumb to potato poisoning even when no green potatoes have been fed. Symptoms include salivation, diarrhoea, colic, thirst, depression, weak, incoordinated movements, paresis (slight or incomplete paralysis), laboured breathing and dehydrated injected (livid) mucous membranes. The best course is not to feed potatoes of any sort to horses.

Onion poisoning   Onions contain a volatile oil (n-propyl disulphide) which can cause severe damage to horses and cattle fed large numbers of waste onions. The signs include inappetence, tachycardia (rapid heart beat), staggering, jaundice, haemoglobinuria and haemolytic anaemia. It is unwise to feed onions and similar vegetables to horses.

Bacteria and bacterial toxins in feed Disease caused by pathogenic enterobacteria such as pathogenic species of *Salmonella* cause a chronic diarrhoea in horses which is difficult to eliminate. Sources of these organisms include dead rodents and rodent droppings and badly, or incorrectly, processed animal protein sources, particularly meat meal and meat and bone meal. Rodent infestation of cereal grains should be kept to an absolute minimum and there is no need to feed horses any form of meat or meat and bone meal.

Feed contaminated by the soil-borne, pathogenic species of *Clostridium* can lead to the proliferation of *C. perfringens* in the intestines of horses, causing a severe gas colic. Large intake of succulent forages increases the likelihood of this type of infection, which can lead rapidly to death. Only small meals of cut fresh forage or silage should be permitted for horses.

A number of cases of **botulism** (see p. 415) have occurred in horses as a consequence of the consumption of insufficiently fermented haylage or silage. *C. botulinum* will grow under anaerobic conditions in a silage clamp where the pH is above 4.5 or where the silage contains less than about 25 per cent dry matter. Only a very small quantity of this toxin is required to kill a horse. Both growth of the organism and toxin production in the gut seem to occur only in young animals.

It is important that green feed and silage provided for horses should be contaminated as little as possible with soil, and that silage has a sufficiently high proportion of dry matter (over 30 per cent) and a sufficiently low pH (below 4.5). Lush forage and silage should be fed to horses only in small quantities at each meal.

Poisonous seeds contaminating vegetable protein concentrates In the past cases of poisoning occurred as a consequence of feeding horses imported vegetable protein concentrates which contained highly toxic seeds, including castor seed, croton seed and certain species of tropical peas and beans. This problem does not now occur, although cheap protein concentrates of unknown origin should always be viewed with suspicion.

Miscellaneous farm poisons Concentrated sources of herbicides, insecticides, fungicides, rodenticides and molluscicides should be kept well away from livestock. Horses should not have access to sheep dips, and care should be taken to keep tractor paraffin, diesel oil, sump oil, disinfectants (mainly phenols) and antifreeze (ethylene glycol) well away from feed and horses.

Snake bites and stings by bees, wasps and spiders The horse is very susceptible to bites from venomous snakes. However, because of a horse's size, a bite that would kill a small domestic animal may only injure a horse. Such bites might be recognized by the fang marks in the centre of a swollen area. Where species of poisonous snakes are known to inhabit an area, it is wise to keep a supply of the appropriate serum for immediate use and also to keep a supply of antivenin from the serum of horses that have been immunized.

The horse should be kept quiet to reduce the rate of absorption of the venom and, in addition to serum, it is normally given cortisone or other anti-inflammatory steroids, an antibiotic and possibly antitetanus. The latter two are required to counteract bacterial contamination of the fangs and subsequent infection of the wound. Similarly, where known species of poisonous spiders inhabit a particular area, specific antivenin should be kept on hand.

When bee or wasp stings occur, the sting should be removed and an effective antihistamine administered generally and locally around the site of the sting.

Moulds and mould toxins Certain species of mould can cause serious damage to livestock through the production of toxins which may either be present in the feed together with the active mould or simply be left as a residue in the feed after the mould has been largely destroyed. Two or three species of mould, however, may damage horses by an entirely different mechanism, and that is by setting up a respiratory allergy (see chronic obstructive pulmonary disease, p. 48).

The mould particles and spores are inhaled during the consumption of mouldy hay. They may also be present in the atmosphere of badly contaminated and poorly ventilated stables. Some horses are more likely than others to develop symptoms.

The damage may be partly repaired or the problem avoided by ensuring that buildings are properly ventilated and that very dusty hay is not used – it should either be soaked before feeding or replaced with properly fermented silage. Dusty, mouldy straw bedding should also be avoided.

The most notorious mould toxin is produced by ergot of rye (*Claviceps purpurea*). This mould also infects several species of pasture grass, although it is unlikely that horses will become seriously intoxicated during grazing. Horses given 500 g ergot showed only transient symptoms and even heavily contaminated pastures are unlikely to contain more than approximately 0.3 per cent ergot. The most likely cause of intoxication by this source is badly infected rye grain.

A number of other mould species found on cereal grain (including *Puccinia graminis*) can cause fatal poisoning in horses, but the most poisonous mould toxin produced in badly stored oil seeds and cereals is aflatoxin. The horse seems to be more susceptible to this than most other domestic species of animals.

Many similar mould toxins can develop when cereal grain is stored in silos at a moisture content above 14 per cent. All such feed stored in bulk should have a moisture content of no more than 13 per cent and the storage facilities should be well ventilated and not subject to any wide daily variations in temperature.

Several species of mould grow on forage crops and are a cause of intoxication of grazing animals. **Lupinosis** is caused by the ingestion of toxins produced by a fungus growing on lupin plants which causes damage to the liver. The only solution to this is to remove horses from pasture where lupins are found and to feed hay and concentrates. Another toxin – sporodesmin – is produced by a mould which grows on rye grass and which causes facial eczema in sheep. This toxin has also caused photosensitization reactions in horses in Queensland.

Bacterial and fungal toxins may account for the pasture toxicity of ryegrass and fescue. For example, in some cases ataxia and convulsions have been associated with seed galls of annual ryegrass (*Lolium rigidum*), ergot alkaloids of *Sphacelia typhina* (not *Claviceps*) seem to cause summer tall fescue (*Festuca arundinacea*) toxicity, especially following high nitrogen fertilization, and staggers has been caused by perennial ryegrass (*L. perenne*) neurotoxins. The only solution is to remove horses from pastures where the conditions are known to occur. It is likely that grass sickness seen in the UK and Europe is also caused by a fungal toxin, and removal of stock from pastures causing the condition seems to be the only solution at the present time.

Photosensitization reactions   In bright sunny weather horses with un-pigmented skin, and with white or grey coats in particular, may be subject to photosensitization. This causes a form of dermatitis that arises particularly in horses with damaged livers. Unwanted toxic compounds absorbed from the intestine are normally degraded by the liver and excreted. This process is obviously less efficient when there is a measure of liver dysfunction and when light-sensitive compounds reach subcutaneous tissues.

Toxins contained in St John's wort, buckwheat, bog asphodel and sometimes lucerne, and alsike and red clovers have been imputed as a cause. Several forage species of *Vicia* and *Lathyrus* (grazing species of legume) may also cause sensitization reactions.

Dermatitis is normally preceded by swelling on the muzzle, around the eyes and on various places of the body. Presenting horses should respond to hydrocortisone and diuretics. They should be removed from areas where the causitive species of plant occur in the pasture. Furthermore care should be taken that implicated species are not present in meadow hay fed to horses.

Poisonous shrubs and trees   The leaves and seeds of a number of species of shrubs and trees are poisonous in varying degrees. All parts of the yew are highly toxic to horses. Laburnum is also toxic in all parts, especially the flowers and seeds. Privet leaves are said to be toxic but are clearly less so than the first two species. Among forest trees, both beech and oak leaves and acorns contain several marginally toxic substances. Unripe acorns are said to be the most dangerous. They contain large amounts of tannic acid. Some animals develop a liking for them and should not have access to areas where oak trees are present. Dullness, inappetence and diarrhoea may occur, although horses may be less susceptible than cattle. Treatment includes administration of liquid paraffin or purgatives.

POISONS FOUND IN VEGETABLE PROTEIN SOURCES

Tannins Many common plants contain tannins (weak acids) which depress both protein and carbohydrate digestion and cause colic in horses when present in high concentrations in the diet. Autoclaving or pressure cooking destroys these tannins, but at lower temperatures prolonged treatment is required. Brown varieties of sorghum grain are rich in tannins and therefore only the white grain varieties should be used. Field beans (*Vicia faba*), particularly the coloured-flower varieties, also contain tannins, and again prolonged cooking to a great extent rectifies the problem. The pasture legume marsh bird's-foot trefoil (*Lotus pedunculatus*) is rich in condensed tannins when growing on poor soil. Other related species found in pastures also contain tannins.

Lectins (proteins) Lectins seem to disrupt the brush borders of the small intestinal villi and hamper the absorption of nutrients. Apparently they also allow the absorption of certain toxic substances which increase tissue breakdown and urinary nitrogen and thus depress growth in young stock.

Field or horse beans (*Vicia faba*) contain small quantities of lectins, and relatively larger amounts are contained in black grams and kidney, haricot or navy beans (*Phaseolus vulgaris*). Horse grams, moth beans (*Phaseolus aconitifolius*), certain pulses, cow peas, lima beans (*P. Lunatus*), butter-beans and winged beans, groundnuts or peanuts (*Arachis hypogaea*), soya beans and rice germ also contain these substances. Most rice bran fed to horses has had the germ removed, although some residual activity is normally found.

The susceptibility of lectins to destruction by heat varies with the plant source and therefore the safety of certain vegetable protein sources may not be guaranteed even after cooking. The lectin content of kidney beans is very stable: treatment for two hours at 93° C (199.4° F) is necessary for adequate destruction. Kidney beans are therefore generally unsuitable for non-industrial processing and should not normally be fed to horses. Recent evidence has shown that steam flaking of field beans is more effective in the destruction of the trypsin inhibitor and lectin activities than is micronization at 150° or 100° C (302° or 212° F).

Enzyme inhibitors Many of the vegetable proteins already listed contain substances which depress the digestion of protein and in some cases of carbohydrate. These substances are considered to be somewhat less toxic than lectins and by and large are more susceptible to destruction by wet heat. Where a bean or pea of unknown origin is available, it should only be used in horse feed after prolonged cooking by steaming or boiling.

Lathyrogens   The horse is particularly and characteristically affected by lathyrism or poisoning by lathyrogens. This is a condition in which there is a sudden and transient paralysis of the larynx with near suffocation, brought on by exercise. This is associated with a degenerative change in the nerves and muscles of the larynx and profound inflammation of the liver and spleen. A number of species of pea of the family *Lathyrus* contain lathyrogenic agents, including the Indian or grass pea (*L. sativus*), the sweet pea (*L. odoratus*), the wild winter pea (*L. hirsutus*), the singletary pea (*L. pusillus*) and the everlasting pea (*L. sylvestris*). Although the whole plant contains the toxin, the seeds appear to be the most potent source, and it is only partly destroyed by heat.

Gossypol   Cotton seeds contain the yellow pigment gossypol which is toxic to horses and which is only partly destroyed by heat. It depresses appetite and protein and iron utilization. Its toxicity can apparently result in death from circulatory failure. Fairly large additions to the diet of iron in the form of ferrous sulphate will partly suppress the adverse effects of gossypol. Owing to differences in temperature achieved during manufacture, expeller meals contain less gossypol activity and are therefore less dangerous than solvent-extracted meals. High-quality cotton-seed meal is palatable to horses and varieties which contain low amounts of gossypol or which have had the germ removed can be usefully included in mixed feeds. Cotton-seed meals derived from the safe varieties are generally not available in the UK; feeds containing more than 60 mg free gossypol per kilogramme are unsatisfactory for horses.

Cyanogenetic glycosides   Certain glycosides (sugar compounds) present in lima beans, sorghum leaves, linseed (*Linum usitatissimum*) and cassava (tapioca – *Manihot esculenta*) will generate hydrogen cyanide (HCN) when acted on by specific enzymes contained in the plants. HCN can cause respiratory failure, but as the poison is released by enzyme activity, heat treatment will ensure safety so long as prolonged storage of moist seeds or roots has not led to an accumulation of free HCN. Thus it is important that raw, uncooked materials should be stored in dry conditions. HCN can also react with any thiosulphate present in the material to produce thiocyanate, which is responsible for thyroid enlargement after prolonged feeding.

Linseed is unique in so far as it contains a relatively indigestible mucilage. This can absorb large amounts of water, producing a thick soup during cooking, and its lubricating action regulates faecal excretion and sometimes overcomes constipation without causing looseness. The cooking of linseed also destroys the enzyme linase, which would otherwise release HCN if the linseed was merely soaked. For this reason linseed should be added to boiling water rather than to cold water and then boiled. However, HCN is volatile and a proportion of any already present will be driven off by subsequent boiling. UK law states that linseed cake or meal must contain less than 350 mg HCN per kilogramme, although this takes no account of the effect of any linase that may be present.

Anti-thyroid substances A large number of vegetable protein sources, particularly those in the genus Brassica, contain thyroactive substances. When consumed persistently, particularly by young stock, these substances can cause goitre. Both the seeds and the vegetative parts of cabbages, rape, mustard and kale are incriminated. The effects of goitrins are not counteracted by additional dietary iodine, although further metabolism of certain of them can release isothiocyanates and thiocyanates. The anti-thyroid effect of these on young horses can be overcome by additional dietary iodine. Goitrins are released by enzymes contained within the plant and these can be destroyed by heat treatment. However, this is impractical with the vegetative parts of plants.

Kale contains a goitrogenic substance but is relatively low in iodine content. The effect of the plant on sheep can be partly overcome by supplementary iodine. Kale also contains a sulphur compound metabolized by rumen bacteria to form dimethyl sulphide, which causes haemolytic anaemia. This particular substance, however, is not likely to be of great significance in horse feed. For the same reasons cruciferous vegetables are not recommended for feeding to young or lactating horses in other than small quantities.

Among the brassicas the principal seed byproduct available as a vegetable protein source is rapeseed meal, which contains large amounts of goitrogens. In recent years varieties of rapeseed have been bred which contain low quantities of goitrogens, therefore making the rapeseed meal derived from them suitable for feeding to horses. Unfortunately the safety of rapeseed meal cannot be guaranteed in the UK, although it is in Canada, and consequently it is an unreliable source of vegetable protein and should not be fed to horses in Europe. Nevertheless, prolonged heat treatment of rapeseed during processing decreases the hazard by destroying the enzyme which releases the goitrogens. However, it is difficult to justify the cost of additional heat treatment given the availability of other, more reliable protein sources.

Poisonous pasture plants A large number of plant species available to the grazing animal in various parts of the world are poisonous. The degree of toxicity varies considerably from species to species.* Many of the toxic substances present in pasture plants are alkaloids, which are organic basic compounds, and their toxic effects on the horse vary widely. Alkaloids are rare in grasses.

One of the commonest causes of poisoning amongst all grazing animals, including horses, in the British Isles is common ragwort (*Senecio jacobaea*), which causes permanent liver damage. Elevated plasma gamma glutamyl transferase activity is a useful early indicator of the damage. Despite claims that horses will not eat this plant, many outbreaks of poisoning have been found to have followed the consumption of growing ragwort. Intoxication can also result if ragwort is present in hay as the poison remains stable after the hay has been made.

Horses with ragwort-damaged livers should be given a well-balanced diet, containing good-quality protein supplemented with B vitamins and trace elements. They should not be given access to pasture infested with either ragwort or groundsel (*Senecio vulgaris*), which contains the same toxin as ragwort but at lower concentrations.

Other plants causing a similar liver condition include heliotrope (*Heliotropium*) and the legume crotalaria, numerous species of which have proved very poisonous to horses in South Africa, America and Australia. One species of this legume causes Kimberley horse disease. In some species the highest concentration of poison is present in the roots, which are normally inaccessible. However, roots of water dropwort (*Oenanthe crocata*) may be unearthed during ditching operations and be consumed by horses.

Horses usually avoid alkaloid-containing pasture plants unless there is a major shortage of palatable grazing as a result of overgrazing or drought. However, they sometimes develop a predilection for bitter or unusual flavours.

Many leguminous plants contain a variety of poisons. Some have already been mentioned, such as laburnum, but others include broom (*Cytisus scoparius*) and lupin (*Lupinus*). The toxicity of the latter species is principally confined to the seeds and the different strains vary in their potency. Sweet lupin (*L. luteus*) has a low alkaloid content and is grown on poor land as a source of fodder.

Occasionally horses eating lupins have died from respiratory paralysis, whereas the chronic and progressive liver damage associated with lupinosis in horses and sheep is caused by an associated fungus growing on the lupins (see p. 516).

A number of pasture legumes, particularly subterranean clover (*Trifolium subterraneum*) grown on light soils, contain appreciable amounts of oestrogens. These substances are known to affect fertility in other domestic livestock, although their influence on the breeding mare has not been determined.

---

*For a complete list of plant species thought to be the cause of poisoning in horses, see D. L. Frape, *Equine Nutrition and Feeding*, Longman, 1986.

Photosensitization associated with certain pasture species of *Vicia* and *Lathyrus* has already been referred to. Two genera of vetch in North America, milk vetch or locoweed (*Astragalus*) and the related *Oxytropis*, are implicated in several abnormal conditions of horses. One caused by locoweed is recognized as eliciting irreversible nervous signs. None of the poisonous members of these genera is found in the British Isles. Where they exist in the USA, their growth begins in late summer and they remain green in the winter. They must be grazed for a period before poisoning is obvious.

Some plant poisons remain active after drying during haymaking. These species include horsetails (*Equisetum*), bracken (*Pteridium aquilinum*), hellebores (*Helleborus*), larkspurs (*Delphinium*), poppies (*Papaver*), greater celandine (*Chelidonium majus*), St John's worts (*Hypericum*), pimpernels (*Anagallis*), henbane (*Hyoscyamus niger*), black nightshade (*Solanum nigrum*), foxglove (*Digitalis purpurea*), meadow saffron (*Colchicum autumnale*) and black bryony (*Tamus communis*). Sweet clover or melilot (*Melilotus*) contains coumarin, which is broken down to dicoumarol in hay made under bad harvesting conditions or during moulding. Dicoumarol prolongs blood-clotting time. Sweet clover hay made during inclement weather develops mouldy patches and should not be used in horse feeding.

Poor pasture management, including overgrazing by horses, the absence of ruminants and lack of pasture cultivation, the failure to use appropriate fertilizers and to manage pasture as a crop leads to its general decline both in terms of productivity and the ingress and dissemination of poisonous, and therefore unwanted, plants. The reader should acquire the ability to recognize the most important of these species in his or her area. Their spread can be prevented by increased competition from productive pasture species and by preventing them from seeding. The encroachment of bracken may be difficult to counter in areas of marginal land, but today the enormous spread of ragwort is simply a reflection of neglect. The removal of these and other pernicious weeds can be achieved by spraying clumps at the appropriate time with herbicides and a knapsack sprayer or by digging them out before the plants have a chance to seed. Many other poisonous plants are much less likely than ragwort to cause poisoning of a serious kind and their beauty should be allowed to decorate hedgerows and copses from which the horse can be kept at bay by adequate fencing.

38
PREVENTIVE MEDICINE

Preventive medicine is the use of environmental measures and veterinary treatment to control the development and build-up of disease. Preventive medicine and good management are interrelated and inseparable, and they provide a challenge both to stud managers and owners and to veterinarians.

The objectives of preventive medicine are: to keep all animals in good health and condition and to maintain a steady rate of growth and development in young stock; to minimize the possibility of disease entering the studfarm or stables from outside; to minimize the build-up of disease; to identify individuals especially at risk for special care; and to control the spread of infection after an outbreak of infectious disease.

Keeping animals in good health

Housing   Poor housing is stressful to all animals and will result in a build-up of respiratory and intestinal disease. The most important factor is ventilation, which should be variable to provide a maximum flow of air to reduce temperature and a minimum flow of air to reduce humidity; a ratio of 10:1 between maximum and minimum flows is desirable. Horses kept in a dry environment can tolerate very low and very high temperatures so, control of humidity is much more important than control of temperature. However, in providing ventilation it is important to avoid draughts at ground level which will chill stabled animals.

All housing should have ventilation inlets and outlets and the most common method of air circulation uses the 'stack' effect. This relies on the principle of cold air entering through the side inlets, warming as it filters through the building, and rising in the centre to be drawn out through the roof. The roof outlet may be boosted by extractor fans. The minimum requirement for ventilation has been estimated at 1 sq ft per horse outlet and 3 sq ft per horse inlet.

The other major influence on ventilation and air movement in buildings is insulation. Insulation reduces condensation on the side walls and roof and increases air movement through the building. Many buildings can be greatly improved by the appreciation of these basic principles.

Bedding Bedding should be dry and dust-free. A thick, dry straw bed allows a foal to keep warm when the environmental temperature is low. Dusty straw increases the incidence of chronic obstructive pulmonary disease and a variety of materials have been used as alternatives. Peat moss is dust-free but cold and tends to soften the feet. Wood shavings and chopped paper are clean and dust-free, but not as warm as straw, and the soiled bedding is difficult to dispose of.

Deep-litter bedding has the advantages of keeping dust to a minimum while, at the same time, reducing labour costs. The disadvantages are that moulds may form in deep-litter straw or wood shavings and cause allergic reactions such as chronic obstructive pulmonary diseases. In addition, deep-littering leads to moist conditions underfoot and may cause thrush unless the feet are cleaned regularly.

Figure 153   A correctly laid bed

banking bed

Nutrition Nutrient requirements and levels of feeding are discussed in chapter 43. However, there are a few basic considerations which are of importance in relation to disease.

Clearly, inadequate nutrition, resulting in weight loss and debility, makes animals susceptible to disease of all kinds. However, more frequently there is a tendency to overfeed high-energy and protein feeds to growing horses and this can result in an unusually high level of limb abnormalities in foals and yearlings (see chapter 19).

Overfeeding also results in damage to the growth plates producing enlargements of the epiphyses (physitis – see p. 163). Such reactions may result in gross deformity of the limbs, such as medial or lateral deviation of the carpus (knee). The importance of severely reducing the total food intake to control such abnormalities cannot be overstressed. The total calcium intake and the ratio of calcium to phosphorus in the diet must be checked and corrected if necessary (see p. 586).

In recent years it has become clear that trace elements also are of importance in the feeding of stud animals. Zinc, copper and selenium have all received attention and may be important in relation to abnormal bone and muscle development.

Pasture management   Horses are notoriously bad grazers and all readers will be familiar with the untidy appearance of paddocks persistently grazed by horses; some areas will be grazed to the ground while other areas grow coarse and long. These grazing patterns are controlled by faecal contamination of the pasture rather than by urine excretion. The grazing patterns can only be eradicated by regular removal of droppings or by allowing other herbivores such as cattle or sheep to graze the land. Ploughing and reseeding pastures will not remove established grazing patterns.

Vaccination   Vaccination of all stock against commonly occurring diseases is clearly desirable. In the UK and Ireland vaccination is frequently carried out against three common diseases – tetanus, influenza and rhinopneumonitis. The principle of all vaccination is to administer an initial course and to follow this with booster doses at various intervals, depending on the nature of the vaccine and the immune response for each product.

Permanent vaccination with tetanus toxoid can be started at any age from three months onwards and consists of a primary vaccination of two doses separated by two to four weeks. A booster vaccination is then given a year later and the manufacturers recommend boosters every other year thereafter.

Pregnant mares are often given a tetanus toxoid booster shortly before foaling to increase the level of tetanus antibodies passed in the colostrum to the newborn foal. To supplement this many foals are given tetanus antitoxin soon after birth to provide temporary cover for three to four weeks. A further dose of antitoxin may be given at a month old.

Tetanus vaccination is often coupled with vaccination against influenza, and several drug companies now produce combinations of influenza and tetanus vaccine.

Vaccination against influenza is highly effective and is now mandatory for all racehorses and for all horses using racecourse premises. The vaccination requirements are strict and tightly enforced. A primary course of two injections, 21–90 days apart, must be followed by a booster 150–215 days later. (Manufacturers may differ as to timing but this does not matter to within a couple of months.) Subsequently a dose may be given annually within twelve months of the last injection. Some manufacturers recommend a further primary vaccination six months after the first booster and annual vaccination thereafter. This vaccine covers against all the commonly occurring strains of influenza (see p. 422). However, it should be remembered that influenza viruses vary periodically and are subject to a phenomenon known as antigenic drift and such variations may result in a breakdown in immunity. (For Jockey Club Rules on vaccination, see p. 423.)

Vaccination against rhinopneumonitis or virus abortion (see p. 339) is more contentious. Vaccination is widespread in the USA and is becoming more common in the UK, where a live and a killed vaccine are now available and licenced for use. The killed vaccine is recommended for the control of virus abortion and the live vaccine for the control of the respiratory form of the disease.

The principles of vaccination are similar to those for other diseases and consist of a primary vaccination course of two injections followed by regular boosters. The frequency of these boosters is open to question but many people recommend vaccination every three months because the immune response to this herpesvirus is very short-lived.

The regimen of vaccination for the control of virus abortion in pregnant mares is more exact and the manufacturers recommend injection of the dead vaccine at five, seven and nine months of pregnancy. There is little doubt that some animals will abort despite vaccination, but the more widespread use of the vaccine in this country will provide evidence of its effectiveness in the control of this potentially disastrous infection.

Teeth All horses should have their teeth examined at least annually to check for the development of abnormally sharp edges on the outside of the upper molar teeth and the insides of the lower molar teeth. These edges can be removed easily by rasping.

Two-, three- and four-year-old animals may be shedding temporary incisor and premolar teeth (caps) and these can be removed by routine dentistry at the time of examination. In older animals the molar teeth must be examined for signs of abnormal wear or overgrowth which requires more vigorous attention. For more details, see chapter 33.

Feet Good farriery and regular trimming of the feet of all young stock and broodmares is essential. Changes in the shape of the feet can occur very rapidly, and unless the animals are carefully inspected and walked up in hand, important changes may be missed.

It is helpful to record the observations made at these examinations for future reference; changes in diet and levels of exercise can also be recorded. Many studs rely on monthly visits from the farrier, but at certain times of the year, particularly through the grazing summer months, foals and yearlings may benefit from attention at shorter intervals, even down to fortnightly, in order to prevent the development of sandcracks and splits in the walls of the feet (see chapter 20).

Minimizing the introduction of disease

Most disease enters a studfarm or stables through the arrival of an animal which is already infected or one which is a carrier. It is therefore essential to ensure that all animals which join a resident group should be carefully screened for the presence of disease. During this period they should be isolated from the resident animals. Good isolation facilities are therefore necessary.

New arrivals should enter the isolation premises where they can be inspected for overt clinical disease, such as respiratory disease or ringworm. At this time tests can be carried out for any diseases for which special precautions are needed. An example is the collection of dung samples for a worm egg count to enable any necessary worming treatment to be carried out. Animals should be kept in for twenty-four to forty-eight hours after such treatment to ensure that the parasite eggs being expelled from the alimentary tract are not voided onto pasture. If such droppings are allowed to contaminate the pasture, they should be collected within forty-eight hours of being passed.

Screening for more unusual infectious diseases should be carried out before a horse arrives at a stud. In particular, blood samples can be collected from mares from high-risk areas for serum antibody levels against equine infectious anaemia (Coggins test) or equine arteritis. These two diseases do not, under normal circumstances, occur in the UK and their likely route of entry into the country is through the importation of horses from the United States and South America, although both diseases occur in other parts of the world.

It is also advisable to screen all mares for venereal disease, and this can be done by taking a sample for bacterial culture from the clitoris, particularly from the clitoral sinuses based on the upper border of the clitoris. This site harbours the common venereal bacteria. This test may be performed before or immediately upon arrival at the studfarm because evidence of spread other than at mating is minimal. Samples should also be taken from the cervix when the mare is in oestrus.

Minimizing the build-up of disease

Where animals are kept in a stable or an intensive stud environment, the bacterial population will increase. This is not necessarily harmful, although a newborn foal or a debilitated or sick adult will be more susceptible to disease when challenged by large numbers of organisms. Thus, some basic principles should be followed to reduce the build-up of infective microbes.

It is advisable to maintain separate groups of animals so that the interaction and mixing of mares, yearlings and foals are kept to a minimum. Barren and maiden mares should be kept separate from pregnant mares, and mares with foals at foot and yearlings should be kept in separate buildings from adult animals.

The build-up of bacterial contamination in the environment is perhaps most serious in the foaling unit. It is essential that the newborn foal, and particularly its navel, is not exposed to more organisms than necessary in the crucial first twenty-four hours of life.

To achieve this, occupation of the foaling boxes should be kept to a minimum and bedding should be scrupulously clean. Between foalings the box should be cleaned out completely and the floors and walls disinfected, using Ministry of Agriculture-approved disinfectants.

Healthy foals can be removed from the foaling unit, but each foal should then be kept in the one box and moved as little as possible because each time it is moved it is exposed to new microbes, both viral and bacterial, encouraging the outbreak of respiratory disease and diarrhoea.

Parasite control   The biggest single cause of poor growth and intestinal disease is a build-up of roundworm infection. Strongyles (redworms) contaminate horses of all ages, while ascarids (whiteworms) tend to cause unthriftiness in foals (see chapter 32). Parasite control represents the most important form of preventive medicine in any horse establishment where animals are grazing, and paddock management is the first and essential step in any programme of parasite control. The need to alter established grazing patterns has already been discussed (see p. 524 above), particularly the use of sheep and cattle to clear rank patches of grass which horses will not touch. Only one relatively insignificant roundworm infects both cattle and horses, and therefore cattle grazing also reduces significantly the number of infective larvae on paddocks.

It is also important to avoid overgrazing. Ideally the stocking density should not exceed one mare and her foal per hectare. Where stocking densities are high, removal of droppings is a particularly necessary part of pasture management. Paddocks where young foals and yearlings are to be grazed must be cleared of all faecal contamination, the droppings being removed within forty-eight hours of being passed. Fortunately machines for collecting droppings are now available, making this routine chore less arduous.

Regular dosing of animals of all ages with a dewormer (anthelmintic) every four to six weeks is a crucial aspect of worm control. This topic is dealt with in full in chapter 32.

Identifying individuals at risk

Careful observation of all the animals on the premises will reveal some that have problems which require special attention.

With adult horses, particular problems may be associated with the conformation of the feet or dental irregularities. These abnormalities must be carefully noted and special care taken.

Mares going to stud should be subjected to a veterinary examination by rectal palpation and vaginal examination to establish the normality of the genital tract. Swabs may also be taken from the cervix for bacterial culture and the examination of cells (cytology).

If these tests are unsatisfactory a clearer picture of the condition of the mare's uterus can be achieved by taking a uterine biopsy for histological examination. On the basis of these tests individual mares may be separated from the band for special care using management procedures which minimize the contamination of the reproductive tract at mating.

The newborn foal is especially at risk both to infectious and non-infectious problems. Considerable physiological and anatomical changes take place in the neonatal period. Detailed knowledge of behaviour of young foals is necessary in order to be able to detect deviation from normal patterns (see chapters 26 and 27).

Following birth attention to the umbilical cord is important to reduce occurrence of infection through the navel. The cord is usually dressed with antiseptic or antibiotic powder or solution. For discussion of the advantages and disadvantages of this practice, see p. 370.

It is essential that the newborn foal rapidly ingests good-quality colostrum from the mare. Colostrum is the secretion present in the udder at the time of birth and is rich in antibodies. These are absorbed through the intestine of the foal if ingested within twelve hours of birth (see p. 372).

However, the earlier this colostrum is given or sucked by the foal the more certain is its adequate uptake. Mares which run milk before foaling or foals which are slow to suck must be identified and treated accordingly.

A supply of donor colostrum collected from other mares at the time of foaling is very useful. Such colostrum can be kept in a deep freeze for long periods but must be thawed slowly before being fed to a newborn foal. Temperature in excess of 60° C is thought to damage the immunoglobulins present in the colostrum.

Blood samples taken from the foal on the second day of life will give a good indication of the colostral transfer of immunity. It is necessary to measure the globulin and particularly the immunoglobulin level in the serum. At the same time routine haematology may be used to pick up signs of infection or haemolytic disease (neonatal jaundice).

It is usual to give newborn foals an injection of tetanus antitoxin (see p. 415), although this may not be necessary if the mare is vaccinated with tetanus toxoid because antibodies should be transferred in the colostrum. To increase the levels of tetanus and influenza antibodies, pregnant mares should be given a booster influenza and tetanus toxoid vaccination four to six weeks before foaling. Primary vaccination against influenza and tetanus may be started at three to six months of age. It is important to remember to give the third influenza vaccination 150–215 days later.

It is common practice to start worming foals at six to eight weeks of age and the anthelmintic may be given as paste or by nasogastric tube. Worming should be continued monthly thereafter. Worm egg counts should be carried out twice a year to ensure that parasite control is adequate.

Young growing horses are highly susceptible to alterations in the conformation of the limbs. Acquired deviations in the forelimbs are common. Lateral deviation from the knees, the development of club feet and going straight through the fetlocks are the most common abnormalities seen (see chapter 19).

It is very important that these changes should be seen as early as possible, at a time when the abnormalities can often be corrected by rapid change in management such as reducing exercise and feed levels. Once the abnormalities have become established they are extremely difficult to correct.

Controlling the spread of infection

The most common epidemic infections to strike groups of horses are the respiratory virus infections, particularly rhinopneumonitis (see p. 425) and influenza (see p. 422), and the bacterial respiratory disease strangles (see p. 411). Epidemics of venereal disease (see p. 419) may be associated with infections such as *Taylorella equingenitalis* organism, *Klebsiella pneumoniae* and *Pseudomonas aeruginosa*. Ringworm (see p. 95) is a highly contagious disease caused by a variety of fungi and is most commonly seen in stabled horses.

Once an infectious disease has become established in a group of horses it is necessary to introduce control measures to prevent the spread of infection to other animals on the same premises and to other premises. Certain principles should be followed.

1. In the more serious conditions all movement of horses on or off the premises must cease.
2. The affected group of animals must be isolated as far as possible and treated for the infection from which they are suffering.
3. Personnel should not move from this group of affected animals to other animals. The latter must be regarded as 'in contacts' and should be kept under constant observation for any sign of the disease.
4. In the case of venereal infection mating should cease until the situation has been thoroughly investigated and infected animals treated.
5. Vaccination of in-contact but unaffected animals may be considered if an effective vaccine is available. However, once a disease is present in a community it is often too late to vaccinate because of the interval between administration and development of the individual's immune response.

39
SURGERY

The horse is kept primarily for athletic prowess and anything which diminishes its ability to perform successfully will, of necessity, affect adversely its usefulness and value. Thus the demands made of surgery in the horse are very exacting.

The success of any surgical procedure may be qualified as follows: complete success with return to soundness; partial success whereby the horse's eventual soundness is compromised although an improvement in the condition may have been achieved; or failure to restore soundness. Partial success may allow the horse to perform at less demanding levels than before, whereas failure to permit a return to work might not necessarily be deemed a technical failure if surgical intervention has been life-saving. In this respect the salvage of severely injured fillies and occasionally colts by surgical intervention may be undertaken despite a poor prognosis for a functional recovery. These animals may subsequently be used for breeding purposes. However, surgery of this nature would only be undertaken in exceptional circumstances on geldings as they have no value for breeding.

Limitations

Before we embark on a course of surgical treatment we should be realistic in our expectations of surgery. Old or debilitated animals are not suitable candidates for general anaesthesia or major surgery, and those animals with an underlying defect or disability may subsequently develop complications, sometimes insuperable, in the post-operative period.

Another facet to be considered carefully is that of economics. In the case of an animal of relatively little value, all due consideration should be given to the financial cost of surgery and post-operative attention.

We should also be aware that no guarantee of success can be given for the outcome of any operative procedure, even for the treatment of cases in which there is a high success rate. Any number of eventualities or complications may arise, not necessarily associated with the surgery itself, but sometimes as a consequence of the individual animal's temperament or an underlying inherent defect, possibly congenital or acquired, structural or physiological.

Surgical success is ultimately dependent on accurate diagnosis, technical expertise, correct management and realistic but optimistic prognosis. As well as recognition of the disease itself, an understanding of its pathogenesis (natural development) and its relationship to disturbance in function is essential.

Surgical success rate depends on the surgeon's competence and ability to handle tissues and, in addition, the availability of equipment and materials essential to the surgical techniques employed. Surgical success rate is also, to a large extent, affected by case management and therapeutics in the post-operative period whereby complications are dealt with. This frequently depends on anticipating a problem before it arises.

Progress

The field of equine surgery has expanded dramatically over the last twenty-five years due to the great advances made in the biological and technological sciences. Our greater understanding of biological structure and function has given us a new insight into the means of treatment and refinement of established techniques. Technology has risen to the demands made on it by our increased awareness. It produces equipment necessary for basic scientific investigation, which in turn can be used by clinicians for diagnosis and treatment.

The discovery of safe and effective methods of general anaesthesia in the horse has had a profound effect on surgery of the horse, enabling prolonged invasive surgery to be undertaken with the development of more refined techniques. Two prominent examples are orthopaedic and abdominal surgery. The application of the principles of engineering has resulted in very great advances in fracture repair work by the implantation of bone screws and plates as developed on the internal fixation principle. Newer forms of casting materials have major advantages of lightness, great strength, ease of application and water resistance, and have all but superseded the use of plaster of Paris casts.

The advent of antibiotics has made a major contribution to the overall success rate of surgery by the prevention and treatment of post-operative infection. Historically, wound infection was by far the biggest single cause of surgical failure and death. Non-steroidal anti-inflammatory drugs have also made a significant contribution to the control of post-operative tissue reaction and oedema, as well as improving post-operative mobility.

Surgical success rate has climbed in parallel with the development of more refined methods of diagnosis, examples of which are radiography, ultrasonic echography, thermography, nuclear scanning techniques, and the use of the flexible endoscope and the operative arthroscope. In line with these has been the development and advanced treatment methods, including high-power lasers, electromagnetic stimulation of tissue healing, cryotherapy, radio-frequency-induced hypothermia, and the advent of inert synthetic materials which are non-antigenic (in other words, they do not stimulate an immune-type rejection response) and may be permanently implanted in the body with a minimum risk of rejection.

MAJOR SURGICAL TECHNIQUES

In the following section a variety of surgical techniques are described in relation to the different organ systems.

RESPIRATORY TRACT

Surgery is almost entirely confined to the head and neck and involves either the paranasal sinuses and guttural pouches or the airways.

The paranasal sinuses (see p. 26) are not commonly the seat of infection which results in the accumulation of pus. This may arise as a primary infection or secondary to tooth root disease. Cysts may form during the development of the tooth or in the surrounding bone; tumours may also occur at these sites.

Simple infection has a good prognosis and is readily treated by flushing the sinuses using a catheter placed through the overlying skull. Cysts or tumours of the nasal sinuses or nasal passages and ethmoid haematoma, that is, blood blisters around the ethmoid bones which form part of the nasal passages, all require more radical surgery and carry a poorer prognosis because of risk of recurrence. The four rear upper molar teeth have their roots within the maxilliary sinus, and dental disease is treated surgically through the sinus.

The guttural pouches (see p. 26) may develop empyema (accumulations of pus) subsequent to infection. Treatment consists of surgical drainage and frequently carries a good prognosis. Fungal infection (mycosis) of the guttural pouch is a much more serious problem as there is a risk of fatal haemorrhage. The condition is caused by the formation of a fungal plaque and erosion of the arterial wall of the internal carotid artery within the guttural pouch. Treatment is by ligation of the artery to prevent haemorrhage. The fungal infection is treated locally.

Laryngeal hemiplegia, usually left-sided, is manifested in the exercised horse as roaring or whistling (see p. 35). Surgical treatment to relieve obstruction to the airflow carries a good prognosis. The standard method of treatment for many years past has been stripping of the laryngeal ventricle (Hobday operation), but this technique has been further refined in the treatment of pronounced hemiplegia by the insertion of a supra-laryngeal prosthesis.

Horses affected with persistent pharyngeal or laryngeal conditions not amenable to surgical treatment may have their respiratory function improved by a tracheostomy operation. In this procedure a fistula is created between the windpipe and the front upper neck and a metal tube inserted. The tubing of animals with respiratory difficulties has a high success rate. However, the management of the fistula is important and complications may arise (see p. 35).

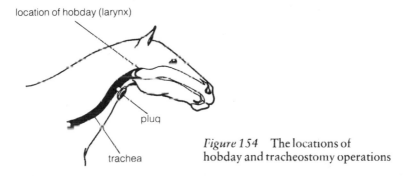

location of hobday (larynx)

pluq

trachea

Figure 154   The locations of hobday and tracheostomy operations

GASTRO-INTESTINAL TRACT

Gastro-intestinal disorders have always been of major importance in the horse. The sheer size and complexity of the organs pose great difficulty for the clinician. Diagnosis of the underlying cause of colic, poor access to a large part of the abdomen and the difficulty of handling such heavy, bulky structures pose particular problems for the surgeon.

As practical experience has been gained in operation techniques and improved methods of diagnosis have been developed, there has been a gradual but steady increase in the success rate of the surgical treatment of colic.

The outcome of surgery depends on many factors. Simple obstructions and malpositions, including torsion of the large colon, carry a relatively good prognosis, as does simple resection of fibrous bands.

The prognosis is less favourable in cases where enterotomy (incision into the intestine) is carried out to relieve obstruction, or bowel resection is undertaken to remove devitalized tissue secondary to the loss of its blood supply.

Conditions of the small intestine are usually more acute and frequently fatal unless rapid intervention takes place. Disorders of the large intestine may also be acute in onset with early death; however, most conditions of the large intestine tend to be of a more chronic nature.

Any situation involving volvulus or torsion of the bowel, with strangulation and loss of blood supply, results in tissue death, leading to absorption of toxins from the devitalized bowel and the development of peritonitis. Any procedure involving resection of devitalized tissue, prolonged manipulation of the bowel, lengthy surgery or late presentation carries a poor prognosis.

Control of shock is essential, both during surgery and in the post-operative period. In the post-operative period paralytic ileus (failure of the gut to establish normal motility) is a major problem, as is the development of peritonitis and post-operative intra-abdominal adhesions. The long-term prognosis may be poor, with significant damage to the blood supply associated with migratory larval worms. This also applies to cases in which extensive adhesions have formed.

URINOGENITAL SURGERY OF THE MARE

CASLICK AND POURET OPERATIONS

There are a number of surgical procedures related to restoring reproductive performance and fertility in mares. The most frequently employed and best known of these is the Caslick operation, which is named after an American veterinarian. This involves suturing the upper part of the vulval lips together, thus reconstituting the valve formed by the vulva and its surrounding tissues, the perineum, which prevents air being sucked into the genital tract (pneumovagina) (see Figure 117 on p. 319).

The operation is performed under local anaesthetic. A small strip of skin is removed from each side of the vulva and the two areas are then brought together by suturing. They heal within about a week of the operation.

The essential object of the operation is to suture the upper part of the vulva so that it is closed to the level of the brim of the pelvis. The results are effective but, because the vulval aperture is artificially reduced, it is necessary to cut the sutured part to open the way for the foal at birth (the approach to this procedure is described on p. 357). After the foal has been born, the wounds on the vulva are resutured to restore the vulval seal.

In recent years an increasing number of individuals, especially older mares, require a further operation to restore the conformation of the vulva and perineum. This operation has been named after the veterinarian who introduced it, Dr Edouard Pouret of France. The Pouret operation involves a more radical approach to restoring the normal conformation. It is required when the Caslick operation has, of necessity, been extended to such a degree that the lower aperture in the vulva is too small for a stallion to penetrate at mating.

The surgery is performed under a combination of spinal and local anaesthesia. A dissection is made between the rectum and the roof of the vagina. This frees the vulva from the pull exerted by the rectum either because it has been drawn forward with age or because of poor conformation. The vulva then returns from its abnormal horizontal inclining position to the normal verticle situation. After the dissection the wound is sutured and heals within two to three weeks.

The advantage of this operation compared with the Caslick is that it reduces the amount of suturing of the vulval lips, thus giving a larger aperture at the lower part of the vulva.

The disadvantage of both the Caslick and the Pouret operations is that they overcome a defect which has an inherited basis. The more the operations are performed, the greater the number of individuals likely to require the procedure. Discerning breeders should reject mares with poor conformation for breeding and thereby improve the fertility of their herd.

OPERATIONS TO OVERCOME URINE POOLING

In some young mares the pooling of the urine on the floor of the vagina occurs as a result of poor perineal conformation or other features which allow the cervix and entrance of the urethra into the floor of the vagina (see p. 323) to be drawn forward, while at the same time the floor of the vagina between these two openings becomes depressed below the pelvis. Urine emerges from the urethra and, instead of being voided posteriorly, drains forward and collects in the pouch formed by the depressed vaginal floor.

Surgery to correct this abnormality includes the Pouret operation, which allows the vagina to move back so that the urethra is restored to its proper position. In addition, plastic surgery to the floor of the vagina around the opening of the urethra can be attempted in order to draw the urethra back into its normal position.

RECTOVAGINAL FISTULA

Tears in the vagina may occur during foaling if the foal's limbs or head are forced through the roof of the vagina into the rectum. The injury is seen most often in mares foaling for the first time and is due to the violent expulsive efforts of the mare in combination with some degree of malalignment of the foal.

The condition can only be rectified by surgery. The technique consists of a first operation in which a shelf is constructed between the rectum and the vagina, followed by a second operation which reconstructs the perineum and vulva. The procedure is usually carried out with the mare tranquillized and placed in stocks, using epidural and local anaesthesia.

CALCULI

The urethra in the male and female can be blocked by a calculus (stone). The surgical procedure to relieve this condition in the mare consists of dilating the urethra with forceps and removing the stone. In the male it may be necessary to cut into the urethra at the level of the pelvic brim as it passes around this area from the bladder to the penis. An incision is made through which the stone is removed.

HERNIA (RUPTURE)

A hernia (rupture) is a protrusion of bowel, omentum or any organ through a natural or an artificial opening in the walls of the cavity within which the organ is contained. Strictly speaking, a hernia is a displacement, perhaps congenital, through a natural opening. However, very often the term is applied to what is correctly referred to as a rupture, i.e. the passage of an organ through an artificial opening.

Rupture of organs such as the lungs or the eyeball do occur, but hernias are generally found in connection with abdominal organs. The protrusion may be bowel, omentum or both. In some cases the bladder is involved and, in other cases, the uterus (womb). In the horse inguinal (scrotal), umbilical and ventral hernias are quite common. Hernias are also encountered in the mesentery (causing colic), the diaphragm and the perineum.

Causes

In congenital cases a natural opening – for example, the umbilicus – is abnormally large. In cases of scrotal or inguinal hernia in newborn foals, there is usually a large opening in the abdominal wall in the groin through which the testes descend (see p. 308 and Figure 116, p. 311) during development.

Hernias acquired after birth are commonly caused by rearing, kicking, jumping or straining; they may also occur when a horse is cast for a surgical operation. Ventral rupture may arise from an external injury, such as staking or being horned by cattle. In the mare an accident producing a hernia may occur at foaling or during the later stages of pregnancy due to the weight of the foetus. In the male it may occur after castration or after an operation for scirrhous cord.

The severity depends on the age of the animal, the condition and size of the opening, whether it is natural (i.e. congenital) or acquired, and the volume of the protrusion. In some cases, for example, small congenital umbilical, ventral and, occasionally, scrotal hernias, recovery takes place spontaneously. If the hernia is due to displacement of part of the bowel, it is quite likely to disappear as the animal becomes older.

In acquired cases hernias do not disappear spontaneously. However, they can often be rectified, but seldom without some form of surgical intervention.

Most congenital cases, when first seen, are reducible. The volume of the swelling varies and may be more pronounced at some times than at others.

When the animal lies down, the swelling tends to disappear, only to reappear or increase in volume when the horse gets up.

Umbilical, inguinal and even a few ventral hernias may be reducible when first seen, but over time there is a danger of them becoming irreducible due to the formation of adhesions. Sometimes there is an alteration in the contents of what is termed the sac, that is, the pouch containing the herniated organ. For example, a loop of bowel may become filled with food, which then prevents reduction.

STRANGULATED HERNIA

This is always a serious condition. It is caused by a narrowing of the hernial ring (the mouth of the sac) or by changes occurring in the hernia itself. Changes in pressure alter the blood supply to the herniated tissues, causing swelling, pain, haemorrhage, exudation, peritonitis and, if not relieved, necrosis. In most cases of necrosis death follows. A strangulated hernia requires immediate surgical correction.

VENTRAL HERNIA

Initially the swelling is compressible but may not be very evident. Sometimes a hard swelling may be seen, the result of blood extravasation from haemorrhage arising from the cause of the hernia. In most cases it is compressible, and coughing will produce a vibration. The ring may be felt, but not always. In some cases of ventral hernia the ring may be situated some distance from the swelling. The discovery of the ring may take a little time, because the bowel is flattened as it escapes through the opening and cannot be traced easily.

INGUINAL HERNIA

Hernias coming under this designation are not always easily discernible and there may be no external evidence of their existence. However, if an adult animal is at all restless and shows signs of colic, a rectal examination may reveal the presence of a hernia. In some cases this examination is the only method by which to discover the opening through the abdominal wall. By moving the hand towards the swelling, the part of the intestine will be felt to be very tense; by tracing the course of the tenseness, it is possible to discover the opening through which the hernia has passed.

UMBILICAL HERNIA

If a swelling is noticeable at the navel, nine times out of ten it is a hernia (Figure 155). A hernia in this position is nearly always compressible. By thrusting a finger towards the centre of the swelling, a hole or opening in the abdominal wall, the so-called hernial ring, can be easily detected.

Treatment

It should be remembered that umbilical hernia in foals usually resolves spontaneously with maturity. However, in practice, cases in which the hernial ring is more than 2 cm in diameter should be treated to speed up resolution of an abnormality which may become strangulated.

Traditional methods of treatment involved the use of blisters, skewers, clamps and trusses. Such methods have now been superseded and two methods are commonly used by veterinarians:

Rubber rings   Elastrator rings, normally used for docking lambs' tails, may be applied to the skin over the hernial sac. Two or three rings are usually applied in succession.

Care in placement is essential to avoid strangulating a section of bowel or mesentery in the hernial sac. Such a mishap would produce pain, necrosis and death if not corrected rapidly.

The technique is simple and can be performed in the standing position, although sedation may be necessary with fractious foals. The rings should be placed as close to the abdominal wall as possible, in effect holding the contents of the hernial ring, which will then close spontaneously. The necrotic tissue below the rings will shrink and drop off in three to four weeks.

As with any surgical procedure, it is vital that the foal be vaccinated against tetanus or given antitoxin before this treatment is undertaken.

Surgical closure   Surgical closure of the hernial ring under general anaesthesia is the method of choice when the defect is too large for the application of rubber rings or when the hernia is irreducible or has strangulated. Modern surgical techniques and anaesthetics render the operation simple and routine.

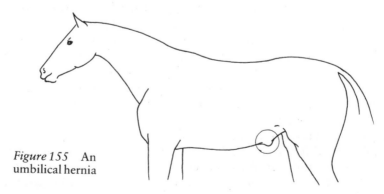

Figure 155   An umbilical hernia

CASTRATION

The removal of the testes, an operation known as castration or gelding, is carried out to render the animal more docile and to facilitate control in the presence of mares. It also renders the animal sterile.

Castration may be performed at any age. The main problems in castrating a foal are the testes are small and more difficult to grasp and the foal is not so used to being handled. Advocates of castration of foals have maintained not only that the operation is quite successful and has no effect in retarding development, but that there are fewer accidents and complications. Nevertheless most authorities would not advocate castration prior to a year of age, and the heavy breeds, especially those like hunters destined for prolonged hard work, are often left until they are three or even four.

When a horse is castrated many of the characteristics of a stallion fail to develop or regress if they have developed. The crest does not appear and the neigh becomes more like that of a mare. Changes in temperament vary with the breed, though most geldings are more docile than stallions. Whether or not a stallion is aggressive often depends on his management – Standardbred stallions are often extremely docile and the author's children ride his pony stallions in hand with aplomb.

Castration can be carried out at any time of year, but the custom is to do it in the spring or autumn. Spring is generally preferred because there are fewer flies about and the animal can be turned out afterwards and so reduce the swelling that is otherwise likely to develop.

The operation must, in the United Kingdom, be performed with adequate anaesthesia or analgesia and must be performed by a veterinarian. It may be carried out with the animal standing (in which case anaesthetic is injected deeply into the testis) or with the animal recumbent. (There are so many good anaesthetic agents available today that there can be little justification for casting the horse with ropes.)

Both methods have their advocates and the choice should be the result of a consultation between owner and veterinarian. The advantage of the standing method is that all the risks of a recumbent animal are avoided. Its disadvantage is that it is more risky to the operator, especially if the animal does not respond to sedation or restraint.

Castration by emasculator is the most popular method today; the older methods involving clamps, cautery, torsion and ligation having almost disappeared.

Most castrations are performed 'open', which means leaving open the wound through the scrotum. If the inguinal ring is abnormally large, bowel may leave the abdomen, pass through the inguinal canal and protrude through the scrotal wound. Some vets, therefore, employ a closed technique for castration which seals off this opening. For such a technique to be employed successfully, general anaesthesia, clean surgical conditions and a ligature are obligatory.

Complications of Castration

HAEMORRHAGE

Dripping of blood after castration is common and of no significance, provided the drips are not running into one another and the rate of drip is slowing down. Applying cold water to the scrotum, either from a bucket or a hose pipe is often apparently effective, although there is a danger that the bleeding vessels may retract further into the wound and the bleeding continue internally. Lay persons should not therefore interfere.

Streaming of blood, however, is a matter of considerable concern and veterinary advice should be sought. Some advocate packing the wound and waiting, but the author's preference is to anaesthetize the animal again, find

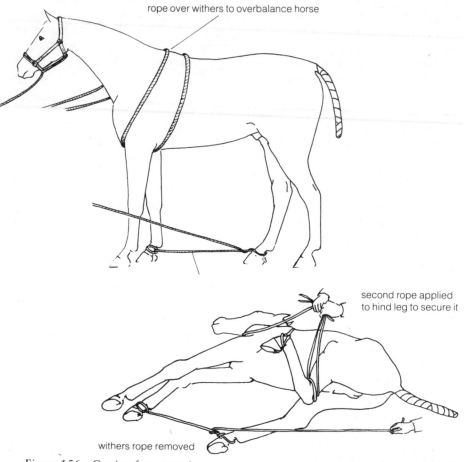

rope over withers to overbalance horse

second rope applied to hind leg to secure it

withers rope removed

Figure 156   Casting for castration

the bleeding point and ligate it. Haemorrhage can be prevented by the use of an adequate, well-maintained emasculator.

Haemophilia is very rare in horses, but the author has seen two horses bleeding profusely after castration, both of which had unidentified clotting defects.

A rare complication of profuse haemorrhage is irreversible blindness due to damage to the retina.

PROLAPSE OF THE BOWEL

Passage of a loop of bowel down the inguinal canal and through the castration wound can occur while the castration is being performed, as the horse stands up (or attempts to) after a general anaesthetic, or up to forty-eight hours after castration. This is the complication of castration most likely to be fatal because the bowel becomes dry and dirty or may get torn or damaged by the horse's feet. Moreover, the bowel gets trapped in the canal, its blood supply is severely reduced (strangulation) and this causes colic.

Veterinary advice should be sought immediately if it is not already present. Prior to arrival of the professional, the best action for a lay person is to use a clean towel or sheet to keep the bowel off the ground. Sometimes heroic surgery is required to save these animals but, in the author's experience, it is often successful.

SWELLING

Some swelling of the scrotum and sheath almost invariably accompanies castration and is best controlled by daily forced exercise – no recently castrated horse should ever be turned away and forgotten. The swelling usually reaches its maximum by four days and should have resolved by twelve. The author does *not* advocate the practice of artificially keeping the scrotal wound open by putting fingers into it daily – this is likely to result in infection, unless carefully done, and is best avoided.

If the swelling persists or seems excessive, veterinary advice should be sought. In such a case it is likely that infection has supervened and the establishment of adequate drainage and injections of antibiotics are required.

If swelling develops some time after castration, it may be due to a number of other conditions which are listed below.

ABSCESS

A scrotal abscess is characterized by a spherical, fluctuating, painful swelling, and the horse can sometimes be quite ill from poisons produced by pus in the abscess. Abscesses usually develop within a few weeks of castration. The abscess should be opened by a veterinarian and drained, and the cavity kept open until healing has advanced. Occasionally an infected ligature will be at the root of an abscess and resolution will only occur if the whole abscess is surgically removed.

CHAMPIGNON

This condition derives its name from the French word for 'mushroom' and is characterized by a mushroom-like growth of proud flesh from the scrotal wound. It develops a few weeks after castration and must be cut out under general anaesthetic. Fortunately, it is quite rare today.

LIGATURE SINUS

This condition is characterized by the development of a small opening in the scrotum which discharges pus and of a hard lump in the groin. It usually takes several years to develop and the animal may present as lame on that side before the discharge is noted. The cause is an abscess developing round a ligature used for castration. The abscess and the sinus tract leading from it to the outside must be excised.

SCIRRHOUS CORD

Like ligature sinus, this condition develops years after castration and is characterized by a large hard lump in the groin, sometimes with multiple openings discharging pus. It is caused by chronic infection with a staphyloccocal organism and is extremely difficult to treat. Occasionally it can have spread into the abdomen before it is recognized; the prognosis is then hopeless. Surgical excision should be attempted, perhaps after a long course of suitable antibiotic treatment has reduced its size.

CYSTIC ENDS

Soft, fluctuating swellings can develop in the scrotum of castrated horses, months or years after castration. They are very soft, fluid-filled cysts and can appear and disappear, sometimes quickly, sometimes slowly. They cause the horse no trouble, but can be surgically removed if they are considered a blemish.

CRYPTORCHIDISM (RIG, RIDGELING)

Cryptorchids are animals with improper testicular descent and the condition may be bilateral or unilateral (see p. 311). The retained testicle may lie high up within the inguinal canal but external to the body wall, or it may lie within the abdomen internal to the inguinal ring. General anaesthesia is essential when castrating to allow exposure of and exploration for such hidden testicles.

OTHER TECHNIQUES

Cryosurgery

Cryosurgery is the technique of destroying tissues by the local application of intense cold. The tissue is rapidly frozen to a temperature of $-20°$ C $(-4°$ F) or lower, then slowly thawed and subsequently refrozen. The number of freeze–thaw cycles used depends on the type of tissue under treatment, the depth of penetration required and overall area to be destroyed.

Tissues contain large amounts of water, both extra- and intracellular, and thus ice formation within the tissues can readily be induced. Freezing causes the cells to swell, followed by death and rupture of the cell membranes. The frozen tissues die and gradually slough off to leave a well-demarcated, healthy, granulating wound.

Cryotherapy is most frequently utilized for the removal of skin tumours (see chapter 41), especially squamous cell carcinoma, sarcoids, cutaneous granuloma and exuberant granulation tissue. It has been found that the technique, used alone or in combination with prior surgical excision, has improved the overall success rate by decreasing the number of treatments per case and reducing the incidence of recurrence at the original site.

Cryosurgery is also used in ophthalmic surgery for cataract extraction. Latterly it has also been developed as a technique for neurectomy of the lower limb; it is said to reduce the risk of secondary neuroma formation (see p. 250).

Lasers

Lasers are a relatively recent addition to the surgeon's armamentarium. At the present time there are two main types of laser: the high-energy ('hot') laser and the low-energy ('cold') laser.

The former produces a high energy 'lightbeam', capable of both cutting and burning tissues, which is used to treat the base of a wound after surgical excision of a tumour or tissue mass. Hot lasers are most frequently used in the removal of skin tumours, epithelial carcinomas, sarcoids and to treat beds of granulation tissue. They are also used in the more refined techniques of ophthalmic surgery for treating retinal detachment.

Cold lasers are a more recent innovation and have been used mainly in the fringe areas of physiotherapy, cosmetic surgery and acupuncture. At the present time there has been little published scientific data to substantiate the claims made for the therapeutic benefits of this tool.

Currently in the veterinary field these lasers are being used for management of specific soft-tissue injuries, such as sprained tendons, ligaments, tendon sheath injury, haematomas and open wounds. It is not known how the laser beam affects tissue response or assists the rate of healing of different tissue types, which is said to follow treatment.

It is claimed that this class of laser can significantly reduce the healing time for open wounds of soft tissue. Practical experience has shown that recent tendon injuries may be cosmetically improved, but that the underlying structural damage remains materially unaffected. This may lead to a horse being returned prematurely to work, only to break down (see p. 208ff).

Different types of lameness have been treated with the cold laser both locally and at sites distant from the injury, the laser being applied over the nerves supplying the injured area. Benefits from this technique may be related to a desensitizing or local anaesthetic effect, as can be seen with acupuncture.

Note: Lasers produce a concentrated beam of light which can be reflected from glass or metal surfaces and the operator should be aware of this risk. The laser should never be pointed at the eye, either directly or indirectly.

Electromagnetic stimulation

The application of an electrical current across the fracture site of a bone injury stimulates bone repair under certain circumstances. Under normal conditions unstressed bone has a static surface electrical potential, which alters in response to mechanical stress (i.e. loading). If the bone is fractured, the inherent electrical charge of the bone becomes rearranged, with a negative polarity induced at the fracture site. It has been found in cases of non-union of fractures and pseudoarthrosis that application of an electrical charge across the fracture site stimulates repair.

Direct current may be applied via implated electrodes (an invasive technique which has inherent problems with electrolysis). Another method is by electromagnetic induction of current in the tissues under treatment. Pulsing electromagnetic fields (PEMFs) are produced by passing pulsed electrical current through special circular coils placed on either side of the bone under treatment. The tissue between the coils is thereby exposed to an electromagnetic field which induces changes in the electrical potential of that tissue and modifies cellular activity. By varying the electrical pulse in size, shape and rate, it is possible to produce the ideal electrical conditions for the particular tissue type under treatment.

PEMFs are commonly used for treatment of stress fractures of the anterior cortex of the cannon bone, bucked shins, sesamoid bone fractures and as an adjunct to standard orthopaedic surgical procedures. Both sesamoid fractures and cortical fractures of the cannon bone have a tendency to heal slowly, frequently with non-union; it is thought that PEMF therapy can significantly reduce the healing time and improve the final union.

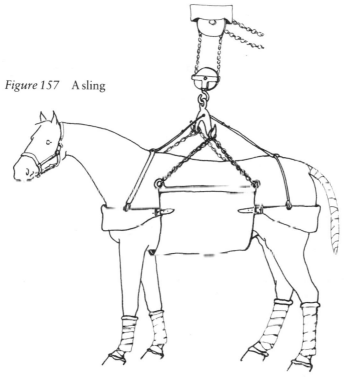

Figure 157 A sling

At present there are several systems on the market. The Blue Boot, which is designed to be strapped to the leg, is completely portable and contains a rechargeable energy pack. There are other rechargeable portable systems and also larger, mains-operated systems which give the operator a choice of pulses.

Slinging as an aid to surgery

A sling is employed as a means of support to an injured horse when it is essential that it be kept in the standing position, as, for example, in cases of pelvic fracture, which may become displaced with serious complications under the strain of the animal lying down or getting up. The apparatus may also be used for lifting recumbent animals.

A patent sling consists of a middle piece or suspender which supports the body and is attached on each side by a metal ring to a bow (a metal tree), which is in turn attached to a strong overhead support by an endless-chain pulley.

Breast straps at the front of the bodybelt prevent the horse from falling forwards, and breechings at the rear afford support if the horse sits back.

The sling should be adjusted to a height at which the horse may stand unsupported of its volition. It should also be able to lean backwards against the breechings and thereby derive postural support. On no account should the horse be suspended without its feet touching the ground, unless it is being raised from a recumbent position.

A horse in a sling should be checked regularly to make sure that the apparatus is properly adjusted and that pressure sores do not develop. Extra padding may be needed at potential pressure points. A laxative diet is essential.

Some horses, by their very nature, are unsuitable candidates for slinging. To prevent recumbency, such cases should be tied up by the head collar with a loop of string connecting the stable chain to the ring of the head collar.

Firing

Firing is the application of hot irons to the area of a damaged tendon, bone or joint with the purpose of inducing a severe inflammation (a counter-irritation) in an attempt to effect a cure. It is a procedure virtually confined to the horse and has been handed down over centuries.

In the present day it has been superseded as a means of therapy by the introduction of more refined treatments developed from a newer under-standing of pathology and carried out with equipment developed as a result of technological advance.

Recent scientific research has been unable to demonstrate any benefit from firing damaged tendons and, despite some dissenting views, veterinary opinion is against its use.

Blistering

This is the term for the application of a chemical irritant to produce vesication (blisters) and counter-irritation, in other words, to induce an inflammatory response as a therapeutic measure.

The use of vesicants (blistering agents) is a contentious subject and is not advocated by the veterinary profession. The efficacy of blistering is likely to remain based on subjective opinion rather than on scientific fact.

40

WOUNDS; THE FIRST-AID KIT

Wounds are commonly seen in horses as a result of falls, being kicked or bitten by other horses, colliding with or getting entangled in fencing, hitting jumps, etc. A wound, is defined as 'an injury to the body caused by physical means with disruption of normal continuity of body structures which is followed by healing.'* A wound may be closed, that is, the skin remains intact as in bruising, sprains and ruptures, for example, or open with various degrees of skin damage.

OPEN WOUNDS

Open wounds can be grouped according to the nature of the damage.

Incised wounds   These wounds have clean straight edges and often bleed quite freely. There is usually very little associated bruising and they normally heal quickly and simply. Examples are surgical incisions using a scalpel and cuts caused by sharp pieces of metal or glass.

Lacerations and tears   These wounds have torn rather than cut edges and may be irregular in shape. There is usually some associated bruising and the amount of bleeding is variable. These wounds often result in tags or flaps of skin, the blood supply of which is compromised, resulting in death of the skin (necrosis) at a later stage. Lacerated wounds are the result of getting caught on protruding nails or posts and sometimes wire.

Puncture wounds   These can be more serious than they appear and are characterized by a small skin opening with soft-tissue penetration to a variable depth. They are caused by bites, being staked on fences or jumps, treading on nails, pieces of wire, pitchforks, and so on.

* *Darland's Illustrated Medical Dictionary*, 26th edn.

The object causing the puncture wound can carry with it, to the depth of the injury, either foreign material (for example, a splinter) or bacteria, which can become established and cause deep infection. The skin wound may be so small as to not be seen.

Puncture wounds should not be probed or explored excessively because such action may disrupt blood clots or force any foreign body deeper. This type of wound always requires the administration of tetanus vaccination and antitoxin. Drainage must be established and encouraged so the wound can heal from the inside out. A poultice (e.g. Animalintex) can be applied to try to draw out any contaminating material and help keep the wound open.

Penetrating wounds   These are wounds which penetrate into one of the body cavities, such as the thorax or abdomen, and are very serious. There may or may not be injury to internal organs.

Emergency first aid in these cases involves covering the wound with sterile gauze or bandage to prevent further contamination and/or the escape of organs or tissues, and to reduce the amount of air sucked into the body cavity and hence prevent infection.

Abrasions   These are very superficial skin wounds, resulting from rubbing or scraping against an irritant surface. Examples are saddle chaffs and shoulder rubs from ill-fitting saddles and rugs respectively. Abrasions may also result from falling on the road, but, although the skin injury may seem superficial in these instances, the bones of the limbs which have poor protection may be damaged even if not exposed through the wound.

These wounds should be gently but thoroughly cleansed and, if possible lightly bandaged.

Treatment

Open wounds involve damage to some of or all the following: skin, muscles, nerves, blood vessels, tendons, bones, internal organs. All wounds, unless incurred during aseptic surgery, are contaminated by bacteria, which may become established and result in an infected wound.

The main aims in wound treatment are: to control haemorrhage; to turn the contaminated wound into a clean one; and to promote rapid healing.

Haemorrhage to a limited degree helps to flush a wound free of contaminating material, and it may be difficult to decide whether it is more important to try to control the haemorrhage or cleanse the wound. This depends on the degree of haemorrhage and the degree of contamination. If bleeding is minor, cleanse the wound and apply a dressing, preferably sterile, which will help to control the bleeding. If bleeding is more extensive, there are several methods available to reduce or stop it completely.

Control of bleeding

Ligature   If a large vessel is severed, it must be ligated before excessive blood loss occurs. If an artery is involved, bright red blood will be escaping in spurts. If it is a vein, the blood is darker and flows continuously. The damaged ends of the vessel should be grasped in a forceps and a ligature of sterile catgut or other sterile absorbable material placed around them and tied tightly so that it does not slip.

Clamping with and without torsion   Smaller vessels, especially arteries, will seal if clamped for several minutes with an artery clamp or forceps. Twisting the clamp or forceps (torsion) until the vessel stretches and breaks causes elastic recoil and can be used to seal many smaller arteries and veins, although veins lack the full elasticity of arteries and may not seal without being ligated.

Pressure   This may be applied directly by placing a clean dressing to the wound and holding it firmly in place until bleeding stops. On the limbs a pressure bandage with several layers of absorbent material or a wad of material underneath can be applied over the wound. This must be left in place until bleeding has stopped.

The pressure bandage must be applied tightly but should be removed once haemorrhage has ceased to avoid interfering with the circulation. Tourniquets should not be used unless haemorrhage is severe, as they can, if incorrectly applied, exacerbate the bleeding by interfering with venous drainage from the area.

Topically applied substances   Some chemicals can be applied to the bleeding surfaces to control haemorrhage. They include silver nitrate, ferric chloride, ferric sulphate, alum and tannin. These substances work by precipitating proteins in the damaged vessel to block it and allow clotting to occur. Pressure should be used to reduce haemorrhage and the wound should be cleansed before the substance is applied, as excessive amounts of blood or a blood clot will interfere with the effectiveness of the chemical.

Locally applied materials   These are used surgically to encourage clotting and include oxidized cellulose, calcium alginate and absorbable gelatin sponges. They act as a framework on which a clot can develop. They can be left in a clean wound as they are absorbable.

Electrocautery, diathermy, electrocoagulation   These methods use heat or electric current to seal vessels or coagulate tissues to stop haemorrhage.

Cleansing and débridement

Simple hosing is the best way initially to cleanse many wounds, especially if they are large or heavily contaminated (dirty), because it produces a constant flow of water in large volumes and under variable pressure. Excessive pressure should be avoided as it may force foreign material deeper into the wound or open up new tissue planes, allowing spread of infection. The skin surrounding the wound should also be hosed clean of mud and debris.

Smaller wounds, and larger ones after initial hosing (performed for up to fifteen or twenty minutes), should be gently cleansed with a *dilute* solution of a mild skin antiseptic in *warm* water using either a syringe or a hand pump and pieces of clean cottonwool or Gamgee. Suitable solutions can be made up using iodine-based washes such as povidone iodine, chlorophene, cetrimide and chlorhexidine. If possible, the surrounding area should be clipped or shaved before cleansing, care being taken that hair does not enter the wound by packing it with clean gauze.

After a wound has been cleansed the remaining, often embedded, foreign material and dead or damaged tissues may need removing (débridement). Physical or chemical restraint (tranquillization or general anaesthesia), with or without the use of local anaesthesia, may be needed, depending on the nature of the wound, the amount of contamination, the facilities available and the temperament of the patient. A pair of tissue forceps, a sharp pair of scissors and a scalpel are essential instruments for débridement. If the wound is extensive, this procedure may have to be repeated at a later date as some tissues will die despite correct treatment. During débridement all care must be taken to preserve tendons, nerves and blood vessels, but tags of skin or other damaged or dead tissue should be removed.

Drainage

Some wounds, especially puncture wounds or wounds in which there is a large gap left due to loss of normal tissue, will require drainage which must be maintained for a variable period of time to allow healing. This may be achieved either by leaving the wound open, with or without enlarging the skin opening, or by creating a second skin opening and establishing drainage with or without the use of drains.

These drains are pieces of latex or plastic which are sutured into the wound with one or both ends communicating with the outside. They allow the passage of fluid and debris from the depth of the wound. Care should be taken, however, over placement and protection to prevent drains being torn or acting as routes for infection to enter the wound. They should not exit through the wound itself as this will interfere with healing.

Healing

A clean wound will begin the process of healing immediately after the injury. Wounds heal in several ways depending on the nature and site of the injury.

Healing by first or primary intention can only occur in non-contaminated incised wounds where the edges are or can be brought together. For this type of healing to occur, the wound must also be fresh and sutured to bring the skin edges into direct contact with each other.

The wound should be stitched as soon as possible after the injury has occurred. If the skin edges are not under tension, a simple pattern of interrupted sutures or a continuous suture may be used. The former permits better apposition of skin edges than the continuous pattern; also if a knot comes untied, only one suture is lost. The continuous suture can be inserted more quickly.

Subcutaneous and deeper tissues may be brought together using an absorbable suture material before the skin is closed. However, if structures such as tendons and ligaments need to be sutured, stainless steel should be used for its strength and durability as these tissues need a long time to heal.

If the edges of a wound can only be brought together under tension or if extensive swelling is likely, tension sutures, using either buttons or tubing to spread the tension over a larger area, or a vertical mattress suture pattern may be used. Sutures should remain in place at least for ten days, and longer if necessary.

If the wound cannot heal by primary intention, it must undergo the processes of granulation, contraction and epithelial cell multiplication and migration. This is called healing by second intention.

Large skin and tissue defects on the body tend to heal with relatively little scarring because the skin is loose and wound contraction can occur readily. On the limbs, however, there is little or no loose skin and wound contraction is limited. The formation of excessive granulation tissue (proud flesh) in wounds to the limbs also interferes with healing, as the epithelial cells cannot migrate over the proud flesh to create a new skin covering. Little can be done to facilitate wound contraction on horses' limbs and skin grafting may be necessary to complete healing. The forces of wound contraction are so great that, if scarring occurs over or near a joint, the skin may be pulled so tight as to prevent proper joint movement.

Proud flesh can be kept to a minimum by the use of pressure bandaging and immobilization. However, once present, it must be removed either surgically or by the use of caustic powders or solutions. These substances include copper sulphate (bluestone) and silver nitrate. Care should be taken when using these to ensure that the delicate band of advancing epithelial cells around the edges of the wound is not damaged. Formalin may also be used to reduce excessive proud flesh, but, again, this must not come into contact with healthy tissue.

Dressings

Bandaging wounds serves many purposes. One is the immobilization of the region to aid healing. Another is to keep the wound clean and protect it from infection and to prevent further trauma. Pressure, as applied through a bandage, can aid in reducing swelling and oedema and in controlling haemorrhage. Not all wounds require or are suitable for bandaging. Some are best left open, kept clean and free from debris, and treated with either a wound powder or spray and allowed to granulate. Wounds on many parts of the body and upper limbs must be treated in this way. On the other hand, where rigid immobilization is necessary, for example, with leg wounds where a tendon is exposed or damaged or with some wounds around the joints, the limb should be placed in a cast to allow tissues to heal.

All dressing should be non-adhesive and may be impregnated with sterile petroleum jelly (Vaseline) or antibiotics. They should preferably be sterile but at the very least clean. Padding, such as cottonwool, combine or Gamgee should be used to help distribute the pressure of the bandage and absorb any discharge from the wound. There are many types of bandages available, from light stretch crepe through stable bandages to adhesive elastic bandages. Care must be taken with the stretch bandages not to apply them too tightly as this may interfere with the blood circulation to the area and below.

Drugs

Systemic antibiotic treatment may be necessary in serious or heavily contaminated wounds. Penicillins, sulphonamides and trimetho-prin-sulphonamide combinations are most frequently used. Anti-inflammatory drugs are also occasionally indicated as they help to reduce pain, inflammation and swelling.

Factors affecting healing

There are not many ways to stimulate healing to progress faster than it does in a clean, 'healthy' wound, and the rate of healing is the same in a large as in a small wound. However, many factors interfere with and delay healing. The most important of these is infection, which results in further tissue damage, discharge and inflammation. An infected wound must be thoroughly cleaned, drainage established and antibiotics administered. Topically applied antibiotics are often unable to reach the bacteria in infected wounds because of the barrier produced by dead tissue and discharges, and systemic antibiotics must be used instead.

Other local factors which may affect healing include blood supply to the wound, associated soft-tissue damage such as bruising and haematomas (blood sacs), skin temperature, and the availability of loose connective tissue to allow wound closure. Many systemic disorders may also interfere with wound healing: these include protein or vitamin A or C deficiency, zinc deficiency, age, and some hormonal, cardiac, liver and kidney abnormalities.

CLOSED WOUNDS

Closed wounds include bruises, contusions, sprains, and muscle and tendon rupture. Contusions result from a blunt force causing haemorrhage, bruising and oedema without breaking the skin. Signs of contusion include swelling, heat and pain at the site of injury, and discolouration of the overlying skin if it is pink (or depigmented). Kicks from other horses often result in contusions with the formation of haematomas under the skin due to leakage of blood from damaged vessels. Treatment of contusions involves initial immobilization of the region and cold hosing, or the application of ice packs to reduce heat and swelling. Subsequently applying heat to the area encourages the absorption of excessive fluid.

Large haematomas often require draining, but this is best left for two or three days to allow haemorrhage to cease. The drainage hole should be made in the most dependent (lowest) point of the haematoma and should be kept open by vigorous cleaning until there is no more discharge from it. If allowed to close early, the haematoma sac may refill with blood or fluid and require redraining.

Other closed wounds include sprains, ligament tears and ruptures, and muscle tears and ruptures (see chapters 14 and 15).

BURNS

Burns may be caused by excessive heat – for example, flame, hot solids, steam or water or other hot liquids; excessive cold or freezing, such as frost bite; electric currents; substances such as acids and alkalis; or radiation. They are classified as follows:

First-degree burns These involve only the very superficial epithelial layers of the skin and result in temporary reddening and loss (sloughing) of these layers, which are rapidly replaced from deeper layers. Mild to moderate sunburn is a first-degree burn.

Second-degree burns These involve almost the full thickness of the epidermis and damage some of the accessory skin structures such as sweat glands and hair follicles. They heal by the multiplication of surrounding cells, which migrate into the tissue defect, usually under a scab.

Third-degree burns These cause damage to the full thickness of the skin and some of the subcutaneous tissues, and result in ulceration and sloughing of the full thickness of the skin. They often require skin grafts to complete healing.

Very deep burns may also affect the muscles and tissues underneath. The hair coat of mammals protects them, to a small extent, from burns by flames or hot objects, but may also act to mask the full extent of an injury. The reddening of skin in a first-degree burn may go unnoticed, especially where the skin is pigmented.

In second degree burns there is damage to the dermis and loss of the epidermal layers, resulting in leakage of serum from blood vessels the development of oedema in surrounding tissues and a crust on the surface. Third-degree burns result in the coagulation of the skin, thrombosis (blocking) of vessels and subsequent obstruction to the nutrient supply to the upper tissue layers, resulting in the formation of a black, leathery scar (an eschar). Damage to nerve endings results in loss of sensation. These burns, if large in area, often require skin grafting.

Electric burns appear as cold, pale yellow, bloodless, painless lesions. These are worse if the hair is wet because wet tissue conducts electricity more efficiently. There may only be a small skin lesion, but a much larger area of damage may have occurred under the skin. These wounds generally heal slowly and there may be some tissue sloughing.

Although the wounds themselves can appear dramatic, burns can have more serious effects on the whole body. In burns due to fire or steam, swelling and oedema of the nasal passages and pharynx may result in death from asphyxiation. Shock may develop immediately or as a result of the loss of large amounts of fluid from the damaged area. This can be fatal.

Another long-term effect of severe burns is the development of anaemia due to depression of red blood cell formation in the bone marrow. Infection is common after serious burns, and toxaemia may develop and result in the death of the animal within a few days or some time later.

Treatment

Treatment of burn victims must take into account both the local and the systemic consequences of the injuries. Burns are extremely painful and the affected animals should be handled quietly and gently at all times. If the burns are extensive or severe, your veterinarian should be called immediately. Fluid replacement and maintenance therapy is most important. Fluids may need to be administered intravenously at first, although, once the animal has stabilized, giving water by stomach tube and encouraging the horse to drink may be adequate. Painkillers may also be necessary to reduce the chance of shock and make the animal more comfortable. Useful painkillers are the narcotics (e.g. pethidine) and certain anti-inflammatory drugs. The horse should be kept quiet, warm and comfortable.

Local treatment of the burned or scalded area involves *gently* washing the area with a very dilute antibacterial solution or wash (e.g. povidone iodine). Avoid the use of oily or greasy ointments, tannic acid, silver nitrate, iodine, methylated spirits or other household remedies. Wet dressings consisting of sterile gauze soaked in warm isotonic saline or surgical chlorinated soda solution should be applied to the area. Water-based creams with antibiotics may be applied to the wounds and covered with a sterile dressing.

Treatment of burns due to chemicals

The most important initial step is to rinse the area free from any remaining chemical. If the burn is caused by an acid, bath the area with an alkaline solution such as baking soda in warm water. If the burn is caused by an alkali, e.g. quicklime, bath the area with a fifty-fifty vinegar and water mixture. In either case, or if the causative chemical is unknown, the area should be rinsed freely with clear water and then treated as any other burn.

Burns due to cold

Fortunately burns due to excessive cold are uncommon although freeze branding is becoming increasingly popular as an aid to identification of horses in some countries. In temperate climates frostbite may occur if a horse is allowed to stand in mud and water during very cold weather. This results in damage to the superficial skin layers, leakage of serum from the capillaries and oedema of the affected areas, which become swollen and painful. The skin may appear cracked and the condition is often called cracked heels or mud fever in its milder form (see p. 255).

Treatment consists of keeping the affected areas clean and dry and applying a soothing, non-greasy cream to soften the scabs. The cream may contain an antibacterial substance such as a sulphonamide to prevent infection. It is better to try to prevent cracked heels either by not washing a horse's legs in winter or by thoroughly drying them immediately if washing is necessary or if the animal has been standing in cold water or mud. Do not allow horses to stand for any period in mud or water in cold weather and ensure they are kept in good health and condition throughout the year.

LIGHTNING STRIKE AND ELECTRIC SHOCK

Both these events usually result in death with little external evidence of injury apart from a line of singed hair or burned skin along the course of the current. Occasionally more obvious evidence of lightning strike is present, such as a struck tree nearby or a branching pattern on the hair from the point of strike. Rigor mortis is usually present for a very short period only and the carcase decomposes rapidly. Post mortem reveals widespread petechial (pinpoint) haemorrhages throughout the intestine, endocardium (lining of the heart), meninges, central nervous system and viscera (internal organs). It may be difficult to differentiate between septicaemia, anthrax, lightning strike and other causes of sudden death unless further tests are performed.

Surviving animals appear dazed or unconscious, with severe depression of both cardiac and respiratory functions. Respiration is slow, laboured or gasping. The pulse is weak and slow. The pupils may be dilated or constricted, and convulsions are common. A varying degree of paralysis is also common; its disappearance is a good sign of recovery. Recovery may take hours or days, but in some cases permanent paralysis or blindness follows.

Electric shock arises from contact with overhead cables, wire fencing or other sources of electric current, particularly if the immediate area is wet. At post mortem the heart appears flabby and there is marked congestion of the lungs, heart and other organs.

Treatment for a surviving victim of electric shock or lightning strike is largely a matter of good nursing. Plenty of bedding, food and water should be available and the animal's condition constantly monitored. Support bandages on all limbs may be useful if the animal is weak or is paralysed in one leg.

THE FIRST-AID KIT

Every responsible horse or pony owner should have a basic first-aid kit in the tack room. It is best kept in a small, clean, preferably waterproof box (a plastic sandwich box is ideal). This ensures that the kit remains clean and dry, and can be taken with the horse whenever it travels away from home.

The contents of the box are for dealing with any minor injuries which may occur either in the stable or paddock or while out riding. These are usually superficial cuts and grazes, such as those resulting from kicks, wire cuts, overreaching, thorns, etc.

If the injury is severe, first aid should only be a temporary procedure and a veterinarian contacted as soon as possible.

The contents of a basic first-aid kit are as follows:

Antiseptics

An antiseptic cleansing agent, such as Pevidine or Savlon (diluted for use), is essential for cleaning wounds. Hosing is generally a very good way of flushing out debris from the wound area (see p. 550) and then the antiseptic solution can be applied at the final stage. If a hose is not available, the antiseptic should be added to a bucket of clean, preferably warm, water. The wound should be cleaned thoroughly, starting at its centre and working outwards.

Wound powders and sprays

After cleaning a wound which is not going to be bandaged (either because it is in an area which is impossible to bandage or because it is very superficial), a dressing of either powder or spray should be applied to help prevent infection and aid in the drying of the wound.

Powders such as acrimide are antibacterial and those such as aureomycin contain antibiotics. During the summer fly-repellent powder containing coumaphos should be used. This is to prevent fly strike (flys laying eggs in the open wound).

Some horses object violently to sprays. If this is the case the spray should be squirted onto cottonwool at some distance from the horse and then dabbed on the wound. Some antibiotic sprays contain gentian violet (purple spray), which is an effective antifungal agent. These sprays are particularly useful when treating areas on and around the feet.

Never use powders or sprays on or around the eyes of a horse.

Creams and ointments

An antiseptic ointment such as Fucidine is useful for applying to mild skin problems such as cracked heels and mud fever, and a light healing cream such as Dermisol can be used on dry non-adherent dressings before bandaging.

Bandages

It is useful to have a good selection of open-weave, adhesive and crepe bandages. These can be obtained from most chemists or from a veterinarian.

Dressings are employed after the injured area has been cleansed to control haemorrhage, to keep an open wound clean, and also for support and protection. Most wounds which involve the full thickness of the skin should be bandaged if possible because this prevents dirt from entering and helps to hold the edges of the wound together.

Crepe bandages give support and slight pressure without restricting movement. Adhesive bandage such as Elastoplast helps to hold a bandage onto a difficult area such as the knee or hock and should be applied directly to the skin above and below the bandage and over the bandage itself.

All bandages must be applied with care. It is important that there is adequate padding (such as Gamgee) underneath and that they are kept flat and not wrinkled. Except in cases of severe haemorrhage, when they may be used tightly for short periods (not more than fifteen minutes at a time), bandages should be applied with a light, even pressure. Overtight bandaging can cause disruption to the blood circulation of the skin and underlying tissues and result in necrosis and sloughing.

Sterile, non-adherent dressings

These are applied where the surface of the skin is broken and are placed over the wound before bandaging. Some of these dressings are impregnated with antibiotic and are either greasy or have a non-adherent surface. The greasy form should only be used when the wound is fresh, as it will keep it moist and

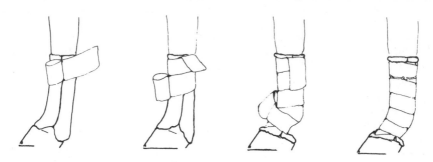

Figure 158   Stable bandage

encourage excessive granulation tissue if used over an extended period of time. When the wound has nearly healed it should not be bandaged but treated with wound spray or powder (see above) to encourage it to dry and scab over.

Cottonwool and Gamgee

Cottonwool is useful for cleaning wounds, but should not be applied directly as it will stick to an open wound. A non-adherent dressing should be applied first, and covered with a layer of Gamgee before bandaging. This will absorb any discharge and protect the wound from trauma.

Scissors

Curved, blunt-ended scissors will be needed for cutting hair away from a wound and straight ones for cutting tape and bandages.

Poultices

Poultices may be hot or cold. Hot ones are used either to increase the blood supply to an area, to draw out infection as with pus in the foot, or to encourage an abscess to burst; cold ones decrease inflammation associated with swelling and bruising caused by blows or kicks.

A proprietary of gauze and wool impregnated with boracic powder (Animalintex) is widely used for hot poultices. Kaolin is excellent for foot

Figure 159   Exercise bandage

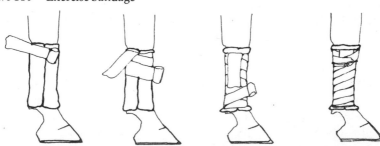

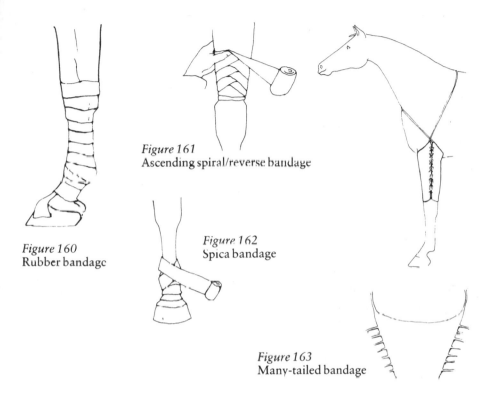

Figure 161
Ascending spiral/reverse bandage

Figure 160
Rubber bandage

Figure 162
Spica bandage

Figure 163
Many-tailed bandage

problems as it has good heat-retaining properties and an antiseptic action. If nothing else is available, bran may be used mixed with an antiseptic and hot water. However, this is not really recommended as the wet bran is a good culture medium for moulds and bacteria.

There are several types of cold poultice on the market which are cooled in the fridge before use, but the best way to reduce inflammation is by cold hosing or by applying ice cubes between layers of Gamgee.

Thermometer

A clinical thermometer should be used to take a horse's temperature if it is showing symptoms of any illness. The mercury is shaken down and the bulb end of the thermometer placed in the horse's rectum for at least one minute. The normal temperature variation for the horse is 38–38.2°C (100.4–100.8°F). A rise in temperature of 0.7–1°C (2°F) or more above normal should be considered cause for concern and a vet should be consulted.

41

GROWTHS AND CYSTS

Any swelling of an abnormal or unusual character on the body may be described as a tumour, a cancer, a growth or a cyst. The same terms are used to describe internal swellings, although as these are usually unobserved, they are not appreciated to the same extent as those occurring on the surface of or just below the skin.

To the horseman it does not really matter what term is used, provided it is clear that not all lumps are cancers and that not all cancers produce lumps. The important practical matter is the nature of the condition and whether or not it causes minor, major or fatal harm.

Medical and veterinary scientists refer to these swellings as neoplasms, meaning literally 'new growth of cells' (tissue). This term expresses the essential, practical and clinical importance of the distinction between new growth which is orderly and that which is disorderly. Orderly growth which underlies the increase in size of the body as an animal matures is not neoplasia; nor is the orderly repair of damaged tissue, such as the skin, when healing takes place, perhaps with the formation of a scar.

A neoplasm is disorderly growth and therefore causes swellings referred to as cancer, tumours or growths. This disorderly increase in tissue may none the less be either restricted or invasive. Restricted growth is usually referred to as benign, whereas new growth of an invasive character is termed malignant (see below).

Uncontrolled growths (neoplasia)

Growth of cells serving no purpose and largely outside the body's control acts as a kind of parasite. The growth obtains nourishment from the body but provides nothing in return.

In order to understand the subject the reader must appreciate that all cells in the body have, to a greater or lesser extent, a specialized purpose. At one end of this spectrum of specialized function are nerve cells, for example, which fulfil a definite and specific task of transmitting nerve impulses (see p.

108). At the other end of the spectrum are cells which serve a more nebulous and broader-based function. These cells, such as those which form fibrous tissue, have a general supportive role as scaffolding. Their form and nature tend to be dictated by the needs of the moment in the context of where they develop and the stimulus that brings them to a particular part. Thus fibroblasts (i.e. fibre-producing cells) may be found in wounds as they repair, or in any other part or organ of the body, such as muscle cells and tendons, requiring repair or support for other tissue.

Neoplasms (tumours) are always composed of cells resembling those of one or another body tissue. For example, a bone tumour is composed of cells resembling those of bone, a nerve tumour contains nerve cells, and a fibrous tumour contains fibroblast or similar cells.

However, tumour cells tend to be somewhat less specialized than their normal counterparts, and they are very much more active and multiply frequently by simple division, one into two into four and so on. Thus, if we examine tumour cells, we find a much higher proportion of actively dividing cells than would be the case if we examined normal tissue.

This underlines one of the features already described of neoplasms, i.e. their growth is uncontrolled. However, a further feature characteristic of tumours is that the way in which the cells are arranged is usually disorderly compared with normal tissue. This feature can be identified by the pathologist examining tissue prepared with special stains under the microscope. We might summarize the situation by comparing cells which point in one direction in normal tissue but point in all directions in a tumour.

Tumours arise in any part of the body. The skin is the most common site in horses, but tumours may also occur in bone, liver and the lining of mucous membrane and other surfaces, such as those that line the air sinuses of the head.

Names of tumours

Tumours derive their name from the tissue of which they are composed and from which they generally take origin. The more common varieties are listed in Table 19.

Tumours are classed by the way they behave. The tumour that grows in one position and does not spread to other parts of the body is called benign. This type of growth rarely causes death unless it happens to obstruct some other function. For example, a benign growth attached to part of the gut might cause strangulation and death from colic.

Benign growths are usually easy to remove surgically and do not recur. They do not form seedlings or metastases, which are typical of malignant growths.

Malignant growths are serious because they spread locally by invading the tissues in which they grow as well as forming seedlings (metastases). These seedlings may be carried in the blood or lymph stream to other parts, where

Table 19   Some Common Tumours

Tumour	Site	Character
Adenocarcinoma	Glands	Malignant
Adenoma	Glands	Benign
Carcinoma*	An epithelial surface	Malignant
Fibroma	Beneath the skin	Benign
Fibroma	Fibrous tissue	Benign
Fibrosarcoma	Fibrous tissue	Malignant
Granulosa cell tumour*	Ovary	Benign
Haemangioma	Blood vessels	Benign
Hepatoma	Liver	Benign
Intersitial cell tumour	Testicle	Benign
Lymphoma	Blood-forming tissues (lymph nodes)	Malignant
Lipoma	Fat in abdomen	Benign
Melanoma	Skin	Benign
Melanosarcoma*	Skin	Malignant
Osteoma	Bone	Benign
Osteosarcoma	Bone	Malignant
Papilloma (wart)	Skin	Benign
Polyp (papilloma)	Nasal passage or alimentary canal	Benign
Sarcoid (angleberry)*	Skin	Semi-malignant†
Squamous cell carcinoma*	Skin, sinus	Malignant
Teratoma*	Ovary, testis	Benign

*Relatively common in hores.
†Grows rapidly, recurs after removal, but does not form seedlings.

they form similar growths. The term 'cancer' is often used in connection with these malignant type of growths, which grow rapidly and spread extensively.

The name given to tumours usually reflects the type of tumour and whether it is benign or malignant. For example, 'adeno-' refers to a glandular type of growth (see Table 19), 'carcino-' or '-sarc-' refers to malignancy. Using these derivations, an adenocarcinoma is a malignant glandular growth, where an adenoma is a benign glandular growth. Similarly, a fibroma is benign but a fibrosarcoma is malignant.

In the horse the most common malignant growths are carcinoma, lymphosarcoma and melanosarcoma.

A carcinoma is a growth originating from an epithelial surface (skin, mucous membrane) or which is composed of epithelial-type cells. It is malignant because it grows rapidly and forms seedlings which grow in other parts and organs of the body.

The melanosarcoma is so-called because it contains the pigment melanin. It too is malignant and spreads rapidly to many parts of the body, although its origin is usually in skin. Grey horses are particularly susceptible, although the lumps which are found around the anus are often benign melanomas and not the malignant melanosarcomas.

Another example of a malignant growth which is quite common in horses is the lymphosarcoma. This takes a number of different forms. It may be found in a skin, a blood or an alimentary form, causing symptoms of colic, wasting, diarrhoea or even sudden, unexpected death.

Diagnosis

Benign and malignant growths may be distinguished by biopsy specimens. These are obtained by taking small portions of growths and examining them in the laboratory. Malignant growths contain many cells which split into two (mitosis). Benign tumours are less active and cell division more difficult to identify. The diagnosis is completed by distinguishing the type of cell (e.g. glandular or fibrous).

From this information the pathologist and the clinician may base their advice for action, namely, whether the tumour should be removed by surgery, sometimes using the special technique of cryosurgery (freezing), or whether it should be treated by the application of radioactive or chemical anti-neoplasia drugs. If a particular growth is incurable the need for euthanasia must also be considered following a diagnosis.

Symptoms and Treatment of Some Common Horse Tumours

WARTS

Warts grow from the skin. They can, therefore, be observed and this is one of the reasons why they are classed as the most common growth of horses.

There are three types of warts. The first are **milk warts**, which occur on young horses, usually around the muzzle. These are caused by a virus and spread from one horse to another and sometimes from a horse to a human, although this is not common.

This type of wart usually disappears spontaneously after about two months, when an immunity develops in the same way as the body receives protection from other infectious diseases. Various remedies are used to remove them, some people even claiming that they have passed a charm on the way. But because the warts inevitably disappear any treatment which is applied about two months after the warts appear is the one most likely to be successful!

Milk warts serve as a blemish but do not usually present a problem, unless they are close to the angle of the lips or in some other position where harness may rub and cause them to bleed. In these cases treatment may be necessary and removing them with laser or cryosurgery (see p. 543) is probably the most effective, although other surgical or medical remedies may be used.

The second type of wart is a simple firm single protuberance from the skin which causes no problem and, if left undamaged, may remain for years without any alteration in its character or features. This type of growth is less common than its close counterpart, the sarcoid.

The **sarcoid** is a growth which is also thought to be caused by a virus. It may be referred to as an **angleberry** because of its large and multiple nature. It grows from skin, particularly on the inner aspect of the thighs, but may occur on the ear or any other part of the body.

It has the characteristics of a benign tumour because it does not form seedlings except in the immediate surroundings; but it also has malignant properties because it invades the skin and tends to recur after surgical removal. It also grows rapidly, although it may have quiescent periods during which it remains static for months or years.

Angleberries have most significance when they occur on stallions, especially if they are situated around the sheath or on the chest. They then become damaged during mating and may subsequently increase substantially in size because of the stimulus to the growth that this provides. They may also bleed profusely. The same problems arise in mares when the angleberries occur close to the mammary gland and become knocked when the foal sucks.

Removal by simple surgical means is usually followed by recurrence of the growth, often with more vigorous growth than previously. A number of therapies are now available, including cryosurgery, laser-beam surgery and radioactive implants.

Angleberries and simple warts may be confused with proud flesh, which is a reaction to penetrating wounds or to the presence of small foreign bodies such as splinters

CARCINOMA

The most common carcinoma in the horse is that affecting one or more sinuses of the head. Symptoms include a one-sided nasal discharge and pain over the affected sinus. The growth usually increases in size dramatically and causes a softening of the bones of the skull above the affected sinus. Eventually seedlings form in other parts of the body and may cause symptoms related to the part in which they form.

There is no effective treatment at the present time and once the growth is active and spreading euthanasia on humane grounds is usually advised.

GRANULOSA CELL TUMOUR

This is a common tumour of the ovaries of mares. It may occur at any age following puberty. It usually affects one ovary only. The tumour is composed of cells growing from the lining of the follicle.

The cells are secretory and produce oestrogen and/or testosterone. The symptoms are therefore masculine male behaviour or a continuing state of oestrus or anoestrus. The ovary increases in size and may be felt per rectum as a hard enlarged organ with a smooth surface or with small protuberances like a bunch of grapes. The unaffected ovary is small and inactive.

Confirmatory diagnosis may be made by echography, which enables the numerous small follicles containing blood-stained fluid which are a feature of the growth to be identified.

Treatment consists of removing the affected ovary surgically. The mare usually returns to normal breeding soundness, based on the other ovary, within three to twelve months.

LYMPHOSARCOMA

Lymphosarcoma or malignant lymphoma is one of the most common tumours. It arises in blood-forming tissue and may develop in any site of the body where this tissue exists. The gut and chest are two of the more common regions, but it may also occur in any of the lymph glands or in such parts as the roof of the mouth and the throat.

Weight loss, inappetence, lethargy and chronic colic are signs seen singly or in combination. Other symptoms include swellings (oedema) on the undersurface of the chest and abdomen, coughing, difficulty in breathing, fluid in the pleural cavity of the chest and distension of the jugular vein, and enlarged lymph glands in the throat, between the lower jaws, at the front of the shoulder or deep within the chest or abdomen. Nasal discharge, difficulty in breathing and diarrhoea may also occur in some cases. All symptoms depend on the location of the tumours in any given case.

Diagnosis is made in the laboratory from biopsy specimens taken from tumour sites. Once major symptoms appear, death usually occurs eventually as a result of the spread of malignant cells. Sudden death, although rare, may occur as a direct result of the tumour. There is no known effective treatment that can be used in practice and the horse should be killed on humane grounds.

CYSTS

The term cyst is reserved by veterinarians and pathologists to describe a closed cavity lined by a membrane which secretes contents that may be liquid or semi-solid. A cyst may be produced by an obstruction to the outflow of a normal secretion, as in the case of a sebacious cyst. This type of cyst has a soft, inelastic, putty-like consistency and when cut is found to be filled with a whitish or dirty white tallow material.

DERMOID CYSTS

These cysts arise because embryonic skin cells are displaced into the subcutaneous layers beneath. They develop within a firm capsule in which there are single or numerous hairs, together with cells and a sticky fluid. They mostly occur on the back, on the base of the ear and occasionally on the surface of the eye.

They are painless except where harness causes them to become sore. They may occur singly and may reach 0.5 cm in diameter, but they are usually much smaller.

Management and Husbandry

How we manage, feed and maintain our horses is one of the most important subjects for the lay reader. It is very much a part of the responsibility of owners, managers, trainers and lay personnel associated with horses.

Sue Dyson discusses a number of behavioural problems frequently encountered by horse owners and Harold Hintz describes diets and feeding of horses for various puposes. Energy to support performance and work is necessary if we are to achieve the objectives for which we keep our horses; and the inclusion in the diet of basic substances required for growth is essential, especially for young horses. At the end of this chapter is a table of causes and symptoms of malnutrition, compiled by Rob Pilsworth.

The description by Harold Dawes on the relationship between soundness and conformation has been retained from the previous edition of this book. The assessment of conformation is a subjective matter and the older veterinary practitioners had probably greater insight into the subject than their present-day counterparts.

Equus caballus, the modern horse, has been bred by man into types as different as the Falabella and the Shetland, the Clydesdale, the Shire and the racehorse. These differences have been produced by selection based on the genetic composition of what we now describe as breeds. Susan Long contributes a chapter on this subject which will undoubtedly be of interest to anyone responsible for and interested in the breeding of horses. The subject is also taken up by Hilary Legard, in relation to the performance horse.

Finally in this section William Morgan has a number of practical comments to make about the care and management of the hunter.

42

BEHAVIOURAL PROBLEMS

There are a number of problems encountered in the day-to-day management of horses which can be grouped together loosely as behavioural problems. These include weaving, windsucking, crib-biting, excessively mareish behaviour, unusual aggression, rearing, bucking, nappiness, extreme cold-back behaviour, unwillingness to work on the bit, headshaking, unwillingness to load into a trailer or horsebox, and travelling badly. This is by no means a complete list but it encompasses the most common problems. Some of these problems may have a primary veterinary cause, for example, back pain causing nappiness or a nutritional deficiency predisposing to wood-chewing. However, many of the problems are true behavioural problems, perhaps related to previous or current management practices, or are of unknown cause.

It is important to recognize that horses and ponies vary considerably in their temperaments, their willingness to oblige and to submit to handling and working. Although not exceptionally intelligent animals, they are strong, much stronger than any person, and readily recognize a handler who is apprehensive or not a strict disciplinarian, and many will be inclined to try to take advantage of such a situation. Once a horse has got away with unruly behaviour it will often try to do so again. What starts as a very minor problem can become a major problem which may make, for example, the horse unsuitable to be ridden by that particular rider or somebody of similar experience and ability. That is not to say that the problem is incurable – given the right handling the horse may become extremely amenable – but generally a difficult horse will always need skilful (not necessarily forceful) handling. Some problems may be persistent despite expert handling: for example, there have been a number of top-class international showjumpers which have been extremely difficult to mount.

One particular horse–rider combination may be totally unsuited. A rider must be prepared to recognize this and at times be ready to admit defeat and sell the horse to a more suitable rider. Another problem can arise if a relatively inexperienced rider is receiving advice from an expert in whom he or she understandably has faith. Occasionally this so-called expert is not such an expert (he or she may be very competent to handle easy horses, but may have limited experience with a large variety of difficult horses). It can be very difficult for an independent adviser to convey this diplomatically to the rider and to advise that the rider seeks the help of a different expert.

It is also important to realize that sometimes it is necessary to be quite aggressively firm in order to get a horse to submit to discipline. Quiet kindness certainly has a role in horse management and must not be undervalued, but this is not always the most appropriate method.

An objective assessment of some behavioural problems is not easy. Ideally it requires a thorough understanding of horses' temperaments and psychology, a knowledge of veterinary medicine and an ability to recognize good and bad handling and riding of horses, and to identify when there is a mismatch between horse and rider. The aims of investigation of a behavioural problem include identifying whether the problem has a painful or other medical cause, or is purely behavioural or related to the relationship between the horse and its rider or manager.

REARING, BUCKING, NAPPINESS

A horse which repeatedly bucks, rears or naps may become a potential danger to the rider, particularly if the behaviour is unpredictable and may occur on a road. A similar approach is adopted to the investigation of all these problems. First it must be established how long the horse has been in the owner's possession. Does it have a history of awkward behaviour? How soon after purchase did the problem arise? Could the onset be related to any specific incident – a fall, for example? Does the horse act similarly on the lunge or only when ridden? Does it behave the same with different riders? It is also important to learn whether the behaviour occurs only under certain circumstances – for example, only at a competition; if this is the case, it is unlikely to be related to a medical problem. Then the temperament of the horse and of the rider is assessed and the ability of the rider and or manager. Does, for example, the rider sit straight or put weight heavily on one side, predisposing to the development of back muscle soreness? The fitting of the saddle and bridle and the suitability of the bit are assessed. It is also useful to review the feeding of the horse – it may be receiving too much food and may be much more manageable when receiving considerably less.

A complete physical examination of the horse is performed to try to identify any medical problems. Special attention is paid to the mouth – the presence of sores in the corners, sharp edges on the teeth, an oddly positioned tooth, especially if it is slightly movable and the bit is likely to come in contact with it. Wolf teeth rarely cause a problem unless they are movable or positioned abnormally far forward. Other areas meriting particularly careful attention are the back, sternum and ribs, and, of course, the limbs. A horse with a low-grade bilateral lameness may be unwilling to go forward and may nap.

It is important to evaluate the horse not only at rest and in hand, but also ridden, both by the regular rider and by a genuine expert – a horseman rather than somebody who may have official qualifications but may lack widespread experience of problem horses. In some cases it may be necessary for that person to ride the horse for several days in succession before an answer can be reached.

Based upon the results of all these investigations additional diagnostic tests may be indicated, for example, radiography, assessment of concentrations of serum muscle enzymes in the blood before and after exercise. In some cases it can be very useful to treat the horse with a painkiller such as phenylbutazone to assess whether the problem is pain-related. The horse must be treated at a sufficiently high dose for its bodyweight, and for long enough in order to make a proper judgement of the drug's efficacy. The horse must also be maintained in work. The author usually recommends that a horse of 500 kg bodyweight should be treated with 2–3 g phenylbutazone daily for at least four weeks.

Possible causes

Underlying medical problems which may cause this type of behaviour include back pain, neck pain or a mouth or tooth problem. The reader is advised to refer to the relevant chapters in this book for further information. Other causes include poorly fitting tack, a rider problem, overfeeding and a genuinely difficult horse. The question 'Is the horse suitable for the rider?' must be asked.

Treatment

If a medical cause is found this can be treated accordingly. If no underlying cause is identified, then it is usually worthwhile seeking the help of a genuinely expert horseman. This may simply be with a view to improving the horse so that it is suitable to be sold to a more experienced rider. If the horse is nappy it may benefit from a complete change of job for a while: for example, a horse that has become nappy in the show ring may benefit tremendously from spending a season hunting or being turned out for several months.

THE HORSE THAT WILL NOT WORK ON THE BIT

The horse is said to be working 'on the bit' if it is pushing evenly with its hind limbs, with impulsion, is reasonably relaxed in the back, and is accepting the bit so that the head is positioned slightly in front of a vertical line. The conformation of the horse may limit its ability to do this properly and to maintain it throughout all movements. Many inexperienced riders do not appreciate the importance of the horse pushing properly from behind: unless the horse is moving freely forward with adequate hind-limb impulsion it cannot be said to be on the bit. In order to achieve this the horse must be pushed forwards – it is not achieved by pulling the horse's head into the appropriate position and restricting its forward movement. This tends to create stiffness and possibly an irregular hind-limb rhythm. There is a certain knack in encouraging horses to work on the bit and this is probably one of the most elusive skills for inexperienced or uneducated riders, or for those who lack real feel for the way the horse is responding to the aids. There are medical causes for a horse's reluctance to work on the bit, many of which are shared with the horse that naps, so the reader is advised to refer to the preceding discussion.

Treatment

If a medical cause is identified it must be treated appropriately if possible. Conformational abnormalities which make it mechanically and physically difficult for the horse to work on the bit must be recognized and the shortcomings of the horse appreciated. It may be suitable for many purposes other than dressage. A change of rider may provide the key to success: a horse which is difficult to get on the bit may be improved dramatically by an experienced, skilled rider, and when worked in this way for several weeks may begin to find it easier. It will develop strength in the appropriate muscles and may become appreciably easier for the regular rider to cope with. Work on the lunge with the horse in a Chambon or running (draw) reins may serve the same purpose provided the horse is encouraged to work sufficiently hard from behind. If done carefully, it may also be helpful to ride the horse in draw reins. It must always be remembered that the engine is in the rear of the horse and that the horse must be pushing properly from behind if it is to be on the bit.

EXCESSIVELY COLD-BACK BEHAVIOUR

Cold-back behaviour refers to the horse which tenses abnormally or sinks (lowers) the back either when tacked up, when the girth is tightened or when the rider mounts. Some horses arch the back and buck repeatedly. A few horses throw themselves to the ground, which can be very alarming and is potentially dangerous.

Causes

In many horses there is no underlying cause. The horse performs quite normally in all other respects so it may seem illogical to presume that something hurts only when the saddle is placed on the horse's back or when the rider mounts. Nevertheless this is not true of all cases. Causes of cold-back behaviour include poorly fitting tack resulting in a sore back (for example, a saddle with too narrow a tree causing undue pressure on the areas on either side of the withers), an overtight girth (especially if the girth has an elastic insert), other causes of back pain, a previous fracture of a rib or the sternum, and girth galls.

Investigation

Investigation of this problem follows much the same pattern as that for napping. Particular attention is paid to the back and chest, the fitting of the tack, the way the horse reacts when the saddle is lowered into place, when the girth is tightened and when the horse first moves forward, the way in which the rider mounts (whether he or she pulls excessively on the saddle, sticks a toe into the horse's side, sits down heavily onto the horse) and whether or not the rider sits straight. The reaction to a roller being placed on the back is compared.

Treatment

If an underlying cause can be identified appropriate action can be taken. If no cause can be identified there are several approaches which may help. The saddle can be placed on the horse several minutes before the girth is fastened. A clean, thick, well-fitting numnah may be used beneath the saddle. The girth is done up loosely at first, the horse is walked forwards and the girth is then tightened slowly. Although superficially it would seem that a girth with an elastic insert would allow more give, and would thus be better tolerated by the horse, such a girth tends to be done up more tightly than non-elasticated girths; some horses may resent this but behave normally if a non-elasticated girth is used. Some horses benefit from being lunged for a while, with the saddle on, before the rider mounts. The rider may either be given a leg up or use a mounting block so that the girth need not be excessively tight and the saddle is not unduly pulled as the rider mounts. Initially it may be necessary for the horse to be led. Some horses remain very difficult, and although this may be acceptable in a competition horse, managed by a professional, such a horse is generally unsuitable for an amateur who rides for pleasure.

HEADSHAKING

Headshaking is a poorly understood syndrome in the horse which occurs most frequently during the summer months and is often worst when the weather is sunny, rather than overcast, and warm. Headshaking behaviour varies from a slight twitch of the head from side to side, or a slight nod, to vigorous up-and-down movements of the head. The horse may repeatedly try to rub its nose against one of the forelimbs, or may strike out repeatedly with its forelimbs. In the majority of affected horses the behaviour occurs only when the horse is ridden, but a few horses demonstrate headshaking at rest or when worked on the lunge. The problem may be sudden in onset and disappear just as suddenly, or it may be persistent or intermittent, occurring only during the summer. Some horses may be severely affected if worked outside but much better if worked indoors, suggesting that exposure to high concentrations of ultraviolet light may be an inciting factor.

Causes

In the majority of horses it is not possible to identify a cause despite an intensive investigation. Possible causes include poorly fitting tack, lameness, a tumour or other type of growth in the head, the presence of mites in the ears, vision difficulties, infection of a tooth root and an allergic type of reaction or undue sensitivity to something in the environment.

Investigation

A complete physical examination must be performed, paying especial attention to the head, neck and back. The eyes are examined carefully (see chapter 9) and an endoscopic examination of the upper respiratory tract is performed. Radiographs of the head are obtained. It is worthwhile treating the ears with a drug that kills mites (an acaricide). It is sometimes helpful to see if the behaviour is altered by painkilling or tranquillizing drugs.

Treatment

If an underlying cause is identified this can be treated appropriately, but in the vast majority of cases the cause remains obscure. Some horses improve if a stocking is placed over their nose when ridden. Others are helped by a change of occupation. Many horses show total remission of clinical signs during the winter, only for the problem to recur the following summer. It has been suggested that neuralgia of the facial nerve (pain associated with the facial nerve) might be a cause, and cutting the nerve has been performed with generally poor results. A drug used in people to help sufferers of facial-nerve neuralgia has had similarly disappointing results. This is an extremely frustrating condition to deal with because so little is known about why it happens, so there is no logical method of approach to treatment.

EXCESSIVELY MAREISH BEHAVIOUR

Some mares are very unpredictable in their performance especially when in season. They may show reluctance to go forward freely, swish the tail excessively, repeatedly pass small volumes of urine or wink the clitoris, or uncharacteristically refuse to jump. The exact underlying cause remains uncertain but presumably it is the result of variations in the concentrations of certain hormones at different stages of the oestrous cycle. In many mares the problem is controlled by suppression of oestrus, which can be achieved by the administration of a prostagen drug, allyl trenbolone. This drug is administered in the feed, and while the mare is being treated the oestrous cycle will be suppressed; after cessation of treatment the mare will return to oestrus in approximately eight days.

AGGRESSION

Abnormally aggressive behaviour may be seen in mares, entire males and castrated males. Aggression may be directed towards other horses or towards handlers. In some instances this type of behaviour may reflect poor handling or be a response to fear. In other circumstances the horse may be trying to establish its dominance in the social hierarchy in which it is placed. In a mare the underlying cause may be hormonally related: a mare with a granulosa cell tumour of an ovary usually has abnormally high levels of the hormone testosterone in the blood. If the ovary is removed, testosterone levels decline and the aggressive behaviour disappears. Entire males may show aggression and following castration often become easier to handle. Some rigs (see p. 311) show aggressive behaviour, but a recent study comparing behaviour before and after castration showed that there was only limited improvement in aggressive behaviour postoperatively.

THE HORSE THAT IS DIFFICULT TO CLIP

Some horses will not tolerate part or all of their body being clipped. This may be manifest as an unwillingness to stand still, shaking or twitching the skin and kicking with both the fore- and hind limbs. The problem may arise because the horse has been badly handled in the past, or is unduly sensitive to the noise of the clippers, or the clipper blades have been blunt and pulled the skin, or the clippers have become excessively hot.

Some horses can be satisfactorily controlled by the use of a nose twitch, an ear twitch and/or a lip shank, provided they are skilfully handled. It is important that sharp clipper blades are used, that the clippers are not allowed to overheat, and that the job is performed as quickly as possible. In the past tranquillizers were of little use: acepromazine produced minimal sedation and the horse was more likely to kick unpredictably; xylazine was more potent but horses often tended to sweat, which made clipping difficult, and could still kick unexpectedly. The drug had a useful effect for only fifteen to twenty minutes, therefore repeated doses were often necessary. The introduction of a relatively new drug, detomidine, represents a considerable advance. This has a very powerful effect, lasts for up to an hour (depending on the initial dose) and does not encourage the horse to sweat. However, difficult horses may still kick. Detomidine can be used in combination with butorphanol, an opiate-like drug, and this combination produces excellent results – the horse stands immobile with the limbs planted on the ground and seems unaware of what is going on.

Figure 163a Enticing with food often succeeds in getting the pony on the ramp but no farther. The open jockey door gives a sense of space and light

Figure 163b A helper stands to the side and behind the pony, carrying a lungeing whip but not actually using it. The pony capitulates

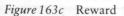

Figure 163c Reward

Figure 163d The partition is in place and the breeching strap is in position to prevent a hasty backward exit

TRANSPORTATION PROBLEMS

Transportation problems include the horse that will not load into or, less commonly, walk out of a trailer or horsebox, the horse that 'scrambles' when the trailer is in motion, and the horse that worries excessively and develops loose faeces, sweats a lot or goes off feed.

UNWILLINGNESS TO LOAD

Unwillingness to load may reflect stubbornness or be the result of previous bad experiences (travelling too fast, especially around corners, poor balance between the trailer and towing vehicle so that the trailer shunts the towing vehicle, falling off the ramp during loading or unloading) or be genuine apprehension. It is usually not related to a pathological problem.

The problem must be approached thoughtfully. The trailer or horsebox should be positioned so that the slope of the ramp is as slight as possible, either with the ramp resting on a slope or on a loading bay. If possible the sides of the ramp should be enclosed so that the horse is unable to swing from one side to the other. The ceiling of the trailer should be as high as possible and the interior as light as possible. The walls should be a pale colour and if possible the front doors should be open. The horse should be allowed as much room as possible in the trailer, so the partition should either be removed or tied back. The horse must be held by a strong, experienced handler and be adequately restrained using a chain shank over the nose, or applied as a lip chain, or as a bit, or using a bridle or Chiffney. Whichever method is adopted, it is useful to have a lunge rein or a long lead rope so that if the horse does pull back the handler will not lose hold. The handler should wear gloves to protect his hands. The limbs of the horse should be protected with boots or bandages because serious injuries can result from a horse scraping a leg against the ramp of a trailer or horsebox. The handler should offer the horse a bowl of feed as a reward. At least two extra people are usually necessary. In some cases it is useful to put a rope around the hindquarters and pull the horse forwards. Sometimes the horse can be encouraged forward with the bristles of a broom prodded into the hindquarters but great care must be taken in case the horse kicks back. Restrained force may include cracking a lunge whip behind the horse or hitting it on the hindquarters with a broom, but it is important to remain calm and disciplined.

Whatever method of approach is adopted, it is important to have plenty of time available and to remain as calm as possible. With a difficult loader the calm, quiet, enticement approach is sometimes successful. This requires a great deal of time and patience but is definitely the way to start with a horse which has not travelled previously. The horse is enticed with food and rewarded when it makes progress. However, this approach often succeeds in getting the horse onto the ramp with its head just over the threshold, but no farther. More often restrained force is necessary, the horse only being rewarded once it is safely locked inside. It is useful to repeat the loading procedure on several occasions, to feed the horse in the trailer, and not to travel anywhere. In some cases it is helpful to load another horse first or to load the horse from the front of the trailer if that is possible. Occasionally sedation of the horse is beneficial.

THE BAD TRAVELLER

If the horse is going to maintain its balance when travelling it must straddle all four limbs. If apprehensive or claustrophobic it may not do this. If the limbs are not straddled the horse will tend to fall either to the left or to the right, especially when going around corners, and may lean against the side or the partition of the trailer and kick. This behaviour may persist even when the vehicle has come to a stop. Apprehension must be overcome and feeding the horse in the trailer a number of times without travelling anywhere can be helpful. Some horses travel badly on their way to competitions but are much better on the home journey. With such horses it can be helpful to break the routine and travel to a place and just go for a hack. It is vitally important that the trailer does not shunt the towing vehicle and that the horsebox or trailer is driven slowly, especially around corners. Some horses will travel perfectly calmly if they are allowed more room, for example, if the partition of a double trailer is removed. Other horses travel better facing backwards rather than forwards (this can be done in a trailer); in a horsebox, they can stand crosswise (diagonally).

STABLE VICES

The most common stable vices are crib-biting (wood-chewing), windsucking and weaving. Windsucking is the aspiration of air, done by the horse arching its neck and sucking in air. Some horses do this while holding onto something with their teeth; others do it unaided. It results in a grunting type of noise. Weaving is swinging the head and neck from side to side, rocking on the front feet. These vices can also be called stereotypies – repetitive behaviours, constant in form, that serve no real purpose. Most arise from boredom and are probably the result of horses being maintained in an unnatural environment.

CRIB-BITING

Crib-biting or wood-chewing occurs in both stable-kept and grass-kept horses. It tends to be an infectious habit, copied by other horses. Although a nutritional deficiency may be an underlying cause, if the horse is being fed a balanced diet and has free access to a mineralized salt block this should not be the case. A chronic crib-biter will develop abnormal wear of the incisor teeth.

The problem can be controlled by minimizing the number of surfaces which the horse has available to chew: for example, removing the manger, placing a strip of metal over the top of the door or placing a grille on the door. Any surfaces which remain should be painted or covered in a noxious substance such as creosote. Some horses are helped if they have a companion – a small pony, a sheep or a goat. Others are improved if a solid object, such as a rubber ball, is hung from the ceiling.

WINDSUCKING

Traditionally windsucking has been described as a cause of recurrent colic or of failure 'to do well', but the vast majority of horses that windsuck suffer no adverse effects at all. If the habit is severe the muscles on the underside of the neck, which the horse contracts when it arches its neck to suck in air, may hypertrophy (get bigger) and this might be regarded as unsightly. In the majority of horses the habit can be effectively controlled by placing a tight leather strap around the top of the neck; this seems to prevent the horse from arching its neck. Various surgical procedures have been tried, the most successful of which involves removing a piece from several of the muscles on the top of the underside of the neck (the omohyoideus and sternothyro-hyoideus muscles) and cutting their nerve supply (the accessory nerve). Although this operation is successful in some horses, others subsequently relapse and some are not improved at all. It also results in a slight cosmetic defect where the muscles have been removed. The author would not recommend the procedure if the habit can be controlled by a leather strap, and would also not be averse to buying a horse with this problem although it is a habit which should be declared at the time of sale.

WEAVING

Weaving is usually a sign of boredom or anxiety – some horses will only do it when they are about to be fed – and it may result in excessive wear of the front shoes. In a few cases the horse rocks from side to side to relieve the weight on painful feet. It is a problem rarely seen in a horse kept at grass. It is usually controlled by placing a V-shaped grille on the stable door.

43
THE NUTRITION AND FEEDING OF HORSES

Horses must be fed a diet which supplies the necessary ingredients – energy, protein, vitamins and minerals – in order to perform at their best. Many different rations can be used to supply these nutrients. There is no one best diet. The ingredients of a diet depend on many factors, such as availability of feedstuffs, economics, palatability and, of course, tradition.

The following chapter is divided into four sections. The first deals with the digestive system. Nutrient requirements are discussed in the second section. The characteristics of various feeds are given in the third and feeding programmes are discussed in the fourth.

Although I have attempted to base all recommendations on scientific studies, there remains a great deal of art to feeding horses. The following words, written by Professor William Henry in 1901, are still true: 'The skill of the artist horse feeder enters into the very life of the creature he manages along with the food he supplies.'

Digestive physiology

Understanding the digestive system of the horse is essential for proper feeding and management. The horse and its relatives have a unique system among domestic animals (Figure 165). Cattle, sheep and goats have a large rumen (or specialized 'first' stomach) in which bacteria digest fibre. The horse also has bacteria which digest fibre, but they are located in the large intestine (colon and caecum). Pigs, dogs and cats have much simpler digestive tracts and therefore do not digest fibre as efficiently as the horse.

Some of the differences between the horse and the ruminant are advantageous to the horse and some are disadvantageous. For example, the ruminant can utilize the products of bacterial metabolism more efficiently than the horse can. The bacteria of the rumen pass into the small intestine, where digestive efficiency is high. The horse has its bacterial population in the large intestine, which is beyond the primary site of digestion and absorption. It has a much higher incidence of colic than other domestic

Figure 164 Digestive system of the cow

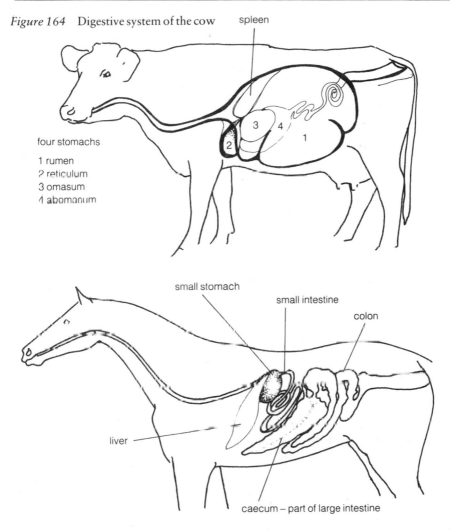

spleen

four stomachs

1 rumen
2 reticulum
3 omasum
4 abomasum

small stomach

small intestine

colon

liver

caecum – part of large intestine

Figure 165 Digestive system of the horse

animals because of the complicated structure of the intestine. The horse is more susceptible than a ruminant to mould and many other toxins because the bacteria in the rumen can detoxify some compounds before they are absorbed. However, if a horse had a large rumen, its speed of flight would be decreased.

The rate of passage of digesta is faster for horses than for cattle. Thus horses do not digest fibre as efficiently as do ruminants because the intestinal bacteria do not have as much time to act on the fibre. On the other hand, the faster rate of passage of digesta allows the horse to eat larger amounts of poor-quality feed than the ruminant, and thus the horse is more likely to survive when fed poor-quality roughage than is the ruminant. For example, studies in Africa with zebra and antelope indicate that zebra do better than antelope when only poor-quality roughage is available because the rumen of the antelope becomes filled with poorly digested material. The zebra does not digest fibre as efficiently but, because more food passes through, more energy is obtained. Of course, this does not mean it is a good idea to feed poor-quality roughage containing low concentrations of nutrients to horses. Most owners want more from their horses than survival. Poor-quality roughage is also more likely to lead to impactive colic than is good-quality roughage.

The digestive tract

The digestive tract extends from the mouth to the anus and can be divided into different components:

Mouth Correct dental care is essential for good nutrition. If the horse cannot chew properly, food intake and efficiency of food utilization may decrease. Poor teeth are a major cause of thin horses. Improperly chewed food can also lead to choke or impactive colic. For information on dental care, see chapter 53.

Oesophagus This tube is 120–150 cm long. Choke (see p. 11) is the most common nutritionally related problem. It is most often seen in animals which do not moisten feed adequately when chewing. Thus greedy eaters are prone to choke. Preventive measures in such cases can include moistening the feed, feeding small amounts several times a day or the age-old trick of putting smooth, large stones in the manger to decrease the rate of intake.

Stomach The horse's stomach is relatively small and the horse seldom vomits. Thus overfeeding may cause gastric distension and even rupture of the stomach. Horses fed significant amounts of grain should be fed two or more times daily.

Food normally does not remain in the stomach for a prolonged period but passes into the small intestine. However, the digestive process starts in the stomach. Some fermentation and digestive actions occur.

Small intestine This is the primary site of digestion and absorption of soluble carbohydrates (such as starch), protein, lipids, vitamins and many minerals. Parasite control is essential for the health of the small intestine. Heavily infested animals have greatly reduced capacity to utilize nutrients.

Large intestine This is a very large organ consisting of the caecum and colon. The colon has several sections. Bacteria similar to those found in the rumen of cattle live in the large intestine. Bacteria produce enzymes which digest fibre, the end products of which are volatile fatty acids (acetate, propionate and butyrate), which are absorbed and used by the horse as energy sources. Horses fed high-fibre diets may obtain one third or more of their energy from volatile fatty acids. Some of the bacterial protein can be used to supply amino acids, but the efficiency of utilization is not high.

The bacteria also supply some water-soluble vitamins but, as with the protein, utilization is not great. Therefore the diet of horses with great demands, such as rapid growth, must contain the essential amino acids and water-soluble vitamins, whereas the ruminant can survive without either if nitrogen and carbohydrates are supplied for the rumen bacteria to use.

Nutrient requirements

Water This is the nutrient required in largest amounts. It comprises about 70 per cent of the body. It has many important functions, being involved in digestion, body-temperature regulation, lubrication and metabolism. Water, however, is often neglected. For example, it is thought that the incidence of impactive colic increases during winter because owners neglect to provide water for their horses or because the horses will not drink extremely cold water. Automatic water bowls are often neglected and become fouled.

The requirement for water depends on many factors: environmental temperature, amount of work performed (i.e. sweat production), level of milk production, rate of bodyweight (bwt) gain, and faecal and urinary loss. The estimates vary from 20 to 60 litres per day, depending on conditions. If possible, the best policy is to allow the individual to drink all it wants. If the horse has reasonable and consistent access to water, it can regulate its own intake. As Dr Hinton writes: 'The simplest and most obvious way to prevent dehydration is to allow horses to drink whenever they wish. However, it would appear that this is not a universally recommended practice.' Hinton suggests that 'working horses be given the opportunity to drink every hour or so. They should be allowed sufficient time to take what they require and it must be remembered that they may pause and lift their heads during the course of a drink.' Of course, if a horse is very hot and thirsty, it may need to have its water intake limited to a series of small drinks because a single large intake is thought to cause laminitis and colic.

Energy A deficiency of energy can diminish growth rate, reproductive performance, athletic performance, resistance to disease, parasites or other stress and can affect the appearance of the horse. Excess energy causes obesity, laminitis, colic, reduced resistance to some diseases, and perhaps skeletal problems. It also involves the owner in unnecessary expense.

The energy content of feeds can be expressed in many different ways. The digestible energy system, expressed in megajoules (MJ), is used in this chapter. Digestible energy is determined by measuring the gross energy in feed and faeces with a special device known as a bomb calorimeter. Intake

Table 20 Daily Energy and Protein Requirements of Various Classes of Horse*

| | Expected mature weight (kg) | | | | | |
| | 400 | | 500 | | 600 | |
	DE (MJ)	Protein (kg)	DE (MJ)	Protein (kg)	DE (MJ)	Protein (kg)
Maintenance, mature	58	0.55	69	0.63	79	0.73
Mares, last 90 days of gestation	65	0.64	77	0.75	88	0.87
Lactating mare, first 3 months	96	1.12	118	1.36	138	1.60
Lactating mare, 3 months to weaning	84	0.91	102	1.10	118	1.29
Weanling	54	0.66	65	0.79	71	0.86
Yearling	58	0.60	70	0.76	78	0.90
Two-year-old	58	0.52	69	0.63	81	0.74

*From the National Research Council, *Nutrient Requirements of the Horse*, National Academy of Science-National Research Council publication, Washington, DC, 1978.

Table 21 Digestible Energy Requirements above Maintenance for Horses at Various Activities*

Gait	DE (KJ) hour per kg bwt†
Slow walk	7.1
Fast walk	10.5
Slow trot	27.1
Medium trot	39.7
Fast trot/slow canter	57.3
Medium canter	81.5
Gallop	96.1
Strenuous effort	163.0

*Adapted from J. D. Pagan and H. F. Hintz, 'Equine Energetic II. Energy expenditure in horses during submaximal exercise', *Journal of Animal Science*, vol 63 (1986), pp. 822–30.
†Weight of horse plus rider and tack.

minus faecal loss equals digestible energy. If it is preferred to use total digestible nutrients (TDN), 1 kg TDN equals approximately 18.4 MJ digestible energy.

Estimates of energy requirements are provided in Tables 20 and 21. The figures show how work and lactation can greatly increase the requirement. For example, let us assume that a horse weighing 500 kg is worked 60 minutes at a fast walk, 60 minutes at a medium trot and 15 minutes at a gallop and that the weight of tack and rider is 70 kg. The maintenance requirement would be 69 MJ (Table 20).

Table 22   Condition Score for Horses*

Score

1   *Poor.* Animal extremely emaciated. Spinous processes, ribs, tailhead and hooks and pins projecting prominently. Bone structure of withers, shoulders and neck easily noticeable. No fatty tissues can be felt.

2   *Very thin.* Animal emaciated. Slight fat covering over base of spinous processes; transverse processes of lumbar vertebrae feel rounder. Spinous processes, ribs, tailhead and hooks and pins prominent. Withers, shoulders and neck structures faintly discernible.

3   *Thin.* Fat build-up about halfway on spinous processes; transverse processes cannot be felt. Slight fat cover over ribs. Spinous processes and ribs easily discernible. Tailhead prominent, but individual vertebrae cannot be visually identified. Hook bones appear rounded, but easily discernible. Pin bones not distinguishable. Withers, shoulders and neck accentuated.

4   *Moderately thin.* Negative crease along back. Faint outline of ribs discernible. Tailhead prominence depends on conformation, fat can be felt around it. Hook bones not discernible. Withers, shoulders and neck not obviously thin.

5   *Moderate.* Back level. Ribs cannot be visually distinguished but can be easily felt. Fat around tailhead beginning to feel spongy. Withers appear rounded over spinous processes. Shoulders and neck blend smoothly into body.

6   *Moderate to fleshy.* Slight crease down back. Fat over ribs feels spongy. Fat around tailhead feels soft. Fat beginning to be deposited along the sides of the withers, behind the shoulders and along the sides of the neck.

7   *Fleshy.* Crease down back. Individual ribs can be felt, but noticeable filling between ribs with fat. Fat around tailhead is soft. Fat deposited along withers, behind shoulders and along the neck.

8   *Fat.* Prominent crease down back. Difficult to feel ribs. Fat around tailhead very soft. Area along withers filled with fat. Area behind shoulder filled in flush. Noticeable thickening of neck. Fat deposited along inner buttocks.

9   *Extremely fat.* Extremely obvious crease down back. Patchy fat appearing over ribs. Bulging fat around tailhead, along withers, behind shoulders and along neck. Fat along inner buttocks may rub together. Flank filled in flush.

* D. R. Hennecke, G. D. Potter, J. R. Kreider, 'A condition score relationship to body fat content of mares, during gestation and lactation', *Proceedings of the 7th Equine Nutrition Physiology and Symposium*, 1981, p. 105

The energy above maintenance for the work would be (570 kg × 1 hr × 10.5 KJ/kg/hr) + (570 kg × 1 hr × 39.7 KJ/kg/hr) + (570 kg × 0.25 hr × 96.1 KJ/kg/hr) or 5985 + 22,630 + 13,694 = 42,309 KJ or 42.3 MJ. The total requirement would be 69 + 42.3 or 111.3 MJ daily.

Of course the energy requirement depends on the desired body condition. the values in Tables 20 and 21 are only guidelines. If the horse is too lean, provide more energy; if it is too fat, decrease energy intake.

Body condition can be evaluated by visual appraisal, by weighing the horse or by more sophisticated methods such as ultrasound. Routine evaluation is helpful in the assessment of management practices, feeding and health programmes. It is recommended that horses be visually evaluated according to body scores such as those listed in Table 22 and also weighed monthly. If scales are not available, tapes which are placed around the heart girth can be used to estimate weight. Properly formulated tapes are reasonably accurate for most types of animal. Mares in middle to late pregnancy are obvious exceptions.

Protein   Proteins are chains of amino acids. Amino acids which cannot be synthesized by the body and must be supplied in the diet are called essential amino acids. The requirements for essential amino acids have been studied extensively in many species, but knowledge about the horse's requirements is limited.

It is known that the weanling requires 0.7 per cent dietary lysine for a reasonable rate of growth, but there are no recommendations for the other amino acids. A deficiency of protein causes a decrease in food intake and rate of gain, foals that are small for dates and affects the quality of the coat, making it rough. Protein intake above the requirement is utilized for energy but with less efficiency than carbohydrates or fats. Nitrogen is excreted in the urine. Thus overfeeding of protein increases urinary excretion and water intake. Because protein sources are usually more expensive than energy sources, overfeeding of protein is uneconomical. Estimates of protein requirements are shown in Tables 20 and 27.

Minerals   The horse requires at least twenty-one different minerals. Calcium, phosphorus, magnesium, sodium, chloride and potassium are called major minerals because they are required in large amounts. The other minerals are called trace minerals because they required in smaller amounts, not because they are less important.

Calcium is required for muscle function, blood clotting and bone development. A deficiency of calcium in a young animal causes rickets, a condition in which the bone is not fully hardened. The bones become weak and the long bones may bow.

Bone is a dynamic tissue. It is constantly being remodelled and calcium removed and replaced. The condition known as **nutritional secondary**

hyperparathyroidism (NSH) causes more calcium to be removed than is deposited, weakening the bones. In some bones, particularly those of the skull, connective tissue invades the affected bone, which actually increases in size. Hence a common name for the condition is **big-head disease.**

NSH usually results when a diet containing low levels of calcium and high levels of phosphorus is fed. The high level of phosphorus impairs the utilization of calcium, the blood level of calcium drops, stimulating the parathyroid gland to release a hormone which increases the rate at which calcium is removed from bone. The condition is often caused by feeding high levels of wheat bran, which has a calcium to phosphorus ratio of 1:12. Hence NSH is also called **bran disease.**

The role of bran in the aetiology of the disease was first described in the scientific literature by Dr Varnell, an English veterinarian, in 1860. In spite of the fact that the dangers of feeding high levels of wheat bran without calcium supplementation have been known for many years, the condition is still occasionally reported by veterinarians.

Table 23 Daily Calcium (Ca) and Phosphorus (P) Requirements for Various Classes of Horse*

| | \multicolumn{6}{c}{*Expected mature weight (kg)*} |
| | 400 | | 500 | | 600 | |
	Ca (g)	P (g)	Ca (g)	P (g)	Ca (g)	P (g)
Maintenance, mature	18	11	23	14	27	17
Mares, last 90 days of gestation	27	19	34	23	40	27
Lactating mare, first 3 months	40	27	50	34	60	40
Lactating mare, 3 months to weaning	33	22	41	27	49	30
Weanling	27	20	34	25	37	27
Yearling	24	17	31	22	35	25
Two-year-old	20	13	25	17	31	20

*National Research Council, op. cit.

Table 24 Calcium (Ca) and Phosphorus (P) Content of Some Mineral Supplements

| | \multicolumn{2}{c}{*Percentage*} | \multicolumn{2}{c}{*Amount contained in 1 tablespoon (g)*} |
	Ca	P	Ca	P
Calcium carbonate	34	0	10	0
Defluorinated phosphate	32	15	10	5
Bone meal	30	14	9	4
Dicalcium phosphate	27	21	8	6
Monocalcium phosphate	17	21	5	6
Monosodium phosphate	0	22	0	7

Calcium requirements are listed in Table 23. The amount of calcium needed in the diet depends on its availability. As mentioned, high levels of phosphorus decrease the utilization of calcium. Studies in Australia demonstrated that many tropical forages contain oxalate, an organic compound, which can bind calcium and decrease utilization.

Legumes such as lucerne are excellent sources of calcium. Grains have very low levels of calcium. Inorganic materials, such as those listed in Table 24, are excellent sources of calcium.

Phosphorus is also involved in bone formation. About 80 per cent of the body's phosphorus is in bone and a phorphorus deficiency can also result in improper mineralization of bone. A deficiency of phosphorus also causes the blood level of phosphorus to decrease but, unlike the case of calcium, the decrease does not stimulate the parathyroid hormone to release phosphorus from the bone.

Phosphorus requirements are shown in Table 23. The phosphorus content of forage depends on the soil. The phosphorus content of grains is much higher than that of hay. Grains, however, have a significant percentage of phosphorus in the phytic form, which is not utilized efficiently by horses. Several inorganic sources (Table 24) are effectively utilized by horses.

Magnesium is required for bone formation and for many enzymes. If the blood level of magnesium greatly decreases, the animal develops **tetany** (muscle spasm). The condition is usually associated with stress, such as being transported.

Electrolytes (potassium, sodium and chloride) are important in osmotic pressure regulation and acid-base balance. Forages usually contain high levels of potassium. Potassium nutrition can be of concern, however, when horses sweat profusely because sweat contains a high concentration of potassium. Sodium is lacking in most conventional feeds. Thus free choice intake of salt is recommended.

The function and deficiency signs of trace minerals are summarized in Table 25. The trace mineral content of foodstuffs depends on several factors such as the mineral content and pH of the soil where the crops were grown.

Vitamins   Vitamins are divided into two categories: fat-soluble and water-soluble. Vitamins A, E, D and K belong to the former. Fat-soluble vitamins (with the exception of vitamin E) are more likely to be stored in large amounts in the body and are more likely to be toxic when fed in excessive amounts than are water-soluble vitamins. The functions requirements and signs of deficiency and toxicity are listed in Table 26.

Green, leafy plants and high-quality hay are excellent sources of many vitamins. Vitamin supplements are more likely to be needed when large amounts of grain and poor-quality hay which has been stored for longer than a year are fed. Biotin is not included in Table 26 but it has been found that 10–15 mg supplemental biotin daily may help repair cracked and/or poor-quality hooves.

Table 25 Summary of Trace Mineral Functions, Deficiency Signs and Requirements

Mineral	Some functions	Some deficiency signs	Requirement*
Iron (Fe)	Part of the haemoglobin molecule and therefore involved in oxygen transport; part of some enzymes which speed up important bodily chemical processes	Anaemia: lack of stamina, poor growth	40 mg/kg feed for maintenance; 50 mg/kg for growth
Copper (Cu)	Iron absorption, haemoglobin synthesis, skin pigments, collagen metabolism	Anaemia, hair pigment loss; bone disease, swollen joints, deformed thin bones	9 mg/kg feed
Zinc (Zn)	Activator of many enzymes	Skin problems: hair loss, scaly skin, poor wound healing; reproductive, behavioural and skeletal abnormalities	40 mg/kg feed
Iodine (I)	Thyroid function	Goitre, poor growth, low body temperature, impaired development of hair and skin, foals weak at birth	0.1 mg/kg feed
Manganese (Mg)	Synthesis of bone and cartilage components, cholesterol metabolism	Reproductive problems: delayed oestrus, reduced fertility, spontaneous abortion, skeletal deformities in the newborn	40 mg/kg feed
Potassium (K)	Maintenance of acid-base balance	Decreased rate of growth, reduced appetite and hypokalemia (decreased serum level of potassium)	
Selenium (Se)	Removal of peroxides from tissues	White muscle disease, low serum selenium and serum glutathione peroxidase concentration	0.1 mg/kg feed

*Based on National Research Council recommendations.

Table 26 Summary of Vitamin Functions, Deficiency Signs and Requirements

Vitamins	Some functions	Some deficiency signs	Requirements*
Vitamin A	Growth and development of bone and epithelial cells, night vision	Night blindness, corneal cloudiness; impaired growth; reproductive problems: poor conception rate, abortion, loss of libido, testicular degeneration; convulsions, elevated cerebrospinal fluid pressure; decreased vitamin A in tissues and serum	1400 IU/kg feed for maintenance and working horse; 1800 for growing horses; 2500 for reproducing or lactating mares
Vitamin D	Absorption of dietary calcium and phosphorus	Skeletal disease: poor mineralization of bone, bone deformities; impaired growth; low blood calcium and phosphorus	275 IU/kg feed
Vitamin E	Antioxidant in tissues	Decreased serum tocopherol, increased red blood cell fragility, elevated serum glutamic-oxalic transaminase (SGOT); muscular dystrophy	15 mg/kg feed
Vitamin K	Blood clotting	Haemorrhagic disease in species that require the vitamin	Unknown
Thiamin	Co-enzyme in energy metabolism	Accumulation of acids in tissues; loss of appetite and weight, impaired growth; incoordination, muscular weakness and twitching; hypoglycemia	3 mg/kg feed
Riboflavin	Co-enzyme in many enzyme systems	Impaired growth and feed efficiency; eye problems: conjunctivitis, lacrimation, aversion to bright light	2 mg/kg feed
B_{12}	Co-enzyme in several systems	Deficiency signs have not been described in horses	Probably synthesized in the intestine

IU = international unit
*Based on National Research Council recommendations.

Table 27 Nutrient Concentration in Diets for Horses and Ponies Expressed on 90 Per Cent Dry-Matter Basis*

	Digestible energy (MJ/kg)	Crude protein (%)	Ca (%)	P (%)	Vitamin A activity IU/kg	IU/lb
Mature horses and ponies at maintenance	8.4	7.7	0.27	0.13	1450	650
Mares, last 90 days of gestation	9.4	10.0	0.45	0.30	3000	1400
Lactating mare, first 3 months	10.5	12.5	0.45	0.30	2500	1150
Lactating mare, 3 months to weanling	9.6	11.0	0.40	0.25	2200	1000
Creep feed	13.2	16.0	0.80	0.55		
Foal (3 months of age)	12.1	16.0	0.80	0.55	1800	800
Weanling (6 months of age)	11.7	14.5	0.60	0.45	1800	800
Yearling (12 months of age)	10.9	12.0	0.50	0.35	1800	800
Long yearling (18 months of age)	9.6	10.0	0.40	0.30	1800	800
Two-year-old (light training)	10.9	9.0	0.40	0.30	1800	800

Ca = calcium, P = phosphorus

*National Research Council, op. cit.

Table 28 Estimates of Composition of Foodstuffs for Horses (Dry-Matter Basis)*

	Dry matter (%)	DE (MJ/kg)	Crude protein (%)	Ca (%)	P (%)	Mg (%)	K (%)	Cu (mg/kg)	Zn (mg/kg)
Cereals									
Barley	86	15.0	10.8	0.08	0.40	0.13	0.45	9	17
Maize	86	16.1	9.8	0.05	0.26	0.12	0.35	4	20
Oats	86	13.5	11.0	0.09	0.37	0.17	0.44	6	30
Rye	86	14.7	13.3	0.07	0.36	0.12	0.42	8	36
Sorghum	86	15.5	10.8	0.04	0.33	0.20	0.39	12	12
By-products									
Brewer's grains, dried	90	11.3	22.4	0.30	0.60	0.17	0.09	24	30
Distiller's grains, dried	90	12.1	30.1	0.11	0.44	0.10	0.20	48	35
Sugar-beet pulp	90	12.2	9.0	0.75	0.10	0.30	0.20	14	10
Sugar-beet molasses	75	12.9	7.4	0.12	0.03	0.30	6.20	22	18
Sugar-cane molasses	75	12.9	4.1	1.05	0.15	0.47	3.80	80	30
Wheat feed, middlings	88	11.9	17.6	0.10	0.90	0.60	1.40	10	106
Wheat feed, bran	88	11.1	17.0	0.12	1.45	0.60	1.60	14	120
Miscellaneous									
Locust bean plus pods	86	13.0	6.9	–	–	–	–	–	–
Peas, dried	89	13.8	26.5	0.13	0.47	–	1.14	–	–
Oil cakes									
Cotton-seed meal	90	13.3	45.7	0.20	1.20	0.50	1.40	20	70
Groundnut meal	90	14.0	48.1	0.29	0.68	0.17	1.25	17	22
Linseed meal	90	12.5	40.4	0.40	0.89	0.66	1.53	29	36
Soyabean meal	90	14.0	50.3	0.31	0.70	0.30	2.20	30	50
Sunflower cake (no hulls)	90	12.9	48.3	0.41	1.10	0.81	1.10	4	–
Roots									
Carrots	13	12.8	9.2	0.40	0.35	0.20	2.80	10	–
Turnip	9	11.2	12.2	0.60	0.26	0.14	2.90	21	–

Grasses									
Cocksfoot, young	23	8.6	18.4	0.55	0.29	0.30	2.50	12	—
Cocksfoot, mature	27	8.2	10.0	0.35	0.23	0.20	2.00	10	—
Rye-grass, perennial, mature	25	8.4	10.5	0.50	0.25	0.20	1.65	10	—
Timothy, in flower	25	8.5	9.6	0.45	0.25	0.14	1.65	5	17
Green legumes									
Clover, early flower	19	8.6	18.0	1.90	0.30	0.40	2.20	9	17
Lucerne, early flower	23	8.8	19.0	2.00	0.30	0.50	2.25	9	18
Hays									
Clover, good	86	8.4	16.1	1.50	0.25	0.40	1.70	11	18
Clover, poor	86	8.0	12.0	1.00	0.21	0.30	1.50	7	14
Grass, early cut	86	8.5	13.0	0.55	0.25	0.20	1.35	7	18
Grass, late cut	86	8.0	8.5	0.30	0.19	0.15	1.00	5	14
Lucerne, half flower	86	9.0	18.0	1.60	0.25	0.29	1.90	9	16
Lucerne, full flower	86	8.3	15.5	1.20	0.21	0.28	1.75	8	14
Oats, milk stage	86	8.3	9.0	0.30	0.24	0.60	1.20	4	—
Straws									
Barley	87	5.8	3.4	0.27	0.07	0.19	2.0	5	7
Oat	87	6.2	3.4	0.25	0.09	0.17	2.3	9	6
Rye	87	5.8	3.7	0.25	0.09	0.07	1.0	5	6
Wheat	87	5.8	3.7	0.21	0.08	0.12	1.4	4	6

Ca = calcium, P = phosphorus, Mg = manganese, K = potassium, Cu = copper, Zn = zinc

*The values are from several sources. The dashes indicate that no values were found. The values are expressed on a dry-matter basis in order to compare feeds that contain different amounts of water. As mentioned earlier, the energy and protein content of forages depends greatly on the stage of maturity and time of harvesting. The mineral content of plants depends on several factors such as the genus, species and variety, the type of soil on which the plant was grown, the weather during the growing season and the stage of the maturity of the plant at harvest. The values in the table should be considered as guides or general indicators. If possible, the balancing of rations should be based on analysis of your foodstuffs.

Nutrient requirements can be expressed in two ways, units per day or percentage of the ration. Many horse owners prefer the latter system. The requirements for several nutrients expressed as percentages of the ration are shown in Table 27.

Feed

Grains, succulents such as pasture and roughages such as hay are the most commonly used sources of energy. Grains (also called concentrates) usually contain 85–95 per cent dry matter. They contain high levels of digestible starch, thus providing a high level of digestible energy (Table 28). Any of the common grains can be fed if their characteristics are taken into account. Owners usually prefer oats to the other grains because they are safer due to the higher fibre content and because the horse finds them palatable. Maize is a very good energy source and is widely used in many parts of the world but requires more careful management than oats because of its high energy concentration. Barley has a digestible energy content somewhat between that of maize and oats.

Pasture and other succulent foods contain high concentrations of water. Thus the energy content is usually expressed on a dry-matter basis, that is, MJ per kilogramme dry matter. The types of pasture plants desired depend on many factors such as soil, climate, drainage and traffic patterns. Therefore it is impossible to make specific recommendations without knowledge of local conditions. A general recommendation is that the mixture be about one third legume if possible.

Hays have a much higher fibre content than do grains. Fibre is not digested as efficiently as starch. Thus the digestible energy concentration in hay is not as great as that in grains (Table 28). The energy concentration in hay depends on several factors, but the most important is the stage of maturity at harvesting. The fibre content increases as the plant matures, thus older plants contain lower concentrations of digestible energy.

Legume or grass hays can be fed to horses. Legumes such as lucerne usually provide more protein than is needed by mature horses, causing them to urinate more in order to excrete the unneeded nitrogen. The greater excretion, however, does not cause kidney damage as is frequently suggested. Legume hays also usually provide more energy and vitamins than grass hays. As mentioned earlier, legumes contain much more calcium than grasses.

Many of the protein supplements used in livestock feeds are by-products of vegetable oil production. The composition of several oil meals is listed in Table 28.

As mentioned earlier, some classes of horse require specific amino acids in the diet. The level of lysine is of particular concern. Of the commonly used meals, soyabean meal has the greatest lysine content – 3 per cent, compared with 1.7, 1.6, 1.2 and 1 per cent for cotton seed, groundnut, linseed and sunflower meals respectively. Dried peas can also be an effective protein source. They contain less protein (26 per cent) but have 1.8 per cent lysine. Thus the protein:lysine ratio is better than for many of the other vegetable proteins. Any legume seeds such as soyabeans and peas must be heat-treated to destroy components which inhibit utilization. Over-long heating can also decrease protein utilization.

Animal products such as dried skimmed milk and fish meal are excellent sources of amino acids and can be fed to horses (see, however, p. 514), but they are much more expensive than plant sources. Locust beans are not high in protein but are considered to be very palatable.

Feeding programmes

Mature horses at maintenance This class of horses is usually the least demanding. Average- to good-quality hay consumed at a rate of 1.5–1.75 kg per 100 kg bwt, water and trace mineralized salt fed free choice should supply all the necessary nutrients. If the soil is lacking in trace minerals, additional minerals may be needed. During cold weather the energy requirement will be increased and some grain may be helpful.

Working horses A primary concern for working horses is energy intake (Table 21). Horses at the racetrack may need 1.5 kg hay and 1.5 kg grain per 100 kg bwt or more. The source of energy can be important. If the hay is of very poor quality, intake may be limited. Maize, oats and barley can all be used as energy sources. The advantages and disadvantages are discussed above.

The addition of fat increases the energy density of the ration. Several studies indicate that the addition of 6–10 per cent fat such as vegetable oil or animal fat may have some benefits for endurance horses but spectacular results should not be expected. There is no substitute for good training practices.

The protein requirement is not greatly increased by work. It is true that some nitrogen is lost in sweat, but as the general intake is greatly increased to meet the energy needs, so protein intake is also increased. Thus there is no need to increase the protein concentration of the diet. In fact excess protein can decrease performance. Recent studies at Washington State University demonstrate that conventional feed – hays and grains – contain adequate protein and no protein supplement is needed for working horses.

Work increases the mineral requirements because of the losses in sweat, but, as with protein, if the diet contains a percentage of minerals adequate for maintenance, the horse will, in most cases, obtain additional minerals when eating to meet energy needs. There are exceptions, however. Electrolyte losses may be of particular concern in horses which sweat profusely, such as endurance horses or three-day-event horses. **Synchronous diaphragmatic flutter (thumps)** has been related to low serum calcium and potassium levels in endurance horses. Several commercially packaged electrolyte supplements are available.

Selenium might also be of concern because selenium is required for muscle function. The diet should contain about 0.1–0.2 parts per million (ppm) selenium. Excess selenium can be toxic (see p. 510), thus supplementation by addition to feed or by injection should be done very carefully.

As energy intake increases, the requirement for B vitamins increases because the B vitamins are cofactors necessary for energy utilization. Reports have suggested that some racehorses have marginal intakes of thiamin, one of the first signs of which is anorexia. If a supplement is desired, it should provide about 25 mg thiamin daily.

Stabled racehorses may require a folic acid supplement, but horses on pasture apparently do not. Stabled horses utilize folic acid more effectively when large doses are given weekly than when smaller doses are given daily. If poor-quality hay is fed, a vitamin A supplement may be needed. A supplement of 13,000 IU vitamin A in such cases would not be unreasonable. Horses with lower than normal levels of vitamin A in the blood perform poorly.

Broodmares   Energy is also of great concern when feeding mares. Underfeeding of fillies can delay the onset of first heat. Severe underfeeding of pregnant females can cause embryonic death. Overfeeding has also been implicated as a cause of infertility but it is difficult to determine if some mares are barren because they are fat or fat because they are barren. If a mare does not have a foal, her energy requirement is greatly reduced and she is much more likely to gain weight. It is better to have the mare a little heavy than too thin at breeding time.

The pregnant mare early in gestation does not have nutrient requirements greatly different from those of the non-pregnant mare. During the last ninety days of gestation the foetus is developing rapidly and the mare's needs are increased. The energy requirement of the mare during the period of rapid foetal growth is about 12 per cent greater than for maintenance.

The energy needs of the lactating mare are a function of the level of milk production. The amount of milk produced varies greatly among mares, but some mares will produce amounts of milk equivalent to 3 and 2 per cent of their bodyweight during early lactation (one to twelve weeks) and late lactation (thirteen to twenty-four weeks) respectively. A 450-kg mare producing milk at these levels would require about 70 per cent more energy during early lactation and about 48 per cent more energy during late lactation than for maintenance.

The pregnant mare's need for protein, as for energy, is increased significantly over that for maintenance only during the last ninety days of gestation. At least 10 per cent dietary protein is needed at that time. Even though the increase is 20 per cent above maintenance, the actual amount needed is not really high. Mares fed legume hays such as lucerne or clover (usually 11–15 per cent protein) and grain such as oats (12 per cent protein) or maize (9 per cent protein) would not need a protein supplement. When a grass hay such as late-cut timothy hay is fed, a protein supplement may be needed. For example, if a grass hay contains only 8 per cent protein, and if 5.5 kg hay and 1.5 kg grain are fed, the grain mixture should contain about 16 per cent protein. The lactating mare needs about 12.5 per cent protein in her ration. As with the pregnant mare, the need for a protein supplement depends on which hays and grains are used.

The calcium and phosphorus requirements, when expressed as percentages of the diet, are similar for pregnant and lactating mares. Of course, total intake of minerals is much greater for the lactating mare because she eats more food.

Orphan foals An adequate intake of colostrum or another source of antibodies is essential for survival of the foal (see p. 372), but good nutrition is also important. A foster mare can be a very effective source of nutrients. The least troublesome type of mare is probably an older, cold-blooded one, and the worst type is a young, flighty Thoroughbred. A foster mare should be checked for disease, milk samples should be taken following examination of the udder, and her tail should be thoroughly washed and disinfected. She should be brought to the stable and hooded so that she can not see, and a strong-smelling substance placed on her muzzle. The same substance can be used on the foal's head, neck and tail. A fostering gate will allow the foal to suck without danger of being kicked. It can be very simple but the construction should be sturdy.

Nanny goats can also be very effective nurses, particularly during the first few days. Foals at the Critical Care Center at the University of Florida are routinely fed goat's milk. Mare's milk in early lactation usually contains 10.5–11 per cent total solids, 1.4–1.8 per cent fat, 2–2.3 per cent protein and 6.5–7 per cent lactose. Goat's milk usually contains 14 per cent total solids, 4 per cent fat, 3.6 per cent protein and 5 per cent lactose and therefore is slightly richer than mare's milk.

Mare's milk replacers are now available, but they can cause diarrhoea in some foals. In such cases it may be necessary to thicken the replacer.

When milk replacer is fed in a bottle, the foal should be fed near another horse, which acts as a decoy, and never at the doorway of the stable. If fed at the doorway, the bottle-fed foal will spend all its time inside the door waiting for the human voice and the next feeding.

Creep feed, milk pellets and good-quality hay or grass should be provided by the time the foal is seven days of age.

It is important to monitor carefully the weight changes of the foal in order to evaluate the feeding programme.

Weanlings   Weanlings are much more susceptible than older horses to nutritional problems. For example, the protein requirement, expressed as a percentage of the diet, is almost twice that of the mature horse at maintenance. Of course, the requirements are dependent upon the desired rate of growth. More attention must be given to balancing the ration when rapid rates of gain are desired. Rapid growth and overfeeding can cause severe skeletal problems. Osteochondrosis (see p. 173), flexural deformities (see chapter 19) and physitis (see p. 163) are often claimed to be induced by overfeeding. Genetic factors are also probably involved.

Table 29   Estimates of Bodyweight at Various Ages in Relation to Mature Bodyweight

Age (months)	Mature weight (kg)					
	200	400	500	600	800	1000
2	60	105	130	155	180	210
4	85	150	180	220	250	315
6	110	185	230	275	340	420
8	125	220	275	320	400	500
10	140	245	301	360	450	565
12	150	270	335	400	500	630
14	160	290	360	435	540	670
16	165	305	380	460	580	730
18	170	320	400	480	620	780

Table 30   Estimates of Daily Feed Requirements (kg) for a Growing Horse

Age	Feed	Expected mature weight (kg)		
		400	500	600
4	Hay	1.4	1.5	1.8
	Grain	3.0	3.5	4.2
6	Hay	1.6	1.8	1.9
	Grain	3.2	3.8	4.3
8	Hay	1.9	2.2	2.5
	Grain	3.4	4.1	4.7
12	Hay	2.7	3.2	3.7
	Grain	2.8	3.4	3.9
14	Hay	3.2	3.7	4.3
	Grain	2.7	3.3	3.7
18	Hay	3.7	4.3	4.9
	Grain	2.4	2.9	3.3

The optimal growth rate is not known, but the results of several surveys suggest that the average light horse might be expected to obtain about 47, 67 and 80 per cent mature weight and about 83, 91 and 95 per cent mature height at the withers by six, twelve and eighteen months respectively. Estimates of bodyweight at various ages in relation to mature bodyweight are shown in Table 29. Estimates of food intake are shown in Table 30.

Nutrition is more than just balancing the nutrients in the diet. There are many aspects involved. Proper selection of feeds that are palatable is important and parasite control is essential as the benefits of a balanced diet are greatly reduced by a heavy infestation of parasites. Horses should be fed at regular times – they are creatures of habit and regular feeding times help to reduce stress and digestive problems.

Horses are susceptible to poisoning by mouldy feed (see p. 515). Although moulds cannot always be detected by eye, tests are available for the detection of many mycotoxins. Mangers, buckets and feed tubs should be kept clean, not only to deter the spread of disease, but also to decrease waste, improve feed intake and prevent the formation of mould.

Feed by weight not by volume. There are considerable differences in density among horse feeds. Wheat bran weighs about 225 g per quart whereas maize weighs 775 g per quart.

Abrupt changes in the type of feed should be avoided. Colic, inappetence or diarrhoea may result when horses are changed abruptly from a low-energy feed to a high energy one. Reasonable levels of fibre should be provided. There is no established requirement for fibre, but a level equivalent to at least 0.22 kg hay per 100 kg bwt seems to be adequate.

In conclusion, the eye of the master remains important in the feeding of the horse. Fortunately the master also has more scientific help at his disposal than ever before.

Malnutrition

Malnutrition is defined as an abnormal intake of nutrients. Although we usually think of this term in relation to starvation and underfeeding, it applies equally well to excessive intake of nutrients, which, in many cases can be just as harmful.

Below are outlined the most common states of malnutrition seen in practice. Deficiencies of minerals and vitamins are dealt with in chapter 43 and poisoning by excess of the same in chapter 38.

Nutrient	*Shortage*		*Excess*	
	Condition	*Symptoms*	*Condition*	*Symptoms*
Carbohydrate	Weight loss	Poor covering of bones, prominent ribs and pelvis, hollow neck	Obesity	Ribs not palpable. Development of crest in all sexes. Sluggish exercise tolerance
	Milk shortage in lactating mares	Foal sucks for longer than usual. Does not sleep after feeds. Poor growth	Obesity with laminitis	Bilateral lameness. Stiff gait in front. Stands rocked back from front feet. Hot feet (feel near coronet). Lameness worse on gravel or stones
	Poor fertility	Repeated return to stud (other factors often involved)	Azoturia	Severe cramping of muscles after short bursts of exercise. Hind limbs very stiff. Severe pain, sweating, etc. Overfeeding while in irregular work
	Stunted growth	Underweight, small yearlings	Flexural limb deformities in foals	Club feet, upright pasterns in rapidly growing foals (other factors also involved)

Protein	Protein starvation	Muscle wasting associated with fat belly. Often linked to poor worming programme in face of *apparently* adequate feeding programme. Neck hollow at sides, quarters sunken behind bony pelvis
	Milk shortage in lactating mares	See above
	Poor fertility	See above
	Susceptibility to disease	Low protein levels in blood may reduce immune system's ability to fight infection
	Poor performance	Overzealous use of protein supplements can occasionally lead to poor athletic performance
	Diarrhoea	Loose, often dark-coloured, foul-smelling faeces. May follow sudden introduction or overuse of high-protein supplements such as soyabean meal and milk powder
	Flexural limb deformities in foals	See above
Roughage or fibre	Spasmodic colic (caused by poor gut movement associated with low-fibre diet)	Pain, sweating, rolling, looking at flank
	Laminitis (caused by overeating cereal to satisfy bulk intake)	See above
	Impaction colic (often linked with sudden fall in regular exercise)	Small, hard or absent droppings. Low-grade, dull pain. Horse lies down a lot. May roll onto back and lie still. Can progress to severe pain. Often linked to horse eating bedding or straw being used as feed
	Nutritional secondary hyperparathyroidism ('bran disease' – see p. 586)	Swelling of joints and bones of head. Shifting lameness. Brittle bones, leading to pathological fracture

44

THE RELATIONSHIP BETWEEN SOUNDNESS AND CONFORMATION

The examination of horses as to soundness and their selection as to suitability are part of the work of veterinarians which requires sound judgement and the employment of knowledge tempered with experience. The relationship between soundness and conformation has long been recognized.

A horse is sound when he is free from hereditary disease, is in the possession of his natural and constitutional health and has as much bodily perfection as is consistent with his natural formation.

The rule as to unsoundness is, if at the time of sale or examination, the horse has any disease, which either actually does diminish the natural usefulness of the animal, so as to make him less capable of work of any description, or which in its ordinary progress will diminish its natural usefulness; or if that horse has, either from disease (whether such disease be congenital, or arising subsequently to birth) or from accident has undergone any alteration of structure that either does at the time or in its ordinary course will diminish the natural usefulness of the horse, such horse is unsound.

Conformation is the manner in which the horse is formed or put together. Bad conformation may not be unsoundness in itself, but it may often lead to unsoundness. The study of conformation should consist of the appraisement of points of structure and the estimation of their significance in the horse as a whole. Let us now consider what we require as broad principles of conformation.

In the first place the horse, whatever its breed or job, should convey to the eye suitability in make and shape, with no obvious fault which would upset the whole make-up. In short, the horse must have presence – that undefinable something which, at first impact to the eye, impresses one with the suitability of the horse for its particular work. If the horse meets you well and, on a cursory inspection, shows no outstanding faults of conformation, it is more than likely that on further examination it will be found to be more or less sound. It is presence, allied with good movement, which enables one

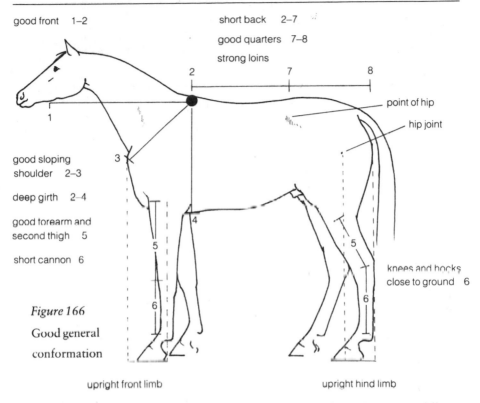

good front   1–2

short back   2–7

good quarters   7–8

strong loins

good sloping
shoulder   2–3

deep girth   2–4

good forearm and
second thigh   5

short cannon   6

point of hip

hip joint

knees and hocks
close to ground   6

Figure 166

Good general

conformation

upright front limb   upright hind limb

to pick out the first half dozen in a strong class in the show ring, or rapidly to select a few animals of the right type in the busy atmosphere of a crowded sale yard and then proceed to a more detailed examination.

Head and neck

The head should be of a size proportionate to the size of the horse itself, with a straight face line and well-defined features. The forehead should be broad, full and flat, and the ears of medium size, finely pointed and carried alertly. The eyes should be prominent, clear and large, with eyelids of uniform curvature. The muzzle should not be too fine, the nostrils large but not dilated, with thin lips and the incisor teeth sound and regular. The lower jaw should be well defined, clear at its angle, and the space between the two branches of the lower jaw should be wide in order that the larynx may be fully accommodated, with room for large muscular attachments. Any deformity of the jaw, such as a parrot mouth or an undershot jaw, is an unsoundness depending entirely on a fault of conformation. Such horses are bad doers as a rule, and require additional care in feeding. In the case of breeding animals a faulty conformation of the jaw may be passed on to their progeny. The width between the branches of the jaw is an established feature of the Arab horse and one to which great importance is attached.

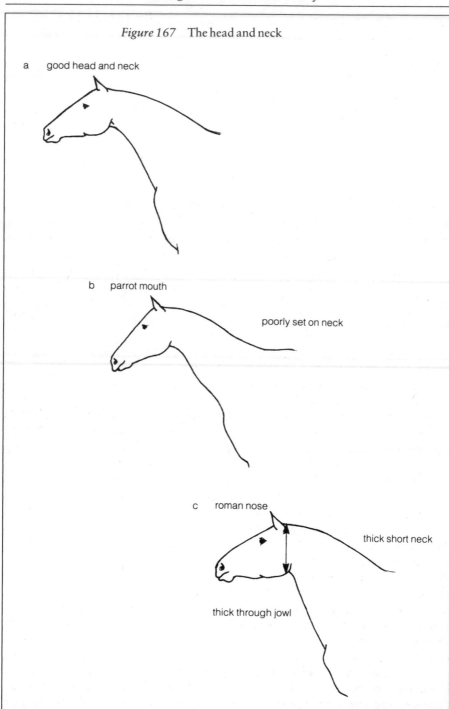

Figure 167 The head and neck

a good head and neck

b parrot mouth

poorly set on neck

c roman nose

thick short neck

thick through jowl

The angle at which the head meets the neck is one of the most important features of conformation. If this angle is too acute, the head and neck are not well set on; in the extreme, a 'cock-throttled' appearance is shown. By the acuteness of this angle there is the possibility of compression of the layrnx, with consequent interference with respiration. When, in such a case, the depth from ear to throat is also marked, it is suggestive of commonness or jowliness and such a horse is not likely to bridle well or to carry its head kindly when ridden or driven. An overlarge head places a strain upon the forehead, and means that more muscular power from the great muscles of the neck is required to maintain it in position. Such horses often tire easily and die on the hand when ridden or driven.

The neck should be of proportionate length, reasonably crested but not too heavy, and its muscular development should be in proportion to the work the horse has to do. A long, lean neck on a Thoroughbred or riding horse is desirable; a shorter, well-muscled neck is an essential part of a draught horse and prepares the collar area for the reception of the draught. The carriage of the head is very largely determined by the shape and nature of the neck and, moreover, the junction of the neck with the body determines, very largely, the slope and carriage of the shoulder. Actually, the neck of the draught horse is rarely very short, but the muscular development of the neck and crest may make it appear to be somewhat shorter in proportion, for example, to that of the riding horse. The jugular groove should be easily determined, and in the well-bred horse the trachea should be well marked out.

The withers should be of good height and well defined. Withers which are too high are undesirable and are sometimes associated with deficient spring of the chest, while low, thick, heavy withers are undesirable in the light horse and interfere with the free mobility of the shoulder. In the Hackney, low, thick withers are usually associated with deficient action and a bad shoulder, and while strong withers are desirable in the draught horse, withers which are too low and fleshy result in the saddle not maintaining its correct position and, in the draught-horse, there is a tendency for the collar to rock. It should be noted, however, that some very good Arab horses may be found to have rather low withers.

Chest

The chest should be deep and full, the ribs should be long, well sprung and spaced well back, so that the edge of the last rib is not too far away from the point of the hip. Flat, narrow ribs are undesirable and tend to reduce the capacity of the chest. Such horses are often poor doers, due to there being insufficient room for the heart and lungs. If too narrow, not only will the horse have no heart room, but the two forelegs will emerge from the body too close together and give rise to the dealer's expression 'both legs coming out of the same hole'. If the chest is too wide, the horse will be found to have

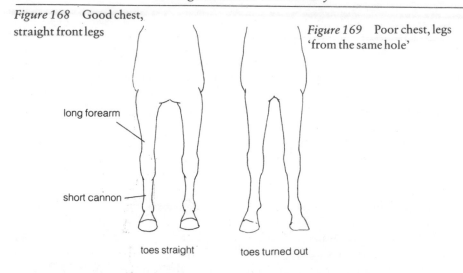

Figure 168 Good chest, straight front legs

Figure 169 Poor chest, legs 'from the same hole'

long forearm

short cannon

toes straight

toes turned out

a rolling gait, will paddle with its forelegs, and will be found to waste a considerable amount of muscular action when endeavouring to walk freely.

Measurement of girth is of the greatest importance, and in a horse of 16 hands the girth measurement should be at least 6 feet. At one time, when purchasing a large number of horses for travelling long distances daily in double harness, I was instructed by the director of the firm that I must never purchase a horse that did not have 6 feet of girth. It was maintained, quite rightly, that this was the minimum measurement that gave the heart and lungs room to function adequately when the horse was in hard work.

A prominent sternum is sometimes encountered. This is a conformation which I dislike intensely: it gives the horse a pigeon-breasted appearance and is often seen in ill-balanced horses whose forefeet are too much under them. It is often associated with a flat chest and insufficient heart room, and such horses are often bad doers when put into hard work.

Figure 170 Pigeon breast

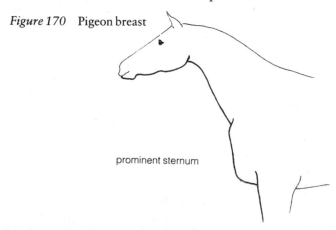

prominent sternum

Figure 171   Wide chest, bench knees and pigeon toes

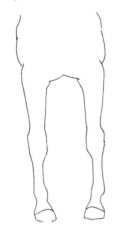

Figure 172   Narrow chest, small knees and feet turned out

Back

The back should be short and strong, but it must be remembered that the relative shortness of the back must be governed by the work the horse has to do. The Thoroughbred and the riding horse must have some length of back if they are to travel quickly, while the draught horse must be short of back and closely coupled. The term 'long back' is often used loosely. A horse for fast work must have some length of back and the confusion arises when the length of the back and the length of the loin are not defined. It is the loin which must be as short as possible in all circumstances; the loin is the least supported portion of the back and it is the horse with the length of loin which particularly gives the impression of slackness and too much length behind the saddle.

In the conformation of the back one may have a hollow back, in which the back is unduly dipped (and which must not be confused with the hollowing of the back with old age); and the roach back, in which there is an upward curve of the back and loin. Both are undesirable, and in my time I have noted a number of roach-backed horses which have eventually turned out to be shiverers. Horses with odd conformation of the back very often do not lie down regularly when in the stable and so shorten their working life.

Particular care should be taken when examining so-called 'cold-backed' horses (those that dip their back as the saddle is put on – see p. 572). Some of these horses may have an abnormality of the withers and saddle-bearing area and only very careful examination will reveal this. Often such an abnormality may not be noted on palpation of the withers and saddle area, but only be discovered by standing behind the horse and viewing along the back to the base of the neck. Any alteration in the shape of the withers or saddle-bearing area is then more easily detected.

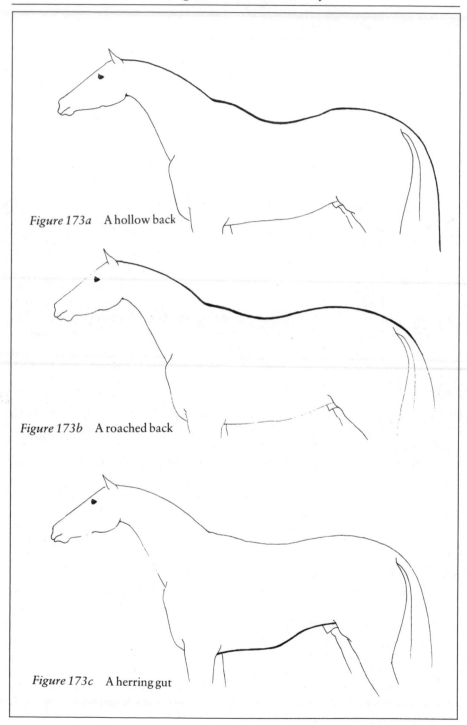

Figure 173a   A hollow back

Figure 173b   A roached back

Figure 173c   A herring gut

The belly should be proportionate to the size of the horse, but not too big. The horse in training will show a tendency towards lightness of the abdomen, particularly as it approaches the peak of its work, but this must not be confused with the very sharp narrowing of the belly known as herring-gutted, which usually indicates poor condition, with insufficient room for the abdominal contents. Such horses are often of a nervous temperament, difficult to get fat, and often tend to scour when at work. In the draught horse a good capacious belly – or, as it is sometimes termed colloquially, bread-basket – indicates a good constitution and a good feeder; when needed for long hours of work such a conformation is essential.

In all geldings of any breed, always look for a well-developed sheath. It is a practical point that lack of development of this appendage usually indicates a weak constitution and, again, such animals are often bad doers.

The croup is an area of great importance in conformation. It comprises that part of the body between the loins and the setting of the tail. The pelvis and sacrum are involved in its formation and so effect a compact connection between the hind leg and the trunk. In most cases a nearly horizontal croup is ideal and, indeed, is requisite for the development of great speed; but in the draught horse a more inclined croup will fill the requirements of ability to shift weight. In a nearly horizontal croup, the tail is well set on, whereas in the draught horse the tail may appear to be somewhat lower owing to the inclination of the croup.

Forelimbs

The shoulder, in proportion to good withers, should be of ample length and slope. No other portion of the horse's anatomy comes under greater criticism than the shoulder, and opinions on the type and suitability of the shoulder may vary with different individuals. Ample slope is essential in any breed of horse and a good shoulder is as essential in the draught horse as in the Thoroughbred. Ample length in the shoulder is required in order that there be plenty of room for the insertion of large and powerful muscles. Moreover, full action of the shoulder cannot be attained unless there is sufficient length of back to accommodate its obliqueness. Upright shoulders give rise to a shortened gait and, indeed, to undue concussion of the whole of the foreleg, while in many cases an upright shoulder is associated with a horse standing over in front – a combination which will eventually diminish its usefulness. The arm should be suitable for the attachment of its large muscles and, in all cases, should be as long as is proportionate to the shoulder, while the elbow should stand clear of the body and be well defined. Elbows that are turned in are objectionable, as they result in the feet being turned out, and, in the opposite tendency, the feet are turned in. In both cases undue strain is directed to the fetlock and feet; both conditions tend to produce lameness in the lower part of the leg and speedy-cutting and interference are common faults.

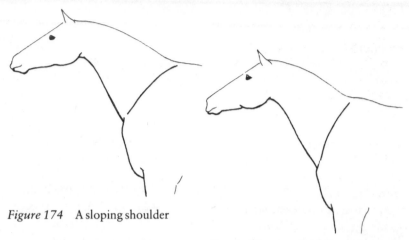

Figure 174   A sloping shoulder

Figure 175   An upright shoulder

The forearm should be long, wide, thick and well developed. From the point of view of speed, the conformation should be such as to present a long forearm and a comparatively short cannon. In the Hackney with high knee action, the forearm will be found to be comparatively short, but it should be remembered that if the forearm is too short, the action will be of a choppy nature and will not produce sufficient freedom to allow the horse to move with pace *and* action and to reproduce that impressive one, two, three, four, which is so desirable and essential.

The knee should be as large as is compatible with the size of the horse and it should be flat and free from any suggestion of roundness. In reason, the larger the knee the better – more articular surfaces are provided and

Figure 176   From left to right: correct forelimb conformation, forelimb set too far back, forelimb sloping back from the vertical, forelimb set too far forward

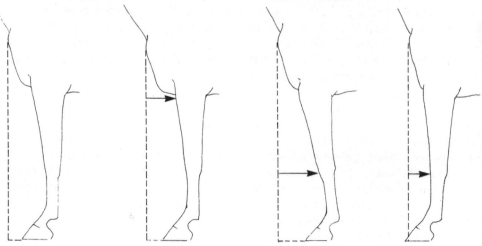

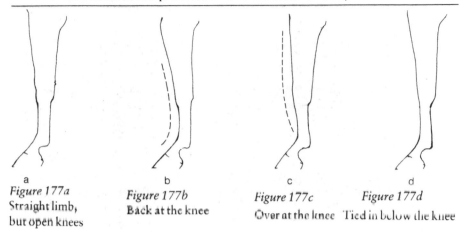

a
Figure 177a
Straight limb,
but open knees

b
Figure 177b
Back at the knee

c
Figure 177c
Over at the knee

d
Figure 177d
Tied in below the knee

concussion is absorbed. Small round knees are very objectionable and cannot play their part in absorbing the weight of the horse and the concussion of the ground. The knee may show several objectionable aspects of conformation. For example, a calf knee is undesirable and does not absorb concussion; additionally the calf knee is ill-fitted to resist the overextension of the knee which occurs in fast work. The amount of overextension of the knee which may occur during a 'chase or a fast-run hurdle race is amazing and, in the fraction of a second, when the horse is alighting, an enormous strain is temporarily thrown upon the knee, which may be in a position of overextension. Calf knees are often tied in below, with insufficient room for the flexor tendons. Any lateral deviation of the knee is a serious breach of conformation. Such conditions give rise to unequal distribution of the bodyweight and tend to produce injuries to the supporting and connecting ligaments as a whole.

A markedly forward direction of the knee is known as 'over at the knee' or 'knee-sprung' and it may be congenital or acquired. Many young horses with slightly forward knees are very sure-footed and have great freedom of movement. When acquired, this conformation is usually the result of excessive work combined with contraction of the tendons, and such horses will frequently stumble and be unsafe to ride.

The cannon should be short and strong with width from front to back, and this gives a good measurement of bone below the knee. Nevertheless, it should be remembered that in the long run it is not the amount of bone, but the quality of it which really counts. The cannon of the draught horse is shorter than that of the Thoroughbred, and in all well-formed animals the metatarsus is always longer than the metacarpus. The tendons must be clearly defined, with no suggestion of gumminess, and, when viewed from the front, cannon, fetlock and pastern must be in a straight line. No conformation is more likely to lead to unsoundness than a round cannon bone with fleshy tendons; such legs will not stand up to hard work.

The fetlock should be wide, thick and free from blemishes. When the fetlock is narrow in the antero-posterior direction, the tendons are always closer to the cannon bone and become more subject to strain at work.

The pastern should be of medium length and slope and both extremes have their drawbacks. The excessively long pastern, which is often low-jointed, is weak, and not only does it throw great strain on the tendons but it is an important factor in the production of sesamoiditis. The short, upright pastern is very strong, but it absorbs concussion to a greater extent and may result in the early formation of ringbone *if* associated with an indifferent foot. There is no doubt that the worst combination met with in the pastern is that of excessive length and low-jointedness. This conformation in the hind limb is sometimes associated with a straight hock and stifle and is one of the worst conformations of the draught horse that I know of. It leads to trouble with the hock joint, which is subjected to excessive strain above and below, while the tendons of the hind limb rapidly show evidence of strain. In such a conformation the hind leg, throughout its length, has no mechanism for relieving the concussion of the ground.

Feet

Perhaps in no other part of the body is conformation related to soundness more closely than in respect of the feet. Xenophon, centuries ago, pointed out the importance of the foot in the horse and insisted that in all cases of examination of the legs, one should look first at each foot. With defective feet the usefulness of the horse is diminished, and whatever the job it does its working life is limited, and eventually disease or inability will make its appearance. Feet must be of a similar size and odd feet must arouse suspicion at once. Occasionally a horse may be found which has had odd feet since birth, but for all practical purposes the odd-footed horse is an unsound horse. A good foot must be well shaped, not too large or too small, with a strong, deep, wide heel and a well-developed frog, and the colour of the horn should be dark or blue. Seen from the front, a well-developed foot should present a level surface, free from rings or grooves, and showing no tendency to contraction at the quarters. Any form of contraction is an unsoundness. When lifted, the foot should present a deep, wide heel with a good frog having a shallow, medium lacuna. Any difference of the angle of the slope in the wall of either foot should be regarded with suspicion.

McCunn has drawn attention to the important significance of any 'waisting' of the hoof, accompanied by a lateral groove in the wall on either side. Such a foot is almost invariably unsound and a horse with such a foot usually develops some form of pedal osteitis.

I dislike a frog with a deep, split-up cleft, particularly in the draught horse; such feet, in my opinion, frequently develop thrust or canker.

Of all faults in conformation of the feet, a weak heel is the worst, because without sufficient depth and width of heel, no horse will remain sound for long. Such a conformation exposes the navicular area to injury and particularly encourages injury to the wings of the pedal bone, resulting in osteitis.

The foot may appear to be an excellent one when viewed from the front, but the real test of its value is to see whether it possesses sufficient depth of heel. A narrow hoof head should be avoided and in this connection it is always essential, in heavy horses, to raise the hair at the coronet in order to examine the top of the hoof. A horse with a narrow hoof head, with a tendency to bulge slightly on its anterior aspect, is likely to develop pyramidal disease or low ringbone when put to hard work. Flat feet are weak feet, and horses with such rarely remain sound for any length of time.

It should always be remembered that on the foundation of the horse's feet rests its upper structure. In many cases the horse with indifferent feet will begin to prefer the centre of the road and will avoid the extreme camber of the near side.

Hind limbs

The hind limbs are the essential elements of propulsion in the horse and are associated with groups of muscles larger and more powerful than those of the forelimb. It has been pointed out that the greater obliquity of the shoulder and the more horizontal position of the croup in horses of speed tend to diminish the scapulo-humeral and coxofemoral angle, and so facilitate the forward and backward movement of the limbs. The thigh

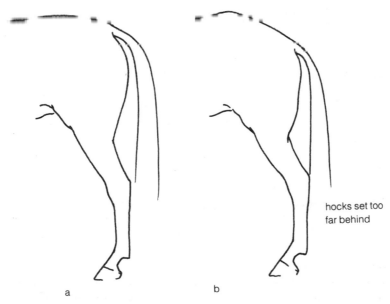

hocks set too
far behind

a

b

Figure 178a   Horizontal croup   *Figure 178b*   Goose or apple rump

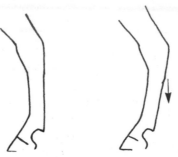

Figure 179a Normal hock a   b *Figure 179b* Sickle hock

should be long, well-muscled, deep and well let down. Looked at from behind, it should be thick, with ample muscular development; above all, it must not show any signs of a split-up appearance. In this respect one should remember the old axiom of 'a head like a duchess and a bottom like a cook'. The second thigh should be well developed, and the stifle should be well forward in position.

Hocks

The hock constitutes the most important joint in the process of propulsion, and a good, well-developed, well-positioned hock is essential for soundness. The hock should be big in proportion to the size of the horse, wide and deep, with a well-marked point and, above all, well supported beneath and with no tie-in immediately below. Above all, the hocks must be a pair and remember that the strong hock found in the young horse may fine down with increasing age. A slender, narrow hock is bad, just as a full, round, fleshy hock must be disliked.

The true value of the hock, apart from its size, depends upon the greater or less inclination of the tibia above and the cannon below. The so-called sickle hock results in the cannon bone taking an inclination forward so that the hind leg is brought under the body. Such a conformation is most undesirable. It leads to excessive strain of the hock joint above and of the tendons below, and usually results in unsoundness. In all cases, however, it must be remembered that for draught horses the hock may have a little forward inclination compared with that of the riding horse. This sickle-hock conformation is sometimes found in a big horse which stands over in front. Such a horse will usually be a source of trouble, either from overreaching or pulling off his foreshoes when galloped.

The condition known as cow hock is objectionable and is often associated with other defects of conformation. As a result, the toes are turned out and loss of power and movement occurs as the limbs are moved outwards instead of forward in a straight line.

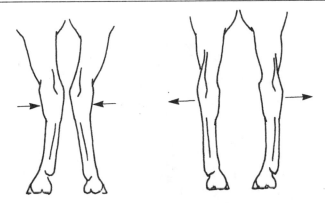

Figure 180a Cow hocks   *Figure 180b* Overwide hocks

Bowed hocks are equally objectionable, the hocks being set wide apart and the toes turned in. In this conformation the animal will be noted to twist the hock out as the foot comes to the ground and the foot develops a screwing movement as it touches the ground. In such animals the hocks tend to develop thoroughpin and bog spavin, while the coronet and feet become upright. Such animals are very hard wearers on their shoes and the toe is invariably knocked out too soon. The screwing action of the foot on reaching the ground is particularly likely to produce lameness. A good hock should be large and well directed and in its relation from the point through the back of the cannon to the ground should be vertical.

With regard to the limbs as a whole, in the forelimb, looked at from the front, a perpendicular line dropped from the point of the shoulder should divide the leg and feet into two lateral halves. Viewed from the side, a perpendicular line dropped from the tuberosity of the scapular spine should pass through the centre of the elbow joint and meet the ground at the centre of the foot. In the hind limb, viewed from the rear, a perpendicular line dropped from the point of the buttock should divide the leg and foot into two lateral halves. Viewed from the side, a perpendicular line dropped from the hip joint should meet the ground midway between heel and toe.

The horse's action

Good conformation is associated with correct movement. A horse must walk well, and if this movement is carried out correctly the horse will usually be satisfactory in his other paces. Action should be straight and true, with no dishing, brushing or interfering, and the toe should be well extended, especially in the riding horse. In the active draught horse and the Hackney, the knees and hocks should be well flexed and carried from the forearm and thigh in a straight and forward direction. In these breeds the horse must move over the ground and not pick the feet up and put them down in the same place again.

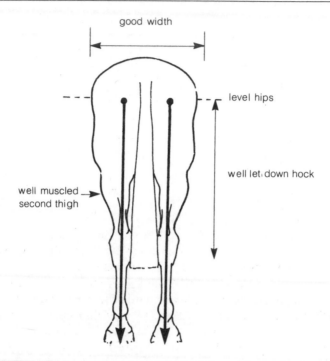

Figure 181 Good hindquarters and straight limbs

The action of the Thoroughbred and riding horse should be low and sweeping, with extension of the toe and a good carry forward of the hind leg. Avoid a horse that goes on its heels – this is bad movement and will usually be found to be associated, sooner or later, with unsoundness.

Wind

Lastly, soundness of wind and conformation. That conformation may influence soundness of wind is, to my mind, undeniable. From the point of view of size and height alone, it is well known that a big horse, e.g. a heavyweight hunter with height, is more likely to be unsound in his wind than a horse of moderate size. How many times do we examine a big, good-looking hunter and immediately in our mind wonder if he will prove to be a roarer or a whistler? The relative immunity of the pony breeds from roaring and whistling and the marked tendency of the fat, short-backed, wide-barrelled pony to become broken-winded is, indeed, well known.

As already noted, the set of the head upon the neck also has some influence. Not every whistler or roarer will have paralysis of the recurrent nerve, and conformation may, and in my opinion does, play a part in the production of such unsoundness.

Finally, 'a good horse is one with many good, few indifferent and no bad points'.

Never hesitate to buy a sound, well-made horse because it is in poor condition. Such horses, under good management and feeding, grow just as you would wish them to; and remember that fat or gross condition may hide a multitude of faults.

Without an understanding of conformation no one can develop that knowledge of soundness and unsoundness which is desirable in those who undertake examinations of the horse. It must never be forgotten that within the framework of its conformation lies the horse's essential soundness.

45

GENETICS OF THE HORSE

Genetics is the science of heredity, the study of how characteristics or traits are transmitted from parents to offspring. Animals and man inherit their characteristics via genes. Genes are chemical groups arranged in a specific pattern in the deoxyribonucleic acid (DNA) chains which form chromosomes. Chromosomes are found in the nucleus of every cell. The horse has a total of sixty-four chromosomes, made up of one pair of sex chromosomes (these are XX in a female and XY in a male) and thirty-one pairs of autosomes (chromosomes that are not sex chromosomes) (Figure 182). An individual receives one of each pair of chromosomes from each of its parents.

Each gene has its own position, or location, on a specific chromosome; this is called the gene locus. Since the chromosomes come in pairs, it follows that an individual can have two copies of a gene, one on each of a chromosome pair. If a gene occupying a locus exists in more than one form, these genes are said to form an allelic group. No animal can inherit more than two alleles from any allelic group. When the alleles on the same locus of a chromosome pair are different, the animal is said to be heterozygous for that gene. When the two alleles are the same, the animal is said to be homozygous for the gene.

A gene can be dominant, recessive or additive in respect to its effect on its allelic partner. In other words, a dominant gene will always be expressed even when it is only present in the heterozygous state. However, a recessive gene is only expressed when it is present in the homozygous state. When the gene is neither dominant nor recessive, the effect produced is the sum of the effects of the two alleles. This is said to be additive gene action. Some genes can affect the action of genes on a different locus (i.e. genes that are not members of the same allelic group). This is said to be an epistatic effect.

Those genes whose loci are on the sex chromosomes are said to be sex-linked genes. Since the Y chromosome is very small and carries very few genes, sex-linked genes are usually found on the X chromosome. Those characteristics which are only expressed in one sex are said to be sex-limited

Figure 182 Karyotype and chromosome spread from mare: $2n = XX$

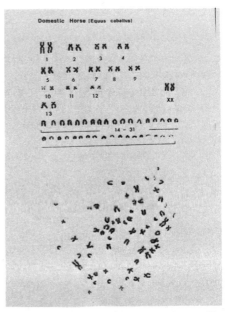

characteristics. For example, a male carries genes which code for milk quality, but these genes cannot be expressed in the male sex. However, the male can pass on the genes to female offspring.

The genetic make-up of an animal, that is, the number and type of genes it is carrying, is said to be its genotype. The outward appearance of the animal is its phenotype. The animal's phenotype is always known, but its genotype may be obscure because of recessive genes and epistatic effects. As a general rule, inbreeding increases the amount of gene homozygosity and so the genotype more closely relates to the phenotype. Inbreeding is the mating of individuals more closely related than animals chosen from the population at random. Line breeding is a form of inbreeding with one individual recurring in the pedigree. The degree of inbreeding can be calculated from a pedigree and is called the coefficient of inbreeding (Table 31). The coefficient of inbreeding is the probability that two genes at any locus in an individual are alike by descent (i.e. have been inherited from a single ancestor). In order to avoid problems from deleterious recessive genes the coefficient of inbreeding should not exceed 6 per cent.

The coefficient of inbreeding can be reduced by outbreeding or outcrossing, that is, breeding from individuals that are less closely related than animals chosen from the population at random. The effect of outbreeding is to increase gene heterozygosity and so mask the effects of some recessive genes. This leads to heterosis or hybrid vigour.

Blood typing

A good example of normal genetic variation (or genetic polymorphism) is

Table 31 Coefficient of Inbreeding

$$F_x = (\tfrac{1}{2})^{n_1 + n_2 + 1} (1 + F_a)$$

where F_x = coefficient of inbreeding of individual x.

n_1 = the number of generations between one parent and a common ancestor.

n_2 = the number of generations between the other parent and the same common ancestor.

F_a = coefficient of inbreeding of the common ancestor. (When this is not known F_a is given an arbitrary value of 0.)

Table 32 Blood Group Systems in the Horse

Antigen type	Alleles
A	A^a, A^b, A^c, A^{bc}, A^-
C	C^a, C^-
D	D^{bc}, D^c, D^{ce}, D^{cef}, D^d, D^{ad}, D^{de}, D^{df}
K	K^a, K^-
P	P^a, P^b, P^-
Q	Q^a, Q^R, Q^{RS}
U	U^a

Table 33 Protein Polymorphism Used in Blood Typing in the Horse

Protein/Enzyme	No. of alleles
Albumin	3
Transferrin	10
Prealbumin (Pr)	9
Prealbumin (XK)	3
Esterase	7
6 Phosphogluconate dehydrogenase (PGD)	3
Phosphoglucomutase (PGM)	3
Phosphohexose isomerase (PHI)	3

the series of genes which control the red blood cell antigens and the different serum proteins. Depending upon their different cell surface antigens, red cells can be divided into groups and this is what is meant by the term 'blood group' (Table 32). In addition, present in serum and within red cells, there are a number of different proteins and enzymes which are polymorphic and therefore can be used to identify individual horses (Table 33). The protein complement plus the red cell antigens make up the blood type of the horse.

The efficiency with which blood typing can be used to categorize an individual depends upon the number and frequency of alleles for each system. Different breeds have different alleles or a different frequency of alleles in the population. For example, the red cell factors D^{df} and K^a have not been found in Arabs but are present in Thoroughbreds, while the enzymes PGM and PHI are found in Arabs but not Thoroughbreds. The greater the number of characteristics tested, the larger the number of alleles at each locus; and the broader the spread of frequency of each allele within a population, then the less likely it is that any two individuals will be found to have exactly the same genotype. This is important because blood typing is mainly used as an individual's 'fingerprint' and hence utilized in questions of doubtful parentage. Whereas an animal can be excluded as a parent by means of blood typing, it can never be proved to be the parent.

Developmental abnormalities

When abnormalities are present at birth, these are said to be congenital. Such abnormalities may be caused by deleterious genes and therefore are heritable. However, they could also be caused by other agents during pregnancy, such as virus infections, drug administrations, extremes of temperature and exogenous chemicals. Such abnormalities would not be passed on to the next generation, but they might look exactly like those anomalies which are genetic in origin. It is therefore often not easy to determine whether or not a specific abnormality is caused by deleterious genes. Even when a genetic cause is strongly suspected, it may not be possible to define the mode of action and inheritance of the gene or genes involved. For this reason definitive advice on development anomalies is often not possible.

A number of congenital abnormalities are recognized in the horse but only a very few have been proved to be genetic in origin.

REPRODUCTIVE SYSTEM

Developmental abnormalities of the reproductive tract occur due to single gene anomalies and also to whole chromosome abnormalities.

TESTICULAR FEMINIZATION

This condition is due to an X-linked gene, the testicular feminizing gene (tfm), which renders the target organs incapable of responding to testosterone. The result is that, during embryogenesis in a genetic male, the gonads differentiate to form testes but the testosterone-dependent male duct system fails to develop. The female duct system is inhibited in the normal way and the uro-genital sinus, being unable to respond to testosterone, develops as a blind-ending vagina. Externally the animal is a phenotypic female, while internally there are abdominal testes and little or no tubular genitalia.

Inheritance and recommendation

Females carry the tfm gene in the heterozygous state and 50 per cent of their offspring will receive the tfm gene. All male offspring receiving the gene will be affected and will present as infertile 'females'. Female offspring receiving the gene will be reproductively normal but may pass the gene to their offspring. If an affected animal is diagnosed, the dam should not be used for rebreeding. The sire will not have contributed to the condition and can safely be re-used.

XY GONADAL DYSGENESIS

This condition is superficially similar to testicular feminization. The animal is a genetic male but presents as an infertile 'female'. Internally there is normally some development of the Mullerian duct system with a cervix and a uterus. However, there is always a complete absence of normal gonadal tissue.

Inheritance and recommendation

Gonadal dysgenesis is thought to be due to an autosomal gene, but the mode of inheritance is not known. It may be that both parents have contributed to the condition (autosomal recessive) or that it is passed on only through the dam (male-limited autosomal dominant). In either case it is advisable not to repeat the mating.

XY SEX REVERSAL

This is a condition seen in Arabs, Quarter horses and Paso Fino breeds. The animals again present as infertile 'females' although genotypically they are male. Phenotypically they can range from 'mares' showing oestrous cycles and sporadic follicle production to 'mares' that are overtly masculinized.

Inheritance

This varies. In most cases it appears as an X-linked or autosomal sex-limited dominant trait. In one case there was inheritance through the male either as an autosomal sex-limited dominant trait or as a Y chromosomal mutation with the carrier having some germ cells with the normal gene and other germ cells with the mutant gene.

XO SYNDROME AND XO/XX MARES

Some mares have only sixty-three chromosomes because one X chromosome is missing. These are described as 63 XO mares.

Pure XO mares tend to be small in stature with an infantile uterus and small, underdeveloped, fibrous gonads. They present as animals which fail to cycle. Clinical symptoms in cases of mares which have both abnormal (XO) and normal (XX) cells are more varied. There is often some development of the ovaries with irregular signs of oestrous behaviour, while others show no signs of oestrus at all.

Inheritance and recommendation

It is not known whether it is the maternal or paternal X that is missing in these cases, which are rare. There is no record of any mating having produced more than one abnormal offspring, therefore no particular breeding policy is necessary.

INTERSEXES

Intersexuality (part male, part female) in the horse can be due to an autosomal gene. In these cases the animal is a genotypic female but externally there is an enlarged clitoris which may be rather penis-like. There is often an increase in the distance between the anus and vulva. Internally the gonads are testicular and may lie anywhere along the line between the normal ovarian position and the inguinal ring.

Other intersex types have had abnormal chromosome complements (e.g. 63XO/64XX/65XXY, 63XO/64XY, 64XX/65XXY) but their phenotype is very similar to the 64XX intersexes.

Treatment

The problems associated with these animals are behavioural. Most have some male characteristics and may try to mount other females. Removal of the gonads solves this problem but requires major surgery. Secondly, because of the position of the penis-like organ, the animal will urinate backwards in an arc, even although it will squat like a female. This may create problems for the unwary.

CRYPTORCHIDISM

Cryptorchidism (see p. 311) is hereditary but the mode of inheritance is not always clear. In the Welsh Mountain pony it is thought to be due to an autosomal recessive. Unilateral cryptorchids should not be used for breeding, and mares producing a cryptorchid foal should be eliminated from the breeding stock.

HAEMATOPOIETIC AND LYMPHATIC SYSTEMS

HAEMOLYTIC DISEASE (NEONATAL ISOERYTHROLYSIS)(see also p. 393)

This is a condition seen in young foals of any breed after they have suckled the dam's colostrum. It is characterized by an acute jaundice and may result in death if not treated.

The condition is caused by the production by the mare of antibodies to the foal's red blood cells. These antibodies pass into the foal via the colostrum. The mare only produces antibodies if her blood group and that of the foal are incompatible and she has been previously sensitized. Hence it is usually only seen in mares which have already produced a number of normal foals.

Treatment

This consists of replacement blood transfusions to the foal with blood from a compatible donor. It is advisable to remove some of the foal's blood to limit damage to the kidneys due to haemolysis (see p. 394).

Preventive measures

Before mating takes place the mare and stallion should be checked for blood group compatibility. Serum from the mare is mixed with erythrocytes from the stallion and if these haemolysize any offspring may develop haemolytic disease if it inherits an incompatible blood group from the sire. The mating may be abandoned at this stage.

Alternatively the mating can proceed and the foal's blood checked at birth before it suckles the colostrum. If the foal's blood is compatible with the mare's, suckling can take place as normal. However, if the foal's blood is incompatible with that of the mare, colostrum from a compatible nurse mare should be given for forty-eight hours and the foal prevented from suckling its own dam. After this period antibodies are not absorbed from the digestive tract, so suckling can be permitted.

HAEMOPHILIA

This is a rare condition in which the normal clotting mechanism is impaired. In the horse it is due to a deficiency of Factor VIII. Only male foals are affected. They appear normal at birth but within a few days develop haematomas.

Inheritance and recommendation

The inheritance is a sex-linked recessive gene.

The condition is passed on by the mare since females are heterozygous carriers, and males are affected hemizygotes. Thus the dam of an affected animal and any of her daughters should not be used for breeding.

STRUCTURAL ABNORMALITIES OF THE HEART

A number of congenital abnormalities of the heart are thought to be genetic in origin but the mode of action and inheritance are not known. These include interventricular septal defect, patent ductus arteriosus, patent foramen ovale, persistent right aortic arch, and the tetralogy of Fallot.

IMMUNODEFICIENCY

There are three similar conditions which are due to a failure of the normal immunological defence systems of the horse.

COMBINED IMMUNODEFICIENCY (CID)

This is a condition seen in Arabian-bred foals and which is due to a simple autosomal recessive gene. There is a combined B- and T-lymphocyte deficiency, and affected foals are markedly lymphopaenic (that is, there is a marked decrease in the proportion of lympocytes in the blood), with less than 1000 peripheral blood lymphocytes/mm^3 blood. The foals are incapable of responding to immunization and produce no immunoglobulins of their own.

Affected foals develop clinical infections, usually a pneumonia, due to adenoviruses with secondary bacterial invasion, which are always fatal. The life expectancy depends upon the amount of passive protection the foal receives from the dam's colostrum, but to date all foals have died within five months of birth.

Recommendation

Because both the mare and the stallion are carriers of the recessive gene, they should not be used for breeding.

PRIMARY AGAMMAGLOBULINAEMIA

This condition was seen in a male Thoroughbred foal. The T-lymphocyte levels and functions were normal but there was a complete absence of functional B-lymphocytes. The animal eventually died at the age of seventeen months after repeated infections causing pneumonia and arthritis. It is suggested that the condition is similar to the sex-linked disorder in humans.

SELECTIVE IgM DEFICIENCY

Low or complete absence of serum IgM has been seen in foals of Arabian and Quarter horse breeding. The T- and B-lymphocyte counts were normal as were the levels of other immunoglobulins. It is not known whether this is a primary, genetic-based condition.

EYE

ANIRIDIA

Aniridia is an absence of the iris and is usually associated with cataract.

Inheritance and recommendation

The condition is due to an autosomal dominant gene. Since the gene is dominant, discarding all affected animals will eliminate the condition.

OTHER ABNORMALITIES

A number of other congenital abnormalities occur, though rarely (see Table 34). Many are thought to have a genetic component in their aetiology but the modes of inheritance are not known.

Table 34   Congenital Eye Abnormalities in the Horse

Aniridia (known to be due to an autosomal dominant gene)
Anophthalmia (complete absence of an eye)
Atresia of the naso-lacrimal duct (blockage of the tear duct)
Cataract (see p. 133)
Coloboma iridis (abnormal development of the iris resulting in part of it missing)
Congenital keratopathy (developmental abnormalities of the cornea usually resulting in loss of opacity)
Corneal dermoids (opaque, skinlike growth on the normally opaque cornea)
Detached retina (detachment of the retina from the back of the eyeball resulting in blindness)
Ectropion (eversion of the eyelids exposing the mucous membranes)
Entropion (see p. 130)
Glaucoma (swelling of the eye due to increased fluid pressure)
Melanosis of the cornea (black pigmentation on the cornea)
Microcornea (abnormally small cornea)
Night blindness (inability to see in weak light because of a defect in the retina)
Optic nerve hypoplasia (incomplete development on the optic nerve resulting in blindness)

Recommendation

When inheritance is suspected but not proven, the safest procedure is to refrain from breeding from stock that have produced an affected foal.

NERVOUS AND MUSCULOSKELETAL SYSTEMS

CEREBELLAR HYPOPLASIA (CEREBELLAR DEGENERATION)

A hereditary form of cerebellar hypoplasia is seen in Arabians. In this condition the animal is unable to control the extent or degree of muscular action, which results in overreaching (hypermetria), paddling and head tremors. Signs usually appear at four to six months of age.

Inheritance and recommendations

The condition is thought to be genetic in origin, although possible viral causes have not been excluded. It is advisable not to rebreed from parents of an affected foal.

HEREDITARY ATAXIA

A form of ataxia (incoordination) seen in the German Oldenberg breed is genetic in origin. Symptoms appear from three weeks onwards, when the foal shows loss of muscular coordination. The animal is iiable to fall and is unable to rise. Death usually occurs within two weeks of symptoms first appearing.

Inheritance and recommendation

The ataxia is due to a single autosomal recessive gene. Both parents of an affected animal are carriers and should not be used for breeding.

WOBBLER SYNDROME (see also p. 274)

Wobblers are young horses, more commonly males, between the ages of six and twenty-four months, which show signs of ataxia, weakness and spasticity of the pelvic limbs. It is a complex syndrome with more than one aetiology. In one form the symptoms are due to a compression of the spinal cord due to cervical vertebral malformation. There is thought to be a genetic component to the syndrome in that there is a predisposition to a narrow vertebral canal and susceptibility to bone and cartilage disease.

OCCIPITO-ATLANTO-AXIAL MALFORMATION (OAAM)

A familial abnormality of the atlas, with fusion to the occiput, is seen in Arabians. Foals may be born dead because of medulla oblongata compression. Alternatively, the less severe cases range from tetraplegia to abnormal head and neck carriage.

Inheritance and recommendation

It is suggested that in Arabs this is due to a simple autosomal recessive. Parents of an affected foal should not be used for breeding.

TORTICOLLIS (WRYNECK)

Affected animals have a twisted neck due to involuntary contraction of the cervical muscles. In the congenital form the condition is due to an autosomal recessive, and thus both parents are carriers and should not be rebred.

OTHER ABNORMALITIES

Other congenital abnormalities of the musculoskeletal system are listed in Table 35. Evidence of any genetic component and mode of inheritance for these conditions is weak.

Table 35   Congenital Abnormalities of the Musculoskeletal System

---

Arthrogryposis (literally 'crooked joint'; abnormal contraction of the muscles causing crooked, fixed joints)
Contracted flexor tendons (see p. 278)
Multiple exostosis (see p. 170)
Patella luxation and fixation (see pp. 202–3)
Polydactyly (see p. 171)

DIGESTIVE SYSTEM

ATRESIA COLI

This is a closure or lack of development of the ascending colon in the region of the pelvic flexure. Death will occur due to an inability to defaecate unless the condition is corrected surgically.

The condition is due to a simple, autosomal recessive gene, so neither parents should be used for breeding.

PARROT MOUTH AND SOW MOUTH

Parrot mouth is when the lower jaw is shorter than the upper, while sow mouth is when the lower jaw is longer than the upper. Both conditions are considered an unsoundness.

Both conditions are believed to be genetic but the mode of inheritance is not known.

WHITE FOAL SYNDROME

There are a number of different genes which produce the white coat colour. One, which produces a white foal with blue eyes, is recessive. The foals are born alive but die within a few days because of a large constriction of the large intestine.

Neither parent of affected foals should be used for breeding.

MISCELLANEOUS

EPITHELIOGENESIS IMPERFECTA (HAIRLESSNESS)

Affected foals have patches of skin which lack hair and in these areas the skin is leathery. Sometimes one or more hooves are missing. Most foals die within a few days of birth.

The condition is due to an autosomal recessive gene, so neither parent should be rebred.

UMBILICAL AND INGUINAL HERNIAS

Males tend to have inguinal hernias more commonly than umbilical, while in females it is vice versa. Quarter horses seem more prone to umbilical hernias than other breeds.

The mode of inheritance is not known but affected animals should not be used for breeding.

LETHAL DOMINANT WHITE

As the name suggests, this is a dominant gene that produces a white foal with blue or hazel eyes. Homozygous foals die *in utero* and all white horses with the dominant white gene are heterozygotes. When such horses are mated, 25 per cent of the embryos will be homozygous for the white gene and will therefore die *in utero*. The cause of death is not known.

46
THE IMPORTANCE OF
SELECTIVE BREEDING

In Great Britain there is a growing awareness that the time has come to reassess attitudes towards competition horse breeding and the requirements of contemporary riders and their sports. The growth in popularity of dressage, showjumping and riding club activities has created a greater demand for an athletic horse with substance and an equable temperament.

Although thousands of unwanted horses and ponies are bred, there is a steady trade in importing horses from the Continent. Gelderlanders, Hanoverians and Danish horses, for example, appear to find greater favour with many riders today, especially with dressage competitors.

Many Continental countries promote and monitor the breeding of a national riding horse, often with financial aid from their governments, and these horses are developed through crossbreeding native horses with the Thoroughbred. Here, in Britain, we have no one organization devoted to the production of such a riding horse.

We do, however, have the necessary stock to cross with the Thoroughbred: for example, the Cleveland Bay, the Welsh Cob, the Connemara, the Irish Draught, and also the Shire and the Clydesdale (popular for showjumping). A strong first-class mare makes an ideal foundation mare from which to breed potential competition horses.

The breeding of horses, particularly competition horses, is an expensive, time-consuming and often very disappointing occupation. It is one which necessitates considerable financial input, however small your set-up, and probably no financial return. It is a calling not to be taken without careful thought.

However, should prospective breeders be undaunted by these observations, there are a number of considerations to be taken into account to tilt the odds in their favour.

Selection of breeding stock is, of course, a prime factor when breeders initially contemplate the subject. Far too often mares lamed through congenital weakness of one form or another are bred, and often, by so doing, an inherited weakness is passed to their offspring. There are heritable traits such as parrot mouth, dipped back and crooked legs to be avoided in breeding stock (see chapter 45).

There are certain conformational defects which are also best avoided in breeding stock, because defects in conformation can lead to unsoundness (see chapter 44). Also, because it is an athlete that is ultimately being bred, the guidelines of conformation are an indication of the make and shape from which a horse is able to perform its work with the minimum of stress to its body. Together with conformation, a horse's performance capabilities also depend on its temperament and attitude to discipline.

There are, today, a far greater number of competition stallions from which breeders can choose to suit a particular mare. However, there is a great shortage of proven competition mares with good temperaments, soundness, ability and conformation from which to breed.

It is important to remember that the sire and dam each contribute 50 per cent inheritable material to the foal. It should also be taken into account that, not only does the mare provide half the foal's genes, but she also carries, nourishes and subsequently rears the foal. Along with the parental influence, the genetic influence of the antecedents – grandparents, great-grandparents, etc. – up to four or five generations back must also be considered. Certain traits and characteristics miss a generation or so and reappear at a later time, which is why it is so important to use the best possible stock to breed from and to learn as much as possible about their breeding and relative performance records.

Unfortunately, at the present time there is little or no data for the serious breeder to study the form – i.e. performance, soundness – especially of mares in areas of equestrianism such as eventing, showjumping and dressage.

A foal needs to be looked on as a patchwork of its parents, and the final element which plays its part in the foal's make and shape is chance. This fact makes the case of discriminative (selective) breeding all the more valid. There are no guarantees with breeding that astute selection will make for the perfect foal. However, it raises the odds in favour of the breeder. For example, breeding from two parents with good hocks does not absolutely guarantee a foal with good hocks as one grandparent may have had poor hocks. But to do the reverse and breed from two parents with bad conformation in that regard would almost certainly result in a foal with poor hocks.

In the past it has been thought that the age of the foal's parents had a direct bearing on the size and strength of subsequent foals. There is no scientific evidence to prove this is the case, although fertility may lessen with age, particularly with mares.

Once a breeder has decided what it is that he/she is trying to breed, a standard needs to be set and adhered to. It is not easy to look at home-bred youngsters objectively: all too often they look like swans, not geese, to their owners. Culling is an important part of breeding. Unsuitable colts should be gelded, to be ultimately sold as riding horses, and fillies which do not come up to the breeder's standard should not be kept on as breeding stock.

The important criteria for the competition horse breeder is a horse's performance record and prepotency for certain traits in its breeding stock. Prepotency is partly the ability of a mare or stallion consistently to produce offspring of considerable talent, conformation and excellent disposition.

It is considered that movement is a fairly inheritable quality, as is height. The Continental horses – for example, the Westphalian – have a naturally elevated, rounded action, which is much sought after by dressage riders. Their action is different to the lower, straighter action of the Thoroughbred. By crossbreeding with the Thoroughbred and with such breeds as the Welsh Cob, the Cleveland Bay and the Connemara, it is possible to achieve this elevated action. However, a skilled trainer can improve greatly the way in which a horse carries itself, whatever its breeding.

It is also considered among some riders, particularly showjumpers (and breeders for that matter), that proven jumping mares should be used to breed showjumping stock. This adds credibility to the thought that the aptitude for jumping is an inheritable trait, not solely through conformation, but also through an inherited temperament, musculature, heart rate, etc.

Prospective breeders would find it helpful to observe the horses which are successful in the various equestrian sports today and learn how they are bred. Having seen which types prove consistently successful, breeders could experiment with crossbreeding, noting which types blend well together.

There is a demand for a 160–170-cm (16-17-hand) athletic horse with substance. Recently there has been a trend for horses over 172-cm (17.2 hands) high; however, there now appears to be a swing back to smaller horses, which are often tougher and more durable, and able to withstand the severe tests which contemporary sports such as eventing place on them. Height in a horse does not denote strength, only a greater likelihood of wind and leg problems, especially if the height is achieved by the length of the horse's legs and not by the depth of his body. A well-proportioned (deep-bodied, short-legged with the appropriate amount of bone) 170-cm (17-hand) horse has all that is needed to carry a big heavy man, 16 stone and over, across country. This type of horse is still in very short supply.

The attitude of the horse to its work is what ultimately makes it the right type for whatever discipline it is required. The critical initial schooling by an experienced trainer plays an important part in channelling the young horse's physical and mental capabilities.

A breeder can assess, to a degree, his young stock's potential by observation. This ability is partly a gift, but a great deal can be learned by studying as many young horses as possible in their training and following up their success or failure.

Environmental influences on heredity are an extremely relevant factor which must be taken into account when deciding to take up horse breeding, whether it be one foal or many. All the planning and selection carried out by the breeder will be to no avail if the maintenance of the mares and youngstock is neglected. The youngster may carry a potentially highly successful combination of genes from its sire and dam, but unless the medium – its environment – is suitable, this may never be realized.

Whether it is bred for sentiment or ultimately to sell on as a potential competition horse, no young horse can be left to cope for itself in man's artificially induced environment and expectations. In the natural state the horse would range free, moving on as the food supply was exhausted, and the weaker animals would be killed off by the natural process of survival of the fittest, the stronger ones being able to outrun predators and survive on less food. The domestic horse is dependent on man for its maintenance: consequently it is the responsibility of breeders to see that their horses receive the necessary food, worming, foot care and correct handling to prepare them for their future work.

The influence of the environment starts with the foetus. Therefore the care and feeding of the in-foal mare is very important. The mares should be fed a balanced, nutritional diet according to their size, type and requirements (see chapter 43). Are they living out all the year round, for instance? If so, they will require more food to keep them warm as well as feeding the unborn foal.

The mare's intake of food has a direct bearing on the welfare of the unborn foal. Undernourished mares cannot normally be expected to produce strong, healthy foals. Weak foals from poor mares will have a greater susceptibility to disease and parasites. Crooked legs in young horses – not the natural weakness often seen in new foals – can frequently be due to a nutritional imbalance in the mare while she carries the foal. (Crooked legs are seen frequently in horses and must be considered to be congenital – i.e. inherited – in cases in which the breeding stock receives the best attention; see chapter 19.) Given favourable surroundings, a foal from an undernourished mare can make up strength once it is born and realize its genetic potential. However, an owner who allows a mare to decline during pregnancy would not necessarily be expected to produce the ideal environment for the birth of the foal.

Fertility of broodmares is quite largely dependent on environmental factors, although there is no doubt that mares with low conception rates will pass on this condition, whatever the causes, to their offspring.

Overweight mares are considered to be less likely to conceive than a mare which is putting on weight and condition. In-foal mares should receive regular exercise, such as being turned out in the field. They can also be lightly ridden for the first four months of their pregnancy.

The mare and her new foal will need good grazing and the continuance of food and mineral supplements (see chapter 43), depending on the breed and physical type of mare.

Once the foal has been weaned from the mare it will need a balanced, high-protein diet with added minerals, taking into account that approximately 75 per cent of a young horse's growth takes place during this first year. As we are the result, in a large part, of what we eat, the extreme importance of feeding the young horse will be appreciated. Lack of suitable feeding during the formative years can lead to stunted growth, lack of substance and bone, and general weakening of the limbs, which are a vital aspect of the potential athlete.

During the foal's and young horse's early years (up to about four years of age) regular worming is a very high priority (see chapter 32). Incalculable internal damage can be done by severe infestations of worms to the lining of the intestines and stomach. This damage can express itself in later life: the horse may never thrive and may even die prematurely. The importance of regular worming cannot be stressed too strongly, particularly where there is limited, horse-sick pasture, as worms breed in greater density under such conditions.

The ideal pasture, although not always available for the horse breeder, is one which is well supplied with limestone or chalk of varying types, for example, the carboniferous limestone found in parts of northern England and Derbyshire or the chalk formation in Norfolk. It is interesting to note that over the years many famous Thoroughbred studs have been established in limestone or chalk regions, the Royal Stud at Sandringham in Norfolk being just one example.

It has been noted by breeders over the years that limestone or chalk land tends to produce better horses with good strong bone and height, than, say, a soil heavy with clay. Ireland exports many of its riding horses to England, and these horses are bred on limestone pastures. In the USA, Kentucky, the Blue Grass state, where limestone underlies the pasture land, is renowned for the horses it produces.

This should not deter breeders situated on other types of soil. Careful pasture management to suit your land can improve the quality of grazing. Calcium additives can also be included in feedstuffs for breeding stock.

Horse breeding can be viewed as a calculated game of chance, governed in varying degrees by fate. For those absorbed in the subject, it is both a fascinating and compelling occupation and the breeding of competition and riding horses has a significant part to play in the equestrian world in Britain. It should receive the recognition it deserves.

47
THE HUNTER

Finding the right horse

Buying a horse can involve a great deal of money nowadays, but selling horses is a very old business with its own set of customs and its own particular traps for the unwary. Basically there are three different ways of buying a horse: by private treaty, at public auction or through a dealer.

A great many riding horses are bought privately and this method has certain advantages for both parties. The seller can be more certain of finding a good home for his or her horse and has a chance to assess the suitability of the prospective rider. The buyer can ascertain details of the horse's history and often have the animal for a trial period. However, it is wise not to become too friendly with the vendor – it is surprising how easily ethical considerations are abandoned when there is a need to be rid of a troublesome beast.

Public auction is the method of sale most popularly associated with horses. Auctions have a vivid atmosphere and are frequented by characters as entertaining and as various as those in a Dickens novel.

For the vendor the auction has the advantage of widening the field of purchasers: more people will attend an auction than will reply to an advertisement. In addition they are collected together in a specific place for a specific length of time, with no opportunity to go away and think about whether or not to buy. However, because there are a number of horses to choose from, presentation is all-important.

For a buyer, however, an auction is a difficult path to tread, where his or her judgement is put to the test in the instant. On no account should an inexperienced person buy a horse at an auction without help. The overriding rule of all auctions, however reputable they might be, is *caveat emptor* (see p. 672), apart from some basic conditions. These vary from place to place, but they usually exclude from the sale ring, unless declared, whistlers or roarers and horses prone to such vices as crib-biting. Some auctions may give a guarantee that a horse is a good hunter, but such conditions offer but a meagre safety net.

Most hunters are in an auction for a good reason, which the purchaser must endeavour to find out. By no means all horses are bad ones, however. A master of hounds may be selling up or perhaps an owner simply cannot get on with his or her mount and wishes to be rid of it quickly. A good judge of a horse and, sometimes more importantly, of the person selling it can often pick up a bargain. In addition, there is a variety of horses to choose from. In essence an auction presents the biggest risks and potentially the biggest gains.

A middle course is the dealer. By going to a dealer a purchaser can see a number of horses at leisure and also has some of the advantages of buying privately, such as a trial day's hunting. The key lies in choosing the dealer: a good dealer will have reliable sources of horses and, with an eye to his reputation and perhaps a second sale, will do his best to match rider and horse.

A bad dealer will be professional at lying and cheating, and can survive for many years doing so. There is no federation or association of dealers to protect a purchaser, but reputation is a good yardstick, and it is always worth asking knowledgeable friends whom they would recommend. The dealer's attitude is all-important: if he is willing to allow a prospective purchaser to ride the horse thoroughly, then he is probably quite reputable. However, he cannot be expected to run down his own horse.

For the buyer a policy of reticence without being rude is wise. A stream of trumpeted assertions and stipulations will not only annoy a vendor who may otherwise be helpful, but it will also allow him or her to say less. An experienced dealer in particular will soon stress the horse's good points which match the purchaser's opinions. Reticence, on the other hand, will often draw the truth and give you a chance to learn more and make a better assessment.

There are many points to bear in mind when buying a horse, some of which should not be compromised while others are more flexible. The most important point, which must never be compromised, is to insist on a horse that is quiet in traffic. Modern roads make a badly behaved horse a constant danger. Many are a little nervous of large lorries and may shy slightly when one goes by, which is just about tolerable with an experienced rider, but it is a vital principle to have a horse that is quiet in traffic.

Beyond this, good manners are important, but they are more a matter of personal taste than absolutes. By manners I mean that the horse should stand still when required, that it should be able to go away from other horses, that it should be kind in the box, and so on. Many experienced riders will put up with a fidget, but will get very annoyed if a horse will only follow other horses, whereas other riders are happy to go in a crowd but, as they like to chat, would get cross if their mounts were to keep going round in circles.

Soundness is also a prerequisite in a good hunter. It is surprising how some purchasers will be carried away by ability – or talk of it – and will overlook even glaring unsoundness. They may think they are buying a horse on the cheap, but it is a false economy for there is nothing more expensive or frustrating than a lame horse.

Hunting puts great stress on a horse, particularly on its legs. Not only is it asked to carry large weights over jumps at speed – a job for which it is in no way designed – but it has to cross plough, grass and metalled road in quick succession, standing one moment, going flat out the next.

A hunter which has done some work will not be without blemish. Knocks, scars and cold lumps on knees are rarely of consequence; nor are windgalls, though they are a sign of wear. The foot, the seat of 90 per cent of lameness, is most vulnerable in a hunter, and any wear such as ringbone (see pp. 182 and 252) or sidebone (see p. 253) – any bony growth in fact – should rule out a horse.

The thickening of a tendon (see pp. 211 ff.) should also be viewed with great suspicion. This is usually the result of either having been ridden over plough for a period, or having tripped in a hole, or poor conformation. Tendons can recover and may never give trouble again, but it is worth getting professional advice.

This brings me on to my next point: the importance of having a horse vetted (see chapter 49). The veterinarian is not responsible for selecting a good horse, but he or she can save you from buying a wreck. It is advisable to consult a veterinarian experienced in purchase examinations because such a person will be able to spot quickly the most important points.

There is disagreement as to the value of radiography when having a horse vetted, but if you are spending several thousand pounds on a horse, a radiographic view of the foot may save you from wasting your money by revealing the start of osteitis or navicular disease.

As to ability, a horse must suit the rider and the country in which he or she hunts. Someone who is seventy and hunts over Lincolnshire plough hardly wants to buy a Thoroughbred that is excellent over fly fences and gallops on. He or she would be better advised to buy a steady half-bred which can jump safely and find its own way out of trouble, and which probably costs far less.

Basically the horse should be able to jump the local obstacles. An inability to do so will soon leave you far behind and miserable. The need for speed varies, from the shires – Leicestershire and the like – where quick runs over hedges and ditches make a good galloper desirable, to plough country, where a broad, sure foot rather than speed is the order of the day.

Horses which follow a shire pack will tend to be Thoroughbreds and quality half- or threequarter-breds. The Irish Draught is marvellous for producing good sense and an instinct for self-preservation, which compensates for the lack of speed and better action of the pure-bred horse.

In plough country you will find many different types of horse, Irish Draught, cobs and native crosses, all of which are excellent in tricky situations. A touch of Thoroughbred is desirable in such horses, as the breed imparts an ability to last and try when tired.

As for other countries, a half-bred horse is generally considered best for hilly country, while the followers of the moorland hunts often use native ponies or crosses.

In the foregoing discussion I do not mean to define types absolutely because some Thoroughbreds are marvellously clever across ditches, for example, and, just as importantly, some riders get on better with one type rather than another. Also the amount of time available to devote to the horse must be taken into account: a half-bred or a cob can take much rougher treatment and be hunted from less exercise than a Thoroughbred.

A rider should buy a horse of appropriate size for his or her needs. There is a growing preference for big horses, perhaps to make the fences look smaller. However, the bigger the horse the greater the likelihood of problems in wind and limb.

Training a hunter

It is impossible to describe in full detail how to get a hunter fit, but, although you should bear in mind that every horse is different, starting right is half the battle won.

After a season's work hunters are turned out to grass to rest and put on condition, and also to rest their legs, but they should not be allowed to get fat, because this may strain the heart and legs on restarting work. Cubhunting starts after harvest, so every horse should be in work by August at the latest.

There is no harm bringing a horse in from the field, riding it and turning it out in July up to the time when it is in serious work and the nights are drawing in. The object of exercise is to build up muscle. If a horse starts to lose condition without gaining muscle, it should be brought in whatever the weather.

Others can stay out for some of the day, coming in at night. Some indeed are better out for an hour, under rugs, each day well into the winter to keep them keen and fresh.

It is tempting for a rider who likes leaping over fences at the gallop to hurry a horse, but every hunter should be walked for at least two weeks, starting with half an hour and working up to an hour or so. Jogging can then be introduced, initially with little bursts, using gentle hills, building up to two hours or so.

After about another two weeks a hunter will usually be ready for cubbing. At this stage you can canter a little, so that by six weeks of work your horse will be nearly fit to hunt. Again it must be stressed that the time taken to reach fitness will vary according to the individual.

There are three main dangers to look out for when getting a horse fit: coughs, back soreness and leg trouble. A cough in a horse which has just come up from grass is often due to dust in straw and hay, which should be damped; a good airflow without a draught will help. This can be achieved by leaving open the top door of the stable.

Back sores are caused by rubbing tack, particularly the saddle. Leather linings, as opposed to old-fashioned serge, and girths are the usual culprits, so the best solution is to use a numnah under the saddle and candlewick or webbing girths (girths should always be used in pairs, because they can occasionally break).

Many an old groom would be horrified at the use of numnahs, but they save wear on back and saddle, and even the best saddle will not fit a fat horse well. The back can be hardened with lead lotion, salt water or rubbing alcohol. If a sore develops, it should be protected by felt with a hole cut out over the area of the sore to prevent further rubbing.

Swelling in the legs which is not painful, hot or bowed (a sign of tendon trouble) is usually due to the effect of corn on the blood and is common. Such swelling can be walked off by and large, but it is best to reduce the grain ration until the legs are normal and the horse doing work.

Once a horse is being hunted regularly it will need relatively little work, unless it has a tendency to stiffen up. If a horse is hunted on Mondays and Fridays, it should be walked out on the following days. On Thursdays it should again be walked out with perhaps one half-speed canter. You should aim to be out for between one and two hours – the more walking the better. This is as much to keep the horse interested as anything else.

Feeding

The theory of feeding is discussed at length in chapter 43, but it is worth looking at how feeding works in practice in relation to a specific example, namely, the hunter.

First, it has to be remembered that every horse is different and, given the endless variety of feeds available, feeding an individual animal is a matter of skill, sensitivity and experience, a matter of art, in fact, as much as science. It is an irony that the rise in research into and knowledge of nutrition has been matched by a decline in the quality of feed for horses, mainly due to the emphasis on quantity in farming.

Feed is divided into two sorts: hard (concentrates) – oats, bran and so on – and soft – hay and grass. As a horse becomes fitter, you should feed more of the former and less of the latter.

Oats are the main source of protein and they should be plump, heavy – a 55-kg bushel is ideal – hard and sweet-smelling. To help digestion they should be bruised or rolled – not more – if possible on the day of use, though this is not vital.

Of the alternative grains, the best is barley, which is used in many parts of the world and was often the basic diet of army horses. Barley is a harder grain than oats, and should be well rolled or boiled whole as a substitute for part of the oat ration. It is better at keeping on flesh than oats, but horses unused to it can often show adverse reactions, such as swollen legs.

Wheat used to be fed a good deal to carthorses and, being high in vitamin E, is thought by some to be good for young showjumpers. However, it is not a good feed for horses. Maize, which is fed flaked to keep on flesh, is more likely to produce an empty saddle than anything else as it is high in energy but relatively low in proteins and vitamins.

The pure digestible protein level for a hunter should be 12–14 per cent, and oats and barley often contain only 8 or 9 per cent nowadays, so you may also have to give a higher-protein food. Beans used to be fed in small quantities, and they are indeed very high in protein, but they are also full of carbohydrates, producing energy and fat.

Far more worthwhile (but expensive) is linseed, with 35 per cent pure protein, or soyabean meal, with 45 per cent. Linseed should be soaked overnight, and then boiled to a jelly or heated with more water to produce a nutritious tea. This is not a tidy process, but the result is very popular with the horse.

Soyabean meal is easier to use because it needs no cooking, but it is less palatable and needs mixing well, up to about one part soyabean meal to twelve parts oats (the ratio should be slightly higher for linseed).

The other main constituent of a feed is wheat bran. Bran should generally be fed damped (it can be fed dry, especially after a physic, but can cause choking). Broad bran should have large flakes, be full of flour and perfectly dry, not musty. Nowadays so-called broad bran has lost all its flour and is steamed and rolled heavily to reconstitute the broad flakes; it will provide bulk but not much else.

Such a diet would, of course, be very boring and there are several other foodstuffs that add interest, the most common of which is sugar-beet pulp or nuts, the residue of processed farming beet. It should be soaked for twenty-four hours before feeding and has an appetizing sweetness. Like all foods rich in carbohydrates, it is good at keeping flesh on a horse. Although it is not too heating, it does little to promote fitness and should be used in smallish quantities. Another appetizer is palm kernel, which is high in oil and good for the coat and digestion.

Carrots, which are easily digestible, are good for cooling the blood and a help with poor-winded horses. Other roots such as swedes and turnips are also palatable sources of vitamins and bulk, but need to be introduced gradually because horses can be put off them if overfaced.

Extreme luxuries are eggs, which can be fed six at a time for four days and no more to a horse in strong work, and beer at the rate of two bottles a day for, say, seven days when leading up to a competition. However, this should be stopped three to four days before competing.

Of course, the fun of creating concoctions is lost if you feed nuts (cubes), but they have their advantages, as do all convenience foods. They are easy to feed and there is no waste; the mix is likely to be consistent, though some of the constituents are not ideal – wheat and fish meal, for example, which is excellent protein but indigestible. You should only use reliable manufacturers who have a proven reputation, because they can be relied on to use good-quality foodstuffs.

Some horses, including top-class racehorses and yearlings, do very well on nuts, but they can become boring and, as they have less bulk, can be less filling. Horses, like any other animal, prefer to feel full, whatever their requirements.

So much for the concentrates; the rest of the feed for hunters is grass and its derivative, hay.

The two main classes of hay are seed hay and meadow hay, the former grown as a crop in rotation over three years or so, the latter cut from permanent pasture. Seed hay is more controlled and contains desirable grasses such as timothy, which is high in fibre and carbohydrates but low in digestible protein and minerals, clover, which is rather the opposite and a laxative, and the staple rye-grass. The best seed hay is generally second-year lay, as it will contain a wider variety of herbs.

Meadow hay, consisting of older grasses, will be far more variable in every way and its quality will depend on the grassland management of the farmer. It is likely to be lower in protein but may contain a variety of herbs which are both nutritious and highly palatable.

For a hunter, good meadow hay is the most desirable. Good hay should smell sweet and be free from dust. The most common fault with meadow hay is that it hangs onto flowers, especially clover. It should be crisp to touch and a soft green, neither yellow, which is a sign of dampness, nor bottle green, which indicates excessive nitrogen and overproduction of grass. The latter is not so serious, but such hay is less digestible and less palatable.

Lucerne hay (alfalfa) can be fed, but with caution as it can be very high in protein, but its role is limited in England, which is not its natural environment.

A new sort of forage feed has come onto the market under various brand names. Basically it is vacuum-packed hay or silage, often enriched by molasses, and is known as haylage. Depending on the type of grass from which it is made, it can be high or low in protein; the former is claimed to be virtually a complete food. Time will tell if this is true for a hunter in full work, though it might well be the case. Variable quality and unpalatability to a horse unaccustomed to such feed can be problems. It is free from dust but expensive compared with hay and prone to mould if not stored carefully.

With the advent of research and the decline in the quality of foodstuffs, mineral and vitamin supplements have become very popular. If high-quality foodstuffs are available such expensive additives are unnecessary, but they can be useful and harmless if given as the manufacturers direct.

Cod-liver oil is also a useful supplement, enabling a horse to convert vitamins and giving it a shiny coat. Salt is also important and can be added to the feed, but a permanently available salt lick is preferable.

The following is an example of a diet for a stabled middleweight hunter, 163 cm (16.1 hh) This is only a guide. One should look carefully at the individual horse and the work it is doing, and vary the feed accordingly. Feeding, in the end, is an art.

Early morning (an hour and a half before exercise)

2 lb oats
½ lb soaked sugar-beet pulp

Midday

3 lb oats
½ lb bran
½ lb soaked sugar-beet pulp
1 lb barley
¼ lb soyabean meal

Night

6 lb oats
½ lb bran
½ lb soaked sugar-beet pulp
½ lb soyabean meal or cooked linseed

Hay (up to 18 lb per day) should be fed throughout the day and water should be freely available.

On a hunting day the early-morning feed should be replaced by the following fed at 7–8 a.m.:

3 lb oats
3 lb bran
½ lb soyabean meal (this should be quite wet and warm)
½ lb soaked sugar-beet pulp

The evening ration of sugar beet can be increased to $\frac{2}{3}$ lb if the feed is regularly eaten up.

The diet should also contain mineral supplements, salt, cod-liver oil and carrots. In addition, three times a week 2 × 15 ml of the following mixture may be mixed into the feed:

7 oz saltpetre
7 lb Epsom salts
7 lb bicarbonate of soda

Horses generally do better if fed at night but as their stomach is small they should be fed little and often. It is important to keep to a routine both in feeding and exercising, as horses have a very well-adjusted clock in their head.

Harness

A great many people, perhaps impressed by the magnificent sight of a saddler's shop, keep far too much equipment for a hunter. The most basic needs are, of course, a saddle and a bridle.

The important aspects of fitting the saddle are that the shoulders should be free to move without hindrance and the spine and withers untouched. The weight of the saddle should be borne by the ribcage and not by the loins, which are prone to soreness and least able to bear weight.

The best way to buy a saddle is to take several and try them on the horse. Failing this, one can simulate the withers and ribcage with a stout but pliable cable moulded to the horse's shape. This can then be taken to the saddlers.

These days the great majority of saddles are lined with leather. Leather linings are longer lasting and easier to use than linen or serge linings, but are much harder on the horse's back, necessitating the use of numnahs. However, a leather lining is easier to clean.

Numnahs are saddle-shaped pads made of sheepskin, felt or synthetic fibre. They fit underneath the saddle to which they are attached by straps. They should be kept clean and uncreased, otherwise they will cause soreness rather than prevent it. They are particularly useful on thin-skinned horses.

There are various types of girths. Leather girths have the same benefits and drawbacks as leather linings, whereas webbing girths are serviceable but encourage sweating. My own favourite is candlewick, which has to be scrubbed clean and changed if fraying occurs, but which is tough, kind to the horse and smart.

The bridle, like the saddle, should be fitted carefully, but is easier to adjust. The most important element is the bit, which lies between the canine and molar teeth and acts on the lips, the bars of the mouth, the tongue and the jaw to help stop and balance the horse. If it is sitting right, a bit should cause, at most, one wrinkle in the side of the horse's mouth, while the ends of the bar of the bit should be about 1 cm free of the mouth at each side – not more and not less, otherwise it will pinch the mouth.

There are innumerable types of bits. Some horses pull and need a strong bit. However, a horse often pulls because the rider uses the bit too much. In addition, a more severe bit will work only for a short time, until the nerves in the mouth deaden further and leave the rider with a worse problem. Ironically stronger bits, such as gags and curbs, need much more careful handling and far more skill, especially when jumping, because being caught in the mouth will cause a horse to rush its jumps. It also has to be remembered that excitement can cause a horse to pull, a problem no bit will solve, but a good seat and quiet voice might.

I believe a snaffle is usually best, but if a severe bit is required, the double bridle, with two bits, is the most satisfactory because the horse can be ridden on the snaffle bit most of the time and on the curb when necessary. Both horse and rider need to practise its use, especially as there are four reins, but it is an art well worth learning.

There are also several types of noseband available. Again, the noseband should be chosen with thought and, with the majority, fitted high enough so that pressure is applied to the bone of the nose and not to the air passages.

The other method of constraint is the martingale, the running version of which is often part of the hunter's kit, even if it is not tight enough to do its job. However, the neck strap in dire circumstances may be useful.

Clipping

In cold weather any horse in hard work should be clipped, because the long hair will make a horse sweat and then take chill. There are three main types of clip: a full, which leaves only a saddle patch and legs; a trace, which takes off below where traces would come: the belly, lower neck and jaw but excluding the legs; and a blanket, which takes in the neck, head and shoulders as well, leaving a blanket shape.

The first is the one for a stabled hunter in hard work, but a trace clip is useful, especially if one wants to turn a horse out during the day under a rug.

Some people clip all over the first time (a horse will need clipping at least twice in a season), but this is unnecessary and robs the horse of valuable protection, as does clipping the inside of the ears.

Clipping is an art gained by practice. You should start with a clean, dry horse and clip against the coat in as broad a sweep as possible, without forcing. It helps to tense the skin lightly and to keep the clipper blades sharp and well oiled. Some horses dislike being clipped, so it is advisable to let them hear the clipper beforehand so they become accustomed to the noise and to do the sensitive areas last. In extreme cases it is best to ask your veterinarian to administer a tranquillizing drug (see p. 575). When clipping or pulling manes (which are never cut) it is better to resort to a twitch or a tranquillizing drug rather than engage in a brawl.

Clothing

Clothing is a major item of expense with a hunter. There are many kinds of rugs to choose from, but the jute night rug is still the most useful. This is a top rug, under which one can put any number of blankets, either purpose bought or made from old bed blankets. Underblankets should be folded back over the jute rug at the withers to prevent chafing and to keep them in position. All of these should be surrounded by a webbed surcingle with a pad to protect the horse's withers. This strap should be done up snugly, but not too tightly, as it will be there for long periods. There should also be a strap and buckle at the front to prevent the rug slipping.

hunter

blanket

trace high

Figure 183   Types of clip

Some rugs have one or two straps instead of a surcingle. If this is the case they should be wide, so that the rug is not pulled down on the withers, which would cause pinching.

The jute rug is also perfectly adequate as a day rug; light day rugs are an unnecessary luxury.

If a horse is turned out with a rug or if it is being roughed off, a New Zealand rug is generally used. This is made of tough canvas with a soft lining, and has a surcingle and leg straps to keep it in place. These are necessary because the horse may roll and move around its paddock at speed.

Synthetic rugs have come to the fore recently. They are easy to look after, to dry and to clean, and are light, but they are not cheap, can rip easily and do not breath as well as rugs made from natural fibres. However, they are very handy in a variety of situations, especially outdoors.

The other rug which is indispensable is the sweat rug. Basically this is a string vest for use, as its name implies, immediately after a horse has worked, to let him dry without chilling.

Boots and bandages

The extremities of the horse have attracted all sorts of garments. The most important extremity is the leg, for which, without trying, I can think of fifteen types of boots and five types of bandage. Most of these are designed in response to particular problems.

Some owners take out their horses wrapped up like mummies, with enough boots to equip a football team. The two basic bandages necessary for a hunter are the stable bandage, which is used on the legs for warmth and to foster good circulation, and the tail bandage, which is used for protection when travelling.

The stable bandage is broad and long, and covers the leg from the knee to the coronet. The leg should be wrapped in Gamgee and the bandage bound evenly (most important) and not too tight. Most bandages have tapes which should be tied at the side of the leg, not at the front or back, in a bow, with the ends tucked in.

Nowadays there are soft synthetic bandages which can be used without Gamgee and which have Velcro fastenings. The latter are very convenient, but tend to wear out.

Bandaging every night is not necessary with a normal horse, but it is useful for tired limbs after hunting, both for support and warmth as legs lose heat rapidly after the pores have opened during work.

The tail bandage is used not only to protect the tail when travelling, but also to shape it. It is made of stretch fabric, 3 inches or so wide, and should be applied to a lightly damped tail – never the other way round because the bandage will shrink.

The procedure is: place the left hand under the tail, holding the end of the bandage, and wrap the bandage round with the right. Keep the left hand in place until the end is secured, and then wrap several turns at the top to catch the top hairs and give the bandage an anchor.

You should bandage to the end of the dock bone and then back up, tying the tapes about a third of the way down, again in a bow.

Figure 184a Protective or brushing boots – these boots do not prevent a horse from striking into itself, but do minimize the damage incurred

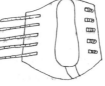
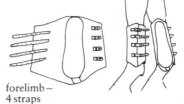

forelimb – 4 straps

hind limb – 5 straps

Figure 184b Tendon boots are fitted to the forelimb with the straps in front. They provide support to the tendons when jumping.

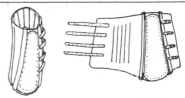

Figure 184c A felt Yorkshire boot, tied around the hind fetlock, protects the fetlock and upper pastern region of a horse which moves closely behind. It is an alternative to a fetlock boot

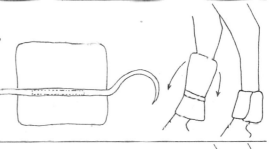

Figure 184d A hind fetlock boot protects the fetlock and part of the pastern region of a horse which moves closely behind

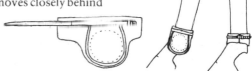

Figure 184e A sausage boot, placed around the pastern of a forelimb, prevents the heel of the foot coming in contact with the elbow when the horse lies down. It may help to prevent a capped elbow developing

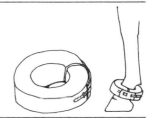

Figure 184f A rubber ring. The ring is placed around one or both hind pasterns to protect the insides of the pasterns

Figure 184g An overreach boot, which protects the pastern and heel regions provided that the boot fits correctly. If the boot is too big, it may be easier to put on but will sit too low and not completely protect the pastern

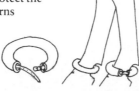

To remove the bandage, undo the ties, grasp the top in both hands and slide it down. When applied every day for several hours, it will give the tail a pleasing shape.

Exercise bandages are designed to give support to tendons and protect legs from knocks. They are unnecessary, indeed undesirable, for normal horses, whose legs should be strong enough without support. Indeed, they are only of limited use with bad-legged horses. They are made from stretch fabric, like tail bandages, but shorter, and should be put over Gamgee, between the knee and the fetlock joint.

Unroll 6–8 inches and, having taken one wrap round, hold the bandage obliquely. Then, letting the spare hang down, wrap the bandage around the legs, keeping it fairly firm but even. Having reached the fetlock, work back up the leg, tying as for stable bandages. The ends may be secured by sewing if hard work is envisaged.

Grooming

Grooming is performed mainly for our benefit, although it may improve the horse's circulation. For the most part we like to see clean horses, but horses themselves like to roll in the mud, acquiring an effective duvet against the weather.

A basic grooming kit consists of a dandy brush to remove the mud, a body brush, which is used in circular sweeps to remove dust and to brush the tail, a curry comb, which is pulled across the body brush to clean it every few sweeps, a rubber curry comb, which is excellent for removing tough mud, a water brush for laying the mane and tail, a mane comb, used when pulling a mane, two sponges for cleaning the nose and the dock, a stable rubber – a cloth – for the final polish, a hoofpick, to clean out the foot (away from the frog), and oil for moistening the foot and sole.

This is not the place for a detailed discussion of grooming, but one should be wary of washing large areas of the horse without the facility to dry it in the warm. Surplus water should be removed with a scraper and the horse rubbed and walked under a light rug until dry.

In addition to a grooming kit, you will also need a first-aid kit (see chapter 40).

Injuries

A horse is a highly complex animal and prone to injury when asked to do things not suited to its frame, such as carry weight at speed over fences. It is remarkable indeed that horses do so much with injuries similar to those we experience when playing a contact sport. For the most part these will be knocks, bangs or cuts, with only the occasional disaster, but a lot depends on the horseman.

'Horseman' is a word I use with care: many good riders never make successful followers of hounds because they fail to be observant stablemen, judging a horse's health, or prudent pilots, spotting wire on a hedge or a hole in the ground. It is surprising how some people always seem to be in the front rank but rarely lame a horse, while others are frequently on their feet at the meet, their horses at home.

Every owner should be aware of his or her horse's character and appearance when it is healthy; it should be keen in its work, eating well, bright-eyed and with a shiny coat and loose skin. The most obvious sign that a horse is unwell is deviation from the norm – failure to eat, listlessness or a dull coat.

The most common illnesses with hunters – generally pretty tough characters – are colds, which they can catch when meeting so many other horses, and colic (see p. 11), rarely seen in the wild but common enough when a horse is receiving relatively little natural roughage and large amounts of concentrates. An owner should be alert to a persistent cough, listlessness, a runny nose or, worse, fever, and should keep an eye on the horse's droppings, which should be distinct but not too firm.

The most common injuries to a hunter are cuts on the legs. With luck these will be superficial, in which case treatment with antiseptic powder or spray will be sufficient. Alternatively the wound can be wrapped with a bandage soaked in salt water (1 teaspoon salt to 1 pint water). This dressing should be renewed every twenty four hours until the wound is healed.

Some horses have actions that make them liable to injury. An extravagant hind action may cause a horse to overreach; some horses move close in front and will brush (hit their fetlocks). Overreaching can also come about by accident, particularly on heavy ground, if a front foot is held by the mud.

Such accidents have to be solved mechanically. All hunters should have their hind shoes set so that the toe of the hoof is slightly prominent, as it is the metal shoe that does the most damage. Also overreach and brushing boots will afford good protection.

With an overreach the bulb of the heel is usually cut and may only require treating with sulphanilamide powder to prevent excess scar tissue forming. More care should be taken with a deeper cut. The hole should be washed and filled with a poultice of brewer's yeast until it has nearly healed. This should take a week or so, although complete healing will take a week longer.

An overreach higher up on the fetlock joint is more serious because the tendons may be affected even if the cut is small. Any swelling indicates bruising and fluid escaping from the sheath. Poultices may be applied to draw any moisture and keep the wound clean, but in case of doubt about the seriousness of the injury, you should call your vet. When the swelling has subsided you can start walking the horse if it is not lame.

Another wound which may appear small but which sometimes can be more serious results from a kick. The underlying bone may be affected, especially in the thigh. Rest and advice from the veterinarian are recommended in these circumstances.

Puncture wounds are common, especially in the foot. With any puncture wound there has to be free passage for the serum to drain, and this can be done by either a blacksmith or a vet. For details of treatment, see p. 550.

Wounds in the leg caused by thorns and the like should be treated with poultices, either Animalintex or one made from Epsom salts and glycerine on lint and covered by greaseproof paper to hold in the heat. Success in treatment is indicated by a clean area, with several small points of blood, denoting a good supply.

In all cases of wounding vaccinations should be taken against tetanus (see p. 414). Indeed, all hunters should be vaccinated annually; a small cut, which may easily be missed, may otherwise prove fatal.

There is another type of injury found in older hunters, the result of wear and tear over the years. It includes chronic osteitis, sidebone, ringbone, navicular disease and pedal osteitis. These manifest themselves in various forms of lameness and hard, bony swellings. All will require diagnosis by a veterinarian and are described in detail in the section on the musculoskeletal system.

Preparing for a hunter's day

The etiquette of hunting has been dealt with at length in other books, but enjoying the day and surviving intact to enjoy another are the most important points of all. Several days before going hunting the horse's shoes should be checked. On the day, the heels should be greased to keep the wet out of sensitive areas, especially if the horse is prone to cracked heels.

A hunter should travel in a tail bandage and whatever rugs are necessary to keep him warm without sweating. Night rugs should not be used if possible, as they may get wet or dirty in the general scramble.

It is best to put the tack on before going, with the girth done up loosely, because it is awkward to fiddle with an excited horse in the confined space of a horsebox or trailer.

Unbox a mile or two away from the meet, walk a little way and then trot on gently to loosen horse and rider. So often horses get out at the meet, stand, getting cool, while their owners chatter, and then are asked to set off at speed.

During the day the rider should observe the hounds and the going, and take care of the horse. These can be done at one and the same time. This does not mean you have to display excessive caution, just alertness and common sense. For example, it is pointless to clatter down a road when hounds are not running or when there is a decent verge, yet so many do just that.

Seeing what others do is helpful but it is far more satisfying to take your own line, watching the direction of the hounds not the field. This may be possible even in small ways: a long queue may form to jump and leave other parts of a hedge clear simply through lack of confidence.

The next problem is when to go home. It is far better to do two half days than one full day in a week. The important point is not to exhaust the horse; it is for an owner to know his or her horse well enough to judge when to go home. A horse may stop pulling or fidgeting , or it may slow down markedly or start hitting fences.

The horse should be walked to the box and cooled off as much as possible, then untacked, rugged up to keep warm without sweating, and then taken home.

Most people wash off their horses vigorously when they return home, but this is unnecessary. Brush out saddle sweatmarks and feel down the legs carefully for thorns, chips of wood or stone flakes. A tired horse likes to be warm and dry and prefers to eat in peace rather than be clean.

This does not imply leaving it unobserved. The horse should have a good deep bed, be bandaged and have its rugs changed; this latter point may need fine judgement. Frequent observation is necessary, especially if a horse is trace-clipped, in case it gets cold under the lighter rugs or gets too hot and breaks out in a sweat again under heavier rugs. Some horses are prone to sweating but generally a dry horse is fit to be rugged up.

If you have many horses to do, then some will have to be cleaned that night. If possible this should be done with a brush and cool water; hot water opens the pores and increases the chance of a cold. A sponge is preferable to a hose, because the water will not then penetrate the coat and chill the horse so much, but the latter is commonly used in livery yards.

After a day's hunting I like to use a mixture of methylated spirit, vinegar and water in equal quantities to wipe on the legs at night in fact a daily application will do no harm. The mixture is a good cooling agent and astringent. A stronger version, for a horse with windgalls or slight heat in the legs, is fuller's earth soaked with vinegar as a mudpack, under Gamgee and bandage or a flannel soaked in Epsom salts. This should be changed every few hours.

It is also a good time to check again for thorns and so on. By the next day most of the mud will have dropped off, but the remainder should be brushed off and the tail washed if necessary. The horse should then be checked for soundness and allowed to pick grass and relax.

Miscellaneous

This section includes a chapter by David Snow on exercise physiology, a relatively new development in the field of veterinary studies. Then come two chapters which deal with considerations relating to the purchase of horses: the first, by Nicholas Wingfield Digby, discusses examining the horse for veterinary certification, and the second, by Simon Hopes, examines the legal implications of buying and selling horses. These are followed by two chapters on aspects of the veterinary service: the role of the State Veterinary Service by Ian Dick and the training of the veterinary nurse by Jennifer Dykes. The final chapter, on colours and markings, has been contributed by Janet Anderson.

There is also a chapter which has been retained from the previous edition of the book, that by Donald Tutt on ageing a horse by examining its mouth. Although little new has been added to the subject in recent years, it is still important, especially for non-Thoroughbred breeds of horses.

48
EXERCISE PHYSIOLOGY

In the last twenty-five years great advances have been made in human athletic achievements. Arguably much of this improvement has been gained from a scientific approach to training, the result of detailed studies by exercise physiologists of the various factors that determine performance. In the broadest sense exercise physiology encompasses the disciplines of physiology (that is, how the different body systems function and their integrated response), biochemistry (the chemical reactions which occur within cells and which are essential for the maintenance of life) and biomechanics and kinesiology (the study of motion).

In the horse advances have lagged behind those in man, except for excellent pioneering work carried out by veterinarians at the Swedish University of Agricultural Sciences at Uppsala. It has only been in this decade that an impetus to such research activities has occurred, especially with the recent establishment of equine exercise units in a number of universities and institutes around the world. The possibility of carrying out such research is due to a large number of technological advances in engineering, instrumentation and computerization which permit the monitoring of horses at work. Today the cost of much of this equipment means that its use is restricted to specialized laboratories and the wealthier patrons of racing. However, in the future it is likely that more sophisticated equipment will become available to the veterinarians in practice.

It is the purpose of this chapter to describe briefly the areas of research presently being undertaken and how they may be of relevance to both owners and trainers, as well as to veterinarians. The knowledge acquired has potential benefit in a number of ways, in particular in assessing potential and fitness; in improving athletic performance by defining appropriate training methods for specific tasks (it should be stressed that the aim is not just to improve race records by enhancing performance in the elite animal, but also to improve overall performance no matter what class of animal. This also occurs in human athletics where scientific advances have aided and reduced the risks of those competing in leisure activities. It should also be realized that the scientist is not trying to supplant the rider or trainer, but rather to establish guidelines which can then be adjusted to the requirements of the individual horse); and in the prevention, early detection and/or evaluation of injuries or disease. In addition what constitutes an adequate recovery period before training recommences can also be evaluated.

It should be appreciated that these benefits are not just directed towards owners; much more importantly they are concerned with the welfare of the horse by ensuring that risks to its health are kept to a minimum. For example, correct training to develop adequate fitness reduces the chance of fatigue during competition and, therefore, the risk of being injured, for example, by falling at a fence.

Effective and maintained movement is dependent upon integration between all the body's systems, including the muscular, nervous (central and peripheral), cardiovascular and respiratory systems. The first two are essential for effective movement, while the latter are of vital importance in maintenance, as they are responsible for assisting in the fuelling of working muscle, as well as the disposal of waste products and the dissipation of heat generated during intense muscular activity. In addition, psychological factors (i.e. the mental attitude of the horse) are important in helping to optimize training effects. Unfortunately this aspect is almost impossible to evaluate scieetifically, and is, therefore, dependent on the rapport between owner/trainer/rider and horse.

The responses to exercise can be investigated by monitoring horses while they are being ridden in the open. Devices enabling the examination of the different systems have been developed which can be applied non-invasively, safely and atraumatically to the horse. Information from these devices can be either recorded onto a cassette recorder carried by the rider and later decoded, or transmitted by radio signals to a receiver located at distances of up to half a mile or more away and a printout of the signal obtained. An alternative method is to monitor horses while exercising on a treadmill (Figure 185). Although treadmills have been available for a number of years for training horses, their construction has only allowed horses to be worked at a walk and slow trot. However, machines have recently become available which allow horses to be trotted, cantered or galloped at near race speeds. This means that conditions encountered in racing can be simulated in a controlled reproducible manner, and in some laboratories in a constant environment. Therefore, a better comparison both between animals and within an animal at different stages of training can be investigated. Horses adapt very quickly to working on a treadmill, even at higher speeds. Their ready acceptance to walk onto the machine on repeated occasions indicates that they are not distressed by exercising in this manner. With treadmills installed in laboratories, very expensive monitoring equipment can be attached to the horse to evaluate the functioning of the different systems.

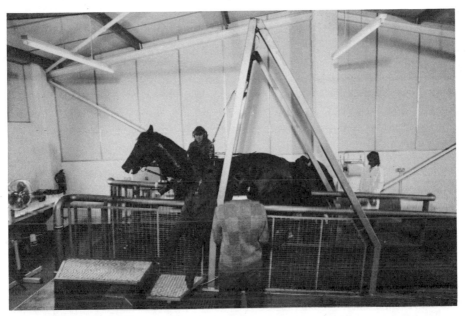

Figure 185 A treadmill

The capacity to monitor horses at exercise, whether it be in the field or on a treadmill, is not only of great assistance in enabling us to develop a better understanding of the horse's responses and to determine an animal's potential, but should also prove of great use in assessing exercise-related clinical problems. No matter how proficient the veterinarian, minor ailments (often classed as subclinical diseases) can be missed when the horse is examined at rest. It is often only during hard exercise that problems affecting, for example, a portion of the lungs become evident, because at rest only a fraction of the total capacity is utilized, while at maximal work all reserves are called upon. In the past evaluation has had to be largely subjective. Today the monitoring equipment available allows an objective evaluation to be made.

A variety of studies have been undertaken to find out how different systems function during exercise, and this knowledge can be utilized by the veterinarian.

Muscular system

An understanding of the changes that occur within muscle during training and the causes of fatigue have been brought about by the ability to collect small pieces of muscle from horses following exercise. This has helped in prescribing training programmes for specific equestrian disciplines and the correct diets to enhance performance. For example, the muscular adaptions necessary for endurance are different from those necessary for sprinting.

Such information is not only of use to the trainer/rider, but is also vital for the veterinarian trying to understand the cause of exertional rhabdomyolysis (azoturia – see p. 226). By monitoring the levels of certain enzymes (creatine kinase, CK, lactic dehydrogenase, LDH, and aspartate aminotransferase, AST or GOT) in the blood it is possible to evaluate fitness, as well as to diagnose exertional rhabdomyolysis. As an animal becomes fitter, strenuous exercise is less likely to cause minor damage, so that measurement of the above enzymes approximately six hours after exercise can be a useful guide to fitness. Generally once a horse is fit, these enzymes remain remarkably constant from month to month.

Cardiovascular system

Recent research has shown how the heart can increase its rate very markedly during exercise. Heart rates of 220–250 beats/minute occur during racing. This increased pumping of blood to the working muscles ensures that their elevated oxygen demands are satisfied. For the trainer/rider a major advance in this field has been the commercial availability of an instrument to monitor accurately a horse's heart rate during exercise and recovery. This device is called an 'on board' heart-rate meter. Two small electrodes are placed over the heart, one under the saddle near the withers and the other on the belly under the girth strap, and connected by leads to a small meter which can be attached to the rider's wrist or thigh. A digital readout of the heart rate is displayed (Figure 186). The heart-rate meter can be used like a rev counter

Figure 186   A jockey's watch to show the heart rate

(tachometer) in a car, enabling the effort expended by the horse to be measured accurately. This means that training programmes can be designed so that the horse is working at fixed heart rates, depending on the training effect required, and always within its capacity. The horse's fitness can be assessed both by the heart rate attained during exercise and by the rate of recovery when the animal is at rest. A horse will develop a lower heart rate for the same amount of work as it becomes fitter and recovery will be quicker.

The ability to record electrocardiograms (ECGs – electrical signals from the heart indicating events occurring within it) while horses are working is especially useful to the veterinarian. These tests can be best performed using a treadmill. Abnormalities of heart function are sometimes evident only when a horse is working. This is true of certain arrhythmias (abnormal rhythms in the heart beat). Examples of such arrhythmias which are of clinical interest to a veterinarian are paroxysmal atrial fibrillation and extrasystoles (heart beats which originate from non-pacemaker cells of the myocardium). Both these arrhythmias are known to be associated with diminished performance, but they are not always evident in the resting ECG; it may require an exercise ECG recorded at a fast work rate to clinch the diagnosis. On the other hand, irregularities such as dropped heart beats can occur at rest but if they do not occur at exercise they can then be considered of little significance.

Blood   Changes in both the cellular and water fractions of blood during exercise and training have been studied extensively. The information gained has been of great benefit to the veterinarian. For example, it has been shown that exercise itself produces alterations in the number and proportion of the different types of white cells. These changes are similar to those seen in certain diseases. Therefore it is important that, when blood samples are taken to help in a clinical diagnosis, they should not be collected within eight hours of exercise, especially if it has been strenuous. Although it is often claimed that a horse's poor performance may be due to anaemia, in fact true anaemia is uncommon in Europe. Because of the horse's capacity to store red blood cells in the spleen, the best way of detecting anaemia which may affect performance is by measuring the horse's blood volume and red blood cell count after emptying the spleen's reserves with maximal exercise. Using this method, it is possible to discover whether poor performance is due to a low red count or to too high a count (referred to as polycythemia), which is associated with overtraining, leading to hormonal disturbances.

Respiratory system

All owners and riders are concerned about the soundness of their horse's wind. In scientific terms this refers to how the airways from the nose to the lungs and the millions of small sacs within the lungs are functioning. The major role of this system is to allow the passage of oxygen into the blood and the removal of the waste product carbon dioxide arising from cellular metabolism. In the airways themselves conditions can occur which limit the effective flow of air.

Until comparatively recently a veterinarian's assessment of respiratory conditions depended upon a physical examination of a horse at rest and exercise. Although such methods can disclose frank respiratory disease, they do not measure how well a lung or an airway is functioning, nor do they always indicate the nature of a malfunction. Disturbances in airflow caused by constrictions of the airways in the lungs or by paralysis of the larynx can be detected by radiostethoscope. This can be applied over the windpipe so that recordings can be made while the horse is exercising. Other devices to record chest expansion and various other changes within the lungs that may indicate how the lungs are coping at exercise and possible disease are also being developed. These can be applied while the horse is exercising on a treadmill, and some even when the horse is worked in the field. The ability of the veterinarian to detect changes in how the lungs are functioning should be greatly enhanced, although the old, everyday methods will still be of major use. The development of the endoscope has also greatly facilitated the veterinarian's ability to examine the upper and lower airways of the horse. Its full potential is realized when examination is carried out immediately after exercise, when disturbances in the larynx can be best assessed. It is also used to evaluate the degree of bleeding from the lungs after exercise, as well as the production of material that may indicate infection within the lungs.

Locomotion

Until recently there has been a general lack of quantitative methods to analyse effectively gait and locomotory pattern and to ascertain how small differences, whether inherent or disease-induced, may affect performance. However, advances are now being made in developing often very sophisticated systems which permit gait analysis for assessment of performance potential, as well as improving the diagnosis of lameness. Gait and locomotory analysis is based upon the evaluation of limb placement, movement and coordination, and the forces acting on the limb. For analysis of locomotion, high-speed cinematography is used, the data from the different phases being fed into a computer. Such equipment has provided detailed insights into the phases of the locomotory cycle, and has also been used to relate respiratory and locomotory patterns. It has been found that, once into a steady canter or gallop, the healthy horse has linked respiration and gait patterns, breathing once every stride. In respiratory conditions this normal pattern is upset.

Forces acting between the hoof and the ground can now be analysed by the use of measuring shoes and force plates, the sophistication of these depending on in how many directions the forces can be measured. Therefore both marked and subtle changes in the pressures exerted by each limb during locomotion can be determined. At the present time most of these devices can only be used in the standing or slowly moving horse, but developments should soon allow effects to be measured at a fast trot or gallop.

Until now much of the new equipment has been used mainly to study actions in the normal animal, essential if clinical problems are to be assessed correctly. However, it is likely that in the next five years or so these techniques will become available to the veterinarian for diagnosis. They should also help us establish which conformational problems are significant to performance, and show that a number of traditional ideas are incorrect. They will also provide information which will result in better-designed shoes for both the normal and, more importantly, the abnormal animal, as well as racetracks that impose less risk of injury.

Dietary requirements

Unfortunately, at the time of writing, very little work has been done to determine the dietary requirements of the exercising horse. This has led to many misconceptions and myths, often fuelled by companies selling feed and supplements, in which the benefits of adding certain compounds to the diet having been stressed without any scientific backing. In this the situation is no different to that for man. However, the possibility of carrying out controlled nutritional studies in conjunction with horses working in a regulated manner should result in better information being available to the horse owner on what additional, if any, vitamins, etc., should be fed to an animal during training. This will also be of great assistance to veterinarians, as often, when horses are not doing as well as expected, they are asked if supplements should be given. Whether there is a place for such things as 'glycogen loading', increasing the fat content of the diet and other manipulations, which are used to help generate energy in human athletes, is currently being evaluated. However, early results indicate that, as would be expected, the responses of humans and horses are not identical.

49
THE PURCHASE OF HORSES AND VETERINARY CERTIFICATION

It cannot be emphasized too strongly that would-be purchasers of a horse should, whenever possible, have it examined by a veterinarian, and should not complete the purchase until they have in their possession the certificate indicating the result of this examination.

A buyer may not consider this necessary when the seller can produce a recent certificate of such an examination, but nevertheless the wisest plan is to obtain an independent opinion because the animal may not have shown symptoms of a serious defect previously.

Should the buyer wish to have the animal on trial, he must remember that nothing must be done to it, such as removing a mane or replacing the shoes (even if those the animal is wearing require removal) until he has made up his mind whether to retain or return, because should he do so, it constitutes 'purchase' and legally the seller is entitled to refuse return.

The buyer must understand that, from the standpoint of the veterinarian, the animal can only be classified as suitable or unsuitable for purchase. The veterinary certificate will list the defects detected in the horse and offer an opinion on the significance of the fault in relation to the purpose for which the animal is being purchased – for example, racing, dressage or breeding.

Very often a prospective buyer may have noticed a particular vice, and he should always mention this to the veterinarian because some vices or bad habits are not always found at the time of an examination for purchase. He should also remember that a veterinary certificate does not indicate freedom from vice. Nevertheless the seller is under an obligation to disclose to the buyer any vice or bad habit that is within his knowledge as failure to do so can nullify the transaction and the animal can be returned.

Traditionally the maxim *caveat emptor* (see p. 672) has been the rule of the law, and a party who has bought a defective horse has no remedy, unless there is evidence either of express warranty or of fraud. In the general sale of a horse the seller only warrants it to be an animal of the description it appears to be and nothing more; if the purchaser makes no inquiries as to its qualities and it turns out to be unfit for use, he cannot recover against the seller.

Recently consumer legislation has altered this situation and sales have been nullified on the basis of manifest or 'hidden' defects being shown to have been present before or at the time of sale. The current situation, including the professional liability of a veterinarian who undertakes an examination for purchase, is discussed in chapter 50.

Common conditions rendering a horse unfit for purchase

It is impossible to lay down rules for conditions that render horses fit or unfit for purchase. All decisions must take account of the future use for which the horse is required and, to a certain extent, the value placed on the individual. For example, a horse with partial vision may be suitable for purchase for breeding while being unsuitable for all athletic duties. Similarly, a horse with total laryngeal hemiplegia (paralysis) will usually be considered unfit for purchase for racing or breeding, but will be capable of use as a hack or even as a hunter.

However, it is helpful to consider the most common defects of the organ systems which are likely to appear on veterinary certificates.

Defects of eyes   Absence of an eye, collapse of an eye, any form or size of corneal opacity, lenticular or capsular cataract, paralysis of the iris, or blindness from any cause constitute serious defects. Inflammation or injury of the iris and pupil (iridocyclitis) and loss of orbital pressure may be an indication of periodic ophthalmia and should be considered a serious defect. Photophobia and conjunctivitis may be temporary or indicative of a more serious problem. Other more subtle abnormalities detected with an ophthalmoscope are rare but usually serious – for example, retinal atrophy.

Defects of wind (the respiratory system)   The chief abnormalities of wind are laryngeal hemiplegia (whistling or roaring), chronic obstructive pulmonary disease (COPD, broken wind), coughing and bleeding.

The main respiratory disorders are discussed in detail in chapter 2. However, in relation to purchase the condition of laryngeal hemiplegia, frequently demonstrated clinically as an abnormal inspiratory noise described as a 'whistle' or a 'roar', has been the cause of great controversy in recent years. Examination of the upper airway of horses has been greatly facilitated by the introduction of flexible fibre-optic endoscopes which allow visual examination of the larynx before and after exercise. Thus, the examination of wind of highly priced horses will often involve exercise and endoscopic tests. The results of such examinations have not always been simple to interpret. The laryngeal paralysis (usually left-sided) may be partial or complete. Cases of partial paralysis may or may not produce abnormal inspiratory noises and detectability of the noise may be altered by the fitness of the horse or concurrent respiratory infection.

There is little doubt that many horses with partial paralysis perform satisfactorily. However, the progressive nature and probable heritability of the defect make unreserved recommendation of affected horses impossible.

Other respiratory sounds are emitted under exertion by some horses, but unless they are connected with disease, injury, operation or acquired alteration of structure, they should not be regarded as unsoundness of wind. High-blowing may be due to excitement (showing condition or freshness). It should, and often does, disappear with exercise or as the horse settles down to steady work.

The term 'bleeding' is more correctly called exercise-induced pulmonary haemorrhage (EIPH – see p. 51; see also epistaxis – p. 32). As this name suggests, affected horses bleed into the substance of the lung during strenuous exercise and this may adversely affect their performance. After exercise blood passes into the respiratory tract and may appear at the nostrils, particularly as the horse lowers its head. Endoscopic examination of horses worldwide shows that a high percentage of horses have blood in their trachea (windpipe) after exercise. A smaller number show bleeding at the nostrils. Nevertheless, clinical evidence or a history of bleeding constitutes a serious abnormality sufficient to advise against purchase for strenuous athletic duties.

Persistent purulent nasal discharges may be bilateral, related to infectious bacterial or viral diseases, or unilateral in cases of sinusitis or guttural pouch disease. Coughing is a common sign of respiratory disease and may be related to infection or allergy and may be temporary or persistent. Purchase should be delayed until coughing has ceased or the condition investigated to the purchaser's satisfaction.

Defective limb or action Lameness, if present in any degree is a serious abnormality. The cause is immaterial. The action may be peculiar or objectionable, such as dishing, but when due to conformation it does not amount to lameness. Stringhalt is a definite defect and shivering a serious one, which is often rapidly progressive.

Thickening or inflammation of tendons, especially the flexor tendons of the forelimbs, must always be considered a serious defect when purchasing a horse for athletic duties. Such tendon strains are frequently recurrent despite treatment. Osteoarthrosis of joints is of great significance when related to lameness or pain, but many mature horses may be unaffected by old injuries and even fractures. In these cases the examining vet's opinion is all-important.

Incoordination of the hindlimbs or all four limbs must always be regarded as a serious defect. The most common cause in young horses is pressure on the spinal cord in the neck region (the wobbler syndrome – see p. 274). Other causes are traumatic injuries to the head and neck and certain infections such as the neurological form of rhinopneumonitis and protozoal encephalomyelitis (seen in horses imported from the USA).

Existing disease or effects of disease or accident   Diseases of the heart, respiratory and digestive systems, urinary and genital organs, skin, feet and eyes all constitute serious abnormalities. Dribbling of the urine may be due to a calculus or sabulous (gritty) accumulation in the bladder or congenital malformation. If diarrhoea is present, it must be noted; it may be temporary but the purchaser should await its disappearance. Sometimes profuse staling occurs when the animal is being ridden: this may be only a peculiarity of temper, but must be mentioned. For disorders of these systems, see the relevant chapters.

Blemishes   Any blemish, such as scars or firing marks, devalue a horse but may be of no consequence if the animal is not lame. Broken knees may indicate a tendency to fall in some cases, the significance of which will depend upon the work the horse may have to perform. All blemishes must be mentioned. Capped hocks and elbows do not interfere with work but some people object to them as an eyesore.

Vices and bad habits   When these impair the natural usefulness of the animal, they will render it unfit for purchase. Several may pass unnoticed at the time of the examination, for example, windsucking. A horse that is a crib-biter or a windsucker must be rejected. A windsucking horse is said to 'crib in the air', that is, without seizing any object or supporting the chin, and the habit produces no abnormal wear of the teeth as in crib-biting. Weaving wears out the forelimbs and leads to an unsteady gait. Box walking and weaving may cause horses to lose body condition rapidly. These vices may be temporary, associated with a change of environment or separation from companions. A distinction must be drawn between vice and mere force of habit. It is sometimes the case that a horse may prove unsuitable to the new owner and may develop bad habits as a result of this (see chapter 42).

Defective conformation   This is largely a matter of taste or opinion: a horse should not be rejected because of 'bad shape'. Naturally there is a great difference of opinion among veterinarians, judges and owners, and reference should be made to chapter 44.

Responsibility of the examiner for purchase

The responsibility is to the one who pays the fee and the opinion given after the examination may be oral or written. The latter is preferable.

   The veterinary profession has received very clear instructions on both the method of examination and the type of certificate to be used. The procedure is laid down in the Royal College of Veterinary Surgeons/British Veterinary Association Joint Memorandum, *The Examination of Horses on Behalf of a Purchaser* (revised edition), BVA Publications, London, 1974. All veterinary certificates should be issued on these forms; where insufficient space is

available on the sheet, additional sheets may be attached to the official form.
The format of the certificate is shown on p. 667.

Procedure to be adopted when examining a horse for purchase

Before the animal is brought out of the loosebox or stable, it should be
observed, undisturbed, by the examiner. Very often a vice such as crib-biting
or wind-sucking will be spotted which might escape notice later on. Its
attitude while resting should receive particular attention. Standing with one
forefoot in advance of the other or frequent shifting of the weight from one
forefoot to the other is suggestive of foot lameness or disease. Having
watched the animal for a few minutes, the examiner should enter the box or
stall, approaching the animal on its left (near) side and making it move over
to its right (off) side, paying particular attention to the movement of the tail
and hind limbs for signs of stringhalt, shivering and incoordination.

The teeth can now be examined for age, the pulse taken and the heart
auscultated (this must be done again later after testing for wind), and a
preliminary examination of the eyes can be made (this again to be repeated
after testing for wind when the pupils will be well dilated). The horse is then
led out quietly with a bridle or halter and stood in a convenient spot to
enable the examiner to walk around it. During this preliminary inspection
the colour, markings (natural and any acquired such as firing marks) and sex
can be written down. In addition the following defects may be seen: nasal
discharge, deformity of the face, lips or nostrils, corneal opacities, scars, skin
eruptions, bursal distensions, marks of brushing, speedy-cuts, capped
elbows and hocks, bowed or thickened tendons, odd feet, sandcracks,
asymmetry of the pelvis, muscle wasting, thoroughpin, spavin, curb,
windgalls and so on.

The person in charge of the horse should now be asked to walk it away
from the examiner, giving it full use of its head, i.e. *not* holding the bridle or
halter close to the head, for a distance of not less than 30 metres, and then
back. It should be trotted over the same distance. It is a rather common
fallacy that any lameness will become more apparent the faster the animal
moves.

Each veterinary examiner has his or her own method for the next
procedure. Some prefer to examine both fore and hind limbs, for example, in
sequence, but personally I prefer to start on the horses left (near side) and,
having finished here, proceed to the right (off side), working backwards
from the hind limb to the front leg, the same examination being identical on
both sides.

Starting at the head, I examine the eyes, teeth (the tongue is grasped and
the condition of the cheek teeth noted on both sides), nostril, the
submaxillary space, parotid gland, poll, throat, larynx, trachea (at this stage
it is convenient to make the animal cough by squeezing the trachea and note
the tone of the cough). I note if there is any sign of a jugular pulse, then raise

CERTIFICATE OF VETERINARY EXAMINATION OF A HORSE ON BEHALF OF A PURCHASER

Description of horse:

LEFT SIDE / COTE GAUCHE

WHORLS MUST BE SHOWN THUS - 'X' AND DESCRIBED BELOW IN DETAIL

RIGHT SIDE / COTE DROIT

FORE ANTERIEURS

HIND POSTERIEURS

Please ensure that diagram and written description agree. Also type or use block capitals

MUZZLE   NEZ

WHITE MARKINGS TO BE SHOWN IN RED

Name of Horse (or Breeding)	Breed or Type	Colour	Sex	Age or Year of Birth	Approximate Height

Head ....

....

Limbs:
    L.F. ....

    R.F. ....

    L.H. ....

    R.H. ....

Body ....

....

Acquired marks ....

REPORT
This is to certify that at the request of (name and address).........................

....

I have examined the horse described above, the property of (name and address) ....

....

at (place of examination) ....

and I find no clinical signs of disease, injury or physical abnormality other than those here recorded.

Signs of disease or injury: ....

....

....

Other Observations: ....

....

....

Opinion:
(a) On this examination I find no clinical signs of disease, injury or physical abnormality likely to affect the animal's usefulness as a

(b) In my opinion, on this examination, the conditions set out above are not likely to affect the animal's usefulness as a

(c) In my opinion, on this examination this animal is not suitable for purchase as a ....
This clinical examination was carried out in accordance with the standard procedure recommended by the Royal College of Veterinary Surgeons and the British Veterinary Association (Joint Memorandum on the Examination of Horses, 1976). Veterinarians have developed a general routine of examination which has been found to be satisfactory as a means of detecting signs of disease and injury. The examination is conducted in five stages and all the stages should be completed. If this has not been possible, it should be made clear on the certificate in what way the examination has been varied, and that any opinions are based on this restricted examination.

| Stage 1 Preliminary examination | Stage 3 Strenuous exercise | Stage 5 The second trot and foot examination |
| Stage 2 Trotting up | Stage 4 A period of rest | |

The opinion hereinbefore expressed is based solely on the clinical examination conducted substantially in accordance with the aforesaid procedure and is made and given subject to the qualification that the said animal may be presently subject to some previously administered drug, or medicament intended to, or having the effect of masking or concealing some disease, injury or physical abnormality which would otherwise presently be clinically discoverable.

Warranty
If a purchaser wishes to obtain a warranty covering such matters as exact height, freedom from vices, the non-administration of drugs prior to examination, or the animal's existing performance as a hunter, show-jumper, riding pony, eventer, etc, he is advised to seek such warranty in writing from the vendor, as these are matters between vendor and purchaser and are not the responsibility of the veterinarian..
*No radiological or other specialised techniques were included. The certificate does not cover an examination for pregnancy.

*Owing to .... it was not possible to carry out stage(s) .... of the standard procedure recommended by the RCVS and the BVA (Joint Memorandum on the Examination of Horses 1976). My opinion is therefore subject to my having been able to carry out a partial examination only and I have been unable to ascertain whether any clinical signs of disease, injury or abnormality would have manifested themselves in the course of that part/those parts of the standard procedure which I was unable to carry out.
*Amend as required.   Time and date of examination:...

Veterinarian's name:...................................   Address:..

Signed:..   ....

the jugular. Then I examine the withers, shoulder point, forearm, knee, cannon, flexor tendons, fetlock, pastern and coronet; next, the elbow, back of forearm, knee, cannon, fetlock, and suspensory and sesamoid region, pastern and foot, testing the lateral cartilages for their elasticity. Holding the foot in the left hand, I press with the fingers of the right into the hollow of the heel, and flex the foot, noting any evidence of pain such as flinching. The foot is then examined for any signs of corns, thrush, seedy toe or canker. Whenever possible, the shoes should be removed if a really satisfactory examination is to be made; if the seller objects, this cannot be insisted upon, but a note should always be made to this effect.

Having finished here, I proceed to the chest, back, loins and croup, crural (leg) region, stifle, front of leg, hock, cannon, fetlock, pastern and coronet; next the quarter, buttock, thigh, back of leg, point and sides of hock, flexor tendons, suspensory, fetlock, heels and hind foot, which is to be raised, the hock flexed and the limb abducted. Next I raise the tail and inspect the anus, vulva, perineum and dock. While the fore and hind limbs are being examined, the inner side of the opposite limb should be carefully inspected, paying special attention to the groin, sheath, scrotum and testicles if entire and in the mare the udder. The inside of the groin is frequently a site of sarcoids (warts or fibrous tumours) which can cause trouble (see p. 564).

The wind should now be tested, and this is guided, to a certain extent, by the breed and condition of the animal. For example, if the animal is a mare advanced in pregnancy, this may be neither practicable nor advisable. In the case of the lighter breeds it is customary for the animal to be ridden, starting off with a slow canter round the examiner and then, at a signal from him or her, the animal is put into a gallop, to be finally pulled up (preferably after coming up an incline) beside the examiner when he or she so indicates. Alternatively, and this is usually employed with all stallions and yearlings, the animal should be lunged until sweating occurs.

After testing for wind, the heart should be re-examined. It should not be forgotten that an unfit horse, in some instances being fed for sale, may take as long as half an hour after a wind test before his breathing and heart settle down. A normal heart should settle in about six to eight minutes after any but the most excessive exercise. Also the respiratory system cannot function efficiently in the presence of a diseased or disordered heart, and a careful examination of the respiratory movements should enable the examiner to detect a defective heart. When carrying out an examination for wind, if it happens to be a windy day, proximity to trees should be avoided and the examiner should stand with his back to the wind. Every precaution must be taken to avoid extraneous noises.

The eyes should be examined directly after the test for wind and while the pupils are dilated, preferably in a shady spot, loosebox or stable. In the event of the examination being made inside, be careful to avoid white-washed walls behind the animal. These may cause a reflection in the eyes, giving the external appearance of cataract. The examination of the eyes should be made with an ophthalmoscope.

The height is taken at the highest point of the withers, ensuring that the animal is standing on level ground and with all four feet in alignment. The shoes, where practicable, can now be removed, the feet examined, and the soles pressed with the pincers to detect any sensitivity. Thin soles increase an animal's susceptibility to bruising. The animal should now be rested for half an hour and then led out and trotted away from and back to the examiner.

In the case of a harness horse it is important that the purchase is not completed until the animal has been driven for a few miles; the journey should include an ascent and a descent of a hill. This may identify any faults which would render it useless for the purposes for which it is being bought and which would not be detected in the customary examination for purchase. If possible, the person who is going to drive it later on should do so now.

The following recommendations are taken from an unpublished paper prepared by Major A. C. Fraser, BVSc, PhD, MRCVS, on the subject of examination of wind. He emphasizes that, when examining a horse for wind, the object is to exert him, not to exhaust him.

1. With Thoroughbred horses in training the pace given should be a half-speed canter over 3–4 furlongs, followed by a faster gallop over a distance agreed upon with the trainer.
2. Hacks, hunters and polo ponies should be tried more slowly over a longer distance.
3. Draught animals should be harnessed and driven uphill with a wheel locked.
4. Untrained animals or those too young or too small to be ridden may be lunged at this stage.

In summary, the animal should be given sufficient exercise to achieve the following objects: to make him breathe deeply and rapidly so that any abnormal breathing sounds may be heard; to cause his heart to beat strongly so that any abnormalities may be detected; and to tire him somewhat so that any strains or injuries may be revealed by stiffness or lameness after a period of rest.

The use of special techniques

Advances in veterinary science have led to the use of various techniques to extend the scope of the standard examination for purchase. Particularly, radiographic examination of the lower limbs, fibre-optic endoscopic examination of the upper respiratory tract and blood sampling have become popular in cases of expensive racehorses, eventers and showjumpers. Rectal palpation and vaginal examination of the internal genital organs of fillies going to stud and bacterial cultures of the external genital organs of mares and stallions prior to purchase have become commonplace. Collection of semen samples for quality evaluation from stallions and colts out of training is sometimes required.

These techniques may be useful when correctly applied by a veterinarian and used in conjunction with his clinical examination. The danger of all such tests is that they become fashionable and may be requested by the purchaser without full appreciation of the limitations of the particular test. This can lead to problems of interpretation. Such extra tests should be performed whenever the examining veterinarian feels that they would be helpful, and the implications of the results of such tests should be discussed in advance with all parties. The permission of the vendor to carry out these tests must be sought in advance. The problems associated with the use of radiographs are well expressed by Peter Webbon, BVetMed, DVR, MRCVS, in *Equine Veterinary Journal* (1981), vol. 13, pp. 15–18:

Radiographs of a diagnostic quality need to be taken and interpreted by a veterinarian who is reasonably well versed in radiological interpretation. Occasionally a lesion will be overlooked or misinterpreted and the radiographs will be retained so that the veterinarian's judgement can be challenged. Nevertheless, if the examination is properly conducted, it is the prospective purchaser who must accept the inherent limitations of the technique, not the examining veterinarian.

The results of all radiographic examinations should be viewed in the light of the clinical and other findings. As part of a clinical investigation radiography is a precise procedure providing detailed information about an area to which attention has already been drawn.

In diagnostic work a lesion is likely to be found and each radiograph is inspected with this in mind. When several areas of a clinically normal horse are radiographed the veterinarian not only has to recognize any changes which are present but also has to assess their present and future significance in the absence of any clinical abnormality.

Reasons for radiography as part of an examination for a purchaser

There are three main reasons for radiography (almost invariably of the limbs):

1. The veterinarian may wish to radiograph a specific area of the horse because of observations made during the clinical examination. In this instance radiography is performed as in any other clinical investigation and the problems which confront the veterinarian are no more than those of any other case of lameness. If confirmation of the clinical suspicion is obtained radiographically, an opinion can be given depending on the intended use of the horse.

2. The purchaser asks that radiographs should be taken of a clinically normal horse. It is under these circumstances that radiography is often used as a prognostic screening device. Such radiographs will occasionally be of assistance to show (or at least appear to show) that a lesion which subsequently is diagnosed was not present at the time of examination. On balance more problems will be caused for the veterinarian by the radiography of clinically normal horses than will be averted.

3. A third possible reason for radiography is at the request of a vendor who wishes, provided that the result is favourable, to warrant the horse sound. Chandler (1978)* considers that a vendor is entitled to such specialist advice from the profession, but warns of the inherent dangers, particularly in the manner in which the opinion is given. In all such instances a verbal report is to be preferred.

The examination itself should consist of producing an adequate number of technically adequate radiographs of the appropriate areas and presenting the facts in the form of a report. This report can then be incorporated into the general examination before an opinion on the horse is given. The requirement, as for a clinical examination, is simply that the veterinarian should exercise reasonable care in producing the radiographs and commenting on them.

The date of the examination should be marked on the film, together with a positive means of identification such as the name or brand mark, preferably not in code form.

The veterinarian is required to identify any variations from the normal state and to assess their significance. There are undoubtedly difficulties associated with an assessment of the present or future significance of a radiographic change. If the initial radiographs reveal an abnormality on which the veterinarian is not prepared to comment without further films, these should be taken at the purchaser's request and expense.

---

* N. Chandler (1978), 'Certification of Horses for Change of Ownership', *Equine Veterinary Journal*, vol. 10, pp. 75–7.

50

THE LEGAL IMPLICATIONS OF
THE PURCHASE OF A HORSE

The starting point when discussing the purchase of a horse can be found in the maxim *caveat emptor* or let the buyer beware. This rule, at common law, led to the position that when a buyer of goods required no warranty he took the risk of quality upon himself and had no remedy even if he could show that the representation had been fraudulent. *Caveat emptor* places the purchaser in the position whereby either he must rely on his own skill and judgement in assessing the horse or he may require the vendor to give a condition or warranty on the horse. If the former, he may have the horse examined professionally, thereby giving him some redress in law if the examination is performed negligently.

The old maxim has, to some extent, been mitigated in its severity by the intervention of statute, essentially by the Sale of Goods Act 1893, which codified the preceding common law, and the Sale of Goods Act 1979, which, while repealing the 1893 Act, largely re-enacts the pre-existing law. It is worth noting that horses are regarded in law as 'things' and their ownership is transferred by ordinary contracts for sale with no special features.

By order of section 14(2) of the 1979 Act, where a vendor sells goods in the ordinary course of business, there is an implied condition that the goods supplied under the contract are of merchantable quality, except that there is no condition with regard to (a) defects specifically drawn to the buyer's attention before the contract is made, or (b) defects which, if the buyer examines the goods before the contract is made, that examination ought to reveal. Goods will be of merchantable quality if they are fit for the purpose for which goods of that kind are commonly bought, as is reasonable to expect, having regard to any description applied to them, the price (if relevant) and all other relevant circumstances.

Fitness for purpose and its requirements are contained in section 14(3), which states that if the seller of goods is selling in the course of a business and the buyer, expressly or by implication, makes known to the seller any particular purpose for which the goods are being bought, there is an implied condition that the goods supplied under the contract are reasonably fit for that purpose. This applies whether or not the purpose is one for which such goods are commonly supplied, except where the circumstances show that the buyer does not rely, or that it is unreasonable for him to rely, on the seller's skill or judgement.

The purchaser frequently requires a condition or warranty to be attached to the horse before purchase, and a breach of the former by the seller entitles the purchaser to return the horse and be restored to the *status quo ante* by the return of his or her money and any costs incurred.

However, more frequently a horse is sold as 'warranted' and a breach of such warranty entitles the purchaser to claim monetary damages. Often horses are warranted with no further details as to what the warranty actually covers, and such warranties are deemed in law to cover the horse's soundness only.

The expression 'soundness and freedom from vice' is a time-honoured expression commonly used, and judicial interpretation has, in the past, been fraught with difficulties.

In *Riddell* v. *Burnard* (1847) Parke B stated that 'soundness' implies the 'absence of any disease or seeds of disease in the animal at the time of sale which actually diminishes or, in its progress, would diminish its usefulness in the work it would normally and properly be applied.'

The case of *Coates* v. *Stephens* (1838) held that even a temporary injury amounted to unsoundness and the onus of proof is on the defendant to show that it is only temporary. Judicial findings of unsoundness have been, for example, a cough (*Coates* v. *Stephens* (1838)).

The phrase 'freedom from vice' has been held to mean either a defect in temperament which makes the horse dangerous or diminishes its usefulness, or a bad habit which is injurious to its health (such as crib-biting) (*Scholefield* v. *Robb* (1839)).

When a warranty is made after the sale there must be a new consideration to support it (*Roscorla* v. *Thomas* (1942)). The reason for this is the general rule that past consideration is no consideration. Therefore where a horse is sold and at a later stage the seller gives a guarantee as to its quality such consideration is deemed insufficient as it is past.

The intention of the party making the statement and whether it was part of the conditions of sale will be a question of fact. If the word 'warranted' is used, it will extend only to whatever terms are governed by the word: in *Antony* v. *Halstead* (1877) the statement 'a black horse rising five years, quiet to ride and drive and warranted sound' was held to be merely a warranty as to soundness. Where the word 'warranted' is used alone, it refers only to soundness and not to any description preceding it: in *Richardson* v. *Brown* (1823) a horse was described as 'a black gelding, five years old, has been constantly driving in the plough, warranted'.

Commonly horses will be sold by auction and an auctioneer is regarded as an agent to sell primarily for the vendor. However, upon the horse being knocked down, the auctioneer becomes the agent of the buyer also, but only for the purpose of signing the memorandum sufficient to satisfy section 40(1) of the Law of Property Act 1925.

The auctioneer has authority to sell but not to give warranties as to the horse sold unless he is expressly authorized to do so by the vendor (*Payne* v. *Lord Leconsfield* (1881)). The seller will be bound if the auctioneer acts within his ostensible authority even though he may disobey the specific instructions which were primarily given by the seller.

Auctioneers' catologues may contain distinct statements of fact which are intended to confer additional value on the horse sold and are consequently to be regarded as warranties (*Gee* v. *Lucas* (1867)), but in the case of *Harling* v. *Eddy* (1951) it was held that where an auctioneer gives an oral assurance inconsistent with the printed conditions of sale the oral promise will prevail.

In the case of a complaint concerning a stipulation in a warranty, it is usual at a sale by auction for there to be a condition that the horse should be returned within a signified time, and if this stipulation is not complied with no action can be brought (*Hinchcliffe* v. *Barwick* (1880)).

The purchaser should give notice to the vendor as soon as possible of any alleged breach of warranty, and if there is no time limit in the contract, the purchaser is not prejudiced by anything done by him before he discovers the defect.

The purchaser is not bound to return the horse as soon as he discovers the defect, so that, as in the case of *Head* v. *Tattersall* (1871), if an injury happens to the horse while in the buyer's possession, and without his fault, he is not liable for it and may still return the horse within the specified time.

By virtue of Section 11(4) of the 1979 Act, the buyer will be deemed to have accepted the horse if he intimates to the seller that he has accepted or if, after delivery and after the buyer has had an opportunity to inspect the horse, he either does some act in relation to the horse which is inconsistent with the seller's ownership or retains the horse for more than a reasonable time without intimating his rejection of it (Section 35). In cases falling under Section 11(4), although the buyer's action is still technically for breach of condition he can only recover damages (*Wallis* v. *Pratt* (1911)).

If there has been a breach of warranty, the amount of damages will be the difference between the value of the horse with the warranty and without (*Loughlan* v. *McDonnell* (1903)). The damages awarded can be considerable: in the case of a breach of warranty it has been held to include the loss of stud service fees. This case may, however, be doubted on the authority of *Sapwell* v. *Bass* (1907) in which it was held to be too remote and contingent.

An innocent misrepresentation by a vendor which has the effect of inducing a person to enter into a contract means that the contract may be rescinded by the buyer, and the court has a discretion to assess damages in lieu of recession (Section 2(2), Misrepresentation Act 1967). A person induced into a contract by a negligent misrepresentation is entitled to rescind that contract, as is the case with fraudulent misrepresentation; however, the remedies and measures of damages are tortious (*Esso Petroleum* v. *Mardon* (1976)). The consequence of this is that the remedy available to the buyer is that he may sue under Section 2(1) of the Misrepresentation Act 1967 whereby if he has suffered loss after a misrepresentation has been made to him and the person making the misrepresentation would be liable had the misrepresentation been made fraudulently, the person making such misrepresentation shall be liable notwithstanding that it had not been made fraudulently unless he proves that he had reasonable grounds to believe and did believe up to the time the contract was made that the facts represented were true; the buyer may also rescind the contract. The buyer may alternatively sue in court under the rule in *Hedley Byrne & Co. Ltd* v. *Heller & Partners Ltd* (1964) whereby the tortious duty of reasonable care will be applied to a statement made in the ordinary course of business and the person making the statement must exercise a reasonable degree of care if he knows or ought to have known that the other person was relying on the statement.

The courts have always sought to restrict the operation of exclusion clauses in contracts and, when the contract is not in writing, have required that the terms should be adequately drawn to the attention of the party agreeing to them. Where the contract is in writing notice is presented.

Concerning exemption clauses, the English courts have not, as a matter of common law, developed any general rule that exemption clauses must be fair or reasonable, but they have lain down a number of specific limitations on their efficacy. An exclusion clause must be clear and unambiguous and must cover the event which is alleged to have been excluded (*Photo Productions* v. *Securicor Transport* (1980)). The most important limitations are now to be found in the Unfair Contract Terms Act 1977 whereby some clauses are simply ineffective *ab initio* while others are made subject to the requirement of reasonableness. It will generally be for the party seeking to rely upon the clause to prove damages and to satisfy the requirement of reasonableness.

The ultimate question when considering an exclusion clause is, therefore, to what extent it is fair and reasonable to allow a party to rely on it; and the ability to exclude or modify the terms implied by the Sale of Goods Act is largely restricted by the Unfair Contract Terms Act.

Professional liability

Because of the probable high costs involved in purchasing a horse and the rule *caveat emptor*, prospective purchasers are well advised to consult a veterinarian before completing the sale. The professional liability of the vet is of great importance because if the vendor obtains a certificate of inspection the purchaser could have a claim against the veterinarian for negligence, as the certificate can be viewed as a form of limited guarantee.

The law whereby only a contractual client could sue his professional adviser for misrepresentation or negligence has changed, originally with the inroad made upon it by *Donoghue* v. *Stevenson* (1932) per Lord Atkin, and extended by *Hedley Byrne & Co. Ltd* v. *Heller & Partners Ltd* (1964).

The current situation is summarized by David Clark QC in the *Equine Veterinary Journal* (1984), vol. 16, no. 5, pp. 411–13, in an article entitled 'The Law and the Veterinarian':

It is well recognized in the veterinary profession that examinations for purchase should only be carried out on behalf of a prospective buyer and not on behalf of a seller. When a contract of sale of a horse is made, the deciding event is the decision of the buyer to buy; the decision of the seller to sell has been made at an earlier stage. It is, therefore, principally the buyer who will be relying on the veterinary advice in the certificate, whether the examination was, in fact, carried out on his behalf or on behalf of the seller.

Yet the veterinarian who examines on the instructions of the seller does not know who the buyer will be or the purpose for which the horse is required. It is clearly far safer and more satisfactory for the examination to be carried out for the buyer and for the certificate given to him to reflect the horse's suitability for the particular purposes and uses for which he, the buyer, requires it.

In the case of private individuals, we have seen that where, in the absence of specific express terms of contract, there are no warranties of quality or of suitability for any particular purpose, the maxim *caveat emptor* prevails.

However, as we have also seen:

When the seller sells in the course of a business, such as a horse dealer, the position is somewhat different in that the [Sale of Goods] Act [1979] provides certain implied conditions as to quality and suitability: these are of fairly limited effect in the case of a horse examined by a veterinarian for the purpose of purchase. In practice the buyer who has had a veterinary examination performed on his behalf will rely on his remedy against the professional person rather than against the seller. Hence it is the veterinarian who is more likely than the seller to be sued in the event of anything going wrong.

There are three essential classes of case in which complaints against the examining veterinarian are made. The first is where he has failed to detect a defect which existed and was apparent at the time of his examination and which any competent veterinarian should have detected. He has no defence to an action brought by the buyer, who will recover the purchase price as well as any further expenses (such as livery charges and subsequent veterinary fees) as damages for breach of contract and negligence.

The second case is where the buyer complains of a defect which the examining veterinary surgeon claims was not present at the time of examination but must have developed subsequently. Such an issue has to be resolved by the judge as a question of fact based on available evidence as to where and in what circumstances the defect first became apparent; also on expert evidence as to the way in which, and the speed with which this sort of defect can develop. In the examining veterinarian's defence, it is of course very valuable if the seller gives evidence that there was no such defect at the time of sale.

The third case, which gives rise to serious difficulty, is where the horse has a permanent or long-standing defect, perhaps of a congenital nature, which must by definition have been present at the time of the examination. The only available defence is that the defect was not one which ought reasonably to have been detected by an examination of the type undertaken. Hence the importance of having a set procedure for carrying out examination of horses for purchase and of not departing from that procedure [see chapter 49 above]. An unnecessary extra element of uncertainty would be introduced if the court had to decide between differing views as to what should or should not be included in the examination and what procedures should or should not be used [Clark, op. cit.].

Veterinarians have a duty to use reasonable care, the same duty as is owed by every person towards others who might be affected by his or her acts or omissions. However, that duty requires further elaboration regarding persons professing to exercise some professional skill because, as stated by Lord Justice Edmund-Davis in *Whitehouse* v. *Jordan* (1981): 'When you get a situation which involves the case of some special skill or competence, then the test as to whether there has been negligence or not is not like the test of the man on top of the Clapham omnibus because he has not got this special skill.'

The case of *Whitehouse* v. *Jordan* is of great importance in the field of medical negligence and the nature of the duty owed by a medical practitioner as contained in the words of Edmund-Davis L. J.

It may be said that, because of the duty owed to a third party and the higher standard of care which a veterinarian must show, as liability exists whenever it is reasonable for one party to rely on another's skill and judgement in making a statement, a veterinarian will very rarely, if ever, warrant a horse as to soundness. This is because the definition of soundness is so wide in ambit, and because the judicial interpretation afforded the word over the years has led to the position whereby a dissatisfied party may prefer to resort to litigation as against the possibility that he or she has made a bad bargain.

51

THE ROLE OF THE STATE
VETERINARY SERVICE

The Veterinary Department – now known as the State Veterinary Service – was set up by the Privy Council in 1865 to deal with cattle plague, one of the most devastating diseases ever to affect livestock in this country. Veterinary opinion of the day favoured the slaughter of infected and in-contact animals.

This was strongly opposed by various interested parties and it was only the continued ravages of the disease that finally altered public opinion and resulted in the disease being eradicated in 1867. In addition to the slaughter of infected animals, other control measures were introduced which today seem obvious, but in 1865 they were the subject of much ridicule by other professions and the public. These control measures have stood the test of time and are still being practised, albeit in a more refined form.

In Great Britain the State Veterinary Service is one of the many sections of the Ministry of Agriculture Fisheries and Food. In 1985, of the 13,384 veterinarians registered with the Royal College of Veterinary Surgeons, 672 were employed by the state. Assistance is given to veterinary staff by scientific, technical and administrative staff.

The structure of the State Veterinary Service can be summarized briefly as follows: the country is divided into eight regions and sixty divisions. There are twenty-two Veterinary Investigation Centres and a Central Veterinary Laboratory at Weybridge. The Chief Veterinary Office has a headquarters staff and advisers at Tolworth, Surrey, and is also supported by the staff of the Central Veterinary Laboratory in reaching policy decisions in respect of disease control, imports, exports, welfare of animals, etc. In England and Wales there are six regions, each in the charge of a Regional Veterinary Officer, who is responsible for implementing headquarter's policy decisions in his region. The Regional Veterinary Officer is assisted by one or more Deputy Regional Veterinary Officers, staff in the divisions and the Veterinary Investigation Centres. Most general practitioners in large-animal practice are employed by the Ministry on a part-time fee-paying basis and are known as Local Veterinary Inspectors (LVIs). In Scotland there are two regions with a similar staffing arrangement, but the Veterinary Investigation Centres are not under Ministry of Agriculture control. Veterinary officers are attached either to an Animal Health Office (field office) or to a Veterinary Investigation Centre (laboratory staff). The latter provide a diagnostic, investigative and advisory service to owners of agricultural animals through the veterinarian practising in the private sector. Over the years there has been an increase in laboratory backup for official health schemes, exports and statutory disease-control work, which are carried out by the field veterinary staff. Centres have an important function in national disease surveillance: to note and record new or emerging diseases, and to monitor and interpret this information so that further advice, research or regulations can be made for the benefit of agriculture. In addition centres are on the alert for notifiable disease which may not have been recognized and reported.

At the Central Veterinary Laboratory at Weybridge the major part of the work is applied to research into conditions of economic importance in regard to livestock. The remainder of the work is of a service nature, including confirmation or negation of notifiable disease, laboratory testing of samples submitted by the field staff in respect of various health schemes, and carrying out various tests for export purposes. Weybridge is well equipped to investigate and advise on various disease matters, having departments of bacteriology, virology, biochemistry, breeding, biological products and standards, epidemiology, parasitology, pathology, poultry, animal production and maintenance and a medicines unit.

The main functions of the field State Veterinary Service are:

1. To prevent and control those diseases of animals which are notifiable and, as far as is possible, to eradicate them. Diseases which have been made notifiable comprise those which spread rapidly, involve serious economic loss to agriculture or have some public health significance. Before a disease is made notifiable, which means an owner has a legal obligation to report the presence of certain symptoms in his stock, the Ministry must be satisfied that the owner can reasonably be expected to notice such symptoms and the disease must be capable of accurate diagnosis. Although still notifiable, epizootic lymphangitis was eradicated in 1906 and glanders in 1928, parasitic mange (sarcoptic and psoroptic mange – see pp. 469 and 470) in 1948 and equine infectious anaemia (see p. 430) in 1976. Anthrax still occurs occasionally in horses, while African horse sickness, dourine (see p.435) and viral encephalomyelitis of horses (see p. 430) have not been recorded in Great Britain. Glanders, anthrax, rabies (see p. 432) and viral encephalomyelitis are also of public health significance in that infection may occur in man.

It should not be forgotten that there are a number of other notifiable diseases which are of considerable economic importance, for example, foot and mouth disease, which occur in species other than the horse, and much time and effort are spent in implementing preventive measures to avoid outbreaks of these diseases. Contagious equine metritis (see p. 420) is now a notifiable disease.

2.   To protect the human population from disease contracted from animals or animal products, including meat and meat products. To achieve this objective all cattle in the country are tested at regular intervals to ensure freedom from tuberculosis and brucellosis.

3.   To keep a watching brief on the housing, rearing, management, transit, marketing and slaughter of animals to ensure that their welfare is safeguarded and that they are not exposed to unnecessary pain and distress.

4.   To ensure the safety, efficacy and efficiency of veterinary medicines.

5.   To prevent the importation of diseases of animals which do not already exist in Great Britain. Infection may be introduced by the live animal, meat or meat products, or mechanically by other means. Preventive legislature measures may include a total ban on imports from certain countries or importation under specified conditions. For example, the importation of horses into Great Britain is prohibited from any country where African horse sickness and/or Venezuelan equine encephalomyelitis (see p. 430) has occurred during the twenty-four months prior to export, or where vaccination against African horse sickness has been practised during the preceding two years. Import of horses may be allowed by special or general import licences which lay down the conditions that must be met before an import can take place. This invariably involves a veterinary health certificate which specifies that the animal of any species is healthy and, in the case of horses, that they have not been exposed to certain specified diseases during a prescribed period prior to import. In addition, they are required to pass certain biological and laboratory tests. Additional requirements may be laid down to prevent a disease being imported, even though a particular disease may be present in the exporting country. A recent example of such a measure concerned equine viral arteritis (see p. 428): there was a total ban on American horse imports until the national picture of the disease became clear. Subsequently, horses being exported to Great Britain were required to have originated from premises which were free from specified diseases including viral arteritis for the preceding three months. Additionally, they must not have been vaccinated against viral arteritis and must be quarantined on premises under the control of a United States Department of Agriculture (USDA) veterinarian, and must have passed various laboratory and biological tests.

6.   To provide the necessary documentation and assistance to foster exports. The majority of horses for export require certification carried out by local veterinary inspectors. Certain countries, for example, Japan, Australia and New Zealand, require ministry inspection and approval of

isolation/quarantine premises prior to horses entering such premises. The United States import regulations require that ministry veterinary staff carry out the final inspection and certification of horses entering the country. Where swabs are required for contagious equine metritis certification, these are collected by the general practitioner and sent to a ministry-approved laboratory.

The export protocol laid down by the USDA for mares (female horses over 731 days which are not in training) is rather lengthy and takes approximately fifty days if all tests are negative. The American authorities insist that the clitoral sinuses are surgically removed and the sinuses sent to an approved laboratory for CEM culture. A week later the mares external genital organs are treated with 2 per cent chlorhexidine solution and 0.2 per cent nitrofurazone. After a further week three sets of swabs are taken at not less than seven-day intervals. Where stallions are involved, treatment involves the application of 2 per cent chlorhexidine and 0.2 per cent nitrofurazone to the penis, prepuce, fossa glandis and urethral sinus while the penis is in full erection. Subsequently three swabs are taken at weekly intervals.

The Canadian authorities impose a very similar regime to that laid down by the Americans.

Following surgery healing tends to form depressions in the clitoral mucous membranes and invaginations on its surface. These can be mistaken for retained sinuses and in a number of cases, this confusion has been the subject of dispute between the USA and British veterinary authorities concerning the efficiency of the procedure.

On 1 November 1974, Great Britain, France and the Irish Republic established a common policy for the importation of horses. The purpose of this tripartite agreement was to facilitate the movement of horses from one participating country to another while ensuring that all necessary disease precautions have been taken. The countries which are party to this agreement undertake to prohibit the import of horses from countries considered to be infected with African horse sickness and Venezuelan equine encephalomyelitis, and to ensure that horses exported to the other participating countries fulfil the conditions specified in the agreement. The following diseases are subject to compulsory notification in the participating states: anthrax, African horse sickness, dourine, equine encephalomyelitis, epizootic lymphangitis, glanders or farcy, infectious equine anaemia and rabies.

It was hoped that other European countries might participate in this agreement to facilitate the movement of horses within Europe, but to date no other country has joined the three founder states.

There is a multiplicity of acts, orders, regulations and codes of practice laid down by Parliament for the control of animal disease in its broadest sense within Great Britain; for the welfare of animals while being reared, marketed, transported by road, rail, sea or air, or being slaughtered; for the import of various species of animals and the conditions under which imports may take place; and similarly for the export of animals. It is not proposed to deal with this vast subject, which covers over 2000 pages, but to refer any interested reader to Her Majesty's Stationary Office where copies of any legislation may be purchased.

Useful addresses

Central Veterinary Laboratory
New Haw
Weybridge
Surrey

Ministry of Agriculture, Fisheries and Food
Animal Health Division
Hook Rise
Tolworth
Surbiton
Surrey

Scottish Office
Department of Agriculture
Chesser House
500 Gorgie Road
Edinburgh
EH11 3AW

Welsh Office
Department of Agriculture
Crown Buildings
Cathays Park
Cardiff
CF1 3NQ

52

VETERINARY NURSES IN PRACTICE

Anyone wanting to specialize in working with animals will find many opportunities open to him or her. Riding schools, boarding kennels, catteries, veterinary practices and grooming parlours employ young people, with little experience, to assist in the daily routine work. The work can be tiring and dirty and will usually include working weekends because animals require looking after seven days a week.

Larger established veterinary practices employ trainee or qualified veterinary nurses. The latter have been trained to a standard which enables them to assist and carry out nursing procedures and are able to assist veterinarians with more competence and less explanation than untrained staff. This chapter outlines the training and work involved in becoming a qualified veterinary nurse (VN).

Entry requirements

The academic requirements necessary before you can be accepted as a trainee veterinary nurse are a minimum of GCSE grades A, B or C in four subjects (or equivalent O-Level or CSE grades). They should include English language and a maths or a science subject. The applicant should have reached the age of seventeen and should be in full-time employment (thirty-five hours per week) in a practice which is an approved training centre.

Qualifications

The veterinary nursing course lasts for two years, with a preliminary and a final written and oral exam. The exams are held twice a year and the written section has to be passed before the practical examination can be taken.

The preliminary examination is taken at the end of the first year of training and includes the anatomy and physiology of the cat and dog, nursing, first aid, animal management, nutrition and feeding.

The final examination is a more practical exam and includes medical nursing, laboratory work, radiography, surgery and anaesthesia, obstetrics and paediatric nursing.

Practice organization

A daily routine should be encouraged so that clients know when a veterinarian is available. In this respect the nurse can be very helpful. Nurses are often the first person the client meets and the impression he or she receives will usually be a lasting one. An efficient, understanding and polite manner must be maintained at all times. The telephone will also play an important role, with owners phoning for advice and appointments. The nurse should be able to give advice on general matters, such as worming, routine vaccinations and operations, without having to call for the veterinarian.

Operating theatre The nurse will be in charge of the operating theatre, and this usually includes making sure that it is run efficiently and carrying out the sterilization of surgical drapes, gowns and instruments. Stocks such as sutures, sterile packs and dressings must be maintained. Instruments must be checked as they can bend, break or become blunt and need to be replaced. The theatre must always be ready for action and, after surgery has taken place, everything must be cleaned and returned to its proper place.

Anaesthesia Although all anaesthetics are supervised by a veterinarian, the nurse must be aware of all the risks of anaesthesia and have a good knowledge of the action of the drugs and gases used in that particular practice. The anaesthetic machine should be regularly serviced and always checked before each operation to ensure that the gas bottles contain sufficient gas for the next operation and that a spare oxygen cylinder is available.

Radiography The dangers of radiation must be recognized before taking any radiographs (x-rays). All staff assisting with this procedure should wear a monitoring badge, and it is usually the task of the veterinary nurse to ensure that these badges are replaced at regular intervals and the old films sent away for assessment. Protective lead clothing should be worn by all persons attending a radiographic examination and no pregnant women or people under the age of eighteen years should be allowed to remain in the area.

The nurse will be able to assist or, if sufficiently trained, to take the radiographs and/or position the patient correctly. The nurse must be proficient in the development of the radiographs – more faults occur in the darkroom than anywhere else!

Laboratory work The laboratory is an important area in most practices and nurses are trained to carry out routine tests on samples such as blood, urine and faeces. A diagnosis of a patient's problem can be made with the help of the results of laboratory tests and laboratory work is therefore a specialized area requiring accuracy.

Patient care No day is the same in a veterinary practice and a wide variety of jobs are dealt with throughout the day. Nurses should be able to cope under pressure, especially as it is often after a very busy day that the inevitable emergency arises.

Being involved with animals often means working outside normal hours to look after and monitor a patient's progress. Even a sleepless night can be very rewarding if an animal is seen over a crisis and on the way to recovery. The patient receiving treatment should have a card to record all drugs and fluids given. This will enable other veterinarians and nurses to see when a drug was administered. The patient's temperature, pulse and respiration, and urine and faecal output should be recorded because these can be guides to the condition of the patient. These records may be critical when nursing a very sick animal with intensive care.

Medical nursing The nurse will be responsible, under the vveterinariian in charge, for the patient's care during its stay at the surgery. An understanding of the various treatments given, and for what reason, will enable the nurse to look after his or her patients to the best advantage.

The care of wounds, by daily cleaning if necessary, and changing bandages if they have become loose, tight or contaminated are all part of the nurse's responsibility, which depends enormously on common sense.

The veterinary nurse must have some knowledge of all the species of animals which come under his/her care as it is important that their normal basic behaviour patterns are known to enable the abnormal to be recognized. Some abnormal behaviour noticed during nursing care and passed on to the veterinarian can be very important and may affect the diagnosis and subsequent care of the animal.

Although the veterinary nursing syllabus is based mainly on dogs and cats, there is no reason why nurses cannot be involved with other species. There are many veterinary practices which specialize in certain areas, such as horses, zoology or farming, and there are also opportunities for working abroad.

Nurses have a great responsibility, and a high standard of behaviour and attention to duty is required of them. They should be able to work as members of a team and should be people of reliability, trust and responsibility.

The veterinary profession as a whole has benefited from the vocation of animal nursing and it is to be hoped that many more veterinarians will see the need for employing trained nurses in their practice.

Further information and a list of training centres for veterinary nursing can be obtained from:

Royal College of Veterinary Surgeons
32 Belgrave Square
London SW1 8QP

53

THE EXAMINATION OF THE HORSE'S MOUTH FOR AGE

The horse's life expectancy

It cannot be stated with any degree of accuracy to what age a horse would live if not subjected to domestication. However, a horse is generally considered to have reached old age at seventeen. Changes in their teeth, such as the wearing away of the molars, appear to prevent many of them from reaching a ripe old age. Instances are on record of horses attaining the age of thirty-five or fifty, and one animal is known to have lived to sixty-three years of age. Bracy Clark (1771–1860), a well-known veterinary surgeon in practice in London, knew a hunter of fifty-two years of age. Youatt (1776–1847), another veterinary surgeon with a high reputation and also in practice in London, knew an owner who had three horses which died at the ages of thirty-five, thirty-seven and thirty-nine; and a colleague of his knew one that received a ball in his neck at the Battle of Preston in 1715, which was extracted at his death in 1758. Another well-known veterinary surgeon of this period, Percivall, gives an account of a barge horse that died in its sixty-second year. The age at death of some famous racehorses is cited by F. Smith in his *Veterinary Physiology*:

Eclipse	26 years	Ladas	23 years
Touchstone	30 years	Collar	19 years
St Simon	27 years	Pocahontas	33 years
Marcion	23 years	Melton	29 years
Cherry Tree	26 years	Bend Or	26 years
Parrot	36 years	Queen's Birthday	26 years
Hermit	29 years	William III	19 years
King Tom	27 years		

Blaine (1770–1845) in *Outlines of the Veterinary Art* appears to have gone very carefully into the question of old age in horses and he drew the following comparison, which is doubtless very close to the truth:

The first 5 years of a horse may be considered as equivalent to the first 20 years of a man. Thus a horse of 5 years may be *comparatively* considered as old as a man of 20; a horse of 10 years as a man of 40; a horse of 15 years as a man of 50; a horse of 20 as a man of 60; of 25 as a man of 70; of 30 as a man of 80; and of 35 as a man of 90.

The indications of advanced age in horses are well marked, apart from those connected with the length, shape and colour of the teeth: the edge of the lower jaw becomes sharp, there is a deepening of the hollows over the eyes (supra-orbital fossae), and the eyelids become wrinkled. Grey hairs may appear on the face, particularly over the eyes and about the muzzle, and elsewhere, while black horses may turn 'white', although this is unusual. There is a thinness and a hanging down of the lips, a sharpness over the withers, a sinking of the back – a hollowed back is very greatly intensified with age. The joints of the limbs show the effects of work, and the gait loses its elasticity. In Thoroughbred stallions and mares the mean age of death is a little under twenty years. An interesting fact is that horses seldom die quietly.

The teeth

Parts of a tooth   A tooth is made up of two parts, one of which is firmly implanted in the socket (alveolus) in the bone which carries it; this part is called the root. The other portion is exposed and its base is surrounded by the gum. The surface of this portion, which is subjected to wear on account of the friction during mastication, is called the table of the crown. The constricted portion of the tooth which separates these two parts is the neck. The extremity of the tooth shows a small perforation opening into a cavity which extends for some distance up the middle of the tooth. This is the pulp cavity.

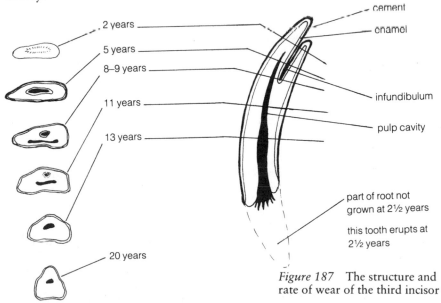

Figure 187   The structure and rate of wear of the third incisor

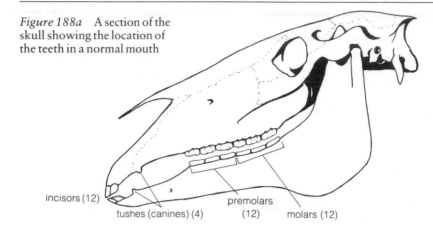

Figure 188a A section of the skull showing the location of the teeth in a normal mouth

incisors (12)

tushes (canines) (4)

premolars (12)

molars (12)

Three substances enter into the composition of all teeth, namely dentine, enamel and cement. Dentine is the yellowish-white, bone-like material which makes up the greater part of the tooth, and surrounds the pulp cavity. Enamel is the shiny white layer which extends over the exposed portion of tooth, and which is seated upon the underlying dentine. Cement is simply connective tissue converted into bone; it is spread over parts of the exterior of the tooth.

A peculiar feature of the teeth is that as the table of the tooth becomes worn out by friction, the alveolar cavity becomes gradually filled up, so that the tooth is slowly pushed out from its socket. This goes on throughout life, and thus we have, at successive periods of the animal's existence, at first the crown, next the neck, and lastly the root actually in wear. Although in an aged animal the incisors appear to be very long owing to the increase in length of their visible portion, the actual length of the tooth has diminished on account of the diminution in length of the root. The maximum length is attained when the animal is about five years old.

Temporary and permanent teeth   Two sets of teeth are developed, namely the temporary, milk or deciduous teeth, and the permanent or persistent teeth.

In the horse the upper and lower jaws carry the same number of teeth. In each jaw of the adult male there are twelve molars, six incisors, two canines or tushes and, occasionally, one or two so-called wolf teeth. In the temporary dentition, however, there are six incisors and only six molars – the first three on either side. The incisor teeth are situated in front; the canine teeth or tushes are situated a little farther back, interrupting the space between the incisors and the premolar or cheek teeth. Canines are usually present only in the male, though small rudimentary ones are quite common in the female, and appear at three-and-a-half to four years; they are fully

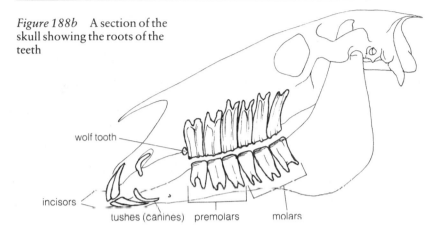

Figure 188b   A section of the skull showing the roots of the teeth

wolf tooth

incisors

tushes (canines)   premolars   molars

developed at four-and-a-half to five years. They are absent in a two-year-old. The premolar and molar teeth form the sides of the dental arch and are commonly referred to as the cheek teeth.

Incisors   These are in three pairs, termed respectively the centrals, laterals and corners. They are named incisors because they are adapted for cutting. Each is made up of a crown, which is depressed from front to back, and a root, the upper portion of which is somewhat three-sided. A little lower down the root becomes circular, while near the apex it is in the form of an ellipse, the long axis of which lies in an antero-posterior direction. These differences in the shape of the tooth are used as an indication of the age of the animal, because the outline of the free wearing surface will vary according to the part of the tooth which is in use. The table of the crown presents a marked depression called the infundibulum. This was formerly used as an indication of the animal's age, since its gradual disappearance was supposed to occur at a definite rate during the life of the animal. This theory is negated by the fact that considerable variations are met with in the depth of the cavity. The enamel covers the exposed portion of the incisor and also in part the root. It also dips into and lines the infundibulum. Thus when the table has been slightly worn, two rings of enamel are visible on its surface, namely an outer ring by which the whole surface is surrounded and an inner ring surrounding the infundibulum. The cement is deposited in a layer, which presents considerable variations in thickness over the enamel.

Temporary or milk incisors are much smaller and whiter than permanent incisors. They possess a well-defined neck, the anterior part of the crown presents a faint striation and the infundibulum is present at first, but it is very shallow and, as a result, soon disappears as the tooth is worn.

Permanent incisors, on the other hand, are much larger, and on the anterior surface of the crown there is present a well-marked vertical groove.

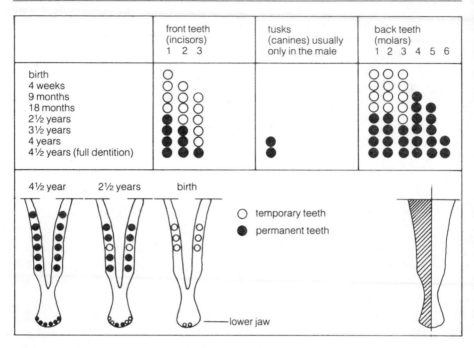

	front teeth (incisors) 1 2 3	tusks (canines) usually only in the male	back teeth (molars) 1 2 3 4 5 6
birth 4 weeks 9 months 18 months 2½ years 3½ years 4 years 4½ years (full dentition)			

Figure 189   Teeth eruption on one branch of jaw (lower) i.e. × 4

The tooth tapers gradually from the crown to the root, so that there is no well-defined constriction or neck. The infundibulum is wide and deep, and surrounded by a fairly thick layer of enamel.

Molars   In the permanent dentition there are twelve of these in each jaw, six on either side. The two rows in the upper jaw are more widely separated from one another then are those in the lower. Moreover, the tabular surfaces of the former are directed obliquely downwards and outwards, while those of the latter take an oblique direction which is upwards and inwards. The inner edge of the lower molars is therefore higher than the outer, and the outer edge of the upper molars extends to a much lower level than the inner edge. The roots of some of the molars project into the maxillary sinuses where they are covered by a thin layer of bone. Hence, when diseased and removal is necessary, trephining of the sinus has to be carried out.

Wolf teeth   Four teeth are frequently present which are placed one in front of each first molar. These are the wolf teeth. Their exposed portion presents considerable variation in shape: usually they are somewhat tubercular but occasionally one is observed with a crown which resembles a small molar. They are interesting as being the remnants of teeth which were well developed in the eocene ancestors of the horse. A wolf tooth may erupt during the first six months, and is often shed about the same time as the milk tooth behind it, but it may remain indefinitely. The occurrence of a similar tooth in the lower jaw, and which rarely erupts, increases the permanent dental formula to forty-four, which is considered the typical number for mammals. To which set these teeth belong is an open question.

Canine teeth or tushes   There are four of these, two in each jaw, and they are frequently referred to as tusks, tushes or fangs. They are characteristic of the male and are usually absent in the female, though it is not uncommon to encounter small, rudimentary ones. Those of the upper jaw are much more posteriorly placed than are those of the lower. There is, therefore, no friction, and in consequence no change in the teeth due to wear of their exposed surfaces. The canine teeth are not replaceable and, as previously noted, are absent in the mouth of a two-year-old (male).

The teeth as evidence of age

Although the time of eruption of the teeth is subject to considerable variation, depending upon the habits and uses of the animal, the nature of the food and so on, the examination of the teeth remains, nevertheless, up to a certain period of life one of the most potent methods we possess of determining the age. The times given below are of course only approximate, but they may be reasonably accepted as being the most constant:

At birth   Two central incisors. These may not appear until the seventh or tenth day. Three cheek teeth are present.

At 4–6 weeks   The lateral incisors.

At 6–9 months   The corner incisors.

Figure 190   Teeth at 1 month

Figure 191   Teeth at 6 weeks

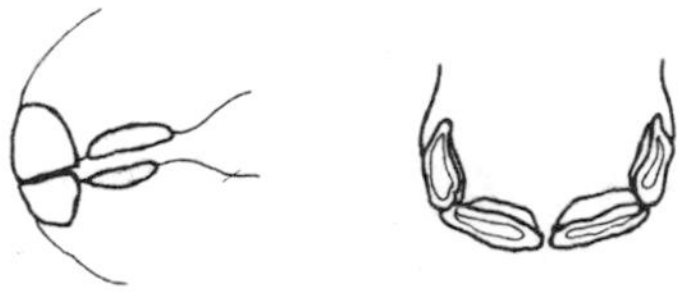

Figure 192   Teeth at 9 months

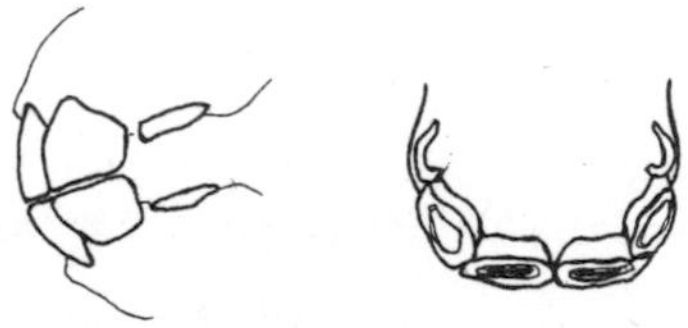

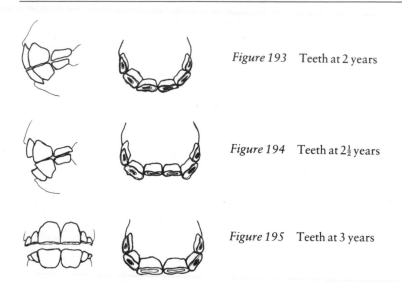

Figure 193   Teeth at 2 years

Figure 194   Teeth at 2½ years

Figure 195   Teeth at 3 years

At 1 year   All six temporary incisors are present, and four cheek teeth: the three premolars and the first permanent molar. The latter has made its appearance through the gum, but is not so well developed as the other three.

At 2 years   The animal's mouth may present some little difficulty. The incisors are showing signs of wear. The cup-like cavities on their tables have disappeared and the tables themselves are flat and present a faint striation. It is most important to be on one's guard in distinguishing between these and permanent incisors. At this age the molars form the better guide, for an additional permanent molar has made its appearance, so that we now have five present, three of which are temporary and two permanent. In his book *The Examination of Animals for Soundness* R. H. Smythe, MRCVS, states:

The tail of a 2-year-old is usually shorter than that of a 5-year-old, reaching to just above or level with the hocks. In a 5-year-old it usually reaches to well below the hocks. Even this is a variable feature, and in any case, tails may be pulled or trimmed. Tail length is often a useful guide in moorland ponies running out. Tails are apt to grow faster with good feeding and housing. Tushes or canine teeth in the case of the male will be absent in a 2-year-old but fully developed in a 5-year-old.

At 2 years 6 months   The central temporary incisors are cast and the first pair of permanent incisors burst through the gums.

At 3 years   The two permanent central incisors are up and in wear. The first and second (in position counting from the front, but numbers three and four in age) permanent molars cut through the gums, pushing before them the first and second temporary teeth beneath which they have erupted. These of

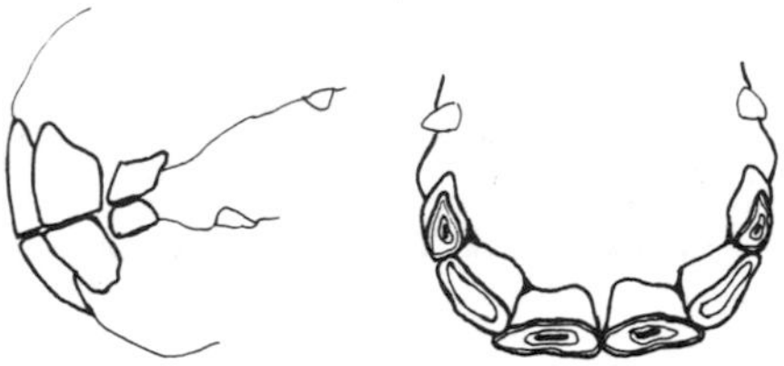

Figure 196   Teeth at 4 years

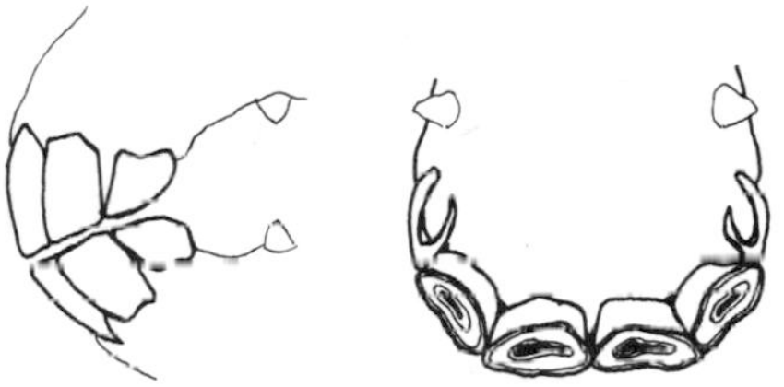

Figure 197   Teeth at 5 years

Figure 198   Teeth at 6 years

Figure 199   Teeth at 7 years

Figure 200   Teeth at 8 years

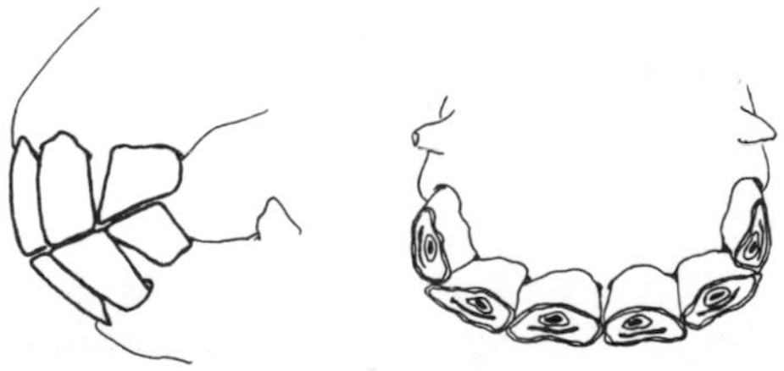

Figure 201   Teeth at 9 years

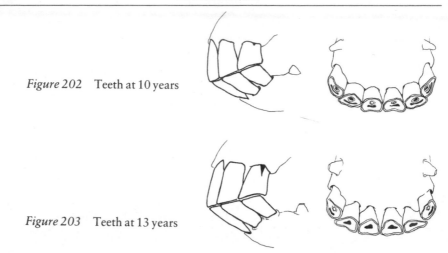

Figure 202   Teeth at 10 years

Figure 203   Teeth at 13 years

course are not yet the height of numbers four and five. The supplementary molars, or wolf teeth, are most frequently cast simultaneously with the shedding of these two temporary molars.

At 3 years 6 months   The second pair of permanent incisors (the laterals) appear through the gums and are on a level with those of the first permanent pair when the horse attains the age of four years.

At 4 years 6 months   The corner permanent incisors are cut, and when these teeth are well up and the inner and outer edges of their tables are level, the horse is five years old. The last two permanent molars (numbers 3 and 6 in position) in each jaw are cut between the ages of four and five.

At 6 years   The corner incisors are exhibiting evidence of wear. The infundibula of the two lateral incisors may have entirely disappeared. This disappearance was formerly regarded as constant at this age, but, for the reasons which have previously been stated, such is not the case and some trace of them is frequently found to remain, although the depressions are much shallower than those in the lateral, or corner, incisors. At this age, in addition, a new feature presents itself on the tabular surface of the central incisors in the form of a blackish or brownish line which runs transversely between the disappearing infundibulum and the anterior edge of the tooth. This is the first appearance of what is known as the dental star, and it indicates the fact that so much of the tooth has been worn away as to bring the upper extremity of the pulp cavity filled with dentine into appearance on the table.

At 7 years   The infundibula have disappeared from the central and lateral incisors. The dental star is much better marked in the centrals, and at eight

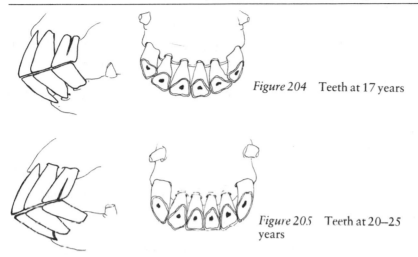

Figure 204   Teeth at 17 years

Figure 205   Teeth at 20–25 years

there should be no difficulty in seeing it. At the age of seven a useful guide is furnished by the top corner incisor tooth which does not wear evenly throughout its length, and as a result a projection or hook (sometimes called a dovetail) develops at its posterior edge. As the tooth wears from front to back without reducing the length of the hook, one gets the impression that the tooth carries a projection downwards from its rear edge.

This hook and accompanying notch first appear at seven years. At eight years the hook has worn away a little, and by eight-and-a-half to nine years has disappeared and the surface of the tooth is again level.

At eleven years the hook reappears and the notch becomes successively deeper, so that by the time the horse reaches thirteen years of age it is very noticeable and then usually persists for the rest of the horse's life.

From 8 years onwards   Very little definite evidence can be obtained, but there are a number of changes which assist in arriving at an approximate estimate. At eight the infundibulum has disappeared from all the incisors, and the dental star is clearly apparent in the central incisors. At nine years it appears in the laterals, and at ten to twelve it is present in all the incisors. Attention should also be directed to the shape of the tables, which varies from oval to triangular and then to round as the horse becomes older. In horses up to seven years they are oval, from nine to thirteen triangular, and after thirteen years rounded with a central pulp mark. Once again, the upper corner incisor tooth comes to our assistance by the appearance of a well-marked longitudinal groove, which first appears as a notch at the outer side of each upper corner tooth just below the gum. As the horse ages, it travels down the tooth as a narrow longitudinal furrow, which is sometimes discoloured (yellow or brown). This is the so-called Galvayne's groove after the well-known horse expert who first drew attention to it, and who is the author of *The Twentieth-Century Book of the Horse*.

This groove makes its appearance at ten years, but quite often its faint commencement can be seen on close inspection at nine years. When it reaches halfway down the tooth the horse is regarded as a fifteen-year-old, and when it has reached the bottom of the tooth, twenty years old. At twenty-five years it has disappeared from the upper half of the tooth, and at thirty years it has disappeared completely.

Treatment and care of the horse's teeth

Regular attention to a horse's mouth ensures healthy teeth and gums, normal mastication, which is essential for good digestion and the assimilation of food, and a responsive mouth. A horse which has difficulty in chewing, drinking or swallowing may be experiencing problems with its teeth. Other signs of dental problems are quidding or the dropping of food,

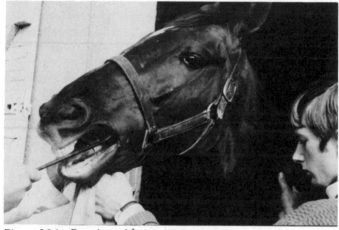

Figure 206   Rasping without a gag

Figure 207   A gag for rasping

the drooling of saliva, loss of condition, and oral or facial pain, which may be accompanied by facial swelling and frequently a fetid odour.

As already explained, the horse's incisor and molar teeth continue to grow throughout its life. The rate of growth is normally balanced by an equal rate of wear. However, if the upper and lower tables are not in opposition, there may be loss of grinding action and consequently uneven wear, with unrestricted growth of the unopposed tooth. In cases in which a horse has undergone extraction of a lower permanent molar tooth, it will require regular attention throughout its life to prevent the unopposed molar in the upper arcade becoming overgrown.

The temporary teeth are relatively soft and readily form sharp points along the length of the outer edge of the upper premolars of cheek teeth, particularly the second, and of the inner edge of the lower premolars. With a young horse in the process of mouthing, it is helpful if these sharp edges are smoothed off, thereby reducing the risk of the horse becoming resentful of the bit or hanging on the bit because of oral discomfort. In addition, the action of the snaffle bit forces the cheeks against the leading edge of the upper premolars, and if these have sharp points, the undue pressure will result in bruising and laceration of the inner surface of the cheeks.

It will be seen from Figure 189 that the troublesome period of tooth eruption occurs between two and four years of age. During this period it is a good idea to have the horse's mouth examined two or three times a year and, if necessary, the premolar caps and wolf teeth should be removed and any sharp edges rasped. On conclusion of molar eruption at four years of age and with the development of a level arcade of permanent molar and premolar teeth, regular dental attention may be only necessary once every nine months, unless there are anatomical irregularities such as a narrow mouth, leading to sharp points on the unopposed edges of the molar arcades, or a parrot mouth, leading to excessive growth of the incisors.

Examining the mouth and rasping

Examination of the horse's mouth is performed by grasping the horse's tongue with the left hand through the mandibular space, retracting the tongue, then rotating hand and tongue dorsally. In most instances this causes the horse to open its mouth. The right hand can then be used to draw back the top lip so that the incisor tables can be examined. If a second person holds the horse's head, the operator can inspect all the teeth, using a torch if necessary, and feel for sharp edges. Care should be taken when palpating molar teeth that you do not get your fingers trapped – this is always painful and potentially serious.

If the teeth need rasping, a gag should be used. Sometimes, with difficult subjects, a twitch may also be necessary, but as this tends to interfere with the use of the rasp, it is often better to sedate or tranquillize the patient. The dental rasp is held obliquely against the sharp edges of the molars and parallel to the upper arcade; it is then moved backwards and forwards under pressure to rasp off the excess tooth. When sufficient tooth has been removed the rasping sound will change and the rasp itself will move easily against the teeth.

Overgrown points on upper and lower second premolars and lower third premolars may be removed with a chisel. This procedure should be carried out by a veterinarian.

Major dental operations, such as extractions or the removal of protuberances, require general anaesthesia.

54
COLOURS AND MARKINGS OF
BRITISH HORSES FOR
IDENTIFICATION PURPOSES

In 1930 the Royal College of Veterinary Surgeons published a report of a subcommittee set up by the Council in 1928 to prepare a system of description of colours, markings, etc., of horses for identification purposes. Since that date there have been several revised editions, the latest issued in 1984. The following is abstracted from that edition:

The following list of names of body colours and markings is recommended as sufficient. It is further recommended that the use of colloquial names not included in the following list should be discontinued. The Royal College is strongly of the opinion that the use of the terms 'near' and 'off' for identification purposes should be discontinued and that the terms 'left' and 'right' should be used exclusively. Care should be taken that the terms refer to the left and right side of the horse.

Body colours

The principal colours are black, brown, bay and chestnut. Where there is any doubt as to the colour, the muzzle and the eyelids should be carefully examined for guidance.

This section has been divided into two parts:

A: colours acceptable to Thoroughbred authorities
B: additional colours accepted by non-Thoroughbred authorities.

It should be noted that the Thoroughbred authorities now call for the foal to be identified by colour and markings shortly before it attains four months of age, or earlier if it is to be exported.

Section A Colours acceptable to Thoroughbred authorities

Black – Where black pigment is general throughout the coat, limb, mane, and tail, with no pattern factor present other than white markings.

Brown – Where there is a mixture of black and brown pigment in the coat, with black limbs, mane and tail.

Bay brown – Where the predominating colour is brown, with muzzle bay, black limbs, mane and tail.

Bay – Bay varies considerably in shade from dull red approaching brown, to a yellowish colour approaching chestnut, but it can be distinguished from the chestnut by the fact that the bay has black on the distal parts of the limbs, a black mane and tail, and often black tips to the ears.

Chestnut – This colour consists of yellow-coloured hair in different degrees of intensity, which may be noted if thought desirable. A 'true' chestnut has a chestnut mane and tail which may be lighter or darker than the body colour. Lighter coloured chestnuts may have flaxen manes and tails.

Grey – Where the body coat is a varying mosaic of black and white hairs, with the skin black. With increasing age the coat grows lighter in colour. As there are many variations according to age and season, all of them should be described by the general term 'grey'. The flea-bitten grey may contain three colours or the two basic colours, and should be so described.

Section B Additional colours accepted by non-Thoroughbred authorities

Blue dun – The body colour is a dilute black evenly distributed. The mane and tail are black. There may or may not be a dorsal band (list) and/or withers stripe. The skin is black.

Yellow dun – There is a diffuse yellow pigment in the hair. There may or may not be a dorsal band (list) and/or withers stripe and bars on the legs. The striping is usually associated with black pigment on the head and limbs. The skin is black.

Cream – The body coat is of a cream colour with unpigmented skin. The iris is deficient in pigment and is often devoid of it, giving the eye a pinkish or bluish appearance.

Piebald – The body coat consists of large irregular patches of black and white. The line of demarcation between colours is generally well defined.

Skewbald – The body consists of large irregular patches of white and of any definite colour except black. The line of demarcation between the colours is generally well defined.

Odd coloured – The body coat consists of large irregular patches of more than two colours, which may merge into each other at the edges of the patches.

Whole coloured – The term 'whole coloured' is used where there are no hairs of any other colour on the body, head or limbs.

Palomino – Newly-minted gold coin colour (lighter or darker shades are permissible), with a white mane and tail.

Appaloosian – The body colour is grey, covered with a mosaic of black or brown spots.

Roans – Roans are distinguished by the ground or body colours, all of which are permanent.

Blue roan – Where the body colour is black or black-brown, with an admixture of white hair, which gives a blue tinge to the coat. On the limbs from the knees and hocks down the black hairs usually predominate; white markings may be encountered.

Bay or red roan – Where the body colour is bay or bay-brown with an admixture of white hairs which give a reddish tinge to the coat. On the limbs from the knees and hocks down black hairs usually predominate; white markings may be encountered.

Strawberry or chestnut roan – Where the body colour is chestnut with an admixture of white hairs. On the limbs from the knees and hocks down chestnut hairs usually predominate; white markings may be encountered.

Markings

The variations in markings of horses are infinite and cannot be described accurately by a limited number of terms without certain arbitrary groupings. In some cases a combination of the terms given below must be employed. It is stressed that all certificates of identification should, in conformity with later remarks, consist of a narrative accompanied by a sketch on which the markings are indicated accurately.

Whorls

Whorls are formed by changes in direction of flow of the hair. Their recording is one of the oldest methods of identifying horses from birth, since their site and character vary to some degree in every animal. They may take various forms, depending on the interface at which two or more flows of hair meet, e.g. simple, tufted, linear, crested, feathered, and sinuous, and should be so described in the narrative. A guide to the recognition of the various types of whorl is:

Simple – a focal point into which the hairs seem to converge from different directions; this requires only the term 'whorl' in the narrative.

Tufted – as for a simple whorl, but the hair converges and piles up into a tuft.

Linear – two opposing sweeps of hair meet from diametrically opposite directions along a line.

Crested – as for linear, but the hair from each of the two directions rises up to form a crest.

Feathered – two sweeps of hair meet along a line but the direction of flow of each sweep is at an angle to the other so that together they form a feathered pattern.

Sinuous – two opposing sweeps of hair meet along an irregular curving line.

In all cases, whether there are white marks or not, the whorls on the head and crest should be described in the narrative and indicated in the sketch. If there are few or no white markings, at least five head, neck or body whorls must be noted.

The position of head whorls should be clearly specified with reference to the midline and eye level, to white markings, and to each other if two or more occur in close proximity. The description invariably begins at the forehead.

White marks

If the boundary of a white mark is not clearly defined, one of the following descriptions should be used.

Mixed – To be used to describe a white marking which contains varying amounts of hairs of the general body colour.

Bordered – to be used where any marking is circumscribed by a mixed border, e.g. 'bordered star', 'bordered stripe'.

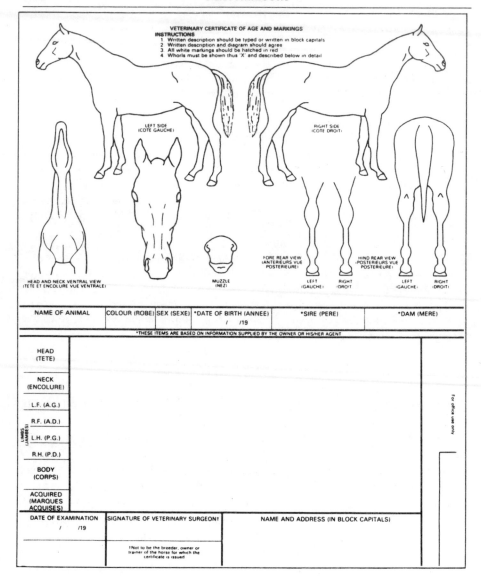

VETERINARY CERTIFICATE OF AGE AND MARKINGS

INSTRUCTIONS
1 Written description should be typed or written in block capitals
2 Written description and diagram should agree
3 All white markings should be hatched in red
4 Whorls must be shown thus 'X' and described below in detail

LEFT SIDE
(COTE GAUCHE)

RIGHT SIDE
(COTE DROIT)

HEAD AND NECK VENTRAL VIEW
(TETE ET ENCOLURE VUE VENTRALE)

MUZZLE
(NEZ)

FORE REAR VIEW
(ANTERIEURS VUE
POSTERIEURE)
LEFT   RIGHT
(GAUCHE)   (DROIT)

HIND REAR VIEW
(POSTERIEURS VUE
POSTERIEURE)
LEFT   RIGHT
(GAUCHE)   (DROIT)

NAME OF ANIMAL	COLOUR (ROBE)	SEX (SEXE)	*DATE OF BIRTH (ANNEE)	*SIRE (PERE)	*DAM (MERE)
			/ /19		

*THESE ITEMS ARE BASED ON INFORMATION SUPPLIED BY THE OWNER OR HIS/HER AGENT

HEAD (TETE)		
NECK (ENCOLURE)		
L.F. (A.G.)		
R.F. (A.D.)		
L.H. (P.G.)		
R.H. (P.D.)		
BODY (CORPS)		
ACQUIRED (MARQUES ACQUISES)		

LIMBS (JAMBES)

For office use only

DATE OF EXAMINATION	SIGNATURE OF VETERINARY SURGEON†	NAME AND ADDRESS (IN BLOCK CAPITALS)
/ /19		
	†Not to be the breeder, owner or trainer of the horse for which the certificate is issued	

Flesh marks – Patches where the pigment of the skin is absent should be described as 'flesh marks'.

Head

Star – Any white mark on the forehead: size, shape, intensity, position and coloured markings (if any) on the white to be specified. Should the marking in the region of the centre of the forehead consist of a few white hairs only it should be so described, and not referred to as a star.

Stripe – The narrow white marking down the face, not wider than the flat anterior surface of the nasal bones. In the majority of cases the star and stripe are continuous and should be described as star and stripe conjoined. Where there is a gap in the length of the stripe it should be described as an interrupted stripe. Where a stripe is separated from the star it should simply be noted that a stripe is present and where no star is present the point of origin of the stripe should be indicated. The termination of all stripes and any variation in breadth, direction and any markings on the white should be so stated, e.g. broad stripe, narrow stripe, inclined to left, terminating at upper left nostril, etc.

Blaze – A white marking covering almost the whole of the forehead between the eyes and extending beyond the width of the nasal bones and usually to the muzzle. Any variations in direction, termination and any markings on the white should be stated.

White face – Where the white covers the forehead and front of the face, extending laterally towards the mouth. The extension may be unilateral or bilateral, in which case it should be described accordingly.

Snip – An isolated white marking, independent of those already named, and situated between or in the region of the nostrils. Its size, position and intensity should be specified (see **Flesh marks**).

Lip markings – Should be accurately described whether embracing the whole or a portion of either lip (see **Flesh marks**).

White muzzle – Where the white embraces both lips and extends to the region of the nostrils.

Other characteristics

Acquired marks – There are many adventitious marks (i.e. not congenital marks) which are permanent, e.g. saddle marks, bridle marks, collar marks, girth marks and other harness marks, permanent bandage marks, firing and branding marks, surgical scars, tattoo marks. Wherever these occur they should be described in the narrative and their location indicated in the sketch by an arrow. The presence of white hairs should be mentioned. If a horse is docked or has nicked ears this fact should be mentioned.

Congenital abnormalities – Any congenital marks or other abnormalities should be clearly described in the certificate and indicated on the sketch where possible, e.g.:

Wall-eye – This term should be used exclusively where there is such a lack of pigment, either partial or complete, in the iris as usually to give a pinkish-white or bluish-white appearance to the eye. Any other important variations should be noted.

Showing the white of the eye – Where some part of the white sclera of the eye shows between the eyelids.

The Prophet's Thumb Mark – This is a muscular depression seen usually in the neck, but sometimes in the shoulders and, occasionally, in the hindquarters – more often found in Arabs and Thoroughbreds. It should be indicated on the sketch by a triangular mark and mentioned in the narrative.

Body

Grey-ticked – Where white hairs are sparsely distributed through the coat or any part of the body.

Flecked – Where small collections of white hairs occur distributed irregularly in any part of the body. The degrees of flecking may be described by the terms 'heavily flecked', 'lightly flecked'.

Black marks – This term should be used to describe small areas of black hairs among white or any other colour.

Spots – Where small, more or less circular, collections of hairs differing from the general body colour occur, distributed in various parts of the body. The position and colour of the spots must be stated.

Patch – This term should be used to describe any larger well-defined irregular area (not covered by previous definitions) of hair differing from the general body colour. The colour, shape, position and extent should be described.

Zebra marks – Where there is striping on the limbs, neck, withers or quarters.

Mane and tail – The presence of differently coloured hairs in mane and tail should be specified.

List – A dorsal band of black hairs which extends from the withers backwards.

Limbs

Hooves – Any variation in the colour of the hooves should be noted. If a horse has few other identifying characteristics the hoof colour should be specified, even if black. In the case of grey the colour of each hoof should be stated.

White markings on limbs – White markings on limbs should be accurately defined and the extent precisely stated, e.g. 'white to half pastern', 'white to below the fetlock', etc. The use of such terms as 'sock' and 'stocking' is not acceptable.

APPENDIX 1:
PROPRIETARY MEDICINES

Listed below is a selection of drugs mentioned in the text together with their trade names.

acetylpromazine: ACP Injection or Tablets
acriflavine: Diacrid
adrenaline: Adrenaline 1–1000
allyl trenbolone: Regumate
aluminium hydroxide: Diampron
amikacin: Amikin
aminacrine: Acrimide
amoxycillin: Clamoxyl
ampicillin: Penbriten
anthracenes: Danthron, Altan
antimony trichloride: Antimony Trichloride Collodion
arsenic: Arsenical Solution (Fowler's Solution), Arsenic Trioxide
ascorbic acid (vitamin C): Ascorbic Acid Injection or Tablets
aspirin (acetylsalicylic acid): Aspirin Capsules, Tablets or Mixture
atropine: Atropine Sulphate Injection BVet C

benzyl benzoate: Ascabin, Temadex
benzyl penicillin: Crystapen
betamethasone: Betsolan
bromocyclen: Alugan
butorphanol: Torbugesic

calcium alginate: Ultraplast Dressings
calcium disodium versenate (see sodium calcium versenate)
camphechlor: Toxaphene, Coopertex
carbenicillin: Carbenicillin Injection
cetrimide: Cetrex
charcoal, activated charcoal: Forgastrin
chloramphenicol: Chloromycetin
chlorhexidine: Hibiscrub, Hibitane
chlorinated soda: Dakin's Solution
chlorpyrifos: Dursban, Killmaster
chlortetracycline: Aureomycin
clenbuterol: Ventipulmin Injection or Granules
cloxacillin: Orbenin
codeine: codeine
cortisol (see hydrocortisone)
cortisone: Cortelan
coumaphos: Asuntol, Negasunt (topical)
cypermethrin: Rycopel, Cyperkill

dantrolene: Dantrium
detomidine: Domosedan
dexamethasone: Azium
diazapam: Valium
dichlorvos: Astrobot, Equigard

digoxin: Lanoxin
dimethyl sulphoxide (DMSO):
    Demovet
dioxathion: Tick Dip Liquid, Bercotox
dipyrone: Buscopan
doxapram: Dopram

erythromycin: Erythrocin
etamiphylline: Millophyline
ethion: Cooperthion, Diethion

febantel: Bayverm
fenbendazole: Panacur
fenchlorphos: Ronnel
fenithrothion: Durakill, Cooper's
    Residual Spray
fenthion: Tiguvon
flunixin meglumine: Arquel, Finadyne
framycetin: Framomycin
furosemide: Lasix

gamma-HCH: Lindane, Gamma-BHC,
    Cooper's Lice and Mange Dressing
    Skin Dressing No. 3
gentamycin: Gentacin
glycosaminoglycan: Adequan
gonadotrophin releasing hormone
    (GnRH): Receptal
griseofulvin: Fulcin

haloxon: Equilox
human choronic gonadotrophin
    (hCG): Choronic Gonadotrophin BP
    (Vet), Chorulon
hydrochlorothiazide: Vetidrex
    Injection or Tablets
hydrocortisone: Cortocaps (with
    neomycin)
hyocine (hyocine-n-butyl bromide):
    Buscopan

imidicarb: Imizol
iodine (strong iodine, weak iodine):
    Aqueous Solution of Iodine
iodofenphos: Nuvanol
isoxsuprine hydrochloride: Circulon
ivermectin: Eqvalan

kaolin: Kaogel
ketamine: Vetalar

lincomycin: Lincocin

mebendazole: Telmin
meclofenamic acid: Arquel
mefenamic acid: Ponstan
metriphonate: Neguvon
metronidazole: Torgyl
monensin: Rumensin, Elancoban

nandrolone: Nandrolin
naproxen: Equiproxen
neomycin sulphate: Vonamycin
niclosamide: Mansonil, Yomesan
nitrofurazone: Furacin Ointment

oestradiol benzoate: Oestradel
orgotein: Palosein
oxfendazole: Systamex, Synthetic
oxibendazole: Equitac, Equidin,
    Rycovet Wormer
oxyclozanide: Zanil
oxyphenbutazone: Tanderil
oxytetracycline: Terramycin
oxytoxin: Oxytocin

penicillin: Mylipen Duphapen
pentobarbitone: Sagatal
permethrin: Stomoxin, Coopex
phenamidine: Phenamidine
phenylbutazone: Equipalazone
pirevan: Piroparv, Babsan
povidone iodine: Pevidine
praziquantel: Droncit
prednisolone: Solu-Medron
proflavine: Proflavine Cream
prostaglandin: Estrumate
pyrantel embonate: Strongoid P
pyrethrin: Flyban, Cooper's Veterinary
    Insecticide

rafoxanide: Flukanide
resorantel: Terenol

sodium calcium versenate, sodium
    calcium EDTA: Calcium Disodium
    Versenate, Ledclair

sodium cromoglycate: Cromovet Forte
sodium fucidate: Fucidine
sodium hyaluronate: Hylartid
streptomycin: Streptovex
suramin: Suramin Injection

tannin, tannic acid: Phytex
testosterone: Testoral, Androject

thiabendazole: Thibenzole, Equizole
triamcinolone: Panolog Veterinary
   Cream
trimethoprim (trimethoprin):
   Duphatrim

vasopressin: Pitressin

xylazine: Rompun

APPENDIX 2:
FEI PROHIBITED SUBSTANCES

FEI prohibited substances are substances originating externally whether or not they are endogenous to the horse.

drugs acting on the central nervous system
drugs acting on the autonomic nervous system
drugs acting on the cardiovascular system
drugs affecting the gastro-intestinal function
drugs affecting the immune system and its response
antibiotics, synthetic anti-bacterial and anti-viral drugs
antihistamines
anti-malarials and anti-parasitic agents
anti-pyretics, analgesics and anti-inflammatory drugs – other than phenylbutazone and oxyphenbutazone
diuretics
local anaesthetics
muscle relaxants
respiratory stimulants
sex hormones, anabolic agents and corticosteroids
endocrine secretions and their synthetic counterparts
substances affecting blood coagulation
cytotoxic substances
any substance other than a normal nutrient which could by its nature affect
   the performance of the horse as a whole

APPENDIX 3:
NOTIFIABLE DISEASES

The following diseases in horses are notifiable as laid down by the Ministry of Agriculture, Fisheries and Food in *Infectious Diseases of Horses*, 1987. This means that horse owners have a legal obligation to report the presence of the relevant symptoms in their animals:

African horse sickness
contagious equine metritis
dourine
epizootic lymphangitis
equine infectious anaemia
equine viral encephalomyelitis
glanders (including farcy)

In addition, anthrax and rabies, which occur in humans as well as horses, are also notifiable.

GLOSSARY

The following is not intended to be a comprehensive list, but a useful guide to the terminology commonly used throughout the book. More detailed definitions can be obtained by reference to a veterinary dictionary.

Acute Sudden in onset

Aerobe A micro-organism which requires oxygen to exist

Aetiology The causes of disease

Anaemia Reduction of red cells and/or haemoglobin within the blood

Anaerobe A micro-organism which is able to exist without oxygen

Analgesic An agent which alleviates pain without causing loss of consciousness

Anaphylaxis Immediate hypersensitivity to a foreign protein or a drug

Anterior Towards the front

Arrhythmia Variation from the normal rhythm of the heart beat

Ataxia Incoordination of muscular activity

Atelectasis Incomplete expansion of the lungs

Atrophy Wasting; reduction in size

Azoturia Excess nitrogen in urine, associated with destruction of skeletal muscle

Biopsy The removal of a portion of tissue for diagnostic purposes

Bradycardia Decreased heart rate

Carcinoma A malignant tumour, consisting of epithelial cells

Cardiovascular Relating to the heart and blood vessels

Congenital Existing at, or before, birth

Chronic Of long duration

Diuretic A substance that promotes the excretion of urine

Dysrhythmia Disturbance of rhythm

Dystocia Difficulties associated with birth

Ectoparasites Parasites which live on the exterior of their hosts

Empyema The presence of pus in a body cavity, e.g. guttural pouch

Endocrine Relating to the glands of internal secretion

Endoscope An instrument for visualizing the inside of cavities

Enterotomy An incision into the intestine

Epiphysis Portion of bone separated from the main bone by cartilage

Epistaxis Bleeding from the nose

Excoriation Abrasion of a portion of the skin

Exostosis A cartilage capped protuberance from the surface of bone

Fibrosis An increase in fibrous connective tissue

Globulins A group of proteins which are insoluble in water

Haematology The nature, functions and diseases of blood

Haematoma A collection of blood which forms a mass

Hemiplegia Paralysis affecting one side only

Immunoglobulin A protein with antibody activity

Laparotomy An incision through the abdominal wall

Lateral Towards the side

Lesion Any alteration caused by disease or injury

Leucocyte One of the white cells of the blood

Lymphangitis Inflammation of vessels

Medulla The innermost portion of an organ or structure

Micturition Urination

Necrosis The death of cells

Nephritis Inflammation of the kidney

Neuritis Inflammation of nerves

Neuroendocrine Involving the relationship of the nervous and endocrine systems

Neuroma A tumour of the nervous system

Oedema Swelling, caused by an accumulation of fluid

Ophthalmia Inflammation of the eye

Ophthalmoscope Instrument for examining the interior of the eye

Osteochondritis Inflammation of bone and cartilage

Osteocytes Bone cells

Paresis Partial paralysis

Pathogenesis The development of disease

Pathogenic Capable of producing disease

Pathology The study of the nature of disease

Periosteum Connective tissue covering bone surfaces

Periostitis Inflammation of the periosteum

Peristalsis Muscular movement consisting of successive wave-like contractions

Physiology The study of functions of the living organism

Plasma Portion of blood which is straw-coloured prior to clotting

Posterior Towards the back

Prognosis Prediction of the course and outcome of a condition

Prophylaxis Measures to prevent the development or spread of disease

Pyrexia Abnormal elevation of body temperature

Resection Removal of a portion of organ or tissue

Serum Amber-coloured liquid which separates from clot when blood coagulates

Sloughing Casting off necrotic tissue

Synovia Clear fluid found in joints, bursas and sheaths of tendons

Systemic Involving the whole body

Tachycardia Increased heart rate

INDEX

Note: numbers in bold refer
to illustrations

abdomen, 6, 22
   abscesses in 15, 401, 406,
      416–17
   conditions of 14–16
   dermatophilus of 94
   distended 87
   nerves 113
   oedema of 19
   pain in *see* colic
   wall muscles of 80, 353
abdominal cavity 322
abducens nerve 110
abomasum 581
abortion 20, 42, 116–17,
      337–9
   causes of 338–9
   and infection 338
   non-infection causes 338
   twisting of umbilical cord
      and EHV–1 339–43,
      425–6
abrasions 548
abscessation 505
abscesses
   abdominal 15, 401, 406,
      416–17
   from bacterial respiratory
      conditions 44, 46
   and castration 541–2
   dental 406
   in foot 242–3
   of gut 406, 416
   in lungs 411, 413, 416
   in lymph glands 68, ch29
   of neck 267–8
   pelvic 406
   of pharynx 32, 33
   skin 95
   spinal 86

of throat 31
of trachea 36
in umbilical area 88
acaricides 409
   table of 463
acariasis (mange, scab, itch)
      98–9, 100, 101
accessory glands
   of digestive system 16–24,
      78
   of reproductive system 79,
      313
accident effects, rendering
      horse unfit for purchase
      665
accommodation (focusing)
      128
acepromazine 227
acetylpromazine 483
acidemia 71
acidity 71–2, 74
acidosis 71
acne (saddle boils, heat rash)
      93–4
acoustic nerve 110
acquired/false bursae 186–7,
      207–8
   see also hygroma
acquired marks 703
acridine dyes 483
acriflavine 483
ACTH hormone 115, 122
actinic sunlight 102, 104
Actinobacillus equulli 43,
      379, 380–4, 404, 410
action of horse 615–16
acute renal failure *see under*
      kidneys
adenovirus 429
adhesions 45
adnexa, functional anatomy
      307–10

adrenal cortex 18, 115, 119
adrenal gland 118
adrenal exhaustion 113
adrenal medulla 121
adrenaline 63, 121, 483–4
adrenocorticotrophic
      hormones *see* ACTH
aerobe 401
aerosol transmission of
      infection 402
African horse sickness 679–
      81, Appendix 3
afterbirth *see* placenta
air sacs 135
Agglutinade-Strongyle 441
aggression 575
airways 38
   obstruction 39, 49, 51
age *see* examination of
      mouth for age
aimless walking 19
albumin 18, 71, 76
alimentary tract 113, 410
   excretion, foetal *v.*
      newborn 368
alkalinity 71, 72, 74
allanto-amnion 332, 332,
      347
allantoic fluid 332, 332
allantois 332, 332
allergens 34, 42
allergic dermatitis 103
allergies 42, 48, 67, 77, 92,
      100, 103, 138
allyl trenbolone 117
aloes 484
alpha globulin 71
alveolar emphysema *see*
      chronic obstructive
      pulmonary disease
alveoli 36, 49
American Quarter horses
      144, 246

amicarbalide 434
amino acids (organic acids) 17, 18, 22, 71, 72, 124, 238, 245
aminocrine 483
aminoglycosides 485
ammonia 18, 484
amnion 332, **332**, 333, 349, 351
amniotic fluid 332, **332**, 369
ampulla gland **308**, 313
anabolic steroids 118, 484
anaemia 21, 70, 73, 83, 394, 434
  see also equine infectious anaemia
anaerobic bacteria 243, 401
anaesthesia 10, 12, 29, 30, 87, 88, 89, 129, 131, 132, 166–7, 179, 483–4, 497–500
  general 498–500
  local 149, 197
  and regional 497–8
  and veterinary nurse 684
analgesics 145, 178, 191, 204, 227, 248, 250, 483
anaphylactic shock 484
anaphylaxis 103
angleberries 564
angular limb deformity 183, 280–91
animal bites 401
animal products, nutritional 595
aniridia 626
annular ligament **206**
  of carpus **x**
  constriction of tendon sheath by 184, 210
  of fetlock **xi, xii**,
anodynes 484–5
anoestrus 116, 117, 318, 330
Anoplocephala magna (tapeworm) 456–7
Anoplocephala perfoliata (tapeworm) 456–7
anterior chamber (of eye) 127, **128**, 129, 130, 132
anterior pectorals **x**
anterior segment (of eye) 127
anterior vena cava 60
anthelmintics 46, 409, 442–55 *passim*
  resistance of strongyles to 446
anthracene purgatives 484
anthrax 413, 679
antibacterials 485

antibiotics 30, 69, 82, 83, 84, 88, 94, 95, 131, 164, 179, 211, 243, 244, 261, 263, 370, 383–4, 405, 414, 417, 419, 420, 485
  as poison 513
antibodies 71, 372, 379
anticoagulants 75
antidiuretic hormone 122, 123
  deficiency 22–3
antifungal drugs 30, 32, 490
antigens, organic dust 48, 49, 50–1
antihistamines 483, 486
anti-inflammatory drugs 32, 145, 158, 176, 191, 198, 204, 208, 209, 215, 227, 250, 261, 486
antimicrobials 69
antimycotic agent 96
antiparasitic
  dressing 99
  drugs 137
antiprostaglandins 69
antiprotozals 409
antisepsis 93
antiseptics 556
antiserum 19, 83
antithyroids 519
antitoxin 415, 416
anus 8, **8**, 100
  irritation 448–9
anvil 135
aorta **54**, 54, 56, 58, 59, 60, 62
apnoea 390
appetite 40, 49
  lack/loss of 83, 411, 417, 434
apocrine gland 91
aqueous humour 127, 132
arachnid 409
Arab horses 113, 275–6, 429
arachnoid mater 108
arbovinus 431
arrhythmia 63
arsenic 21, 510
arterial bleeding 74
arterial oxygen pressure 391
arteries 38, 53, 54, 55, 55, 56, 59, 60, 70
  damage to 441
  rupture of 60, 74–5
arterioles 59
arteritis 338
arthritis *see* secondary joint disease

arthrogryposis 628
arthropods 409, 459–74
arthroscope 152
arthrosis of coffin joint 251
articular cartilage 153, 172, **172**, 195
articular windgalls 174, 181, 208–9 *see also* windgalls
arytenoid cartilage 112
aspartate aminotransferase 151, 226–7
Aspergillus fumigatus 48, 408
asphyxia neonaturium 389
  resuscitation 390–1
aspiration of food 27, 35
aspiration pneumonia 31, 32, 411
aspirin 228, 486
assistance with newborn foals 366–77
astringents 101
ataxia 110
  hereditary 627
    inheritance and recommendations 627
  see also incoordination
atlantal bursa 267
atlas 267
  wing of **x**
atresia coli 628
atria 53, 54, 55, 56, 57, 58, 59, 60, 63
atrial filibration 63
atrio-ventricular tricuspid valves 56
atropine 481, 490
auctions 635–6
aural problems *see* ear(s)
aureomycin spray 234
auricles 53, 56, 62
auricularis muscle **x**, 136
auriculoventricular node 57
auscultation 57, 61–3
autogenous vaccine 93
autonomic nervous system 113
axis 267
axon **108**
azoturia 82, 226–8, 483

Babesia caballi (piroplasmosis) 433–5
Babesia equi (piroplasmosis) 433–5
babesiosis (piroplasmosis) 77, 433–5
back **ix** 147, 148
  broken 111, 271

conformation 607, **608**
fracture 111, 271
functional anatomy 264–8
nerves 109
pain 266, 268–71
short **603**
sore ix
soundness and
conformation 607–9
back-at-the-knee
conformation 214
bacteria
discoveries of 398
diseases caused by 411–21
and haemolytic disease 21
and lower respiratory
conditions 41, 43
toxins in feed 514
bacterial pathogens 432
bacterial infections 30, 43,
67, 68, 82, 84, 92, 110,
163–4, 379
Group I (breakdown of
skin) 400–1
Group II (access to
sensitive body tissue)
402–5
Group III (present within
normal flora) 405–6
Bacterium viscosum equi see
Actinobacillus equulli
bad birth *see* birth, abnormal
bad habits rendering horse
unfit for purchase 665
bad traveller 578
balance 135
loss of 138, 143
poor 222, 246
balancing foot when shoeing
297–302
bandages 166, 210, 218–19,
231, 262, 286, 288,
557–8, **558, 559**
blow 213–14
for hunters 646–8
pressage 208
pressure 549
barker *see* neonatal
maladjustment
syndrome
bars (shoe) **297**
basophils 74
bay **700**
bay brown 699
bedding 40, 44, 103, 244,
365, 523, **523**
for newborn foals 371,
374–5
straw, and urination 79

substitutes for hay and
straw 50
bee stings 514–15
behavioural problems 20,
133, 569–79
aggression 575
bad traveller 578
cold-back behaviour 572–
3, 607
crib biting 678–9
difficult to clip 575
gross disturbances 384–91
headshaking 573–4
'mareishness' 574–5
not working 'on the bit'
571–2
rearing, bucking,
nappiness 570–1
stable vices 578–9
transportation problems
577–8
unwillingness to load 576,
577–8
weaving 579
windsucking 579
bench knee 155, **155**, 157
berry bug *see*
neotrombiculosis
Besnoita bennetti 437
beta globulin 71
betamethasone 118
bicarbonate 71
biceps brachii muscle 190
biceps femoris muscle x
bicipital bursitis 207
big-head disease (NSH) 587
bilateral cryptorchidism 311
bilateral nasal discharge 30,
33
bilateral nosebleeds 33
bile 17
pigment 20, 21, 73
secretion 18
biliary fever *see babesiosis*
bilrubin 18, 19, 20
biopsy 93
biotin 238, 245, 302
birth 39, 69, 75, 83, 87, 110,
113, 123, 344–6
abnormal 360–5, 391
foetal preparation for 345
forces of 347–8
induced 118
initiation of 346–7
maternal preparation for
344–5
readiness for 345–6
of sick foal 342–3
see also foaling

bladder 78, **78, 79,** 79, 80,
81, **308,** 319
inflammation of *see* cystitis
obstruction of neck 82
paralysis 84, 86, 271
rupture of 82, 86–7
stones *see* cystic calculi
tumours 86
black 699
black marks 703
blankets (rugs) for hunters
644–6
blastocyst, attachment of
331–3
blaze (head marking) 702
bleeding
from ear 138
from lungs 51–2
from nose (epistaxis) 30,
32–3
from wounds, control of
549
blemishes rendering horses
unfit for purchase 665
Blenkinsop shoe 299–300
blindness ix, 30, 112, 132–3
periodic ophthalmia
(moon blindness) 132
blind splints 159
blind staggers 510
blistering 546
blisters 145, 245, 428
blood 137
blood 16, 17, 22, 37, 70–7,
119, 151
conditions of 77
examining 77
see also haemotopoietic
system; heart
blood blisters 137
blood cells
red 56, 70, 72–3, 79, 81,
132, 393–4, 433–4
white 70, 73–4, 118, 132,
418
blood circulation 53–65, **54,**
70
defects in 82
blood clotting 18, 71, 74–6,
77, 246, 250
blood content stability *see*
homeostasis
blood enzymes 19
blood and exercise 659
blood-fluid balance 76–7
blood loss, 27
see also haemorrhage
blood osmolality 123
blood plasma 70–2

blood pressure 59–60, 74, 82, 113, 122
see also hypertension
blood samples 41, 81, 82, 83, 87
bloodstream 67, 71, 113–15, 117, 120
blood sugar 22, 121
blood tests 238–9, 429, 430, 442
blood transfusion 434
blood typing 619–21
blood vessels 36, 37, 53, 59–60, 66, 67, 71, 74, 79, 113, 122, 128, 129, 131, 132
bloody sweat 455
blow flies see myiasis
blue dun 700
blue roan 700
body marking 703
body temperature
high 42
increased 15, 27
bodyweight estimates (table) 598
see also weight
bog spavin ix, 144, 174–5, 198–9, 200, 210, 224
bolus doses 121
bonding at birth 371–4
bone 139
conditions of 153–71
fractures 218
functional anatomy 153–4
bone cell metabolism 246
bone marrow 20, 73
bone scanning 29, 151
bone spavin ix, 144, 143, 177, 193–8, 291
clinical signs 194
diagnosis 194–5
nerve blocks 196–7
radiographic examination 195–6
treatment 197–8
boots 218
for hunters 646, 647
bordered marking 701
Bordetella bronchiseptica 43
boric (boracic) acid 486
bot larvae 21
bots see *Gastrophilus intestinalis*; *Gastrophilus nasalis*
bottle feeding of newborn foal 372, 386
botulism 10, 406, 415–16, 514

bowed tendon ix
bowel
prolapse of 541–2
ruptured 48
bowel worm see *Oxyuris equi*
box rest 176, 181, 216
brachial plexus 230
brachialis muscle x, xi
brachiocephalic muscle xii
brain 20, 26, 107–12 *passim*, 120–3 *passim*, 129, 135, 137
brain cells 122
brain haemorrhage 384–6
brain lesions 277
bran 227
bran disease (NSH) 586–7
branches of suspensory ligament to extensor tendon xi, xii
breast ix
breathing 76, 109
difficulties 7, 31, 34, 87, 411, 417
failure after birth see asphyxia neonatorum
irregular 39
mechanics of 37
over- 72
breathing system see respiratory system
breathlessness 49
breeding 92, 145, 170
selective 630–4
and environment 633–4
brewer's grain 12
bridle lameness 149
brittle feet 245
broad ligament 319, 322
broken knee(s) ix, 141, 261–2
broken wind see chronic obstructive pulmonary disease
bromosulphthelein 19
bronchi 36
bronchilitis 425
bronchodilating agents 44, 50, 51
bronchopneumonia 43–4, 417
broodmares see mares
brown 699
Brucella abortus (brucellosis) 404, 413
brucellosis 404, 413
bruising 149, 161
of shoulder region 191

of sole 233–5
of spinal cord 276–7
of stifle region 204–5
of vagina 363
buccinator muscle x
bucking see rearing, bucking, nappiness
buckthorn 21
buffalo flies 461
bulbar conjunctiva 126
bulbo-urethral gland 308, 313
Bundle of Hiss 57, 63
burns 401, 553–5
from chemicals 555
from cold 55
degrees of 553–4
treatment 554–5
bursa(e)
acquired/false 186–7, 207–8
bicipital 207
infection of 211
bursitis
inertubercular (bicipital) 191, 207
trochanteric 207
bute see phenylbutazone
buttock(s) ix, 100, 616
buying horses
for hunting 635–8
legal implications of 672–7
with old tendon injury 219
and veterinary certification 662–73

cadmium 511
caecum 7, 8, 8, 581
calcaneus 220, 223
calcium 75, 79, 81, 157, 227, 284
and nutrition 586–8
-phosphorus ratio 164
tables of requirements 587, 591, 592–3
calcium carbonate 85
calcium phosphate 155
calculi (stones) 82, 83
surgery to relieve 535–6
see also cystic calculi
calluses 166
camphor 486
Campylobacter 405
cancellous bone (trabecular) 153, 153
cancer see tumours
cancerous thickening 14
canine teeth (tushes) 5, 688, 689

cannon bones ix, xi, 154–5, 220
  fracture of 168, 183–4
  short **603**
cantering **141**, 142, 220
capillaries 53, **54**, 56, 59, 60, 70, 73
capped elbow *see* elbow, capped
capped hock *see* hock, capped
capsule 127, 172–6
capsulitis 175–6
capture myopathy 226
carbohydrate 18, 22, 72, 121
carbon dioxide 37, **38**, **54**, 72, 73
carbon fibre implants 217, 219
carbon tetrachloride 21
carbonate calculi 85
Carborundum 293
carcinomas 130, 564
cardiac arrest 121
cardiac failure 389
cardiac output 64
cardiac veins 60
cardiovascular system and exercise 658–9
carotene 284
carpal bones 282–9, **288**
carpus (knee) **ix**, 143, **185**
  arthritis of 185–6
  chip fractures of 144, 146
  conditions of 154–60, 184–7
  distension of tendon sheaths of 187
  fracture of 167, 186, 291
  functional anatomy 184–5
  hypoplasia of 289–90
carpus valgus 288–9, **281**, **283**, 289
carpus varus **281**, **283**, 289
cartilage 126, 151, 172–4, 189
  damage to 177
cartilaginous flaps 26, 135
Cash, Robert 345
Caslick (sutured vulva) operation 356, 534–5
castration 310–12
  operation 539
    complications 540–3
casts 166, 290, 291
cataracts 133
catechu 486
catheterization 80, 85, 86
catarrh 425

caudal articular process **265**
caustics 486–7
cauterizing agent 88
cell body **108**
cell membranes 18, 72
cellulitis 505
CEM (*Taylorella (Haemophilus) equigenitalis* infection, CEMO, equine metritis) 402–4, 420–1
cement **687**, **688**
CEMO *see* CEM
central nervous system *see* nervous system, central and peripheral
cephalosporins 485
cerebellar hypoplasia (cerebellar degeneration) 113, 277, 627
  inheritance and recommendations 627
cerebellum 109
cerebral nerve trunk 108
cerebral spinal fluid 108, 109
cervical nerves 109
cervical vertebrae **xi**, **265**
  congenital malformation of 275–6
  fractures of 267, 276
  transverse process of **267**
cervix 118, 318, 319, 322–3, **348**, **349**
cestodes 409, 455–8
Cetavlex 256
chalk 487
chambers (of heart) 53–7, **55**, **57**, 61
champignon 542
check ligament **212**
  sprained **144**
  see also deep digital flexor tendon
cheek ix
check teeth 8, 9, 25, **688**, 690, 696
chemical(s)
  restraint by 496
  treatment of burns due to 555
chest 36, 41, 62, 67
  injury to wall 40
  nerves 109, 110, 113
  oedema of 18
  pleuritis and 45
  soundness and conformation 605–6
chestnut **ix**, **700**
chestnut roan **701**

chewing difficulties 9
chin ix
chip fractures in fetlock joint 183
chlamydia 407
chloral hydrate 487
chlorhexidine 487
chloride 58
chlorophyll 104
chlorpromazine 483
choke 32
choking up 34–5
cholesterol 18, 116
choline 18
chorio-allantois **332**, 349–50, **349**, **351**
chorion 120, **332**, 332, 333
Chorioptes equi (leg mange) 98, 469
choroid 127–8, **128**
chronic dilatation of oesophagus 11
chronic obstructive pulmonary disease (COPD) 29, 35, 42, 48–51, 408
chronic renal failure *see under* kidneys
chronic uterine endometritis 381
CID *see* combined immunodeficiency
cilia 37
ciliary body 128, **128**
circulation *see under* blood; heart
cirrhosis of liver 19
clamping 549
Claviceps purpurea 515
cleansing of wounds 550
cleft palate
  foals with 11, 31, 393
clenbuterol 487
clipping 644
  problems with 575
clitoral sinuses 421
  removal of 681
clitoral winking 84
clitoris 79
Clostridium botulinum 405, 415–16, 514
Clostridium tetani (tetanus) 400, 414–15
closed wounds 553
clothing of hunters 644–6
clotting *see* blood clotting
club foot *see* distal interphalangeal joint flexural deformity

coat, foetal *v.* newborn 369
coccygeal nerves 109
coccygeal vertebrae 264–77, 265
cochlea **136**, 136, 137
coconut matting 187
codeine 487, 497
coffin bone 232
coffin joint **x**, 211, 232, 246
    arthritis of 252
    arthrosis of 251
Coggins blood test 430, 526
coital exanthema *see* equid herpesvirus
cold-back behaviour, excessive 572–3
cold burns due to 555
cold compresses 215
cold hosing 209
cold lasers 543–4
cold treatment 145, 181
cold virus 43, 429
colic (abdominal pain) 11–13, 14, 15, 16, 33, 60, 83, 84, 85, 87, 89, 418, 434, 484–5
collagen(s) 176
collagen fibrils 213–17
collapse 36
    of carpal bones 289–90
collateral ligament **172**, 175, 180
    of navicular bone **233**
    of third and/or central tarsal bones of hock 201, 291
colon 7, **8**, 8, 581
    impaction of 14
colostrum 20, 82, 345, 528
cots 118, 274
colours
    and markings of British horses for identification 699–704
        body colours 699–701
        markings 701–3
        other characteristics 703–4
    and newborn foals 374
combined immunodeficiency (CID) 625
common digital extensor **xi**, **221**, **233**
    distension of tendon sheaths of 187
communication systems 106–24
competition horses 298
compression on umbilical cord 362

compressive lesions 36
    and lymphosarcoma 15
conception 116, 120
concussion 112, 149
condition
    rapid loss of 14, 15
    score (table) 585–6
condylar fractures 183–4
conformational
    abnormalities 144, 146, 178, 283
    rendering horse unfit for purchase 665
    see also soundness and conformation
congenital abnormalities
    of ears 137
    of eyes 134
    of flexor tendons 278
    of joints 173
    of markings 703
    of mouth 8, 703
    of neck 275–6
    of teeth 10, 137
    see also genetics; heritability
congenital luxation of patella 203
congestive heart failure 260
conjunctiva 126, 129, 131
conjunctivitis 131
consciousness, loss of 431
constipation 14
constriction of tendon sheath 184
    by annular ligament 210
contagious equine metritis *see* CEM
contracted tendons *see* distal interphalangeal joint flexural deformity
contractions, birth **347**, 347–8
convulsions 20, 110, 112, 384–9, 352–3, 415
convulsive syndrome *see* neonatal maladjustment syndrome
coordination 110
copper 21, 589
copper deficiency, induced 510
copper sulphate 487
cornea 126–32, *passim*, **127**, **128**
corns 147, 149, 233–5
coronary corium 233
coronary disease 60
coronary sinus 60

coronary vessels 60
coronet **ix**
corpora nigra 127
cortex 118, 121, **153**
corticosteroids 138, 145, 158, 198, 211, 256, 267, 427, 487–8
cortisol 115, 118, 347, 488
cortisone 116, 118–19, 122, 487–8
Corynebacterium equi infection *see* *Rhodococcus equi* infection
cottonwool and Gamgee 558
coughs 10, 11, 29, 32, 411, 417, 425, 426, 447, 450
    in COPD 40
    in lungworm infection 46
    mixtures 188
    paroxysmal 33
    as sign of respiration malfunction 39, 40, 42
coxofemoral (hip) joint, arthritis of 273
cow-hocked conformation 291
cracked heels 255–7
cranial articular process 265
cranial thoracic region *see* withers
cranial vault 26
cranial vena cave 55
cream (colour) 700
creams and ointments 557
creatine kinase (CK) 151, 226–7
creatinine (waste products) 81, 82, 87
    clearance test 227
cremaster muscle **309**
crena 161
crepitus 271–2
crest **ix**
crested whorl 701
crib-biting 578–9
crimp 211–12, **212**
croup **ix**, 109, 608, 613
    nerves 109
cruciate ligaments 201
cryosurgery 93, 543
Cryptococcus neoformans 408
cryptorchidism 309, 311–12, 542–3, 623
    castration and 312
crystals 81
Cuboni test 117, 337
Culicoides (sweet itch) 100, 453, 462

cumulus oophorus 320
curb ix, **144**, 200, **224**
cyanogenetic glycosides 518–19
cystic calculi (bladder stones) 84, 85–6
cystic ends 542
cystic lining 10
cystitis 83, 84–5, 86, 88, 271
cysts 347, 566
  dentigenous 10, 137
  dermoid 137, 566
  hydatid 457–8
  maxillary 30, 33
  pharyngeal 34
  sebacious 566
  subchondral bone 174
cytomegalovirus 380–4

daily nutritional requirement tables 584–98
  calcium and phosphorus 587
    content of mineral supplements 587
  digestible energy 584
  energy and protein 584
  feed for growing horse 598
  foodstuffs 592
  malnutrition (table) 600–1
  nutrients 591
  trace minerals and deficiencies 589
  vitamins and deficiencies 590
Damalinia equi (lice) 97, 467–8 *see also Haematopinus asini*
dandruff (pityriasis) 104
danger, response to 135
dantrolene 228
daylight 121
deafness 138
dealers 636
debilitation 104
débridement of wounds 261, 550
debris, inhalation of 36
decubitus ulceration 103
deep digital extensor muscle **xi**, 206
deep digital flexor tendon **xi**, 180, 211, **221**, **228**, 232, **233**, 237, 243, 246, 278–9
  enlargement of *see* thoroughpin
  sprain of accessory ligament of 223

deep distal sesamoidean ligament 221
deep going 143
deer flies 461
defaecation 7
defective conformation rendering horse unfit for purchase 665
deferent duct **308**, **309**, **311**
deficiency, vitamin and nutrient (tables) 589, 590
deformity 183, 392–3
  see also development abnormalities
degenerative cataracts 133
dehydration 70, 82, 91
delivery
  of afterbirth 349–51
  post- 366–71
deltoideus muscle **x**
demodectic mange 471
Demodex equi (demodetic mange) 471
dendrite 108
dental abnormalities 29, 30
dental care 525, 582, 676–7
dental disease 10
  see also teeth
dentigenous cysts 10, 137
depression 15, 19, 83, 87, 434
Dermacentor andersoni 474
dermatitis 100
dermatophilosis (greasy heel) 94–5
Dermatophilus congolensis (dermatophilis) 94
dermatophyte skin infections 408
dermis 91, 92, 103, 104
Dermobion 256
dermoid cysts 137, 566
desensitization 247, 251, 252
desmotomy 250, 280
development abnormalities 284, 379, 391–3, 621–9
  table 392
  see also genetics
developmental cataracts 133
dexamethasone 118
diabetes insipidus 22–3
diabetes mellitus 22, 81, 121
diagnostic medication 152
diaphragm 8, 36, 37, rupture of 15
diaphyseal angular deformity 289
diaphysis **153**, **281**, **288**

diarrhoea 13, 14, 15, 18, 70, 71, 85, 236, 379, 405, 418–9, 432, 442, 451, 459
diastole 57, 58, 59, 62
diathermy 549
dichlorvos 446, 488
Dictyocaulus arnfieldi (lungworm) 449–50
  see also lungworm infection
diets
  and exercise 661
  for hunter 642
  low nitrogen 83
  restricted 236–7
  see also nutrition and feeding
digestible energy requirements table 584
digestive system 5–24, 79
  accessory glands of 16–24
  congenital abnormalities of 628–9
  foetal *v.* newborn 368
  disturbance of 14–16
  physiology 580–2
  tract 583–4
digital cushion 233
digital extensor muscle **xi**
digital flexor tendon 297
  sheath, distension of 144, 147
digital palpation 157–8
dimethyl sulphoxide (DMSO) 158, 211, 267, 488
dioestrus 116, 324–30, **325**
discharge
  of sinus 10
  nasal 10, 27, 29–31
disease
  minimizing build-up of 526–7
  minimizing possibility of 525–6
  rendering horse unfit for purchase 664
disinfection for EHV-1 341
dislocation *see* luxation
displacement *see* luxation
distal annular ligament 212
distal interphalangeal (coffin) joint flexural deformity 161, 257, 278–9
distal intertarsal joint 193
distal sesamoid (navicular) bone **x**, 232

distal sesamoid (navicular)
   ligaments 222–3
distension
   of fetlock joint capsule *see*
      articular windgall
   of hock joint capsule *see*
      bog spavin
   of tendon sheaths 187,
      208
diuresis 82, 83
diuretics 82, 488
DMSO *see* dimethyl
   sulphoxide
dock ix
dogs 436–7, 457–8
dollar spots 435
donkeys 46, 135
dorsal midline 100–1
dorsal sacroiliac ligament
   268
dorsal spinous process
   fractures of 271
   impingement and
      overriding of 269–70
double lift (heave) 40, 43
dourine (*Trypanosoma
   equiperdum*) 316, 435
doxapram 121
*Draschia megastoma see
   Habronema*
drainage
   of guttural pouch 31
   of pus in foot 242–3
   of wounds 550
dressage horses 144, 162
dressings
   for wounds 551–2
   sterile non-adherent 557–8
drink
   inability to 80
   need to *see* thirst, excessive
drinking water 85
driving horses 300
dropped heart beat 63
drug(s)
   reactions 82, 103
   routes of administration of
      477–82
   for treatment of parasites
      in horses (tables) 444–5
   veterinary 483–93
   for wounds 552
drug therapy 50, 51, 119
duodenum 8, 22
   inflammation of 21
draughts, avoidance of 376
dummy *see* neonatal
   maladjustment
      syndrome

dura mater 108
dust and newborn foals
   374–5
dysmaturity 391
dysrhythmia *see* arrhythmia
dystocia *see* birth, abnormal

ear(s) 33, 98, 104, 135–8
   bleeding from 138
   canal(s) 136
      infection of 137
   conditions 137–8
   discharge 137
   drooping 110
   functional anatomy 135–7
   mange *see Psoroptes
      cuniculi; Psoroptes equi*
   mites 137, 470–1
   paralysis of 137–8
   plaques 102, 137
   pricking of 414
   shyness 137
   tumours 137, 138
   waxy 470–1
eardrum 135, **135**
Eastern encephalomyelitis
   (EE) 111, 430–1
eating problems and weight
   loss 14
E. coli see Escherichia coli
ECG *see* electrocardiograph
eCG *see* equine chorionic
   gonadotrophin
Echinococcus granulosus
   (hydatid cyst) 457–8
echocardiography 64
echography *see* ultrasound
   scanning
ectoparasites 94, 95, 104
EHV-1 *see* equid herpesvirus
   1
EHV-3 *see* equid herpesvirus
   3
EIPH *see* exercise-induced
   pulmonary haemorrhage
ejaculation 118
elasticity of skin, decreased
   91
elastin 56, 59
elbow ix, x
   capped ix, 187–8, 207
   conditions of 187–9
   dropped 111
electric shock 55–6
electrocardiograph (ECG)
   57, 58, 61, 63–4
electrocautery 549
electrocoagulation 549
electrolyte(s) 92, 488–9, 588

electrolyte-water balance 67,
   70, 76, 79, 82
electromagnetic therapy *see*
   pulsating
   electromagnetic field
   (PEMF) therapy
emasculator 539
emboli 69
embryo 333
emotions 109
empyema of guttural pouch
   31, 411
enamel 687, 688
encephalitis 111
encephalomyelitis 111
endocardium 56
endocrine gland 22
endocrine system 113–21
endocrinology 123
endogenous infection 405–
   10
endolymph 136, 137
endometrial cups 120, 131
endometrium 322
endoscopic examination 10,
   11, 27, 28, 29, 32, 41
endotracheal intubation 391
enemas 481–2
   for newborn foals 375
energy and nutrition 583–6
   daily requirement tables
      584
enlarged tonsular tissue 33–4
enteric disease 417–19
enteritis (inflammation of
   intestines) 13–14, 418
   and peritonitis 15
enterocolitis 417
entropion 130–1
environment 91
   control of 50–1
   internal 121
   and newborn foals 374–5,
      380
   and selective breeding
      633–4
enzyme(s) 22, 71, 151
   blood 92
enzyme inhibitors 518
eosinophils 74, 77
epidermis 90–1, 92
epididymis 307, **308**, 309,
   309, 311
epiglottis 6
epiphyseal growth *see*
   imbalance of
   metaphyseal or
   epiphyseal growth
epiphysis 153, **281, 288**

epiphystisis *see* physitis
epistaxis *see* nasal
  haemorrhage
epithelial cells 320
epitheliogenesis imperfecta
  92, 629
Epsom salts 491
equenine 117
equid herpesvirus 1 (EHV-1;
  rhinopneumonitis) 19–
  20, 42, 86, 379
  abortive strain 339–43,
  425–6
  respiratory strain 425,
  426–7
  Thoroughbred Breeders'
  code of practice 341–3
  vaccination and 427,
  524–5
equid herpesvirus 3 (EHV-3)
  428
equilinin 117
equine adenovirus 43, 429
equine arteritis 428–9
equine asthma *see* chronic
  obstructive pulmonary
  disease
equine chorionic
  gonadotrophin (eCG)
  119, 120, 331
equine coital exanthema
  (horse pox) 315–16
equine degenerative
  myeloencephalopathy
  276
equine infectious anaemia
  21, 77, 430
equine influenza 42, 422–4
  Jockey Club Rules and
  423–4
  vaccination against 525
equine metritis *see* CEM
equine picornaviruses 429
equine protozoal myelitis
  277
equine rhinovirus 1 (ERV-1)
  43, 429
equine sarcoid 93
ergot ix
erythromycin 417, 485
erythrocytes 72
Escherichia coli 338, 380–4,
  405, 420, 432
eucalyptus oil 489
Eustachian tubes 26, 135,
  136
event horses 214
examination
  of eye 129–30

of heart 60–4
for lameness
  at exercise 147
  at rest 145
of mouth, for age 686–98
for respiratory problem 40
of skin 92
for soundness *see*
  veterinary certification
  and purchase of horses
of teeth *see* teeth as
  evidence of age
*Examination of Animals for
  Soundness, The* 691
excitement 38
excretion 17, 79, 104
exercise 27, 34–5, 38–9,
  51–2, 60, 67, 68, 70,
  145, 197–8, 204–5,
  216, 249, 284–5
  examination at 147–8
  intolerance 23, 27, 35, 36,
  40, 42
  newborn foal and 376–7
exercise-induced pulmonary
  haemorrhage (EIPH)
  51–2
exercise physiology 655–61
  blood 659
  cardiovascular system
  658–9
  dietary requirements 661
  locomotion 660–1
  muscular system 657–8
  respiratory system 659–60
exercise psychology 65
exfoliative dermatitis 104
exhalation 37
exocrine gland 22
exostosis 154, 160
expectorant drugs 44
expiration 40–1
extension 294
extensor carpi obliquus
  muscle xi
extensor carpi radialis
  muscle **x, xi**
  distension of tendon
  sheaths of 187
extensor process **xi, 212**
  fracture of 252
extensor tendon **xii**
  of carpi obliquus muscle **xi**
external abdominal oblique **x**
external intercostals **x**
extracellular fluid 76
extrauterine *v.* intrauterine
  life (table) 368–9
exuberant granulation tissue
  102

eye(s) 1, 29, 33, 121, 124–34
  birth defects 133
  chambers and segments of
  127
  conditions of 130–4
  congenital abnormalities
  626–7
  defects rendering horse
  unfit for purchase 663
  discharges 129, 130, 131,
  132
  examination of 129–30
  lotions 489
  sore 130
  tumours 129, 130
  ulcers 130, 132
  see also blindness;
  conjunctivitis; ocular
  abnormalities; optic
  system
eyeball 125, 127, 132
eyelashes 126, 130
eyelid(s) 102, 110, 126, 128,
  129, 132
  injuries to 129, 130, 132
  retraction of 414

face flies 101–2
facial catheter 30
facial crest **x**, 125, **126**
facial nerve 110, 137–8
facial paralysis 111, 138
facial swelling 10, 29, 31
faecal egg counts 442
Fallopian tubes 318, **319**,
  322
  infundibulum of **321**
false bursa *see* acquired/false
  bursae
false rig 312
faradism 145, 151
farm poisions 514
farrier-made shoes 297–302
fascile 211, **212**
fascicular membrane **212**
Fasciola hepatica 459
fat 15, 17, 18, 22, 125
fatigue fractures 160
fatty liver syndrome 236
feathered whorl 701
feed 594–5 *see also* food;
  nutrition and feeding
feeding horses 44
  excessive 67, 103
  hunters 639–43
  and NMS 388–9
feeding programmes 595–9
  broodmares 596–7
  mature horses at
  maintenance 595

orphan foals 597
weanlings 598–9
working horses 595–6
see also food; nutrition
and feeding
feeling 109
loss of 110, 111–12
feet 232–57, **233**, **237**
conditions of 233–57
examination of 525
functional anatomy of
232–3
infection in 242–3
lameness of 141, 143, 144,
147, 151
of newborn foals 377
pain in 146
poor trimming of 143
preparing for shoeing
296–7
sore 233–5
soundness and
conformation 612–13
weightbearing surfaces of
295–6
female genital organs 318–23
feminization, testicular 621–2
femoropatellar joint 203
femur x, **164**
fractures of 170
fenbendazole 46, 450, 451
ferric/ferrous compounds
489
fertility 317, 420
fetlock
conditions of 180–4
distension of *see* articular
windgall
notching of contour 210
sinking of 219
fetlock joint ix, x, 148, 162,
208, 294
angular deformity 281,
281
arthritis of 181–2
chip fractures in 183
condylar fractures 183
flexural deformity of
279–80
sprain of 181
fetlock varus 281, **281**
fever 425, 434
neonatal 380–4
fibre (dietary) 594
fibre-optic endoscopy 11, 27,
28, 35, 41
fibres, nerve *see* nerve fibres
fibril **212**, 213–17, 219
fibrin 75

fibrinogen 18, 71, 75
fibroblasts **212**, 213, 215–17
fibroplastic sarcoid 93
fibrosis 19
fibrous adhesions 210
fibrous band **228**
fibrous strings 45
fibula xii
fractures of 170
fibular tarsal **192**, 192–3
fibularis tertius, rupture of
228, **228**
filarial worms *see Onchocera*
cervicalis
filled leg 260
fillies 272
fimbriae 321
firing 145, 216, 546
first-aid 131, 166
first-aid kit 556–9
first phalanx x
first-stage labour 123, 352–3
fistula 505
fistulous withers ix, 453, 504
flank(s) ix, 40
flat-race horses,
Thoroughbred 144
flecked 703
flesh mark 702
flexion 181, 186, 294
flexion tests 148–9
flexor carpi radialis muscle x
flexor carpi radius muscle xi
flexor carpi ulnaris muscle x,
xi
flexor tendon sheath 184,
294
strain of 209–10
flexural deformities 183,
278–80, 628
acquired 278–80, 451–3
congenital 278
flies 100–2, 409
biting *see* biting and
nuisance flies
black 461–2
blow *see* myiasis
bot *see Gastrophilus*
buffalo 461
deer 461–2
horn 461
horse 461
house 460
prevention of irritation by
463–4
screw-worm *see* myiasis
stable 103, 460–1
fluid-blood balance 76
fluid-electrolyte balance 149

fluid line 45
fluid therapy 227
flukes 409, 458–9
flunixin meglumine 178,
237, 489
fluorine 510
foaling 352–60
duties of personnel present
at 356–60
first stage 352–3
induced 118
second stage 353–5
third stage 356
see also, birth; foals,
newborn
foaling boxes 381
foals 11, 13, 15, 31, 34, 43,
46, 48, 68, 82, 83, 95–
6, 113, 123, 163, 164,
189, 203, 272, 284–91,
416, 432, 446, 447–8,
451
newborn 18, 19–21, 39,
42, 44, 73, 76, 87, 92–
3, 120, 130–1, 171,
173, 308, 333, 410, 414
adaptive behaviour
366–7
conditions of 378–94
development
abnormalities 391–3
gross behavioural
disturbances 384–91
immunological
reactions 393–4
infective 380–4
dealing with 367–77
v. foetal life (table)
368–9
in health 366–77
nutritional requirements
of 598
positioning of, for
delivery 348
at risk 528
sick 342–3
nutritional requirements of
597–8
tables 587, 591
premature 119
focal necrosis 20
focusing 128
foetus 19–20, 117, 120, 123,
332, **347**
abnormalities 361–2
contribution to abnormal
birth 360–1
death of 20
membrane, development
of 33

preparation for birth 345
follicle(s) 320, **321**
    development of 120, 320
    inducing 329–30
follicle-stimulating hormone
    see FSH hormone
fomentation 490
food
    composition of (table)
        592–3
    nasal discharge of 31
foodpipe *see* oesophagus
    see also nutrition and
        feeding
foot *see* feet
'footy' horse 246
forage mites 99
forage poisoning (botulism)
    415–16
forceps 92
forearm **xi, 603**
forebrain 110
fore cannon ix
forehead ix
forelimbs 98, 141–9 *passim*,
    160, 182, 183, 214, **603**
    soundness and
        conformation 609–12
foreign bodies 74
    in nasal passages 30, 32
    in pharynx 11, 33
    and pneumonia 43
forging **142**, 143
foul smell
    of breath 9, 10
    of nasal discharge 29, 30,
        31, 33
fractures 165–71
    of cannon bones 168
    of carpal bones 167, 186,
        291
    of cervical vertebrae 267,
        276
    chip
        in fetlock joint 183
        of small bones of knee
            144, 146
    classification 165
    condylar 183
    diagnosis 165
    of extensor process 252
    of femur 170
    first aid 166
    healing of 166–7
    of hock 170, 200
    of humerus 167, 191
    of navicular bone 170
    of patella 170
    of pelvis 170, 272

of phalanges 169–70, 184
of proximal sesamoid
    bones 169, 184
of radius 167
of sacrum 272
of scapula 167, 191
of skull 33, 112, 138
of splint bones 168–9
of stifle joint 204
of supraglenoid tubercle
    190, 191
of thoracolumbar spine
    271
of tibia 170
of wing of pedal bone
    252–3
of withers 272
fright 119
frog **233**, 243–4, 293–302
    passim, **297**, **299**
front **603**
FSH hormone 113, 117,
    119–23 *passim*, 324–30,
    325
fungal infection 30, 50–1,
    338, 408
    of guttural pouch 10, 11,
        30, 32, 33, 137, 138,
        408
    ringworm *see* ringworm
fungi 407–8
fusion
    of bones 196
    of joint 183, 197

gait, abnormal 19, 85, 111,
    113, 142–3, 189, 190,
    220, 232–57 *passim*,
    275, 291, 416
galloping 27, 130, **141**, 145,
    220, 272, 377
Galvayne's groove 694
gamma camera 151
gammaglobulin 71
ganglia 108
gangrene 505
gangrenous pneumonia 10
gaseous distension (tympany)
    of intestines 12
gas exchange 37, 38, 39, **54**
gastric distension 14
gastrin 124
gastrocnemius muscle **x**
gastrocnemius lateral head
    xiv
gastrocnemius tendon **206**
Gastrodiscus aegyptiacus
    458–9
gastro-intestinal tract surgery
    533–4

Gastrophilus
    haemorrhoidalis 464–6
Gastrophilus intestinalis (bot
    flies) 464–6
Gastrophilus nasalis (bot
    flies) 464–6
geldings 312
general anaesthesia 498–500
genetics 122, 618–29
    and blood typing 619–21
    and digestive system 628–
        9
    other development
        abnormalities 629
    and eye 626–7
    and haematopoietic system
        624–5
    and immunodeficiency
        625–6
    and lymphatic system
        624–5
    and musculoskeletal
        system 627–8
    and nervous system 627–8
    and reproductive system
        621–3
genital inflammation 420
gentamytcin 485
GH (growth hormone) 122
girth, deep **603**
girth itch *see* ringworm
glanders 404–5
glands 107, 113
globin 20
globulin 18, 19, 71
glossopharangeal nerve 110
glucagon 124
glucose 22, 81, 121
glucosoria 22
gluteal superficial muscle **x**
gluteal fascia **x**
glycogen 17
glycosaminoglycen 178
GNRH (gonadotrophin
    releasing hormone) 119,
    120–1
gonadotrophic hormones
    324
goose rump **613**
gossypol 518
grains 588, 592–3, 504–5
granules 73–4
granulosa cells 320
granulosa cell tumour 565
grass 138, 236
grasscrack 244–5
grass sickness 14, 15, 60,
    124
grazing, mixed 445

grazing patterns 524
greasy heel *see*
dermatophilosis
greater trochanter x
grey 138, 700
grey-ticked 703
griseofulvin 490
grooming
of hunters 648
lack of 93
gross behavioural
disturbances, neonatal
384–91
growth hormone *see* GH
growth plate (physis) 280–9,
281
growth rates 598–9
see also nutrition and
feeding
gubernacular bulb, 311
gullet *see* oesophagus
gut 16, 18, 21, 22, 70, 72,
113, 123, 124
guttural pouch 6, 26, 135
empyema of 31, 33
obstruction of 26
tympany of 33
see also fungal infection of
guttural pouch

Habronema (summer sores)
451–3, 461
Habronema majus 451
Habronema muscae 451
Haemapinus asini (lice) 97,
467–8
Haematobia (deer flies) 461
Haematobia irritans (horn
flies) 461
Haematobia stimulans (horn
flies) 461
haematocrit 21, 70
haematology 92
haematomas 137, 363
haematopoetic system,
development
abnormalities of 624–5
haemoglobin 18, 20–1,
72–3, 81
haemolysis 20, 73
haemolytic disease 20–1, 73,
77, 393–4, 624
diagnosis and symptoms
394
prevention 624
treatment 394, 624
haemophilia 76, 624–5
Haemophilus equigenitalis
infection *see* CEM

haemorrhage 28, 33, 74, 81,
82, 110, 112, 214, 362,
548–57
and castration 540
hair 90, 91, 92
loss of 92, 95–104 *passim*,
126, 262
see also epitheliogenesis
imperfecta
matted 94
hammer 135
hamstrings ix, x
handling methods *see*
restraint and handling,
methods of
hard ground 234, 236, 292–
302 *passim*
hard palate 6
harness
badly fitting 104
for hunter 643–4
harvest mite *see*
neotrombiculosis
hay 228, 236–7
and nutrition 594
and straw, mould in 48,
50–1
hCG *see* human chorionic
gonadotrophin
HCN (hydrogen cyanide)
518–19
head 19, 29, 109, 125, 135,
137, 147, 148, 604
injuries to 122
markings of 702–3
soundness and
conformation 603–4
tremors 113
headshaking 573–4
headshyness 30, 31, 137
healing of wounds 550–1
factors affecting 552
health, keeping animals in
good 522–5
hearing *see* ear(s)
heart 8, 36, 37, 53–65, 64,
66, 70, 79
abnormalities 34–5
structural 624
auscultation 61–3
and circulation 59–60
see also under blood
conclusions on 64–5
disease 60, 76
examination 41, 60–4
failure 82
murmurs 60, 62–3
muscles 113
heart attack 60

heart-beat rate 61–4, 87, 369
heat, localized 145, 146
heat rash *see* acne
heave(s) ix, 40
heaveline 49
see also, chronic
obstructive pulmonary
disease
heavy draught horses 300
heavy hunter horses 260
heavy metals as poisons
509–12
heel ix, 146, 233, 239, 294–
302, *passim*, 299
heel bug 471–2
see also neotrombiculosis
collapsed 246
cracked *see* cracked heels
helminths 409, 438–59
heparin 75–6
hepatic artery 16
hepatic jaundice 73
hepatitis 20, 21, 104
hereditary ataxia 627
hereditary multiple exostosis
170, 263
see also genetics
heritability of lameness 144
see also congenital
abnormalities
hernia ix, 15–16, 536–8
causes 536–7
inguinal 537, 629
rubber rings 538
strangulated 557
surgical closure 538
treatment 538
umbilical 537–8, 538, 629
ventral 537
herpesvirus 42
see also equid herpesvirus
1; equid herpesvirus 3
herring gut 608
hidebound 91
high articular ringbone 144,
182
hind brain 109
hind cannon ix
hind limb(s) 146–9 *passim*
ataxia 427
impulsion 572
lameness 141–9 *passim*,
193–8
paralysis of 111, 427
shivering of 112
soundness and
conformation 613–14
hindquarters ix, 111, 148
hip 147, 603

hip joint x, 148, **603**
hippomanes 332
histopathological
    examination 93
hives *see* urticaria
hobday *see* larynx
Hobday, Sir Frederick 35
hock(s) **ix**, 69, 144, 148,
    154, 159, **603**
    arthritis of 193–8
        clinical signs 194
        diagnosis 194–5
        nerve block 196–7
        radiographic
            examination 195–6
        sprain of 199
        treatment 197–8
    capped **ix**, **144**, 207
    conditions of 192–201
    distension of capsule *see*
        bog spavin
    fractures of 170
    functional anatomy 192–3
    soundness and
        conformation 614–15
hollow back **608**
homeostasis 389
hook bones 585
hooks (on teeth) **9**
hooves 292–302 *passim*
    horn 76, 243
        growth and function of
            293–5
        markings on 704
        wall of 243–5, 293–302
            passim, **297**
        cracks 244–5
hoof dressing 302
hoof testers 147
hormonal control 307
hormonal system *see*
    endocrine system
hormones 71, 79, 107, 110,
    113–24
    function during birth
        346–7
    measurement of 113
    therapy 123
horn 120, 243, 293–302,
    passim, **299**
horn flies 461
horny sole **233**
horsebox 145
horse flies 461
horse pox 315–16
horseshoe *see* shoes/shoeing
hot lasers 543
house flies *see Musca
    domestica; Musca
    sorbens*

housing 522–3
human chorionic
    gonadotrophin (hCG)
    119, 312
humerus **x**, **xi**, 153, 187,
    189, 207
    fracture of 167, 191
humidity 38
humour 67
hunter-chasers 214, 300,
    635–51
    boots and bandages 646–8
    buying 635–8
    clipping 644
    clothing 644–6
    feeding 639–43
    grooming 648
    harness 643–4
    injuries 648–50
    preparing for hunting
        650–1
    training 638–9
husbandry 94, 95
hyacine 21
hyaluronic acid 172, 178
Hybomitra (buffalo flies) 461
hydatid cyst 457–8
hydrocortisone 118
hydrogen cyanide (HCNB)
    518–19
hydrogen ions 71
hydrogen peroxide 243, 491
hygiene 94
hygroma 186–7, 207
    see also acquired/false
        bursae
hyoscine (hyoscine-n-butyl
    bromide) 490
hyperextension 214
hyperflexion 195, 393
hyperglycaemia 22
hyperirritability 110
hyperlipaemia 22, 23, 121
hypersensitivity 48, 103, 409
hypertension 60, 384–6
hypoflexion 393
hypoglossal nerve 110
hypoplasia of carpal bones
    186, 284, 289–90
    treatment 290
hypoplastic joint 173
hypostome 100
hypothalamus 122
hypothermia 389
hypoxia (oxygen shortage)
    374, 379, 384–6

ileocaecal valve 6
iliolumbar ligament **269**

ilium **x**, 264
    fractures of 272
imbalance of metaphyseal/
    epiphyseal growth
    280–9, 290
    cause 281–2
    conclusion 284
    deceleration of growth on
        convex side 287–8
    development abnormalities
        284
    location 281
    nutrition 284
    removal of implants 289
    stimulation of growth on
        concave side 285–7
    trauma 282–3
    treatment 284–5
    wedge osteotomy 289
imidicarb 434
immaturity 391
immunity 74, 120
    of newborn foal 379
immunodeficiency
    combined (CID) 625
    congenital 625–6
immunoglobulins 381
immunological reactions
    between maternal and
    foetal tissues 393–4
impactive drug 12
impingement and overriding
    of dorsal spinous
    process 269–70
inappetence
    and equid herpesvirus 42
    and guttural pouch
        empyema 31
    and liver disease 19
    and upper airway disease
        27
incised wounds 547
incisor teeth 3, 5, **688**
    malocclusion 8
incomplete development of
    small metacarpal (splint)
    bones 290
incomplete ossification
    (collapse) of carpal
    bones 289–90
incontinence 86, 271
incoordination 110, 112,
    113, 138, 431
    of back and pelvis 274–77
    hind limb 427
    causes of 274–7
incus *see* anvil
induced copper deficiency
    510–11

in-dwelling catheter 31
inertubercular (bicipital)
    bursitis 191
infection(s) 42, 74, 77, 95,
    103, 110, 111, 118,
    119, 129, 131, 137,
    147, 163–4, 179–80,
    242–3, 338, 339–43,
    378–9
  controlling speed of 529
  see also bacterial
    infections; virus
    infections
infectious diseases 395–474
  bacterial 411–28
  causes of 397–410
  parasitic 438–74
  protozoan 433–7
  viral 422–32
infective arthritis ('joint ill')
    179, 379
infective conditions
    (neonatal) 380–4
  table of causes/symptoms
    382
inflammation 74, 119, 131,
    132, 157–9, 181, 214,
    501–6
inflammatory oedema 217
influenza *see* equine influenza
infraspinatus muscle 229
infundibulum 687, 689
inguinal areas 98
inguinal canal 311
inguinal hernia 537, 629
inguinal ring 308
inhalation 38
  of vapours 481
  of debris 37–8
initiation of birth 346–7
injuries 68, 111, 112, 192,
    219, 222
  to hunters 648–59
  see also first-aid
inner ear 135, **136**, 136, 138
insect(s) 409
insect bites 103, 430
insecticides 409
  table of 463
inspiratory sound, abnormal
    34, 35
instability of shoulder 192
insulation of housing 522–3
insulin 22, 121
intermittent upward fixation
    of patella 202
interosseus ligament 154,
    157
intersexes 623

interspinous ligament 267,
    269
interstitial cell(s) 119
interstitial cell tumours 310
interstitial fluid 66, 76
intertransverse ligament 269
intervertebral disc 265
intervertebral foramen 265
intestinal blockage 15, 21
intestinal parasitism 14
intestinal wall (lining)
  catastrophy *see* twisted gut
  damage to 432
    and colic 12
  and prolapse of rectum 16
  and weight loss 14
intestinal worms 46, 48
intestines 7–8, 8, 37, 47, 76
  gaseous distention
    (tympany) of 12
  infections of 13
  inflammation of (enteritis)
    13–14
intra-articular anaesthesia
    149, 182, 183
intracellular fluid 76
intramuscular administration
    of drugs 480–1
intraspinatis muscle xii
intra-uterine administration
    of fluids 482
intra-uterine *v.* extrauterine
    life (table) 368–9
intravaginal administration
    of fluids 482
intravenous administration
    of drugs 480
intussusception 13
in utero feeding 367
involucrum 163
involuntary activity 113
involution 364
iodine 244, 370, 490, 589
iris 127, 128, **128**, 129, 130,
    132
iron 20, 589
irritation
  ear 137
  skin 91, 92, 97–104
    passim
ischium x, 264
  fractures of 272–3
Islets of Langerhans 22
isolation facilities (for EHV-
    1) 341
isoxuprine 250
isoxuprine
  hydrochloride
    162

itch *see* acariasis
itchiness 91, 92, 97–104
    passim
ivermectin 46, 442, 446,
    450, 451
Ixodes holocyclus (ticks) 474
Ixodes ricinus 99
Ixodes rubincundus 474

jaundice 18, 19, 20, 73, 394
jaw(s) ix, **x**
  muscles 125
  overshot (parrot mouth) 8,
    9, 393, **604**, 629
  undershot (sow mouth) 8,
    629
Jenner, Edward 398
Jockey Club Rules 118
  on equine influenza 123–4
jockey itch *see* ringworm
joint(s) 88, 139, 172–205
  conditions of 172–84
  damaged 119
  disease, secondary 151
  infection 179–80
  laxity 283
  sprain 175
  structure/function 172–3
joint capsule **172**
  distentions and
    enlargement of 174
joint 'ill' (infective arthritis)
    179, 379
jowl ix
jugular groove ix
jugular vein viii
jumper's bump 264
jumping horse 144–5, 204,
    214
  hunters and 636–7
  problems 234
  see also showjumpers

keratin 90, 92, 238
keratitis 131–2
keratoma 253–4
kidneys 18, 37, 71, 72, 76,
    78, **78**, **79**, 79, 122,
    123, 124, 227, **308**, **319**
  acute renal failure 82
  chronic renal failure 83
  conditions of 81–3
  infection of pelvis of
    (pyelonephritis) 83
kidney stones (calculi) 83
kissing spines 269–70
Klebsiella 314, 338
Klebsiella pneumoniae 380–
    4, 404, 413, 419–20

knee *see* carpus

laboratory work, and
    veterinary nurse 684
labour
    first-stage 123, 352–3
    second-stage 353–5
    third-stage 356
labyrinth (of ear) 136
lacerations 547
    lacrimal duct **xii**
        blocked 131
lacrimal gland 126
lactic acid 71–2, 227
lameness 110, 141–52, 283
    and bone conditions 153–
        71
    bridle 149
    defects rendering horse
        unfit for purchase 664
    diagnosis of 145–6
    examination
        at exercise 147–8
        at rest 146–7
        incidence of 144
    and feet 231–57
    after foaling 364
    and joints 172–205
    miscellaneous conditions
        of 258–63
    and muscles 225–31
    and performance 144–5
    and shoulder 189
    and swellings 144
    tests for 148–9
    and tendons and ligaments
        206–24
    treatment 145
    see also paralysis
laminae 232, **233**, 236–8,
    237, 239, 241, 244, 297
laminitis **ix**, 60, 83, 146,
    236–8, 363, 365
    causes of pain 236
    clinical changes 236
    chronic 238
    treatment 236–8
laparotomy 12
large colon 7, 12
large intestine 7, **581**
    impaction of food in 12
    and nutrition 582–3
    rupture of 362
large metatarsal (cannon
    bone) **xii**
large roundworm *see*
    Parascaris equorum
larvae (lungworm) 47, 449
laryngeal hemiplegia 35, 112

larynx 6, 25, 27, 34, **533**
    conditions of 35–6, 112
    paralysis of 35, 112
laser therapy 217, 543–4
lateral canthus **126**
lateral digital extensor
    tendon **x, xi, 212**
    distension of tendon
        sheath of 187
lateral femoral fascia muscle
    xii
lateral ligaments of carpus
    xiii, 192
lateral nostril dilator muscle
    x
lathyrism 518
lathyrogens 518
latissimus dorsi muscle **xii**
laziness 143
lead 21, 511
lectins 517
Leewenhoele, Antonine van
    398
legal implications of buying
    horse 672–7
leg(s) 80, 99, 111, 113,
    147–9
    filled 260
    mange *see Chorioptes equi*
    oedema of 19, 71, 83
legumes 588, 594
leishmania 408
lens 127, 128, **128**, 130,
    132, 133
lesions
    chest 41
    skin 94, 95, 96, 100, 101
lethal dominant white 629
lethargy, neonatal 380–4
leucocytes 73, 118
leukoderma 104
levator muscle
    of nasolabialis **x**
    of upper lip **x**
LH (luteinizing) hormone
    117–23 *passim*, 324–30,
    325
libido 118, 119
lice 92, 97, 409, 467–8
life expectancy 686–7
ligaments 151, 160, 161–2,
    220–4
    functional anatomy 220
    laxity 290–1
    sprain of 223
    strain of 221–4
    suspensory apparatus
        220–1
ligamentum nuchae 453

ligature 549
ligature sinus 542
light 127, 128–30
    and newborn foals 374
lightning strike 555–6
limbs, markings on 704
    see also forelimbs; hind
        limbs
limbus 126
linamycin 485
lincomycin 513
linear whorl 701
line firing 216
lip(s) **x**
    markings 703
    sagging 110, 138
lipomas (tumours of fat) 15
list (dorsal identification
    mark) 704
Lister, Joseph 398
listlessness 42
liver 7, 8, 16–21, 70, 75, **581**
    cells, degeneration of 19
    cirrhosis of 19
    conditions of 18–21, 91
    damage *see* hepatitis
    disease, chronic 260
    functions 17–18
    poisoning 19
    weight of 16
liver fluke 459
lochia 364
lockjaw 110, 111, 414–15
locomotion and exercise
    660–1
loins **ix**
long digital extensor muscle
    x, 206, 212, 228
long flexor muscle **xii**
long intestine **581**
long pastern bone, fractures
    of 169
lousiness *see Haematopinus
    asini*; lice; pediculosis
lower jaw 5, 688, 689
    discharging wound on 10
    swelling on 10
lower limbs 98, 99, 177
lower lip, drooping 138
lower respiratory tract 25,
    36–52
    conditions of 42–52
    functional anatomy 36–8
    methods of examining
        40–1
    respiration and factors
        affecting adversely 39–
        40
    healthy 38–9

signs of malfunction 39
lower urinary tract 79
lumbar nerves 109
lumbar vertebrae xii, 82,
  264–77, **265**
lumbodorsal fascia muscle
  xii
lung(s) 36, **37**, 37, **47**, 56,
  70, 72, 74, **479**
  abscessation of 45
  disease *see* chronic
    obstructive pulmonary
    disease
  function
    abnormal 39–40, 41
    and EHV-1 20
    and lack of oxygen 18
    see also lower
    respiratory tract
  haemorrhage 51–2
lung tissue
  infection from bacteria 44
  inflammation of 43
lungworm infection 42, 46,
  47, 449
lupinosis 516
luteinizing hormone *see* LH
luxation 173, 178–9
  congenital, of patella 203
  of superficial digital flexor
    tendon 200, 220
  traumatic, and fracture of
    carpal bones 291
lymph fluid 66
lymph glands 68, 69, 111,
  414
lymphangitis 68–9, 259–60
lymphatic diseases 67–9
lymphatic enlargement 27,
  29, 34
lymphatic system 1, 36, 66–9
  development abnormalities
    of 624–5
lymphatic tissue 34
lymphatic vessels, blockage
  of 69
lymphocytes 67, 74
lymphoid hyperplasia 34
lymphosarcoma 15, 563,
  565–6

machine-made horseshoes
  297–302
magnesium 588, 589
magnesium suphate 491
Magnetopulse 218
mal de caderas 435, 436
malignancy 91
malignant tumours of
  stomach 15

malleus *see* hammer
malnutrition 260
  causes and symptoms
    (table) 600–1
malocclusion 8
maltose 23
mammary development 69
mammary glands 90
management and husbandry
  567–651
mandibular gland 68
mane and tail marks 704
manganese 589
mange
  demodectic 471
  ear *see* *Psoroptes cuniculi*;
    Psoroptes equi
  leg *see* *Chorioptes equi*
  mites 468–72
  nodular 471
  psoroptic *see* *Psoroptes*
    cuniculi; *Psoroptes equi*
  see also acariasis
mangers 99
manure removal 443, 524,
  526, 527
'mareish behaviour',
  excessive 574–5
mare(s) 13, 79, 83, 84, 115,
  116–17, 118, 120, 123,
  318–23, 335–43, 419–
  21, 428
  feeding programmes for
    596–7
  tables 587, 591
  immunological pregnancy
    test *see* MIP test
  and newborn foal 366–94
  and parturition 344–65
  see also birth; foaling
  pregnant *see* pregnancy
  urinogenital surgery of
    534–8
markings
  head 702–3
  other characteristics 703–4
  white 701–2
  whorls 701
  see also colours and
    markings of British
    horses for identification
masseter muscle xii
mast cells 75
mastication 8
  difficulties in 9–10
maternal contribution to
  abnormal birth 362–5
maternal preparation for
  birth 344–5

mature horses at
  maintenance, feeding
  programmes for 595
maxillary cysts 30, 33
mebenazole 450
mechanical dysfunction 144
mechanical irritants 42
meclofenamic acid 178, 250
meconium and newborn
  foals 375, 378
meconium colic 87, 378
mecrolides 485
medial canthus **126**, 126
medial collateral ligament of
  carpus xi
medial splintbone xi
medical nursing, and
  veterinary nurse 685
medicines, veterinary 483 93
medullary cavity 153
mefenamic/meclofenamic
  acid 491
melanoma 138
melanosarcomas 563
menace response test 134
meninges 108–9
meningitis 111, 380–4
menisci 201
mercury 512
mesorchium **309**, 311
mesosalpinx 322
metabolism 17–18, 22–3,
  78 81, 118, 375 6
metacarpophalangeal joint
  see fetlock joint
metacarpus xii, 143, 153,
  154–60, 164, 168, 172,
  220, **288**
  periostitis of 143, 159–60
metals, heavy 82
metaphyseal growth *see*
  imbalance of
  metaphyseal/epiphyseal
  growth
metaphysis 153, **281**, **288**
metatarsals x, 143, 154–60
  periostitis of 143, 159–60
metatarsus 206
methionine 238, 245, 302
metritis 84
  see also CEM
metronidazole 243
microbes 74, 93
micro-organisms, infectious
  42, 397–409 *passim*
Micropolyspora faeni 48
microscopic examination 92,
  397
Microsporum 95, 408

Microsporum canis 408
microtyledons 333, 351
micturition 79, 80
mid-brain 109
middle annular ligament xii, 212
middle distal sesamoidal ligament 221
middle ear 26, 135, 136, 137
midges 100, 103, 462
migrating parasites 277
milk 123
  goat's 597
  post-foaling 388, 596–7
  pre-foaling 344–5, 596
milk teeth 9, 688, 689
milk warts 92–3, 563
minerals 85, 164, 288
  daily requirements (tables) 587, 589, 591, 592–3
  and nutrition 586–8
minimal-dust environment 50
MIP test 336–7
mites 409
  ear 137
  mange 438–762
  skin 92, 99
mitral valve 54, 55, 56, 58, 62
mixed grazing 445
mixed marking 701
mixed sarcoid 93
molar teeth 5, 5, 68, 689, 691–4 *passim*
molybdenum 510–11
monensin 513
monocytes 74
moon blindness (periodic ophthalmia) 132
Morgans 276
morphine 21, 491
motilin 124
motor activity 110, 111
motor nerves 111
mould, in hay and straw 48, 515–16
  in rye 515
mould toxins 515-16
mouth 5–6, 10, 25, 104
  examining *see* examination of mouth for age
  and nutrition 582
  parrot (overshot jaws) 8, 9, 393, 604, 629
  sow (undershot jaws) 8, 629
movement 109
  problems 236

mucosal linings 118
mucus 29, 37–8, 41
mud fever *see* cracked heels; dermatophilosis
multiple exostosis 170
murmurs *see* heart murmurs
Musca domestica 460
Musca sorbens 460
muscle(s) 70, 71, 111, 118, 139, 151, 211
  abnormal function secondary to nerve injury 229–31
  atrophy 191, 225
  enzymes 151
  fatigue 214
  heavy 283
  inflammation (myositis) 226
  loss of 147
  problems 225–31
  sprain 270
  stiffness 414
  strains 145, 151, 160–1, 191-2, 226
muscular contractions, controlled 145
muscular spasms 414
muscular system and exercise 657–8
musculoskeletal system 139–302
  common problems 303–4
  congenital abnormalities 627–8
  other congenital abnormalities (table) 628
muzzle ix, 99, 104, 138
Mycobacterium bovis 404
Mycobacterium tuberculosis 404
mycoplasma 407
mycosis 338
mycotic dermatitis *see* dermatophilosis
myiasis 453, 466–7
myocardium 56, 60
myoglobin 82
myometrium 322
myopathy 226
myositis 226

nagana 435, 436
nail bind 241
nail holes 300–1
nail prick 241–2
nailing on shoes 302
nandrolone 484

nanny goats 597
nappiness *see* rearing, bucking, nappiness
naproxen 491
nasal aperture 126
nasal bones 125, 126
nasal chamber 6
nasal discharge 10, 27, 29–32, 33, 39, 44, 137, ch29, 425
nasal granuloma 408
nasal haemorrhage (epistaxis) 30, 32–3
nasal mucuous membrane 26
nasal tumours (cancer) 30, 32, 33
nasal twitch *see* twitch
nasolabialis muscle x
naso-lacrimal duct 126
nasopharynx 6, 25, 26, 32, 34
National Stallion Approval Scheme 178
navel 43
navel stump 370–1
navicular (distal sesamoid) bone ix, x, 232, 233, 246–50
  fractures of 170, 251
  functional anatomy 246
navicular bursa 243, 246
navicular syndrome 143, 144, 146, 147, 239, 246–50, 248
  clinical signs 246
  diagnosis 247
  exercise for 249
  treatment 247–50
  trimming and shoeing 247–9
neck ix, 112, 125, 147, 148, 267, 453–5, 604
  abscess 268
  broken 111, 267–8
  conditions of 266–8
  injuries 192
  muscle damage 267
  nerves 109
  soundness and conformation 603–5
  stiffness 33
  wry neck *see* torticollis
necrosis 87, 250, 289–90, 291, 310, 505
nematodes 409, 438–55
  life cycle 438–9
neomycin 256, 485
neonatal infective conditions 380–4

neonatal isoerythrolysis *see* haemolytic disease
neonatal maladjustment syndrome (NMS) 384–9
neoplasia 102–3, 560–1
  see also tumours
Neotrombicula autumnalis 99; *see also Trombicula*
neotrombiculosis 99
nephrotoxins 82
nerve
  cervical 109
  spinal 109
nerve blocking 110, 149, 182, 196–7, 204, 252
nerve cells 107, 108–9, 122
nerve damage 10, 110
nerve fibres 107–9, 122
nerve ganglion 107
nerve injury, abnormal muscle function secondary to 229–31
nervous system 79, 121
  autonomic 113
  central and peripheral 107–13
    brain 109–10
    conditions of 110–13
    congenital abnormalities of 627–8
    infection of 432
    nerve cell 108–9
    spinal cord 109
nettle rash *see* urticaria
neural arch 265
neural paralysis 137–8
neurectomy 250, 251
neuritis 111
  of cauda equina 86
neuroaxonal dystrophy 276
neuroendocrine system 113, 121–4
neurohormone 122
neurological disease 437
neurological function, foetal *v.* newborn 369
neurological symptoms
  of liver disease 18–19
  of diabetes 22
neuromas 250
neuromodulators 122
neurone 122
neutrophils 74, 77
newborn foals *see* foals, newborn
nipple 123
nitrates/nitrites 512
nitrogen 82, 83, 118
nits 98

nodular mange 471
nodular necrobiosis 102
noise, abnormal during exercise 34–5, 36
non-adherent sterile dressings 557–8
noose twitch *see* twitch
normal flora 398–40
  infections of bacteria within 405–6
nose ix, 7
  roman 604
noseband, dropped 35
nosebleed 27, 30, 51–2
  bilateral 33
nostril(s) ix, x, 25, 29, 40, 104, 126
  collapsed 110
  dilation 415
  foul-smelling discharge from 10
notifiable diseases 679–80, Appendix 3
noxious chemicals 21
NSAID (non-steroidal anti-inflammatory drugs) 119
NSH (nutritional secondary hyperparathyroidism) 586–7
nuchal ligament 267, 269
nuclear medical technology 29
nuclear scintigraphy 131
numbness 110, 111–12
nurses, veterinary *see* veterinary nurses
nursing 44, 46, 83, 84, 683–5
nutrient requirements *see under* nutrition
nutrition
  and angular limb deformities 284, 523
  and feeding 580–99
    bodyweight estimate table 599
    causes and symptoms of malnutrition (table) 600–1
    daily calcium/phosphorus requirements (table) 587–8
    daily energy requirements (table) 583–5
    digestive physiology 580–2

    digestive tract 582–3
    exercise 661
    feed 592–5, 598
    feeding programmes 595–6
    foals 597
    mares 596–7
    minerals 586–7, 589
    nutrient requirement 583–94
    requirements 583–8
    vitamins 589–90
    weanlings 598–9
nutritional secondary hyperparathyroidism (NSH) 586–7

obdurator 111
obesity 38
oblique carpal extensor muscle x
obstacle course 134
obstructions
  to airflow 34
  by impacted food (choke) 11
  of throat 31
obstructive jaundice 21
obstructive pulmonary disease *see* chronic obstructive pulmonary disease
occipito-atlanto-axial malformation 275–6, 628
occiput xii
occupation of horse 144
OCD *see* osteochondrosis
Octobius megnini 472–3
ocular abnormalities 30
  see also eye conditions
ocular motor nerve 110
odd coloured 700
oedema 19, 67, 71, 83, 103, 104, 384–6
  inflammatory 157
oedematous swellings 69
oesophagus (gullet) 6, 6, 7, 11, 27, 36, 47, 479
  chronic dilatation of 11
  and nutrition 582
  rupture of 11
oestradiol 117
oestradiol benzoate 118
oestrogen 115, 117–18, 119, 324–30, 325, 347
oestrone 117
oestrone sulphate 117, 309, 312
oestrus 79, 116, 117, 118, 119, 121

oestrus cycle 123, 324–8
  advancing onset of 327–8
  controlling 326–7
  inducing 329
  physiology of 326
  use of treatments 330
ointments 557
olecranon **xi**
  fractures of 187, 188–9
olecranon process **x**
olfactory nerve 110
omasum **581**
'on the bit', horse not
  working 571–2
Onchocerca cervicalis
  (filarial worms) 453–5
Onchocerca reticulata 453
onchocerciasis 453–5
onion poisoning 513
oogonium 324–30
open wounds
  abrasions 548
  cleansing/debridement 550
  control of bleeding 549
  drainage 550
  dressings 550–2
  drugs 552
  healing 550–1
  incised 547
  lacerations 547
  penetrating 548
  puncture 547–8
  treatment 548
operating theatre for
  veterinary practice 684
ophthalmia, periodic 132
ophthalmoscope 129, 132,
  133
opium 491
optic atrophy 134
optic nerve 110, 112, 121,
  128, **128**, 129, 134
optic pallida **128**
optic system 125–34
  see also eye; ocular
  abnormalities
oral administration of
  medicines 477–8
orbit **x**, 125
orchitis 310
organic acids *see* amino acids
organic dust antigens 48
organophosphorus 98
organ system 3–138
orgotein 178
oropharynx (back of mouth)
  6–7, 25
orphan foals *see* foals
osmolality, blood 123

osmotic gradient 71, 76
osteitis 160–2
  pedal 160–1
  sesamoiditis 161–2
osteoblasts 154
osteochondrosis (OCD) 144,
  163, 173–4, 189–90,
  199, 200–1, 203, 275
  clinical signs 189–90, 203
  diagnosis 190, 203
  treatment 190, 203
osteocytes 153
osteomyelitis 163, 168
osteophytes 177, 195
osteoporosis 290
outer ear 135, **136**, 137
  tumours 137
ovaries 113, 116, 119, 120,
  318–20, **319**, **321**, **325**
overactivity 283
overcrowding 381, 445
overfeeding 13, 523
overgrazing 527
overlong feet 143
overreaching **142**, 143,
  254–5
overshot jaws (parrot mouth)
  8, **9**, 393, **604**, 629
overweight horses 236
oviduct **321**
ovulation 117, 119, 120
  incidence of 328–9
oxalates 83, 512–13
oxfendazole 442
oxibendazole 451
oxygen
  and cardiac function 60
  and COPD 49
  lack of *see* hypoxia
  and lung function 18, 37,
  38, **54**, 70
  and red cells 72
oxyhaemoglobin 72–3
oxyphenbutazone 18
oxytocin 118, 122, 123, 325,
  347, 360
Oxyuris equi (pinworm)
  100, 448–9

pace 142
paces, normal 141–2
packet-cell volume (PCV) 70
pads 235, 247
pain 80, 119, 129, 132,
  144–50 *passim*
pain-relieving drugs 69, 152
palate 6–7, **6**
palmar carpal ligaments 223
palmar vein 221

Palomino 700
palpation 147, 151
  renal 82, 86
pancreas 7, 8
  conditions 22–3
  function 22
panniculus muscle 91
papules 103
Parafilaria multipapillosa
  455
paralysis 110–11, 414–15,
  425, 431, 435
  of bladder 84, 86, 271
  facial 10, 110, 138
  hind-limb 427
  laryngeal 35, 112
  neural 137–8
  pharyngeal 11
  radial 111
  respiratory 416
  of tail 271
  of tongue 10
paramastgoid process **267**
paraphymosis 89
Parascaris equorum 20, 48,
  447–8
parasites 42, 91, 92, 97–8,
  409–10
  migrating 277
parasitic conditions 13, 21,
  46–8, 77 433–73
parasiticides 98, 409–10
parasitic larval migration,
  and peritonitis 15
parasympathetic nervous
  system 113
paratenon 211, **212**
parenteral administration of
  drugs 479
parotid duct **8**
parotoid gland **x**, 8, 23
  swollen 138
paroxysmal coughing 33
parrot mouth (overshot jaws)
  8, **9**, 393, **604**, 629
parturition 344–65
  see also birth
pastern–foot axis 162, 294–5,
  294
pastern joint 232, 294
  arthritis of *see* ringbone
  conditions of 180–4
Pasteur, Louis 398
Pasteurella 43
pasture and nutrition 594
pasture management 524
pasture plants, poisonous
  520–1
patchy sweating 33

patch 703
patella xii, 144, 148, **164, 201**
  delayed release of 202
  fractures of 170, 205
  luxation and fixation 628
patent urachus 88
pathogenicity 397
pathogens 92
patient care, and veterinary nurse 685
PCV *see* packet-cell volume
pectorals xii
pedal bone 232, **237**, 243, 293, **297**
  fractures of 169–70
pedal osteitis 161–2, 235–6
pelvis 78
  conditions of 171–4
  fractures of 170, 272
  functional anatomy 264–6
PEMF *see* pulsating electromagnetic field therapy
penetrating wounds 548
penicillin 414, 415, 420, 485
penis 78, 79, 84, 118, 307, **308**, 313–14
  conditions of 314–16
  prolapsed 314–15
  tumours 88, 315
  and urethral obstruction 88–9
peptidergic nervous system 124
peptides 123–4
percussion 41, 45, 147
performance 133
  and lameness 144–5
periarticular bone spurs 177
pericardium **37**, 56
perineal irritation 100
perineum **319**, 322
permanent teeth 688, **690**
periodic ophthalmia 132
periosteum 153, 154, 157, **172**, 173, **281**, 288
  proliferative reactions 222, 236
  stripping 285–7
periostitis 143, 154, 157
  secondary to muscle or ligament strain 160
  of third metacarpal/metatarsal bones 159–60
peripheral nervous system (PNS) 107–13
Periphigus foliaceous 104

peristalsis 113
peritendinous adhesions 216
peritoneal fluid 15
peritonitis 15, 406
peroxide 491
pethidine 491
pH 71, 81
phalanges xii, 161–2, **164**, 180, 211, **221**, 232, 235
  fractures of 169–70, 183, 184
pharyngeal cysts 32
pharyngeal wall 26
pharyngitis 411, 426
pharynx 7, 10–11, 25, 135
  abscesses of 11, 31–3
  diseases of 10–11
  foreign bodies in 11, 33
  muscles of 7
  paralysis of 11, 32
  swelling of 31, 33
  tumours of 31, 33
phenamidine 434
phenylbutazone (bute) 18, 69, 119, 145, 152, 158, 178, 181, 183, 197, 209, 215, 227, 237, 250, 252, 491–2
phonocardiography 61
phospholipids 18
phosphate 81
phosphorus 18, 21, 157, 284
  and nutrition 586–8
  requirement (tables) 587, 591, 592–3
photosensitization (blue nose) 91, 104–5
physical restraint 494–5
physiotherapy 145
physis 163, **281**
physitis 163–4, 186, 282
phytate 227
pia mater 108
Piefferella mallei 405
pigeon breasted 606
pigeon toes **607**
pigment 104
piebald 700
pin bones 585
pin firing 216
pineal body 121
pinna 135, **136**, 137
  tumours of 137
pinworm *see Oxyuris equi*
piroplasm 409
piroplasmosis 77, 433–5
pisiform x, xi
pitressin 23

pituitary gland 23, 110, 113, 118–23 *passim*, 324–6
pituitary hormones 117
pityriasis (dandruff) 104
placenta 116, 119, 120, 123, 331–3, **334, 351**
  delivery of 349–51
  development and structure 333
  expulsion of 356
placentation 331–4
placentitis 379
plaiting 143
plantar ligament **192**
plantar tarsal ligament, strain of 223–4
plant toxins 21, 82, 83
  see also poisoning in horses
plasma 70–2, 73, 75, 76
plasma cells 74
platelets 74, 75
PMN *see* polymorphonuclear neutrophils
PMSG (pregnant mare's serum gonadotrophin) 119, 120, 327, 331
  detection of 336
pneumonia 379, 404, 422–3
  aspiration 31, 32, 43–4, 46, 74
  summer *see Corynebacterium equi*
pneumonitis 425
point-to-pointers 214, 222
poisoning in horses 507–21
  diagnosis 508
  heavy metals 509–12
  other poisons 512–17
  routes 507
  symptoms 509
  toxicity 507–8
  treatment 509
  vegetable protein sources 517–21
poll ix
poll evil ix, 504
pollen 48
polydactyly 171, 628
polymorphonuclear neutrophils (PMN) 74
polyvalent equine antitoxin 416
ponies 60, 100, 236–8, 339, 591
pons 109
pooling *see* urine pooling
portal vein 16
position, delivery 349

posterior chamber (of eye) 127
posterior deep pectoral x
posterior segment (of eye) 127
posterior vena cave 60
post-operative treatment 30, 88, 286, 288
postrenal failure 82
posture, delivery 348
potassium 71, 76, 81, 227, 238, 588
potato poisoning 513
poultices 234, 492, 559–60
Pouret operation 534–5
powder, wound 556–7
prednisolone 256
pregnancy 69, 81, 116–17, 119, 120, 331–43
　conditions of 337–43
　diagnosis 335–6
　feeding programmes 596–7
　length of 335
　states of 335–43
pregnancy test 117, 120
pregnant mare's serum gonadotrophin (PMSG) 120
premature foals 119, 381, 391
premature rupture of umbilical cord 367, 381
premolars 5, 688, 691
preparturient loss of colostrum 381
prerenal failure 82
pressage bandage 208
pressure bandage 549
pressure sores 103
preventive medicine 522–9
primary agammaglobulinaemia 625
primary oocytes 320
primordial follicle 320
primordial germ cell 320
proflavine 483
progesterone 115, 116–17, 119, 324–30, 325, 347
prohibited substances Appendix 2
prohormones 122
prolactin 122
prolapse
　of bowel 541
　of penis 314–15
　of rectum 16
promethazine 483
Prophet's Thumb Mark 703

proprioception 112
prostaglandins 118, 123, 324–30, 325, 347
prostate gland 308, 313
protective immune response 409
protein(s) 81
　allergic reaction to 103
　balance 67
　high-, diets 67–8
　and liver function 17, 18
　and nutrition 584, 586
　and pancreas function 22
　plasma 71, 76
　requirements (table) 584
proteoglycins 176
prothrombin 75
protozoa 408–9
　diseases caused by 433–7
proud flesh 102
proximal annular ligament 212
proximal interphalangeal joint *see* pastern joint
proximal intertarsal joint 193, 198
proximal sesamoid bones x, 161–2, 180, 221
　fracture of 169, 184
pseudomonas 314
Pseudomonas aeruginosa 401, 404, 419–20
psittacosis 407
Psoroptes cuniculi (psoroptic mange) 470–1
Psoroptes equi (psoroptic mange) 470–1
psoroptic mange *see Psoroptes cuniculi; Psoroptes equi*
pubis 264
　fractures of 272–3
Puccinia graminis 515
pulmonary artery 53, 54, 55, 56, 59
pulmonary disease *see* chronic obstructive pulmonary disease
pulmonary valve 62
pulmonary vein 54, 55, 56
pulp cavity 687
pulsalite doses 121
pulsating electromagnetic field (PEMF) therapy 145, 218, 544–5
pulse xiii
puncture wounds 547–8
punkies 462
pupil 127–30 *passim*, 133

contracted 132
dilated 416
purchasing horse *see* buying horses
purgatives 484
purpura haemorrhagica 260, 411
pus 29, 31
　in foot 242–3
pyaemic nephritis 83
pyelonephritis 83
pyrantel 446
pyrethroids 101, 102
pyrexia 429

QRS waves 57
Quarter horse 144, 246
quarters 603
Queensland itch 462
quidding 8, 697
Quinnapyramine 435
quittor 253

rabies 111, 432
racehorses 33, 34, 118, 119, 146, 167
　Thoroughbred flat- 144, 160, 176, 177
radial nerve paralysis 187, 189, 230–1
radiographic examination 11, 27, 28–9, 61, 87, 149–51, 158, 161–2, 168, 174, 176, 177, 190, 195–6, 235, 247, 417
　reasons for, in soundness examination 670–1
　and veterinary nurse 684
radius x, xi, 153, 163, 164, 164, 187, 288
　fracture of 167
ragwort (*Senecio jacobaea*) 21
rain scald *see* dermatophilosis
rasping 9, 9, 698
rattles *see Corynebacterium equi* infection
rearing, bucking, nappiness 570–1
receptors 115
rectal examination 335
rectovaginal fistula 535
rectum 8, 8, 79, 308, 319
　manual examination via 12, 83, 84
　palpation of 80–1, 85
　prolapse of 16

red roan 700–1
reflex(es) 107, 125
relaxant drug 12
removing permanent teeth 10
renin 124
repair of tendon tissue 215–16
reproduction 305
reproductive system 305–94
  development abnormalities 621–4
requirement, nutritional *see* daily requirement tables; nutrition
respiration
  factors affecting adversely 39–40
  foetal *v.* newborn 368, 369
  healthy 38–9
  signs of malfunction 39
  see also respiratory system
respiratory disease 429
respiratory distress 43, 103, 386–91, 411–14, 447
respiratory failure (neonatal) *see* asphyxia neonaturum
respiratory obstruction 32
  at exercise 33–5
  infection 425
  at rest 33
respiratory paralysis 416
respiratory rate 38–9
  increase in 42, 44, 49
respiratory sounds, abnormal 39, 41
respiratory symptoms, of *parascaris equorum* infection 48
respiratory system 7, 25–52
  defects rendering horse unfit to purchase 663–4
  exercise and 659–60
  soundness and conformation of 616–17
  surgery on 532–4
respiratory tract *see* lower respiratory tract; upper respiratory tract
rest
  examination at 146–7
  true 145
restraint and handling, method of 494–500
  anaesthetic 497–500
  chemical 496
  physical 494–5
resuscitation 390–1

reticular membrane 212
reticulo-endothelial (RE) system 17
reticulum 581
retina 121, 127, 128, 128
  degeneration of 134
rhabdovirus 432
rhinitis 411
rhinopneumonitis *see* equid herpesvirus 1
Rhodococcus (Corynebacterium equi) infection 46, 378, 402, 404, 480
rhomboideus muscle x
ribonucleic acid *see* RNA
ribs ix, x, 36, 37, 78, 170
rickets 284
rickettsia 407
ridgeling *see* cryptorchidism
riding horse 144
rifampin 417
rig *see* cryptorchidism
ringbone ix, 144, 182
ringworm 92, 95–6, 408
risk, identifying individuals at 527–9
RNA (ribonucleic acid) 122
roach back 99, 608
roans 700
roaring (laryngeal hemiplegia, whistling) ix, 35, 112
rolled-toe shoe 299
rotavirus 432
roughage 85
round ligament of liver 17
roundworms 409, 438–55
routes of medical administration
  enema 481–2
  inhalation 481
  intramuscular 480–1
  intrauterine 482
  intravaginal 482
  intravenous 480
  oral 477–8
  parenteral 479–80
  stomach tube 478–9
  subcutaneous 481
  topical 482
routes of poisons 507
rubber ring 538
rugs (blankets) for hunter 644–6
rumen 580, 581
Rumensin 513
rupture
  of large intestine 362

  of uterus 362
  see also hernia

sacral nerves 109
sacral (pelvic) segment of spinal cord 86
sacral vertebrae x
sacroiliac 264, 265
sacroiliac articulation 269
sacroiliac disease 225, 273
sacroiliac joint 269
sacroiliac ligament 269, 274
sacrosciatic ligament 269
sacrum x, 86, 109, 264–77, 265
  fractures of 271
saddle boils *see* acne
saddle gairs (sores) 103
saddle for hunters 643
salivary glands 8, 23–4, 113
  parotid, swollen 138
salivation 10, 23–4, 115
Salmonella 13, 380–4, 405, 417–19, 514
Salmonella typhimurium 418, 432
salmonellosis 417–19
salmonycin 513
salt, as first-aid 131, 227, 365
salt licks 82
salts 18, 71
sandcrack ix, 244
sarcoid 564
  see also skin tumours
Sarcoptes scabiei (scabies) 469–70
sarcoptic mange 98
  see also Sarcoptes scabiei
Sarcocystic bertrami 436–7
Sarcocystic fayeri 436–7
saucer fractures 160
sausage boot 188
scab *see* acariasis
scabies 98
  see also Sarcoptes scabiei
scalding tears 126
scalding urine 84, 86, 88
scaliness of skin 91, 96
scapula x, 189, 191, 229
scapular fracture of 167
  cartilage xii
scar collagen 216
scirrhous cord 542
sclera 126, 127, 127, 128, 128
sclerosis of subchondral bone 177

scratches *see* cracked heels
screening for infectious
    diseases 525–6
scrotal hernia 310
scrotum 307, 308, **311**
    abscess of 541–2
seated out shoe **297**, 298
sebaceous gland 91
secondary joint disease 151,
    165, 169, 174, 175–8,
    272, 290, 291
    of carpus 185–6
    clinical signs/diagnosis 177
    of coffin joint 252
    of fetlock joint 181–2
    of hip joint 272–3
    of hock *see* bone spavin
    of pastern joint 182
    treatment 177–8
second-degree burns 553
    phalanx x
second-stage labour 353–5
secretory cell 122, 124
secretory glands 113
sedation 28, 179
sedatives 415, 483
seeds, poisonous in vegetable
    protein concentrates 514
seedy toe 244
selective breeding 630–4
selective IgM deficiency 626
selenium 226, 509–10, 589
self-abrasion 94
self-excoriation 97–104
    passim
semen 316–17
    examination of 317
seminomas 310
semitendinosus muscle x
sensation, loss of 111–12
senses, foetal *v.* newborn 368
sensitive body tissue, access
    of bacteria to 402–5
sensitive laminae **233**, 236–8,
    237, 239, 241, 244, **297**
sensitive sole **233**
sensitivity 104
sensory activity 110, 111
sensory nerves 111
septicaemia 82, 380–4, 404,
    410
septic arthritis *see* joint
    infection
septum 25
sequestrum 164
serological test 434
serratus dorsalis caudalis
    muscle x
serratus muscles 189

serratus ventralis cervicalis x
serratus ventralis thoracis x
Sertoli cells 309
serum 71, 74, 75
serum gonadototrophin 119
Serum hepatitis see Theiler's
    disease
sesamoiditis 160, 161–2, 184
sesamoids **xii**, 161–2, **164**,
    180–4, 201
setfast *see* azoturia
severence 110
sex gland(s) 18
    accessory 313
sex hormone 118
sexual activity 121, 308–17
    passim, 318–23 *passim*
shaker foal syndrome 415–
    16
sheath **ix**, **308**
sheep tick 99–100
Shetland pony 144
Shigella equirulus see
    Actinobacillus equulii
shigellosis 404
shins, sore **ix**, 159–60
Shire horse 144
shivering 112, 148, 259
shock 82, 119
    see also trauma
shoes/shoeing 143, 144, 147,
    197, 202, 252–7 *passim*,
    292–302
    fitting 301–2
    manufacture of 297–300
    nailing on 302
    and navicular disease
    247–9
    preparing foot for 296–7
    problems 239–41
short-backed horses 269
short pastern bone 211, **297**
    fractures of 169
shoulder **ix**, **xii**, 111, 189–
    92, **610**
    bruising of 191
    functional anatomy 189
    instability of 192
    joint 230
    lameness 187, 189
    sloping **603**
showjumpers 133, 162
shrubs, poisonous 516–17
shyness,
    ear 137
    head *see* headshyness
sickle-hocked conformation
    291
sidebone **144**, 232, 253

sight 109
    see also eye; ocular
    abnormalities; optic
    system
Silver, Professor 216, 217
silver nitrate styptic 88
simple whorl 701
Simulium 461–2
sino-auricular node 57
sinuous whorl 701
sinuses 26, 163–4, 505
    discharging 137
sinusitis 10, 29–30, 32, 33
sitfast 103
skeleton 139
skewbald 700
skin 73, 90–105, 107, 145
    conditions 92–105
    cracked 255–7
    examination and
        diagnostic aids 92
    infections caused by
        physical breakdown of
        400–1
    lesions 453–4, 469–70,
        471
    numbness in 111
    swelling beneath 71
    tumours 93, 130, 137
    see also itchiness;
        scaliness, of skin
skull **xii**, 109, 125, 135, 136
    fractures of 33, 138
sleepiness, and liver disease
    19
sleepy foal disease 380–4,
    404, 410
slinging as aid to surgery
    545–6, **545**
small colon 8
small intestine **8**
    and nutrition 589
small metacarpal bone,
    incomplete development
    of 290
small metatarsal (splint)
    bone x
small stomach **581**
smell 109
snake bites 514–15
snip (head marking) 703
snoring 29, 31
snotty nose *see* equid
    herpesvirus 1
sodium 71, 76, 81, 227, 588
sodium bicarbonate 492
sodium cromoglycate 51
sodium hyaluronate 176,
    182, 186, 251

soft palate 6, **6**, 7, 25
  disease 34
  obstruction **26**, 27
soft-tissue swelling 220
solanine 513
soleus muscle **212**
sole(s) 232, 237, 295–302
  passim, **297, 299**
  paint 235
somotostatin 124
sore(s) 451–3
  pressure 103
  summer *see Habronema*
sore back **ix**
sore feet 233–5
sore shins **ix**, 159–60
sound and newborn foals
  374
soundness and conformation
  602–17
  back 607–9
  chest 605–6
  feet 612–13
  forelimb 609–12
  head and neck 603–5
  hind limbs 613–14
  horse's action 615–16
  procedure for examining
    666–8
  responsibility of examiner
    for certifying 665–6
  wind 616–17
  see also conformational
    abnormalities
sow mouth (undershot jaws)
  8, **629**
spasm 110
spasmodic colic 12
spasmolytic drug 12
spavin
  bog *see* bog spavin
  bone *see* bone spavin
  test 195
special techniques for
    soundness examination
    669–70
speedy-cutting 143
spermatic cord 309
sperm 307, 309
sperm count 317
sperm duct **79,** 308
spider stings 514–15
spinal abscesses 86
spinal accessory nerve 110
spinal column 37, 78, 86
spinal cord 107, 108–9, 111,
  112, 123, 264–77
  bruising of 276–7
spinal fluid 109

spinal nerves, local 86, 108,
  109
spinal tumours 86
spine **267, 269,** 322
spinose ear tick *see Octobius
  megnini*
spleen **8,** 22, **37,** 70
splenius muscle **xii**
splint **ix,** 143, **144,** 154–9
  blind 159
splint (small metatarsal)
  bone **ix, x, xi,** 14, 143,
  154–9, **156**
  functional anatomy 154–6
  fracture of 168–9
  incomplete development of
  290
splinting 290
spores 407–8, 416
spots
  as identification marks 703
  see also equid herpesvirus
  3
sprays, wound 556–7
squamous cell carcinoma
  102
stable cough *see* equid
  herpesvirus 1
stable fly 103, 460–1
stable vices 578–9
stables, and virus infections
  42
stabling, COPD and 48, 50
staggering 112
stall box 79
Stallion Licensing Act 178
stallions 118, 307–17, 419–
  21, 428
stapes *see* stirrup
staphylococci 338
Staphylococcus areus 93,
  380–4
star (head marking) 702
starches 22, 23
starvation 91
State Veterinary Service
  functions 679–81
  role of 678–82
  useful addresses 682
steeplechasers 222
sterile non-adherent
    dressings 557–8
sternocephalic muscle **xii**
sternum **xii, 606**
steroid hormones 116–19
stethoscope 63
stifle joint **xii,** 148
  bruising of 204–5
  conditions of 201–5

sprain of 204
stilboestrol 118
stillbirth 342, 391
stings (bees etc.) 514–15
stirrup 135
stomach 8, 98, **479, 581**
  and nutrition 582
  rupture 14, 15
stomach tube, administration
    of drugs by 478–9
Stomoxis calcitrans (stable
    fly) 103, 460–1
strain of flexor tendon sheath
  184
strangles infection 11, 31,
  43, 68, 95, 402, 411–14
strangulated inguinal hernia
  310, 537
  see also hernia
stratum corneum 91
stratum germinativum 91
straw bed 79, 271, 371–5
  damage from 365
strawberry roan 701
streptochricosis *see*
    dermatophilosis
Streptococci 338
Streptococcus equi
    (strangles) 411–14
Streptococcus pneumoniae
  406
Streptococcus pyogenes
  380–4
Streptococcus zooepidemicus
  380–4, 404
streptomycin 485
stress 43, 45, 77
  and birth 380
  and infection 405
stress fractures 160
stride length 148
stringhalt 112, 258
stripe (head marking) 702
strip test, for foaling 345
strongyles (roundworms)
  clinical signs 441–2
  diagnosis 442
  life cycle 439–41
  prevention 443–6
  resistance to anthelmintics
  446
Strongyloides cocentatus
  439, 440, 441
Strongyloides equinus 439,
  441
Strongyloides vulgaris 439,
  440, 441
  treatment 442–3 *see also
    Strongyloides westeri*

Strongyloides westeri
(threadworm) 450–1
strychnine 21
stumbling 143, 262
stump, naval 370–1
subchondral bone 172
subchondral bone cysts 174,
203–4
subcutaneous administration
of drugs 481
subcutis 91
subfibrils 212
subluxation 179
sublingual glands 23, 24
subsolar haemorrhage 234
Substance P *see* peptide
suckling 93
impaired 372–5, 380–4,
386–9, 416
submandibular glands 23, 24
sugar 17, 22, 121
sulphanimalide 244, 256
sulphonamides 82, 485,
492–3
sulphur 493, 510–11
summer eczema 462
summer pneumonia *see
Corynebacterium equi*
infection
summer sores *see
Habronema*
superficial digital flexor
tendon xiii, xiv, 185,
206, 211, 212, 213–14,
218, 219, 221, 233
luxation of 200
superficial distal sesamoidean
ligament 221
superficial gluteal muscle xii
superior check ligament 217
suppuration 504
supraglenoid tubercle,
fracture of 190, 191
supraorbital fossa 126
process 125, 126
suprascapular nerve 111,
229
supraspinatus muscle 229
supraspinous bursa 267, 269
supraspinous ligament 264,
267, 269
strain of 270–1
suramin 435
surfactant 346
surfeit (excessive feeding)
103
surgery 15, 111, 198, 285–9
castration 539
complications of castration
540–3

limitations 530–1
major techniques 532–4
other techniques 543–6
progress 531–2
slinging as aid to 545–6
urinogenital, of mare
534–8
surgical exploration 152
surra 435–6
suspensory desmitis 168,
169, 221–2
suspensory ligament x, 127,
154, 162–3, 168, 208,
212, 220–4, 221, 228,
246
sprains of 144, 223, 239
strains of 221–4
swabs 92
swallowing 6–7, 10, 11, 14,
27, 31, 32, 415, 416
tongue *see* soft palate
disease
sway back 608
sweat glands 90
sweating 12, 14, 76, 85,
226–8, 415
patchy 33
sweeny ix, 111, 192, 229
sweet itch 100–1, 462
swelling(s) 119, 145, 146,
147, 154, 157–8, 303–4
and castration 541
on face 10
of joints 174
and lameness 143
of ligaments 224
on lower jaw 10
of lymph nodes 411–14
of tendons 214–16, 220
in throat region 33
sympathetic nervous system
113, 121
synovial bursa 206
synovial joint fluid 172–84
passim, 172, 199, 206
synovial membrane 206, 246
synovial sinus 262
synovitis 175, 176
synthetic pyrethoids 98
syringe 478–81
systemic factors 91
systemic infections *see
septicaemia*
systole 57, 58, 59

Tabanus (horse flies) 461
tack 92, 96
tail 80
nerves 109

paralysis of 271
tannin/tannic acid 493, 517
tapeworms 409, 435–8
*see also Anoplocephala
magna; Anoplocephala
perfoliata*
tarsal bone, collapse of third
and/or central 201, 291
tarsal tendon of hamstrings x
tarsometarsal joint 192–201
passim
tarsus 206
Taylorella equigenitalis see
CEM
tear(s) 126
tear ducts 126, 129
blocked 131
tears as lacerations 547
technetium 151
teeth 5, 5, 8–10, 137, 690–7
canine (tushes) 690
as evidence of age 690–5
examination 525, 687–98
incisors 689
molars 689
parts of 687–8
rasping 698
removing permanent 10,
698
temporary and permanent
688
treatment and care of
696–7
temperament of horse 144,
147
temporary (milk) teeth 9,
688, 689, 690
temperature, body
control of, foetal *v.*
newborn 368
increased 15, 27, 417
loss of 389
see also hypothermia
regulation of 90
temperature, environmental
high 38, 42
and newborn foal 374–7
tenderness around flanks 15
tendinous windgalls 143,
181, 208–9
tendon(s) 151, 154, 160,
211–20, 212
acute injury 215
bowed ix
conditions of 213–20
displacement of 220
distension of sheath 187
of extensor carpi obliquus
xi

of extensor carpi radialis
xi, 187
of flexor carpi radialis xi
functional anatomy 211–
13
lacerations 219–20
laxity 290
of lateral extensor muscle
187
prevention of injury
218–19
repair 215–16
rupture 219
sheaths
conditions of 208–11
constriction of 210
infection of 211
strain of 209–10
splitting 217
sprained 144
strain 218
tensor fascia latae muscle x,
228
teratomas 310, 311
testes 79, 118, 119, 308,
309, 311
conditions of 310–12
functional anatomy 307–
10
normal descent and
growth 308–10
testicular feminization 621–2
testicular torsion 310
testicular tumours 310
vessels 309
testosterone 116, 118, 119,
484
tetanus 243, 400, 406, 414–
15
prophylaxis 262, 263
vaccination 415, 524
tetany 588
tetracyclines 485
theca 320
Theiler's disease (*Serum
hepatitis*) 19
thermometer 559
thermoregulation 376
thiabendazole 46, 451
thigh ix, 603, 616
third-degree burns 553
third phalanx x
see also pedal bone
third-stage labour 356
thirst, excessive
and diabetes 22–3
and respiratory problems
40
thoracic cavity, penetration
of 40

thoracic nerves 109
thoracic spines 270
thoracic vertebrae x, 264–
77, 265
thoracolumbar spine
conditions of 268–72
thorax, abscess in 411
Thoroughbred Breeders
Association 340
1986 code of practice (for
EHV-1) 341–3
Thoroughbred racehorses
144, 160, 169, 173,
177, 179, 183, 186,
189, 228, 269, 272,
274–5, 335, 359, 372,
630–4
thoroughpin ix, 144, 210
threadworm *see*
Strongyloides westeri
throat *see* pharynx
thrombi *see* blood clots
thrombin 75
thrombokinase 74, 75
thrush 243–4
prevention/treatment 244
thyroid-stimulating hormone
see TSH
tibia x, 164, 192–201,
passim, 201
fractures of 170
tibialis anterior muscle x
tibiotarsal joint (of hock) 111,
164, 174, 192–201
passim, 192
enlargement of *see* bog
spavin
tick 409, 433–5, 472–4
spinose ear *see Octobius
megnini*
tick-borne babesia 409
tick infestation 99–100
tick paralysis 473–4
tiredness 143
tissue infections, bacterial
402–5
tissue spaces 76
toes 294–302 *passim*, 299,
606, 607
dragging 143, 148, 194–5,
203
long 162, 238, 241, 246,
296
lowerung/shortening 296
seedy 244
toe-in, toe-out conformation
180–1, 180
togavirus 428
tongue 6, 6, 7

tongue strap 35
tonsils 33–4
topical administration of
medicines 482
for haemorrhage 549
torsal tendon of biceps
femoris muscle 212
torsion 549
torticollis 268, 628
toxaemia 236
toxicity 507–8
see also poisoning in
horses
toxin 406
toxoid 415
trachea ix, 6, 25, 37, 47,
479, 533
breathing sounds in 41
conditions of 36
hole in 36
obstructions of 33, 35
tracheostomy 35, 36, 414
trachoma 407
tracking up 142
traction 167
traffic 636
training a hunter 638–9
tranquillizer 227, 415, 483
transphyseal bridging 286,
287–9
transportation 42, 44, 166,
227
transportation problems
577–8
unwillingness to load
577–8
transverser process 265
trapezius muscle x
trauma 93, 96, 102, 109,
110, 119, 157, 168, 188
and angular deformities
282–3
general, with secondary
infection 263
repetitive 207
severe 36, 138
see also shock
traumatic luxation and
fracture of carpal bones
291
traveller, bad 577–8
tread 143
trees, poisonous 516–17
trematodes 409, 458–9
trembling, and grass sickness
14
tremors 416
head 113
trenbolone 484

triceps muscle x, xi
Trichophyton (ringworm) 95, 408
Trichophyton equinum 408
Trichostrongylus axei 445, 455
tricuspid valve 54, 55, 62
trigeminal nerve 110
trimming of hoof 232, 238–57 *passim*, 292–302 *passim* *passim*
  and navicular disease 247–9
  poor foot 143, 144, 147, 283, 285
  problems 239–41
trochanter, greater x
trochanteric bursitis 207
trochlear nerve 110
trochlear ridges 201–3
Trombicula (heel bug) 471–2
trombiculosis *see* neotrombiculosis
trotting 141–2, 141, 143, 148, 216
true bursae *see* bursae(e)
Trypanosoma 316, 408, 435–6, 461
Trypanosoma brucei (nagana) 436
Trypanosoma congolense (nagana) 436
Trypanosoma equinum (mal de caderas) 436
Trypanosoma equiperdum (dourine) 435
Trypanosoma evansi (surra) 435–6
tsetse fly 436
TSH (thyroid-stimulating hormone) 122
tubbing the foot 242
tube, stomach 478–9
tuber calcis xii, 206, 223
tuber ischii coccygeal vertebrae x
tubera coxae 225, 264, 273–4
tubera sacrale 225, 264, 273–4
tuberculosis 404
tufted whorl 701
tumours (cancer) 21
  bladder 86
  diagnosis 563
  ear 137, 138
  eye 129, 130
  kidneys 83
  name of 562–4

nasal 30, 32, 33
  penis 88, 315
  pharyngeal 31, 33
  skin *see* skin tumours
  symptoms and treatment of 563–6
  see also keratoma; neoplasia
turbinates 25
  fungal infection of 30
turn, reluctance to 15
tushes (canine teeth) 2, 5, 688, 689, 690
T wave 57
twin conception 338
twinning 333, 334
twisted gut (intestinal catastrophy)
  and colic 13
  and lipomas 15
twisting
  of intestines (volvulus) 13
  of umbilical cord, and abortion 338–9
twitch 28, 494–5, 495
tying up *see* azoturia

udder 123
ulcerations 89, 92, 95, 103, 130, 504
ulcers 129, 428
ulna x, 187
  fractures of olecranon of 188–9
  head of deep flexor muscle x
ulnaris lateralis muscle x, xi
ultrasound scanning 61, 64, 145, 151, 176, 181, 191, 215, 222,
  in pregnancy 335–6, 417
umbilical cord 332–3, 349, 351, 414
  breaking of 370
  compression in 362
  infected stump of 83
  hernia 537–8
  and patent urachus 88
  premature rupture of 367
  twisting of, and abortion 338–9
unbalance *see* balance, loss of
uncontrolled growth *see* neoplasia
underrun sole 242–3
undershot jaws (sow mouth) 8, 629
unilateral cryptorchidism 311–12

unlevelness 142, 149
unthriftiness *see* weight loss
unwillingness to load 576, 577–8
upper airway disease 27
upper jaw 5, 26
upper limbs 98
upper respiratory tract 25–36
  conditions of 29–36
  functional anatomy 25–7
  methods of examining 27–9
urachus 87, 88
  patent *see* patent urachus
urea 18, 78, 81, 87
ureters 78, 78, 79, 319
urethritis 89
urethra 78, 78, 79, 80, 82, 83, 84, 308, 319
  conditions of 88–9
  obstruction of 88–9
  ulcerations and urethritis 89
urethral calculi 84, 88
urethral fossa 308
urinary disease 80
urinary system 78–89
  conditions of
    bladder 84–8
    kidney 81–3
    urethra 88–9
  foetal *v.* newborn 368
  functional anatomy 78–81
  methods of assessing 80–1
urinary tract 83
urinary tract tissue (casts) 81
urine/urination 22–3, 79–89 *passim*, 119, 123
  infected 428
  pooling, operation to overcome 535
  scalding 84, 86, 88
  tests 239
urinogenital surgery of mare 534–8
urticaria 103
uterine contraction 352–3, 353
uterine haemorrhage 363–4
uterine horn 322
uterine inertia 362
uterine infection 420–1
uterine prolapse 364
uterine tortion 362
uterine wall 351
uterus 75, 79, 81, 115–23 *passim*, 318, 319, 322–3, 347, 348

malpositioning in 283
rupture of 362

vaccination 40, 42, 103, 414,
    415, 426, 427, 429,
    431, 524–5
  for EHV–1 341
vagina 78, **78**, 79, 318, **319**,
    323
  bruising of 363
vaginal discharge 420
vaginal speculum 80
vaginal tunic **309**, 310
vagus 110, 113
vascular turbinates 26
Vaseline 84
vasoactive inhibitory protein
    (VIP) 124
vasopressin (vp) 122, 123,
    325
vegetable protein sources,
    poisons in 517–21
veins 53, 60, 70
vena cava **54**, **55**, 60
venereal disease 316, 402,
    419–21, 428, 435
Venezuelan
    encephalomyelitis (VE)
    111, 430–1
ventilation of housing 526–3
ventral abdomen 78, 83, 99
ventral crest **265**
ventral hernia 537
ventral longitudinal ligament
    269
ventral sacroiliac joint **269**
ventricles 53, 54, 57, 58, 59,
    61, 63, 109
verrucae sarcoid 93
vertebrae, fractures of 86
vertebral body **265**
vertebral canal 264–77
vertebral column 108, 109
vertebrate 409
vertigo 138
vesicles 122, 428
vesicular gland **308**, 313
vesicular lesions 315
vesiculitis 313
vestibular seal **319**
vestibule 136
vestibulitis 313
veterinary assistance with
    newborn foals 374
  and preventive medicine
    522–9
veterinary certification and
    purchase of horses
    637–8, 662–71

conditions rendering horse
    unfit for purchase 663–5
  examining for soundness
    666–9
  procedures to be adopted
    666–9
  and radiography 670–1
  reasons for radiography
    670–1
  responsibility of examiner
    for soundness 665–6
  special techniques 669–70
veterinary medicines 483–93,
    662–71
veterinary nurses in practice
    683–5
  entry requirements 683
  practice organization
    684–5
  qualification 683
veterinary service *see* State
    Veterinary Service
vices rendering horse unfit
    for purchase 665
villi 432
  foetal 333
violent behaviour
  and colic 13
  and Theiler's disease 19
VIP *see* vasoactive inhibitory
    protein
viral encephalomyelitis 111,
    430–1
  papillomata (milk warts)
    92–3, 563
  treatment 93
virulence 397
virus(es) 21, 42, 407
  diseases caused by 422–32
  and haemolytic disease 21
virus abortion *see* equid
    herpesvirus 1
  infections 67, 77, 110,
    111, 338, 339–43, 379
visceral peritoneum **309**
vision, anatomy of 128–30
  see also eye; ocular
    abnormalities; optic
    system
vitamin(s) 71
  A 284, 588, 590
  D 78, 284, 588, 590
  E 226, 588, 590
  K 75, 588, 599
  and nutrition 588, 599
  requirements (table) 590
vitiligo 104
vitreous humour 127, 128,
    134

vocal cords 112
volvulus (twisting of
    intestines) 13
vulva 78, **79**, 79, 80, 318,
    319
  inflammation of 86

walking 141, **141**, 148, 216,
    237
  in paddock 377
wall eye 703
wall of hoof **233**
  separation of 244
wanderer *see* neonatal
    maladjustment
    syndrome
warfarin 250
warts 92–3, 563–4
wasp stings 514–15
waste products *see* creatinine
wasting and liver disease 18
water, as nutrient
    requirement 588
water-electrolyte balance 23,
    70, 76, 79, 82
water loss 85
water-soluble medicines 477
weakness 23, 83
weaving 579
wedge osteotomy 289
weanlings, feeding
    programmes for 598–9
Webbon, Peter 670
wedged tooth 9, 10
weight-bearing 294
weight-bearing surfaces of
    foot 295–6
weight loss 10, 14, 15, 22–3,
    48, 83, 417, 436, 459
Western encephalomyelitis
    (WE) 111, 430–1
wheezing 40, 49
whistling (laryngeal
    hemiplegia, roaring) 35,
    112
white of eye, showing 703
white face (head marking)
    702–3
white foal syndrome 629
white line of foot **233**, 244
white marks 701
white muzzle (head marking)
    703
whole coloured 700
whorls 701
wild pea 21
wind *see respiratory system*
windgalls ix, **144**, 184
  articular *see* articular
    windgalls

tendinous *see* tendinous windgalls
windpipe *see* trachea
windsucking 579
windswept deformity 283, 290
wing, of atlas x
wing fracture 252–3
withers ix, 264, 608
  fistulous ix, 453, 504
  fractures of 271–2
wobbler syndrome 112, 274–5, 627
wolf (first premolar) teeth 5, 9, 10, 689, 689
  removal of 10

womb *see* uterus
working horses, feeding programmes 595–6
wounds 43, 74, 163, 400, 466–7, 547–59
  closed 553
  first-aid 556–9
  open *see* open wounds
wound powders and sprays 556–7

XO syndrome and XO/XX mosaics 622–3
X-rays *see* radiographic examination
XY gonadal dysgenesis 622

inheritance and recommendation 622
XY sex reversal 622

yearlings 48, 68, 164, 272, 446
yeasts 408
yellow body (YB) 320–1, 321
yellow dun 700

zebra marks 705
zinc 493, 589
zygomaticus muscle xii